NOTABLE PLAYWRIGHTS

NOTABLE PLAYWRIGHTS

Volume 2

Johann Wolfgang von Goethe –
Edmund Rostand
373 – 750

Edited by
CARL ROLLYSON
Baruch College, City University of New York

SALEM PRESS, INC.
Pasadena, California   Hackensack, New Jersey

All the essays in this set originally appeared in *Critical Survey of Drama,
Second Revised Edition*, 2003, edited by Carl Rollyson. Some new material
has been added.

∞ The paper used in these volumes conforms to the American National
Standard for Permanence of Paper for Printed Library Materials, Z39.48-1992
(R1997)

Library of Congress Cataloging-in-Publication Data

Notable playwrights / editor, Carl Rollyson.
    p. cm. – (Magill's choice)
  Includes bibliographical references and indexes.
  ISBN 1-58765-195-5 (set : alk. paper) – ISBN 1-58765-196-3 (vol. 1 : alk. paper) – ISBN 1-58765-197-1 (vol. 2 : alk. paper) – ISBN 1-58765-198-X (vol. 3 :
alk. paper)
  1. Drama–Bio-bibliography–Dictionaries. 2. Drama–Biography–Dictionaries. 3. Drama–History and criticism–Dictionaries. I. Rollyson, Carl E.
(Carl Edmund) II. Series.
  PN1625.N68 2005
  809.2'003–dc22

                                                                    2004011762

First Printing

PRINTED IN THE UNITED STATES OF AMERICA

Contents – Volume 2

Complete List of Contents

Contents–Volume 1

Contents–Volume 2

Contents—Volume 3

NOTABLE PLAYWRIGHTS

Johann Wolfgang von Goethe

Born: Frankfurt am Main (now in Germany); August 28, 1749
Died: Weimar, Saxe-Weimar-Eisenach (now in Germany); March 22, 1832

Principal drama • *Die Laune des Verliebten*, wr. 1767, pr. 1779, pb. 1806 (*The Wayward Lover*, 1879); *Die Mitschuldigen*, first version wr. 1768, pr. 1780, pb. 1787, second version wr. 1769, pr. 1777 (*The Fellow-Culprits*, 1879); *Götz von Berlichingen mit der eisernen Hand*, pb. 1773, pr. 1774 (*Goetz of Berlichingen, with the Iron Hand*, 1799); *Götter, Helden und Wieland*, pb. 1774; *Clavigo*, pr., pb. 1774 (English translation, 1798, 1897); *Erwin und Elmire*, pr., pb. 1775 (libretto; music by Duchess Anna Amalia of Saxe-Weimar); *Stella*, first version pr., pb. 1776, second version pr. 1806, pb. 1816 (English translation, 1798); *Claudine von Villa Bella*, first version pb. 1776, pr. 1779, second version pb. 1788, pr. 1789 (libretto); *Die Geschwister*, pr. 1776, pb. 1778; *Iphigenie auf Tauris*, first version pr. 1779, pb. 1854, second version pb. 1787, pr. 1800 (*Iphigenia in Tauris*, 1793); *Jery und Bätely*, pr. 1780, pb. 1790 (libretto); *Die Fischerin*, pr., pb. 1782 (libretto; music by Corona Schröter; *The Fisherwoman*, 1899); *Scherz, List und Rache*, pr. 1784, pb. 1790 (libretto); *Der Triumph der Empfindsamkeit*, pb. 1787; *Egmont*, pb. 1788, pr. 1789 (English translation, 1837); *Torquato Tasso*, pb. 1790, pr. 1807 (English translation, 1827); *Faust: Ein Fragment*, pb. 1790 (*Faust: A Fragment*, 1980); *Der Gross-Cophta*, pr., pb. 1792; *Der Bürgergeneral*, pr., pb. 1793; *Was wir bringen*, pr., pb. 1802; *Die natürliche Tochter*, pr. 1803 (*The Natural Daughter*, 1885); *Faust: Eine Tragödie*, pb. 1808, pr. 1829 (*The Tragedy of Faust*, 1823); *Pandora*, pb. 1808; *Die Wette*, wr. 1812, pb. 1837; *Des Epimenides Erwachen*, pb. 1814, pr. 1815; *Faust: Eine Tragödie, zweiter Teil*, pb. 1833, pr. 1854 (*The Tragedy of Faust, Part Two*, 1838)

Other literary forms • Johann Wolfgang von Goethe made substantial contributions to German letters in almost every genre. He is generally recognized as one of the world's greatest lyric poets. Especially important in a vast array of powerful and diverse poems styled in many meters and forms are his *Römische Elegien* (1793; *Roman Elegies*, 1876), the exuberant love lyrics of *Westöstlicher Divan* (1819; *West-Eastern Divan*, 1877), and the magnificent ballads that he created during his association with Friedrich Schiller. With *Die Leiden des jungen Werthers* (1774; *The Sorrows of Young Werther*, 1779), Goethe achieved international fame as a novelist. His most important later narratives, *Wilhelm Meisters Lehrjahre* (1795-1796; *Wilhelm Meister's Apprenticeship*, 1825) and *Wilhelm Meisters Wanderjahre: Oder, Die Entsagenden* (1821, 1829; *Wilhelm Meister's Travels*, 1827), became models for the development of the *Bildungsroman*.

In addition to fiction, Goethe wrote nonfiction throughout his life, and many of his nonfiction works became landmarks of German thought and intellectual expression. The early essay *Von deutscher Baukunst* (1773; *On German Architecture*, 1921) is a key theoretical document of the Sturm und Drang movement. His autobiography, *Aus meinem Leben: Dichtung und Wahrheit* (1811-1814; *The Autobiography of Goethe*, 1824), has special significance in the history of letters for what it reveals of the creative literary process.

Among Goethe's writings, several volumes of scientific and technical treatises, including *Versuch die Metamorphose der Pflanzen zu erklären* (1790; *Essays on the Metamorphosis of Plants*, 1863), *Beyträge zur Optik* (1791, 1792; contributions to optics), and

Zur Farbenlehre (1810; *Theory of Colors*, 1840), were of particular import to Goethe himself. In later life he often regarded them as more meaningful than his literary work. The extensive correspondence with Schiller is only one of many revealing volumes of letters collected and published both during his lifetime and after his death.

(Library of Congress)

Achievements • From the beginning, Johann Wolfgang von Goethe's success as a playwright depended not on his skill in creating drama per se, but rather on the manner in which his works communicated to the audience a sense of history and human experience that emphasized the special individuality of characters and the times in which they lived. The key to his artistic greatness was an unprecedented mastery of language. It gave his writings an intensity, a dynamic power of expression, and a new insight into life that set a pattern for psychological and social plays from Goethe's time forward. Lines and scenes notable for their renewal of the language of antiquity with lightness, grace, naturalness, and eloquently blended rhythms earned for his mature works recognition as pinnacles of musically poetic dramatic literature. Goethe's ability to cast in language timeless universal symbols for the diversity of human experience, achieved especially in his famous masterpiece *The Tragedy of Faust*, elevated him to the stature of a giant of world letters.

The instant overwhelming acclaim for Goethe's *Goetz of Berlichingen, with the Iron Hand* advanced him to the forefront of the Sturm und Drang (literally, "storm and stress") movement and made him its standard-bearer. The propagators of the Sturm und Drang movement, in reaction to the rationalism of the Enlightenment, placed high value on the individual and his power to take moral action despite—and often against—repressive society. Under the tutelage of Johann Gottfried Herder, who was the chief theoretician of Sturm und Drang, Goethe created models that exerted powerful influence on works written for the German stage throughout the nineteenth century.

Despite the attractiveness and intellectual power of their content, characterization, language, and ideas, Goethe's dramas were not immediately successful as theater. They were difficult to stage, and deviations from norms of dramaturgy left weaknesses that stimulated negative response from critics. Nevertheless, guided by Schiller during the decade of their collaboration in Weimar, Goethe eventually rendered his most important works sufficiently playable to win for them a place in the standard repertory of the German stage.

By 1808, Goethe was still most recognized by theatergoers for *Goetz of Berlichingen, with the Iron Hand*. The publication of the first part of *The Tragedy of Faust* together with the production of works revivified by Schiller reestablished Goethe's image with the public. In later years, he enjoyed the status of an internationally renowned figure and received visits from influential people from all over the world. It was not until many years after his death, however, that he surpassed Schiller in popular estimation to assume his position as the man most representative of German literature.

Biography • The early life of Johann Wolfgang von Goethe was shaped by cultivated middle-class and patrician surroundings. An emotionally complex relationship with his sister Cornelia had significant impact on many of his creative works, while the contrasts in temperament and worldview of his parents fostered a rapidly developing awareness of German cultural polarities: northern intellectual and moral intensity and southern artistic sensuousness and sensitivity.

From the autumn of 1765 until serious illness forced him to return home in 1768, Goethe studied law in Leipzig. Stimulated by encounters with popular rococo culture, a love affair with the daughter of an innkeeper, and university exposure to the ideas of Christian Fürchtegott Gellert, Johann Christoph Gottsched, Adam Friedrich Oeser, and Christoph Martin Wieland, he began creating poetry and light pastoral plays that were intended only to be socially entertaining. The poems of *Neue Lieder* (1770; *New Poems*, 1853) are his most important literary accomplishment of this period.

After a slow convalescence in Frankfurt, during which he studied the writings of Susanne von Klettenburg and the natural philosophers Paracelsus von Hohenheim and Emanuel Swedenborg, Goethe entered the university at Strasbourg. Under the influence of Herder, whom he met during the winter of 1770-1771, and other Sturm und Drang figures, the young poet turned away from the cosmopolitan tendencies of Leipzig and declared allegiance to a German gothic ideal. Homer, William Shakespeare, and the Ossian poems of James Macpherson provided the literary models for changes in creative approach that mark Goethe's subsequent writings. On the level of personal experience, his love for the pastor's daughter Friederike Brion informed his best lyrics of the time.

On completion of his studies, Goethe practiced law in Frankfurt. While at the Imperial Chancelry in Wetzlar during the summer of 1772, he fell in love with the fiancée of a friend—a situation that provided the basis for *The Sorrows of Young Werther*. In Frankfurt cultural circles, he became acquainted with Karl August, duke of Weimar; their ensuing friendship shaped the rest of Goethe's life.

The unbearable restrictions of an engagement to a wealthy banker's daughter, Lili Schönemann, caused Goethe to flee to Weimar, where he established his permanent home in 1776. During the next decade two major influences molded his personal and creative existence. Charlotte von Stein, the wife of a court official, taught him social graces, organized his daily routine, and provided him with intellectual stimulation during the course of a lengthy, frustratingly platonic love affair. The continual burden of a variety of official duties in the service of Karl August broadened Goethe's public experience but severely limited his artistic productivity. Neither a patent of nobility, which he received in 1782, nor his scientific studies provided him with the personal fulfillment that his nature demanded.

A hasty departure to Italy in 1786 was in part an escape from the pressures of life in Weimar, in part a search for renewal and rejuvenation as a writer. The two years that Goethe spent in Italy gave him the peace, freedom, and inspiration necessary to complete three of his most important plays, *Iphigenia in Tauris, Egmont*, and *Torquato Tasso*, and to make substantial progress in the writing of *The Tragedy of Faust*. His experiences also yielded substance for significant works of poetry, especially *Roman Elegies* and *Epigramme: Venedig 1790* (1796; *Venetian Epigrams*, 1853). The former collection, however, was also informed by his love for Christiane Vulpius. After his return to Weimar from Italy, she lived with him for many years and bore him several children before he finally married her during the French invasion of 1806.

Goethe's affirmative response to Schiller's invitation to assist him in editing a new journal led to the most productive artistic friendship in the history of German letters. It is impossible to measure the full impact of reciprocal influence of ideas on the development of their poetry, dramas, and prose writings during the decade of their association. In the case of Goethe, neither *The Tragedy of Faust* nor the Wilhelm Meister novels would have attained their ultimate form and stature without Schiller's influence.

After Schiller's death, experience of many kinds contributed substance and essence to Goethe's mature works. The German Romantics stimulated him to a wider view of literature as a world phenomenon. His insatiable curiosity about life abroad led him to new friendships. Late love affairs with Marianne von Willemer and Ulrike von Levetzow moved him to write the most profoundly beautiful love lyrics of his career. In the completion of the second part of *The Tragedy of Faust* during his final years, he culminated his existence in the creation of a grand symbol for a life that saw him become, in the words of Thomas Carlyle, "the universal man."

Analysis • Like his poetry and prose narratives, Johann Wolfgang von Goethe's dramas are powerful documents of personal introspection, evaluation, and interpretation of experience. Even the plays that are based on historical and earlier literary models derive their special character from their reflection of intimate feelings, concerns, passions, and perceptions that informed the author's being. In defining the relationship between his works and his life, Goethe said that everything that he wrote was part of a grand confession. Examination of his creative growth and development, especially as mirrored in his dramatic writings, uncovers the rich and colorful panorama of his personal response to stimuli from people, both contemporaries and influential personalities of the past, directly and vicariously experienced events, traditions, issues, philosophies, cultural and social heritage, ideals, science, and confrontations with self.

The basic characteristics of Goethe's dramaturgy include episodic form, focus on cultural and existential polarities, emphasis on strong and careful characterization more than on the traditional external dramatic conflict and action, treatment of problems related to social and human ideals, and externalization of psychologically complex tensions arising from encounters between the individual and the surrounding world. Well defined in Goethe's earliest successful plays, these features mark especially his theatrical masterpieces and set them apart from works by other playwrights of the time.

Goethe's successful career as a serious creator of dramatic literature did not actually begin until he came under the influence of Herder in Strasbourg. Before then he had experimented with light, undemanding plays written in the popular anacreontic style of the day and comedy in the manner of the classical French theater, but the results had not been very impressive. *The Wayward Lover*, his first pastoral work, is interesting for its revelation of an early command of sensitive, natural, graceful lyricism, yet has little to recommend it as stageworthy. *The Fellow-Culprits*, a comedy reflecting Goethe's intense study of Molière, is a more demanding product of concrete observation of middle-class society, but a certain harshness in the portrayal of acts against law caused it to be rejected in the German theater.

Involvement with Herder and the Sturm und Drang movement in Strasbourg was the first of three major intellectually formative experiences that triggered and gave direction to the most important stages in Goethe's evolution as an internationally known dramatist. Herder introduced him to Shakespeare as a representative of a natural ideal that was preferable to the artificiality of French classicism as a literary model. Shakespeare's approach to history, the realistic content and tragic nature of his art, and his emphasis on situations centered on the personalities of powerful individuals became patterns whose lasting impression is clearly visible in Goethe's most famous plays, from *Goetz of Berlichingen, with the Iron Hand* through the final version of the second part of *The Tragedy of Faust.*

Goethe's special interpretation of Shakespeare's motives and intentions provided him with the timeless dramatic situation that is central, in one guise or another, to all of his best-remembered plays: the conflict between the particular nature of the individual—his specific needs, freedom of will, natural ideals, creative genius—with the demands of the social establishment. In *Goetz of Berlichingen, with the Iron Hand* and the original fragmentary version of *The Tragedy of Faust,* the most significant dramatic products of the Strasbourg influences, a strong element of subjectivity prevails, in that the treatment of this problem of individual freedom corresponds to Goethe's perception of his own struggle between an inner law of creativity and the external order of society's institutions.

By introducing in his Sturm und Drang plays a previously unattained richness and depth of individuality combined with a picture of life as organized around a definite focus, Goethe created a pattern that allowed his subsequent dramas to mature as symbolic and general statements about life. These artistic utterances are at once powerful in what they communicate and weak in traditional theatrical impact. Their great strengths are vivid characters who are alive in language and psychological presence; substantial, captivating situations; colorful scenes with intense representational quality; and effective dramatization of conflicting attitudes and worldviews. In his best plays, these factors outweigh significant weaknesses of plot and a persistent failure to develop dramatic situations to the full.

For more than a decade after the appearance of *Goetz of Berlichingen, with the Iron Hand,* Goethe was unsuccessful in completing any new play of comparable artistic merit. In some cases, potentially powerful projects were left incomplete because of the struggling playwright's inability to master the chosen substance; still other works foundered on their internal weaknesses or on general mediocrity. As Goethe turned away from the influences of Sturm und Drang, he attempted to emulate Gotthold Ephraim Lessing in the development of middle-class tragedy as a viable stage form. In *Clavigo,* he achieved a strong depiction of contemporary bourgeois society, its moods and spiritual attitudes, but could not compete with Lessing in dramatic technique or proper organization and orientation of plot. Like *Clavigo, Stella,* with its elegiac tone and its emphasis on the problems of the inner man, remained a secondary accomplishment in which the author captured social reality without attaining the literary power and originality that made *Goetz of Berlichingen, with the Iron Hand* dynamically appealing. Only in specific manifestations of the writer's facility with language, especially his lyric virtuosity, do any of the completed plays of this period display substantial literary artistry.

The second upswing in Goethe's advancement as a dramatist occurred as a direct consequence of the process of rebirth and reorientation that he experienced in Italy between 1786 and 1788. Specific renewal of his creative approach featured a return to the elaboration of individual characters for their own sake, combined with expansion of the dramatic framework to give it the breadth and reality of history. At the same time, new awareness of models provided by the art of classical antiquity moved him toward strictness of form and organization, simplicity of plot and action, and pure, refined, stylized language. In the resulting completed works, including *Iphigenia in Tauris, Egmont,* and *Torquato Tasso,* the external conflict between individual will and the dominant order of the social whole is subordinated to the ideals of harmonious self-education and self-fulfillment governed by the principles of pure humanism. Action and plot are minimized in favor of portraiture, psychological penetration, and revelation of the central character's internal dilemma in a situation that forces him to confront his own nature.

Following the appearance of a fragmentary version of the first part of *The Tragedy of Faust* in 1790, the quality of Goethe's completed productions again waned. Although the association with Schiller was fruitful in its impact on the technical aspects of his dramaturgy, it did not immediately stimulate the creation of new plays of lasting import. Among the writings completed before Schiller's death, only *The Natural Daughter*—the first part of a planned, unfinished trilogy and the last of four plays in which Goethe came to grips with the phenomenon of the French Revolution—exhibits elements of potential greatness. These are visible especially in its cool, formal perfection; its carefully formed, elevated language; and the richness of its disputation.

Finally, however, Schiller's influence *was* the formative impulse that moved Goethe into his last and greatest period of dramatic-literary achievement. It was Schiller who encouraged him to complete *The Tragedy of Faust,* providing him with ideas and direction that in part enabled him to master seemingly insurmountable problems that had troubled him since he began the project during his Sturm und Drang years.

The two parts of *The Tragedy of Faust,* which Goethe finished in 1808 and 1831 respectively, represent a summation, a synthesis, and a culmination in the development of the most representative characteristics of Goethe's dramatic work. The episodic form that dominates *Goetz of Berlichingen, with the Iron Hand* and *Egmont* is carried to its greatest extreme in *The Tragedy of Faust.* Lyric language and portraiture, the major strengths of earlier works, attain new heights. The standard conflict of the great individual at odds with his social context finds logical resolution in Faust's transformation from a seeker of experience into a man who accepts limited fulfillment in constructive human service.

Goetz of Berlichingen, with the Iron Hand • Exposure to the Sturm und Drang enthusiasm for Shakespeare in Strasbourg caused Goethe to seek out identifiably German material for his plays, comparable to the English national material used by Shakespeare. In the autobiography of Gottfried von Berlichingen, a robber baron of the sixteenth century, Goethe found suitable subject matter which he adapted to his own purposes in *Goetz of Berlichingen, with the Iron Hand,* his first truly successful drama.

The portrayal of Goetz in his role as Sturm und Drang hero—a man of natural genius, a great, free, creative personality—established the pattern for a completely new kind of dramatic literature. *Goetz of Berlichingen, with the Iron Hand* is not a play centered on a tension-filled situation. It is the dramatized chronicle of an entire life. In its abandonment of the traditional unities of time, place, and action; its panorama of disjointed yet often strikingly original scenes; its varied, colorful, vital dialogue; and its natural, vigorous tone, it shattered the barriers of the French classical theatrical heritage and anticipated the ultimate course of Goethe's dramaturgical development.

Central to the play's exposition of Goetz's existence is the confrontation and inevitably destructive conflict between an old, natural, free human order and the artificial institutions of a changing, ever more restrictive society—the opposition between individual will and the unrelenting progress of history. This conflict—couched in the story of Goetz's feud with the bishop of Bamberg, his betrayal by a childhood friend, Weislingen, and his disastrous involvement in the historical backdrop of the peasant wars—serves to convey the tragedy of a man who has outlived his times. He can no longer be the free knight that he once was, because the impersonal political configurations of the dawning era make it impossible. Faced with the necessity to choose between inner collapse resulting from the resignation of freedom, and external destruction as a consequence of maintaining his integrity, Goetz stays true to himself and perishes.

Goethe's major achievement in the writing of *Goetz of Berlichingen, with the Iron Hand* was his success in creating the totality and fullness of a life that is its own reason for being. The lack of an organized thread of action and a uniform plot, often cited as the play's most significant weakness, is more than balanced by the powerful authenticity of the characters, the successful portrayal of a complete social-historical reality, and the new and vital language that changed German theater forever.

Iphigenia in Tauris • During his early Weimar period, Goethe became concerned with the creation of drama on the highest possible artistic level. Proceeding from the perception that only in the patterns and spirit of antiquity can aesthetic perfection be achieved, he sought to create a literary unity that combined beauty of form with a thematic content advocating humanistic idealism. The most important result of this endeavor was *Iphigenia in Tauris*. A prose version of the play was completed and performed in 1779, with Goethe himself playing the role of Orest, but the ultimate recasting in blank verse was not accomplished until 1786, when he went to Italy.

Although based on Euripides' model, *Iphigenia in Tauris* treats the existing elements of legend with a free hand, creating a synthesis of the classical and the modern. Goethe developed the tragic situation of antiquity from the perspective of the eighteenth century, replacing the ancient pagan religious motif with the concept of pure humane action. The central issue is expanded from the limited, localized situation of Euripides' play to the entire history of the family of Tantalus, presented as a symbol for the historical progress of humankind. All the harshness and terror of her ancestors' fate is brought to focus in Iphigenia, who must reexperience and suffer everything, not physically but psychologically.

Like Goetz of Berlichingen, Iphigenia is faced with a moral dilemma. She matures through having to choose between lying, and thereby betraying the trust of Thoas, and telling the truth, thus placing the lives of herself, her brother, and his companion in jeopardy. Her victory over the tragic situation is a direct result of having exercised her own free will to maintain her personal integrity—a choice consistent with Goethe's belief in the inherent goodness of humanity.

Iphigenia in Tauris, like most of Goethe's major dramatic works, is lacking in external action. Its artistic success derives, rather, from masterful lyric language, as well as a penetrating portraiture that reveals the title figure as the focus of a variety of complex themes. The latter include feminine ambition, isolation, evil and guilt, virtue, and humanity as a preserving and exalting force. The play is especially significant for a moral idealism that combines Christian and classical values in glorifying the possibility of absolute human goodness.

Egmont • Although the final version of *Egmont* was completed and first published after *Iphigenia in Tauris*, making it at least technically a product of Goethe's visit to Italy, it is primarily a document of transition from Sturm und Drang to classicism. In many respects it is the least satisfying of the major plays, exhibiting a lack of unity that is partly the result of the fact that it was written piecemeal, in the course of four distinct attempts made in the years 1775, 1778-1779, 1782, and 1787. Unsuccessful integration of surviving Sturm und Drang elements with new elements of classicism renders the presentation spotty and unconvincing, and the extreme emphasis placed on portraiture gives the work a static quality that caused even Schiller to criticize its lack of action. One result of this intensity of characterization is that secondary figures, especially Margaret of Parma, William of Orange, and the duke of Alba, are ironically more realistic, more vividly alive, than the central character.

The main dramatic concerns of *Egmont* are quite similar to those of *Goetz of Berlichingen, with the Iron Hand*. In Egmont, as in Goetz, Goethe intended to present a powerful figure with a will to maintain his personal liberty. Set against the historical background of Spain's tightening political and religious hold on the Netherlands, the conflict is again a confrontation between the individual and a repressive social establishment—in this instance an environment dominated by fanaticism and mistrust of any freedom. To some extent, Egmont is also a Sturm und Drang hero whose behavior is governed by instinct and impulse. The problem is—and this is the critical point— he appears passive because his character is illuminated primarily from outside. The spectator is told of Egmont's achievements, virtues, strengths, and successes, but they are not confirmed directly in what Egmont does within the movement of the play. He fails to act to avert destruction and therefore perishes because of a blind, heedless confidence in himself. For that reason, he comes across as shallow, ordinary, and unworthy of sympathy.

Despite the obvious weaknesses of *Egmont*, the work is important to the development of German drama for several reasons. By transforming the historical Egmont, a middle-aged husband and father, into a youthful, carefree lover, Goethe made of him an original character and broke with the tradition that the playwright could be only the dramaturgical processor of given material. At the same time, Goethe remained faithful to the spirit of the historical record, evoking the era of religious strife with telling details. Finally, by supplementing his historical sources with personal material from his daily routine—as, for example, in certain dialogues that reflect his ministerial experience—Goethe gave the play an unprecedented realism.

Torquato Tasso • Aside from *The Tragedy of Faust*, the most deeply personal play that Goethe wrote was *Torquato Tasso*. It is the only drama in which he attempted to come to grips directly with the polarities and dilemmas of his vocation as a writer. Like *Goetz of Berlichingen, with the Iron Hand* and *Egmont*, *Torquato Tasso* derives its basic substance from the life of a real, historical person, in this case a famous Italian poet of the late Renaissance. In aspects of Tasso's situation at the court of his mentor Alfons II, Goethe saw mirrored the problematic elements of his own life in Weimar—from the frustrating relationship with Charlotte von Stein to the spiritually conflicting demands of his art and his political-social responsibilities. The result was a kind of dramatic confession, a justification of the existence of the artist in which Tasso emerges as a symbol both for Goethe himself and for the poet in general.

Tasso's fate is related to that of earlier Goethean heroes in that it dramatizes the conflict between the will and nature of the individual and the demands and expectations of his or her society. Again, the play features little external action, and the dramatic tension is a function of the central figure's inner being. The title character struggles to become a whole man, one who is at home in both the imaginative world of the poet and the practical, material realm of social intercourse and commitment. His counterpart is Antonio, Alfons's state secretary, a genius of political reality with no meaningful artistic-creative dimension. They become enemies because, as one character observes, nature did not forge them into a single being. As more cultivated, refined versions of Faust and Mephistopheles, they symbolize the existential dichotomy that Goethe perceived as the very essence of his own (and modern humankind's) nature.

In its harmonious interplay of motifs and ideas relating to individual and social behavior, ideals and etiquette, freedom and self-control, *Torquato Tasso* eloquently illuminates timeless principles of moral philosophy. Yet at the same time, the play is deeply and personally human. Its treatment of life's central ethical questions—culture and wisdom, humanism and civilization, idealism and reality—is part of one of the most profoundly moving portrayals of suffering in all German literature. Tasso's final achievement of reconciliation serves to celebrate the vitality of both the physical and the moral person.

The Tragedy of Faust • The two plays that constitute *The Tragedy of Faust* are, as a unit, universally regarded as Goethe's greatest masterpiece and one of the most important artistic accomplishments of world literature. *The Tragedy of Faust* is the poetic-dramatic summation of Goethe's career as a writer and thinker. It is also a powerful, perceptive, intricately modeled, symbolic representation of the vast spectrum of the human condition.

The legend of Faust occupied Goethe's creative attention off and on from his Sturm und Drang years through his old age. The work that finally emerged is both the drama and the product of an entire life. Its two parts are framed and joined in the metaphysical relationship of the human to the divine in a way that justifies the work's portrayal of human progress as a positive process of eternal development.

Part one of *The Tragedy of Faust* is a nontraditional, lyricized Sturm und Drang production, consisting of short, rapidly changing scenes that carry Goethe's early episodic technique to its extreme. The action's focus is Faust the seeker. A pact that the traditional Faust made with the Devil is transformed by Goethe into a wager between the protagonist and a cleverly, cynically human Mephistopheles, with Faust's eternal soul at stake. The essence of the bet is that Mephistopheles may claim Faust's soul if he can fully satisfy Faust's insatiable thirst for new experience. Proceeding from this agreement, the drama unfolds in two intertwined threads of plot: the tragedy of the intellectual who fails to find in knowledge true meaning for his life, and that of Gretchen, the innocent girl whom he destroys through his inability to attain lasting contentment in love.

The central concern of the plot strand that illuminates the main character in his role as scholar is the existential definition of Faust as a symbol for humanity in the modern world. In the first scene that follows the "Prologue in Heaven," the famous opening monologue communicates Faust's frustration at the lack of fulfillment provided by his one-sided search for personal meaning in the acquisition of knowledge for its own sake. Failure to find a satisfactory solution in magic, subsequent contemplation of suicide, and the reawakening of his thirst for life in an almost mystical encounter with Easter and spring are the formative elements of experience that at last generate within him an awareness of the duality of his own nature. In a profound self assessment in the second scene, Faust acknowledges that his soul consists of two opposing parts: one that draws him unrelentingly toward the things of the real, physical world, and another that urges him upward into an ideal, spiritual domain that holds the key to boundless existence. The internal conflict created by these two forces is what motivates him to forge the agreement with Mephistopheles and is the basis for all that follows. It leads him to new avenues of sensation and learning, including sensual, emotional gratification in the love affair with Gretchen, and the attempt to penetrate the secrets of nature through scientific investigations in renewed isolation from the world.

By presenting in the character Faust the concept of polarities within the human spirit, Goethe created the basis for a general interpretation of humankind's being. With the appearance of the two plays, the Faustian man—an individual torn between his simultaneous inclinations toward the real and the ideal sides of life—immediately became a symbol for basic mortal struggle and progress. This symbol had enormous impact on German literature in the works of the most important authors of the nineteenth and twentieth centuries.

Within the first part of *The Tragedy of Faust*, the tragedy of the intellectual serves as a frame for the self-contained, linearly developed Gretchen material. The quest for new experience in the real world leads through a magical restoration of youth to a seeking of satisfaction in the universal experience of love. Faust's seduction of the innocent Gretchen; the resulting deaths of her mother, brother, and baby; Faust's betrayal of their relationship; Gretchen's final insanity; and Faust's failure to find lasting purpose in the alliance are the particulars of a timeless story that lays bare the fundamental psychological and emotional processes that govern the interaction of people.

More important for the general conception of *The Tragedy of Faust* as a whole, however, is the fact that Faust's destructive encounter with Gretchen, with all of its ramifications, has uniquely powerful symbolic value in its representation of a primary, potentially dangerous conflict that tears at the fabric of humanity's social development. Specifically, Faust is the embodiment of cultivated civilization, while Gretchen is the essence of naïve, simple, natural being. The inherent tension between the two abstracts, culture and nature, is for Goethe the nucleus on which is centered the ultimate strain that dominates the internal world of the individual. Faust's meeting with Gretchen and its attendant consequences thus become an admonitory representation of the sacrifice of natural human beings to the growing dominance of culture, and the temporal loss of elemental purity and goodness that can be regained only in the realm of divine absolutes.

The second drama, largely a product of Goethe's old age, is a highly stylized, often weighty, symbolic idea play that is connected to the first part only by the cosmic frame and occasional faint allusion to earlier events. In spite of its five-act form, part 2 is not a unified dramatic work. It, too, consists of self-contained episodes that are often only loosely related to one another. Emphasis is on the mature Faust and his search for existential consummation in the ideal realm of aesthetics, the social context of political manipulation, and the personal achievement of great deeds, symbolized respectively in his liaison with Helen of Troy, his service in the emperor's court, and his final commitment to human service in the winning of land from the sea. Although it appears that Faust loses the wager with Mephistopheles, in that he feels a degree of fulfillment in his land-reclamation project, his ultimate redemption in the final scene of the play conveys the message that as long as people never quit striving, they will in fact achieve the divine destiny of their existence.

Other major works

LONG FICTION: *Die Leiden des jungen Werthers*, 1774 (*The Sorrows of Young Werther*, 1779); *Wilhelm Meisters Lehrjahre*, 1795-1796 (4 volumes; *Wilhelm Meister's Apprenticeship*, 1825); *Die Wahlverwandtschaften*, 1809 (*Elective Affinities*, 1849); *Wilhelm Meisters Wanderjahre: Oder, Die Entsagenden*, 1821, 1829 (2 volumes; *Wilhelm Meister's Travels*, 1827).

SHORT FICTION: *Unterhaltungen deutscher Ausgewanderten*, 1795 (*Conversations of German Emigrants*, 1854); *Novelle*, 1826 (*Novel*, 1837).

POETRY: *Neue Lieder*, 1770 (*New Poems*, 1853); *Sesenheimer Liederbuch*, 1775-1789, 1854 (*Sesenheim Songs*, 1853); *Römische Elegien*, 1793 (*Roman Elegies*, 1876); *Reinecke Fuchs*, 1794 (*Reynard the Fox*, 1855); *Epigramme: Venedig 1790*, 1796 (*Venetian Epigrams*, 1853); *Xenien*, 1796 (with Friedrich Schiller; *Epigrams*, 1853); *Hermann und Dorothea*, 1797 (*Herman and Dorothea*, 1801); *Balladen*, 1798 (with Schiller; *Ballads*, 1853); *Neueste Gedichte*, 1800 (*Newest Poems*, 1853); *Gedichte*, 1812, 1815 (2 volumes; *The Poems of Goethe*, 1853); *Sonette*, 1819 (*Sonnets*, 1853); *Westöstlicher Divan*, 1819 (*West-Eastern Divan*, 1877).

NONFICTION: *Von deutscher Baukunst*, 1773 (*On German Architecture*, 1921); *Versuch die Metamorphose der Pflanzen zu erklären*, 1790 (*Essays on the Metamorphosis of Plants*, 1863); *Beyträge zur Optik*, 1791, 1792 (2 volumes); *Winckelmann und sein Jahrhundert*, 1805; *Zur Farbenlehre*, 1810 (*Theory of Colors*, 1840); *Aus meinem Leben: Dichtung und Wahrheit*, 1811-1814 (3 volumes; *The Autobiography of Goethe*, 1824; better known as *Poetry and Truth from My Own Life*); *Italienische Reise*, 1816, 1817 (2 volumes; *Travels in Italy*, 1883); *Zur Naturwissenschaft überhaupt, besonders zur Morphologie*, 1817, 1824 (2 volumes); *Campagne in Frankreich*, 1792, 1822 (*Campaign in France in the Year 1792*, 1849); *Die Belagerung von Mainz, 1793*, 1822 (*The Siege of Mainz in the Year 1793*, 1849); *Essays on Art*, 1845; *Goethe's Literary Essays*, 1921; *Goethe on Art*, 1980.

MISCELLANEOUS: *Works*, 1848-1890 (14 volumes); *Goethes Werke*, 1887-1919 (133 volumes).

Bibliography

Bishop, Paul, ed. *A Companion to Goethe's "Faust": Parts I and II.* Rochester, N.Y.: Camden House, 2001. This collection of essays covers both parts of Goethe's *The Tragedy of Faust*. Contains essays on the character of Faust and Mephistopheles and on the production of the play. Bibliography and index.

Boyle, Nicholas. *The Poetry of Desire (1749-1790).* Vol. 1 in *Goethe: The Poet and the Age.* New York: Oxford University Press, 1991. The first volume of a projected three-volume biography of Goethe. A monumental scholarly work. Covers the first forty years of Goethe's life, including the writing and publication of his early works.

_____. *Revolution and Renunciation (1790-1803).* Vol. 2 in *Goethe: The Poet and the Age.* New York: Oxford University Press, 2000. This second volume covers only the next thirteen years of Goethe's life. Boyle's extensive discussion of the Wilhelm Meister novels and Goethe's drama *The Tragedy of Faust* is set amid a period of radical political and social change, fallout from the French Revolution.

Boyle, Nicholas, and John Guthrie, eds. *Goethe and the English-Speaking World: Essays from the Cambridge Symposium for His 250th Anniversary.* Rochester, N.Y.: Camden House, 2002. A collection of sixteen papers presented at a September, 1999, symposium at the University of Cambridge discuss Goethe's literary and other achievements. Bibliography and index.

Brough, Neil. *New Perspectives on "Faust": Studies in the Origins and Philosophy of the Faust Theme in the Dramas of Marlowe and Goethe.* New York: Peter Lang, 1994. Brough compares and contrasts the portrayal of the Faust story in the works of Goethe and Christopher Marlowe. Bibliography and index.

Kerry, Paul E. *Enlightenment Thought in the Writings of Goethe: A Contribution to the History of Ideas.* Rochester, N.Y.: Camden House, 2001. A examination of the philosophy that filled Goethe's writings. Bibliography and index.

Swales, Martin, and Erika Swales. *Reading Goethe: A Critical Introduction to the Literary Work.* Rochester, N.Y.: Camden House, 2002. A critical analysis of Goethe's literary output. Bibliography and index.

Wagner, Irmgard. *Critical Approaches to Goethe's Classical Dramas: Iphigenie, Torquato Tasso, and Diet Natürliche Tochter.* Columbia, S.C.: Camden House, 1995. Literary criticism of Goethe's dramas, in particular *Iphigenia in Tauris, Torquato Tasso*, and *The Natural Daughter.* Bibliography and index.

_____. *Goethe.* New York: Twayne, 1999. A basic biography of Goethe that covers his life and works. Bibliography and index.

Williams, John R. *The Life of Goethe: A Critical Biography.* Malden, Mass.: Blackwell Publishers, 1998. A biography of Goethe that presents his life as well as critical analyses of his works. Bibliography and index.

Lowell A. Bangerter

Oliver Goldsmith

Born: Pallas, County Longford(?), Ireland; November 10, 1728 or 1730
Died: London, England; April 4, 1774

Principal drama • *The Good-Natured Man*, pr., pb. 1768; *She Stoops to Conquer: Or, The Mistakes of a Night*, pr., pb. 1773

Other literary forms • Although best remembered as a dramatist, Oliver Goldsmith is also known for his work in several other genres. His only novel, *The Vicar of Wakefield* (1766), the comic and sentimental tale of a village curate's attempts to guide his children through the tribulations of growing up, remains a minor classic. *The Citizen of the World* (1762), a recasting of Charles de Montesquieu's *Lettres Persanes* (1721; *Persian Letters*, 1722), is a collection of fictitious letters, purportedly written by a Chinese philosopher who is living in London, describing English customs and English society from an outsider's point of view.

Goldsmith's poetry was often comic as well (as in his parodies of "An Elegy on the Death of a Mad Dog," of 1766, and "An Elegy on the Glory of Her Sex: Mrs. Mary Blaize," of 1759), but when his sympathies were touched, he produced some creditable serious poems, the most notable of which is *The Deserted Village* (1770), a protest against the economic and social conditions that were forcing a massive shift of the populace from small villages to cities.

Like other eighteenth century authors, Goldsmith earned his living by writing whatever publishers thought would sell: histories of Rome and England, biographical sketches, epilogues for the plays of others, translations, and introductions to the natural sciences as well as plays, novels, and poems. The best modern edition of Goldsmith's varied canon is *The Collected Works of Oliver Goldsmith* (1966), in five volumes, edited by Arthur Friedman for Oxford University Press.

Achievements • Oliver Goldsmith's success rate as a dramatist is virtually unmatched: two plays written, the first very good, the second a masterpiece. Goldsmith was the preeminent English comic dramatist in the period of almost two centuries between William Congreve and Oscar Wilde. Only his contemporary Richard Brinsley Sheridan—who wrote more plays and had better theatrical connections—came close to matching Goldsmith's talent.

The qualities that make *The Good-Natured Man* and *She Stoops to Conquer* wonderful theater are the qualities that mark all Goldsmith's writings: an eye for human foibles, a knack for creating the scene or situation in which such foibles can best display themselves, and a willingness to laugh at folly rather than to be irked by it. Goldsmith expresses his comic vision of human experience in language that induces the reader's continuing attention and seduces the reader's affection.

Goldsmith was a writer who believed that it was his duty to entertain his audience. Like a stage performer, he used every device, trick, and resource that gives pleasure. No reader finds Goldsmith's prose a chore to read; no theatergoer finds his plays too long.

Biography • Tony Lumpkin in *She Stoops to Conquer* is one of those classic ne'er-do-wells in English literature who would rather eat, drink, and play a merry prank than work for a living. Tony may have been Oliver Goldsmith's favorite male character in the play; at the very least, he was a kindred spirit, because the playwright himself had lived a ne'er-do-well's existence before successful authorship brought him some stability and an income, however irregular it may have been.

Goldsmith began life as the second son in the large family of an Anglo-Irish clergyman. What limited wealth the family had was destined to become part of his older brother's inheritance or of the dowry for an older sister who "married above herself"; nothing much was left for Oliver. Goldsmith seems to have been equally slighted by nature: He was a sickly child, badly disfigured by smallpox contracted at age seven, and he was considered dull by his first teachers. From this inauspicious background, it took a number of years for Goldsmith to discover his niche in the world as a writer.

Goldsmith was graduated from Trinity College, Dublin, in 1749, after fitful periods of study that were punctuated by riotous parties and pranks, clashes with administrators, and attempts to run away. Two years later, he applied for ordination in the Church of England, but the red trousers he wore to the interview seem not to have made a favorable impression on the local bishop. Goldsmith's uncle, the Reverend Thomas Contarine, gave him the money to study medicine, first at the University of Edinburgh and then at the University of Leyden, but the fledgling physician preferred to spend the time and money otherwise, wandering the Continent as a tourist. In 1756, when Goldsmith returned to London, he found it hard to support himself. His casual medical knowledge was no help in obtaining a doctor's commission in the Royal Navy (which at the time appointed as "surgeon" almost anyone who could wield a scalpel without self-mutilation). Goldsmith tried teaching, but he proved less disciplined than the young boys he was supposed to instruct.

Not until he began work as a proofreader for novelist-printer Samuel Richardson did Goldsmith find a task that focused his energies. Drawing on his Continental wanderings, the proofreader turned author in 1759 when his *An Enquiry into the Present State of Polite Learning in Europe* was published with some success. His achievement brought Goldsmith freelance assignments from other publishers, and he contributed essays, reviews, and poems to several periodicals. From these, Goldsmith gained popular applause, the recognition of fellow writers, and a modest though unsteady income. The most notable sign of his success was his admission to the Literary Club in the early 1760's. There, Goldsmith dined and conversed with the most prominent London intellectuals, among them the painter Sir Joshua Reynolds, the politician Edmund Burke, the actor David Garrick, and the writer-critic Samuel Johnson. In the Literary Club, Goldsmith found and immersed himself in a sophisticated version of the lively fellowship Tony Lumpkin enjoys at the Three Pigeons Tavern.

Club members helped channel Goldsmith's efforts in new literary directions. When Goldsmith was threatened with arrest for nonpayment of rent, Samuel Johnson sent the unfinished manuscript of *The Vicar of Wakefield* (on which Goldsmith had been working intermittently for several years) to a publisher, who bought it for sixty pounds. Because Goldsmith did not get along with David Garrick, who was manager of the Drury Lane Theatre, Reynolds wrote a letter of recommendation to Garrick on behalf of Goldsmith's recently finished first foray into drama, *The Good-Natured Man*. Though Goldsmith was no doubt eager to become a playwright, with a chance of making hundreds of pounds if his play ran until the third night (which was the performance known as the "author's benefit"), *The Good-Natured Man* was not produced until two years later. Garrick and Goldsmith had argued over revisions and payments; eventually, Goldsmith had to take the play to another theater.

The profits from his first play were enough to provide Goldsmith with new quarters, new furnishings, and several new coats; they also whetted his desire to repeat his success. By 1771, he had finished a second comedy, *She Stoops to Conquer*, which was produced by a recalcitrant theater manager who procrastinated over the production for more than a year until Johnson again intervened. Through his reasoned arguments and bearlike presence, Johnson persuaded the manager to put the play into production, and from the moment it opened on March 15, 1773, it was a huge success. Goldsmith, however, would have only thirteen months left in which to enjoy these financial rewards.

Even after he turned novelist and dramatist, Goldsmith never stopped racing from literary project to literary project. He continued to write essays, biographies, and general histories as well as to compile translations and anthologies. Despite his remarkable output in the last decade of his life, he was never far out of debt. Fortunately, publishers were always eager for his services, because they knew that Goldsmith's name on the title page increased their chances of a brisk sale.

Goldsmith wrote almost until the hour of his death. His last effort was the poem "Retaliation," a verse response to Garrick's epigrammatic remark (that Goldsmith "wrote like an angel, but talk'd like poor Poll"). Goldsmith died on April 4, 1774, the victim of both a fever and the remedy prescribed to cure it.

Analysis • Oliver Goldsmith wrote *The Good-Natured Man* and *She Stoops to Conquer* to spite the prevailing taste in comedy. In an essay written just after he completed the second play, he explained that the comedy of his time, which he called sentimental comedy, was a degeneration of a genre that had been clearly defined since the days of Aristotle. Comedy, Goldsmith lamented, had become a kind of tragedy that sought to influence the audience by appealing to its sympathy.

(Library of Congress)

Sentimental comedy was a dramatic subgenre that developed at the beginning of the eighteenth century. The Restoration comedy of manners, which had delighted audiences with contrasting manners, sharp wordplay, and sexual innuendo, had been attacked by Jeremy Collier and others as immoral.

To save drama, some writers began to make sure that every rake reformed by the fifth act and that sober, sensible lovers got as much attention as witty, scandalous ones. Sir Richard Steele, in the influential *The Conscious Lovers* (pr. 1722), had shown that lovers could be entangled in plots of parental opposition and mistaken identities so complicated that only the playwright could untie the fifth-act knots. Audiences, it seemed, would watch good people suffer through complex but manageable difficulties and would cheer when the protagonists swept all before them. Sentimental comedy was a part of Sensibility, a movement that characterized much literature after 1740. Sensibility invited readers and audiences to prove their humanity by sympathizing with the plight of fictional or dramatic heroes and heroines; it promised that their sympathy would be rewarded because all would work out in the end, leaving viewers with emotions stirred, teased, and satisfied.

In his essay on "laughing comedy," Goldsmith described the typical sentimental play

> in which the virtues of private life are exhibited . . . and the distresses rather than the faults of mankind made our interest. . . . In these plays almost all the characters are good, and exceedingly generous; they are lavish enough of their *tin* money on the stage; and though they want humor, have abundance of sentiment and feeling.

Whatever claim to merit such plays have is reduced by the fact that they—like modern television situation comedies—are too easily written. Goldsmith scoffed that in sentimental comedies, it was enough

> to deck out the hero with a riband, or give the heroine a title; then to put an insipid dialogue, without character or humor into their mouths, give them mighty good hearts, very fine clothes, furnish a new set of scenes, make a pathetic scene or two, with a sprinkling of tender melancholy conversation through the whole. . . .

The essay concludes with a lament on the art of making audiences laugh, an art that Goldsmith thought had disappeared with plays of Sir John Vanbrugh and Colley Cibber at the start of the eighteenth century. Determined to show that whatever delight sentimental comedies gave, laughing comedies gave better, Goldsmith submitted his own two plays as evidence.

Even without the historical interest, many readers still find Goldsmith enjoyable for his prose style and his sense of humor. He is one of the masters of the middle style; his informal, almost conversational prose and his humane and humorous observations of individuals make his work accessible and pleasurable even to those who have never met a lord or made the Grand Tour. Goldsmith's characters and comments are rooted in universal experience.

The Good-Natured Man • *The Good-Natured Man*, which debuted while Hugh Kelly's latest sentimental play, *False Delicacy* (pr. 1768), was dominating theatrical London, teased contemporary taste in two ways. First, Goldsmith created scenes that are ironic, farcical, or witty enough to generate laughter. Second, he delineated—that is, in traditional terms, offered up to ridicule—the folly of a culture hero of the age, the "good-natured man." The good-natured man is the sentimental hero, the one who thinks with his heart rather than his head and who leaps to help solve life's smallest distresses. This generous instinct, Goldsmith's good-natured man discovers, has its limitations: One so inclined to sympathize with others may be in danger of losing himself. The twin purposes of the play—literary and moral—actually work together because the laughter that the play generates makes the lesson easier for the audience to accept.

The Good-Natured Man traces Sir William Honeywood's attempt to test and reform his nephew and heir, whose easy generosity (that is, good nature) has led him into extravagance and foolishness. Sir William's plan is to involve young Honeywood in enough fictitious distresses that he will be jailed for debt. Young Honeywood, then, the uncle reasons, would learn a valuable lesson by seeing which of his friends come to his assistance and which of them have only been taking advantage of his generosity. Sir William willingly admits that his nephew's universal benevolence is "a fault near allied to excellency," but as far as Sir William is concerned, it is still a fault to be corrected.

Sir William's plot is intended to demonstrate the need for the sentimental, good-natured man to be shown his follies, and most of the play's other characters reinforce the same idea. Sir William himself is a not very subtle mouthpiece for the dramatist, ex-postulating precisely and exactly on the hero's mistakes. Honeywood's friend Croaker is the exact opposite of Honeywood; as a man who sees everything gloomily and self-ishly, he lets the audience see the defects of the other extreme. Another friend, Lofty, is a character who counterfeits benevolence (pretending to use influence at court on his friends' behalf) in order to puff himself up in the eyes of the world. Lofty is a conscious pretender, while Honeywood is sincere, but the latter comes to see that "in attempting to please all," he "fed his vanity" as much as Lofty did.

Once Honeywood has been arrested for debt, Sir William is pleased to learn, Miss Richland, a woman of independent fortune and a close friend, has secured his release. Honeywood, however, does not need his uncle's conniving to find himself in difficul-ties. His benevolence, good nature, and sensibility generate other problems, one of the most knotty being his relationship with Miss Richland. Honeywood loves her deeply, but he is content to be only a friend. "Never let me harbour," he proclaims sentimen-tally, "a thought of making her unhappy by a connection with one so unworthy her merits as I am." In addition to being modest about his worth to her, Honeywood fears that he could never please her guardians, Mr. and Mrs. Croaker. Rather than tackle such obstacles directly, as would the witty hero of a Restoration comedy, Honeywood is content to sigh and wring his hands in distress.

Circumstances, however, refuse to let Honeywood remain uninvolved. Honey-wood must watch while Croaker tries to marry his son, Leontine, to Miss Richland, de-spite the fact that Leontine is really in love with Olivia, an orphan whom he has brought to England from France in place of the long-absent sister he was sent to fetch. Honeywood must not only watch Croaker's matchmaking, but he must also intercede for Lofty's wooing of Miss Richland. Lofty, pretending to sentimental friendship, calls on Honeywood to court the young heiress for him. Honeywood is on an emotional rack, stretched between the desire to please a friend and the agony of speaking love in another person's name: "What shall I do! Love, friendship, a hopeless passion, a de-serving friend! . . . to see her in the possession of another! . . . Insupportable! But then to betray a generous, trusting friend!—Worse, worse."

Honeywood's dilemmas are solved in the last two acts by accident and by Sir Wil-liam's intercession. He lends money to Leontine and Olivia that they may elope, but when Croaker intercepts what he thinks is a blackmail letter, Honeywood accidentally sends him after the "blackmailer" to the very inn where the lovers are hiding. Catching his son and "daughter," Croaker praises Honeywood for his help and Leontine damns him for his apparent betrayal. Meanwhile, in speaking to Miss Richland on Lofty's be-half, Honeywood coaxes an admission of love from her. Not realizing that the one she confesses to loving is himself, Honeywood decides that "nothing remains hencefor-ward for me but solitude and repentance."

As the characters gather at the inn for the last act, Sir William sets all to rights on his nephew's behalf. First, he persuades Croaker to accept Olivia as Leontine's bride: She is, Sir William testifies, the daughter of an old acquaintance, of good family, and an or-phan with a fortune. Next, Sir William exposes the pretensions of Lofty so that

Honeywood sees he is no friend. Now that his sentimental dilemma between love and friendship is understood to be no dilemma after all, a pleased but surprised Honeywood receives Miss Richland's hand in marriage. The events have been a lesson for the good-natured man, who closes the play with the promise that "it shall be my study to reserve pity for real distress, my friendship for true merit, and my love for her, who first taught me what it is to be happy."

Goldsmith generates "laughing comedy" in the play by several devices: a farcical scene in which a bailiff and his deputy dress as gentlemen, humorous characters such as Croaker and Lofty whose foibles are played on repeatedly, and dialogue at cross-purposes. Dialogue at cross-purposes is one of Goldsmith's favorite comedic devices, one of several dialogue strategies that had made the Restoration comedy of manners so rich in wit. When characters speak at cross-purposes, they manage to hold what appears to be a logical conversation although each is talking about a different subject. The result is confusion among the characters onstage and delight for the audience, which appreciates the ironic interplay of one attitude with another.

The best of these scenes in *The Good-Natured Man* are Leontine's marriage proposal to Miss Richland in act 1, Honeywood's plea on Lofty's behalf in act 4, and Honeywood's interview with the Croakers in act 4. In the first instance, Leontine twists himself into verbal knots as he tries simultaneously to convince his father that he is making an ardent proposal and to make it lukewarm enough to ensure that Miss Richland will reject it. In the second, Honeywood pleads so eloquently for another that Miss Richland is convinced he speaks for himself. In the third, Honeywood counsels Croaker on how to forgive the eloping lovers—counsel that the old man mistakes for advice on how to treat a blackmailer.

She Stoops to Conquer • What Goldsmith does well in *The Good-Natured Man*, he does brilliantly in *She Stoops to Conquer*. The second play dispenses with the mouthpiece figure of Sir William, offers more entanglements more dexterously resolved, and satirizes sentimental comedy more subtly. *She Stoops to Conquer* has no thesis at all in the usual sense. It is a play that is not *about* something; instead, it is a play that *is* something: a recipe for laughing comedy.

Talking about *She Stoops to Conquer* is somewhat like trying to explain a joke. *She Stoops to Conquer* is an inventory of dramatic tricks for making comedy: juxtaposing high-class and low-class characters, creating farcical situations, putting witty dialogue in the mouths of several characters and having them converse at cross-purposes, establishing several good intriguers to initiate the action, and adding a generous helping of mistaken identities. *She Stoops to Conquer* is one of the purest pieces of entertainment ever written; it stands above its time and historical circumstances to such a degree that it has been a theatrical staple since its first production. To enjoy Goldsmith's comedy, an audience needs no special knowledge or moral perspective; it needs only a willingness to react instinctively to high spirits, confusion, and surprise. The play is a delight for actors as well as audience because all the principal characters are good roles; it is a play for an acting company rather than a vehicle for one or two stars. Although there are two plots, they are so nicely balanced that no audience wishes to see one enhanced at the expense of the other.

Goldsmith manages throughout the play to keep the audience informed of all that occurs while the characters onstage usually act under some mistaken impression. By constantly shifting who-knows-what-about-whom, Goldsmith keeps the plot throttle on "full ahead," the characters in unexpected predicaments, and the audience wide awake. Casting the whole in clever dialogue adds to the delight. In the hands of actors capable of playing the physical comedy broadly, *She Stoops to Conquer* becomes three hours of fast-paced merriment.

So much seems to be occurring simultaneously that *She Stoops to Conquer* is a difficult play to summarize. Perhaps reviewing the *dramatis personae* and sketching the action of the two plots best reveals Goldsmith's dexterity at introducing contrasting parts while keeping the whole moving forward. This dramatist is a theatrical juggler of rare skill; once set into motion, no character, action, or situation falls from his hand.

"The mistakes of a night" occur at the country residence of Mr. and Mrs. Hardcastle, a mismatched couple, each of whom is married for a second time. Mr. Hardcastle loves the country and its old-fashioned ways; Mrs. Hardcastle yearns for the city and the latest styles. Like another literary couple grown accustomed to each other's hobbyhorses, Mr. and Mrs. Bennet in Jane Austen's *Pride and Prejudice* (1813), each Hardcastle takes an independent path while poking fun at the spouse's preference.

Living at the Hardcastle residence are three young persons on the verge of independence and love. First, there is Tony Lumpkin, Mrs. Hardcastle's son by her first marriage. He is about to turn twenty-one and come into his own estate. Mr. Hardcastle regards him as a lazy and useless child, while Mrs. Hardcastle dotes on him, one minute sure he has the makings of a scholar and the next worried that he is consumptive. Tony prefers to ignore both parents and to concentrate on drinking and singing at his favorite tavern, the Three Pigeons. Here he entertains his fellows with practical jokes and lyrics that make clear his values:

> Let schoolmasters puzzle their brain
> With grammar, and nonsense, and learning;
> Good liquor, I stoutly maintain,
> Gives genius a better discerning.

Tony, the alehouse hero, is rather a bold protagonist for Goldsmith to portray to audiences accustomed to central male characters dressed in fine linen and attentive to providing themselves with life's essentials: a pretty wife and a sufficient income.

The second resident is Constance Neville, Mrs. Hardcastle's orphaned niece. Constance is treated with as much restraint as Tony is indulged. She is eager to marry George Hastings but cannot, because her dowry, a substantial sum in jewels, is closely kept by her aunt. Mrs. Hardcastle is reluctant to give the jewels into Constance's care because she hopes to force her niece to marry Tony. Mrs. Hardcastle's matchmaking is having no luck: The sober Constance and the lighthearted Tony thoroughly dislike each other. Constance is a typical dramatic heroine of the time: pleasant but not especially bright, rich but without control of her fortune, and restless but not very disobedient.

The third person is Kate, Hardcastle's daughter by his first marriage. She and her father get along much better than do mother and son or aunt and niece. They are honestly affectionate with each other and speak frankly to each other; they care enough for each other to indulge each other's preferences. Kate, for example, who shares her stepmother's interest in fashion, moderates her indulgence by dressing for one half of the day in current styles and the other half in a plain country style that pleases her father. Mr. Hardcastle, in turn, has allowed Charles Marlow, the son of an old friend, to become Kate's suitor only after knowing that he is financially sound, handsome, and modestly spirited. As the play begins, Kate anxiously awaits her first look at this prospecting and prospective husband.

When young Marlow and Hastings (the man Constance loves) arrive at the Hard-castle house, they mistakenly believe that they are at a public inn. This false impression is entirely Tony's fault. Tony recognizes the two London beaux when they stop to ask for directions at the Three Pigeons. Irritated by their affected manners, desirous of playing a trick on his stepfather, and anticipating no consequences but a solid embarrassment, Tony directs them to his stepfather's house, telling them that he is sending them to the best inn of the neighborhood. This first mistake of the night begins a series of events that will turn the household topsy-turvy.

Expecting the modest young men described by his old friend Sir Charles Marlow, Hardcastle greets the two weary travelers generously and familiarly. Surprised at the supposed innkeeper's behavior, Marlow and Hastings react with hauteur and sarcasm. To Hardcastle's every offer of hospitality, they respond with increased demands. This scene (act 2, scene 1) is a classic instance of Goldsmith's spectacular handling of dialogue at cross-purposes.

Soon afterward, Hastings encounters Constance and learns how Tony has deceived him and Marlow. The reunited lovers plan to elope as soon as Constance can gain possession of her jewels; to protect their plot, they decide to keep Marlow in the dark about where he is. They introduce him to Miss Hardcastle as if she had just alighted at the inn. Throughout the play these two couples will maintain distinct characteristics. Constance and Hastings, whose mutual affection is a given, will struggle against external obstacles; Marlow and Kate, having just met, will try to discover what mutual affection, if any, exists between them.

Kate is eager to meet the man who has come to court her. In a complete reversal of the bold, brash character that he showed to Mr. Hardcastle, Marlow becomes shy and stuttering in Miss Hardcastle's presence. It seems that proper young ladies of rank intimidate Marlow with their genteel and sentimental conversation. He bumbles his way through a conversation, saved only by Kate's promptings:

> MISS HARDCASTLE: You were going to observe, Sir—
>
> MARLOW: I was observing, Madam—I protest, madam, I forget what I was going to observe.
>
> MISS HARDCASTLE: . . . You were observing, sir, that in this age of hypocrisy—something about hypocrisy, sir.
>
> MARLOW: Yes, madam. In this age of hypocrisy, there are few who upon strict inquiry do not a-a-a-
>
> MISS HARDCASTLE: I understand you perfectly, sir.
>
> MARLOW (*aside*): Egad! and that's more than I do myself.
>
> MISS HARDCASTLE: You mean that in this hypocritical age there are few that do not condemn in public what they practise in private, and think they pay every debt to virtue when they praise it.

While Constance enlists Tony's help to get the jewels from his mother and thus free both of them from her matchmaking, Kate and Mr. Hardcastle try to decide who is the real Marlow: the overbearing puppy who insulted his host or the tongue-tied dandy who courted the daughter? The mystery begins to clear a little when Kate, now wearing her plain country dress, meets Marlow a second time. The young man makes his second mistake of the night. Not recognizing Miss Hardcastle in what appears to be a barmaid's outfit, Marlow is immediately and frankly attracted to the pretty servant. He proves not shy at all in the presence of lower-class women. With them he can wittily compliment, flirt, and steal a kiss. When Mr. Hardcastle sees Kate receiving this impudent attention, he is ready to order Marlow from his house. Kate, however, having seen what a charming wooer the young man can be, protests that this is the same modest man she interviewed earlier. She asks her father for the chance to show Marlow's real character; he begins to wonder if the usually sensible Kate is not now afflicted by that same malady that makes all young people undecipherable by their elders. At a second interview, Marlow begins to fall in love with the girl he assumes to be a household servant.

For one frantic moment the two plots intertwine before going separate ways. Tony filches Constance's jewels from his mother's bureau and gives them to Hastings. To get them out of sight, Hastings hands the jewels to Marlow. Thinking that such valuable gems must not lie around unguarded, Marlow gives them to Mrs. Hardcastle for safekeeping. Mrs. Hardcastle, alerted by the odyssey of the jewels that something is afoot, is quickly suspicious when her illiterate Tony receives a letter. Neither Constance's extemporaneous excuses nor Tony's obstinacy can prevent Mrs. Hardcastle from snatching the letter and discovering instructions from Hastings about the elopement. Determined to frustrate her niece and Hastings, Mrs. Hardcastle orders her carriage made ready for a trip to London: Constance is going to be taken where she can be better watched.

Thus, by the end of act 4, Goldsmith has every character's fate up in the air. The dramatist who knotted things into such a delightful tangle, however, has enough legerdemain to unravel the confusion. Goldsmith will not have to step in to rescue the characters: Kate by her stooping and Tony by his prankstering will set all to rights.

Kate has quite a tangle to undo: first, her father's impression that Marlow is a rude guest and an inconsiderate lover; second, Sir Charles's fear that the son he thought to be honest and modest is really the lout that Hardcastle has described and an indifferent lover to his friend's daughter; third, Marlow's belief that he can be gallant in the pantry but must act standoffish in the parlor. She accomplishes all three ends by having the fathers witness the third interview of Kate the maid and Marlow. He professes his love for her—and learns to his shock that he has wooed the redoubtable Miss Hardcastle as well as the pliant Kate.

Meanwhile Tony has been frustrating his mother's flight to London. In the darkness, he has led her carriage on repeated rounds of the estate before driving it into a pond; Mrs. Hardcastle is convinced that she is stranded "forty miles from home." Determined to torment her further, Tony leads his mother into a gloomy thicket where even Mr. Hardcastle, out for a walk in his yard, may look like something more sinister. Although Tony's prank is soon exposed, he at least has had the pleasure of exhausting his mother.

Tony has exhausted the eloping lovers as well. Constance and Hastings decide it will be easier to talk Mrs. Hardcastle into compliance than to escape her this evening. All the cold and sore wanderers in the night return to the house and find Kate and Marlow engaged while the fathers stand beaming. When Mrs. Hardcastle threatens revenge on Tony and Constance, Mr. Hardcastle breaks another surprising bit of news: Tony has already reached the age of majority. The Hardcastles had kept this fact secret to keep the irresponsible Tony from squandering his inheritance, but Mr. Hardcastle now resents his wife's misuse of her authority. Tony's first act as an independent gentleman is to renounce any claim to Constance. George Hastings quickly grabs the marriageable hand that Tony surrenders. Everyone except Mrs. Hardcastle now sees that the mistakes of a night have turned out happily indeed.

Even this account of the play omits some of its brighter moments: Hardcastle's amusingly futile efforts to turn rough farm laborers into stylish drawing-room valets, the rousing but innocent debauchery of Tony's friends at Three Pigeons, and Kate's dumb-show wooing that quickly heals Marlow's embarrassment after his mistakes were revealed. Actually nothing but reading or viewing can give a complete idea of the brilliance of *She Stoops to Conquer.* It is a rare play, in which no situation is unexploited, no detail wrong, and no word wasted.

Other major works

LONG FICTION: *The Vicar of Wakefield,* 1766.

SHORT FICTION: *The Citizen of the World,* 1762 (collection of fictional letters first published in *The Public Ledger,* 1760-1761).

POETRY: "An Elegy on the Glory of Her Sex: Mrs. Mary Blaize," 1759; "The Logicians Refuted," 1759; *The Traveller: Or, A Prospect of Society,* 1764; "Edwin and Angelina," 1765; "An Elegy on the Death of a Mad Dog," 1766; *The Deserted Village,* 1770; "Threnodia Augustalis," 1772; "Retaliation," 1774; "The Captivity: An Oratoria," 1820 (wr. 1764).

NONFICTION: *An Enquiry into the Present State of Polite Learning in Europe,* 1759; *The Bee,* 1759 (essays); *The Life of Richard Nash of Bath,* 1762; *A History of England in a Series of Letters from a Nobleman to His Son,* 1764 (2 volumes); *Life of Henry St. John, Lord Viscount Bolingbroke,* 1770; *Life of Thomas Parnell,* 1770; *An History of the Earth, and Animated Nature,* 1774 (8 volumes; unfinished).

MISCELLANEOUS: *The Collected Works of Oliver Goldsmith,* 1966 (5 volumes; Arthur Friedman, editor).

Bibliography

Bloom, Harold, ed. *Oliver Goldsmith.* New York: Chelsea House, 1988. A collection of essays of literary criticism on Goldsmith's writings. Bibliography and index.

Dixon, Peter. *Oliver Goldsmith Revisited.* Boston: Twayne, 1991. A basic biography of Goldsmith that provides coverage of his life and critical analysis of his works. Bibliography and index.

Lucy, Seán, ed. *Goldsmith, the Gentle Master.* Cork, Ireland: Cork University Press, 1984. A group of lectures on Goldsmith that discuss his literary works. Bibliography and index.

Pathania, B. S. *Goldsmith and Sentimental Comedy.* New Delhi, India: Prestige Books, 1988. A study of Goldsmith that focuses on his plays and their relation to sentimental comedy. Bibliography.

Swarbrick, Andrew, ed. *The Art of Oliver Goldsmith.* Totowa, N.J.: Barnes and Noble Books, 1984. This insightful series of essays on Goldsmith's works attempts to restore serious critical attention to those classics created by Goldsmith as well as the certain areas of his life and work previously disregarded. Balances literary criticism with studies of more general aspects of the author, such as his political inclinations, his classical inheritance, his place within certain eighteenth century literary traditions, and his lack of originality. Chronological table.

Worth, Katharine. *Sheridan and Goldsmith.* New York: St. Martin's Press, 1992. Worth compares and contrasts the lives and works of Goldsmith and Richard Brinsley Sheridan. Bibliography and index.

Robert M. Otten,
updated by Genevieve Slomski

Simon Gray

Born: Hayling Island, England; October 21, 1936

Principal drama • *Wise Child,* pr. 1967, pb. 1968; *Spoiled,* pr. 1968 (televised) pr. 1970 (staged), pb. 1971; *Dutch Uncle,* pr., pb. 1969; *The Idiot,* pr. 1970, pb. 1971 (adaptation of Fyodor Dostoevski's novel); *Butley,* pr., pb. 1971; *Dog Days,* pr. 1975, pb. 1976; *Otherwise Engaged,* pr., pb. 1975; *Molly,* pr. 1977, pb. 1978 (revision of Gray's television play *Death of a Teddy Bear*); *The Rear Column,* pr., pb. 1978; *Close of Play,* pr., pb. 1979; *Stage Struck,* pr., pb. 1979; *Quartermaine's Terms,* pr., pb. 1981; *Tartuffe,* pr. 1982, pb. 1990 (adaptation of Molière's play); *The Common Pursuit,* pr., pb. 1984; *Otherwise Engaged and Other Plays,* pb. 1984; *The Rear Column and Other Plays,* pb. 1985; *Plays: One,* pb. 1986; *Melon,* pr., pb. 1987 (revised as *The Holy Terror,* pr. 1989 [radio play], pb. 1990, pr. 1991 [staged]); *Hidden Laughter,* pr. 1989, pb. 1990; *The Definitive Simon Gray,* pb. 1992-1994 (4 volumes); *Cell Mates,* pr., pb. 1995; *Simply Disconnected,* pr., pb. 1996; *Just the Three of Us,* pr. 1997, pb. 1999; *Life Support,* pr., pb. 1997; *The Late Middle Classes,* pr., pb. 1999; *Japes,* pr., pb. 2000

Other literary forms • Simon Gray is primarily known as a stage dramatist, but he began his playwriting career as an author of television scripts, including *The Caramel Crisis* (1966), *Death of a Teddy Bear* (1967), *A Way with the Ladies* (1967), *Sleeping Dog* (1967), *Pig in a Poke* (1969), *The Dirt on Lucy Lane* (1969), *Style of the Countess* (1970), *The Princess* (1970), and *Man in a Sidecar* (1971).

Besides being a successful dramatist, Gray has also published novels: *Colmain* (1963), *Simple People* (1965), *Little Portia* (1967), *A Comeback for Stark* (1968; under the pseudonym Hamish Reade), and *Breaking Hearts* (1997). Gray has also used the pen name James Holliday. Gray became editor of *Delta* magazine in 1964, and he coedited with Keith Walker an anthology entitled *Selected English Prose* that was published in 1967.

In 1975, the playwright wrote the screenplay version of his play for the film *Butley,* directed by Harold Pinter and starring Alan Bates, re-creating his stage role as the title character. The movie was made as part of the American Film Theatre series.

Achievements • Simon Gray has received many of the highest awards for dramatists. *Death of a Teddy Bear* won a Writers Guild Award, *Butley* received the *Evening Standard* (London) Award for Best Play of the Year in 1972, and *Otherwise Engaged* was voted Best Play by the New York Drama Critics Circle. Moreover, the filming of *Butley* and the option taken to film *Death of a Teddy Bear* are indicators of the dramatist's popularity.

Biography • Simon Gray was born on Hayling Island, Hampshire, England, on October 21, 1936, the son of James Davidson and Barbara Celia Mary (née Holliday) Gray. The elder Gray was a pathologist and first-generation Canadian of Scottish ancestry, and when World War II began, Simon Gray was sent from Great Britain to his grandparents' home in Montreal. He returned to the United Kingdom for a while after the war and then moved back and forth between England, Canada, France, and Spain. He married Beryl Mary Kevern, a picture researcher, on August 20, 1964, and they had a son and a daughter. The couple divorced, and in 1997, Gray married Victoria Roth-schild. He has had bouts with cancer and alcoholism. He became a recovering alco-holic in 1996, when alcoholism killed his younger brother, Piers, at the age of forty-nine. This experience shows up in his plays, most particularly in *Japes*.

Gray, a lecturer in English, taught at Trinity College, Cambridge, from 1965 through 1966 and was on the faculty at Queen Mary College of the University of Lon-don from 1965 to 1984. This experience, together with his educational background, serves as the source of many of the dramatist's subjects (and characters) and his literate style. He attended the Westminster School in London, and he received a B.A. (honors in English) from Dalhousie University in Canada in 1958, and another B.A. (again with honors in English) from Cambridge University in England in 1962. Between the awarding of his two bachelor's degrees, Gray served as a lecturer at the University in Clermont-Ferrand, France. He resided in France from 1960 to 1961 and in Spain from 1962 to 1963.

In 1987, Gray's play *Melon* was produced in London, and that same year saw the production of his screenplay *A Month in the Country*. *Hidden Laughter* was produced in Brighton in 1989, and in London a year later. *The Holy Terror*, a revision of *Melon*, was broadcast in 1989 on the British Broadcasting Corporation's radio and was published in 1990. The 1991 Arizona production was its premiere as a stage piece.

Analysis • Two important elements in Simon Gray's playwriting career evolved di-rectly from his educational background. The Cambridge experience was clearly an im-portant one. In a sense, when Gray reports, "I went to university when I was seventeen and I never left," he is speaking metaphorically as well as literally. His postgraduate life has been spent in academia, but it is obvious that there are symbolic connections with his everyday life that reappear in his plays. During Gray's tenure at Cambridge, there was an extraordinarily gifted group of other students also in attendance. The intellec-tual atmosphere was stimulating; a number of undergraduates wrote and acted in satiric revues on campus and then moved on to the London stage immediately afterward (and sometimes even while still pursuing their studies). Peter Cook, a contributor to the im-mensely successful *Beyond the Fringe* (1959), was one such. Novelist Margaret Drabble, television personality David Frost, actor Derek Jacobi, and Christopher Booker, a cofounder of *Private Eye* magazine, were among Gray's contemporaries. Furthermore, director John Barton was a don at King's College and poet Sylvia Plath lived in the town of Cambridge.

Besides the literary climate of the present and the long line of literati connected with the university in the past, Gray was also exposed to literary and dramatic tradi-tions in his course work. Many of his characters, settings, and plot situations derive from this aspect of his life. The numerous literary allusions that are characteristic of his style are direct outgrowths of Gray's Cambridge experience. Finally, the many refer-ences to Cambridge, typically related to the concept of class distinctions, are similarly attributable to this period in his life.

The second element is Gray's experience as a teacher. A number of the aspects of his writing that can be traced to his university days extend to his professional career as well; the origins of several of Gray's dramatic works reflect the attitude of an academic mind.

Unlike many contemporary playwrights who began writing dramas while in col-lege, Gray actually became a dramatist as a young man after he was graduated and while he was trying to write short stories and novels. He had already published two prose volumes, *Colmain* in 1963 and *Simple People* in 1965, when he adapted a short story that was primarily dialogue and sold it as a television script. The piece, entitled *The Caramel Crisis*, was televised in 1966, and within a year *Death of a Teddy Bear*, *A Way with the Ladies*, and *Sleeping Dog* were also televised. *Death of a Teddy Bear* was an award-winning script, and *Sleeping Dog* was well received for its examination of the elements of domination and submission in the British national character (represented by Sir Herbert, a retired colonial administrator, who imprisons Claud, a black homosexual, in the basement of his manor house—the theme of ambiguous sexuality is also introduced).

Gray's plays are interesting, witty, and well structured, and his characters are believably drawn. Furthermore, he uses language well, and it is clear that the use of language in his later works has been influenced by Harold Pinter's dramaturgy, improving an already good product. If Gray's plays lack profound timely significance, they nevertheless excel in stagecraft and technique, and his works have entertained audiences at home in England and abroad. He does not contend that his plays are meant to convey a message, but he does work at his writing rigorously; *Otherwise Engaged*, for example, required thirty-five drafts. Combining this attention to craftsmanship with a flair for witty dialogue, Gray has achieved both critical acclaim and popular acceptance.

Gray has had his difficulties with the theater establishment, despite the abiding commitment that director Pinter and actor Bates have invested in his work. He documents these difficulties in books such as *Fat Chance* (1995), which chronicles his exasperating experience with his play *Cell Mates* when the star actor, Stephen Fry, walked off the cast after the first week of its run in the West End and doomed the play just as it was gaining momentum. In 2001, he published *Enter a Fox*, which details the journey and problems associated with the production of his play *The Late Middle Classes*, killed in out-of-town tryouts. Gray speaks of *Japes*, produced in 2000, as perhaps his last play. He has always moved on to a new play before, but, he says, the drive seems to have gone out of him. Beyond such difficulties, Gray's commitment to a theater rich in language, realistic in style, and highly structured in linear fashion runs counter to trends of the last decades of the twentieth century. Nevertheless, his characters are stunningly spectacular. They are riveting and memorable because of their obsessions, their abuse of one another, their wit, and ultimately their own self-destructive natures.

Wise Child • *Wise Child* was written for television, too, but it was reportedly considered "too bizarre for home viewing," and it became Gray's first play to be staged in the theater (at the Wyndham on October 10, 1967). The play is usually considered Gray's best early effort, and it has been favorably compared with the work of Joe Orton. The plot revolves around a criminal who is wanted for a brutal mail robbery and is hiding from the police by disguising himself as a woman (creating a sort of black comedy version of Brandon Thomas's 1896 farce *Charley's Aunt*) while his accomplice poses as his son. After the pair murder their homosexual landlord, the older man reverts to wearing men's clothing, and the younger man dons the maid's clothes. Gray was fortunate that one of the finest actors of all time, Sir Alec Guinness, took the lead role. The "son's" part was played by Simon Ward, who would appear in later plays by Gray. Harold Hobson, drama critic for the London *Sunday Times*, was impressed by the piece.

Dutch Uncle • *Dutch Uncle* followed *Wise Child* and was considerably less successful. Mounted by the Royal Shakespeare Company at the Old Vic in London, the drama shows the academic turn of mind characteristic of Gray's later works. The play was inspired by the case of police constable Reginald Christie, a mass murderer who did away with his wife, the wife of his upstairs lodger, and several other women. (Christie walled up the corpses in his kitchen. Gray's play *Death of a Teddy Bear*, written a few years earlier, was similarly based on an actual murder case.)

In *Dutch Uncle*, the main character, Mr. Godboy, tries to murder his wife to attract the attention of Inspector "Manly" Hawkins. His motivation is a homosexual obsession for the police officer. Unfortunately for Godboy, he proves ineffectual as a murderer—his wife blissfully and unknowingly avoids his trap—and when the inspector finally becomes interested in the household, it is because the upstairs tenant is the Merritt Street rapist. The play was not well received, and Gray himself described it as a failure "as witless as it was macabre. . . . [It] would goad an audience into an irritated restlessness." He goes on to claim that the London opening was "the worst night in the British theatre." Nevertheless, the husband's distaste for his role as a husband and the dramatist's exploration of the themes of domination and submission (also dealt with in *Wise Child*) mark the play as a contemporary work. It was probably these elements that attracted Harold Pinter to Gray's work.

Spoiled • Next came *Spoiled*, a realistic domestic drama that was televised in 1968 and adapted for the stage in 1970. The play, which premiered at the Close Theatre Club in Glasgow, Scotland, on February 4, moved to London's Haymarket Theatre on October 31 of the following year. It is about the relationships among a high school French instructor, his pregnant wife, and a young male student. While tutoring the teenager, the teacher seduces him, and the play evolves into a straightforward study of the "unthinking abuse of trust and power." *Spoiled* also serves as a companion piece to *Butley*; both plays involve student-teacher relationships in an academic setting as well as failed marriages and homosexual activities. There are also some parallels with *Otherwise Engaged*. In contrast with the latter play, however, in which Simon Hench is too detached to be able to maintain a human relationship, Howarth, the teacher in *Spoiled*, falls tragically because he is too emotionally involved.

Butley • *Butley*, one of Gray's most successful dramas, premiered at the Oxford Playhouse on July 7, 1971, and then moved to the Criterion Theatre in London exactly one week later. The first of Gray's works to be directed by Pinter, it starred Alan Bates in the title role. Subsequently the play moved to the Morosco Theatre in New York City, on October 31, 1972.

All the action in the two-act play takes place in Ben Butley's office in a college of London University. Act 1 opens at ten o'clock in the morning on the first day after the midterm break, and the second act begins about two hours later, "shortly after lunch."

Butley is an English teacher at the university. He shares an office with Joseph Keyston, whom he calls Joey. Joey is also an English instructor, a former student of Butley and his current lover.

From the play's beginning, it is clear what kind of person Butley is—even the office set reflects the nature of his mind. His desk, for example, "is a chaos of papers, books, detritus" in contrast to Joey's neat, almost bare desk. Similarly, Butley's bookcase is "chaotic with old essays and mimeographed sheets scattered among the books." Butley's attitude toward his profession is certainly evident, as is the unsettled state of his mind. The photograph of T. S. Eliot indicates the kind of literature that interests Butley and is a visual reference to the source of some of the literary allusions that embellish Butley's conversations. The smeared and curled corner shows that what was once important enough to Butley that he put it on his wall no longer has his attention and has become damaged (and not repaired) as a result. The lamp that will not work for Butley is further evidence of the lack of connections in his life, the way that things no longer work for him.

Butley's egocentrism and the tactics that he uses to isolate himself from others and from his responsibilities are evident in his very first speech. He tells the head of his department, who has called him on the telephone, that he cannot talk at the moment because he is "right in the middle of a tutorial"—and all the while the audience can plainly see that Butley is sitting alone in his office. In a sense, there is dramatic irony involved here, too, and not only because the audience is aware of something that one of the characters (the caller, in this case) is not.

Throughout the play, people try to get in touch with Butley, and he rejects their attempts; he constantly uses the false tutorial excuse to avoid contact. The comic touch of Butley taking a squashed banana from his pocket and throwing the peel on Joey's desk seems to lighten the effect of Butley's lie, but it soon becomes evident that this is merely another indication of Butley's sloppy habits, his lack of consideration for others, and his conscious attempts to belittle everyone. The piece of toilet paper stuck to his chin to stop the blood from a cut sustained while he was shaving is a parallel to the banana. Obviously Butley does not demonstrate much respect for himself, and he shows even less for those with whom he comes in contact.

In the first act, Gray introduces most of the rest of the characters who play major parts in the protagonist's life. In essence, there is no action and no traditional plot. Joey appears first, and through his conversation with Butley, the various levels of their relationship are exposed, as is Butley's estrangement from his wife and the possibility that Butley is about to be replaced in Joey's life by Reg Nuttall.

The word games, wit, literary allusions (often in the form of direct quotations), and cruelty that characterize Butley are also revealed. Butley emerges as a sad, lonely man who wants some sort of relationship with someone, preferably Joey, but who is unable to give enough of himself or accept enough from anyone else to allow them to penetrate his sarcasm to create a truly emotional relationship. Instead, Butley retreats behind a wall of sterile intellectualism.

Miss Heasman, a minor character, makes an appearance, serving as a bit of comic relief (and creating dramatic irony) when Butley purposely misunderstands her request and then lies about her duties (the audience already knows about his treatment of a student with a similar request previously). There is also a confrontation between Butley and his wife, who informs him that she has decided to take up with an acquaintance of theirs.

In his dealings with all of these people, Butley is consistently sarcastic and offensive, he knows where his victims are most vulnerable, and he sticks the knife in with sadistic pleasure and precision. He jokes about homosexuality, frequently by using double entendres or literary allusions. Other literary allusions (to Eliot, William Blake, Gerard Manley Hopkins, and others) provide further insight into Butley's character (unwittingly on his part), as he uses them as weapons. Butley's use of literary allusions is effective because the other characters in the play recognize their sources; this is an essential part of his game playing.

Also indicated is the probability that patterns are being repeated, implying that they have all engaged in the activity before—and this is reinforced by Butley's expressed appreciation for good comebacks by his targets. One of the games that he plays revolves around Joey's constant use of the tag "in point of fact." When Joey says that Reg's family lives "in a place just outside Leeds, in point of fact," Butley pretends that he thinks that "point of fact" is the name of a suburb. This becomes a running joke in the play and serves a dual purpose by simultaneously drawing attention to Reg's lower-middle-class background. Butley also prepares the audience for the situation concerning Gardner.

In act 2, the only major character not met in act 1 appears when Reg comes to collect Joey (and, incidentally, to make sure that Butley does not adversely influence the younger man's decision to leave). Beyond this, about all that happens is a continuation of the lines self-destructively developed by Butley, leaving him as he was when he first came onstage—alone and ineffectually trying to turn on the lamp. Butley's nonstop allusions (to Eliot, nursery rhymes, John Donne, D. H. Lawrence, John Milton, Sir John Suckling, Richard Lovelace, and Beatrix Potter, among others), his use of a northern dialect to denigrate Reg's social background—all of this epitomizes his hollowness.

In her essay, Sophia B. Blaydes discusses this important aspect of the writer's technique and demonstrates how the allusions may provide insight into Butley's self-image as an individual "beset by betrayal and mediocrity," a tragic figure rather than the pitiable, "irresponsible, wasted man" that the characters in the play perceive him to be. The truth probably lies somewhere between: Butley is, indeed, surrounded by foolish people, but he cannot see beyond their flaws to their common humanity.

Otherwise Engaged • *Otherwise Engaged*, also directed by Pinter and featuring Bates in the part of Simon Hench, was first presented at London's Queen's Theatre on July 30, 1975. In February, 1977, the production was transferred to the Plymouth Theatre in New York City, with Tom Courtenay making his long-awaited Broadway debut in the lead role.

The setting for *Otherwise Engaged* is more elegant than that of *Butley*. As in the earlier play, the action is limited to the events that transpire in one room, in this instance over a period of time equivalent to the running time of the drama. That room is Hench's living room in London. The plot has been described as the depiction of a series of events that occur during an afternoon that Hench wishes to spend listening to a newly acquired phonograph recording of Richard Wagner's opera *Parsifal* and that prevent him from accomplishing his goal; however, this is a bit like saying that *Butley* is about a teacher who is not interested in teaching.

In act 1, Hench, a book publisher, is discovered preparing to listen to his new purchase. He is interrupted by Dave, a dull polytechnic student who is renting a flat from him. This is only the first of a series of interruptions. Hench no sooner gets rid of the young man, who is seeking advice on his love life and money, than Hench's brother, Stephen, enters to expose fears and self-doubts about his professional status. Hench is witty, sociable, and somewhat supportive, but his rather obvious wish is to return to his recording. This pattern is repeated throughout the play.

The next interruption comes in the form of Jeff Golding, a dilettantish literary critic who seems not to be particularly attractive either as a critic or as a person. He confesses, for example, that he does not like literature, and his own description of how he mistreats women is damning. Next, Jeff's current mistress, Davina, appears, searching for her lover, whom she immediately dismisses. After Jeff leaves, Davina tries to seduce Hench. She is unsuccessful, but he does agree to consider for publication a book that she has written.

Hench then records a message on his telephone answering machine to inform anyone who might call that he is "otherwise engaged" for the rest of the day. Bernard Wood enters. Hench and Wood attended Wundale School at the same time, a place where both men engaged in homosexual activities. Wood accuses Hench of seducing his fiancée, Joanna, and Hench admits to the transgression as the curtain falls.

Act 2 opens where act 1 left off; in the continuation it becomes clear that Hench does not consider the seduction as a serious transgression. Wood wants to know if Hench's wife is aware of his activities; the audience soon learns that Mrs. Hench is involved in an affair and that she is considering leaving her husband. Hench finds her choice of partners tasteless but sees the affair, like his, as posing no threat to their marriage. Wood, on the other hand, has a history of being unstable, and he calls to leave a message on the telephone recorder: He is going to shoot himself in the head because he is despondent about the Hench-Joanna affair, and he wants the act recorded so that Hench can hear it. Hench switches the machine off the instant before Wood squeezes the trigger. The play ends with Jeff returning to sit with Hench, listening to *Parsifal.*

The theme of *Otherwise Engaged* is again that of a man incapable of sustaining human relationships. Unlike Butley, however, Hench does not even seem to desire a meaningful relationship. He is comfortable in his marriage—whether he or his wife, Beth, actually have engaged in affairs is less important to him than his desire that they remain together, mainly because breaking up is a tiresome process, and staying together makes life easier, especially since he does not wish to become emotionally involved with anyone, including his wife, anyway.

There are some contradictory pieces of information provided by the dramatist. In act 1, Hench refuses to be seduced by the attractive Davina, even though she is aggressively willing and he admits that "I fancy you because of your breasts" (which she has exposed by removing her shirt). This scene is in direct contrast with Wood's claim that Hench seduced his fiancée. Additionally, in spite of Stephen's protests to the contrary, Hench does seem to have an interest in his brother's well-being. Finally, there is the ironic counterpointing between Hench's apparent attempts to remain emotionally disengaged from those intruders who surround him and his pleasure (and possibly his retreat) into Wagner's *Parsifal.*

Wagner's music is lush and romantic in nature, full-bodied and emotional. If Hench enjoys this kind of music, it would indicate that he, too, has a romantic, emotional nature. His seeming lack of concern for Wood or Beth may stem either from his sense of hurt and betrayal, or from his realization that there may be little that he can do to alter the circumstances, or both. On the other hand, it may well be that he has no feelings for people and that he seeks emotional release in the safety of music—which can make no demands on him and which does not interrupt his privacy. Somewhat like the characters in *Close of Play* four years later, those in *Otherwise Engaged* are so wrapped up in their own problems that they think that all action focuses on them, and they are insensitive to and inconsiderate of others.

Stylistically, the play is entertaining. Gray is at his witty, literate best, and he handles the language masterfully. There are some echoes from Pinter's plays, particularly *The Caretaker* (pr., pb. 1960), *The Collection* (pr. 1961), and *The Homecoming* (pr., pb. 1965), and there are some amusing plot twists. The repetition of certain tags ("Not as stupid as he seems," for example) and other stylistic devices used in *Butley* reappear in *Otherwise Engaged.* Structurally, the interweaving of reappearing characters, motifs (egotism, fidelity, dominance, sexuality, and so forth), and images (drinks thrown in people's faces) all combine to give the play an operatic texture.

Close of Play and **Stage Struck** • Gray's subsequent plays did not immediately develop his earlier themes and style. In *Close of Play* (presented at the National Theatre's Lyttleton Theatre in London on May 24, 1979), Gray returned to an intellectual setting of sorts. Jasper, a retired academic, sits silently while his wife, children, grandchildren, and assorted in-laws reveal the desperate nature of their lives. *Close of Play* is a dark, mature drama, yet it breaks no new ground for the playwright. With *Stage Struck* (Vaudeville Theatre, London, November 21, 1979), the dramatist tried his hand at a stage thriller in the vein of Ira Levin's *Deathtrap* (pr. 1978) and Anthony Shaffer's *Sleuth* (pr., pb. 1970).

Quartermaine's Terms and **The Common Pursuit** • In 1981, *Quartermaine's Terms*, his play about an ineffectual upper-class teacher who is fired by his school's new principal, opened at Queen's Theatre, London, on July 28. In New York, the Long Wharf Theatre presented the drama at Playhouse 91 in February, 1982. *Quartermaine's Terms* earned wide praise; critic John Simon noted the play's powerful mixture of laughter and melancholy and raved over its "understatedly heartbreaking ending." *The Common Pursuit* focuses on a reunion of 1960's campus rebels who have become 1980's sellouts. The play manipulates time in a fashion that reminded some critics of Pinter's *Betrayal* (pr., pb. 1978); Gray, though, explained that his source for the technique was an older television drama.

Japes • Among the very best of Gray's plays is *Japes*, which opened November 23, 2000, in Colchester and opened soon after the new year in the West End. It portrays the bizarre life that two brothers (Jason or Japes and Michael or Mikey) lead over a span of twenty-seven years, as they share a house, as well as sharing the woman Michael marries. It is a poignant and sad display of cruelties and missed directions, mixed with love and mutual devotion.

Other major works

LONG FICTION: *Colmain*, 1963; *Simple People*, 1965; *Little Portia*, 1967; *A Comeback for Stark*, 1968 (as Hamish Reade); *Breaking Hearts*, 1997.

SCREENPLAYS: *Butley*, 1975; *A Month in the Country*, 1987; *Unnatural Pursuits*, 1992.

TELEPLAYS: *The Caramel Crisis*, 1966; *Death of a Teddy Bear*, 1967; *Sleeping Dog*, 1967; *A Way with the Ladies*, 1967; *Pig in a Poke*, 1969; *The Dirt on Lucy Lane*, 1969; *The Princess*, 1970; *Style of the Countess*, 1970; *Man in a Sidecar*, 1971; *Plaintiffs and Defendants*, 1975; *Two Sundays*, 1975; *After Pilkington*, 1987; *Running Late*, 1992; *Femme Fatale*, 1993.

NONFICTION: *An Unnatural Pursuit and Other Pieces*, 1985; *How's That for Telling 'Em, Fat Lady?*, 1988; *Fat Chance*, 1995; *Enter a Fox*, 2001.

EDITED TEXT: *Selected English Prose*, 1967 (with Keith Walker).

Bibliography

Blaydes, Sophia B. "Literary Allusion as Satire in Simon Gray's *Butley*." *Midwest Quarterly* 18 (Summer, 1977): 374-391. Discusses the academic setting of *Butley* and concentrates on explicating some of the more obscure literary allusions. Includes an end note on the making and distribution of the film version in 1975.

Burkman, Katherine H., ed. *Simon Gray: A Casebook*. New York: Garland, 1992. An introduction and a chronology are followed by fourteen essays, a bibliography, and an index. This volume is the first book-length exploration of Gray's work, from *Wise Child* to *Hidden Laughter*. Contains single-work essays, overviews, and articles on adaptations. *The Holy Terror*, a revision of *Melon*, which was produced in Arizona in 1991, is mentioned in the chronology but is not dealt with in the essays.

Nothof, Anne. "The Pictures of Simon Gray: Dramatizing Degeneration." *Modern Drama* 43, no. 1 (2000): 56-65. The essay portrays the artist as a disillusioned idealist whose degeneration (like that of the picture of Dorian Gray) is manifested in his plays, his protagonists, and his autobiographical notes.

Rich, Frank. "Stage: Simon Gray Play, *The Common Pursuit.*" *The New York Times*, October 20, 1986, p. C17. This first play since *Quartermaine's Terms* is about Cambridge "litterateurs from twenty years ago." Rich provides some history of the play's New Haven tryout and change of directors, one of whom is Gray himself. Includes a description of the play's staging.

Shafer, Yvonne. "Aristophanic and Chekhovian Structure in the Plays of Simon Gray." *Theater Studies* 31/32 (1984/1985): 32-40. Deals extensively with *Otherwise Engaged* (whose central character is "a solitary searcher for order and peace in a chaotic world") and *Quartermaine's Terms*, with a Chekhovian atmosphere and a "central character moving through a landscape of incipient disaster, unable to take any action to save himself."

Stern, Carol Simpson. "Gray, Simon." In *Contemporary Dramatists*, edited by Thomas Riggs. 6th ed. Detroit, Mich.: St. James Press, 1999. A thorough account of Gray's work and his relationship with the British theater.

Steven H. Gale,
updated by Thomas J. Taylor,
Robert McClenaghan, and Stanley Longman

Lady Augusta Gregory

Born: Roxborough, Ireland; March 15, 1852
Died: Coole Park, Ireland; May 22, 1932

Principal drama • *Spreading the News*, pr. 1904, pb. 1905; *The Rising of the Moon*, pb. 1905, pr. 1907; *Kincora*, pr., pb. 1905, pr. 1909 (revised); *The White Cockade*, pr. 1905, pb. 1906; *Hyacinth Halvey*, pr., pb. 1906; *The Canavans*, pr. 1906, pr. 1907 (revised), pb. 1912; *The Gaol Gate*, pr. 1906, pb. 1909; *Dervorgilla*, pr. 1907, pb. 1908; *The Jackdaw*, pr. 1907, pb. 1909; *The Workhouse Ward*, pr. 1908, pb. 1909 (with Douglas Hyde; revision of *The Poorhouse*, pb. 1903, pr. 1907); *Seven Short Plays*, pb. 1909; *The Travelling Man*, pb. 1909, pr. 1910; *The Image*, pr. 1909, pb. 1910; *The Full Moon*, pr. 1910, pb. 1911; *Coats*, pr. 1910, pb. 1913; *The Deliverer*, pr. 1911, pb. 1912; *Grania*, pb. 1912; *Damer's Gold*, pr. 1912, pb. 1913; *The Bogie Men*, pr. 1912, pb. 1913; *Irish Folk-History Plays*, pb. 1912; *New Comedies*, pb. 1913; *The Wrens*, pr. 1914, pb. 1922; *Shanwalla*, pr. 1915, pb. 1922; *The Golden Apple*, pb. 1916, pr. 1920; *Hanrahan's Oath*, pr. 1918, pb. 1922; *The Jester*, wr. 1918, pb. 1923; *The Dragon*, pr. 1919, pb. 1920; *Aristotle's Bellows*, pr. 1921, pb. 1923; *The Story Brought by Brigit*, pr., pb. 1924; *Sancho's Master*, pr. 1927, pb. 1928; *Dave*, pr. 1927, pb. 1928; *Selected Plays*, pb. 1962 (Elizabeth Coxhead, editor); *The Collected Plays of Lady Gregory*, pb. 1970 (4 volumes; Ann Saddlemyer, editor)

Other literary forms • Lady Augusta Gregory would have been a significant figure in Irish literature even if she had never written any plays. Her earliest writing centered largely on the life and correspondence of her deceased husband, Sir William Gregory. In 1894, two years after his death, she completed the editing of *An Autobiography of Sir William Gregory*, and in 1898 she published *Mr. Gregory's Letter Box*.

Lady Gregory also did a number of translations, most notably of Molière's plays. Her plays were published in various collections throughout her lifetime and were collected in 1970 in *The Collected Plays of Lady Gregory*. A selection of nine plays can be found in *Selected Plays*, edited by Elizabeth Coxhead.

Lady Gregory's most valuable work for literature and Irish culture, however, was the gathering and publishing of the myths and legends of Ireland, a love for which began early in her life and lasted until the end. Traveling from village to village and cottage to cottage (including trips to the Aran Islands at the same time as John Millington Synge), she devoted herself to the recording of an oral tradition that she felt was central to the future as well as to the past of Ireland. The first of these numerous collections appeared as *Cuchulain of Muirthemne* in 1902, and the last, as *Visions and Beliefs in the West of Ireland* in 1920.

Lady Gregory also wrote for and about the Irish Renaissance itself, particularly about the dramatic revival. In 1901, she edited a book of essays, *Ideals in Ireland*, that called for a renewal of Irish culture and criticized English domination. Her account of the rise of Irish drama and the struggles at the Abbey Theatre is given in *Our Irish Theatre* (1913).

Lady Gregory's other nondramatic writings grow largely out of her personal life. In 1921, she published *Hugh Lane's Life and Achievement*, a memorial to her beloved nephew who died with the sinking of the *Lusitania*, and in 1926 *A Case for the Return of*

Hugh Lane's Pictures to Dublin, part of a futile battle to get his French Impressionist collection returned from England. Others oversaw the publication of some of her private thoughts and reminiscences in *Coole* (1931) and *Lady Gregory's Journals, 1916-1930* (1946).

Achievements • The achievement of Lady Augusta Gregory is not to be found in awards and prizes given to her, but in the gift of her life, possessions, and talents to the literary and cultural awakening of modern Ireland. She would be a significant figure for any one of her contributions, but the sum of them makes her central to one of the most important movements in modern literature.

Lady Gregory's initial contribution to what has been called the Irish Renaissance (or Irish Literary Revival) was the early collecting of the myths and folktales of the Irish people. In so doing, she was participating in the discovery of the richness of so-called primitive cultures that was only beginning at the end of the nineteenth century to engage the interest of the earliest anthropologists and ethnologists. These efforts not only served an important historical function but also became a part of both her own plays and the poetry and plays of William Butler Yeats, and contributed significantly to the Irish people's rediscovery of and pride in their own past.

Lady Gregory's plays, while not greatly influential on other playwrights, were important in their contribution to what has come to be called the Irish dramatic movement (especially in its primary expression, the Abbey Theatre) and as works of art in their own right. They broke new ground, for example, in the mixing of the fabulous with the realistic and in the transformation of peasant speech into successful dramatic dialect. Lady Gregory perfected the one-act play; she also led the way in demonstrating that the lives and speech of peasants could be the stuff of dramatic art—and, in fact, the popular success of her plays helped sustain the Abbey Theatre during years of great struggle.

Perhaps her most important and most widely acknowledged achievement was as a motivating and sustaining force behind the Irish dramatic movement. As cofounder, with Yeats and Edward Martyn, of the Irish Literary Theatre at the turn of the century, later to become the Abbey Theatre, she worked tirelessly as director, fund-raiser, playwright, and defender in what seemed times of endless trouble.

Lady Gregory's contribution, however, extended beyond the dramatic movement itself. She also played the important role of encourager, comforter, guide, provider, and friend to fellow writers and laborers in the cultural renewal of Ireland. The symbol for this was her country estate, Coole Park, near Galway in the west

(Library of Congress)

of Ireland, where she graciously provided spiritual and material sustenance to many, in the best-known instance to Yeats.

Biography • Lady Augusta Gregory was born Isabella Augusta Persse on March 15, 1852, at Roxborough in County Galway, the twelfth of sixteen children. Her staunchly Protestant family was thought to have come to Ireland in the seventeenth century at the time of Oliver Cromwell's suppression of Ireland. The intellectual and aesthetic sterility of her childhood was relieved by the storytelling and quiet nationalism of her Roman Catholic nurse, Mary Sheridan.

An avenue to the larger world of which she longed to be a part was provided by her marriage in 1880 to Sir William Gregory, a man of sixty-three who had recently resigned as governor of Ceylon and returned to his country estate at Coole Park, not far from Roxborough. As the new Lady Gregory, she found a large library, a kind and intelligent husband, and the beginning of an outlet for her incipient talents.

It was to be many years before Lady Gregory would think of herself as a writer. Her first efforts consisted largely of editing the autobiography and letters of her husband, who died in 1892. Of more importance to her career, however, was the publication in 1893 of both Douglas Hyde's *Love Songs of Connacht* and Yeats's *The Celtic Twilight*. These two books sparked her own latent interest in the tales and speech of the Irish peasant. She was drawn to their lyric beauty, imaginativeness, and rich spirituality, and she made it her task for much of the rest of her life to record this rich oral tradition.

Lady Gregory first discussed with Yeats in 1894 the possibility of launching a theater devoted to the writers and plays of Ireland. Their dream became a reality in January, 1899, with the founding of the Irish Literary Theatre. This movement was to be the central concern and accomplishment of her life.

Initially, Lady Gregory's contribution was largely practical. She was an organizer, fund-raiser, encourager, and occasional collaborating playwright; it was she who first argued that the theater should be in Dublin, not London, as Yeats proposed. Within a few years, however, she was writing plays of her own, initially, she said, to provide some brief comic relief from Yeats's more esoteric works. These one-act plays proved to be more popular with the Dublin audiences than were Yeats's, and her career as a playwright was well, if late, begun.

The early years of the literary movement also saw the publication of a series of her collections of Irish myth and folklore, beginning with *Cuchulain of Muirthemne* and followed in rapid succession by *Poets and Dreamers* (1903), *Gods and Fighting Men* (1904), *A Book of Saints and Wonders* (1907), and *The Kiltartan Wonder Book* (1910). These were important books because they offered a single coherent telling of previously scattered tales (especially of the mythic hero Cuchulain) and, in so doing, made this heritage more widely known not only in Ireland but also abroad.

The single phrase that sums up all that Lady Gregory aimed for and achieved was her own oft-repeated observation to her fellow laborers that "we work to add dignity to Ireland," and work she did. As one of the directors of the Abbey Theatre (initially with Yeats and Synge), she was involved in constant battles—artistic, political, financial, and personal—to preserve the dramatic movement. As an Anglo-Irish Protestant with strong nationalistic convictions, she was suspected and attacked by both sides in the increasingly politicized and polarized Ireland.

The symbol of all this was the famous riots early in 1907 over Synge's *The Playboy of the Western World* (pr., pb. 1907). Considered a slur against Ireland by the ardent nationalists, and immoral by some quarters of the Catholic Church, the play evoked a series of riotous confrontations within the theater and an ongoing controversy without. Lady Gregory defended the play with all her energies at the time and during a subsequent tour in the United States in the winter of 1911 to 1912, even though she personally disliked it.

Lady Gregory's skill as a dramatist grew rapidly, and her works were increasingly important to the financial solvency of the Abbey Theatre (especially since she collected no royalties for her plays). The first of a number of collections of her dramas, *Seven Short Plays,* came out in 1909, followed later by *Irish Folk-History Plays* (1912) and *New Comedies* (1913).

The beginning of World War I marks a tragic turn in the life of a remarkable woman who became a central figure in the literary life of a nation, a woman who did not write her first imaginative work until she was fifty. Lady Gregory's beloved nephew, Hugh Lane, died in the sinking of the *Lusitania.* His death left her with the task of trying to get his important collection of French Impressionist art returned from England to its rightful place in Ireland, a battle into which she futilely poured her declining energy until her death. In January, 1918, her only child, Robert Gregory, was killed while flying for the Royal Flying Corps. These personal tragedies, combined with her grief for the suffering of Ireland during the prolonged bloodshed of that nation's struggle for liberation, cast a darkness over Lady Gregory's declining years.

The 1920's were still years of effort on behalf of the Abbey Theatre, however, and they were brightened for a time by Lady Gregory's special role in the discovery and encouragement of Sean O'Casey. That undertaking also took a sad turn, as O'Casey broke relations with her and the Abbey Theatre over their rejection in 1928 of *The Silver Tassie.* Lady Gregory's last years were spent in poor health and growing loneliness, but she maintained her aristocratic dignity up until her death at Coole Park in 1932.

Analysis • Lady Augusta Gregory's beginnings as a dramatist were modest. Her first efforts involved contributions of pieces of realistic dialogue and plot to Yeats's early poetic drama. Even when she began to write her own plays, she claimed that they were only to serve as brief comic relief from the more serious work of the poet. This situation, however, did not last long. Lady Gregory's plays soon became important in their own right to the Abbey Theatre and to the Irish dramatic movement, and they remain a significant part of one of the most seminal periods in modern literature.

The central motivation behind all that Lady Gregory did is found in her statement that she and others worked "to add dignity to Ireland." Some of the ways in which her plays contributed to this lofty goal are suggested in her remarks on the desired impact of her historical plays, comments that at the same time give telling clues to the nature of her own work:

> I had had from the beginning a vision of historical plays being sent by us through all the counties of Ireland. For to have a real success and to come into the life of the country, one must touch a real and eternal emotion, and history comes only next to religion in our country. And although the realism of our young writers is taking the place of fantasy and romance in the cities, I still hope to see a little season given up every year to plays on history and in sequence at the Abbey, and I think schools and colleges may ask to have them sent and played in their halls, as a part of the day's lesson.

One sees here much that finds dramatic expression in Lady Gregory's plays, including the desire to have her work both spring from and appeal to the common people of Ireland; the intention to recover and respect Irish history, particularly as it is found in the stories and songs of the people rather than in the books of academics; the unapologetic combination of didacticism and entertainment; the wish to preserve romance, myth, and imagination in an increasingly skeptical, political, and materialistic age; and the hope that Irish drama could be a natural part of the education and life of the Irish people.

These desires find expression in each of the three categories into which Lady Gregory's plays are usually divided: comedy, tragedy and tragicomedy (including the historical plays), and plays of wonder and the supernatural. Lady Gregory's first plays were comedies. Like most of her drama, they were largely one-act works that combine a skillful command of structure, plot, and dialogue with genuine insight into human nature.

In their formal character, Lady Gregory's plays can most readily be understood, following critic Ann Saddlemyer, as classical treatments of largely Romantic subject matter. The plays demonstrate economy and balance, are very linear and simple in construction, and generally observe the classical unities of time, place, and action. The tendency to sameness and predictability in structure is relieved by her storyteller's gift for local color and suspense, and by her effective adaption to the stage of the Irish-English dialect that she called Kiltartan (after the district in which she and her peasant models lived).

Lady Gregory was not a great playwright. She was not considered so at the time, by herself or by others, and is only in recent years being rescued from the oblivion into which her reputation fell following her death. She deserves great respect, however, as one of a lesser rank who made a significant contribution at a crucial time and in so doing served both her art form and her country well.

Comedies • The recurring locale for Lady Gregory's comedies is the rural community of Cloon, a fictional version of the real town of Gort, near which Lady Gregory lived on her estate, Coole Park. The poor peasants and only slightly less impoverished townspeople with whom she mingled from her earliest childhood became her characters. She tried to capture not only their speech and mannerisms but also the quality of their lives that transcended their poverty and sometime clownishness. That quality had to do with their closeness to the spiritual heart of life, to myth and legend, to a sense of the past and of community, and to other dimensions of reality that Lady Gregory feared were disappearing from Ireland and from the world.

These characters are not idealized. They are often fools, simpletons, and ne'er-do-wells. Hers are not the heroic poor of some literature, yet beneath their gullibility, love of gossip, and simplemindedness is a closeness to the core of life that Lady Gregory admired and tried to capture. This accounts for the consistent sympathy for her comic creations. Lady Gregory laughed with, not at, her characters, and she did not set herself apart from the human foibles that they portray.

One of those foibles, both a weakness and a strength, is the Irish love of talk. This very human desire to share lives manifests itself comically (and sometimes tragically) in Lady Gregory's plays in an unquenchable thirst for gossip, a penchant for exaggeration and misrepresentation, a disposition to argument for its own sake, and an irrepressible urge to know their neighbor's business. This foible is at the heart of two of her most successful works, *Spreading the News* and *The Workhouse Ward*.

Spreading the News • The skillfully structured *Spreading the News* turns on the eagerness of a man's neighbors to hear and believe the worst about him. Poor Bartley

Fallon, a man convinced that if something bad is to happen, it will happen to him, finds that his innocent attempt to do a good deed becomes the basis, through a series of outrageous misunderstandings of everyday speech, of the universally believed story that he has murdered his neighbor and plans to run off with the neighbor's wife. The humor of the situation grows exponentially as each new person who happens on the expanding story embraces it eagerly and adds to its enormity in passing it on. The comic tension builds even beyond where it seems it must be released as the appearance in good health of the supposedly murdered man only prompts the police to arrest him along with Bartley as they set off to find the body of the "real" victim, whom he is assumed to be impersonating.

The Workhouse Ward • *The Workhouse Ward* also turns on the Irish love of talk. Two old men in a poorhouse argue viciously with each other until the sister of one, whom he has not seen for five years, arrives to offer to take him into her home (for largely selfish reasons). He is eager to leave his pitiful surroundings until he learns that his roommate cannot come with him. After the sister leaves, the two old men resume their fighting, hurling objects as well as words at each other.

Both comedies illustrate Lady Gregory's ability to capture the rich dialect of the Irish peasant in all its color, cadence, and natural metaphor. One of the old men in *The Workhouse Ward* responds to the charge of the other in typical fashion: "To steal your eggs is it? Is that what you are saying now. . . . Isn't it a bad story for me to be wearing out my days beside you the same as a spancelled goat. Chained I am and tethered I am to a man that is ransacking his mind for lies!"

As with most of Lady Gregory's comedies, these two reveal her interest in something more than laughter. The condescending and uncomprehending attitude of the English magistrate in *Spreading the News* is a clear if commonplace indictment of Ireland's oppressor, and his repeated references to his earlier duties in the Andaman Islands indicate that Ireland too is simply another of England's exploited colonies. Both plays also reveal Lady Gregory's fondness for symbolism and near allegory. She later said she wanted the two old men in *The Workhouse Ward* to be seen as symbols of Ireland itself, suggesting that the Irish, as with any family, feel free to fight among themselves but do not desire the interference of outsiders, especially hypocritical ones whose apparent benevolence is only thinly disguised exploitation.

Tragedies • Although it was her comedies that were most popular and are most likely to last, Lady Gregory herself preferred to write tragedy. Her work in this form ranges from the highly condensed power of *The Gaol Gate* to one of her most ambitious works, the three-act *Grania*. One finds in the tragedies the clearest expression of the idealism, patriotism, and respect for the noble lost cause that are so much a part of Lady Gregory's own character. The tragedies generally center on people who have refused to be the passive pawns of circumstance, and who, in insisting on acting independently, come to grief against the harsh realities of life.

The Gaol Gate • In *The Gaol Gate*, the man who has acted independently is dead before the play begins. Refusing to inform on his friends, he is hanged for a political murder he did not commit. The action of the play centers on the discovery of his fate by his wife and mother. As they approach the prison, unaware that he has been executed, they agonize over the rumors that he has in fact informed against his friends. His wife makes excuses for him in preparation for the possibility that it may be true, but his mother, with a longer memory of the suffering of the people, will not tolerate the idea of a son who is not faithful to his neighbors. On learning that her son has died for his loyalty, the mother breaks into a shocking celebration that reveals simultaneously the strength of the code of honor of the nationalist, the woman's own selfish desire to triumph over her son's false accusers, and the mental strain of a grief too great to bear; the latter is reminiscent of Maurya's break with reality at the end of Synge's *Riders to the Sea* (pb. 1903).

Grania • Given the nature of Irish history, it is fitting that Lady Gregory's historical plays are found among the tragedies and tragicomedies. This is true both of plays based on Ireland's mythological history, such as *Grania*, and of those based on more verifiable history, such as *The White Cockade*, an idiosyncratic account of James II and that infamous turning point for Ireland, the Battle of the Boyne. In *Grania*, a play that Lady Gregory never allowed to be produced during her lifetime, one finds in the treatment of the legendary love triangle between Grania, Diarmuid, and Finn perhaps her most sophisticated exploration of psychological motivation. As a strong woman whose determination to live intensely rather than conventionally leads her into a lifetime of turmoil to which she never succumbs, Grania perhaps contains more elements of Lady Gregory than she herself was ready to make public on the stage.

Plays of wonder • The third major category consists of the plays of wonder and the supernatural. Here Lady Gregory explored most directly that realm of folk spirituality she loved and valued so much. It was this sense of the spiritual (in both a figurative and literal sense), underlying and giving meaning to the physical, that Lady Gregory feared was disappearing from the modern world. Her plays of wonder and the supernatural, many of them written for children, portray that world where reality is multilayered and the physical world is suffused with beings of another dimension.

The Travelling Man • *The Travelling Man*, in which Lady Gregory gave the Christian tradition of entertaining angels or Christ an Irish setting, is a case in point. Lady Gregory adapted a story told her by an old peasant woman about a destitute girl who had been directed by Christ to the house of her future husband, but who herself failed years later to show charity to Christ in the guise of a traveling beggar. In the play, the woman readies the house, as she does each year on the anniversary of her rescue, for the possibility that her Saviour from long ago, the King of the World, will return as he had promised. She is so absorbed in preparing only the finest for what she assumes will be his dignified and impressive return, that she turns furiously against the poor beggar who interrupts her preparations, and who is Christ himself. In this play, as in many others, Lady Gregory demonstrated her interest in the deeper reality that infused the life of the Irish peasant with a significance that transcended physical deprivation.

This need for a spiritual sustenance to redeem the tragic physical and political burden that had long been Ireland's is the overarching theme of Lady Gregory's plays. She valued, above all, the mythmakers of Ireland, whether the anonymous poets of ancient legend, or Raftery, the blind wandering poet of the early nineteenth century, or a political mythmaker such as Charles Parnell. She wanted the Irish Renaissance to be a revival of mythmakers, herself among them. The potential for all this rested, she believed, in the Irish people themselves, particularly the peasants, with their natural mythmaking reflected in their common stories, their conception of the world about them, and their very speech.

Other major works

NONFICTION: *Our Irish Theatre*, 1913; *Hugh Lane's Life and Achievement*, 1921; *A Case for the Return of Hugh Lane's Pictures to Dublin*, 1926; *Coole*, 1931; *Lady Gregory's Journals, 1916-1930*, 1946 (Lennox Robinson, editor); *Lady Gregory's Diaries, 1892-1902*, 1995 (James Pethica, editor).

EDITED TEXTS: *An Autobiography of Sir William Gregory*, 1894; *Mr. Gregory's Letter Box*, 1898; *Ideals in Ireland*, 1901; *Cuchulain of Muirthemne*, 1902; *Poets and Dreamers*, 1903; *Gods and Fighting Men*, 1904; *A Book of Saints and Wonders*, 1907; *The Kiltartan History Book*, 1909; *The Kiltartan Wonder Book*, 1910; *The Kiltartan Poetry Book*, 1919; *Visions and Beliefs in the West of Ireland*, 1920 (2 volumes).

Bibliography

Kohfeldt, Mary Lou. *Lady Gregory: The Woman Behind the Irish Renaissance.* New York: Atheneum, 1985. A narrative biography that provides information about Lady Gregory's early personal life as well as a thorough account of her involvement with the Irish Literary Revival. While the work's main emphasis is on the literary personalities among whom Lady Gregory spent the influential part of her life, use is also made of archival material.

Kopper, Edward A., Jr. *Lady Isabella Persse Gregory.* Boston: Twayne, 1976. A basic biography of Lady Gregory that covers her private and professional life as well as her writings. Bibliography and index.

Saddlemyer, Ann, and Colin Smythe, eds. *Lady Gregory: Fifty Years After.* Totowa, N.J.: Barnes and Noble Books, 1987. A substantial collection of essays that provide a comprehensive scholarly treatment of Lady Gregory's life and times. Her playwriting and involvement with the Abbey Theatre provide the volume with its central focus. Also included is a considerable amount of material pertinent to an evaluation of the overall cultural significance of Lady Gregory's career.

Stevenson, Mary Lou Kohfeldt. *Lady Gregory: The Woman Behind the Irish Renaissance.* New York: Atheneum, 1984. A basic biography of Lady Gregory that covers her life and works. Examines at length her role in the Irish Literary Renaissance. Bibliography and index.

Tobin, Seán, and Lois Tobin, eds. *Lady Gregory Autumn Gatherings: Reflections at Coole.* Galway, Ireland: Lady Gregory Autumn Gathering, 2000. This collection of essays examines Lady Gregory, her life and friends, her professional life, and her writings. Bibliography.

Daniel Taylor,
updated by George O'Brien

Tawfiq al-Hakim

Born: Alexandria, Egypt; October 9, 1898
Died: Cairo, Egypt; July 26, 1987

Principal drama • *Khatim Sulayman*, pr. 1924; *al-Mar'ah al-jadidah*, pr. 1926, pb. 1952; *Ahl al-kahf*, pb. 1933, pr. 1935 (*The People of the Cave*, 1989); *Shahrazad*, pb. 1934, pr. 1966 (English translation, 1955); *Muhammad*, pb. 1936 (partial English translation, 1955); *Nahr al-junun*, pb. 1937 (*The River of Madness*, 1963); *Shajarat al-Hukm*, pb. 1938; *Piraksa: Aw, Mushkilat al-hukm*, part 1, pb. 1939, part 2, pb. 1960; *Salah al-mala'ikah*, pb. 1941 (*Angels' Prayer*, 1981); *Pijmalyun*, pb. 1942, pr. 1953 (*Pygmalion*, 1961); *Sulayman al-hakim*, pb. 1943 (*The Wisdom of Solomon*, 1981); *Himari qala li*, pb. 1945 (short plays, one translated as *The Donkey Market*, 1981); *al-Malik Udib*, pb. 1949 (*King Oedipus*, 1981); *Ughniyah al-mawt*, pb. 1950, pr. 1956 (*The Song of Death*, 1973); *al-Aydi al-na'imah*, pb. 1954, pr. 1957 (*Tender Hands*, 1984); *Bayna al-harb wa-al-salam*, pb. 1956 (*Between War and Peace*, 1984); *Rihlah ila al-ghad*, pb. 1957 (*Voyage to Tomorrow*, 1984); *al-Sultan al-ha'ir*, pb. 1960, pr. 1961 (*The Sultan's Dilemma*, 1973); *Ya tali' al-shajarah*, pr. c. 1961, pb. 1962 (*The Tree Climber*, 1966); *al-Ta'am li-kull fam*, pb. 1963, pr. 1964 (*Food for the Millions*, 1984); *Shams al-Nahar*, pr. 1964, pb. 1965 (*Princess Sunshine*, 1981); *Masir Sursar*, pb. 1966, pr. 1969 (*Fate of a Cockroach*, 1973); *Kullu shay' fi mahallihi*, pb. 1966 (*Not a Thing Out of Place*, 1973); *al-Wartah*, pb. 1966 (*Incrimination*, 1984); *Ahl al-qamar*, pb. 1969 (*Poet on the Moon*, 1984); *al-Dunya riwayah hazaliyah*, pb. 1971, pr. 1972 (*The World Is a Comedy*, 1985); *Fate of a Cockroach: Four Plays of Freedom*, pb. 1973; *Plays, Prefaces, and Postscripts of Tawfiq al-Hakim*, pb. 1981, 1984 (2 volumes; William M. Hutchins, translator)

Other literary forms • In addition to drama, Tawfiq al-Hakim was active in a number of genres. Among his novels, written rather early in his career, *al-Qasr al-mashur* (1936; the enchanted palace) is notable as a collaborative effort composed with the distinguished man of letters Taha Husayn. His most celebrated work of long fiction, *Yawmiyat na'ib fi al-aryaf* (1937; *Maze of Justice*, 1947), draws on al-Hakim's experience as a legal functionary and deftly combines social commentary with satire. Other novels are significant as indications of al-Hakim's propensity to experiment with this form of fiction. At intervals during his career, al-Hakim wrote short stories, which are most readily accessible through the two-volume collection *Qisas*, published in 1949.

Al-Hakim also published a number of essentially autobiographical works, of which *Sijn al-'umr* (1964; *The Prison of Life*, 1992) deserves particular mention; *Zahrat al-'umr* (1943; life in flower) is a compilation of letters, translated from the French, from al-Hakim's correspondence with those he met during his student days in Paris. Reflections on drama, art, and life are presented in works of literary criticism such as *Min al-burj al-'aji* (1941; from the ivory tower) and *Fann al-adab* (1952; the art of literature), as well as other studies. For a number of years, beginning in 1943, al-Hakim wrote columns for the influential newspapers *Akhbar al-yawm* (news of the day) and *al-Ahram* (the pyramids) of Cairo. His collection of political essays, *'Awdat al-wa'y* (1974; *The Return of Consciousness*, 1985), and a companion volume of documents published the next year, aroused criticism in some circles and wonderment in others, for their unfavorable commentary on the government of Egypt under President Gamal Abdel Nasser.

Achievements • At the beginning of the twentieth century, drama in Egypt and the Arab world remained a derivative and largely secondary form of creative expression. Puppet and shadow plays were produced alongside adaptations drawn for the most part from French and Italian playwrights. Some innovations were introduced on the Egyptian stage with the production of works by Salim Khalil al-Naqqash, Ya'qub Sannu' (James Sanua), and Ahmad Shawqi. After World War I, important new plays were written by Mahmud Taymur, and Najib al-Rihani's performances in comic roles also aroused interest in the theater. Nevertheless, with only an exiguous native tradition, Tawfiq al-Hakim came to the forefront of modern Egyptian dramatists with strikingly original depictions of time-honored Middle Eastern themes.

Al-Hakim's earlier work, particularly that beginning with *The People of the Cave*, achieved the fusion of regional themes with European techniques. More than that, his work came to be classed as pioneering on at least three other fronts as well. He brought to the Egyptian and Arab stage unique and distinctive interpretations of Western works, notably versions of classical Greek drama. Many of his works have a surrealistic bent, suggesting analogies, which he has encouraged, with the Western Theater of the Absurd. He was also among the first Arab dramatists to write dialogue in colloquial language. Purists, who insisted on the use of classical Arabic, were outraged, but others have conceded that the effects may have heightened the contrasts between the timeless and the mundane that are integral concerns of al-Hakim's productions. His efforts to introduce idiomatic usage into the language of the stage were followed by those of other notable playwrights. This trend in itself marks the extent to which, largely as a result of al-Hakim's influence, drama has developed from the stylized, ritualistic forms that characterized the early Arab theater.

Notwithstanding the decidedly mixed reception accorded his works during the early phases of his career, al-Hakim received a number of awards and honors in his native country. In 1951 he was made director general of the Egyptian National Library, and three years later he became a member of the Academy of the Arabic Language in Cairo. He was awarded the cordon of the republic in 1958, and he served as Egypt's representative to UNESCO, in Paris, during the following two years. He received the State Literature Prize in 1961, and in 1963 a theater in Cairo was formally named for him. His position as the preeminent modern dramatist in the Arab world was underscored when a Tawfiq al-Hakim Festival was held at the University of Cairo in 1969.

At that time al-Hakim also presided over a Congress of Arab Dramatists that was held in the Egyptian capital. In 1974, he became president of his country's Story Writers' Club. Although personally at times he may have been inclined to overstate his own importance—during the early 1960's he announced his candidacy for the Nobel Prize in Literature—al-Hakim's stature was imposing among Middle Eastern playwrights, and on the international level his works are almost certainly the most widely recognized of any Arab dramatic productions.

Biography • For some time, the date of Tawfiq al-Hakim's birth was in doubt—in places the year 1902 was cited, but later October 9, 1898, was accepted as proved. It is certain that he was born in Alexandria, Egypt, of an Arab doctor and a mother who was descended from a family of Ottoman officials and army officers. Although his education moved forward slowly during his early years, al-Hakim evinced an early interest in dramatic storytelling. In 1915, he entered the Muhammad Ali Secondary School in Cairo, and he received the baccalaureate in 1921. His youth evidently was marred somewhat by difficult relations with his mother, and a brief, unrequited love affair did nothing to improve his attitude toward women. During the short-lived revolution of 1919, which was provoked by the exile of Saᶜd Zaghlul, a prominent national leader, to Malta, al-Hakim was imprisoned for composing patriotic songs. His incarceration was brief and hardly unpleasant; at about that time he wrote his first play, a work that Cairo producers would not stage because of its defiantly anti-British standpoint.

For four years, until 1925, al-Hakim studied law at the state university in Cairo; increasingly it became evident that his proclivities, and his real calling, lay elsewhere. His further efforts at the writing of drama brought forth *al-Marʾah al-jadidah* (modern woman), which was composed in 1923 and produced on the stage three years later. Three other short plays, including *Khatim Sulayman* (the ring of Solomon), were produced in 1924, shortly after he had committed them to paper.

In spite of an undistinguished academic record—he graduated third from last among those who were promoted in his class—al-Hakim entered the Collège des Lois at the Sorbonne in Paris. At that time he was still guided in part by his father's wish that he should become a lawyer, and evidently he was otherwise undecided about which direction his career should take. During his student years in France—between 1925 and 1928—he spent much of his time reading, sightseeing, and absorbing as much European culture as possible. In addition to philosophy and narrative fiction, he delved at length into published drama and attended performances of major plays.

It appears that al-Hakim was fascinated by the works of Henrik Ibsen, George Bernard Shaw, and Luigi Pirandello. Classical Greek theater also left a lasting impression on him. The lack of an Arab dramatic tradition, which had troubled him during his first efforts in Egypt, was brought home to him more definitely; along the way, two love affairs, which turned out badly, added further poignancy to his outlook. In 1928, having passed all but one of his examinations, he returned to Egypt, ostensibly to commence work within the legal profession, but with his creative aspirations probably now foremost in his mind.

After an apprenticeship of one year in Alexandria, al-Hakim served as a public prosecutor in various rural communities between 1929 and 1934; he then became director of the investigation bureau of the Ministry of Education, and in 1939 he was appointed to a position in the Ministry of Social Affairs. In 1943 he left public service to devote himself entirely to writing. It may readily be inferred from his fictional and autobiographical works that he regarded government positions as sinecures, an attitude he also detected in those around him. The decisive event of his career as a playwright was the publication in 1933 of his *The People of the Cave.* His transfer from legal to bureaucratic responsibilities may have been a result of the uproar that greeted this work.

Although Taha Husayn, a leading critic, and other men of letters praised the play's bold, unconventional approach, others castigated it for its use of informal, even ungrammatical, language. *Shahrazad* had already been published (in 1934) when an outcry broke out over the staged version of *The People of the Cave*; audiences rejected it as far too long and too far removed from the formal routines that they had come to expect from the theater. Typical of other dramatic works from this period are *Muhammad,* a lengthy treatment of episodes from the life of the Prophet, and other works set in classical times. In 1936, al-Hakim, on a visit to Europe, attended the Salzburg Theater Festival, and in 1938 he vacationed in the Alps, in an effort again to maintain cultural contacts abroad.

The next period of al-Hakim's creative life is sometimes associated with the title of his book *Min al-burj al-ʿaji,* which refers to the literary life as being led in an "ivory tower." To be sure, some of his writings expressed concern about Nazi ambitions during World War II; in a more general light, he also wrote about his fears for world peace during an age dominated by brute militarism and technology. Other works explored classical Greek themes or considered episodes from the Old Testament that are also part of Islamic lore. In 1946 he was married, and thereafter fathered a son and three daughters; critics later have tried to determine the effect his family life had on the obvious though sometimes playful misogyny of his literary efforts.

His reputation as a playwright detached from ideological concerns was reinforced during the period surrounding the Egyptian revolution of 1952 and the ultimate withdrawal of British forces from that country in 1956. In 1953, al-Hakim's version of Shaw's *Pygmalion* was staged at the Salzburg Theater Festival; in 1960, *The Sultan's Dilemma* was published simultaneously in Cairo and, in a French translation, in Paris. He was honored by President Gamal Abdel Nasser, who secured official awards for him and attended the production premiere of *Tender Hands* in 1957. The author thus had reason to believe that his renown and acceptance of his works were on the rise. His works were also produced in other Arab countries; some of them were successfully adapted for the cinema. Quite apart from experiments with language, he turned increasingly to futuristic, global concerns or to the bemused contemplation of the absurdities in everyday life. Students of the theater struggled to find political allusions in al-Hakim's later plays; some of them were set in remote historical periods and others took place in future ages.

In January, 1973, the dramatist became directly embroiled in public concerns; he presented President Anwar el-Sadat with a letter on behalf of forty-six writers, protesting the nation's indecisive stance against Israel. Although for a brief period publication and production of al-Hakim's work were suspended, in October of that year war broke out, and the aging author vociferously supported Egypt's military efforts. By 1974 a short treatise that al-Hakim had written that criticized the excesses and extravagances of the Nasser years was cleared for publication, in keeping with Sadat's efforts to chart a political course of his own. Although this work, *The Return of Consciousness,* was denounced by Nasser's remaining supporters (who, among other questions, asked why al-Hakim had remained silent until four years after their leader's death), it became a best-seller for some time. In 1975, it was reported that a companion volume, which presented documents from the author's work, in its turn had become the most popular book in Egypt.

Although he did not go further in his professed intention to open the political files from his country's recent past, al-Hakim remained an important and widely cited newspaper columnist. In line with the nation's foreign policy, at times he suggested that Egypt and Israel may serve as islands of security in the Middle East. He also edited and supervised the collection of the numerous dramatic writings and other works that he composed over the years. Moreover, as the senior representative of an important modern tradition in Arabic and Egyptian literature, his works have been reprinted and have been made available in many parts of the world. Translations of al-Hakim's writings exist in French, Spanish, Italian, German, Hebrew, Russian, and Japanese as well as other Middle Eastern languages; English language compilations of his major plays have also done much to increase his following.

Analysis • Although Tawfiq al-Hakim's dramatic imagination ranged across at least three millennia of human experience, touching down at particularly evocative points along the way, some generalizations may be made about common features in much of his work. Characterization has been important, but something less than a vital issue in his efforts; for that matter some leading personages have been typecast as abstract categories, such as war and peace, while others have been significant not for their intrinsic qualities but as participants in seemingly irrational situations.

Characters in the plays based on medieval themes might possibly be interchanged with others from similar works. The domestic dramas also feature some stock types who seem to appear under various names in works of this kind. The author never claimed to have developed a florid, polished style—indeed, he purposely avoided such tendencies—and his dialogue has a crisp, staccato ring that often serves to heighten dramatic tension. There are, in many of his works, series of exclamations and interjections that, particularly in the absurdist dramas, merge with scenes taken up mainly with the exchange of questions.

Even the most carefully constructed of al-Hakim's plays have been meant as much for the reader as for the theater audience. Although some works have enjoyed considerably more success on the stage than others, the structure of his major dramatic efforts has been determined more by his thematic concerns than by the requirements of actual production. Many plays have long sequences of brief scenes, or sometimes present lengthy acts alternating with short, abrupt transitional passages.

On another level, regardless of whether, during his classical or his absurdist phases, al-Hakim resolved the perennial questions of love, art, guilt, and social division, his works have posed these issues in unusual and distinctively original variations. Although at times he complained that during thirty years he attempted to accomplish for the Arab theater what it had taken Western civilization two thousand years to achieve, the freshness of his works, and the extent to which he has realized the conjunction of diverse aesthetic and moral concerns, should signify the magnitude of Tawfiq al-Hakim's efforts within and indeed beyond the limits of the drama as he had found them.

The drama of al-Hakim displays a remarkable diversity of outlook, and his breadth of vision inspires respect mingled slightly with awe. His cosmopolitan standpoint, coupled with his relentless quest for the new and untried, was in evidence across the span of his career. He was extraordinarily prolific; one recent count yielded eighty-four titles of dramatic works that he has composed, quite apart from his writings in other genres. His plays have been set in historical periods from the times of King Solomon of the Old Testament, through the age of classical Greek drama, across early and medieval periods of Islamic history, on to modern times in Egypt, and beyond, into the space age.

al-Hakim depicted the rustic peasant landscapes of his native country, the courts of great monarchs from the past, and the cosmic scenery of new worlds to come. It may well be argued that his work is uneven, both in its technical execution and where depth of characterization is involved. It would seem that his penchant for the unexpected and the unusual at times may have affected the direction of his dramatic efforts; any facile attempt to devise categories for his works is doomed to frustration. Nevertheless, although even a chronological approach would be subject to anomalies and overlapping impulses may be observed in many areas, there are some broad elements of thematic continuity that may be discerned in the development of al-Hakim's repertory.

The People of the Cave • The historical contexts for major early works were derived from Islamic religious and literary traditions. *The People of the Cave*, the work that in 1933 was hailed as heralding the onset of a new era in Arab drama and that elicited stormy protests on the part of subsequent audiences, deals with the Christian legend of the Seven Sleepers of Ephesus, which is also cited in the Qur'an. In this play, visions of the miraculous, hope, and despair are presented in a light that is broadly consonant with the convictions of Muslim believers, but without prejudice to the Christian values that are also affirmed by Islam.

Shahrazad • *Shahrazad* was al-Hakim's effort to supply a continuation of *Alf layla wa-layla* (15 C.E.; *The Arabian Nights' Entertainment*, 1706-1708); when the fabled storyteller survives and marries the monarch from the tale, some poignant and revealing reflections on nature, beauty, and mortality are recorded.

Muhammad • *Muhammad*, which serves as a sort of Muslim Passion play, is a sweeping pageant that was meant to demonstrate al-Hakim's belief that suitable dramatic forms could be found to evoke themes from the life of the Prophet. This play may also point to the author's contention that the drama is meant to be read as much as it is meant to be viewed: In one edition there are a prologue, three acts, and an epilogue, comprising, in all, ninety-five scenes.

The River of Madness • Absolute power and helplessness are treated in plays taken from past epochs of Oriental despotism. In *The River of Madness*, a one-act production, a monarch's subjects drink mystical waters that render them impervious to his commands. At the end, the unnamed ruler also seeks wisdom in this form of supposed madness. It is not clear who is sane and who is not, or whence real authority springs.

The Wisdom of Solomon • For all of his powers, the biblical King Solomon is unable to win the favor of a beautiful woman, in one of al-Hakim's longer works, *The Wisdom of Solomon*. This effort, which draws on characters depicted in one of the author's earliest plays, *Khatim Sulayman*, opens when a jinni appears to a humble fisherman and informs him of his quarrel with the king. He hopes for reinstatement into Solomon's good graces. When the Queen of Sheba, the most beautiful of all women, is brought before the mighty monarch, Solomon in all of his glory is unable to win her favor. He is tempted to enlist the spirit, but is reluctant to summon unearthly powers. The queen remains demure as ever, and for all of his countless treasures and innumerable wives, the great ruler falls prey to the frailties of the flesh; he becomes old and dies. At the end, the jinni warns that love and power will provoke struggle on this earth for centuries and ages to come.

The Sultan's Dilemma • Themes of punishment and justice converge with concerns about past politics in some of the author's later plays. In *The Sultan's Dilemma*, which is set in late medieval Egypt, a man is sentenced to death for maintaining that the sultan is a slave; a lady intervenes on his behalf, demonstrates that the condemned man is indeed correct, and in the end the ruler's place before the people must be redeemed by a complicated process of manumission. By emphasizing the absurdities of a bygone political system (where in fact under the Mamluk Dynasty the loftiest as well as the lowliest positions were occupied by those who in a technical legal sense were held in bonded servitude), al-Hakim implies that authority and official dignity are transitory attributes that are real only to the extent that society accepts them.

Princess Sunshine • *Princess Sunshine* has an unspecified medieval setting, during the reign of a certain Sultan Nuʿman. He rules over an odd kingdom: Princes from all around are flogged to deter them from courting the princess; executions must be halted because the gallows rope has been stolen. Harmony is achieved, however, when the princess agrees to marry one of her suitors, even after she learns that he is actually a commoner and his real name is the unprepossessing Dindan.

Piraksa • Works that are borrowed from Western traditions exhibit another facet of al-Hakim's conception of the drama. Aristophanes was the original source for *Piraksa: Aw, Mushkilat al-hukm* (Praxagora: or, the difficulties of government). The Egyptian playwright's version turns out to be an exercise in political discourse. Some ludicrous problems arise when the protagonist of the title subjects ancient Athens to a form of feminist communism.

Pygmalion • *Pygmalion*, though suggested by George Bernard Shaw's work, also takes up classical concerns. A Cypriot Greek artist calls on the goddess Venus to endow one of his statues with life; when he falls in love with his creation, Pygmalion, the title character, fears that he will have to abandon sculpture. This work, published in 1942, highlights the conflicting demands of life, love, and art in a felicitous union of several disparate approaches to the drama.

King Oedipus • A major work in al-Hakim's canon is *King Oedipus*, which is an adaptation of Sophocles' *Oedipus Tyrannus* (c. 429 B.C.E.; *Oedipus Tyrannus*, 1715). In this version, the tragic denouement takes place when the monarch learns that he is not of royal birth. He is driven by a zealous pursuit of the truth even beyond the doors that should not be opened. Curiosity is Oedipus's tragic flaw; when he learns that he was adopted, he is blinded. It is noteworthy here that, without introducing overt references to Islam, the pantheon of Greek gods from the original tragedy is replaced with suggestions of a monotheistic purpose. Countervailing concerns with predestination and free will arise when al-Hakim points to problems of divine intentions in this world.

Tender Hands • Contemporary social issues figure in many of al-Hakim's plays, sometimes in a bizarre, mocking sense; but a more straightforward presentation of these themes may be found in *Tender Hands*, which concerns the place in society of university graduates who have more formal learning than practical training. Whether grammatical usage has any relevance to the management of an oil company is a problem that is no more readily resolved than the just division of household tasks for a prospective couple. Nevertheless, all ends happily when a marriage uniting two leading characters is secured.

Himari qala li • Whimsical and broadly comic themes have been pursued in several of al-Hakim's works; this is the case with *Himari qala li* (my donkey said to me). In this group of dramatic sketches, the author's donkey asks him questions about life's predicaments; in some sequences the roles of human and animal almost seem to be reversed, as ordinary logic appears inadequate to explain the anomalies of humankind's condition.

The Tree Climber • In some of his works, al-Hakim acknowledged the examples of European playwrights such as Bertolt Brecht, Samuel Beckett, and Eugène Ionesco; in 1962 he announced that his most recent play had an irrationalist inspiration, and some affinities with the Theater of the Absurd, in the introduction to one of his best-known works. *The Tree Climber* opens as a retired railway inspector is perplexed by the simultaneous disappearance of his wife and a female lizard that had lived under their orange tree. After police interrogation, and with the testimony of a bizarre dervish who appears at the train station, the old railwayman confesses to murder and claims that by burying his wife's body under the tree he had hoped to increase its yield of fruit. The lawmen begin digging, but they uncover nothing; the wife reappears later, and, when her husband questions her about her absence, he becomes enraged by her evasive answers. He strangles her, puts the body in the hole the police have left under the tree, and then is distracted by the mysterious dervish. During their conversation, the wife's body vanishes; in its place they find the body of the lizard, the man's talisman of good fortune.

The Fate of a Cockroach and **Not a Thing Out of Place** • Another notable effort in the same vein is *Fate of a Cockroach*, which commences with a satirical view of order and legitimacy in the insect world. The cockroach king takes precedence over the queen because his whiskers are longer, but the female talks of mobilizing her sex for a war against predatory ants. The two seem to agree, however, that their species is the most advanced on the planet. Unknown to them, a married couple is arguing about the equitable disbursement of household funds. The wife asks the husband to kill a cockroach in their bathtub; when first the man and then the woman begin instead to contemplate the insect in admiration, a doctor is called in. He cannot understand either one of them because he has never been married. For a certain time, the husband and the wife quarrel about rank and obedience in a way that recalls the argument between the cockroach king and queen; relations seem more strained than ever after the maid, in the course of her cleaning routine, drowns the insect without a second thought.

Not a Thing Out of Place is a brisk one-act piece that has villagers talking of melons that resemble human heads and a philosophically inclined donkey when they go off to join a local dance.

The Song of Death and **Incrimination** • Themes of violence and guilt—notably those that elude any judicial resolution—are taken up in certain works. The one-act play *The Song of Death* deals with a blood vendetta between peasant families in Upper Egypt. A young university graduate is unable to persuade them that they would be better concerned with technological means to improve their living standards.

Although power, punishment, and the political order have been considered in plays set in earlier periods, an absurdist treatment of crime during modern times is presented in *Incrimination*. Here a law professor who has written learned treatises on criminal psychology, but has never met any lawbreakers, is introduced to some local gang members. When a policeman is shot to death during a jewel theft, the scholar agrees to defend his acquaintance from the underworld in court. By a strange transposition of the clues, however, the evidence in the end points to the professor. It would seem, then, that in the author's view guilt and innocence have no more fixed constancy than visual illusions.

Voyage to Tomorrow • *Voyage to Tomorrow* begins with a crime story and ends with some of the ironic, futuristic twists that are notable in al-Hakim's later drama. A man who perpetrated murder while in the throes of romantic infatuation is allowed to participate in an experimental, and extremely hazardous, space flight; his companion is a fellow convict who had committed four murders for personal gain. Against all the odds they survive and return to Earth during a future age when all material wants are provided for and people routinely live several hundred years. This state, however, is actually a despotism wherein love and romance are regarded as unwanted, somehow subversive relics of the past. The first convict, after a brief flirtation with a sympathetic brunette, threatens to kill a security guard who tries to separate them. He comes close to committing murder again for the sake of a woman. Here the great themes of conscience and emotional commitment are interwoven with the author's visionary and speculative concerns.

Angels' Prayer • A final grouping of al-Hakim's works might include those that deal with global issues. Here a question that is frequently posed is whether science will benefit humanity or assist in its mass destruction; this issue was taken up at intervals across much of al-Hakim's career. In his attitude toward World War II, and in his considerations on the advent of nuclear weapons and rivalries in space exploration, al-Hakim dealt with important developments in advance of many other Arab authors. The short play *Angels' Prayer* depicts an angel who comes to Earth. He finds a monk and a scientist quarreling over responsibility for the wayward path of the human race. The angel is later captured, tried, and executed at the behest of two tyrants who resemble Adolf Hitler and Benito Mussolini. When he returns to Heaven, still holding his apple of peace, which the dictators have vainly tried to take from him, he urges the other angels to pray for the inhabitants of Earth.

Between War and Peace and **Food for the Millions** • The one-act play *Between War and Peace* has an odd bit of personification: Characters named War and Peace meet in the boudoir of a lady named Diplomacy, where their deliberations resemble the intrigues of a lovers' triangle.

Human issues in the nuclear age are examined in *Food for the Millions.* A scientific prodigy claims to have made a discovery more important than the atom bomb: Food can be produced at an infinitesimal fraction of its original cost, and families everywhere will be able to have it in abundance. Others compare this project to the fond dreams of science fiction, and it falls by the wayside when the youth and other family members learn that their mother, before remarrying, may have acted to hasten the death of their seriously ill father. Toward the end of the drama there are some homely but portentous musings on water stains that repeatedly appear on their apartment walls; these may be symbolic of guilt in the household that has not yet been expunged.

Poet on the Moon • In one of his last plays, *Poet on the Moon*, al-Hakim describes a flight to the moon on which, in spite of some misgivings from the authorities, a poet is allowed to accompany two astronauts. When they arrive, the poet is the only one who can hear the voices of moon creatures, who warn against any attempt to remove precious or hitherto unknown minerals from their domain. On the return of the spacecraft to Earth, the creatures effect the mysterious transmutation of moon rocks into ordinary vitreous earth, thus averting any premature or unprincipled exploitation of outer space.

Other major works

LONG FICTION: *'Awdat al-ruh*, 1933 (*Return of the Spirit*, 1990); *al-Qasr al-mashur*, 1936 (with Taha Husayn); *Yawmiyat na'ib fi al-aryaf*, 1937 (*Maze of Justice*, 1947); *'Usfur min al-Sharq*, 1938 (*Bird of the East*, 1966); *Raqisat al-ma'bad*, 1939; *al-Ribat al-muqaddas*, 1944.

SHORT FICTION: *Qisas*, 1949 (2 volumes); *Arini Allah*, 1953; *In the Tavern of Life and Other Stories*, 1998.

NONFICTION: *Tahta shams al-fikr*, 1938; *Tahta al-misbah al-akhdar*, 1941; *Min al-burj al-'aji*, 1941; *Zahrat al-'umr*, 1943; *Fann al-adab*, 1952; *Sijn al-'umr*, 1964 (*The Prison of Life*, 1992); *Qalabuna al-masrahi*, 1967; *'Awdat al-wa'y*, 1974 (*The Return of Consciousness*, 1985); *Watha'iq fi tariq 'Awdat al-wa'y*, 1975; *Nazarat fi al-din, al-thaqafah, al-mujtama'*, 1979; *Mamalih dakhiliyah*, 1982.

Bibliography

Badawi, M. M. *Modern Arabic Drama in Egypt*. Cambridge, England: Cambridge University Press, 1987. Badawi's study examines the state of Arabic drama in modern Egypt, touching on al-Hakim.

_____, ed. *Modern Arabic Literature*. Cambridge History of Arabic Literature. Cambridge, England: Cambridge University Press, 1992. This history of Arabic literature from the mid-nineteenth century to the late twentieth century contains a long section on al-Hakim as well as a description of many other major dramatists in Egypt and the Arabic world.

El-Enany, Rasheed. "Tawfiq al-Hakim and the West: A New Assessment of the Relationship." *British Journal of Middle Eastern Studies* 27, no. 2 (November, 2000): 165-175. An analysis of one of al-Hakim's early novels on the cultural clashes between the East and the West. Provides insights into the dramatist's views.

Long, Richard. *Tawfiq al-Hakim: Playwright of Egypt*. London: Ithaca Press, 1979. A basic biography of al-Hakim that examines his life and works. Bibliography and index.

Starkey, Paul. *From the Ivory Tower: A Critical Analysis of Tawfiq al-Hakim*. Atlantic Highlands, N.J.: Ithaca Press, 1988. Starkey presents criticism and analysis of the works of al-Hakim.

_____. "Tawfiq al-Hakim." *African Writers*. Vol. 1. New York: Charles Scribner's Sons, 1997. A concise overview of the life and works of al-Hakim.

_____. "Tawfiq al-Hakim (1898-1987): Leading Playwright of the Arab World." *Theater Three* 6 (1989). A look at the life and works of al-Hakim two years after his death.

J. R. Broadus

Peter Handke

Born: Griffen, Austria; December 6, 1942

Principal drama • *Publikumsbeschimpfung und andere Sprechstücke*, pr., pb. 1966 (*Offending the Audience*, 1969); *Selbstbezichtigung*, pr., pb. 1966 (*Self-Accusation*, 1969); *Weissagung*, pr., pb. 1966 (*Prophecy*, 1976); *Hilferufe*, pr. 1967 (*Calling for Help*, 1970); *Kaspar*, pr., pb. 1968 (English translation, 1969); *Kaspar and Other Plays*, pb. 1969; *Das Mündel will Vormund sein*, pr., pb. 1969 (*My Foot My Tutor*, 1970); *Quodlibet*, pr. 1970 (English translation, 1976); *Der Ritt über den Bodensee*, pr., pb. 1971 (*The Ride Across Lake Constance*, 1972); *Die Unvernünftigen sterben aus*, pb. 1973 (*They Are Dying Out*, 1975); *The Ride Across Lake Constance and Other Plays*, pb. 1976; *Über die Dörfer*, pr., pb. 1982 (*Among the Villages*, 1984); *Das Spiel vom Fragen: Oder, Die Reise zum sonoren Land*, pr., pb. 1989 (*Voyage to the Sonorous Land: Or, The Art of Asking*, 1996); *Die Stunde da wir nichts voneinander wussten*, pr., pb. 1992 (*The Hour We Knew Nothing of Each Other*, 1996); *Zurüstungen zur Unsterblichkeit: Ein Königsdrama*, pr., pb. 1997; *Die Fahrt im Einbaum: Oder, Das Stück zum Film vom Krieg*, pr., pb. 1999

Other literary forms • Although Peter Handke first achieved literary celebrity on the basis of his avant-garde plays, he is best known as a writer of fiction, having largely abandoned the theater early in his career. Most of Handke's novels are quite short (several are of novella length), and their language is highly concentrated. As critic June Schlueter notes, while Handke's awareness of the linguistic medium has remained constant, there has been a development in his fiction from an early emphasis on the limits of language and the failure of communication to an emphasis on the "redemptive power of poetic language."

In addition to his novels, Handke has published several books, which are often classified as nonfiction but which he himself regards as of a piece with his fiction. Among these are the much-praised novel *Wunschloses Unglück* (1972; *A Sorrow Beyond Dreams*, 1975), written in response to his mother's suicide, and *Das Gewicht der Welt* (1977; *The Weight of the World*, 1984). Handke has published a small number of short stories, essays, and several slim collections of poetry; he has also written radio plays and has written or co-written screenplays and otherwise collaborated on the making of several films. Since the 1980's, Handke has translated many works of French, Slovenian, English, and Greek writers, among them Marguerite Duras, Bruno Bayen, Aeschylus, and William Shakespeare's *The Winter's Tale* (pr. c. 1610-1611).

Achievements • Despite his rather sparse output, Peter Handke is widely regarded as an important and influential contemporary dramatist. He became one of the first of the generation of German speakers born during World War II to achieve prominence. Unlike many other postwar German and Austrian writers, he does not hark back to the Nazi era, nor does he concern himself with "the past" in any usual way. At the same time, his plays do not follow the example of Bertolt Brecht, so pervasive in the postwar German theater: Handke's plays are not theatrical in the ways Brecht's are, nor do they have Brecht's scope. Rather, they seek to define language as act and language as power.

Three of Handke's plays, *Offending the Audience*, *Kaspar*, and *The Ride Across Lake Constance*, have entered the international repertory; these works made him the most prominent German-language playwright of the 1970's. While Handke was awarded several notable honors and awards—for example, the Gerhart Hauptmann Prize in 1967 and the Schiller Prize in 1972—he refused or returned other prizes, including the Büchner Prize (won in 1973, returned in 1999) and the Kafka Prize (refused in 1979). He accepted the Salzburg Literature Prize in 1986.

Biography • Peter Handke was born in Griffen, Austria, on December 6, 1942. With the exception of a four-year period from 1944 to 1948, when he lived in Berlin, Handke lived in the country in southern Austria. In 1961, he entered the University of Graz to study law. The critic Nicholas Hern argues that this legal training influenced Handke's style: "Most of his plays . . . consist of a series of affirmative propositions each contained within one sentence which is usually a simple main clause on a main clause on a main clause plus one subordinate clause." While he was at the university, Handke published his work in *Manuskripts*, the university's literary review. From 1963 onward, he devoted himself to writing, and his first novel, *Die Hornissen* (1966; the hornets), appeared the year after he left the university.

This novel earned for Handke the chance to read at the prestigious Gruppe 47 conference in April of 1966, held that year at Princeton University. There he read from his second novel, *Der Hausierer* (1967; the peddler), and on the last day of the meeting he delivered a blistering attack on what he saw as the artistic failures of the group's older members. Handke argued that much German postwar writing was too realistic and descriptive and "failed to realize literature is made with language, not with the things that one describes with language."

(Jerry Bauer)

This outburst and the success of his first play, *Offending the Audience*, at the Frankfurt "Experimenta" theater week in June of that year, brought Handke considerable media attention; since he affected a Beatles-like hairstyle and mirrored sunglasses, he was much photographed, interviewed, and read. In 1966, he married actress Libgart Schwarz and moved to Germany from Austria. Over the next seven years, he lived in Düsseldorf, Berlin, Paris, and Kronberg (outside Frankfurt). His daughter, Amina, was born in Berlin in 1969. That same year, he joined with ten other writers to form a cooperative publishing house, Verlag der Autors. In 1979, he returned with his daughter to Salzburg in his native Austria.

In the late 1990's, Handke reestablished himself as one of the enfants terribles of German literature by vociferously taking the side of the Serbs in the Bosnian and Kosovo conflicts, thus finding himself under attack from fellow writers, journalists, and politicians alike. Most of Handke's literary output in the late 1990's is a reflection of and a commentary on the events in the former Yugoslavia. As part of his condemnation of the North Atlantic Treaty Organization (NATO) attacks on Serbia, Handke returned the Georg Büchner Prize, including a substantial stipend, that the German government had awarded him in 1973, and formally renounced his membership in the Roman Catholic Church, which he accused of supporting what he called the genocide of the Serbian people. At the same time, he proudly accepted his elevation to the rank of Knight of Serbia.

Analysis • Peter Handke calls his first three plays–*Offending the Audience, Self-Accusation*, and *Prophecy–Sprechstücke* (literally, speaking pieces). Both "speech" and "piece" are important, for Handke does away with such mundane dramatic considerations as plot and character, replacing them with activities and speakers. Thus, all three plays are made up of speech—pronounced word and rhetorical gesture—which is not involved in imitating an action. The plays examine the power and banality of public and private speech.

Offending the Audience • *Offending the Audience*, the first of these plays to be produced, appeared in 1966 at Frankfurt's Theater am Turm, a theater known for its dedication to the avant-garde. The play was accepted there only after it had been rejected by some sixty other more conservative theaters, and the avant-garde setting may have lessened the play's impact, for it depends on the assumptions and conventions of mainstream theater—a theater in which William Shakespeare, Friedrich Schiller, and more recently Brecht have been the mainstays of the repertory. The play also depends on the predictable reactions of the patrons of such a theater—middlebrow, middle-class, and conservatively dressed.

The audience enters a theater that appears set up for business as usual, complete with assiduous ushers and elegant programs. The usual routine occurs: Doors close and lights dim. When the curtain opens, four speakers are revealed (usually, but not necessarily, two men and two women) on a bare stage. The four ignore the audience and insult one another. Their speeches overlap and blend until at last a formal pattern is established, which culminates in the four saying one word in unison. (Handke has left what they actually say here unscripted.) The four now face the audience and, after a pause, begin to address it directly. Handke has simply broken his text into paragraphs, presumably each one spoken by a different speaker. He has not assigned gestures or speeches, and the script can in no manner be construed as a dialogue among the speakers. Thus, the director has a free hand with the assignment of speeches and movements.

The direct address to the audience concerns four basic themes: the audience's expectations of the theater, the nature of the audience itself, the nature of theatrical illusion and its absence in the current piece, and, by extension, the roles the spectators play in society. These topics are not presented in a logical way but, rather, in a repetitive intertwining of single, declarative sentences. A short sample from Michael Roloff's translation conveys the flavor:

> The possibilities of theatre are not exploited here. The realm of possibilities is not exhausted. The theatre is not unbound. The theatre is bound. Fate is meant ironically here. We are not theatrical.

After some twenty minutes of this, the audience is told, "Before you leave you will be offended." They are then told why they are going to be offended. The piece ends with a decrescendo of silly and vulgar insults. At the end of the play, the curtain closes, only to open again as the four speakers take bows to recorded applause.

So described, one has difficulty seeing why this was a popular play. Handke demonstrates the power of convention by removing it from the context in which it usually exists. He goes further by discussing those same conventions while violating them. The play affirms the power of theater by pointing out that the conventions are mistaken for the reality. When theater imitates, it does so through a structure of conventional movement and language. Handke forces the audience to see how often it confuses the convention with the reality it purports to imitate.

Self-Accusation • Similar themes animate the two other *Sprechstücke. Self-Accusation* has two speakers—one male, one female—who in no sense carry on a dialogue. Rather, speaking alternately and together, they portray an Everyman who spells out the process of growing up civilized. Every sentence in the dialogue has "I" as its subject. Again a short quote will convey more than a description.

> I learned. I learned the words. I learned the verbs. I learned the difference between singular and plural. . . . I learned the adjectives. I learned the difference between mine and yours. I acquired vocabulary.

In this play, the processes of verbal, moral, and physical growth are intertwined by Handke's curiously declarative style. This style seems to imply that verbal growth is the controlling factor in shaping human life: Language civilizes at great cost and it creates our world.

Kaspar • This notion that language creates the individual's world also motivates Handke's first full-length play, *Kaspar*. This play has a historical antecedent. In Nuremberg in 1828, a boy, Kaspar Hauser, was discovered, who—as a result of abuse and sensory deprivation—could, at age sixteen, say only one sentence: "I want to become a horseman such as my father once was." Handke, however, does not write historical drama. He says in the play's introduction that his play "does not show how IT REALLY IS OR REALLY WAS with Kaspar Hauser. It shows how someone can be made to speak through speaking. The play could also be called *speech torture.*"

The play, like the *Sprechstücke*, presents a speaker on what is obviously still a stage, although a much more cultured stage than in the earlier plays. This speaker, Kaspar, is costumed and heavily made up as a Chaplinesque clown. This clown interacts with the voices of four *Einsager*, a neologism that literally means "in-sayers" but implies indoctrinator. (Michael Roloff translates it as prompter.) Later, Kaspar is joined by six other Kaspars all identically made-up and costumed.

Handke lists sixteen stages through which Kaspar must pass, beginning with the question "Can Kaspar, the owner of one sentence, begin and begin to do something with his sentence?" and ending with "What is now Kaspar, Kaspar?" Handke has stressed his concern with identity and individuality by changing Kaspar's only sentence to "I want to be a person like someone else was once."

Basically three main movements constitute the play. Kaspar and the audience learn that his one sentence is inadequate. The *Einsager* teach Kaspar new sentences until he has mastered language. It is at this point that the identical Kaspars appear. Finally

Kaspar discovers that by accepting the *Einsager*'s language he has lost his uniqueness and identity. As Kaspar says, "I was trapped from my first sentence."

Voices heard on the loudspeaker suggest all the voices of coercion one hears in growing up—parents' warnings, teachers' threats, government propaganda. By calling the speakers "in-sayers," Handke demonstrates how quickly humans internalize such voices. The audience is never fully certain where these prompters exist. Are they outside or inside Kaspar's head? Handke might argue that humankind cannot answer that question about its own consciousness and that this inability to answer is the point. Each human being is made up of others' speech that has been internalized.

As the play progresses, the action onstage and the verbal images in Kaspar's speech become increasingly more violent; indeed, there is the sense of a barely hidden threat throughout the play. By the end, Kaspar is left writhing on the ground to a shrill electronic noise, shouting over and over Othello's phrase, "Goats and monkeys."

Writer June Schlueter suggests that *Othello*, like *Kaspar*, is concerned with the "idiocy of language": Othello is led astray by Iago's lines, just as Kaspar is by the *Einsager*'s sentences. A significant difference between the two works, however, is the difference between Renaissance and modern concepts of language. Iago manipulates language to his own ends and violates the moral order by destroying the relation between the world of objects and events and the world of language. Kaspar's *Einsager* use a language that has only a tenuous and conventional relationship to the world of ideas and events. The play seems to argue that this is the only relationship language can have to reality.

Influence of Wittgenstein • In discussing Handke's ideas of language, nearly every critic mentions his countryman, the philosopher Ludwig Wittgenstein (1889-1951), and the group of linguists and philosophers known as the Vienna Circle, who flourished in the 1920's. Although Handke admits to having read Wittgenstein and some of the others, he has not explained the effect of this philosophy on his work, nor have critics satisfactorily suggested what this relationship might be.

Wittgenstein's first major work, "Logischphilosophische Abhandlung," (1921; best known by the bilingual German and English edition title of *Tractatus Logico-Philosophicus*, 1922, 1961), reveals similarities with Handke's understanding and use of language. The first is a stylistic similarity. Both writers use simple declarative sentences, frequently not connected by the usual linguistic connectors to what precedes or follows. In part, the style is a working out of Wittgenstein's dictum: "What can be said can be said clearly, and what cannot be said must be passed over in silence."

The concern with "what can be said" and "what cannot" seems common to both writers. Wittgenstein seeks to put a limit to philosophy, which he defines as "not a body of doctrine, but an activity." One "does philosophy," and its value lies in its doing. Similarly, Handke presents a definition of speech as an activity in which the nature, direction, and energy of the act are all more important than the content conveyed by the speech. That about which "we must remain silent" Wittgenstein calls "the mystical," by which he means not only the subjective religious feelings ordinarily associated with that term but also such normal areas of philosophic inquiry as ethics and aesthetics. Indeed he seems to put ontology (the question of existence) in the realm of the mystical: "It is not *how* things are in the world that is mystical, but *that* it exists."

The notion that humankind infers the existence of the world from language extends throughout Handke's work and even approaches the notion that humans create the world by speaking about it and by hearing elders speak about it. Drama has traditionally dealt with those subjective feelings and expressions about which Wittgenstein says humankind "must pass over in silence." In fact, Handke does pass over them in silence. The expressions of subjective feelings (and they are very rare) are offered as objective statements and have no value beyond themselves.

Thus, one becomes aware of a hole, an absence, in the middle of Handke's work. His dramas seem to be concerned with aesthetics, ethics, and identity—yet there is no language in them that discusses these issues; they are approached through silence. One could argue that Handke parodies a Wittgensteinian universe to show its inadequacies. A more consistent understanding of the plays, however, might be approached through another of Wittgenstein's ideas, the pictorial theory of language, which argues that language can picture reality and that propositions "show what they say." Further, he insists, "What can be shown, *cannot* be said."

This last proposition is extremely important in considering Handke's purpose. Instead of parodying Wittgenstein's universe, he displays its tragicomic nature. Because language is always inadequate, humankind is led to wildly comic errors and actions; because human beings can never speak about that which is most important, they are left alone and twitching at the end of the action.

During his later years, Wittgenstein rethought the *Tractatus Logico-Philosophicus* and challenged his own picture theory. He admitted that language arises out of specific social occasions, and, therefore, words need not always name objects. In his posthumously published *Philosophical Investigations* (1953), Wittgenstein developed the notion of language games and stressed that speech is an activity.

The Ride Across Lake Constance • Handke clearly likes to play language games, but for him, unlike Wittgenstein, they are never innocent. Handke's games are always zero-sum; there is a winner and loser, a master and servant, a speaker and listener. In this, Handke seems to participate in a major theme of German drama, the relation of the individual will to authority. His use of this theme creates a tragic paradox: Language, which enables human beings to conceive of freedom, is the principal force that prevents them from achieving it.

Handke's two full-length plays *The Ride Across Lake Constance* and *They Are Dying Out* explore this paradox and the power relations that it creates. Unlike Handke's earlier plays, *The Ride Across Lake Constance* has a real set—a kind of nineteenth century drawing room with a long double staircase leading into it. There are some suggestions that this may be a madhouse, but Handke, as usual, never specifies. What is apparent is that it is a set. Handke insists on the theatricality of the piece. He arbitrarily assigns the names of famous German actors to his characters, but he suggests that "the characters should bear the names of the actors playing the role . . . the actors are and play themselves at one and the same time." In an interview, Handke said that the play examines "poses" as they are used onstage and in life.

The title derives from a folktale in which the hero, lost in fog, crosses Lake Constance on very thin ice. When learning of his narrow escape, he dies of fright. "To ride on Lake Constance" is the German equivalent for the expression "skating on thin ice." Author Nicholas Hern suggests that the "thin ice" in the play is society itself and that the play explores what society means by the concepts of sense and madness.

This sense of the social definition of madness relates this play to the themes of power and domination in all Handke's work. The familiar images and apparatus of dominance fill the stage. One woman is sold a riding crop and later beaten, another seeks to dominate a man through temptation. Two men are shown in a clear master-servant relationship. Yet the audience feels neither threatened nor enraged by these relationships and acts because they appear as theatrical poses.

A typical first reaction to *The Ride Across Lake Constance* is befuddlement; New York theater critic Clive Barnes admitted that within the first two minutes of the play, he realized that he did not know what was going on. One suspects that Handke wants the audience to see that reality is a mental construction socially imposed and accepted and that madness reconstitutes the world in a socially unacceptable but no less valid way. Again language, sentences, and the place of objects deny the viewer the freedom to recreate reality except through madness.

They Are Dying Out • Handke's next play, *They Are Dying Out*, suggests that humankind's normal construction of the world is equally mad. Its protagonist, Herr Quitt, is a protean, laissez-faire capitalist of the sort who prompted Germany's economic recovery. Throughout the play, he sees into and seems to criticize capitalist society. As Schlueter points out, however, no critic has convincingly given a definition of Handke's politics; she adds that the play "stops considerably short of becoming a Marxist platform." The German title of the play means, literally, the irrational are dying out, and the play seems to be about irrationality. Quitt cannot reconcile his inner sensibilities with his social actions. When he denounces capitalism, another capitalist says, "It was just a game, wasn't it? Because in reality you are. . . ." Quitt cuts him off with, "Yes, but only in reality." This notion that one can choose the irrational world and that it is truer than the rational world motivates one strain of German Romantic thought, especially that of the poet Novalis.

Again, it is unclear where Handke stands. His hero commits suicide at the end of the play by beating his head against a rock to the sound of recorded belching. Is this the defeat of the poet by the modern world? Is it the ultimate image of the failure of civilization? Whatever it is, Handke believes that one cannot talk rationally about it. Handke can only offer the image. Thus Quitt, who is shown as a dominant force throughout the play, destroys himself in part because of society's dominion over him, because of the understanding that society drives human beings away from their true selves.

Because Handke is in this play more concerned with society than language, it is the first of his plays to have conventional characters and something approaching a plot. Narrative seems here to be the appropriate mode. This might suggest that Handke's career as a dramatist began with an examination of language's inability to communicate, passed through an examination of how language forces people to construct reality, and concludes with the acknowledgment that language is only one of the forces that determine humankind. His work centers on force, attack, control, and humans' inability to protect themselves.

1990's plays • Handke's career as a dramatist began with an examination of language's inability to communicate and passed on to an examination of how language forces humans to construct reality. In the plays he wrote in the late 1990's responding to the Balkan conflict, *Zurüstungen zur Unsterblichkeit* (preparations for immortality) and *Die Fahrt im Einbaum* (the journey in the dug-out canoe, or the play about the film about the war), he arrives again at a position first articulated in *Kaspar*: Language is a tool of manipulation and indoctrination. The *Einsager*, the linguistic social engineers of his most famous play, turn into the chorus of the three journalists in *Die Fahrt im Einbaum*.

Other major works

LONG FICTION: *Die Hornissen*, 1966; *Der Hausierer*, 1967; *Die Angst des Tormanns beim Elfmeter*, 1970 (*The Goalie's Anxiety at the Penalty Kick*, 1972); *Der kurze Brief zum langen Abschied*, 1972 (*Short Letter, Long Farewell*, 1974); *Wunschloses Unglück*, 1972 (*A Sorrow Beyond Dreams*, 1975); *Die Stunde der wahren Empfindung*, 1975 (*A Moment of True Feeling*, 1977); *Die linkshändige Frau*, 1976 (*The Left-Handed Woman*, 1978); *Langsame Heimkehr*, 1979 (*The Long Way Around*, 1985); *Die Lehre der Sainte-Victoire*, 1980 (*The Lesson of Mont Sainte-Victoire*, 1985); *Kindergeschichte*, 1981 (*Child Story*, 1985); *Der Chinese des Schmerzes*, 1983 (*Across*, 1986); *Slow Homecoming*, 1985 (includes *The Long Way Around, The Lesson of Mont Sainte-Victoire*, and *Child Story*); *Die Wiederholung*, 1986 (*Repetition*, 1988); *Die Abwesenheit: Ein Märchen*, 1987 (*Absence*, 1990); *Nachmittag eines Schriftstellers*, 1987 (*The Afternoon of a Writer*, 1989); *Mein Jahr in der Niemandsbucht: Ein Märchen aus den neuen Zeiten*, 1994 (*My Year in the No-Man's-Bay*, 1998); *In einer dunklen Nacht ging ich aus meinem stillen Haus*, 1997 (*On a Dark Night I Left My Silent House*, 2000); *Der Bildverlust: Oder, Durch die Sierra de Gredos*, 2002.

SHORT FICTION: *Begrüssung des Aufsichtsrats*, 1967.

POETRY: *Die Innenwelt der Aussenwelt der Innenwelt*, 1969 (*The Innerworld of the Outerworld of the Innerworld*, 1974); *Gedicht an die Dauer*, 1986.

SCREENPLAYS: *Chronik der laufenden Ereignisse*, 1971; *Der Himmel über Berlin*, 1987 (*Wings of Desire*, with Wim Wenders, 1987).

TELEPLAY: *Falsche Bewegung*, 1975.

NONFICTION: *Ich bin ein Bewohner des Elfenbeinturms*, 1972; *Als das Wünschen noch geholfen hat*, 1974; *Das Gewicht der Welt*, 1977 (journal; *The Weight of the World*, 1984); *Das Ende des Flanierens*, 1980; *Die Geschichte des Bleistifts*, 1982 (journal); *Phantasien der Wiederholung*, 1983 (journal); *Aber ich lebe nur von den Zwischenräumen*, 1987; *Versuch über die Müdigkeit*, 1989; *Versuch über die Jukebox*, 1990; *Versuch über den geglückten Tag*, 1991; *The Jukebox and Other Essays on Storytelling*, 1994 (translation of *Versuch über die Müdigkeit, Versuch über die Jukebox*, and *Versuch über den geglückten Tag*); *Eine winterliche Reise zu den Flüssen Donau, Save, Morawa and Drina: Oder, Gerechtigkeit für Serbien*, 1996 (*A Journey to the Rivers: Justice for Serbia*, 1997); *Am Felsfenster morgens: Und andere Ortszeiten 1982-1987*, 1998 (journal).

TRANSLATIONS: *Prometheus, gefesselt*, 1986 (of Aeschylus); *Das Wintermärchen*, 1991 (of William Shakespeare's *The Winter's Tale*).

Bibliography

DeMeritt, Linda. *New Subjectivity and Prose Forms of Alienation: Peter Handke and Botho Strauss*. New York: Peter Lang, 1987. Examines the use of social psychology in German-language twentieth century literature by providing critical interpretation of Handke's and Strauss's prose works.

Firda, Richard A. *Peter Handke*. New York: Twayne, 1993. The most accessible and comprehensive introductory survey of Handke's work up to the early 1990's. Includes a good biography and a jargon-free overview of his major dramatic and prose works. Bibliography and index.

Hern, Nicholas. *Peter Handke*. New York: Ungarm, 1971. One of the first scholarly studies of Handke, particularly useful for a study of his early *Sprechstücke* plays.

Konzett, Matthias. *The Rhetoric of National Dissent in Thomas Bernhard, Peter Handke, and Elfriede Jelinek.* Rochester, N.Y.: Camden House, 2000. Examines the ways in which three authors expose state-directed consensus and harmonization that impede the development of multicultural awareness in modern-day Europe. Explores how Handke focuses on national suppression of post-ideological voices in historians' rendering of marginalized individuals.

Schlueter, June. *The Plays and Novels of Peter Handke.* Pittsburgh: University of Pittsburgh Press, 1983. Concentrates on the use of language in Handke's work. Useful as an update of the Hern book.

Sidney F. Parham,
updated by Franz G. Blaha

Lorraine Hansberry

Born: Chicago, Illinois; May 19, 1930
Died: New York, New York; January 12, 1965

Principal drama · *A Raisin in the Sun*, pr., pb. 1959; *The Sign in Sidney Brustein's Window*, pr. 1964, pb. 1965; *To Be Young, Gifted, and Black*, pr. 1969, pb. 1971; *Les Blancs*, pr. 1970, pb. 1972; *The Drinking Gourd*, pb. 1972 (Robert Nemiroff, editor); *What Use Are Flowers?*, pb. 1972 (Nemiroff, editor); *Les Blancs: The Collected Last Plays of Lorraine Hansberry*, pb. 1972 (includes *Les Blancs*, *The Drinking Gourd*, and *What Use Are Flowers?*)

Other literary forms · As a result of her involvement in the Civil Rights movement, Lorraine Hansberry wrote the narrative for *The Movement: Documentary of a Struggle for Equality* (1964), a book of photographs, for the Student Nonviolent Coordinating Committee (SNCC). Because she died at such a young age, Hansberry left much of her work unpublished, but her husband, Robert Nemiroff, the literary executor of her estate, edited and submitted some of it for publication and, in the case of *Les Blancs*, production. In addition, he arranged excerpts from Hansberry's various writings into a seven-and-a-half-hour radio program entitled *To Be Young, Gifted, and Black*, which was broadcast on radio station WBAI in 1967. This program was later adapted for the stage, opening at the Cherry Lane Theatre in New York on January 2, 1969, and becoming the longest running production of the 1968-1969 season. Many readers know Hansberry through the anthology of her writings edited by Nemiroff, *To Be Young, Gifted, and Black: Lorraine Hansberry in Her Own Words* (1969), a book that has enjoyed very wide circulation.

Achievements · Lorraine Hansberry's career was very brief, only two of her plays being produced in her lifetime, yet she recorded some very impressive theatrical achievements. She was only twenty-nine when *A Raisin in the Sun* appeared on Broadway, and its great success earned for her recognition that continues to this day. When *A Raisin in the Sun* was voted best play of the year by the New York Drama Critics Circle, she became the first black person as well as the youngest person to win the award. In 1973, a musical adapted from *A Raisin in the Sun*, entitled *Raisin* (with libretto by Nemiroff), won a Tony Award as best musical of the year (1974). She was respected and befriended by such figures as Paul Robeson and James Baldwin, and she helped in an active way to further the work of the Civil Rights movement. Though her later work has received far less recognition than her first play, *A Raisin in the Sun* continues to enjoy a broad popularity.

Biography · Lorraine Vivian Hansberry was born on May 19, 1930, in the South Side of Chicago, the black section of the city. Her parents, Carl and Mamie Hansberry, were well-off. Her father was a United States deputy marshal for a time and then opened a successful real estate business in Chicago. Despite her family's affluence, they were forced by local covenants to live in the poor South Side. When Hansberry was eight years old, her father decided to test the legality of those covenants by buying a home in a white section of the city. Hansberry later recalled one incident that occurred shortly after the family's move to a white neighborhood: A mob gathered outside their home, and a brick, thrown through a window, barely missed her before embedding itself in a wall.

In order to stay in the house, to which he was not given clear title, Carl Hansberry instituted a civil rights suit against such restrictive covenants. When he lost in Illinois courts, he and the National Assocation for the Advancement of Colored People (NAACP) carried an appeal to the United States Supreme Court, which, on November 12, 1940, reversed the ruling of the Illinois supreme court and declared the local covenants illegal. Thus, Lorraine had a consciousness of the need to struggle for civil rights from a very young age. Her father, despite his legal victory, grew increasingly pessimistic about the prospects for change in the racial situation, and he finally decided to leave the country and retire in Mexico City. He had a stroke during a visit to Mexico, however, and died in 1945.

Hansberry's uncle, William Leo Hansberry, was also an important influence on her. A scholar of African history who taught at Howard University, his pupils included Nnamdi Azikewe, the first president of Nigeria, and Kwame Nkrumah of Ghana. Indeed, William Leo Hansberry was such a significant figure in African studies that in 1963, the University of Nigeria named its College of African Studies at Nsakka after him. While Lorraine was growing up, she was frequently exposed to the perspectives of young African students who were invited to family dinners, and this exposure helped to shape many of the attitudes later found in her plays.

Lorraine, the youngest of four children, was encouraged to excel and was expected to succeed. After attending Englewood High School, she enrolled in the University of Wisconsin as a journalism student. She did not fare very well at the university, however, and felt restricted by the many requirements of the school. After two years, she left Wisconsin and enrolled in the New School for Social Research in New York, where she was permitted greater leeway in choosing courses.

Once in New York, Hansberry began writing for several periodicals, including *Freedom*, Paul Robeson's monthly magazine. She quickly became a reporter and then an associate editor of the magazine. In New York, she met Robert Nemiroff, then a student at New York University, and they were married in June of 1953. By this time, Hansberry had decided to be a writer, and although the bulk of her energies went into writing, she did hold a variety of jobs during the next few years. When Nemiroff acquired a good position with music publisher Phil Rose, she quit working and began writing full-time.

Hansberry's first completed work was *A Raisin in the Sun*, which, after an initial struggle for financial back-

(Library of Congress)

ing, opened on Broadway at the Ethel Barrymore Theatre on March 11, 1959. The play, starring Sidney Poitier, Ruby Dee, Louis Gossett, Jr., and Claudia McNeil, was an enormous success, running for 530 performances, and in May, winning the New York Drama Critics Circle Award.

Soon thereafter, Hansberry and Nemiroff moved from their apartment in Greenwich Village to a home in Croton, New York, in order for Hansberry to have more privacy for her work. At the same time, her success made her a public figure, and she used her newfound fame to champion the causes of civil rights and African independence. She made important speeches in a variety of places and once confronted then Attorney General Robert Kennedy on the issue of civil rights.

It was not until 1964 that Hansberry produced another play, *The Sign in Sidney Brustein's Window*, and by that time she was seriously ill. The play opened at the Longacre Theatre on October 15, 1964, to generally good but unenthusiastic reviews, and Nemiroff had to struggle to keep it open, a number of times placing advertisements in newspapers asking for support, accepting financial support from friends and associates, and once accepting the proceeds from a spontaneous collection taken up by the audience when it was announced that without additional funds, the play would have to close. On this uncertain financial basis, production of the play continued from week to week.

Hansberry's life continued in much the same way. While the play struggled, she was in a hospital bed dying of cancer. She once lapsed into a coma and was not expected to recover, but for a brief time she did rally, recovering all of her faculties. Her strength gave out, however, and on January 12, 1965, she died. That night, the Longacre Theatre closed its doors in mourning, and *The Sign in Sidney Brustein's Window* closed after 101 performances.

Analysis • Lorraine Hansberry claimed Sean O'Casey as one of the earliest and strongest influences on her work and cited his realistic portrayal of character as the source of strength in his plays. In *To Be Young, Gifted, and Black*, she praised O'Casey for describing

> the human personality in its totality. O'Casey never fools you about the Irish . . . the Irish drunkard, the Irish braggart, the Irish liar . . . and the genuine heroism which must naturally emerge when you tell the truth about people. This . . . is the height of artistic perception . . . because when you believe people so completely . . . then you also believe them in their moments of heroic assertion: you don't doubt them.

In her three most significant plays, *A Raisin in the Sun*, *The Sign in Sidney Brustein's Window*, and *Les Blancs*, one can see Hansberry's devotion to the principles that she valued in O'Casey. First, she espoused realistic drama; second, she believed that the ordinary individual has a capacity for heroism; and finally, she believed that drama should reveal to the audience its own humanity and its own capacity for heroism.

Hansberry claimed that her work was realistic rather than naturalistic, explaining that

> naturalism tends to take the world as it is and say: this is what it is . . . it is "true" because we see it every day in life . . . you simply photograph the garbage can. But in realism . . . the artist . . . imposes . . . not only what *is* but what is *possible* . . . because that is part of reality too.

For Hansberry, then, realism involved more than a photographic faithfulness to the real world. She sought to deliver a universal message but realized that "in order to create the universal you must pay very great attention to the specific. Universality . . . emerges from truthful identity of what is." This concern for realism was present from the very beginning of Hansberry's career and persisted in her work, though she did occasionally depart from it in small ways, such as in the symbolic rather than literal presence of "The Woman" in *Les Blancs*, that character symbolizing the spirit of liberty and freedom that lives inside humanity.

Essential to Hansberry's vision of reality was the belief that the average person has within him or her the capacity for heroism. Hansberry believed that each human being is not only "dramatically interesting" but also a "creature of stature," and this is one of the most compelling features of her drama. Like O'Casey, Hansberry paints a full picture of each character, complete with flaws and weaknesses, yet she does not permit these flaws to hide the characters' "stature." Perhaps she expressed this idea best in *A Raisin in the Sun*, when Lena Younger berates her daughter Beneatha for condemning her brother, Walter Lee. Lena says, "When you start measuring somebody, measure him right, child, measure him right. Make sure you done taken into account what hills and valleys he come through before he got to wherever he is."

For Hansberry, each character's life is marked by suffering, struggle, and weakness, yet in each case, the final word has not been written. Just as Beneatha's brother can rise from his degradation, just as Sidney (in *The Sign in Sidney Brustein's Window*) can overcome his ennui, so each of her characters possesses not only a story already written but also possibilities for growth, accomplishment, and heroism. Hansberry permits no stereotypes in her drama, opting instead for characters that present a mixture of positive and negative forces.

Hansberry's realistic style and her stress on the possibilities for heroism within each of her characters have everything to do with the purpose that she saw in drama. As James Baldwin observed, Hansberry made no bones about asserting that art has a purpose, that it contained "the energy that could change things."

In *A Raisin in the Sun*, Hansberry describes a poor black family living in Chicago's South Side, her own childhood home, and through her realistic portrayal of their financial, emotional, and racial struggles, as well as in her depiction of their ability to prevail, she offers her audience a model of hope and perseverance and shows the commonality of human aspirations, regardless of color. In *The Sign in Sidney Brustein's Window*, she takes as her subject the disillusioned liberal Sidney Brustein, who has lost faith in the possibility of creating a better world. After all of his disillusionment, he realizes that despair is not an answer, that the only answer is hope despite all odds and logic, that change depends on his commitment to it.

So too, in *Les Blancs*, Hansberry gives her audience a character, Tshembe Matoseh, who has a comfortable, pleasant, secure life and who seeks to avoid commitment to the cause of African independence, though he believes in the justness of that cause. He learns that change comes about only through commitment, and that such commitment often means the abandonment of personal comfort on behalf of something larger.

A Raisin in the Sun • Hansberry's earliest play, *A Raisin in the Sun*, is also her finest and most successful work. The play is set in the South Side of Chicago, Hansberry's childhood home, and focuses on the events that transpire during a few days in the life of the Younger family, a family headed by Lena Younger, the mother; the other family members are her daughter, Beneatha, her son, Walter Lee, and his wife, Ruth, and son, Travis. The play focuses on the problem of what the family should do with ten thousand dollars that Lena receives as an insurance payment after the death of her husband, Walter Lee, Sr. The money seems a blessing at first, but the family is torn, disagreeing on how the money should be spent.

The play's title is taken from Langston Hughes's poem "Harlem" and calls attention to the dreams of the various characters, and the effects of having those dreams deferred. The set itself, fully realistic, emphasizes this theme from the first moment of the play. The furniture, once chosen with care, has been well cared for, yet it is drab, undistinguished, worn out from long years of service. The late Walter Lee, Sr., was a man of dreams, but he could never catch up with them, and he died, exhausted and wasted, worn out like the furniture, at an early age. His family is threatened with the same fate, but his insurance money holds out hope for the fulfillment of dreams. Lena and Walter Lee, however, disagree about what to do with the money. Walter Lee hates his job as a chauffeur and plans to become his own man by opening a liquor store with some friends, but Lena instead makes a down payment on a house with one-third of the money, and plans to use another third to finance Beneatha's medical studies.

After the two argue, Lena realizes that she has not permitted her son to be a man and has stifled him, just as the rest of the world has. In order to make up for the past, she entrusts him with the remaining two-thirds of the money, directing him to take Beneatha's portion and put it into a savings account for her, using the final third as he sees fit. Walter Lee, however, invests all the money in a foolhardy scheme and discovers shortly thereafter that one of his partners has bilked him of the money.

The house that Lena has purchased is in a white neighborhood, and a Mr. Lindner has approached the Youngers, offering to buy back the house—at a profit to the Youngers—because the members of the community do not want blacks living there. Walter Lee at first scornfully refuses Lindner's offer, but once he has lost all the money he is desperate to recoup his losses and calls Lindner, willing to sell the house. The family is horrified at how low Walter has sunk, but when Beneatha rejects him, claiming there is "nothing left to love" in him, Lena reminds her that "There is always something to love. And if you ain't learned that, you ain't learned nothing." Lena asks Beneatha, "You give him up for me? You wrote his epitaph too—like the rest of the world? Well, who give you the privilege?" The epitaph is indeed premature, for when Lindner arrives and Walter is forced to speak in his son's presence, Walter gains heroic stature by rejecting the offer, telling Lindner in simple, direct terms that they will move into their house because his father "earned it." It is a moment during which Walter comes into manhood, and if it has taken him a long while to do so, the moment is all the richer in heroism.

The theme of heroism found in an unlikely place is perhaps best conveyed through the symbol of Lena's plant. Throughout the play, Lena has tended a small, sickly plant that clings tenaciously to life despite the lack of sunlight in the apartment. Its environment is harsh, unfavorable, yet it clings to life anyway—somewhat like Walter, whose life should long ago have extinguished any trace of heroism in him. Hansberry gives her audience a message of hope.

Hansberry also reminds her audience of the common needs and aspirations of all humanity, and she does so without oversimplification. None of the characters in the play is a simple type, not even Lindner, who might easily have been presented as an incarnation of evil. Instead, Lindner is conveyed as a human being. When asked why she portrayed Lindner in this manner, Hansberry replied "I have treated Mr. Lindner as a human being merely because he is one; that does not make the meaning of his call less malignant, less sick." Here is where Hansberry calls her audience to action. She reminds the audience of what it is to be human and enjoins them to respect the dignity of all their fellows.

An interesting subtheme in the play, one that would be developed far more fully later in *Les Blancs*, is introduced by Joseph Asagai, an African student with a romantic interest in Beneatha. Some of the most moving speeches in the play belong to Asagai, and when Beneatha temporarily loses hope after Walter has lost all the money, Asagai reminds her of her ideals and the need to keep working toward improvement in the future. When Beneatha asks where it will all end, Asagai rejects the question, asking, "End? Who even spoke of an end? To life? To living?" Beneatha does not fully understand Asagai's argument at the time, but its meaning must be clear enough to the audience, who will see at the end of the play that Walter's victory is not an end, but rather one small, glorious advance. There will be other trials, other problems to overcome, but, as Asagai says, any other problem "will be the problem of another time."

The Sign in Sidney Brustein's Window • Hansberry's second play, *The Sign in Sidney Brustein's Window*, never matched the success of her first, but it, too, uses a realistic format and was drawn from her own life. Instead of South Side Chicago, it is set in Greenwich Village, Hansberry's home during the early years of her marriage with Robert Nemiroff, and the central character is one who must have resembled many of Hansberry's friends. He is Sidney Brustein, a lapsed liberal, an intellectual, a former insurgent who has lost faith in his ability to bring about constructive change. As the play opens, Sidney moves from one project, a nightclub that failed, to another, the publication of a local newspaper, which Sidney insists will be apolitical. His motto at the opening of the play is "Presume no commitment, disavow all engagement, mock all great expectations. And above all else, avoid the impulse to correct." Sidney's past efforts have failed, and his lost faith is much the same as Beneatha's in *A Raisin in the Sun*.

The surrounding environment goes a long way toward explaining Sidney's cynicism. His wife, Iris, has been in psychoanalysis for two years, and her troubled soul threatens their marriage. Iris's older sister, Mavis, is anti-Semitic, and her other sister, Gloria, is a high-class call girl who masquerades as a model. Sidney's upstairs neighbor, David Ragin, is a homosexual playwright whose plays invariably assert "the isolation of the soul of man, the alienation of the human spirit, the desolation of all love, all possible communication." Organized crime controls politics in the neighborhood, and drug addiction is rampant; one of Sidney's employees at the defunct nightclub, Sal Peretti, died of addiction at the age of seventeen, despite Sidney's efforts to help him. Faced with these grim realities, Sidney longs to live in a high, wooded land, far from civilization, in a simpler, easier world.

The resultant atmosphere is one of disillusionment as characters lash out in anger while trying to protect themselves from pain. One of the targets of the intellectual barbs of the group is Mavis, an average, settled housewife who fusses over Iris and pretends to no intellectual stature. When the wit gets too pointed, though, Mavis cuts through the verbiage with a telling remark: "I was taught to believe that creativity and great intelligence ought to make one expansive and understanding. That if ordinary people . . . could not expect understanding from artists . . . then where indeed might we look for it at all." Only Sidney is moved by this remark; he is unable to maintain the pretense of cynicism, admitting, "I *care*. I care about it all. It takes too much energy *not* to care." Thus, Sidney lets himself be drawn into another cause, the election of Wally O'Hara to public office as an independent, someone who will oppose the drug culture and gangster rule of the neighborhood.

As Sidney throws himself into this new cause, he uses his newspaper to further the campaign, and even puts a sign, "Vote for Wally O'Hara," in his window. Idealism seems to have won out, and indeed Wally wins the election, but Sidney is put to a severe test as Iris seems about to leave him, and it is discovered that Wally is on the payroll of the gangsters. Added to all this is Gloria's suicide in Sidney's bathroom. Her death brings Sidney to a moment of crisis, and when Wally O'Hara comes into the room to offer condolences and to warn against any hasty actions, Sidney achieves a clarity of vision that reveals his heroism. Sidney says,

> *This world*—this swirling, seething madness—which you ask us to accept, to maintain—has done this . . . maimed my friends . . . emptied these rooms and my very bed. And now it has taken my sister. *This* world. Therefore, to live, to breathe—I shall *have* to fight it.

When Wally accuses Sidney of being a fool, he agrees:

> A fool who believes that death is waste and love is sweet and that the earth turns and that men change every day . . . and that people wanna be better than they are . . . and that I hurt terribly today, and that hurt is desperation and desperation is energy and energy can *move* things.

In this moment, Sidney learns true commitment and his responsibility to make the world what it ought to be. The play closes with Iris and Sidney holding each other on the couch, Iris crying in pain, with Sidney enjoining her: "Yes . . . weep now, darling, weep. Let us both weep. That is the first thing: to let ourselves feel again . . . then, tomorrow, we shall make something strong of this sorrow."

As the curtain closes, the audience can scarcely fail to apply these closing words to themselves. Only if they permit themselves to feel the pain, Hansberry claims, will it be possible to do anything to ease that pain in the future. James Baldwin, referring to the play, said, "it is about nothing less than our responsibility to ourselves and to others," a consistent theme in Hansberry's drama. Again and again, she reminds the audience of their responsibility to act in behalf of a better future, and the basis for this message is her affirmative vision. Robert Nemiroff says that she found reason to hope "in the most unlikely place of all: the lives most of us lead today. Precisely, in short, where *we* cannot find it. It was the mark of her respect for us all."

Les Blancs • Hansberry's last play of significance, *Les Blancs*, was not in finished form when she died and did not open onstage until November 15, 1970, at the Longacre Theatre, years after her death. Nemiroff completed and edited the text, though it is to a very large degree Hansberry's play. It was her least successful play, running for only forty-seven performances, but it did spark considerable controversy, garnering both extravagant praise and passionate denunciation. Some attacked the play as advocating racial warfare, while others claimed it was the best play of the year, incisive and compassionate. The play is set not in a locale drawn from Hansberry's own experience but in a place that long held her interest: Africa.

Les Blancs is Hansberry's most complex and difficult play. It takes as its subject white colonialism and various possible responses to it. At the center of the play are the members of the Matoseh family: Abioseh Senior, the father, who is not actually part of the play, having died before it opens, but who is important in that his whole life defined the various responses possible (acceptance, attempts at lawful change, rebellion); in addition, there are his sons, Abioseh, Eric, and, most important, Tshembe. Hansberry attempts to shed some light on the movement for African independence by showing the relationships of the Matosehs to the whites living in Africa. The whites of importance are Major Rice, the military commander of the colony; Charlie Morris, a reporter; Madame Neilsen, and her husband, Dr. Neilsen, a character never appearing onstage but one responsible for the presence of all the others.

Dr. Neilsen has for many years run a makeshift hospital in the jungle; he is cut in the mold of Albert Schweitzer, for he has dedicated his life to tending the medical ills of the natives. It is because of him that all the other doctors are there and because of him, too, that Charlie Morris is in Africa, for Charlie has come to write a story about the famous doctor.

Whereas Charlie comes to Africa for the first time, Tshembe and Abioseh are called back to Africa by the death of their father. Abioseh comes back a Roman Catholic priest, having renounced his African heritage and embraced the culture and beliefs of the colonialists. Tshembe, too, has taken much from the colonial culture, including his education and a European bride. He has not, however, rejected his heritage, and he is sensitive to the injustice of the colonial system. Though he sees colonialism as evil, he does not want to commit himself to opposing it. He wants to return to his wife and child and lead a comfortable, secure life.

For both Charlie and Tshembe, the visit to Africa brings the unexpected, for they return in the midst of an uprising, called "terror" by the whites and "resistance" by the blacks. Charlie gradually learns the true nature of colonialism, and Tshembe, after great struggle, learns that he cannot avoid his obligation to oppose colonialism actively.

While Charlie waits for Dr. Neilsen to return from another village, he learns from Madame Neilsen that the doctor's efforts seem to be less and less appreciated. When Tshembe comes on the scene, Charlie is immediately interested in him and repeatedly tries to engage the former student of Madame Neilsen and the doctor in conversation, but they fail to understand each other. Tshembe will accept none of the assumptions that Charlie has brought with him to Africa: He rejects the efforts of Dr. Neilsen, however well-intentioned, as representing the guilty conscience of colonialism while perpetrating the system. He also rejects Charlie's confident assumption that the facilities are so backward because of the superstitions of the natives. Charlie, on the other hand, cannot understand how Tshembe can speak so bitterly against colonialism yet not do anything to oppose it. Tshembe explains that he is one of those "who see too much to take sides," but his position becomes increasingly untenable. He is approached by members of the resistance and is asked to lead them, at which point he learns that it was his father who conceived the movement when it became clear that the colonialists, including Dr. Neilsen, saw themselves in the position of father rather than brother to the natives and would never give them freedom.

Still, Tshembe resists the commitment, but Charlie, as he leaves the scene, convinced now that the resistance is necessary, asks Tshembe, "Where are you running, man? Back to Europe? To watch the action on your telly?" Charlie reminds Tshembe that "we do what we can." Madame Neilsen herself makes Tshembe face the needs of his people. Tshembe by this time knows what his choice must be, but he is unable to make it. In his despair, he turns to Madame Neilsen, imploring her help. She tells him, "You have forgotten your geometry if you are despairing, Tshembe. I once taught you that a line goes into infinity unless it is bisected. Our country needs *warriors*, Tshembe Matoseh."

In the final scene of the play, Tshembe takes up arms against the colonialists, and Hansberry makes his decision all the more dramatic by having him kill his brother

Abioseh, who has taken the colonial side. Yet, lest anyone misunderstand the agony of his choice, Hansberry ends the play with Tshembe on his knees before the bodies of those he has loved, committed but in agony, deeply engulfed by grief that such commitment is necessary.

Les Blancs is less an answer to the problem of colonialism than it is another expression of Hansberry's deep and abiding belief in the need for individual commitment, and in the ability of the individual, once committed, to bring about positive change for the future, even if that requires suffering in the present. Surely her commitment to her writing will guarantee her work an audience far into the future.

Other major works

NONFICTION: *The Movement: Documentary of a Struggle for Equality,* 1964 (includes photographs); *To Be Young, Gifted, and Black: Lorraine Hansberry in Her Own Words,* 1969 (Robert Nemiroff, editor).

Bibliography

Carter, Steven R. *Hansberry's Drama: Commitment amid Complexity.* Urbana: University of Illinois Press, 1991. An examination of Hansberry's plays from the political standpoint. Bibliography and index.

Cheney, Anne. *Lorraine Hansberry.* New York: Twayne, 1994. A basic biography of Hansberry that examines her life and works. Bibliography and index.

Domina, Lynn. *Understanding "A Raisin in the Sun": A Student Casebook to Issues, Sources, and Historical Documents.* Westport, Conn.: Greenwood Press, 1998. A study that places Hansberry's works and life in context and examines her portrayal of African Americans in literature. Bibliography and index.

Effiong, Philip U. *In Search of a Model for African American Drama: A Study of Selected Plays by Lorraine Hansberry, Amiri Baraka, and Ntozake Shange.* Lanham, Md.: University Press of America, 2000. A study of the plays of three prominent African Americans, including Hansberry. Bibliography and index.

Kappel, Lawrence, ed. *Readings on "A Raisin in the Sun."* San Diego, Calif.: Greenhaven Press, 2001. A collection of essays that deal with aspects of Hansberry's most famous work. Bibliography and index.

Keppel, Ben. *The Work of Democracy: Ralph Bunche, Kenneth B. Clark, Lorraine Hansberry, and the Cultural Politics of Race.* Cambridge, Mass.: Harvard University Press, 1995. Keppel examines race relations and the Civil Rights movement, including a discussion of Hansberry's role in the movement. Bibliography and index.

Leeson, Richard M. *Lorraine Hansberry: A Research and Production Sourcebook.* Westport, Conn.: Greenwood Press, 1997. This sourcebook focuses on Hansberry as a dramatist, examining her portrayal of African Americans in literature. Bibliography and index.

Scheader, Catherine. *Lorraine Hansberry: A Playwright and Voice of Justice.* Springfield, N.J.: Enslow, 1998. A biography that examines Hansberry's dual roles as civil rights advocate and dramatist. Bibliography and index.

Hugh Short
updated by Katherine Lederer

Václav Havel

Born: Prague, Czechoslovakia; October 5, 1936

Principal drama • *Autostop*, pr., pb. 1961 (with Ivan Vyskočil); *Zahradni slavnost*, pr., pb. 1963 (*The Garden Party*, 1969); *Vyrozumění*, pr. 1965, pb. 1966 (*The Memorandum*, 1967); *Ztížená možnost soustředění*, pr., pb. 1968 (*The Increased Difficulty of Concentration*, 1969); *Spiklenci*, pr. 1974, pb. 1977; *Žebrácká opera*, pr. 1975, pb. 1977 (adaptation of John Gay's comic opera; *The Beggar's Opera*, 1976); *Audience*, pr. 1976, pb. 1977 (English translation, 1976); *Horský hotel*, pb. 1976, pr. 1981; *Vernisáž*, pr. 1976, pb. 1977 (*Private View*, 1978; also as *Unveiling*); *Protest*, pr. 1978 (English translation, 1980); *Largo desolato*, pb. 1985 (English translation, 1987); *Pokoušení*, pb. 1986 (*Temptation*, 1988); *Asanace*, pb. 1987, pr. 1989 (*Redevelopment: Or, Slum Clearance*, 1990); *Selected Plays, 1963-1983*, pb. 1992; *The Garden Party and Other Plays*, pb. 1993; *Selected Plays, 1984-1987*, pb. 1994

Other literary forms • Known primarily as a playwright, Václav Havel has also written criticism and poetry, plays for radio and television, and essays. Some of his poems (*Antikódy*, 1966) and essays, as well as his first two plays, were published as *Protokoly* (1966). His radio play *Anděl Strážny* was broadcast in 1968, and his television play *Motýl na anténě* appeared in West Germany in 1975. Perhaps Havel's most important essay is "Moc bezmocnych" (1978; "The Power of the Powerless," 1983).

By far Havel's most significant nondramatic work, however, is *Dopisy Olze, 1979-1982* (1985; *Letters to Olga*, 1988), which was first published in a somewhat different version in German translation, in 1984, as *Briefe an Olga: Identität und Existenz—Betrachtungen aus dem Gefängnis*. (The Czech version was issued in Canada by an émigré publisher.) The title of this remarkable book is misleading: Written in prison, these are not personal letters but rather wide-ranging reflections, tracing the author's intellectual and spiritual experience but anchored in harsh realities.

Another noteworthy nondramatic work is *Dalkovy vyslech* (1986; *Disturbing the Peace: A Conversation with Karel Hvížďala and Václav Havel*, 1990). Hvížďala, a noted Czech journalist in exile, wanted to interview Havel on his thoughts at turning fifty, but the politics of the time made it impossible to meet face to face. To work around this, Hvížďala sent written questions for reply. Havel's first attempt, answering in writing, came out too stiff and essaylike. Hvížďala was looking for a more conversational approach, so Havel turned to a tape recorder to capture oral responses, which Hvížďala subsequently transcribed.

Achievements • Václav Havel is the most important Czech playwright of the second half of the twentieth century, acclaimed both in his native land and abroad. His early plays, which established his international reputation, are, as he has modestly said, "plays about bureaucrats." They are, however, much more than that: They are about the mechanism of power, about the dehumanization built into the very institutions that are supposed to serve humanity, about the prison built by the desiccated language of bureaucracy. The fact that he is enthusiastically received in the West suggests that bureaucracy has a momentum of its own and may well be yet another Frankenstein-like offshoot of modernity, whatever its ideological underpinnings may be.

That his plays were allowed to be staged at all is attributable to the relative liberalization or demoralization of the communist control of the arts in Czechoslovakia during the 1960's. Neither the import nor the relevance of Havel's work diminished in the harsher climate of the 1970's and 1980's. As Markéta Goetz-Stankiewicz, the leading Western critic of the Czech theater, has suggested, not all Havel's work has received its due in a world that would benefit from his insight into the roots of the continuing crisis of modernity. His plays offer the sad wisdom of an art born of suffering, tempered by the ironic self-awareness and black humor that he has identified as essential to the "Central European climate."

Havel was honored in 1969 with the Austrian State Prize for European Literature. Twice, in 1968 and 1970, he received the Obie Award. However, Havel's crowning achievement in the post-Soviet era has been in the field of politics. Shortly after the nearly bloodless collapse of the communist regime in Czechoslovakia, he became the nation's first democratically elected president. After the peaceable dissolution of the nation into the Czech Republic and Slovakia, the Czechs elected him their president. His political work has earned for him numerous political awards, including the Averell Harriman Democracy Award, the Raoul Wallenberg Human Rights Award, and the Statesman of the Year Award. He has received honorary degrees from numerous colleges and universities, including an honorary degree of doctor of philosophy from York University, Toronto, Canada, in 1982.

Biography • Václav Havel was born October 5, 1936, the son of a wealthy restaurateur and entrepreneur, Václav M. Havel, himself the author of a voluminous autobiography. Some of Prague's architectural landmarks were built by Havel's father, and an uncle was the owner of Barrandov Studios, the center of Czech filmmaking. Such illustrious connections, decidedly nonproletarian, were held against the young Havel in communist Czechoslovakia, making him ineligible for any higher formal education well into the 1960's. On the other hand, as he was to note later, this very handicap forced him to view the world "from below," as an outsider—a boon to any artist.

After finishing laboratory assistant training, Havel began working in a chemical laboratory, attending high school at night; he was graduated in 1954. Between 1955 and 1957, Havel attended courses at the Faculty of Economy of the Prague Technical College. This was followed by military service and, finally, his work in the theater in Prague: first at the Theater Na Zábradlí and, from 1960, at the Balustrade.

His knowledge of the theater is truly intimate: He entered it as a stagehand, gradually moving to lighting, then to an assistant directorship, and finally becoming the *dramaturg*—that is, the literary manager—of the theater at the Balustrade. When, in the changed atmosphere of political liberalization, he was allowed to study dramaturgy, he took advantage of the opportunity, although he was already a full-fledged playwright and a literary manager, graduating in 1967.

Between 1967 and 1969, Havel became active as the chairman of the Circle of Independent Writers. This, as well as his work at the Balustrade, was prohibited by the authorities in 1969, when his plays were banned and his publications withdrawn from libraries. Officially, he ceased to exist as a Czech playwright.

During the first half of the 1970's Havel worked as a laborer in a brewery. In January, 1977, he reappeared in the public eye as one of the signatories and chief spokespeople of Charter 77, the courageous manifesto of the human rights movement in Czechoslovakia. As a result, he was imprisoned between January and May, 1977. In the same year, he wrote an open letter to Gustav Husák, the president of Czechoslovakia, and was arrested

(Miloš Fikejz)

in January, 1978. Finally, after yet another arrest, in May, 1979, he was sentenced to four and a half years in prison. He was released in 1983, in poor health.

After his release, Havel was subject to intense police surveillance, but he managed to continue meeting with other dissidents and discussing politics. In 1989, he was arrested once again for political activity and was briefly imprisoned. However, on November 17 of that year, events transpired to thrust Havel into the forefront of politics. This was the sudden collapse of communist power in Czechoslovakia, known as the Velvet Revolution (a name derived from the 1960's alternative band The Velvet Underground, but also suggesting softness and civility, as opposed to the coarse brutality of most revolutions). In ten days marked by an astonishing absence of violence, the communist government gave way to a new democratically elected government, and Havel was elected its first president.

Over the next several years, Havel presided over the successful privatization of the Czechoslovakian economy, as well as the "Velvet Divorce" in which the Czech Republic and Slovakia peaceably parted ways to become independent countries, resolving their differences through legal negotiation instead of bloodshed. Unlike other notable dissidents to become their nations' first post-communist leaders, such as Lech Wałesa of Poland or Zviad Gamsakhurdia of the Republic of Georgia, Havel had long-term staying power. He was president of Czechoslovakia from 1989 to 1992 and then was president of the Czech Republic from 1993 to 2003.

Havel's personal life was turbulent throughout the 1990's. He had recurring medical problems, at least partly the result of damage to his health during his years in prison, although his bout with lung cancer was attributed to his heavy smoking. After the loss of his wife, Olga, to cancer, he married a movie actress, Dagmar Veškrnová, a move that opened him to heavy criticism from his opponents.

Analysis • Václav Havel's plays appear in hindsight as crystallizations of the ambiguous time of relative liberalization in a monolithic totalitarian society. This may perhaps also be the reason for their success in the West: Czechoslovakia then, and the West both then and now, seem to share the mood of relativism, uncertainty, and ambiguity characteristic of any transitional period.

Although it is a matter of speculation whether Western society is actually evolving toward full-scale socialism, Czechoslovakia at the time of Havel's greatest successes (between 1963 and 1968) was without any doubt moving toward a less pervasive socialism, at least as it is defined there. The monolith was cracked; the totalitarian machinery was breaking down, though still operating by fits and starts. This created a peculiar atmosphere, exploited by Havel to great effect: What was formerly unquestionably true and clear was suddenly being questioned. The leaders themselves encouraged such questioning by admitting past mistakes that included staged trials and real executions. The followers, on the other hand, could no longer be sure that the present party line would not change shortly and were thus inhibited from acting aggressively on the party's behalf. There were indeed further changes and new revelations of misdeeds. Thus, the political situation acted as a destabilizing force, motivating people to question not only it but also everything else. This was an intense time of debate, of discoveries—and of defeats as well.

The Garden Party • Some of the questions Havel asked in *The Garden Party* could be formulated thus: Is it possible to adjust to the constantly changing policy emanating from above? If so, after all the maneuvering, is the human being still the same as before he started on the tortuous path of adjustment?

The Pludek family, middle-class, solid, and old-fashioned, fears that Hugo, their son, will not be able to make a successful career for himself in the confusing contemporary world with its contradictory signals. The Pludeks, survivors of a bygone era, manage to get by relying on routine, fortified by clichés that they keep repeating, as if trying to anchor themselves in a reality that keeps dissolving around them. In Havel's dialogue, the meaning is hilariously stripped from these clichés and proverbs by deft substitutions, so that while they still resemble proverbial sayings (for such is the form and context in which they are found), their content has been decanted from them, leaving behind an exotic sediment at once both grotesque and absurd. The result is not only absurd but also humorous and vitally meaningful on a higher level: It is immaterial whether the Pludeks' proverbs make sense because even perfect proverbs are irrelevant in the unstable world in which they live.

Hugo surprises his parents when, during and after a garden party, he penetrates an institution, learns its peculiar bureaucratic language, and turns this newly acquired knowledge against the institution and its representatives. His success is unexpected and phenomenal, but so is the price that he has to pay: He becomes a convert to the absurd and thoroughly relativist jargon of the institution, a jargon designed to hide the meaning of one's ideas, for one's commitment cannot be questioned if it is not clear what exactly one stands for. Thus, Hugo becomes an expert Inaugurator and Liquidator at the same time. When liquidation is in, he liquidates, but quickly, on noticing the slightest shift of policy, he begins to inaugurate, and so on. Thus, although Hugo is successful, he is no longer the same Hugo—indeed, his parents at first do not even recognize him. The parents themselves, however, are not immune to the contagion of the debased language, and, after a long harangue by Hugo, they accept him.

It is not necessary to point to the political allusions, because the play of necessity operates on a level of abstraction that universalizes the plight of Hugo and his parents. This quality shows Havel a worthy follower of the great masters of the Theater of the

Absurd, Samuel Beckett and Eugène Ionesco, whom Havel helped to stage at the Balustrade.

The Memorandum • *The Memorandum* is, if anything, a further and quite logical extension of Havel's concern for the debasement of language. Here he expresses this concern through the brilliant satiric device of an artificial language, Ptydepe, which the bureaucracy decides to employ for all communications.

The introduction of the new language strikes terror, not unlike an unexpected change of political line. The question Havel asks is: What happens to an otherwise loyal bureaucrat who knows nothing about the impending introduction of Ptydepe? Can he adjust? Finally, as in the previous play: What is the price of such an adjustment? Thus, some of the concerns with which Havel dealt in *The Garden Party* reappear but in high relief because of the striking effect of the artificial language with its unearthly and perverse sounds, designed to be impossible to learn, and even if learned, impossible to use. Here science makes its entrance, for Ptydepe is a scientifically designed, perfectly rational language. This beautifully implies the "scientifically" designed society of socialism, in which—so the State claims—all the imperfections are caused by the survival of "prescientific" attitudes.

Alas, the converts to the scientific and unnatural Ptydepe are not immune to sudden political change, and no sooner do they "learn" Ptydepe, than another language appears, called Chorukor, based on a diametrically opposed premise: While Ptydepe is based on the principle of maximum differentiation among words, with words increasing in length as their frequency decreases (the word for wombat, for example, is more than three hundred letters long), Chorukor is based on the notion that words with related meanings should sound the same as well, with only slight variations to distinguish them from one another.

The protagonist of *The Memorandum,* Josef Gross, is a humanist battling the opportunist responsible for the introduction of Ptydepe. When Gross's chance to put his humanistic ideals to the test comes, however, he fails, having already accepted Balass, the careerist, and Ptydepe. When Maria, a girl in whom Gross is genuinely interested, is fired by Balass, Gross does not act, for this would mean countermanding Balass's instructions and making himself vulnerable. Gross's breakdown is a tragedy that contrasts with the prodigious ability to adjust found in a man such as Balass—a type that seems to predominate in bureaucracies. It is perhaps on this level, that of the depiction of "organization man," that the play is of most interest to audiences in the West.

The Increased Difficulty of Concentration • After the success of these early plays, Havel made a departure of sorts with *The Increased Difficulty of Concentration.* Gone is the focus on bureaucracy and office intrigue but not Havel's preoccupation with language. Can language survive ethical relativism? Is it possible to have more than one personality: professional and private, with the latter subdivided further into husband and lover?

The protagonist, Dr. Huml, is a social scientist, a victim of the routine forced on him by circumstance and by his own choices. His behavior, robotlike and lacking in human feeling, is echoed by his tautological writings. It is very fitting that Dr. Huml, an intellectual, a member of the elite, becomes by the end of the play an unwitting collaborator in the dehumanizing policies to which he ostensibly objects. His writings and indeed his very life have had an alienating, dehumanizing effect, and it is only just that he in turn should become a guinea pig for others.

The experimental plays • Havel's *Spiklenci* (the conspirators), *The Beggar's Opera*, and *Horský hotel* (mountain resort) are of uneven quality because of their experimental nature and have thus been accorded less attention than his earlier plays. To be fair, one has to stress that two vital elements of the theater, the staging and the reaction of the audience, were no longer available to him, with the exception of *The Beggar's Opera*.

Havel himself is not quite sure about *Spiklenci*, in which he deals with multiple conspiracies, moving from office intrigue to the shadowy world of revolutionary dictators, generals, and prisoners. This is a somber and unreliable world in which loyalty changes as unpredictably as the party line (or official language) did before. Havel is making a point here about the importance of the individual in history. The events of conventional history—the demonstrations, government policies, and so on—are alluded to but always remain incidental and unimportant. The real history is conspiratorial. The implications are astounding: The role of the masses is that of extras; the revolution itself is a deal struck among a gang of power-hungry little people with few, if any, redeeming features. Most ominously, the system of conspiracy neutralizes the good man and gives an unfair advantage to the ambitious clod, the darling of absolute power.

The Beggar's Opera, yet another version of John Gay's masterpiece *The Beggar's Opera* (pr., pb. 1728), suggests that competing establishments, competing centers of power, are essentially the same beneath their surface enmity, as are their victims: the weak, the innocent, the defenseless. The play deserves to be staged, but perhaps Bertolt Brecht's treatment in the 1920's casts such a spell that few dare to stage Havel's version, whatever its merit.

Horský hotel is another matter. Here the problem lies in an experiment that involves, as before, the use of repetition, nonsense, and dislocation based on interchangeability of characters and consequent lack of plot, development, and structure. The play is difficult to read, but may be salvaged, as Markéta Goetz-Stankiewicz suggested, as a film script.

The autobiographical plays • Havel returned to the stage—in the West, if not in his own country—with three one-act plays: *Audience, Private View,* and *Protest*. The plays met with great acclaim in the New York production in 1983 and were well received in Europe, Canada, and Australia as well. The popularity of these linked autobiographical plays, which differ considerably from Havel's early work, is particularly interesting given their genesis: They were originally conceived and performed as private entertainments for Havel's friends in Prague.

All three plays deal with the problems of a playwright, Vaněk, who like Havel is not allowed to publish in his country. In *Audience*, a brewery foreman asks the laborer-playwright Vaněk to inform on himself, since the boss is tired of writing police reports about him. In *Private View*, several friends attempt to bribe Vaněk to give up and make his peace with the regime because surrender pays so well. In *Protest*, Vaněk is called by an old acquaintance who has since accommodated the authorities but who now has a favor to ask. Ultimately, Vaněk refuses to accept the byzantine rationalizations by which men and women excuse their failure to take a stand.

Hugo, Gross, Huml, and Vaněk's tempters have lost or are about to lose something precious. Havel never spells out exactly what it is they are in the process of losing. He only tells the reader how that loss occurs. That seems sufficient in a world little aware of the existence of values that are precious enough to be preserved at any price. Havel's oblique reminder of their existence is a minor triumph in a major struggle in which he has acquitted himself as a master of his art and a hero of his nation.

Temptation • Following his 1978-1983 period of imprisonment, Havel wrote a new play, drawing on the story of Dr. Faustus. *Temptation* tells the story of Dr. Henry Foustka, a scientist in a research institute, who is involved in various experiments of an ethically questionable nature. He also habitually treats his staff in a dehumanizing fashion and makes a great show of the idea that they are producing and protecting the Truth, even as all of them are constantly involved in idle chatter.

The devil is represented by one Fistula, an informer, who seeks to draw Dr. Foustka into his circle by mentoring Foustka in his investigation of black magic. The main action of the play deals with how Foustka struggles to cling to his respectability after his temptation, until he finally realizes that he is ruined and will be punished. Foustka claims that his dabbling in sorcery was solely to discredit it as unscientific. Fistula turns out to be a double agent, and the devil is the pride of the system that uses science for its own ends, a criticism of Soviet-supported and controlled communism. However, the ending of the play is left ambiguous, and the audience is never told precisely what manner of punishment will befall Foustka, since his final immolation onstage is a highly symbolic scene, not to be taken literally.

In leaving Foustka's precise fate unspecified, Havel gives the play its greatest strength because he leaves it up to the reader put the pieces together and realize that while the individual parts may be true, they add up to a lie. Even truth can become demoniac if it is instrumentalized and robbed of its own life.

Other major works

POETRY: *Antikódy*, 1966.

TELEPLAY: *Motýl na anténě*, 1975.

RADIO PLAY: Anděl Strážný, 1968.

NONFICTION: *Dopisy Olze, 1979-1982*, 1985 (*Letters to Olga*, 1988); *Dalkovy vyslech*, 1986 (*Disturbing the Peace: A Conversation with Karel Hvžďala and Václav Havel*, 1990); *Letni premitani*, 1991 (*Summer Meditations*, 1992); *Open Letters: Selected Prose, 1965-1990*, 1991 (Paul Wilson, editor); *Toward a Civil Society: Selected Speeches and Writings, 1990-1994*, 1994 (Wilson, editor); *The Art of the Impossible: Politics as Morality in Practice*, 1997.

MISCELLANEOUS: *Protokoly*, 1966; *O lidskou identitu*, 1984.

Bibliography

Goetz-Stankiewicz, Marketa. *The Silenced Theatre: Czech Playwrights Without a Stage.* Toronto: University of Toronto Press, 1979. Examination of the situation of numerous dissident playwrights under the communist regime, including Havel.

Keane, John. *Václav Havel: A Political Tragedy in Six Acts.* New York: Basic Books, 2000. Although this biography focuses primarily on Havel's political activities, it includes extensive information on Havel's plays and how they reflect the development of his political concepts.

Kriseova, Eda. *Václav Havel: The Authorized Biography.* Translated by Caleb Crain. New York: St. Martin's Press, 1993. Officially authorized biography, using sources provided by Havel that may not be available to other biographers but may be slanted to soft pedal awkward or uncomfortable aspects of his career.

Symynkywicz, Jeffrey. *Václav Havel and the Velvet Revolution.* Parsippany, N.J.: Dillon Press, 1995. Although dealing primarily with Havel's role in the Velvet Revolution, also looks at the role of his plays in forming his reputation.

Peter Petro,
updated by Leigh Husband Kimmel

Lillian Hellman

Born: New Orleans, Louisiana; June 20, 1905
Died: Martha's Vineyard, Massachusetts; June 30, 1984

Principal drama · *The Children's Hour,* pr., pb. 1934; *Days to Come,* pr., pb. 1936; *The Little Foxes,* pr., pb. 1939; *Watch on the Rhine,* pr., pb. 1941; *The Searching Wind,* pr., pb. 1944; *Another Part of the Forest,* pr. 1946, pb. 1947; *Montserrat,* pr. 1949, pb. 1950 (adaptation of Emmanuel Robles's play); *The Autumn Garden,* pr., pb. 1951; *The Lark,* pr. 1955, pb. 1956 (adaptation of Jean Anouilh's play *L'Alouette*); *Candide,* pr. 1956, pb. 1957 (libretto; music by Leonard Bernstein, lyrics by Richard Wilbur, John Latouche, and Dorothy Parker; adaptation of Voltaire's novel); *Toys in the Attic,* pr., pb. 1960; *My Mother, My Father, and Me,* pr., pb. 1963 (adaptation of Burt Blechman's novel *How Much?*); *The Collected Plays,* pb. 1972

Other literary forms · In addition to her original stage plays, Lillian Hellman published original screenplays, a collection of the letters of Anton Chekhov, her adaptations of two French plays (*Montserrat, L'Alouette*) and of an American novel (*How Much?*), an operetta adapted from Voltaire's *Candide: Ou, L'Optimisme* (1759; *Candide: Or, All for the Best,* 1759; also as *Candide: Or, The Optimist,* 1762; also as *Candide: Or, Optimism,* 1947), many uncollected articles, and several volumes of memoirs, the first two of which have received as much acclaim as her best plays.

Achievements · Lillian Hellman was the most important American follower of Henrik Ibsen after Arthur Miller. Like Ibsen in his middle period, she wrote strong, well-made plays involving significant social issues. Like Ibsen, she created memorable female characters, some strong, some weak. Her most important female character, Regina Giddens of *The Little Foxes* and *Another Part of the Forest,* seems at least partially modeled on Ibsen's Hedda Gabler. Both Hellman and Ibsen were exceptional in depicting believable, memorable children. Like him, though more frequently, she used blackmail as a dramatic ploy. Her plays, like Ibsen's, can be strongly and tightly dramatic, and, like his, some, notably *The Little Foxes,* have a question ending: That is, one in which the eventual outcome for the major characters is left ironically uncertain.

Her last two original plays, however, recall Chekhov more than Ibsen in their depiction of feckless characters and, in one of the two, an apparent, though only apparent, plotlessness. She has been blamed for her employment of melodramatic plot elements, but her use of them is often valid and essential and does not interfere with accurate character analysis, convincing dramatic dialogue, and adroit handling of social issues. Hellman was, after Tennessee Williams, the most important dramatist writing primarily about the American South. Two of her plays, *Watch on the Rhine* and *Toys in the Attic,* won the New York Drama Critics Circle Award. Hellman received many other awards, including the Brandeis University Creative Arts Medal and the National Institute of Arts and Letters Gold Medal.

Biography · Lillian Florence Hellman was born in New Orleans of Jewish parents. Her father was also born in New Orleans, and her mother in Alabama, of a family long estab lished there. Part of her mother's family moved to New York, and when Hellman was five years old, her parents moved there and commenced a routine of spending six months of each year in New York and six in New Orleans with her father's two unmarried sisters. As her memoirs make clear, Hellman's plays are strongly influenced by her urban southern background. Her mother's family was a source for the Hubbards in *The Little Foxes* and *Another Part of the Forest*; her paternal aunts, for the sisters in *Toys in the Attic*.

All Hellman's original plays except the first two (*The Children's Hour* and *Days to Come*) are set in the South: in the Washington area, in Alabama towns, or in New Orleans. Hellman was graduated from high school in New York in 1922, attended New York University from 1922 to 1924, and briefly attended Columbia University in 1924, without completing a degree at either school. She worked for a time thereafter in New York and Hollywood in the areas of publishing, book reviewing, and reading manuscripts of plays and movie scenarios. In 1925, she married Arthur Kober; they were divorced in 1932. Two years later, her first play, *The Children's Hour*, was a tremendous hit, achieving a longer original run (691 performances) than any of her later plays. From that success until her last play in 1963, she was primarily a playwright and occasionally a scriptwriter, though she was never really happy in the theater.

Over the years, Hellman made various visits to Russia, to Civil War Spain, and elsewhere in Europe, including a very dangerous visit to Nazi Germany to take money to the underground at the request of a friend. For many years, she was the companion of the novelist Dashiell Hammett, though they lived together only sporadically. Congressional investigations of communism in the United States in the early 1950's caused serious trouble for both her and Hammett, though she denied having sufficiently consistent or deep political convictions to belong to any party.

As a result of the investigations, Hellman and Hammett were both blacklisted in Hollywood, and she lost the home she owned and shared with Hammett in upstate New York, as well as various friends. Hammett was imprisoned. Soon after his release, he became ill, and Hellman took care of him until his death in 1961. In her later years, Hellman devoted herself to her four books of memoirs and taught at Harvard University, the Massachusetts Institute of Technology, and the University of California at Berkeley. She died on June 30, 1984, at Martha's Vineyard.

Analysis • Beginning with her first play, *The Children's Hour*, Lillian Hellman's plays possessed certain dramatic characteristics: crisp, forceful, realistic dialogue; clear character construction and analysis; and a clear-cut plot line in the tradition of the well-made play, with fast movement and adroitly handled suspense that kept (and can still keep) audiences enthralled. Most of her plays can be called melodramatic, because of the suspense, because of the use of violence and of blackmail, and because of obvious authorial manipulation to achieve a neat conclusion. The plays are never, however, pure melodrama because pure melodrama would not include valid, well-drawn characters or significant themes.

The Children's Hour • *The Children's Hour*, like many of Hellman's plays, concerns the destructive power of evil, its ability to erode human relationships and destroy lives. In this play, evil is manifested by a child's malicious lie and its repercussions in the lives of two women. The play, which was based on an actual lawsuit, the Great Drumsheugh Case, opens on a class in progress at a girls' boarding school in Massachusetts. The teacher, Lily Mortar, is the aunt of Martha Dobie, one of the two young women who own and operate the school.

(Library of Congress)

Presently, student Mary Tilford enters—very late for class—carrying a bunch of flowers with which she appeases the teacher. Then the other owner, Karen Wright, enters. Karen has lost her bracelet and asks one of the girls, Helen, if she has found it, an important issue in the play. Karen asks Mary where she got the flowers. Mary repeats her claim that she picked them. Karen, apparently recognizing them, says Mary got them out of the garbage pail and has been lying. Mary's response is, and continues to be, that the teachers are against her, that they never believe her, and that she is telling the truth. Karen grounds her for two weeks. Mary says her heart hurts and pretends to fall into a faint. She is carried to her room.

Martha enters, and she and Karen discuss Mary as a troublemaker, send for Karen's fiancé (Joe Cardin, who is a doctor and also Mary's cousin), discuss getting rid of Mrs. Mortar, and discuss Karen's plans to marry Joe as soon as school is out. Martha is clearly upset at the imminent marriage, although she likes Joe. She hates interference with a friendship that has gone on since college and hates the possibility that Karen might leave the school. Joe arrives and goes off to examine Mary.

At this point in the play, the audience cannot be sure of the meaning of Martha's jealousy, of whether Mary's feelings are in any sense justified, of whether the events thus far are more taut with emotion than what might be expected on a day-by-day basis in a girls' boarding school. Mrs. Mortar, deeply insulted at Martha's desire to get her away from the school and at her offer to send her to London and support her there, indirectly accuses her niece of homosexual feelings toward Karen. Mary's two roommates are caught eavesdropping. Joe has a friendly confrontation with Martha, who apologizes and falls into his arms, weeping. It is reasonably clear that she does not recognize her feelings for Karen as homosexual, if they are. Mary comes in, and it is clear that Joe considers her a troublemaker, as do the women. Then, as the adults leave and the audience sees Mary for the first time alone with other girls, her character becomes only too clear.

Indeed, one becomes more and more convinced that Mary's lies, her manipulation, her dictatorial attitude toward her schoolmates, and presently her outright blackmail of one of them and her cruelty to another represent more than mere naughtiness or adolescent confusion. Mary is psychotic, and dangerously so. Feeling no affection for anyone, she lives for manipulation and power. As soon as the teachers leave the room, she throws a cushion at the door and kicks a table. Apparently, her one genuine feeling other than hatred is the belief that the teachers hate her as much as she hates them. She tells her roommates that if she cannot go to the boat races (since she has been grounded), she will see to it that they do not go either. She forces a girl named Rosalie to do some work for her by hinting of knowledge that Rosalie stole the bracelet that Karen asked about earlier. She forces her roommates to report the conversation that they overheard, and while Mary certainly does not completely understand its import, she nevertheless recognizes it as a weapon she can use. She immediately announces that she is going to walk out and go home, and by physical force, she makes one of the girls give her the money to get there. On this moment of tension, typical of a well-made play, act 1 closes.

The Children's Hour is unusual among Hellman's plays in that it does not all take place in one setting. Act 2 takes place in the living room of the home of Mary's grandmother in Boston. As scene 1 of the act opens, Mary arrives and is admitted by the maid, Agatha, who clearly does not trust her for an instant. Left alone while Agatha goes to fetch Mrs. Tilford, Mary tries with the aid of a mirror to make herself look sick. Mrs. Tilford enters, and Mary dashes into her arms, in tears.

It soon becomes clear that Mrs. Tilford is an intelligent woman but that, unlike Agatha, she can be taken in by her granddaughter. It is an irony of the play, however, that she cannot be taken in easily. Had Mary been able to deceive her by simple lies, there would have been no play. Her usual tricks—tears, stories of being mistreated— do not work. Mrs. Tilford has supported Martha and Karen in their establishment of the school, has encouraged her friends to send their daughters there, and certainly trusts the schoolmistresses. Mary, therefore, begins to use the story she has heard secondhand, mentioning it at first vaguely and uncertainly, but then, as she sees that it is having an effect, more positively and specifically.

Mrs. Tilford is deeply disturbed and obviously finds it difficult to believe that such a story could be invented. She starts to phone Karen but decides against it. She calls Joe and urgently asks him to come over. She calls a friend, perhaps one with a daughter or granddaughter at the school, asking her to come over as well. Scene 2 opens with Agatha telling Mary that Rosalie is coming to spend the night; a few moments later, Rosalie arrives. The audience learns, partly now and fully later, that Mrs. Tilford has communicated with the parents of all the girls and told them Mary's story, with the result that all the girls have been called home. Rosalie is spending the night with Mary because her mother is in New York.

These circumstances represent significant flaws in the structure of *The Children's Hour*, though they are not as noticeable in performance: First, it is difficult to believe that a woman of Mrs. Tilford's maturity and intelligence would take such drastic action on the basis of her granddaughter's word alone; second, it has to be Rosalie, among all the students, whose mother is out of town, or the play would simply grind to a halt. About the first, one might say in Hellman's defense that it would be emotionally and even intellectually difficult for Mrs. Tilford to believe that her granddaughter would have either the desire or the knowledge to invent such a lie; that to seek external verification of the story would be, even if it were true, almost surely fruitless; and that, given the time and place, it would have been irresponsible of her not to inform the other parents. Problems remain, even so. Surely Mrs. Tilford could have spoken with Joe first. True, Hellman arranges that Joe arrives late, on the plausible ground that he had to stop at a hospital, but would one more night have mattered so much?

Doubtless, Mrs. Tilford's urgency is partly emotional, on the ground that most, if not all, of the girls have been at the school on her recommendation. This does not explain, however, her calm assurance later in the play that the story is true. She takes the logical attitude that Martha's, Karen's, and Joe's denials are meaningless, since they are to be expected regardless of whether the story is accurate. She is also a woman who, given her class, her money, and her intelligence, is not prone to being wrong. Perhaps one should regard her attitude as a typical Hellman irony: It is her very sense of responsibility that has made her act irresponsibly. Less defense can be offered for the presence of Rosalie. All one can say is that her presence is essential to the play, and that in a well-made play this represents perhaps the minimum of manipulation.

The scene develops very dramatically. Mary blackmails Rosalie into being prepared to support her lies if necessary. Joe arrives, and very soon he and his aunt are battling. Karen and Martha arrive, and the battle enlarges, with strong emotions on one side and calm assurance on the other. Mrs. Tilford is not even moved by the threat of a libel suit. Finally, Joe insists that Mary be questioned and, against Mrs. Tilford's wishes, brings Mary in.

Mary, genuinely nervous, tells her story, making it more and more circumstantial, until finally the circumstances catch her in a lie. She has said that she has seen things through Karen's keyhole, and Karen announces that her door has no keyhole. Mary is therefore forced to say that it was Martha's room, not Karen's; Martha announces that she lives on a different floor, at the other end of the house, and, moreover, shares her room with Mrs. Mortar. Mrs. Tilford is severely shaken. Backed into a corner, Mary says that it was not she but Rosalie who saw them, and that she saw them because Karen's door was halfway open. Rosalie is summoned and at first denies the story, but when Mary makes it plain that she will, if necessary, expose Rosalie as a thief, Rosalie agrees that the story is true and collapses in tears. The curtain falls.

After so tense a moment, act 3 is almost anticlimactic. It opens on the same scene as act 1. Karen and Martha are alone in the house. They have lost their case; the townspeople are against them; they feel so persecuted that they refuse even to answer the phone; and they have not even dared to leave the house. In a rather surprising anticipation of Samuel Beckett and the Absurdists, Martha says that they are "waiting," with the implication that that is all they—or at any rate, she—will ever do. Martha hopes that Karen will escape through marrying Joe, but Karen seems doubtful. Mrs. Mortar, who had left when told to by Martha, unexpectedly enters, and the audience learns that she would have been the key witness at the trial, that she refused to return, and thus the case was lost. Her failure to return was owing to her reluctance to become involved in such a scandal. She returns now because she has run out of money, but Martha has no more to give her.

Mrs. Mortar leaves the room, and Joe enters. He is planning for the marriage and for all three of them to leave together permanently, even though he would thus be giving up a promising career. Martha leaves, and in his words and attitude toward Karen it becomes clear that Joe is uncertain of the truth. Karen quietly denies any homosexual relationship, and he apparently accepts the denial, but it is uncertain whether his doubts have been laid to rest. Karen asks him to think things over for a day or two and make a decision. He reluctantly agrees and leaves, insisting that he will come back, though Karen is sure that he will not.

Martha returns and, in a scene of high emotion, tells Karen that, though she had not previously been aware of it, the story that has been told about them was, at least so far as her feelings went, true. She loves Karen "that way." She leaves the room, and presently, a muffled shot is heard. Karen opens the door and sees that Martha has killed herself. Mrs. Mortar rushes in, sees what has happened, and expresses her remorse.

The doorbell rings, and she answers it. It is Agatha. Mrs. Tilford is waiting in her car. Mrs. Mortar tries to keep her from coming in, but Karen allows her to enter, and Mrs. Mortar rushes out sobbing.

The final dialogue is between Karen and Mrs. Tilford. Mrs. Tilford has learned the truth. The bracelet was found among Rosalie's things, and Rosalie confessed. Apparently, Mary has confessed, too. The judge at the trial will arrange a public apology and explanation, and Mrs. Tilford will pay the amount of the damages and as much more as they will take. Karen announces Martha's death and expresses her bitter feelings toward Mrs. Tilford and her attempts to relieve her conscience through money. Gradually, however, Karen recognizes Mrs. Tilford's sincerity and sees that the old woman will be the greater sufferer because she has refused to commit Mary to an institution and will hence have to live permanently in her company and because Martha's suicide will inevitably burden her memory. Karen agrees to accept Mrs. Tilford's money. She disagrees with Mrs. Tilford's hope that she and Joe will marry. The two separate amicably, and Karen is left alone at the play's end.

Hellman expressed the feeling later that the final scene was unnecessary, that it was simply evidence of her personal compulsion to spell things out. Certainly none of her important later plays spells things out so thoroughly, but in *The Children's Hour*, the final scene provides desirable satisfaction for the audience. The only valid objection to the scene is that it raises a new possibility: Mrs. Tilford appears soon after Martha's suicide, rather than earlier, perhaps in time to prevent it. Once Martha's feelings are clear, however, it seems doubtful, given the time and circumstances, that anything could have kept her alive, and Hellman properly leaves Karen with an uncertain future. Karen's belief in Joe's permanent defection may be wrong; it may not. The possibility of a happy outcome for her is a valid comfort to an audience after so much bitter emotion, but the certainty of a happy ending would be difficult to accept.

The play was in part a *succès de scandale* on Broadway, since open treatment of homosexuality was very unusual at the time. Hellman wrote the scenario for the first film version, *These Three* (1936), in which the homosexuality was changed to a traditional triangle. A later version restored both title and content.

The Little Foxes • *The Little Foxes* is, and almost surely will remain, Hellman's standard play. It represents significant advances in technique over *The Children's Hour* and is in various ways more typical of Hellman's overall production. First, it is set in the Deep South (small-town Alabama), as are three of Hellman's four most significant later plays. Second, the characters are more sharply distinguished and more deeply realized, and the dialogue is more individualized. Third, Hellman displays three significant qualities that are not fully realized in *The Children's Hour*: compassion, humor, and irony. Fourth, *The Little Foxes* displays more clearly a sociopolitical theme than does the earlier play: These are "the little foxes who spoil the vines" (a quotation from the Song of Solomon), whom Hellman sees as twentieth century capitalists in embryo.

The Little Foxes concentrates on a rapacious small-town Alabama family, the Hubbards, and on some of their victims. The year is 1900. As the play opens, Regina Giddens is giving a dinner party for a businessman from Chicago, William Marshall, with whom her brothers are negotiating to join them in opening one of the first cotton mills in the South. All the characters in the play are present except Regina's husband, Horace, the town banker, long confined at The Johns Hopkins Hospital with a bad heart. The remaining characters are Regina's brothers, Ben and Oscar Hubbard; Oscar's wife, Birdie, the last member of an aristocratic family impoverished by the Civil War; Oscar and Birdie's son, Leo; Horace and Regina's daughter, Alexandra; and the servants, Addie and Cal.

Unlike the Hubbards, Birdie has cultural interests; she is a frightened woman, bullied by her husband. Ben is a jovial hypocrite whose hypocrisy has become so practiced that he is sometimes almost unaware of it. He and Regina are the dominant Hubbards. Oscar is relatively weak, obtuse, and blustery, while Leo is a lesser version of Oscar. Alexandra shares Birdie's cultural interests and seems not at all Hubbard-like. Regina herself is a handsome woman, a smooth and clever conniver, who takes in Marshall to a degree that Ben, for all his hypocrisy, cannot.

When the deal for the cotton mill has been struck, the young couple drive Marshall to the station to return to Chicago. The Hubbards are triumphant, looking forward to being rich. One problem remains: The three siblings are supposed to contribute equal sums to the mill project, enough to make them together the majority shareholders, but while Ben and Oscar are ready to put up their share, Regina must get hers from Horace, who has ignored all letters on the subject. In a piece of typical Hubbard trickery, Regina declares that Horace is holding out because he wants a larger share, and Ben finally agrees that he should have a larger share and that the difference will come out of Oscar's. Oscar is furious, but he is mollified by Regina's quite specious assurance that she will consider something that Oscar very much wants: a marriage between Leo and Alexandra. A plan is then made to send Alexandra, who is devoted to Horace, to bring him home.

Many modern plays, including several of Henrik Ibsen's, involve the return of someone long gone, but the return is almost always early in the play. In *The Little Foxes*, the audience must wait, with anticipation, for what Horace's return in the second act will bring. Before Horace's arrival, Oscar and Leo conceive a plan to steal eighty thousand dollars' worth of bonds from Horace's safety deposit box, to finance their venture. (If they can do this, they will not need Regina as a partner.) Horace then arrives, stiff and ill, accompanied by Alexandra, who has his heart medicine. During the course of the act, it becomes clear that Horace and Regina are, and have been, at odds during most of their marriage, that Horace will not agree to finance the proposed project, and that he will not consent to a marriage between Alexandra and Leo. It is also clear that Regina will not be thwarted and that Horace is too physically frail to withstand her will.

In act 3, Horace, who has discovered the theft of the bonds, informs Regina about the crime and tells her that he will pretend that the theft was a loan. Moreover, he will change his will, leaving Regina the bonds and all his other property to Alexandra. Regina will thus lose the opportunity to invest in the business venture (because the partners will no longer need her money), and she will lose her inheritance from Horace. Furiously, she tells him that she married him only for money. He becomes distraught, reaches for his medicine, spills it, and asks her to get his new bottle. She simply stands there as he collapses and dies. Regina is now in a position to blackmail her brothers into assigning her a 75 percent interest in the mill, lest she prosecute them. Regina is triumphant; nevertheless, she now faces a life of loneliness because Alexandra has discovered her mother's treachery and will leave her.

The play ends with a question and is the better for it. If the ending represented a total and final triumph, it would emphasize the play's kinship to pure melodrama, and given the characters, an ending that had finality would be unlikely. Ben is too clearsighted, too ironically aware, too psychologically healthy to give up. Alexandra's potential for fighting is probably small, but one cannot be sure. Moreover, the Hubbard siblings are more complex than a recital of the plot might make them seem. Ben retains an incompetent servant because she has always been in the family. Ben and Oscar both seem genuinely moved by Horace's death. Ben and Regina are both capable of viewing their own, and others', behavior ironically, and there is humor in some of their dialogue. Regina is frightened at what she has done, or rather not done. Wicked as the two may be, and much as they might remind one of nineteenth century melodramatic villains, they are human beings, complex enough to be believable.

The play, moreover, has other ironies that remove it from total melodrama. It is ironic that Leo should be Birdie's son and Alexandra Regina's daughter, because Leo is an extreme version of Oscar, and Alexandra has the outlook of Horace. For most of his life, however, Horace has been weak, yielding to his wife, as Birdie has to her husband. Birdie, for whom one is made to feel compassion, gains enough strength to tell Alexandra the truth, and Horace gains enough strength to stand up to Regina. These are highly individualized human beings, and the play is skillfully constructed, absorbing, and genuinely insightful.

Watch on the Rhine • Like *The Little Foxes*, *Watch on the Rhine* contains murder and blackmail, but it is a very different kind of play, peopled with a very different set of characters. It takes place entirely in the living room of Fanny Farrelly, in her country mansion near Washington, D.C. Fanny is a wealthy, eccentric matriarch in her sixties, a character typical of comedy of manners: basically good-hearted, sparklingly alert, and accustomed to having her own way. The time of the play is the spring of 1940. Germany is Nazi-ruled, and there is war in Europe in which the United States has not yet become involved.

The pattern of the first two acts of the play consists of alternating conversation of three kinds: humorous and witty, at times gossipy, as is appropriate to comedy of manners; affectionate; and tense, either because of personally threatening political maneuvers or because of the triangle that is a subplot in the play. The shifts from one type to another can be sudden, but they are always appropriate. Tension can lapse into humor, or an unexpected remark can turn humor into tension.

The characters include, besides Fanny, the other permanent residents of the mansion: Fanny's son, David, a lawyer in his deceased father's firm in Washington, in his late thirties; Fanny's longtime companion Anise, a Frenchwoman; and one of the servants, Joseph. There are also two houseguests who have long overstayed their welcome, Marthe de Brancovis, the daughter of an old friend of Fanny, and her husband, Teck, a Romanian count. Fanny's daughter Sara, her husband Kurt Müller, a member of the anti-Nazi underground and a German in exile, and their children arrive. The audience learns that Kurt has collected twenty-three thousand dollars to aid the resistance in Germany. In brief, Teck discovers the money and threatens to expose Kurt to the German embassy officials unless he is paid ten thousand dollars. Kurt is forced to kill Teck and flee the country, aided by Fanny, who during the course of the play has come to realize the Nazi threat and to be lifted above her own private concerns. The killing is presented, strangely, as an absence of the need to fight evil on all fronts, whether on a conventional battlefield or in one's own environment.

Watch on the Rhine is probably the best American play concerning World War II. It demonstrates that war is not limited to battlefronts and that the world is too small for anyone, anywhere, to be unaffected by large-scale violence. It demonstrates that such violence affects the cultured and the humane, whether they are poor, like Kurt, or wealthy, like Sara's family. The play is highly unusual in being a comedy of manners in which the central subject is war. In spite of the attempted blackmail and actual murder that figure prominently in its plot, it is among the least melodramatic of any of Hellman's plays, and to call the murder melodramatic has its own irony because this particular murder constitutes an act of war.

The characters in *Watch on the Rhine* are developed with clarity and depth. Fanny is a far more individualized portrait of a wealthy, dominant older woman than is Mrs. Tilford in *The Children's Hour*. Unlike Mary Tilford or Ben and Regina, Teck is a flaccid, unwilling villain. Unlike Birdie, Horace, and Alexandra, the good people are strong, and for the only time in all her plays, Hellman presents, in Kurt, an admirable hero and a marriage based on strong and permanent love. A believable presentation of either of these is indeed a rarity in modern drama.

The children in *Watch on the Rhine* are more fully portrayed than those in *The Children's Hour*. The theme has universal validity; oppression is indeed a major issue throughout Hellman's plays. In *The Children's Hour*, it is oppression by the established rich, by a psychotic child, by established standards of behavior. In *The Little Foxes*, it is anticipated oppression on a broad scale by a rising class of capitalists, and actual oppression on a narrower scale by moneyed southerners against blacks, poor whites, fallen aristocrats, and one another. *Watch on the Rhine* widens the range in dealing with oppression by Fascists and would-be Fascists. Blackmail itself, in all three plays, is a form of oppression. Later in Hellman's work, in *The Autumn Garden* and *Toys in the Attic*, she showed that even generosity and love can be forms of blackmail; those plays, like *Watch on the Rhine*, give the theme a universality that Hellman's first two successes lack. *The Little Foxes* will probably remain the most popular Hellman play in dramatic repertory, but *Watch on the Rhine* is certainly among her most effective.

Other major works

SCREENPLAYS: *The Dark Angel*, 1935 (with Mordaunt Shairp); *These Three*, 1936; *Dead End*, 1937 (adaptation of Sidney Kingsley's play); *The Little Foxes*, 1941 (with Dorothy Parker, Arthur Kober, and Alan Campbell); *Watch on the Rhine*, 1943 (with Dashiell Hammett); *The North Star: A Motion Picture About Some Russian People*, 1943; *The Searching Wind*, 1946; *The Chase*, 1966.

NONFICTION: *An Unfinished Woman: A Memoir*, 1969; *Pentimento*, 1973; *Scoundrel Time*, 1976; *Maybe*, 1980; *Eating Together: Recipes and Recollections*, 1984 (with Peter Feibleman); *Conversations with Lillian Hellman*, 1986.

EDITED TEXTS: *The Selected Letters of Anton Chekhov*, 1955; *The Big Knockover: Selected Stories and Short Novels of Dashiell Hammett*, 1966.

Bibliography

Feibleman, Peter. *Lily: Reminiscences of Lillian Hellman*. New York: William Morrow, 1988. The author, the son of old New Orleans friends of Hellman, became her close friend and companion in her last years, a relationship he describes in this book. His accounts of renovating the house on Martha's Vineyard inherited from Hellman were first published in his column in *Lear's* magazine. Contains a sadly riveting account of Hellman's illness. Some of the anecdotal accounts of their time together are in Hellman's section of *Eating Together*, a collection of southern recipes selected by both writers, in page proof when she died in 1984.

Griffin, Alice, and Geraldine Thorsten. *Understanding Lillian Hellman*. Columbia: University of South Carolina Press, 1999. A study of Hellman's literary output, including *The Children's Hour*, *Another Part of the Forest*, *The Little Foxes*, *Watch on the Rhine*, *The Autumn Garden*, and *Toys in the Attic*. Bibliography and index.

Horn, Barbara Lee. *Lillian Hellman: A Research and Production Sourcebook*. Westport, Conn.: Greenwood Press, 1998. Provides criticism and interpretation of Hellman's dramatic works as well as plots and stage history. Bibliography and indexes.

Mahoney, Rosemary. *A Likely Story: One Summer with Lillian Hellman*. New York: Doubleday, 1998. A look at Hellman from her friend, Rosemary Mahoney.

Mellen, Joan. *Hellman and Hammett: The Legendary Passion of Lillian Hellman and Dashiell Hammett*. New York: HarperCollins, 1996. The story of Hellman's relationship with author Dashiell Hammett. Bibliography and index.

Rollyson, Carl. *Lillian Hellman: Her Legend and Her Legacy*. New York: St. Martin's Press, 1988. A readable and scholarly biography of Hellman. Photographs, bibliography, index.

Wright, William. *Lillian Hellman: The Image, the Woman*. New York: Simon and Schuster, 1986. A biography of Hellman that covers her life and works. Bibliography and index.

Jacob H. Adler,
updated by Katherine Lederer

Beth Henley

Born: Jackson, Mississippi; May 8, 1952

Principal drama · *Am I Blue*, pr. 1973, pb. 1982; *Crimes of the Heart*, pr. 1979, pb. 1982; *The Miss Firecracker Contest*, pr. 1980, pb. 1982; *The Wake of Jamey Foster*, pr., pb. 1982; *The Debutante Ball*, pr. 1985, pb. 1991; *The Lucky Spot*, pr. 1986, pb. 1987; *Abundance*, pr. 1990, pb. 1991; *Beth Henley: Four Plays*, pb. 1992; *Monologues for Women*, pb. 1992; *Control Freaks*, pr. 1992, pb. 2001; *Signature*, pr. 1995, pb. 2001; *L-Play*, pr. 1996, pb. 2001; *Impossible Marriage*, pr., pb. 1998; *Family Week*, pr. 2000; *Beth Henley: Collected Plays*, pb. 2000-2001 (2 volumes)

Other literary forms · In addition to her works for the stage, Beth Henley has written screenplays, including *Nobody's Fool* (1986); *True Stories* (1986), in collaboration with David Byrne and Stephen Tobolowsky; and the film versions of her plays *Crimes of the Heart* (1986), *The Miss Firecracker Contest* (1989), and *Come West with Me* (1998). She has also written the teleplays *Survival Guides* (1986) and *Trying Times* (1987), both with Budge Threlkeld.

Achievements · Beth Henley is often compared to fiction writers Eudora Welty and Flannery O'Connor for her sympathetic portrayals of eccentric characters who lead deceptively simple lives in small southern communities. Her work has also been identified with the literary traditions of the grotesque and the absurd. Henley's unique achievement, however, is the intermingling of absurdism and realism. Her plays realistically capture the southern vernacular and take place in authentic southern settings, yet they also exaggerate the recognizable and push the bizarre to extremes to reveal the underlying absurdity of the human condition.

Henley's characters are rooted in her southern heritage, but the meaning of their experiences is not limited to time and place. Loss and renewal, the vulnerability of loving, and the frail but indomitable human spirit are among her recurring themes. Henley delivers these serious concerns, however, through unpredictable characters, outrageously witty dialogue, and offbeat humor. It is her insistence on the value of laughter in the face of adversity that places her within the tragicomic tradition of modern dramatic literature.

Another of Henley's strengths is that she approaches her craft with a keen insight into what is stageworthy. This awareness, no doubt, is one of the reasons that her first full-length play, *Crimes of the Heart*, won the Pulitzer Prize in drama in 1981 with the distinction of being the first play to win the coveted award before appearing on Broadway. *Crimes of the Heart* also received the New York Drama Critics Circle Award in 1981, and in the same year, Henley captured the prestigious George Oppenheimer/ *Newsday* Playwriting Award. Experiments with style and theme during the 1990's led Henley away from her southern characters and settings; however, these plays, including *Family Week*, have not received critical or popular acclaim.

Biography · The second of four daughters, Elizabeth (Becker) Henley was born May 8, 1952, in Jackson, Mississippi. Her parents, Charles Boyce and Elizabeth Jose-

457

phine Becker, were reared in the neighboring communities of Hazlehurst and Brook-haven, locales that Henley adopted for two of her plays. Henley's father, an attorney, served in both houses of the Mississippi legislature. A shy child plagued with chronic at-tacks of asthma, Henley, often bedridden, entertained herself by reading play scripts that were in production at the New Stage Theatre in Jackson, where her mother, an am-ateur actress, regularly performed.

Henley attended high school in Jackson. During her senior year, she took part in an acting workshop at the New Stage Theatre, an experience that influenced her decision to become an actress. Selecting drama as her major, Henley enrolled at Southern Methodist University in Dallas, Texas, in 1970. While a sophomore, she wrote her first play as an assignment for a playwriting class. The play, a one-act comedy titled *Am I Blue*, was produced at the university under a pseudonym in her senior year. After grad-uation from Southern Methodist University in 1974 with a bachelor of fine arts degree, Henley taught creative dramatics and acted for the Dallas Minority Repertory Thea-tre. She earned a livelihood at odd jobs as a waitress, file clerk, and photographer of children at a department store. In 1975, she received a teaching scholarship from the University of Illinois, where she taught acting classes while pursuing graduate studies in drama. In the summer of 1976, she acted in the *Great American People Show*, a histori-cal pageant presented at the New Salem State Park.

Hoping to break into films as an actress, Henley moved to Los Angeles in the fall of 1976. Failing to get auditions for parts, Henley turned to writing screenplays as a cre-ative outlet, but without an agent to represent her, the studios would not read her scripts. Thinking that stage plays would have a better chance of getting performed, es-pecially in small theaters, Henley began working on a comedy (set in Hazlehurst, Mis-sissippi) about a crisis in the lives of three sisters. With production costs in mind, she

(AP/Wide World Photos)

deliberately limited the play to six characters and one indoor set. She finished *Crimes of the Heart* in 1978 and submitted it to several regional theaters without success, but Henley's friend and fellow playwright Frederick Bailey had faith in the play. Without Henley's knowledge, he entered *Crimes of the Heart* in the annual drama competition of the Actors Theatre of Louisville, Kentucky, where it was selected as a cowinner for 1977-1978.

In February, 1979, the Actors Theatre produced the play as part of the company's annual Festival of New American Plays. The play was an immediate success. After productions in Maryland, Missouri, and California, *Crimes of the Heart* opened to full houses on Off-Broadway on December 21, 1980. The public's high regard for the play was matched by critical acclaim. In April, 1981, at the age of twenty-eight, Henley was awarded the Pulitzer Prize in Drama for *Crimes of the Heart*, the first woman so honored in twenty-three years. In the fall of 1981, after having been recognized by the New York Drama Critics Circle as the best American play of the season, *Crimes of the Heart* premiered on Broadway; it ran for 535 performances. Subsequent productions were staged in England, France, Israel, and Australia.

Meanwhile, Henley was writing a television pilot entitled "Morgan's Daughters" for Paramount Pictures and a screenplay called *The Moon Watcher* about a historical pageant set in Petersburg, Illinois. She also took a small role as a bag lady in Frederick Bailey's *No Scratch*, produced in Los Angeles in the summer of 1981. In January, 1982, the New York Repertory Company staged Henley's *Am I Blue* with two other one-acts under the collective title *Confluence*. Theater critics found weaknesses in the playwright's student effort but also acknowledged that the comedy showed the promise of her later work.

Within the next three years, two other comedies written before Henley won the Pulitzer Prize were produced in New York City. *The Wake of Jamey Foster* opened on Broadway on October 14, 1982, but closed after only twelve nights. Critics found the play, which was also set in Mississippi, too repetitious of *Crimes of the Heart*. Written before *The Wake of Jamey Foster*, *The Miss Firecracker Contest* was staged in New York in the spring of 1984. Again critics faulted the play for its similarity to her earlier works.

Undaunted by these box-office failures, Henley kept writing for the stage. In the spring of 1985, the South Coast Repertory Theater in Costa Mesa, California, produced her next play *The Debutante Ball*. In the following year, Henley's *The Lucky Spot* (set in a dance hall in Pigeon, Louisiana, in 1934) premiered in New York City. Reviews of the play varied, but one critic considered *The Lucky Spot* to be Henley's best play since *Crimes of the Heart*. In 1990, *Abundance*, Henley's drama about two mail-order brides whose lives become entangled in the American West of the late nineteenth century, opened in New York City to mixed reviews. Later in the same year, the New York Stage and Film Company staged a workshop production of Henley's *Signature* in Poughkeepsie, New York, but the play was not produced until 1995. Set in Hollywood in the year 2052, the play depicts a ruined society in which everyone is obsessed with pursuing fame.

Henley's *L-Play* continued a period of experimentation with style and theme. The play deals with six themes done in six different styles. *Impossible Marriage* marked Henley's return to Off-Broadway theater in 1998. The play is set in Savannah, Georgia, and tells of a young bride-to-be named Pandora whose upcoming wedding is opposed by nearly every other character, including her older, very pregnant sister, Floral (portrayed by Holly Hunter). While Hunter received positive notices, the play was not a success. *Family Week* followed in 2000 and starred another Henley regular, Carol

Kane. The play closed after only six performances. The darkly comic play explores issues of alcoholism, sexual abuse, and murder.

As a Pulitzer Prize winner, the playwright-actress also found herself in demand as a screenwriter. While continuing to write stage plays, Henley wrote the screenplay for the acclaimed film version of *Crimes of the Heart*, released in late 1986; the script for another film, *Nobody's Fool*; and a screenplay based on her drama *The Miss Firecracker Contest*. Henley also collaborated with David Byrne and Stephen Tobolowsky on the screenplay entitled *True Stories* and with Budge Threlkeld on two television scripts, *Survival Guides* and *Trying Times*.

Henley's plays have reached audiences far beyond the regional theaters for which she first wrote, making her a significant contributor to American dramatic literature. Although the plays written after *Crimes of the Heart* have failed to bring her the critical praise she earned with that first full-length comedy, her dramatic output as a whole reveals a consistency in tone and theme unsurpassed by her American contemporaries.

Analysis • While the plays of Beth Henley are well constructed and provide ample conflict and suspense, the playwright's keen sense of place and character and her humorous yet compassionate view of the human predicament most typify her work. Her plays are set most often in her home state of Mississippi, where the innocent façade of friendly small-town life belies the horror and lunacy within. The dark side of humanity—the unpredictable, the irrational, the abnormal—attracts Henley, and her plays abound with stories of sickness, disease, and perversions. Ironically, however, Henley creates comedy out of the grotesque and shapes endearing characters out of eccentricity.

Usually, Henley's plays depict the family in crisis joined by a close circle of friends and neighbors. From this basic situation, Henley makes her case for emotional survival. Guilt, despair, and loneliness are typical experiences of Henley's failed heroines, but each continues to search for some measure of happiness and often finds it, if only momentarily, in the community of others. Whereas Henley doggedly exposes human frailties, in the final analysis, her view is a charitable one and her plays are optimistic, although they offer no lasting resolutions to her characters' problems. The key to understanding Henley's optimism lies in the laughter that her plays evoke; laughter functions to undercut that which is horrifying in life and to render it less horrifying.

Henley's reputation as a major American playwright was established with three full-length plays, *Crimes of the Heart*, *The Miss Firecracker Contest*, and *The Wake of Jamey Foster*. These plays also best illustrate the qualities that shape her unusual talent: a uniquely comic but sad voice, a distinguishing preoccupation with the bizarre, and a gift for working out variations on the themes of loneliness, guilt, loss, and renewal.

Crimes of the Heart • Set in Hazlehurst, Mississippi, five years after Hurricane Camille, *Crimes of the Heart* is about three sisters—Lenny, Meg, and Babe MaGrath. The immediate crisis is that the youngest sister, Babe, has shot her husband, Zackery Botrelle, who is the richest and most powerful man in the community. The plot is fairly easily resolved when Zackery recovers and his threat to confine Babe in a mental institution is thwarted. This, however, hardly accounts for the sisters' bizarre tale, which Henley unravels through exposition that is brilliantly interspersed with the main action.

Babe's trouble is only one more disaster among many that the MaGrath women have experienced, beginning with their father's desertion and their mother's suicide (she hanged herself and the family's cat). The mother's death left the sisters under the supervision of their grandfather, and now the care of the sick old man has fallen to Lenny, the oldest sister, because Babe married young and Meg escaped to California to pursue a singing career. Growing up in the shadow of their mother's inexplicable suicide and the notoriety it brought, each of the sisters suffers silently and alone. Meg was especially affected. Fearing to show pity as a sign of weakness, she tested herself as a youngster by staring at a book full of pictures of people with horrible skin diseases. Remarkably, Henley wrings laughter out of the MaGrath's misfortunes: The sisters suspect that Mama MaGrath killed herself because she was having a bad day; Lenny's prospects for marriage are bleak because she has a deformed ovary; and Babe shoots Zackery because she does not like his looks. To Henley's credit, the laughter is never at the expense of her characters, and there is a kind of bizarre logic to their eccentric behavior that makes the incredible credible. After Babe attempts suicide twice (because she, too, is having a bad day), she learns why her mother hanged the cat: She was afraid to die alone.

The Miss Firecracker Contest • Of the same eccentric mold as the MaGrath women, twenty-four-year-old Carnelle Scott, the central character of *The Miss Firecracker Contest*, seeks to overcome her well-earned reputation as the town trollop by becoming Miss Firecracker at the annual Fourth of July celebration in her hometown of Brookhaven, Mississippi. Because Carnelle's determination to succeed is exceeded only by her lack of talent, the outcome is predictable. Carnelle loses (she comes in fifth in a field of five), but she manages to overcome her despondency over the loss and joins her friends to watch the fireworks display at the close of the play.

Henley enlivens the simple plot with a number of very odd characters, all of whom, like Carnelle, seek redemption from their unhappy pasts. Delmount Williams, Carnelle's cousin, is a former mental patient who wants to be a philosopher; his sister Elain finds it easier to desert her husband and sons than to abandon her clock collection; and Carnelle's seamstress, Popeye Jackson, who learned her trade by making dresses for frogs, hears voices through her eyes.

Henley's propensity for the grotesque is even more marked in *The Miss Firecracker Contest* than in *Crimes of the Heart*. Carnelle recalls a childhood bout with ringworm, the treatment for which was to shave her head and cover it with a disgusting ointment; Delmount's last job was scraping up dead dogs from county roads; and all fondly remember Ronelle Williams, Delmount and Elain's mother, who died looking like a hairy ape after having her cancerous pituitary gland replaced by one from a monkey. Although in *The Miss Firecracker Contest* Henley tries too hard to be amusing at times, her characters are distinctly drawn and believable despite their whimsicality.

The Wake of Jamey Foster • Henley pushes the morbid to extremes in *The Wake of Jamey Foster*, which is set at Easter time in Canton, Mississippi. The inevitability of death, an underlying theme in Henley's earlier work, is the central focus of this very black comedy in which Marshael Foster, the thirty-three-year-old widow of Jamey Foster, endures the embarrassment of holding the wake of her estranged husband in her home. Marshael faces the ordeal with anger and remorse; she has only recently filed for divorce because her alcoholic husband left her for another woman. The widow finds little comfort from the strange group of friends and relatives who gather to pay their last respects to Jamey, who is laid out in the cheapest pine box available and dressed in a bright yellow sports coat.

Among the mourners are Marshael's brother, Leon Darnell, a turkey jerker in a chicken factory; the orphan Pixrose Wilson, Leon's betrothed, who is planning a career washing dogs; Collard Darnell, Marshael's promiscuous sister, whose whole life has been marred by a low score on an IQ test that she took when she was twelve years old; Jamey's brother, Wayne Foster, a successful banker, and his wife, Katie, who turn up their noses at the other guests; and Brocker Slade, a pig farmer who is in love with Marshael.

Very little that is significant happens in the play. As the group waits for morning and Jamey's funeral, they eat, drink, play cards, and take pictures of the corpse, but mostly they talk about gruesome things that have happened to them or others they know: arson, brain damage, miscarriages, automobile accidents, the cow that kicked Jamey in the head and killed him, and exploding pigs. Although plot is subsumed by character and character borders on caricature, *The Wake of Jamey Foster* is both entertaining and convincingly human, especially in the solace the characters find in the calamities of others.

Henley's rise to prominence in the American theater is remarkable considering the regionalism that characterizes her work. The weaknesses of her plays, a penchant for telling tall tales that stretch credulity and a tendency to write gags that force laughter, are overcome by her gift for creating memorable characters. Whereas Henley's most important dramatic material is often confined to small southern towns and the misfits who inhabit them, her humorous but sympathetic treatment of human foibles has a universality and originality that make her one of the most imaginative dramatists writing for the American theater.

Other major works

SCREENPLAYS: *Nobody's Fool,* 1986; *Crimes of the Heart,* 1986 (adaptation of her play); *True Stories,* 1986 (with David Byrne and Stephen Tobolowsky); *Miss Firecracker,* 1989 (adaptation of her play); *Come West with Me,* 1998 (adaptation of her play *Abundance*); *The Shipping News,* 2002 (adaptation of E. Annie Proulx's novel)

TELEPLAYS: *Survival Guides,* 1986; *Trying Times,* 1987 (with Budge Threlkeld).

Bibliography

Betsko, Kathleen, and Rachel Koenig, eds. *Interviews with Contemporary Women Playwrights.* New York: Beech Tree Books, 1987. In an interview, Henley discusses her individual development as an artist, themes, and dramaturgy; gives advice to new writers; and touches on feminist issues, especially the recurring question of a feminist aesthetic.

Bryer, Jackson R., ed. *The Playwright's Art: Conversations with Contemporary American Dramatists.* Brunswick, N.J.: Rutgers University Press, 1995. Chronicles Henley's contribution to contemporary Broadway, Off-Broadway, and regional theater in the United States. Henley discusses the creative process.

Haller, Scot. "Her First Play, Her First Pulitzer Prize." *Saturday Review* 8 (November, 1981): 40-44. Critiques the Off-Broadway production of *Crimes of the Heart* and attempts to account for Henley's idiosyncratic voice. Henley combines elements of the naturalistic play with characters from absurdist comedy and writes "with wit and compassion about good country people gone wrong or whacko." Some attention is given to Henley's biography.

Harbin, Billy J. "Familial Bonds in the Plays of Beth Henley." *Southern Quarterly* 25 (Spring, 1987): 81-94. Examines Henley's plays through *The Debutante Ball* but gives

Crimes of the Heart the most attention. Recurring themes concern "the disintegration of traditional ideas, such as the breakup of families, the quest for emotional and spiritual fulfillment, and the repressive social forces within a small southern community."

Hargrove, Nancy D. "The Tragicomic Vision of Beth Henley's Drama." *Southern Quarterly* 22 (Summer, 1984): 54-70. Analyzes *Crimes of the Heart, The Miss Firecracker Contest,* and *The Wake of Jamey Foster* and finds that the plays "are essentially serious, although they are presented in the comic mode" and that the value of love, especially family love, is Henley's predominant theme. Hargrove's is the first scholarly article to examine Henley's work.

Jaehne, Karen. "Beth's Beauties." *Film Comment* 25 (May/June, 1989): 9-12. Highlights the film version of *The Miss Firecracker Contest* and quotes Henley extensively. Henley's plays analyze "the ways women conform to or rebel against standards of femininity." Although she likes to read tragedies, Henley says "in my own writing I can't see the situations I look at without laughing. I back into comedy. I can't help it."

Jones, John Griffin, ed. "Beth Henley." In *Mississippi Writers Talking.* Vol. 1. Jackson: University Press of Mississippi, 1982. Interviews Henley about her family background, education, and playwriting. Henley says that she likes to write about the South "because you can get away with making things more poetic." About the meaning of her plays, Henley confesses, "I don't think very thematically. I think more in terms of character and story."

McDonnell, Lisa J. "Diverse Similitude: Beth Henley and Marsha Norman." *Southern Quarterly* 25 (Spring, 1987): 95-104. Compares Henley's *Crimes of the Heart, The Miss Firecracker Contest,* and *The Wake of Jamey Foster* and Norman's *Getting Out* (pr. 1977, pb. 1979) and *'night, Mother* (pr. 1982, pb. 1983). Whereas both writers use the family as a framework and employ gothic humor, their plays differ remarkably in tone and style. Henley "writes comedy with serious dimensions, Norman, serious drama with comic overtones."

Simon, John. "Sisterhood Is Beautiful." Review of *Crimes of the Heart. New York* 14 (January 12, 1981): 42-43. Reviews the Off Broadway production of *Crimes of the Heart.* Simon calls Henley "a new playwright of charm, warmth, style, unpretentiousness, and authentically individual vision." His analysis connects Henley's characters to those of Anton Chekhov, Flannery O'Connor, and Tennessee Williams. If Henley "errs in any way, it is in slightly artificial resolutions."

Ayne C. Durham,
updated by Rhona Justice-Malloy

Tina Howe

Born: New York, New York; November 21, 1937

Principal drama • *Closing Time*, pr. 1959; *The Nest*, pr. 1969; *Birth and After Birth*, wr. 1973, pb. 1977, revised pr. 1995; *Museum*, pr. 1976, pb. 1979; *The Art of Dining*, pr. 1979, pb. 1980; *Appearances*, pr. 1982 (one act); *Painting Churches*, pr. 1983, pb. 1984; *Three Plays,* pb. 1984; *Coastal Disturbances*, pr. 1986, pb. 1987; *Approaching Zanzibar*, pr., pb. 1989; *Coastal Disturbances: Four Plays*, pb. 1989; *One Shoe Off*, pr., pb. 1993; *Approaching Zanzibar and Other Plays*, pb. 1995; *Pride's Crossing*, pr. 1997, pb. 1998; *Rembrandt's Gift*, pr. 2002

Other literary forms • Tina Howe is known primarily for her plays.

Achievements • Tina Howe has earned distinction as one of the leading American dramatists of the commercial theater, and she has received some of the highest awards for playwriting. In 1983, largely in response to her most studied and successful play, *Painting Churches*, she captured an Obie Award for Distinguished Playwriting, the Rosamond Gilder Award for Outstanding Creative Achievement in Theatre, and a Rockefeller Playwright-in-Residence Fellowship. In addition to the Outer Critics Circle John Gassner Award for Outstanding New American Playwright in 1984, she has received two National Endowment for the Arts Fellowships, a Guggenheim Fellowship, an American of Arts and Letters Award in Literature, a Tony nomination for Best Play (*Coastal Disturbances*), and an honorary degree from Bowdoin College. *Pride's Crossing* was a finalist for the Pulitzer Prize in Drama and in 1998 received the New York Drama Critics Circle Award for best play.

Biography • Tina Howe, reared in New York City, was born into an aristocratic and celebrated family. Her grandfather, Mark Antony DeWolfe Howe, was a renowned poet and Pulitzer Prize recipient. Her father, Quincy Howe, was an eminent radio and television broadcaster, and her mother, Mary, was a painter. After attending private schools in New York, Howe went to Sarah Lawrence College in Bronxville, New York, where she received a baccalaureate degree in 1959. Howe tried her hand at playwriting during her undergraduate studies and had a play produced (*Closing Time*) at Sarah Lawrence College, with Howe directing and Jane Alexander, Howe's classmate, starring in the production.

Howe did not seriously consider becoming a dramatist, however, until the year after her graduation, when she traveled to Paris and had the opportunity to meet aspiring young writers and, more important, to see various experimental, absurdist theater productions, in particular Eugène Ionesco's *La Cantatrice chauve* (pr. 1950; *The Bald Soprano*, 1956) and *Rhinocéros* (pr., pb. 1959; *Rhinoceros*, 1959). This experience was a turning point for Howe, for the absurdist dramas appealed to her own antic, comic spirit, and these plays would later influence her dramaturgical style. She returned to New York, married writer Norman Levy in 1961, and taught high school English in Maine, where she also served as drama coach for the school's club. This position helped her learn her craft, for the rigors of writing one-act plays for the club's production season helped her gain the discipline and focus that she needed as a writer.

During the late 1960's and early 1970's, Howe and Levy took various teaching positions at colleges in Chicago, Madison, and Albany. Howe continued to write plays, with *The Nest* receiving a professional production. In 1973, the couple settled in New York City with their two children. In 1983 Howe began working as an adjunct professor of playwriting at New York University and in 1990 became a visiting professor at Hunter College.

Analysis • Tina Howe is not only one of the most prominent female playwrights from a new generation of American dramatists who emerged during the second women's movement but also represents a group of dramatists whose works characterize the postmodern theater movement that began in the early 1970's. Her plays blend traditional domestic drama with the experimental techniques that deploy considerable theatricality. On the surface, they appear naturalistic, slice-of-life comedies, but she injects an element of Surrealism throughout her plays by inserting unexpected, outrageous actions: the frenetic destruction of artworks, an old lady jumping on a trampoline.

Like the absurdists, Howe focuses on existential issues, but she lacks their darkness and nihilism, preferring that her characters, and the audience, laugh at life's reversals and accept them with valor and courage. Her language can be, at turns, everyday conversation with dialogue overlapping, or elegantly poetic arias and soliloquies. Through comedy, Howe probes the most basic of human emotions, forces laughter and compassion for those who suffer agonies familiar to all, and reminds viewers that life is full of both tragic and comic events. She celebrates life's everyday, ordinary events—the sunsets, the family vacation, the reunion with relatives—those special ephemeral moments that can be captured perhaps on canvas or with a photograph but can never be relived. Between birth and death is life in process. Howe reminds the audience to live it to the fullest.

Howe's plays are remarkable for their absurdist depiction of life and their female perspective. Her playwriting style closely allies her with the absurdists, to whom she admits her indebtedness. In particular, she borrowed the absurdists' use of surreal details, incongruous actions, bizarre situations, and farcical characters, for these devices suited her interest in exploring the passions, drives, fears, and anxieties that lie below the surface in all persons. As a result, her plays are, on the one hand, wildly comic, replete with pratfalls, sight gags, and much physical and verbal comedy, and yet, on the other hand, are rueful and poignant, exposing the emotional pain of characters who battle life's unavoidable tragedies and suffering.

Howe's tragicomic view of life has sparked comparisons between her work and and that of Russian playwright Anton Chekhov, specifically for Howe's ability to capture "the same edgy surface of false hilarity, the same unutterable sadness beneath it, and the indomitable valor beneath both." Howe presents her absurdist view of life from the female perspective: The central protagonists of her plays are women, and it is through their experiences that Howe explores such universal concerns as the ravages of time, the ineluctable human process of deterioration, the basal anxieties over death, and the human need to find meaning and permanence in an ephemeral world.

The Nest and Birth and After Birth • Howe's first two comedies, *The Nest* and *Birth and After Birth,* are her most overtly feminist and absurdist plays. In these works, Howe draws biting satirical portraits of women as they struggle to find autonomy in a world demanding that they live according to the traditional roles of wives and mothers. *The Nest* depicts a trio of young women battling one another for the prize of an ideal husband, and the inanity of their actions culminates in a highly charged, symbolic moment, when one of the women removes all of her clothes and dives into a seven-foot-tall wedding cake. *The Nest* was panned by critics and closed after one performance.

Birth and After Birth looks at women's choices concerning childbirth. Through Sandy, mother of a four-year-old son with behavioral problems (played by an adult actor), who grows increasingly disillusioned and enraged over the demands that her family places on her, Howe shows the physical and emotional toll that child rearing takes on women and attacks the myth that marriage and motherhood fulfill women's lives. On the opposite pole, Mia, a married anthropologist with no children, fears the physical pain of childbirth, and although she has tried to find personal fulfillment through her job, she feels inadequate as a woman because she has no children. With this play, Howe said she wanted "to show how threatening women on either side of the fence can be to each other." The play implies as well that women, regardless of their choices regarding marriage and children, continue both to define and to judge themselves according to the myths of motherhood and family life. *Birth and After Birth* has proved so incendiary that Howe has had difficulty getting it staged.

A new approach • After the failure of these two plays, Howe made a conscious effort to alter her playwriting style. She took note of the successful Broadway plays at the time and concluded that audiences wanted escape, so she set out to find settings that had not been used onstage before, something that audiences would find novel. More important, she decided to tone down her feminist voice by couching it in less threatening dramatic terms. As a result, Howe took women out of their domestic arena, placed them in such exotic and unlikely locales as museums, restaurants, and beaches, and made her central protagonists women artists.

When Howe hit on this idea and wrote her first successful play (*Museum*) as a result of her new writing strategy, she knew that she had hit her stride: "I had found my niche at last. I would write about women as artists, eschew the slippery ground of courtship and domesticity and move up to a loftier plane." Her later plays are still full of comic exuberance, zany characters, and outrageous situations, but her female characters, in the main, now seek their creative and intellectual potential through nontraditional roles, most particularly as artists.

Museum • As the play's title suggests, *Museum* takes place in a museum gallery with three modernist exhibits: five life-size, clothed figures hanging from a twenty-five-foot clothesline and a basket of clothespins on the floor, a series of sculptures made from animal bones and feathers displayed on pedestals, and a group of three, totally white paintings along one wall. *Museum* has no traditional plot; it is a collage of conversations by some forty gallery visitors who meander about studying the exhibits, some expressing their disgust and confusion over such abstract drivel, others completely enthralled and postulating the meaning of each work and the purpose of art in general.

The climax of the action occurs when Tink Solheim, a friend of Agnes Vaag (the sculptor of the animal-bone exhibit) begins frantically to search for the special secret that Agnes said was hidden in one of the sculptures. Tink finds a hidden switch, and when she turns it, the lights dim, floodlight illuminates the statue, and music by Johann Sebastian Bach swells out from a hidden speaker. The crowd stands entranced for several minutes, experiencing a communal epiphany. This spiritual awakening leads to pandemonium, as the play concludes with the gallery visitors running about in a frenzy, ripping apart the exhibits, and stealing parts of them in their desire to own at least a small part of something artistic, spiritual, and eternal.

The Art of Dining • The communal and spiritual experience brought about by a woman's work of art in *Museum* has its parallel in Howe's next play, *The Art of Dining*. The artist in this play is Ellen, a gourmet chef and partner with her husband in a trendy restaurant. Where people coveted art in *Museum*, in this comedy they wish literally to devour it. Starving diners from the surrounding area come to the restaurant to feast voraciously on Ellen's famous culinary masterpieces.

The symbol of spiritual starvation in the previous play is made more literal in *The Art of Dining*, and, similar to the finale of *Museum*, Howe brings all the visitors together in one communal, ritual moment brought about by the female creator. Everyone huddles together to feast on Ellen's complementary dessert. The symbolism of this closing moment of shared community is articulated by one of the diners, Elizabeth Colt, a young anorexic novelist, who stands apart as the diners eat with gusto and explains that centuries ago people gathered together in a shared celebration to enjoy the feast. Through their collective communion brought about by Ellen's gift, this group of strangers comes together in one common humanity, "purified of their collective civilization and private grief."

Painting Churches • *Painting Churches*, Howe's most successful comedy, returns to the world of the artist. It explores parent-child relationships, children's need to gain parental acceptance and approval, and, especially, the larger and more serious issues of life's inevitable process toward deterioration and the ultimate movement toward death. In this play, Mags Church, an impressionist painter, visits home after a long absence to paint a portrait of her aged parents before their imminent move from their Boston family home and just prior to her first solo show in a famous art gallery.

Mags needs her parents' recognition of her creative genius (something they have never given her), and she hopes that her portrait of them will gain their respect for her as an artist and an adult. Once home, however, Mags sees the debilitating effects of time on her parents; her father, Gardner, once a renowned poet, is now addled, and her mother, Fanny, has been reduced to a life of taking care of her senile husband. Mags must face the shattering reality that all children encounter: Her parents are nearing death.

After some difficulty getting her parents to sit still long enough to pose, Mags finally finishes her portrait, and it is this gift to her parents that brings all three together in a celebratory moment at the end of the play. When Fanny and Gardner look at their portrait, they compare it to one of Pierre-Auguste Renoir's works, and eventually they envision themselves as figures in a Renoir café scene with couples dancing. A Chopin waltz begins to play, and they start to dance about the room, oblivious to Mags, who stands watching them, her eyes filled with tears. Through Mags's painting, her parents have been rejuvenated, if only for a moment, for in effect they have been transformed into the painting. For a brief, magical moment, time stands still. Mags has locked her parents in time, capturing and immortalizing them by her portrait. Although her parents will soon die, they will continue to live not only in her memory but also forever on her canvas.

Coastal Disturbances • *Coastal Disturbances* includes various short scenes that form a collage, a series of impressions about love from different points of view, from an elderly couple who have withstood infidelities and other marital tragedies to a young couple caught up in sexual infatuation. The play's heroine, Holly, is a professional photographer who has come to a private beach in Massachusetts for a two-week vacation to take photographs and to forget a disastrous affair with her agent-boyfriend in New York. Holly becomes enamored of a compassionate and lovable lifeguard, but when her former boyfriend tracks her down and begs a reconciliation, she capitulates to his charm. Although Howe is concerned with the passage of time, which is made quite visible by the ever-changing and gorgeous sunrises and sunsets on the beach, she does not explore this theme as vividly and dramatically as in *Painting Churches. Coastal Disturbances* is atypical of Howe's work; it is a love story that attempts to teach that forgiveness, compassion, and tenderness can calm any emotional disturbance and heal the heart.

Approaching Zanzibar • With *Approaching Zanzibar*, Howe returns to her previous preoccupations with life's ephemerality, death, art, and rebirth. The Blossom family (husband Wally, wife Charlotte, and two children, Turner and Pony) take a cross-country trek from Hastings, New York, to Taos, New Mexico, to visit Charlotte's dying aunt, Olivia. On this two-week trip, the Blossoms enjoy a typical vacation, camping out, fishing, visiting relatives, and meeting some interesting strangers.

At every turn, the realities of life's brevity and ultimate closure through death form a palpable background. Not only is the trip itself a metaphor for the journey of life with its end in death (symbolized by Olivia), but also, throughout, characters make repeated references to the passage of time and the loss of youth and its promise of a future. Charlotte is menopausal, and her anguish over her inability to have more children causes her nightmares about abandoned babies. Wally, once a famous composer, lost his creative energy when his parents' deaths the year earlier traumatized him, forcing him to confront his own mortality.

Howe underscores her theme of the inexorable cycle of life (birth, death, rebirth) not only through dialogue with numerous allusions to evolution and reincarnation but also through the Blossom children. Although Charlotte and Wally face midlife, their children are their source of hope and touch with immortality. Turner is a musical prodigy with great promise of carrying on his father's talent. Pony possesses the most miraculous and powerful counter to death, her potential progeny.

The celebration of the female's ability to create life and rejuvenate her species as the ultimate defense against death forms the play's closing tableau: Pony, alone at Olivia's bedside, rejuvenates the dying woman; soon the two hold hands and begin jumping on Olivia's bed (a trampoline) while crying out "Paradise." All the others rush into the room, freeze at the sight of them leaping into the air, and then gather around the bed to join their euphoric shouts of "Paradise." Here again, Howe ends her play in a highly charged, theatrical moment of spiritual communion, an affirmation of life, nurturing, and humanity, with the female at its core.

Pride's Crossing • In *Pride's Crossing*, Howe wanted fictionally to allow an elderly maiden aunt of hers, a "dutiful Boston daughter" who never rebelled against social mores, to express anger over what she had missed. *Pride's Crossing* explores a powerful woman's passage through a life marred by social constraints. The play's main protagonist is ninety-year-old Mabel Tidings Bigelow, who in her twenties was the first woman to swim across the English Channel.

In the course of the play Mabel's memories take shape and we see the younger

Mabel at ages rangingfrom ten to sixty. The usually rebellious young woman's family were part of a proper Bostonian upper class, and her ties to that society cost her the one great—but socially unacceptable—love of her life; she married an alcoholic Boston Protestant instead of the Jewish doctor who truly loved her. The younger Mabel's athleticism and physical strength contrast with the lost potential of the feisty but aged woman who still clings to social niceties and has lost her physical power. In the end, *Pride's Crossing* expresses the passion of the old woman who looks back and sees the consequences of doing what she thought was right, rather than taking the plunge and following her heart.

Bibliography

Backes, Nancy. "Body Art: Hunger and Satiation in the Plays of Tina Howe." In *Making a Spectacle*, edited by Lynda Hart. Ann Arbor: University of Michigan Press, 1989. Women writers' use of food has become a major area of research, and this essay adds to that body of scholarship by incisively examining Howe's abundant use of food imagery relative to cultural inscriptions about women's bodies, self-image, self-control, and nurturing.

Barlow, Judith E. "The Art of Tina Howe." In *Feminine Focus*, edited by Enoch Brater. Oxford, England: Oxford University Press, 1989. Barlow discusses one of the central motifs in Howe's plays, the importance of art in daily life. Barlow pays particular attention to Howe's use of women as artists, and her insightful comments clarify Howe's interest in celebrating the unique and powerful creativity of women artists.

_____. "Tina Howe." In *Speaking on Stage: Interviews with Contemporary American Playwrights*. Edited by Philip C. Kolin and Colby H. Kullman. Tuscaloosa: University of Alabama Press, 1996. Howe discusses writing comedic plays and the recurring themes in her work.

Betsko, Kathleen, and Rachel Koening. *Interviews with Contemporary Women Playwrights*. New York: Beech Tree Books, 1987. Howe's interview contains a range of biographical information on her, including her writing habits, her view on the arts, her absurdist roots, and her thematic concerns from *The Nest* to *Painting Churches*.

DiGaetani, John L. *A Search for a Postmodern Theater: Interviews with Contemporary Playwrights*. Westport, Conn.: Greenwood Press, 1991. In this interview, Howe discusses her indebtedness to the absurdist playwrights, her concerns as a feminist writer, and autobiographical aspects of her plays and characters. Contains a photograph of Howe.

Howe, Tina. "Antic Vision." *American Theatre* 2 (September, 1985): 12, 14. Although numerous published interviews with Howe provide firsthand information from the playwright, this essay by Howe, written after the success of *Painting Churches*, offers the most insight into her views about comical playwriting, her feminist vision, and her aesthetic voice. Contains photographs from production scenes of *Painting Churches* and *The Art of Dining*.

_____. "Women's Work: White Gloves or Bare Hands?" *American Theatre* 15 (September, 1998): 7. Excerpts from a keynote speech given at the November, 1997, Women's Project Conference. Howe talks about critical responses to her early plays and being both a writer and mother.

Kachur, B. A. "Women Playwrights on Broadway: Henley, Howe, Norman, and Wasserstein." In *Contemporary American Theatre*, edited by Bruce King. New York: St. Martin's Press, 1991. This chapter on four prominent women playwrights includes information on Howe's metadramatic techniques and her feminist perspective, particularly her use of women both as central protagonists and as artists.

Swarns, Rachel L. "New Play, and Old Questions, About Women." *New York Times*, December 7, 1997, Section 2, p. 4. Howe discusses the struggle to find acceptance for women playwrights and feminist topics on Broadway. Other women playwrights and producers offer their perspectives.

Wetzsteon, Ross. "The Mad, Mad World of Tina Howe." *New York* 16 (November 28, 1983): 58. Wetzsteon surveys Howe's plays through *Painting Churches*, discusses biographical details, and provides a brief analysis of Howe's playwriting style and themes.

B. A. Kachur,
updated by Maureen Puffer-Rothenberg

David Henry Hwang

Born: Los Angeles, California; August 11, 1957

Principal drama • *F.O.B.*, pr. 1978, pb. 1983; *The Dance and the Railroad*, pr. 1981, pb. 1983; *Family Devotions*, pr. 1981, pb. 1983; *Sound and Beauty*, pr. 1983 (two one-acts, *The House of Sleeping Beauties*, pb. 1983, and *The Sound of a Voice*, pb. 1984); *Broken Promises: Four Plays*, pb. 1983; *Rich Relations*, pr. 1986, pb. 1990; *As the Crow Flies*, pr. 1986; *Broken Promises*, pr. 1987 (includes *The Dance and the Railroad* and *The House of Sleeping Beauties*); *M. Butterfly*, pr., pb. 1988; *One Thousand Airplanes on the Roof*, pr. 1988, pb. 1989 (libretto; music by Philip Glass); *F.O.B. and Other Plays*, pb. 1990; *Bondage*, pr. 1992, pb. 1996 (one act); *The Voyage*, pr. 1992, pb. 2000 (libretto; music by Glass); *Face Value*, pr. 1993; *Trying to Find Chinatown*, pr., pb. 1996; *Golden Child*, pr. 1996, pb. 1998; *The Silver River*, pr. 1997 (music by Bright Sheng); *Peer Gynt*, pr. 1998 (adaptation of Henrik Ibsen's play); *Aida*, pr. 2000 (with Linda Wolverton and Robert Falls; music by Elton John; lyrics by Tim Rice; adaptation of Giuseppe Verdi's opera); *Flower Drum Song*, pr. 2001 (adaptation of Richard Rodgers and Oscar Hammerstein's musical)

Other literary forms • David Henry Hwang has written a number of screenplays, including *M. Butterfly* (1993), *Golden Gate* (1994), and *Possession* (2001). He has also written for television with scripts that include *My American Son* (1987) and *The Lost Empire* (2001).

Achievements • David Henry Hwang is the first Asian American playwright to bring specifically Asian and American themes to Broadway and Off-Broadway theater. His plays explore issues of ethnic identity, gender, and imperialism, with often stunning theatrical flair. Within the first decade of his career as a playwright, he staged six major productions in New York and abroad, garnering four Off-Broadway "Best Play" nominations and awards. *M. Butterfly*, his first Broadway play, won both the New York Drama Desk Award and the Tony Award for Best Play as well as a nomination for the Pulitzer Prize in Drama. *Golden Child* was nominated for a Tony Award for Best Play in 1998 and earned an Obie Award for Playwriting in 1997.

Biography • David Henry Hwang was born in Los Angeles on August 11, 1957, the son of Henry Yuan Hwang, a banker, and Dorothy Huang Hwang, a professor of piano. His father grew up in Shanghai, China, and emigrated in the late 1940's to California, where he enrolled in the business program at the University of Southern California. His mother, born in southeastern China, had grown up in the Philippines.

Hwang received his A.B. degree in English from Stanford University in 1979, then briefly taught writing in a high school in Menlo Park, California, before attending the Yale School of Drama in 1980 and 1981. His first play, *F.O.B.*, was performed at Stanford University before being accepted for production at the National Playwrights Conference at Connecticut's O'Neill Theater Center in 1979, when he was twenty-one years old. The following year, Joseph Papp brought it to the New York Shakespeare Festival's Public Theatre, Off-Broadway. It won an Obie Award for the best new play of the season.

471

Like *F.O.B.*, Hwang's next two plays focused on the Chinese American experience. *The Dance and the Railroad* depicts two nineteenth century immigrants working on the transcontinental railroad, while *Family Devotions* is a bizarre farce set in contemporary California.

His next two plays, jointly titled *Sound and Beauty*, are stylized one-act plays set in contemporary Japan; they were produced Off-Broadway in 1983. The first, *The House of Sleeping Beauties*, reinvents a novella by Yasunari Kawabata, making the author a character in a version of his own work. The second, *The Sound of a Voice*, involves a conflict between a samurai warrior and a bewitching female hermit whom he intends to kill.

In 1983, Hwang received a Rockefeller playwright-in-residence award and a National Endowment for the Arts artistic associate fellowship. A Guggenheim Fellowship followed in 1984, as did fellowships from the National Endowment for the Arts and the New York State Council on the Arts in 1985. On September 25, 1985, he married Ophelia Y. M. Chong, an artist, from whom he was later divorced.

Rich Relations, produced Off-Broadway in 1986, was his first work not about the Asian experience and his first critical failure, though it recapitulated various themes from his earlier plays. Nevertheless, Hwang has termed this failure exhilarating, freeing him from undue concern about critical reaction.

M. Butterfly, produced in 1988, brought Hwang international renown, a Tony Award for the Best Play of 1988, the Outer Critics Circle Award, and a nomination for the Pulitzer Prize in 1989. Based on a true story of a French diplomat and his Chinese lover who turned out to be not only a spy but also a man, the play explores issues of gender, identity, racism, and political hegemony. The same year, he collaborated with composer Philip Glass on *One Thousand Airplanes on the Roof*, a science fiction work concerning a character who may have been kidnapped by visiting aliens.

In 1992, Hwang's one-act play *Bondage* premiered at the Humana Festival of New Plays at the Actors Theatre of Louisville, Kentucky. Set in a parlor frequented by sadomasochists, its two characters are completely covered in black leather, so that their respective races cannot be discerned.

In 1994, the film *Golden Gate* was released, based on Hwang's screenplay and directed by John Madden. Set in San Francisco in 1952, it depicts the persecution of Chinese Americans by the Federal Bureau of Investigation (FBI) during the Joseph McCarthy era, when they were suspected of having ties to the communist revolution in China. FBI agent Kevin Walker (Matt Dillon) investigates laundryman Chen Jung Song (Tzi Ma), who has collected and sent funds to his and his friends' impoverished relatives in China. Following Song's ten-year imprisonment and subsequent suicide, agent Walker, in disguise, courts the dead man's daughter, who is a law student trying to clear her father's name.

Hwang's play *Golden Child* opened at the Joseph Papp Public Theatre in New York in 1996, directed by James Lapine. Its plot concerned the struggle between tradition and change in a family in 1918 China, when its members encounter a Christian missionary whose values challenge their traditional Confucianism. The play won an Obie Award in 1997.

The Silver River, a "chamber opera" on which Hwang collaborated with composer Bright Sheng, premiered at the Santa Fe Chamber Music Festival in 1997. Based on a beloved Chinese legend, the opera's four characters were intended to be radically different kinds of performers—two "Westerners" and two Chinese, performing in the style of Peking Opera.

In 1998, the Trinity Repertory Company of Providence, Rhode Island, presented Hwang's adaptation and abridgment of Henrik Ibsen's *Peer Gynt* (pb. 1867; English translation, 1892). Described by one reviewer as "Gynt-lite," this version shortened Ibsen's epic drama to two hours (a 50 percent reduction), removing entire scenes and characters while renaming others. It also added pop-culture anachronisms, Freudian symbols, and broad farce.

Hwang next collaborated with Linda Wolverton and Robert Falls in writing the book for the pop musical *Aida*, with music by Elton John and lyrics by Tim Rice. It was first produced in 2000. Like Giuseppi Verdi, whose opera *Aida* premiered in 1871, Hwang and his co-authors drew on a story by nineteenth century Egyptologist Mariette Bey; however, they added characters not present in Verdi's work. These included Mereb, an Ethiopian slave who provides comic relief, and Zoser, who seeks to poison the pharaoh and assume the throne himself.

In 2001, Hwang's radically overhauled version of Richard Rodgers and Oscar Hammerstein's *Flower Drum Song* premiered in Los Angeles, directed by James Longbottom; it was the musical's first major revival since it opened in 1958. During this year Hwang also completed a screen adaptation of A. S. Byatt's novel *Possession* (1990). Now set in a fading Chinese Opera house in Chinatown, the central theme of *Flower Drum Song* is the tension between the older generation's belief in tradition and the younger generation's desire to assimilate into American culture. It also focuses on a young woman's experience after fleeing Mao Zedong's China in 1959.

Analysis • Images of Asians and Asian Americans in modern culture have been relatively rare and often stereotypical; few have been created by Asian Americans themselves. On-screen stereotypes ranged from Charlie Chan (performed by a white actor), an image of wise but humble, ultimately "knowing" inscrutability, to the cook Hop Sing on the television series *Bonanza* (1959-1973). Contact between Eastern and Western cultures had been depicted in such works as David Belasco's *Madame Butterfly* (pr. 1900, pb. 1935, the basis for Giacomo Puccini's opera of the same name), Richard Rodgers and Oscar Hammerstein II's *The King and I* (pr. 1951) and *Flower Drum Song* (pr. 1958), John Patrick's *The Teahouse of the August Moon* (pr. 1953, pb. 1954), and Paul Osborn's *The World of Suzie Wong* (pr. 1958, based on the novel by Richard Mason).

Whatever their merits, however, none of these plays offered a genuinely Asian perspective on the events portrayed. By the early 1970's, literature by and about Asian Americans began to emerge; a decade later, its first critically acclaimed and commercially successful playwright was David Henry Hwang. From his earliest plays about the Chinese American experience to his Broadway hit *M. Butterfly* and the subsequent re-writing of *Flower Drum Song*, he has progressively explored issues of ethnic cultural identity, gender roles, the East/West relationship, and the effects of imperialism—and has done so with deftly constructed plots, a number of which incorporate elements of Chinese opera.

F.O.B. • In his introduction to *F.O.B. and Other Plays*, Hwang identified three phases "in attempting to define [his] place in America," and his early plays correspond to these. The first is an "assimilationist" phase, in which one tries to "out-white the whites" in order to fit in with the majority culture. Dale, the central character of his first play, *F.O.B.*, is a second-generation American of Chinese descent who dresses like a "preppy" and particularly disdains Chinese immigrants who are "Fresh Off the Boat," abbreviated "F.O.B." One such, named Steve, is the target of his scorn throughout the play, in part because he reminds Dale of his ancestry, the nonwhite, non-American past that he prefers to ignore, discard, or deny. Steve's cousin Grace, a first-generation Chinese American, functions as an intermediary between the two men, with insight into the plight of both the newly arrived and the all-too-assimilated "A.B.C.'s," meaning "American-Born Chinese."

Steve announces himself as the great god Gwan Gung, the Chinese folk hero, the "god of warriors, writers, and prostitutes." Grace tells him that in the United States, Gwan Gung is dead; nevertheless, her contact with Steve reawakens her own fantasy, Fu Ma Lan, a great woman warrior. Dale repudiates both myths, having struggled for so long to overcome his Chinese-ness, but Steve's presence forces him to reexamine his values. Following Dale's attempts to humiliate the immigrant, Steve becomes in monologue the embodiment of "ChinaMan," the immigrant Everyman who helped build the American West, particularly its railroads. Such cultural kinship finally binds Steve and Grace, who transmutes him from dead god to living warrior. Dale is left behind at the end of the play, uncomprehending, unrepentant, and alone.

The Dance and the Railroad • Gwan Gung also figures significantly in *The Dance and the Railroad*, Hwang's second play, a product of his "isolationist-nationalist" phase, in which he wrote primarily for other Asian Americans, having rejected "the assimilationist model" as "dangerous and self-defeating." Set in 1867, *The Dance and the Railroad* is a two-character, one-act play whose characters, Lone and Ma, are workers building the transcontinental railroad but are currently on a nine-day laborers' strike.

Although conflicts between white management and Chinese labor underlie the action, personal differences between the characters and the traditions of Chinese opera and culture become increasingly prominent. Lone, a refugee from the Chinese opera, isolates himself from the other workers, practicing his art in solitude on the mountainside, above the strike and commercial toil. Ma, a gullible F.O.B. laborer who believes in the promises of the Gold Mountain in America, ascends in search of Lone, discovers his austere artistic training regimen, and yearns to learn opera to "become" Gwan Gung in the new land. To learn the discipline that artistry requires, Ma maintains the "locust" position all night, a metaphor for immigrant experience. Finally worthy to study Gwan Gung, Ma rejects doing so and returns to the work below when the strike ends. The play's later scenes are performed in the style of Chinese opera. The actor playing Lone—his namesake, John Lone—had trained with the Peking Opera for eight years; he also directed the play, choreographed it, and provided its music.

Family Devotions • Hwang's third play, *Family Devotions*, is a nine-character farce set in contemporary California. The action centers on three generations of a thoroughly "assimilated" Chinese American family satirically based on Hwang's own; they are visited by their "second brother" Di-gou, a doctor and former violinist who has lived for thirty years under the Communist chinese regime. His sisters, ardent fundamentalist Christians, are shocked to find out that he is an atheist and that he rejects the legend of See-Goh-Poh, a Christian "Woman Warrior" who allegedly saved his soul at age eight. He, in turn, is baffled by the family's crass materialism and conspicuous consumption and has come to ask his sisters to renounce their faith and return home with him.

The first act ends with one of the sisters, Ama, delivering a fiery testimonial from a rolling, neon-lit pulpit as the "Hallelujah Chorus" blares away. In the second act, the sisters and their daughters tie Di-gou to a table, assailing him with the word of God and See-Goh-Poh. He breaks his bonds in a holy fit of possession, speaks in tongues, and exposes See-Goh-Poh as a fraud whose crusade was a ruse to conceal an unwanted pregnancy. As the grotesque exorcism proceeds, the sisters die in their chairs as Di-gou continues his vehement speech. Di-gou and the young child of the family depart, leaving the house a spiritual wreck, torn between the Chinese past and the California present, between myth and reality. The play shows the influence of American playwright Sam Shepard, to whom it is dedicated, but many of its thematic preoccupations—assimilation versus origins, lost ethnic awareness, a core conflict of incompatible values—are recognizably Hwang's own.

The House of Sleeping Beauties • In the third phase of his writing, Hwang sought to move beyond his personal experience. *The House of Sleeping Beauties* is an adaptation of a novella *Nemureru bijo* (1960-1961 serial, 1961 book; *The House of the Sleeping Beauties*, in *The House of the Sleeping Beauties and Other Stories*, 1969) by Yasunari Kawabata, who is himself one of the play's two characters. The play is set in a brothel where elderly men learn to accept their mortality by sleeping beside comatose, nude, drugged young virgins. In Hwang's version, Kawabata comes there to research a book but becomes spiritually (platonically) involved with Michiko, the elderly proprietress. The play ends with his suicide by self-poisoning, and he is rocked to his final eternal sleep in her lap.

The Sound of a Voice • The companion piece of *The House of Sleeping Beauties* is *The Sound of a Voice*, a fable of a samurai warrior who goes into a forest to kill a bewitching female hermit but instead falls in love with her. The role of the witch was originally written for an *onnagata*, a male actor specializing in women's parts in Japanese Kabuki theater, but in the initial production it was played by a woman, Natsuko Ohama.

Rich Relations • *Rich Relations*, produced in 1986, was Hwang's first play with all Caucasian characters and his first critical and commercial failure. Like *Family Devotions*, it lampooned evangelical Christianity, deathbed resurrections, and crass materialism within a suburban Los Angeles family, but it offered little that was new in technique or ideas.

M. Butterfly • *M. Butterfly*, two years later, was a commercial and critical triumph on Broadway. The play is based on an article that appeared in *The New York Times* about the conviction for espionage of a French diplomat, who aided the Communist Chinese government by turning over embassy documents to his mistress of twenty years, a Chinese opera singer whom he had mistakenly believed to be an extremely modest woman. Hwang, however, sought no additional details from the actual case so as to avoid writing a docudrama; he was struck by the story as an inversion of the plot of the play and opera *Madame Butterfly*, in which a Japanese woman falls in love with a Caucasian man, is spurned, and commits suicide.

In Hwang's play, the diplomat, René Gallimard, is the counterpart of Puccini's Westerner, Pinkerton, as he falls in love with opera singer Song Liling, unaware that she is the Chinese counterpart of an *onnagata* and an agent of the communist government. The role of Song Liling is played by a man (B. D. Wong in the original production), though this fact is not revealed to the theater audience until the beginning of the third act when, in a moment of startling theatricality, Song Liling removes her makeup and changes clothes onstage, dispelling the illusion for the audience before disclosing her true gender and identity to Gallimard in a nude scene near the end of the play.

In many ways, *M. Butterfly* continues the thematic preoccupations that became apparent in Hwang's earlier plays: the use of Chinese opera from *The Dance and the Railroad*, the role for an *onnagata* and the unorthodox sexuality of *The Sound of a Voice*, and the clash of Asian and Western values that recurred in all of his earlier plays. Incorporating both Puccini's music and Chinese opera, *M. Butterfly* also explores issues of gender and racial stereotyping, of dominance and submission (political as well as sexual), and of the morality of the Western presence in Asia. Furthermore, the play audaciously questions the nature of love and illusion, undermining any certainty about the ultimate knowability of another person or, indeed, of the world itself. While that theme was not new in twentieth century literature—having been particularly prominent in Ford Madox Ford's novel *The Good Soldier* (1915), for example, seldom, if ever, has it been presented with such dramatic effectiveness and theatrical flair.

M. Butterfly also marks a considerable advance in Hwang's dramatic technique over the earlier plays, which were chronologically presented on realistic sets. The play begins with a retrospective monologue by Gallimard in his prison cell; many flashbacks to European and Asian locales are introduced throughout twenty-seven brief scenes in three acts. The stylized set, designed by Eiko Ishioka, is dominated by a gently sloping, curved ramp, enabling a flexible use of the stage space. The original title, *Monsieur Butterfly*, was shortened to *M. Butterfly* (at Hwang's wife's suggestion) to seem more mysterious and ambiguous.

Following the phenomenal success of *M. Butterfly*, Hwang worried that whatever he did next would be considered a disappointment; accordingly, following a collaboration with the composer Philip Glass on a work titled *One Thousand Airplanes on the Roof*, he worked primarily on film scripts, including a screen adaptation of *M. Butterfly*. In 1992, his one-act play titled *Bondage* opened in Louisville, Kentucky. *Bondage*, like *The House of Sleeping Beauties*, is set in an exotic brothel: one that caters to sadomasochists, where a dominating female is paid to humiliate a male clientele. The play begins with Terri, the female dominatrix, in a session with Mark; both are covered from head to toe in black leather so that their faces as well as their ethnic identities are concealed from the audience. The play consists of a fantasy game in which their races continually change, further exploring themes of gender, racial, and political stereotyping, as well as intricate power relationships.

Trends and themes in the 1990's • In the plays and screenplays that Hwang has written after *Bondage*, two major trends have become increasingly apparent. The first is his ongoing interest in the history of the modern Chinese American experience; he has consistently articulated this little-known aspect of American history, as in the award-winning *Golden Child*, set in 1918, and in the critically assailed film *Golden Gate*, which was set during the McCarthy era of the 1950's. In each of these works, questions of allegiance are paramount: The desire to preserve centuries-old cultural traditions and family values proves difficult to reconcile with a desire to become assimilated into American culture. Yet, as *Golden Gate* demonstrates in particular, the extent of one's "American-ness" or "Other-ness" remains dangerously in question, difficult if not impossible to prove to the satisfaction of those in authority. Like V. S. Naipaul, Salman Rushdie, and Buchi Emecheta, among others, Hwang explores the nature of "hybridity," a crosscultural experience that has drawn increasing attention in postmodern and postcolonial literature.

The second major trend in Hwang's later plays is his boldly transformative use of earlier works, particularly (but not exclusively) Western operas. Puccini's *Madame Butterfly* and Verdi's *Aida* both exemplify what the critic Edward Said has termed "Orientalism," the tendency of European (or American) writers and composers to "invent" an "Orient" that is defined by the "other-ness" of its ways, though such presentation may have little or nothing to do with the actualities of life in those non-Western cultures. Hwang's works are often redactions of these classics, deconstructing some of the cultural assumptions that prevailed when they were first produced. Because *Aida* was a collaboration in which Hwang joined two other writers, a composer, and a lyricist, the extent and nature of his specific contributions to the text cannot readily be ascertained.

Flower Drum Song • In his revamping of Rodgers and Hammerstein's *Flower Drum Song*, however, both of the trends cited above receive their fullest elaboration since *M. Butterfly*. The original production, which opened in New York in 1958, was not as successful as *South Pacific, Oklahoma!, Carousel*, or *The Sound of Music*, but it ran for over 600 performances and was made into a film in 1961. Based on a novel by Chin Y. Lee (1957), it told the story of a mail-order bride from China, Mei-Li, who arrived in San Francisco to marry nightclub owner Sammy Fong, who was already in love with Linda Low, a stripper in the club. Although many of its cast members were Asian (including Pat Suzuki as Linda Low and Miyoshi Umeki as Mei-Li), the role of Sammy Fong was played by a Caucasian actor, Larry Blyden, who was made up to appear Chinese.

In Hwang's revision of the story, the character of Sammy Fong has been eliminated. The setting is now a traditional Chinese theater that has presented Chinese opera, but is being transformed by the owner's son into a Western-style nightclub, the Club Chop Suey. The father, Master Wang, is rooted in traditional Chinese culture, while his son Ta is attracted to the more modern and Americanized culture that is represented by the nightclub. The characters of Linda Low and Mei-Li have been retained in Hwang's version, although Mei-Li is now a refugee from Mao's China. The score, though re-orchestrated, retains most of the songs from the original (except "The Older Generation") and restores one that was cut from the original production before its Broadway opening ("My Best Love"). One song ("The Next Time It Happens") from another Rodgers and Hammerstein musical, *Pipe Dream*, was also added. The emphasis on the two styles of theater also allows Hwang to develop the theme of performance and theatricality that also characterized *M. Butterfly*.

Other major works

SCREENPLAYS: *M. Butterfly*, 1993 (adaptation of his play); *Golden Gate*, 1994; *Possession*, 2001 (with Neil LaBute and Laura Jones; adaptation of A. S. Byatt's novel).

TELEPLAYS: *My American Son*, 1987; *The Lost Empire*, 2001.

Bibliography

Bernstein, Richard. "France Jails Two in Odd Case of Espionage." *The New York Times*, May 11, 1986, p. K7. The original news account on which *M. Butterfly* is based. It recounts the sentencing for espionage of Bernard Bouriscot, a forty-one-year-old French diplomat, and Chinese opera singer Shi Peipeu. During their twenty-year relationship, Bouriscot mistakenly believed Peipeu was a woman. He also believed they had a son, Shi Dudu.

Chen, Tina. "Betrayed into Motion: The Seduction of Narrative Desire in *M. Butterfly*." *Hitting Critical Mass: A Journal of Asian American Cultural Criticism* 1, no. 2 (Spring, 1994): 129-154. Analyzes *M. Butterfly* as postmodern drama, focusing on its relationship with the audience.

Gerard, Jeremy. "David Hwang: Riding on the Hyphen." *The New York Times Magazine*, March 13, 1988, pp. 44, 88-89. This biographical profile, preceding the Broadway debut of *M. Butterfly*, focuses on Hwang's crossover from ethnic to mainstream commercial theater with a play that violates conventions of commercial theater in its treatment of sexism, racism, and imperialism, plus its inclusion of Chinese opera, its scandalous plot, and its brief nudity. Hwang comments on the self-doubt that accompanied his sudden fame.

Hwang, David Henry. "Interview with Marty Moss-Coane. Edited with an Introduction by John Timpane." In *Speaking on Stage: Interviews with Contemporary American Playwrights*, edited by Philip C. Kolin and Colby H. Kullman. Tuscaloosa: University of Alabama Press, 1996. Edited transcript of an interview broadcast on National Public Radio in 1993. Hwang discusses the process of adapting *M. Butterfly* for the screen and discusses his family and childhood in more detail than typically found elsewhere.

_____. "*M. Butterfly*: An Interview with David Henry Hwang." Interview by John Lewis DiGaetani. *The Drama Review: A Journal of Performance Studies* 33, no. 3 (Fall, 1989): 141-153. In this extensive interview, Hwang discusses *M. Butterfly*, Edward W. Said's *Orientalism* (1978), the mutual misperceptions of West and East embodied in Giacomo Puccini's *Madame Butterfly*, and his play's implications about homosexuality, heterosexuality, and fantasy in love. He also suggests that René Gallimard knew—at some level—that his lover was a man. Photographs.

Morris, Rosalind. "*M. Butterfly*: Transvestism and Cultural Cross Dressing in the Critique of Empire." In *Gender and Culture in Literature and Film East and West: Issues of Perception and Interpretation*, edited by Nitaya Masavisut et al. Honolulu: University of Hawaii Press, 1994. Discussion of gender issues and the theme of imperialism in Hwang's best-known play.

Pace, Eric. "I Write Plays to Claim a Place for Asian Americans." *The New York Times*, July 12, 1981, p. D4. This biographical profile was published shortly after *The Dance and the Railroad* opened in New York. Among his attributes as a playwright, Hwang discusses his ability to listen to people with opposite views and empathize with both, his interest in myth and legend, and his concern that Chinese American characters be presented not as polemics but as people.

Skloot, Robert. "Breaking the Butterfly: The Politics of David Henry Hwang." *Modern*

Drama 33, no. 1 (March, 1990): 59-66. Skloot discusses the ways in which *M. Butterfly* brings its audience "into complicity with the discovery, dismantling, and reestablishment of theatrical illusion." Though within the limits of "old-fashioned playwriting," it also challenges traditional assumptions about gender politics, cultural politics, and theatrical politics, which are discussed in separate sections of the article.

Street, Douglas. *David Henry Hwang.* Boise, Idaho: Boise State University Press, 1989. This fifty-two-page study, the first book to have been written on Hwang's work, provides a useful introductory overview of his plays through *M. Butterfly* and contains a concise but detailed biography of the playwright. Bibliography.

Weinraub, Bernard. "Fleshing Out Chinatown Stereotypes." *New York Times,* October 14, 2000, section 2, pp. 7, 27. Lengthy interview-based profile of Hwang, emphasizing his reworking of *Flower Drum Song* and its preproduction history.

William Hutchings

Henrik Ibsen

Born: Skien, Norway; March 20, 1828
Died: Christiania (now Oslo), Norway; May 23, 1906

Principal drama • *Catalina*, pb. 1850, revised pb. 1875, pr. 1881 (verse drama; *Catiline*, 1921); *Kjæmpehøien*, pr. 1850, revised pb. 1854 (dramatic poem; *The Burial Mound*, 1912); *Norma: Eller, En politikers kjærlighed*, pr., pb. 1851 (verse satire); *Sancthansnatten*, pr. 1853, pb. 1909 (*St. John's Night*, 1921); *Fru Inger til Østraat*, pr. 1855, pb. 1857 (*Lady Inger of Østraat*, 1906); *Gildet paa Solhaug*, pr., pb. 1856, revised pb. 1883 (verse and prose drama; *The Feast at Solhaugh*, 1906); *Olaf Liljekrans*, pr. 1857, pb. 1902 (verse and prose drama; English translation, 1911); *Hærmænde paa Helgeland*, pr., pb. 1858 (*The Vikings at Helgeland*, 1890); *Kjærlighedens komedie*, pb. 1862, pr. 1873 (verse comedy; *Love's Comedy*, 1900); *Kongsemnerne*, pb. 1863, pr. 1864 (*The Pretenders*, 1890); *Brand*, pb. 1866, pr. 1885 (dramatic poem; English translation, 1891); *Peer Gynt*, pb. 1867, pr. 1876 (dramatic poem; English translation, 1892); *De unges forbund*, pr., pb. 1869 (*The League of Youth*, 1890); *Kejser og Galilæer*, pb. 1873, pr. 1896 (2 parts: *Cæsars frafald* and *Kejser Julian*; *Emperor and Galilean*, 1876, 2 parts: *Caesar's Apostasy* and *The Emperor Julian*); *Samfundets støtter*, pr., pb. 1877 (*The Pillars of Society*, 1880); *Et dukkehjem*, pr., pb. 1879 (*A Doll's House*, 1880; also known as *A Doll House*); *Gengangere*, pb. 1881, pr. 1882 (*Ghosts*, 1885); *En folkefiende*, pb. 1882, pr. 1883 (*An Enemy of the People*, 1890); *Vildanden*, pb. 1884, pr. 1885 (*The Wild Duck*, 1891); *Rosmersholm*, pb. 1886, pr. 1887 (English translation, 1889); *Fruen fra havet*, pb. 1888, pr. 1889 (*The Lady from the Sea*, 1890); *Hedda Gabler*, pb. 1890, pr. 1891 (English translation, 1891); *Bygmester Solness*, pb. 1892, pr. 1893 (*The Master Builder*, 1893); *Lille Eyolf*, pb. 1894, pr. 1895 (*Little Eyolf*, 1894); *John Gabriel Borkman*, pb. 1896, pr. 1897 (English translation, 1897); *Naar vi døde vaagner*, pb. 1899, pr. 1900 (*When We Dead Awaken*, 1900); *Samlede verker, hundreaarsutgave*, pb. 1928-1957 (21 volumes); *The Oxford Ibsen*, pb. 1960-1977 (8 volumes); *The Complete Major Prose Plays*, pb. 1978

Other literary forms • Henrik Ibsen's volume of poetry, *Digte*, was published in 1871; *Ibsen: Letters and Speeches* appeared in English translation in 1964, and *The Collected Works of Henrik Ibsen* appeared between 1906 and 1912 and in 1928.

Achievements • Henrik Ibsen is widely acknowledged as the father of modern drama, but his significance in literature and history overshadows the influence of his revolutionary stage techniques and his iconoclastic concept of the theater. James Joyce observed of Ibsen, his youthful idol, "It may be questioned whether any man has held so firm an empire over the thinking world in modern times." Despite early disappointments, which led to twenty-seven years of self-imposed exile from Norway, Ibsen at last received the acclaim there that he had been accorded previously throughout Europe, and by the end of his long and immensely productive career, the Norwegian government granted him a state funeral as one of its most illustrious, if controversial, citizens. Ibsen's plays continue to be revived throughout the world, and a steady stream of scholarly books and articles testifies to his popularity among critics and readers who appreciate the therapeutic northern blasts of Ibsen's message.

The unvarying setting of Ibsen's quest as a creative artist was the human mind. At first, he concentrated, with little success, on Norwegian nationalistic themes and historical subjects, in opposition to the Danish domination of Scandinavian theater. As he probed increasingly profound psychological themes involving the individual and society, his analytic dramas seemed threateningly radical, largely incomprehensible, or simply obscene to European audiences then content with frothy farce or Scribean melodrama.

Ibsen's first plays written from exile in Italy won for him fame, but their critical reception was mixed. Later, his social problem plays found their greatest contemporary acceptance in England through William Archer's devoted translations and George Bernard Shaw's espousal of Ibsen's work as support for his own Socialist theories. In his next stage, Ibsen concentrated on the individual's psychological condition; his last plays, written after his return to Norway, which deal with the conflict between art and life, exhibited his shift to Symbolism and were greeted with enthusiasm by James Joyce and Thomas Mann, who both learned Norwegian solely to read Ibsen's works. Another lonely thinker, Sigmund Freud, wrote a perceptive essay on the Oedipus complex as motivation in Ibsen's *Rosmersholm*. Much of Europe, especially czarist Russia, saw Ibsen's plays as potentially explosive, but by 1935, the prominent critic Johanna Kröner commented, "Through Ibsen's influence, European drama has experienced a powerful renewal and progress."

Ibsen's technical innovations in the theater have become so widely accepted that it is difficult to grasp the intense novelty that they represented to their contemporary audiences. The strongly realistic and even naturalistic stage settings of his mature plays contain a wealth of closely observed detail that requires a corresponding intensity of attention by actors to the individualized behavior of his characters. His tense, crackling interchanges of dialogue, a dramatic shorthand, often seem to omit more words than they include, conveying highly complex states of mind and passions through implication and demanding a high degree of emotional stamina from his actors.

As Ibsen's American translator Rolf Fjelde has observed, the language of Ibsen's finest plays resembles poetry in its compaction and resonance. Above all, as Henry James noted, Ibsen has a "peculiar blessedness to actors . . . the inspiration of dealing with material so solid and so fresh," an attraction that seems as valid for the careful reader as it is for Ibsen's stage interpreter. Though Ibsen's contributions to dramatic theory and form have been outmoded by many of the very dramatists his work inspired, his insight into the human condition has not dated. Ibsen insisted that he not only "described human beings" but also "described human fates." Such fates, springing from deep conflicts in human personalities, provide both solid and fresh material for endless meditation. In scholar Einar Haugen's words, "Ibsen's plays . . . enable people to look beyond the little cares of the day and . . . give them some glimpses of eternity."

Biography • Henrik Johan Ibsen was born on March 20, 1828, to a well-to-do merchant family of Skien, a small town in the county of Telemark in Norway, whose people Norwegian historians describe as "sanguine but often melancholic . . . proud and stiff . . . afraid openly to surrender to a mood," people who have an apparent lack of spontaneity that Ibsen called "the shyness of the soul." The Ibsens lived well, entertaining lavishly, until Henrik was seven, when financial pressures bankrupted his father, and the family was forced to move to an isolated farm.

Through the next eight years, young Ibsen felt himself an outcast from the provincial, snobbish social clique once eager to savor the family's hospitality. When he was fifteen, Ibsen became apprenticed to an apothecary at Grimstad, a tiny shipbuilding village down the coast, and his poverty was intensified by the necessity of supporting an illegitimate son for the following fourteen years. The boy's mother, a servant of his employer, was ten years older than Ibsen, and there was no thought of marriage. Though he was already writing poetry, Ibsen originally had considered becoming a physician, but the revolutionary fervor in the air in 1848 led him to write *Catiline*, a dramatic treatment in blank verse of the rebellious Roman senator.

After failing his entrance examinations for medicine, Ibsen turned wholeheartedly to literature. In the fearsome struggles that he experienced in the next two decades of his life, Fjelde sees "the seeds of so many of the themes and motifs that found their way into the series of masterpieces composed between Ibsen's forty-seventh and seventy-first years." Having already endured financial ruin and the scorn of "pillars of society," Ibsen next faced the frustrations of an unappreciated author. Selling his painfully financed copies of *Catiline* as scrap paper, he realized only enough funds to buy himself and a friend one decent dinner during his six years as the new Norwegian Theater's stage manager and resident playwright.

From 1857 to 1862, Ibsen abandoned some of his early bohemianism to become artistic director of the poverty-stricken Norwegian Theater in Christiania (now Oslo), which then was a backward, swampy town whose audiences worshiped the dominant Danish theater. Ibsen wrote eight plays there, all stressing Norwegian history and national spirit; all failed. He had married Suzannah Thoreson in 1858, the Norwegian Theater closed in 1862, and in 1864 they left for the Continent with their only child, Sigurd. Ibsen chose not to live in Norway again for twenty-seven years.

The disillusionment that Ibsen must have felt toward his countrymen is clear in the two verse plays that he wrote in exile, *Brand* and *Peer Gynt*. *Brand* involves an unbending country pastor whose ideal is "all or nothing"; he sets out to reform his society but is destroyed. *Peer Gynt*, a folktale drama, chronicles the escapades of a picaresque rascal who wins forgiveness in a woman's embrace. *Brand* earned for Ibsen fame and a modest stipend from the Norwegian government at the same time that it provoked fiery debate at home and abroad, while *Peer Gynt*, a witty criticism of the relatively comfortable life in eastern Norway, eventually became the one book that most Norwegians would take with them if they had to emigrate, according to the Norwegian literary historian Francis Bull.

At the same time, Ibsen was mulling over the implementation of Hegelian idealism in a huge "world-historical" play which evolved into

(Library of Congress)

Emperor and Galilean, an account of Julian the Apostate that depicts the monumental battle of Christianity against paganism in the fourth century Roman Empire. This ten-act play, impossible to stage, was not accepted by Ibsen's contemporaries and remained largely unappreciated.

Beginning in the 1870's, the second half of his exile, Ibsen moved restlessly from place to place in Europe: Rome, Austria, Munich, and Dresden. As he went, he constructed a series of twelve major prose plays that he wanted grasped "as a continuous and coherent whole," the "subtly and significantly interconnected dramatic cycle," as Fjelde describes it, on which Ibsen's artistic reputation chiefly rests. For these plays, he not only drew on the bitter disappointments of his own early life in Norway but also wove the most personal experiences of others' anxiety, frustration, and mental anguish into them.

By 1891, when Ibsen had somewhat hesitantly returned to Norway to stay, Meyer claims that "Christiania was . . . full of people who regarded themselves as the originals of various characters in his plays," not an unmixed blessing. Whatever their social or psychological antecedents, the characters of Ibsen's great prose cycle represent the complex stresses of the modern world, relentlessly exposing such human failings as hypocrisy, moral cowardice, emotional slavery, and deep frustration in marriage.

The conflict between the demands of his life and his art adversely affected Ibsen's own marriage. Often at least geographically separated, he and his wife gradually drew apart emotionally as well. As he aged, Ibsen became increasingly fascinated with the young, and during a holiday to the Tirol in 1889, he had a brief and hopeless affair with an eighteen-year-old Viennese girl, Emilie Bardach, whom he called "the May sun of a September life." Ibsen subsequently formed emotional attachments to three other young women, among them the pianist Hildur Andersen, whom he described in a phrase from *Peer Gynt* as "My Empire and my Crown!" The young women who dominate his last plays—Hedda, Hilde, Rita, and Irene—share passionate, youthful intensity, but their hopes are defeated by the careers of their would-be lovers.

None of Ibsen's late involvements developed into a total sexual relationship. As he wrote in his notes for *Hedda Gabler*, "The great tragedy of life is that so many people have nothing to do but yearn for happiness without ever being able to find it." Meyer cites psychiatrist Anthony Storr's diagnosis of Ibsen as technically "an obsessional character": Such creative people "want to create an imaginary world in which everything can be controlled, and want to avoid the unpredictability and spontaneity of real relationships with real people."

Ibsen's attraction to youth, however, was not limited to young girls. His young French male companion, director Aurélian-Marie Lugné-Poë, noted that Ibsen "had an almost obsessive interest in the rising generation" and took pains to become acquainted with Norway's new writers and artists, "the people who understood his plays most clearly."

During 1891, the year that he returned to Norway to stay, Ibsen attended a performance of August Strindberg's *Fadren* (pr., pb. 1887; *The Father*, 1912) and a lecture by the thirty-two-year-old Knut Hamsun, author of a pain-filled autobiographical novel of the working class entitled *Sult* (1890; *Hunger*, 1899). Hamsun had already given his lecture elsewhere and attacked Ibsen and his work forcefully, particularly "the inherent stiffness and poverty of his emotional life." Hamsun mistakenly saw merely social significance in Ibsen's work, a position of many later critics, but Ibsen attended not only that lecture but also the second and third of the series, finding confirmation there, Meyer conjectures, "of the conviction he himself had already reached that a writer must explore the uncharted waters of the unconscious," the dark arena that Ibsen chose for his last plays.

At seventy-two, as the new century arrived, Ibsen was failing physically. He suffered the first of a series of strokes on March 5, 1890, and never regained full physical health. He hoped to start a new play and perhaps even to travel, but as his condition deteriorated, he was able only to sit at his window gazing vacantly before him; once the renowned actress Eleonora Duse, whose greatest stage triumphs were in his works, gazed in mute tribute at his wintry silhouette from an icy sidewalk. Toward the end, he told his wife, "You were the eagle that showed me the way to the summit." His last word was "Tvertimod!" ("On the contrary!"), a fitting comment, Meyer observes, "from one who had devoted his life to the correction of lies." His state funeral on June 1, 1906, was attended by an immense crowd, and over his grave, the Norwegian people set a column bearing "the simple and appropriate symbol of a hammer."

Analysis • "To be a poet is, most of all, to see," Henrik Ibsen said, and early in his literary career, he had already recognized the hammer as at once the symbol of creation and of destruction, with mythical overtones of the Old Norse thunder god, Thor, who unflinchingly sacrificed his own hand to bind the wolf Fenris and save his world from the unleashed forces of the underworld. Ibsen's early poem "The Miner" shows his gaze fixed firmly into the depths: "Downward I must break my way . . . break me the way, my heavy hammer, to the hidden mystery's heart." Throughout his literary canon, although he is best known for his prose dramas, the rich poetic vein is never far from the working face of Ibsen's creativity.

The constructions and destructions necessary to the realization of Ibsen's vision fall into two distinct categories on either side of the watershed year of 1875. Fjelde differentiates them in apt architectural metaphor, viewing the earlier romantic group of Ibsen's plays as a diverse old quarter, ranging from Roman villa to Viking guildhalls and even a contemporary honeymoon hotel, while glimpsing immediately beyond a small arid space "what appears to be a model town of virtually identical row houses . . . dark and swarming with secret life."

Whatever the outward style of their construction, at the core, all of Ibsen's earlier plays share a basically romantic orientation. Romanticism had already reached its fiery height in most of Europe by the time Ibsen published his first verse drama in 1850, but like the northern summer sun, the German-derived glow of romanticism lingered longer in Norway, where the emerging Norwegian state, lately reestablished, was seeking its national identity in its Viking heritage.

While reviewing a folkloristic play in 1851, Ibsen presented his own characteristically individual theory on nationalism in literature: "A national author is one who finds the best way of embodying in his work that keynote which rings out to us from mountain and valley . . . but above all from within our own selves." Following that precept at the risk of alienating superpatriots, Ibsen wrote three Viking plays, *Lady Inger of Østraat, The Feast at Solhaugh,* and *The Vikings at Helgeland.* In 1862, he made an extensive field trip to gather folklore, which he incorporated with Rousseauistic ideals of the simple natural life in *The Pretenders,* another medieval Viking drama; in the volcanic *Brand,* set in the harsh west fjord country; and in the lighthearted *Peer Gynt.*

An important part of Norway's nationalistic fervor stemmed from its state Lutheranism, in which Ibsen had received a traditionally rigorous grounding as a child, although none of his plays portrays clergymen sympathetically. In *Brand,* Ibsen also seemed to embody Søren Kierkegaard's famous "either-or" in Brand's call for "all or nothing," challenging the institutionalized religion of his day. Haugen has commented that paradoxically "the rascal Peer is saved, but the heroic Brand is sacrificed," seeing therein a reflection of Ibsen's early religious training, similar to his puritanical attitude toward sex and his emphasis on the necessity of confession and atonement for redemption.

The dominant philosophical trend of Ibsen's time and place was the idealism of Georg Wilhelm Friedrich Hegel, who died in 1831. Ibsen's enormous double play, *Emperor and Galilean*, departs from the strictly romantic theories present in his earlier work to take the direction of a Hegelian dialectic conflict between "thesis" and "antithesis," which is resolved by a "synthesis" that itself becomes the "thesis" of a new conflict. Ibsen pits the pagan happiness that he had celebrated in his Viking plays against the spiritual beauty represented by Christ's redeeming sacrifice on the Cross. The failure of Julian the Apostate to bring about the required "third empire," mingling the Christian and the pagan worlds, may be read as Ibsen's rejection, like Kierkegaard's, of the possibility of achieving a synthesis in this life. For Ibsen, duality was inescapable in the human condition, with humanity caught between what it is and what it should be, between the beastly nature and the divine.

In 1875, midway in his literary career, Ibsen struck an "arid place" where he reluctantly had to concede that the rhyme and meter suitable to romantic drama could no longer convey his explorations of "the hidden mystery's heart." The literary trend in Europe, leading toward the realistic and even naturalistic expression of contemporary social problems, came to Scandinavia principally through the critic Georg Brandes, who had become Ibsen's close friend in 1871.

Ibsen's last twelve plays divide neatly into three distinct subgroups of four dramas each, characterized by their dominant thematic elements—social, psychological, and philosophical. This sequence, which Ibsen clearly intended as an organic whole, leads inexorably from social agony to spiritual conflict and at last to an area hitherto unexplored in Ibsen's time, described by Fjelde as an "extraordinary, pre-Freudian sensitivity to unconscious pressures behind the conscious mind—the relationships of motives and conflicts bred in the troll-dark cellar."

In each category, Ibsen employed his personal experiences differently. From *The Pillars of Society* to *An Enemy of the People*, the social plays use contemporary settings that might have been encountered on the streets of Christiania and characters caught up in the new industrialized manifestation of the old conflict between what is and what ought to be. Between *The Wild Duck* and *Hedda Gabler*, Ibsen's hammer broke through to a deeper layer of consciousness beyond the social, forcing away the barriers which the individual erects between his self-image and his ideals.

Finally, from *The Master Builder* to *When We Dead Awaken*, Ibsen probed the clash between his artistic vocation and his responsibility to those who loved him, using in each play a flawed creative personality who at last realizes that the ultimate height of achievement is denied him because he has not been able to merge love with his art. With the twelve plays of his prose cycle, Ibsen adopted what Fjelde calls "a way of seeing, deceptively photographic on the surface, actually a complex fusion of perspectives, which then became his dramatic method," as, even more significantly, he simultaneously reached the summit and the deepest heart of his own experience of life.

To the theater in particular and to literature in amazing generality, Ibsen bequeathed innovations almost as astonishing in retrospect as they must have been to his contemporaries. He was first to involve ordinary human beings in drama, abandoning the old artificial plots and instead creating scenes that might be encountered in any stuffy drawing room or aching human heart. He conveyed for the first time in centuries a depth and subtlety of understanding of human character and relationships, especially those of women, evocative of the height of human tragic experience seen previously among the Elizabethans and the Periclean Greeks. He dared to challenge social abuses, knowing their agonizing sting at first hand. He explored the unconscious mind to an extent unmatched until the promulgation of Freud's theories decades later.

The Vikings at Helgeland • Before Ibsen gained the summit of his creative efforts he participated in the attempt to create a national Norwegian theater by writing plays based on Norwegian folktales. Ibsen gathered his material for *The Vikings at Helgeland* not from the medieval German epic *The Nibelungenlied* but from a much older work, *The Völsungasaga*, itself a derivation of the Elder Edda containing the story of the Valkyrie Brynhild, who destroys her beloved hero Sigurd because he has betrayed her trust. Ibsen chose to base *The Vikings at Helgeland* on the Icelandic family saga, in which, he said, "the titanic conditions and occurrences of *The Nibelungenlied* and the *Volsung-Saga* have simply been reduced to human dimensions." Yet he saw an insoluble incompatibility between the objective saga and the dramatic form: "If a writer is to create a dramatic work out of this epic material, he must introduce a foreign element. . . ."

Ibsen's "foreign element" in *The Vikings at Helgeland* is realism, a rendition of the myth of Brynhild set in tenth century Norway, at the advent of Christianity. The Brynhild-figure is Hjørdis, a merciless visionary, married to Gunnar but in love with Gunnar's close friend, the weak-willed warrior Sigurd, who had won her under the guise of Gunnar and with whom she has had her only satisfying sexual experience. When Hjørdis learns of the deception—Sigurd is married to another woman—she slays her lover, hoping to be united with him in death, but as he dies, Sigurd reveals that his meek wife Dagny has converted him to Christianity. In despair and rage, the pagan Hjørdis hurls herself into the sea. Ibsen's preoccupation in *The Vikings at Helgeland* is not with the fall of mythic goddesses and heroes but with the human tragedy wrought by deliberate falsehood, a theme to which he would often return.

Brand • Ibsen called *Brand* "a dramatic poem." Brand is a stern young pastor who defies both his church superiors and the self-serving local governmental officials, demanding "all or nothing" in the service of his God. Brand even applies his unbending doctrines to his mother, to whom he refuses to grant forgiveness unless she relinquishes all her property, and to his wife and his child, who die because Brand will not take them to a milder climate. Brand then leads his flock to an "ice church" high in the mountains, where he believes that they will all be closer to God, but, daunted by the painful journey, his people at last stone him and return to their valley far below. Brand is finally moved to tears by a vision of his dead wife shortly before he is buried by a mammoth avalanche, above whose roar he hears a voice proclaim, "He is a God of love." In *Brand*, the story of a man whose tragedy is the negation of love, Ibsen not only used the figure of an acquaintance he had met in Rome, Christopher Bruun, a devout reformer who fought the established church as well as the spirit of compromise, but also drew on his own personality. He remarked in an 1870 letter, "Brand is myself in my best moments."

Emperor and Galilean • *Emperor and Galilean*, the double play that stands between Ibsen's two groups of dramas, ranges over much of the fourth century Roman Empire, interpreting successive phases in the life of Julian the Apostate, who tried to replace

Constantine's Christianity with a renewed paganism. In part 1, *Caesar's Apostasy*, the young Julian is disillusioned by Christianity and is influenced by the pagan seer Maximos, who desires a "third empire" uniting classical beauty and Christian ethics. In part 2, *The Emperor Julian*, force proves ineffective in reinstating pagan religious observances; in battle, Agathon, a Christian, slays Julian, who mutters as he dies, "Thou hast conquered, Galilean." Like Cain and Judas, Julian unknowingly changed history in a way he never intended. Ibsen told Edmund Gosse, "The illusion I wanted to produce is that of reality . . . what I desired to depict were human beings." He also said later that *Emperor and Galilean* contained "more of my own personal experience than I would care to admit." He saw Christianity as removing the joy from human life, his own included, encasing people in an emotional confinement from which only violent action could free them. This play marks Ibsen's "farewell to epic drama" and his adoption of prose as his dramatic medium; Meyer calls it the "forerunner of those naturalistic plays which were shortly to explode . . . like a series of bombs."

A Doll's House • The famous slamming of the Helmer front door in *A Doll House* was the second realistic explosion in Ibsen's bombardment of his society's outmoded thought and repressive lifestyle. Significantly, new translations of the play point out the vital difference between the older title, *A Doll's House*, a house belonging to the "doll" Nora, and *A Doll House*, a complex toy, as Fjelde suggests, that itself is "on trial . . . tested by the visitors that come and go, embodying aspects of the inescapable reality outside." At the beginning, Nora is merely a pretty young wife preparing for Christmas, almost a child herself in her eagerness to please her banker-husband as his "squirrel" and "lark."

As Hermann J. Weigand has demonstrated, Nora's love of playacting, her readiness to lie, and her desire to show off make her all the more convincing as she reveals that she has secretly borrowed money needed to save her husband from a physical collapse. Worse, the conventions of the day denied women the right to take out loans in their own names, so Nora was forced by circumstances to forge her dying father's signature to the loan. Her creditor, Nils Krogstad, blackmails her to keep his position at Helmer's bank. When Helmer learns of Nora's debt, he selfishly and brutally declares that she is unfit to rear their children. Nora recognizes the falsity of her position and leaves her husband and children, slamming the door on her life as the toy of Helmer, who is himself a toy of society.

In his "Notes for a Modern Tragedy" (1878), Ibsen wrote, "There are two kinds of moral laws . . . one for men and one, quite different, for women." He knew that in his day, "woman is judged by masculine law," and he used for specifics the contemporary real-life tragedy of Laura Kieler, a friend of Ibsen who had taken out a secret loan so that she could travel with her husband to Italy for his health. The loan went bad; she forged a check; and when the bank refused payment, her husband had her committed to a public asylum and demanded a separation, so that her children would not be contaminated by her presence. Kieler grudgingly took his wife back eventually, but Ibsen's use of her sad story in his play placed additional stress on their already difficult relationship, and Laura Kieler resented *A Doll House* fiercely.

Many interpreters narrowly see *A Doll House* as a plea for female emancipation. Nothing seems further from Ibsen's intention. In 1879, he did strongly support equal voting rights for female members of the Scandinavian Club in Rome, but nearly twenty years later, in 1898, when he spoke to the Norwegian League for Women's Rights, he declared, "My task has been the *description of humanity*," as Fjelde notes, putting the issue of women's liberation squarely in the larger context of "the artist's freedom and the evolution of the race in general."

Ghosts • Ibsen wrote to Sophie Adlersparre in 1882, "After Nora, Mrs. Alving had to come," and he often said that writing *Ghosts* was "an absolute necessity" for him. Mrs. Alving is not simply a Nora grown older, but a character evolved into a vastly more tragic figure. Nora leaves her home, but Mrs. Alving stays with her debauched husband, an irredeemable syphilitic sot. After his death, she builds an orphanage with his fortune and welcomes home their son Oswald, who has been living as an artist in Paris.

A villainous carpenter at the orphanage, Engstrand, tries to entice his daughter Regine, Mrs. Alving's maid, into becoming a hostess (and more) in a seamen's hangout he plans to build, and Engstrand persuades Mrs. Alving's pastor, Manders, to speak to Mrs. Alving in that regard. Manders, once Mrs. Alving's lover, though he counseled her to return to her husband, learns not only that Regine is Captain Alving's illegitimate daughter but also that Mrs. Alving has begun to question her religion. As they talk, they overhear an innocent flirtation between Oswald and Regine in the next room, a "ghost" of a flirtation of years before, when Mrs. Alving overheard her husband and her maid, Regine's mother. After fire destroys the uninsured orphanage, consuming the captain's financial legacy, the ill and exhausted Oswald learns the horrifying truth about Regine's birth and his own inherited venereal disease. Regine consequently leaves to join Engstrand, who blackmails Manders into supporting his new business venture, and Mrs. Alving is left alone with Oswald as he slips into paretic insanity, begging his mother to help him end his life at once.

Ibsen knew that such material could hardly help but inflame Victorian sensibilities. Early in 1882, he wrote, "The violent criticisms and insane attacks . . . don't worry me in the least." As always, Ibsen relished the thrill of the battle, but *Ghosts* aroused more negative sentiment than any of his other plays. Norwegian critics led Europe in dismissing it, Ludvig Josephson calling it "one of the filthiest things ever written in Scandinavia," and Erik Bøgh rejecting it as "a repulsive pathological phenomenon."

Nevertheless, *Ghosts* stimulated the young and the daring. By 1888, some observers noted that the play was comparable to classical Greek tragedy though written about modern people, an opinion still popular today. Whereas in the Greek drama, inexorable Fate brings heroes low, in Ibsen's *Ghosts*, the power of the past devours the central figures. A choice once made must stand, regardless of the consequences, Ibsen is saying, and all the shocks that he delivers to his audience reinforce his basic message. The human choice must be made, in Fjelde's words, "out of the integrity of one's whole being." The ghosts of the past rise to strangle Helene Alving, the hypocritical Pastor Manders, and even the innocent victims of their parents' mistakes, Oswald and Regine. The most powerful of Ibsen's tightly constructed social plays, *Ghosts* also marks an important milestone in dramatic history; according to Meyer, it was "the first great tragedy written about middle-class people in plain, everyday prose."

Rosmersholm • Ghosts of a somber past also haunt the brooding manor house in *Rosmersholm*, the second of Ibsen's psychological dramas and the one that, after *Ghosts*, had the worst contemporary reviews. Among the few who supported it, Strindberg, in a rare tribute to Ibsen, declared *Rosmersholm* "unintelligible to the theatre public, mystical to the semi-educated, but crystal-clear to anyone with a knowledge of modern psychology."

The central problem of *Rosmersholm* is the redemption of a human spirit. A young, liberal-spirited woman, Rebecca West, came to the estate on a western fjord as companion to Rosmer's wife, Beate, and after Beate's suicide stayed on as manager of the household, influencing Rosmer, who feels drawn to her unconsciously. His brother-in-law, the inflexible schoolmaster Kroll, attempts to turn Rosmer back to conservatism, but when he fails, he recalls his late sister's intimations of "goings-on," as does the leader of the radical element, the journalist Mortensgaard. Rosmer tries to quiet the talk by proposing to Rebecca, but she rejects him violently.

After Rosmer's sense of guilt at his wife's despair begins to eat at him, Rebecca openly admits her guilt in urging Beate to death, confessing that she had acted out of love for him. As she prepares to leave the estate, she tells Rosmer that her earlier "pagan" will has fallen under Rosmersholm's traditional moralistic spell, which "ennobles . . . but kills happiness." Rosmer and Rebecca pledge their mutual love, savoring one final moment of bliss before, in atonement, they follow Beate into the white foam of the millrace.

Meyer claims that "in this play Ibsen was, for the first time . . . in any play for over two centuries, overtly probing the uncharted waters of the unconscious mind." Ibsen had given the play the working title "The White Horses," after the ghost reputedly seen frequently on the estate, a white horse, the symbol of irresistible unconscious forces driving the individual to excessive behavior, based on a folktale about a water spirit in equine shape that lures its victims into dangerous depths.

Ibsen gradually reveals that Rebecca came to Rosmersholm as not only the former mistress of one Dr. West but also, as she learned too late, his daughter. Her Oedipal guilt, as Freud observed in 1914, drove her to dispose of Beate, "getting rid of the wife and mother, so that she might take her place with the husband and father." Beate's death in the millrace was only the most recent guilt-inspired act of violence that Rebecca, under the refining, "ennobling" influence of Rosmer, found she must expiate. Ironically, Rosmer himself is weak, and his one act of heroism is performed for Rebecca: "There is no judge over us; and therefore we must do justice upon ourselves."

In his advice to a young actress undertaking the role of Rebecca in Christiania, Ibsen wrote, "Observe the life that is going on around you, and present a real and living human being." He also instructed the head of the Christiania Theater that Rebecca "does not *force* Rosmer forward. She *lures* him." His characterization of Rebecca West, who throughout the play crochets an indefinable white garment, calls up mythic overtones of the Norse Norns, spinning out human destiny in some white-fogged eternal night. Ibsen's revelation of man's destiny in *Rosmersholm* is once more in woman's hands, here lightening the eternal dark with one perfect gesture of sacrificial atonement made ironically for an imperfect lover, an echo of the myth of Brynhild that he had treated earlier in *The Vikings at Helgeland* and to which he would return before long.

With *Rosmersholm*, Ibsen left off political themes as motivation in his drama. The men and women of the Ibsen plays that followed became increasingly aware of what Meyer calls "the trolls within, not the trolls without . . . strange sick passions which direct their lives." Ibsen's earlier plays had portrayed men such as Rosmer undone by their involvement with provincial politics, while his later works stress figures, mostly women such as Rebecca, who feel intense passion but who cannot express it and thus become "ennobled" without some salvific act of atonement requiring the emancipation of self-sacrifice.

Hedda Gabler • In the powerful domestic tragedy *Hedda Gabler*, often considered his most popular play, Ibsen adapted the old myth of Brynhild to startling new uses.

Around this time, he wrote, "Our whole being is nothing but a fight against the dark forces within ourselves," and he began to see that the greatest human resource in that struggle, the will, tended to remain undeveloped in women of his day. As the daughter of General Gabler, Hedda had romantically dreamed of a perfect hero, but her dreams and her physical realization with a man not her equal were quite different. Eilert Løvborg, whose combination of profligacy and brilliant scholarship had originally fascinated her, proved unworthy, and she turned in anger and frustration to mediocre Jørgen Tesman, settling for the weaker man as Hjørdis had done in *The Vikings at Helgeland*. Like Hjørdis, too, Hedda is violently jealous of the gentle girl her first hero seems to prefer.

At the opening of the play, Hedda and Jørgen have returned to their bourgeois home and to Jørgen's bourgeois aunts after a wretched six-month European honeymoon. Hedda is suffering from massive ennui already, compounded by a pregnancy she ferociously denies. When she learns that Eilert Løvborg has reformed under the tutelage of ordinary Thea Elvstad, whose lovely curling hair she has always envied, Hedda exacts a horrifying vengeance. She goads Løvborg to drink again; he loses the only manuscript of the monumental book he has composed with Thea's help, and he later comes to his senses in the boudoir of the redheaded Mlle Diana, a notorious *fille de joie*. Jørgen finds Løvborg's manuscript and gives it to Hedda, but when Løvborg, frantic at the loss of his "child," comes to Hedda for help, she denies all knowledge of it.

Alone, Hedda burns his book, and after a final conversation, she sends him to a "beautiful" death by handing him one of her father's dueling pistols. Hedda's own moment of despair arrives when she learns that Løvborg has botched his suicide disgracefully. She now is trapped not only with Jørgen, and Thea Elvstad, now Jørgen's scholarly inspiration, and his remaining aunt, but also with a blackmail threat from lascivious Judge Brack. Her only escape is to kill herself and Jørgen's despised unborn child.

The portrayal of Hedda Gabler has challenged actresses throughout the play's history, and critics have read her variously as a frustrated feminist, a remnant of the shattered aristocracy, a sadistic psychopath, and even, as Meyer does, as Ibsen's "Portrait of the Dramatist as a Young Woman." No one-sided interpretation seems adequate. Throughout this play, the most claustrophobic of Ibsen's dramas, Hedda Gabler moves in a web of complex symbols, trapped at last, according to Haugen, "between a Christian-bourgeois domesticity and a pagan-saturnine liaison." Her father's pistols, symbols of his rank, his avocation, and his personality, represent both Hedda's entrapment and her release, for the pistol found with the mortally wounded Eilert Løvborg at Mlle Diana's establishment catches Hedda in an unthinkable scandal, while the remaining one allows her to make restitution to the only person who matters now to Hedda Gabler—herself.

Hedda Gabler is appropriately the last of Ibsen's psychological dramas. Ibsen often claimed that "Self-realization is man's highest task and greatest happiness," yet, as he expressed it in *Peer Gynt*, "to be oneself is to slay oneself." Hedda Gabler's tragedy is not merely the selfish act of a spoiled, bored woman, but a heroic act to free herself from a domination she cannot accept. Incapable of selfless love for a fatal multitude of reasons, Hedda Gabler at last even ruefully abandons her youthful dream of "vine leaves in his hair," the pagan ecstasy that had aroused her sensuous curiosity toward Eilert Løvborg. Her self-realization allows her one last moment of paradoxical human life, the moment she leaves it, a poetic truth of "hidden and mysterious power," in

Martin Esslin's words, "which springs from the co-existence of the realistic surface with the deep subconscious fantasy and dream elements behind it."

The Master Builder • Not long after the publication of *The Master Builder*, Ibsen stated, "It's extraordinary what profundities and symbols they ascribe to me. . . . Can't people just read what I write?" Ibsen insisted then, as always, that he only wrote about people's inner lives as he knew them: "Any considerable person will naturally be . . . representative of the . . . thoughts and ideas of the age, so that the portrayal of such a person's inner life may seem symbolic." Having shared experiences, at least to some degree, with many of his characters, Ibsen's last plays, the philosophical garnering of his life's harvest, are in that sense rich in symbol.

The title "Master Builder" has been applied frequently to Ibsen himself in recognition of his mastery of his craft and art, and more perilously, as an identification of the dramatist with the hero of the first of his philosophical plays, Halvard Solness, a talented architect just realizing that he is passing his prime. At the peak of his chosen profession, Solness is gnawed by his wife's unhappiness, a result of his absorption in his work, and obsessed by his strange ability to affect the lives of others, especially his bookeeper Kaja, by the extrasensory projection of his powerful will.

Solness had begun his career with churches erected to the glory of God, though for the last ten years he has defied God by choosing to build only human dwellings. Now Solness is attempting a synthesis, a "third world" of architecture, by building himself a home with a tall spire, like a church. At this difficult moment in his art and life, the passionate young Hilde Wangel enters both. She had become infatuated with Solness ten years earlier when he had daringly hung his last dedication wreath on the tower of her village church. She now urges him to repeat the feat, though he has begun to suffer from vertigo, and, inspired by her youthful ardor, he attempts "the impossible" again. As Hilde waves her white shawl—like Rebecca's, but completed, quivering to unseen harps—Solness plunges to his death.

Critics following William Archer have often played heavily on overt resemblances between Ibsen and Solness. Their ages are similar, their marriages unhappily affected by their devotion to their work, their infatuations with much younger girls notorious. Other commentators stress the resemblance between Solness's three types of building and Ibsen's three types of prose drama. Still others stress the Hegelian thesis-antithesis-attempted synthesis structure of Solness's work and Ibsen's several dramatic versions of that theme.

Meyer cites Ibsen's 1898 lecture to students in Christiania, in which he observed that Solness was "a man somewhat akin to me." In an interview, Ibsen also declared that architecture was "my own trade." His "May sun," Emilie Bardach, was unspeakably grieved to have been identified publicly with the vicious Hilde of *The Master Builder*, and conjectures about Solness's marriage injured Ibsen's relations with his own wife. Haugen suggests that *The Master Builder* "involves the Christian-pagan conflict," since Solness defies God, ceases building churches, and attempts to find his creative outlet solely among "happy human beings." Fjelde convincingly warns against equating Solness's "homes for happy human beings" with Ibsen's *Ghosts* or *Rosmersholm*, and suggests an archetypal reading, in which Solness represents the sacred king who has reached the acme of his powers and must be sacrificed by his own consent to ensure the continued existence of his clan, an impression reinforced, Fjelde claims, when at the close of the play "the young king, Ragnar, brings to the old king, Solness, that ambiguous symbol of victory and death, the ribboned wreath."

Thus, Solness's death, which illuminates the entire play, may be seen on various levels of meaning, as biographically, realistically, symbolically, and mythically significant. *The Master Builder* perhaps more than any other of Ibsen's plays illustrates the immense control that Ibsen could exert over his expressed theme through the limpid prose he used as his dramatic vehicle, which approaches poetry in its compression, imagery, and suggestiveness. Here, too, Ibsen examines not only the workings of the unconscious mind but also mysterious powers beyond ordinary sensory perception, without destroying his chosen naturalistic perspective. Fjelde aptly describes the dramatic method in Solness's tragedy as "Truths beyond, within, outside the self . . . a lyric and seamless unity."

Other major works

POETRY: *Digte,* 1871; *Poems,* 1993.

NONFICTION: *Ibsen: Letters and Speeches,* 1964.

MISCELLANEOUS: *The Collected Works of Henrik Ibsen,* 1906-1912, 1928 (13 volumes).

Bibliography

Bloom, Harold, ed. *Henrik Ibsen.* Philadelphia: Chelsea House, 1999. A collection of criticism regarding Ibsen's plays. Bibliography and index.

Ferguson, Robert. *Henrik Ibsen: A New Biography.* London: R. Cohen, 1996. A basic biography that covers the life and works of Ibsen. Bibliography and index.

Garland, Oliver. *A Freudian Poetics for Ibsen's Theatre: Repetition, Recollection, and Paradox.* Lewiston, N.Y.: Edwin Mellen, 1998. A Freudian approach to examining the psychology that pervades Ibsen's plays. Bibliography and index.

Goldman, Michael. *Ibsen: The Dramaturgy of Fear.* New York: Columbia University Press, 1999. An analysis of Ibsen's plays with respect to his portrayal of fear. Bibliography and index.

Johnston, Brian. *The Ibsen Cycle: The Design of the Plays from "Pillars of Society" to "When We Dead Awaken."* Rev. ed. University Park: Pennsylvania State University Press, 1992. An examination of some of Ibsen's social plays. Bibliography and index.

Ledger, Sally. *Henrik Ibsen.* Plymouth, England: Northcote House in association with the British Council, 1999. A biographical study of the dramatist Ibsen. Bibliography and index.

McFarlane, James, ed. *The Cambridge Companion to Ibsen.* New York: Cambridge University Press, 1994. A comprehensive reference work devoted to Ibsen. Bibliography and index.

Shepherd-Barr, Kirsten. *Ibsen and Early Modernist Theatre, 1890-1900.* Westport, Conn.: Greenwood, 1997. An examination of Symbolism, modernism and Ibsen, focusing on his reception in England and France. Bibliography and index.

Templeton, Joan. *Ibsen's Women.* 1997. Reprint. New York: Cambridge University Press, 2001. A study of Ibsen's drama that examines his portrayal of women. Bibliography and index.

Theoharis, Theoharis Constantine. *Ibsen's Drama: Right Action and Tragic Joy.* New York: St. Martin's Press, 1996. A critical examination of Ibsen's plays, with special emphasis on the themes of joy and dutiful action. Bibliography and index.

Mitzi Brunsdale

William Inge

Born: Independence, Kansas; May 3, 1913
Died: Los Angeles, California; June 10, 1973

Principal drama · *To Bobolink, for Her Spirit*, pb. 1950; *Come Back, Little Sheba*, pr., pb. 1950; *Picnic*, pr., pb. 1953 (expansion of the fragmentary "Front Porch"); *Bus Stop*, pr., pb. 1955 (expanded version of his one-act *People in the Wind*, pb. 1962); *The Dark at the Top of the Stairs*, pr., pb. 1957 (originally as *Farther Off from Heaven*, pr. 1947, pb. 1950); *Four Plays by William Inge*, pb. 1958; *The Tiny Closet*, pr. 1959 (in Italy), pb. 1962 (one act); *A Loss of Roses*, pr. 1959, pb. 1960; *The Boy in the Basement*, pb. 1962 (one act); *Bus Riley's Back in Town*, pb. 1962 (one act); *Summer Brave*, pr., pb. 1962 (revision of *Picnic*); *Summer Brave and Eleven Short Plays*, pb. 1962; *Natural Affection*, pr., pb. 1963; *Where's Daddy?*, pr., pb. 1966 (originally as *Family Things*, pr. 1965); *Two Short Plays: The Call, and A Murder*, pb. 1968; *Midwestern Manic*, pb. 1969; *Overnight*, pr. 1969; *Caesarian Operations*, pr. 1972

Other literary forms · William Inge was fundamentally a dramatist. Atlantic/Little, Brown published two of his novels, *Good Luck, Miss Wyckoff* (1970) and *My Son Is a Splendid Driver* (1971). Bantam published his earlier scenario for *Splendor in the Grass* (1961). The manuscript of his final novel, "The Boy from the Circus," was found on a table in his living room after his suicide. The manuscript had been rejected by a New York publisher and returned to him; he had not opened the envelope containing it. His two published novels and his first screenplay are set in Kansas and are populated by the same sort of lonely, frustrated people found in his major dramas.

Achievements · Although William Inge cannot be said to have advanced the technique of modern drama, as Eugene O'Neill did, he was the first notable American dramatist to write seriously and sensitively about the Midwest, much in the tradition of Theodore Dreiser and Sherwood Anderson among novelists, of Carl Sandburg and Edgar Lee Masters among poets, and of Grant Wood among painters. Inge's first five Broadway plays—*Come Back, Little Sheba*; *Picnic*; *Bus Stop*; *The Dark at the Top of the Stairs*; and *A Loss of Roses*—are set in the Midwest and examine in believable and accurate detail the pent-up frustrations of living in the sort of midwestern small towns that Inge knew intimately from his childhood and youth. The Liberty of some of his plays is the Independence, Kansas, of his childhood; great irony underlies his choice of that place-name.

The decade beginning in 1950 was a remarkable one for Inge. It is unique for an unknown playwright to emerge on Broadway with the sort of critical and commercial success that *Come Back, Little Sheba* commanded and then to be able to produce in rapid-fire succession three more commercial triumphs. Inge did just this, following the 1950 production of *Come Back, Little Sheba* with *Picnic* in 1953, *Bus Stop* in 1955, and *The Dark at the Top of the Stairs* in 1957. *Come Back, Little Sheba* ran for 190 performances; the next three plays ran for more than 450 performances apiece.

Come Back, Little Sheba won for its author an award from the New York critics as the most promising playwright of the season. *Picnic* won the Pulitzer Prize, a New York

Drama Critics Circle Award, and the Donaldson Award, which it shared with Arthur Miller's *The Crucible* (pr., pb. 1953). Even though Inge's next two plays won no awards, they were highly successful. Inge's reputation as a serious dramatist was assured; in addition, his first four full-length plays were made into films that succeeded both critically and commercially.

In 1958, just as Inge crested the wave of popularity to which his first four Broadway plays had brought him, *Four Plays by William Inge* was issued by Random House, which had previously published each of the plays separately. It was followed by Heinemann's British edition in 1960. Inge's next play, *A Loss of Roses*, into whose production the author put a considerable amount of his own money, reached Broadway in 1959 and was rejected by critics and audiences alike. It closed after twenty-five performances, leaving Inge, who was singularly sensitive, severely depressed as well as financially strained.

The failure of *A Loss of Roses* caused Inge to leave New York permanently. At the strong urging of Elia Kazan, who had become a close friend after directing *The Dark at the Top of the Stairs*, Inge moved to the West Coast and turned his talents to screenwriting. His first attempt, *Splendor in the Grass*, which Warner Bros. produced, again focused on small-town midwestern life and was so successful that it received the Academy Award for Best Original Screenplay of 1961.

Splendor in the Grass was to be Inge's last artistic triumph. He followed it in 1963 with *Natural Affection*, which played on Broadway for only thirty-six performances and was the subject of even harsher criticism than *A Loss of Roses* had received. Hurt and distraught, Inge returned to California, where he worked on screenplays. He also did a final original screenplay, based on one of his one-act plays entitled *Bus Riley's Back in Town*, about which he wrote (in a letter to R. Baird Shuman of May 20, 1965): "As for *Bus Riley*, the picture is a loss. I took my name off it. I haven't even seen the version they are showing."

Inge died a broken and defeated man, convinced that he had nothing more to say. His legacy to American drama is nevertheless great. He dealt with the Midwest as had no American playwright before him. As his close friend Tennessee Williams had focused dramatic attention on the South, so had Inge focused dramatic attention on the Midwest. He created a gallery of memorable characters, particularly female characters, because he understood the female mind remarkably well.

Inge's Broadway successes and his screenplay for *Splendor in the Grass* have secured his position as an American dramatist. Although he generally lacked the pioneering genius and willingness to experiment with form possessed by O'Neill, Clifford Odets, and Williams, Inge still ranks high among the significant contributors to American theater in the twentieth century.

Biography • William Inge's understanding of the female personality is not surprising in view of the fact that he came from an emphatically female-dominated home. As the youngest of Luther Clayton and Maude Sarah Gibson Inge's five children, Inge identified more closely with his mother and sisters than he did with males. His father was a traveling salesman who spent little time at home during Inge's formative years. The young Inge, much dominated by his mother, early developed an interest in acting, largely through his initial school experiences with recitation.

Popular as a teenager, Inge was a cheerleader and was active in his high school's dramatic programs. He enjoyed acting and continued his studies after high school at the University of Kansas, where he majored in drama and frequently acted in university productions. Still provincially midwestern at the time of his college graduation, Inge feared going to New York to pursue his first love, acting, and went instead to George Peabody College for Teachers in Nashville to prepare for teacher certification and to take a master's degree in education. Inge taught high school for one year in Columbus, Kansas, where he surely met numerous teachers such as those he depicts with such accuracy in *Picnic* and students such as those in *Splendor in the Grass*. For the next ten years, except for a crucial three years as art, music, book, and drama critic for the St. Louis *Star-Times*, Inge taught English and drama at the college level, first at Stephens College in Columbia, Missouri, and then at Washington University in St. Louis.

It was the crucial years away from teaching, from 1943 to 1946, that led Inge into his career as a playwright. In his position as a three-year replacement for a friend on the *Star-Times* who had been drafted, Inge interviewed Tennessee Williams, who was resting at his parents' home in St. Louis after the 1944 Chicago opening of *The Glass Menagerie*. A friendship blossomed, and Williams persuaded Inge to do some serious writing. *Farther Off from Heaven*, the prototype for *The Dark at the Top of the Stairs*, was the result, and in 1947, Margo Jones, whom Inge had met through Williams, produced the play in her theater in Dallas. The production was well received, and Inge was encouraged by its success to continue writing. By 1949, he had abandoned teaching in order to devote himself fully to his writing.

During this period, Inge had become a heavy drinker, and in 1948, he joined Alcoholics Anonymous. Through his association with this organization, he came to understand much more about alcoholism and about alcoholics, information that finds its way directly into *Come Back, Little Sheba* in the person of Doc Delaney, the play's frustrated protagonist.

Similarly, Inge, continually beset by depression, self-doubt, and concern about his homosexuality, which he was never able to accept, began a course of psychoanalysis in 1949, and he was in and out of analysis through the 1950's. Although one may question whether psychoanalysis made Inge any better able to cope with his own fears and frustrations, its influences and effects are clearly seen throughout his work, particularly in *A Loss of Roses, Natural Affection*, and *Where's Daddy?*

Despite the successes he had known, by 1973 Inge felt that he was "written out," that he had nothing more to say. Although he enjoyed his work in theater workshops at the University of California campuses at Los Angeles and Irvine and was successful in them, he was unable to deal with the artistic frustrations that plagued him, and on June 10, 1973, he took his own life.

Analysis • William Inge understood both the people and the social order of the Midwest, particularly the matriarchal family structure common to much of the area. Inge's midwestern plays reverberate with authenticity. His first four Broadway plays depict their commonplace characters with extraordinary sensitivity, building through accounts of their prosaic lives toward a pitch of frustration that is communicated to audiences with enormous impact. By capturing so deftly this pervasive sense of frustration, Inge presents the universal that must be a part of any successful drama. Audiences left Inge's early plays with an internalized sense of the gnawing isolation and conflict that his characters experienced. This is his legacy to American drama.

Come Back, Little Sheba • All Inge's best instincts as a playwright are at work in *Come Back, Little Sheba*, the story of Doc and Lola Delaney, who are twenty years into a marriage that was forced on them when the eighteen-year-old Lola became pregnant while the promising young Doc was a medical student. Their hasty marriage was followed by Doc's dropping out of medical school and becoming a chiropractor as well as by the loss of the baby through the bungling of a midwife, to whom Lola went because she was too embarrassed to go to an obstetrician. Lola ends up sterile and, as the action of the play begins, fat and unattractive. Doc has become an alcoholic, but as the play opens, he has been dry for a year.

Come Back, Little Sheba is a study in contrasts. It presents thesis and antithesis but seldom any satisfying or convincing synthesis, which makes it a sound piece of realistic writing. Little Sheba is Lola's lost puppy, who "just vanished one day—vanished into thin air." More than representing a surrogate child, Little Sheba represents Lola's lost youth, and only when Lola stops looking for Sheba is it clear that some resolution has taken place, even though the resolution is not presented as a cure-all for Doc and Lola Delaney's problems.

The play revolves largely around four characters: Doc; Lola; Marie, their boarder; and Turk, the recurring priapic figure whom Inge later used to keep the action moving in *Picnic* and in other of his plays. Marie, although she is engaged to someone else, is having a brief affair with Turk (significantly, a javelin thrower) before the arrival of her fiancé from out of town. Lola is titillated by this tawdry affair and actively encourages it, even though she is planning to fix a special meal for Marie's fiancé, Bruce, when he arrives. Doc, who sees Marie as the daughter he never had, is appalled by the whole misadventure. He falls off the wagon and gets roaring drunk. The dramatic climax of the play is his drunk scene, in which he threatens passionately to hack off all of Lola's fat, cut off Marie's ankles, and castrate Turk, but falls into a drunken stupor before he can accomplish any of these vile deeds and is taken off to the drunk tank. So terrified is he by the drunk tank that he returns home chastened, but not before Lola has attempted to go home to her aging parents, only to be rebuffed when she telephones them with her request.

As the play ends, Doc pleads with Lola, "Don't ever leave me. *Please* don't ever leave me. If you do, they'd have to keep me down at that place [the drunk tank] all the time." Doc and Lola are back together, not for very positive reasons, but rather because neither has any real alternative.

The characterization and the timing in this play are superb; the control is sure and steady. The business of the play is well taken care of early in the action as Lola, a lonely woman unhappy with herself and with what she has become, talks compulsively to anyone who will listen—the milkman, the postman, the next-door neighbor, and Mrs. Coffman, who in contrast to Lola is neat, clean, and well-organized, as a woman with seven children needs to be. Lola tells the audience all they need to know about her history while convincing them of her loneliness by reaching out desperately to anyone who comes into her purview. The resolution for Lola comes in the last act, when she begins to clean up the house, pay attention to her appearance, and write a note for the milkman rather than lurk to engage him in conversation.

Lola's dream sequences, which hold up quite well psychologically, are skillfully used to handle more of the necessary business of the play. The final dream has to do with Turk and the javelin, which Turk has already described as "a big, long lance. You hold it like this, erect." In Lola's dream, Turk is disqualified in the javelin throwing contest and Doc picks up the javelin "real careful, like it was awful heavy. But you threw it, Daddy, clear, *clear*, up into the sky. And it never came down." Inge's exposure to Freudian psychoanalysis certainly pervades the dream sequences.

Inge does not give the audience an upbeat or hopeful ending in *Come Back, Little Sheba*; rather, he presents life as it is. Perhaps Lola has matured a little. Perhaps both she and Doc have gained some insights that will help them to accept their lives with a bit more resignation than they might otherwise have, but nothing drastic is likely to happen for either of them. They will live on, wretchedly dependent on each other. If their marriage lasts, as it probably will, the mortar that holds it together will be dependence more than love. At least Lola has faced reality sufficiently to say, "I don't think Little Sheba's ever coming back, Doc," and to stop searching for her.

Picnic • Inge's second Broadway success, *Picnic*, started as a fragmentary play, "Front Porch," that Inge wrote shortly after *Farther Off from Heaven*. The original play consisted of little more than character sketches of five women in a small Kansas town. The play grew into *Picnic*, a much more fully developed play, and finally into *Summer Brave*, which is little different from *Picnic* except in the resolution of the Madge-Hal conflict.

Four of the five women in *Picnic* live in one house. They are Flo Owens; her two daughters, Millie, a sixteen-year-old tomboy, and Madge, the prettiest girl in town; and their boarder, Rosemary Sydney, a schoolteacher in her thirties. Madge is engaged to marry Alan Seymour. Their next-door neighbor is sixty-year-old Helen Potts, who also participates in the action of the play. These women are all sexually frustrated; although Madge and Rosemary both have suitors, the relationships are specifically delineated as nonsexual.

Into this tense setting is introduced an incredibly handsome male animal, Hal Carter, who exudes sexuality. As insecure as he is handsome, Hal is down on his luck and has arrived in town looking for his friend Alan Seymour, who might be able to give him a job. Hungry, he exchanges some work in Helen Potts's yard for a meal. He works bare-chested, much to the consternation of the women, whose upbringing decrees that they feign shock at this display but whose natural impulses are in conflict with their conservative upbringing.

Hal, reminiscent of Turk in *Come Back, Little Sheba*, causes chaos, as might be expected. The play focuses on the women, and Hal serves as the catalyst. Inge's ability to draw convincing characters, particularly female characters, is particularly evident in *Picnic*. He maintains his clear focus on the women in the play, using Hal precisely as he needs to in order to reveal these women as the psychologically complex beings they are. Never does the focus slip; never does the control over material and characters waver.

As the action develops toward a climax in the second act, Hal's physical presence more than anything else pushes the conflict to its dramatically necessary outcome. Millie and Rosemary start drinking from Hal's liquor bottle after Hal turns his attention from Millie to her more mature sister. Both Millie and Rosemary are soon drunk. Flo vents her own frustrations by upbraiding the two of them, but not before Rosemary, humiliated that Hal is not available to her and distressed that she finds him so attractive, shrieks at him that he came from the gutter and that he will return to the gutter. This emotional scene heightens Hal's insecurity, which is necessary if the play is to proceed convincingly to a love affair between Hal and Madge, an outcome that seems inevitable.

The screaming fit also forces Rosemary to face reality and to realize that her erstwhile suitor, Howard, is probably her only realistic out if she is not to continue teaching and if she is not to become frustrated and grow old alone. She goes off with Howard and yields to him, after which she asks, then begs him to marry her. In the play's final version, he will go only so far as to say that he will come back in the morning but when he does, Rosemary has already spread the news that she and Howard are going to marry, so that when Howard arrives, everyone congratulates him, and he has no choice but to leave with Rosemary, presumably to marry her. Inge is intrigued by the theme of forced marriage, which recurs in nearly all his major plays, and *Picnic* offers a striking variation on the theme.

Back at the picnic, Alan and Hal have engaged in fisticuffs and Alan has reported Hal to the police, forcing him to leave town in order to avoid arrest. In *Summer Brave*, Hal leaves and Madge stays behind; at the urging of Joshua Logan, Inge changed the ending of the play, so that in *Picnic*, Madge packs her suitcase and follows Hal a short time after his forced departure.

Bus Stop • *Bus Stop*, despite its popular acceptance, does not have the stature of *Come Back, Little Sheba* or *Picnic*. An expanded version of Inge's one-act *People in the Wind*, *Bus Stop* is set in a small crossroads restaurant between Kansas City and Wichita, where the passengers on a bus are stranded because of a blizzard. Among the passengers is Bo Decker, a twenty-one-year-old cowpoke from Montana who is traveling with Virgil Blessing, a middle-aged father surrogate (suggestive of Pinky in *Where's Daddy?*), and with a brainless little singer, Cherie, whom he met in a Kansas City nightclub, where she was performing. Bo was pure until he met Cherie, but now, in a comical role-reversal, he has lost his virginity to her and is insisting that she return to Montana with him to make him an honest man. Cherie joins Bo and Virgil, and they are on their way west when the bus is forced by the weather to pull off the road.

Cherie has second thoughts about going to Montana, and after thinking the matter over, she accuses Bo of abducting her and the police become involved in the situation. Bo has a fight with the sheriff. He is humiliated and apologizes to everyone in the restaurant, including Cherie. Before the play is over, however, Bo asks Cherie to marry him, she agrees, and they set out for Montana, leaving Virgil Blessing behind and alone.

The development of *Bus Stop* is thin, and the characterization, particularly of Bo, is not close to the high level reached in *Come Back, Little Sheba* and *Picnic*. Although Bo is similar in many ways to Turk and Hal, he is made of cardboard and lacks the multidimensional elements that make Turk and Hal convincing.

The play is stronger in the presentation of its minor characters, particularly the lonely, frustrated Grace, a middle-aged woman who lives at the small crossroads where the bus has stopped and who works the night shift in the restaurant. She has sex with a truck driver not because she loves him but because he keeps her from being lonely. In the end, she and Virgil Blessing are left alone in the restaurant. The bus has pulled out, and one might think that Grace and Virgil are the answer to each other's loneliness, but Inge does not provide a double resolution in this play. He permits Bo and Cherie to leave on a somewhat optimistic note, much as he allowed Hal and Madge a future in *Picnic*, but he wisely backs off from providing the pat resolution that a romance between Grace and Virgil would have provided, because the psychological motivation for such a relationship has not been built sufficiently throughout the play.

The original play, *People in the Wind*, contained two characters who were not included in *Bus Stop*. They are two older women, apparently both unmarried and seemingly sisters, who are going to visit their niece. It appears that they want the niece to take them in in their old age, but they are not sure she will do so. They are nervous, drinking bicarbonate of soda to calm their stomachs. They represent the fate that can befall people who do not form close family ties early in their lives. In dropping them from *Bus Stop*, Inge was clearly opting to make the focus of the later play love rather than loneliness, which was the central focus of *People in the Wind*.

The Dark at the Top of the Stairs • *The Dark at the Top of the Stairs*, the finished version of *Farther Off from Heaven*, is Inge's most autobiographical play. In it, the author returns to a plot centering on a family, and this time, it is clearly Inge's own family that he is writing about. Rubin Flood is a harness salesman who travels a great deal, leaving his children, Sonny and Reenie, in a mother-dominated home. The setting is a small town in Oklahoma.

Inge, who had been in psychoanalysis for several years when he wrote *The Dark at the Top of the Stairs*, paid particular attention to the Oedipal elements of the mother-son relationship in this play and in two subsequent plays, *A Loss of Roses* and *Natural Affection*, although not with the success that he achieved in this earlier presentation.

Rubin Flood and his wife, Cora, were married early, propelled into marriage by Rubin's unmanageable libido. The marriage has encountered difficulties, which come to a head when Rubin, having lost his job—a fact he keeps from his wife—discovers that Cora has bought Reenie an expensive dress for a dance given at the country club by the nouveau riche Ralstons. He demands that the dress be returned for a refund, and a heated argument ensues, during which Cora taunts Rubin to strike her. He obliges and then leaves, vowing never to return. In act 2, Cora's sister, Lottie, and her dentist husband, Morris, have arrived for a visit. Cora hopes that she will be able to persuade Lottie to take her and the children in now that Rubin has abandoned them. In this scene, also, Reenie's blind date for the dance, Sammy Goldenbaum, arrives. A cadet at a nearby military academy, Sammy is meticulously polite and none too secure. His exquisite manners charm Lottie and Morris before he and the pathologically shy Reenie depart for the dance. Once at the dance, Reenie introduces Sammy to the hostess, who is drunk, and Reenie leaves the dance, not telling Sammy she is going. He tries to find her but cannot.

In act 3, Reenie's friend Flirt appears with the news that Sammy took the train to Oklahoma City, rented a hotel room, and killed himself, presumably because the drunken Mrs. Ralston, on discovering that Sammy was Jewish, had asked him to leave the party. Sammy's suicide forces the principal characters to reconsider their lives, and the play ends somewhat on the upbeat. Rubin has returned home. He is tamed, as is evidenced by the fact that he confesses to Cora, "I'm scared. I don't know how I'll make out. I . . . I'm scared," and that he leaves his boots outside, not wanting to dirty up Cora's clean house.

Sonny Flood, who has been an obnoxious child throughout the play, apparently has turned the corner by the end of it. He volunteers to take his distraught sister to the movies, and when his mother tries to kiss him goodbye, he declines to kiss her, giving the audience an indication that his Oedipal tendencies are now coming under control.

Inge tried to do something daring in *The Dark at the Top of the Stairs*, and although he failed, it was a creditable attempt. He juggled two significant conflicts, the Rubin-Cora conflict and the Sammy-society conflict. As the play developed, the conflict involving the suicide was not sufficiently prepared for to be wholly believable. Inge's admitted purpose was to use the suicide subplot to divert the attention of the audience from the conflict between Rubin and Cora, so that they could return to this conflict in the last act with a fresher view.

The suicide subplot has been severely attacked by critics. It is, however, a serious misinterpretation to view the suicide as an event that the author intended to present realistically. It can succeed only as a symbol, serving the useful function of promoting the resolution of the main conflict. This is not to justify the suicide subplot, which is a weakness in the play, but rather to demonstrate the artistic purposes Inge envisioned for it.

Later plays • None of Inge's later plays achieved the standard of his four Broadway successes. Some of his most interesting work is found in his one-act plays, fourteen of which are available in print. Had Inge lived longer, probably some of the materials in these plays would have lent themselves to further development as full-length dramas; particularly notable are *To Bobolink, for Her Spirit, The Tiny Closet,* and *The Boy in the Basement.*

Other major works

LONG FICTION: *Good Luck, Miss Wyckoff,* 1970; *My Son Is a Splendid Driver,* 1971.
SCREENPLAYS: *Splendor in the Grass,* 1961; *All Fall Down,* 1962; *Bus Riley's Back in Town,* 1964.

Bibliography

Leeson, Richard M. *William Inge: A Research and Production Sourcebook.* Westport, Conn.: Greenwood Press, 1994. A study that focuses on the stage history and production of Inge's works. Contains plot summaries.

McClure, Arthur F. *Memories of Splendor: The Midwestern World of William Inge.* Topeka: Kansas State Historical Society, 1989. The focus is the "regional quality" of Inge's work. Unusual features include photographs and posters from stage and film productions and reminiscences from those who served as models for Inge's characters and from actors who played them.

McClure, Arthur F., and C. David Rice, eds. *A Bibliographical Guide to the Works of William Inge, 1913-1973.* Lewiston, N.Y.: Edwin Mellen Press, 1991. An attempt to "present a complete picture of Inge's work as a teacher, journalist and author." Divided into works by Inge, including his journalistic articles and reviews; biographical information, among them obituaries; critical articles and reviews of Inge's work; and brief chapters on his forays into film and television. Sporadic annotations.

Shuman, R. Baird. *William Inge.* Rev. ed. Boston: Twayne, 1989. An updated version of Shuman's 1965 book, this volume focuses primarily on summarizing and analyzing the plays. Shuman's stated goal is "to present a balanced view of William Inge and . . . show the inroads . . . public expectations make upon the private and creative life" of a sensitive artist. Index, select bibliography.

Voss, Ralph F. *A Life of William Inge.* Lawrence: University Press of Kansas, 1989. A carefully researched "reconstruction" of Inge's life, with numerous photographs, most of Inge at various stages of life. Voss's examination reveals a troubled man whose life was a "pattern" of secrecy, especially concerning his homosexuality and alcoholism. Voss concludes, "'Inge Country' was never just the state of Kansas or the midwestern prairies . . . [but] almost always a troubled state of mind."

R. Baird Shuman,
updated by Elsie Galbreath Haley

Eugène Ionesco

Born: Slatina, Romania; November 26, 1909
Died: Paris, France; March 28, 1994

Principal drama • *La Cantatrice chauve*, pr. 1950, pb. 1954 (*The Bald Soprano*, 1956); *La Leçon*, pr. 1951, pb. 1954 (*The Lesson*, 1955); *Les Chaises*, pr. 1952, pb. 1954 (*The Chairs*, 1958); *Victimes du devoir*, pr. 1953, pb. 1954 (*Victims of Duty*, 1958); *Le Maître*, pr. 1953, pb. 1958 (*The Leader*, 1960); *La Jeune Fille à marier*, pr. 1953, pb. 1958 (*Maid to Marry*, 1960); *La Nièce-Épouse*, pr. 1953 (*The Niece-Wife*, 1971); *L'Avenir est dans les œufs: Ou, Il Faut de tout pour faire un monde*, pr. 1953, pb. 1958 (*The Future Is in Eggs: Or, It Takes All Sorts to Make a World*, 1960); *Amédée: Ou, Comment s'en débarrasser*, pr., pb. 1954 (*Amédée: Or, How to Get Rid of It*, 1955); *Jacques: Ou, La Soumission*, pb. 1954, pb. 1955 (*Jack: Or, The Submission*, 1958); *Théâtre*, pb. 1954-1966 (4 volumes); *Le Nouveau Locataire*, pr. 1955, pb. 1958 (*The New Tenant*, 1956); *Le Tableau*, pr. 1955, pb. 1963 (*The Picture*, 1968); *L'Impromptu de l'Alma: Ou, Le Caméléon du berger*, pr. 1956, pb. 1958 (*Improvisation: Or, The Shepherd's Chameleon*, 1960); *Tueur sans gages*, pr., pb. 1958 (*The Killer*, 1960); *Plays*, pb. 1958-1965 (6 volumes); *Rhinocéros*, pr. in German 1959, pb. 1959, pr. in French 1960 (*Rhinoceros*, 1959); *Les Salutations*, pr. 1959, pb. 1963 (*Salutations*, 1968); *Scène à quatre*, pr. 1959, pb. 1963 (*Foursome*, 1963); *Délire à deux*, pr. 1962, pb. 1963 (*Frenzy for Two or More*, 1965); *Le Roi se meurt*, pr. 1962, pb. 1963 (*Exit the King*, 1963); *Le Piéton de l'air*, pr. 1962, pb. 1963 (*A Stroll in the Air*, 1964); *La Colère*, pb. 1963 (*Anger*, 1968); *La Soif et la faim*, pr. 1964, pb. 1966 (*Hunger and Thirst*, 1968); *La Lacune*, pb. 1966, pr. 1969 (*The Oversight*, 1971); *L'Œuf dur: Pour préparer un œuf dur*, pb. 1966, pb. 1970 (*The Hard-Boiled Egg*, 1973); *Jeux de massacre*, pr., pb. 1970 (*Killing Game*, 1974; also pb. as *Wipe-out Games*, 1970); *Macbett*, pr., pb. 1972 (English translation, 1973); *Ce formidable bordel*, pr., pb. 1973 (*A Hell of a Mess*, 1975); *L'Homme aux valises*, pr., pb. 1975 (*Man with Bags*, 1977); *Parlons française*, pr. 1980; *Voyages chez les morts: Ou, Thèmes et variations*, pb. 1981 (*Journeys Among the Dead: Themes and Variations*, 1985)

Other literary forms • Eugène Ionesco was known primarily for his plays. Over the years, however, he published memoirs and fiction worthy of critical attention; most notable are the memoirs *Journal en miettes* (1967; *Fragments of a Journal*, 1968) and *Présent passé passé présent* (1968; *Present Past Past Present*, 1972) and the novel *Le Solitaire* (1973; *The Hermit*, 1974). Successful as a playwright, Ionesco also surfaced occasionally as a theorist of the drama, notably in *Notes et contre-notes* (1962; *Notes and Counter-Notes*, 1964). Several of his better-known plays, including *The Killer* and *Rhinoceros*, were in fact developed from texts originally conceived, written, and published as short fiction; in addition, Ionesco published several highly innovative children's books that prove edifying to the adult reader as well.

Achievements • Eugène Ionesco is rivaled only by Samuel Beckett as the world's best-known and most influential exponent of experimental drama, and he is credited with the development of new conventions according to which serious drama would henceforth have to be written and judged. A number of his early plays, such as *The Bald Soprano*, *The Lesson*, and *The Chairs*, are already established in the "permanent" dramatic repertory, along with Beckett's *En attendant Godot* (pb. 1952, pr. 1953; *Waiting for Godot*, 1954) and *Fin de partie* (1957; *Endgame*, 1958). Although his work differs sharply from Beckett's, both in concept and in execution, Ionesco was recorded as having welcomed Beckett's 1969 Nobel Prize in Literature as applicable partially to himself, in recognition of a kindred spirit. It is clear that, following the emergence of these playwrights, serious drama would never again be the same.

In 1971, two years after Beckett received the Nobel Prize, Ionesco found his own achievement honored by election to the highly conservative Académie Française, a turn of events that only a short time earlier might have seemed equally unthinkable to the playwright and to the institution. Perhaps it appeared for a time that the ultimate artistic anarchist had joined, or become, the establishment; in fact, it was the theater that had changed.

Discovered, according to his own account, by accident, Ionesco's singular approach to dramatic creation ultimately revolutionized the French—and international—stage as thoroughly as the imported work of Luigi Pirandello had a generation earlier. Casting doubt not only on dramatic conventions but also on more fundamental assumptions concerning the nature of language and the nature of humankind, Ionesco's chaotic and tragic vision proved, on reflection, even more anarchic than Beckett's lugubrious pessimism, to which it is frequently compared.

Unlike Beckett, Ionesco mistrusted language to such an extent that it assumes a distinctly minor function in his plays, considerably overshadowed by such visual elements as the gestures and placement of actors. For Ionesco, language was at best the means to an end, certainly never an end in itself. As a result, Ionesco's plays frequently prove unrewarding if they are merely read or considered simply as literature. Arguably, Ionesco's plays are in fact not literature at all, depending as heavily as they do on actors and directors for their completion. Once staged, however, Ionesco's plays turn out to be as profound and intellectually challenging as any drama ever written.

Biography • The writer now known to the world as Eugène Ionesco was born November 26, 1909, as Eugen Ionescu in Slatina, Romania. His father (and namesake) was a Romanian lawyer, and his mother, née Thérèse Ipcar, was the daughter of a French engineer working in Romania. (When fame sought out Ionesco in his early forties, he advanced his publicized birth date to 1912 in an effort to appear younger; as he approached the age of eighty, he reversed his original decision. Many reference sources, however, continue to cite his birth year as 1912 even years after his death at age eighty-four.)

Shortly after Ionesco's birth, his parents moved to Paris, where his father continued the study of law. In 1911 a daughter, Marilina, was born to the couple and in 1912 another son, Mircea, who would die in infancy of meningitis. In 1916 the elder Eugen Ionescu returned to Romania, presumably to take part in World War I, leaving his family in France. It later turned out that instead of serving in the military, he had joined the government police. After the war, even as his wife assumed that he had died in battle, he had used his political power to arrange for himself a convenient divorce and remarriage, adding insult to injury by demanding (and getting) custody of his children by his first wife. Thus it happened that the twelve-year-old Eugène returned with his sister to Romania, where he would continue and complete his studies.

By 1926, Thérèse Ipcar Ionescu had herself returned to Romania, settling in Bucharest where she found work in a bank. Following a dispute with his father and stepmother, young Eugène sought refuge in his mother's apartment, to which his sister had already escaped. By the time he completed his secondary education in 1928, he was living in a furnished room at the home of an aunt, his father's sister. The elder Ionescu, all the while refusing to pay alimony or child support, used his political connections to secure scholarships for his son at the University of Bucharest. Father and son would, however, remain divided on the issue of the son's studies, with the father favoring engineering over literature. Notwithstanding, the future playwright pursued a degree in French and became a regular contributor of poetry and criticism to various literary magazines. In 1934 he created a minor scandal with a volume entitled simply *Nu* (No!), a collection of articles questioning most of the major (Romanian) literary figures and movements of the day.

Married in 1936 to Rodica Burileanu, whom he had met during their student days some six years earlier, Ionesco taught French in various Romanian schools, remaining active as a contributor to literary journals. In 1938, he obtained from the Romanian government a grant to study French literature in Paris. His projected thesis, on the themes of sin and death in French poetry since Baudelaire, would remain unfinished and perhaps unwritten as Ionesco read the writings of such thinkers as Nikolai Berdayev, Gabriel Marcel, and Jacques Maritain.

With the declaration of World War II in 1939, Ionesco returned with his wife to Romania, where he taught French at a Bucharest secondary school. Before long, however, he thought better of his move and attempted to return to France, finally succeeding in May, 1942. A daughter, Marie-France, was born to the Ionescos in August, 1944. For the remainder of the decade, Ionesco earned a meager living on the fringes of literary life, dividing his work among translation, journalism, editorial work, and occasional teaching. During those years, the future playwright recalled, he studiously avoided the theater, dismissing its stock-in-trade as lies or, at the very least, a massive waste of time and energy.

By his own account, Ionesco blundered into playwriting quite by accident when, not long after World War II, he sought to broaden his employment prospects by learning English on his own time, with the help of a popular text-and-record set then readily available in bookstores. As the trained literary scholar and translator applied himself to his task, the seemingly random recital of phrases and phonemes began to make less and less sense. Named characters would, for example, inform one another of their names and relationships, then announce with finality that the floor was down, while the ceiling was up.

Ionesco, soon losing all interest in the acquisition of English, began instead to jot down words and phrases as they rearranged themselves in his mind. When he had finished, the result looked rather like the script of a stage play, albeit a play such as had never before been seen or heard. Revised and reworked well into rehearsal, *The Bald Soprano* was eventually performed in May, 1950, at the Théâtre des Noctambules. The author, meanwhile, had begun to frequent avant-garde artistic and dramatic circles in Paris, most notably the Collège de 'Pataphysique, named in honor of the turn-of-the-century playwright Alfred Jarry, author of *Ubu roi* (wr. 1888, pr., pb. 1896; English translation, 1951).

Understandably reluctant at first, Ionesco soon warmed to the task of writing plays, having at last discovered what was evidently his true vocation; by 1952, he had seen two more of his plays in production, with others already written and waiting to be performed. He also found himself at the forefront of what appeared to be a new kind of theater, soon to be joined by such other middle-aged authors as Samuel Beckett and Arthur Adamov, for both of whom, as for himself, French was essentially an adopted idiom. Incredibly, Ionesco continued to turn out new and baffling plays for years without repeating himself, drawing on a rich store of images and memories that had lain dormant since childhood. Only later did Ionesco's expression begin to seem labored, because, in part, of the consequences of an ill-advised "debate" initiated in the late 1950's by the British critic Kenneth Tynan.

Recalling such controversies of the 1930's as Marxist attacks on Thornton Wilder or Clifford Odets's rebuke of Luigi Pirandello for not openly opposing Benito Mussolini in his plays, Tynan's criticism of Ionesco (whose work he had at first championed) centered on the resolute antirealism and seeming "irrelevance" of Ionesco's dramatic expression, implying that the playwright was derelict in his duties as an artist and that such tendencies as his, if allowed to continue, would distract audiences from social and political problems urgently requiring their attention. Ridiculous though such charges may seem in retrospect, they provoked at the time a vigorous debate involving such peripheral figures as Philip Toynbee and Orson Welles.

Ionesco, in defense of his art, wisely argued that art should serve no particular political creed but should remain a watchdog to all. Indeed, Ionesco's theater had already projected a profound sensitivity to human suffering, beyond politics in its defense of dignity and its aversion to posturing of any kind. Nevertheless, Ionesco proved to be peculiarly sensitive to the charges leveled against him, allowing at least one of his subsequent plays, *Rhinoceros*, to be interpreted as liberal social satire, presumably a bone thrown to pacify his more antagonistic critics. In fact, *Rhinoceros* is little different from Ionesco's other plays, written before or since, and collapses under the freight of political significance applied to it as if by afterthought.

From the early 1960's onward, Ionesco stressed the primacy of art, both in his plays and in his other writings, opposing in particular the Bertolt Brecht style of Social Realism that had asserted itself on the Paris stage. As an artist, however, he became increasingly committed to the cause of intellectual and artistic freedom, particularly in Romania and other nations of the eastern bloc. During the 1970's and 1980's, despite increasingly frail health, he took part in a number of international colloquia both literary and political. He died March 28, 1994, at his home on the Boulevard Montparnasse in Paris and is buried in the Montparnasse Cemetery.

Analysis • Although Eugène Ionesco's dramatic art is often traced to such precursors as the plays of Alfred Jarry and Antonin Artaud, it is essentially *sui generis*, springing primarily from nightmarish visions deeply rooted in the author's own mind and experience. In fact, two of his later plays, *A Hell of a Mess* and *Man with Bags*, can be traced directly to nightmares recorded in his autobiographical writings of the mid-1960's.

As a boy, Ionesco recalled, he frequently attended puppet shows mounted for children in the Jardin de Luxembourg; during the years since, he remained haunted by the reverse relationship of human beings to marionettes, seeing his fellow mortals as puppets pulled by forces unseen and unexplained, prone to violence either as perpetrator or as victim. Puppetry must thus be seen as one of the strongest verifiable influences on Ionesco's theater, as on modern drama in general. Indeed, the grotesquely "flat" characters of *The Bald Soprano*, although immediately drawn from names assigned at random to dialogue in a language textbook, can readily be traced to a deeper, more fecund source in the tradition of the Punch and Judy show.

Critic Martin Esslin hailed Ionesco's theater as a far more effective illustration of Albert Camus's concept of the absurd than Camus himself had ever written for the stage. Forsaking the convenience of rational expression still relied on by Camus, Jean

Anouilh, and even Jean-Paul Sartre, Ionesco—in Esslin's view—presents on the stage the absurd in its purest form, more true to life (if less "realistic") by the mere fact of its apparent gratuity. Indeed, it is difficult to imagine a more effective illustration of dehumanizing habit than is to be found among Ionesco's peculiarly automated characters, whose aspirations (if any) have long since been separated from their lives. When death threatens (as it often does in the later plays), Ionesco's habit-conditioned characters will often proceed as lambs to the slaughter in a manner even more credible than the "philosophical suicide" described by Camus in *Le Mythe de Sispyphe* (1942; *The Myth of Sisyphus*, 1955) as a characteristic human response to the absurd.

Ionesco's memories of puppetry may also account for the strong visual element in his plays, more dependent on gesture and blocking than on the stage set itself, which may range from elaborate to nonexistent. (The most elaborate of Ionesco's stage sets are those that call for enormous quantities of objects, be they household furnishings or eggs, implying that humans are being crowded off the earth by the commodities used for their need or pleasure.) As noted, the spoken text itself is, as a rule, the least significant element of Ionesco's dramaturgy, literally "upstaged" by the posturing and placement of its characters.

Dramatically, Ionesco's most effective use of language occurs in its deformation, with "normal" speech replaced either by incongruous banalities or by equally nonsensical monosyllables. Even so, it is possible to imagine certain of Ionesco's plays performed as pure pantomime; *Exit the King*, for example, was originally written in the form of a ballet. Certain critics, moreover, detected in Ionesco's dramaturgy a strong cinematic influence, primarily from silent films and those of the Marx Brothers.

Considered as a whole, Ionesco's work exhibits a number of different styles, each of them uniquely his own. Although it may be tempting to consider those styles as evolutionary stages, such analysis founders on the simple evidence that the styles do not necessarily occur in chronological order. *The Lesson*, for example, would appear at first glance to be more evolved and "later" than it really is.

There is also the matter of the Tynan debate, or London controversy as it has often been called among students of Ionesco's work. During the late 1950's, perhaps because of the debate, Ionesco began writing plays in which, for the first time, he appeared to be saying something specific; critics, noting the trend either with delight or with alarm, observed that his expression was somewhat weaker than in his earlier efforts. Yet, his expression had not really changed; the best of his apparently "didactic" plays, in retrospect, have much in common with the rest of his theater, both earlier and later. *Rhinoceros*, perhaps the weakest of the lot, is a highly typical Ionesco play, hampered mainly by the commonly held assumption of intended specific meaning.

One of Ionesco's more entertaining and edifying styles, although commonly associated with his shorter plays, involves the characters in aimless speech as the stage gradually fills with objects. In one of Ionesco's earliest plays, *The Chairs*, the two main characters keep bringing out chairs to seat an unseen multitude of guests. Although the proliferation of chairs is hardly the main point of the play, Ionesco clearly appreciated the visual effect and would use it again more than once, most notably in *The New Tenant*, in which furniture is carried onstage with difficulty inverse to its weight. At first, the movers struggle under the weight of bric-a-brac and table lamps; with their task well under way, they balance heavy chests delicately on the tips of their fingers. At the end, not only is the stage filled with furniture, but also presumably the streets and highways outside. The title character, who apparently owns all these things, asks only that the landlady turn out the lights as she leaves him; in a rather obvious effort to

rediscover the prenatal state, he has long since been hidden from view by his possessions.

Easily appreciated or understood at a preconscious level, yet subject to varied interpretations, Ionesco's imagery has brought to the stage sights and sounds that would tax
the ingenuity and imagination of even the most resourceful designers. In a variation on
the proliferation theme, for example, the characters of *Amédée* share the stage with a
growing corpse that is about to crowd them out of house and home; what usually
shows of this monstrosity is a man's shoe, approximately three meters in length, with
sock and trouser leg attached. In *Hunger and Thirst*, the furniture must be specially designed so that it will sink into the floorboards as if into mud. In *Exit the King*, similarly,
the king's throne must simply vanish from the stage while the curtain remains open.
Not all of the headaches fall upon the set designer alone; two of Ionesco's plays call for
an "attractive" female character with multiple noses and breasts.

Whether (as is doubtful) Ionesco's dramaturgy was in any way influenced by
Camus's speculations on the absurd, his writings, both expository and creative, give
evidence of a deep sensitivity and strong moral conscience of the sort commonly associated with *The Myth of Sisyphus* and its author. Although more visceral than cerebral, Ionesco's expression adds up to one of the most deeply humanitarian statements
in contemporary literature, haunted by a nagging doubt that humankind will ever assimilate the evident lessons of history. Ionesco's King Bérenger, the Everyman protagonist of *Exit the King*, meets and surpasses in his life and death the anguished declaration of Camus's *Caligula* (1954; English translation, 1948) that men die and are not
happy; resuming in his modest person the history of all human endeavor, King
Bérenger remains lucid even in his final moments, painfully aware that all has gone for
nought.

Elsewhere in Ionesco's theater, nearly all forms of human behavior are duly
stripped of acculturated meaning, shown to be as absurd and out of phase as they often
seemed to Camus himself. In *Jack: Or, The Submission* and *The Future Is in Eggs*, for example, courtship and marriage are reduced to the least attractive stereotypes, characterized by animal noises, obscene rutting gestures, and a quantitative standard for
human reproduction. In *Amédée*, the telephone-operator wife "goes to work" at a
switchboard in her own apartment while her husband, a writer, labors over the same
phrases that have occupied him fruitlessly for years. The theme of repetition, dominant in several plays that end exactly as they began, bears further witness to the apparent futility of all human endeavor. Beneath it all, however, the viewer can perceive a
strong nostalgia for lost innocence, or at least for things as they ought to be. In each of
his plays, Ionesco seems to be exhorting his audience to "rehumanize" the world before matters get worse than they already are.

Striking in its imagery and resonance, Ionesco's theater remains one of the more
durable bodies of work in twentieth century drama. Although uneven in quality, perhaps least effective when the author seemed to have a specific message in mind, his
theater is nevertheless sufficiently rich and varied to provide rewarding work for future generations of actors and directors. At the turn of the twenty-first century, the
strongest of his plays were in frequent production around the world, performed by
professional and amateur actors alike. In retrospect, it appears fortunate that the playwright never capitulated fully to his detractors' stated demands for relevance; his theater, perennially relevant to basic human needs and tendencies, stands as a useful,
even necessary mirror through which to study human behavior, both individual and
social.

The Bald Soprano • *The Bald Soprano*, Ionesco's first play, served clear notice of a major new talent and remains his best-known effort and the one most frequently performed. Rivaled only by Beckett's *Waiting for Godot* as a classic of the contemporary drama, *The Bald Soprano* (produced in London as the *The Bald Prima Donna*) is neither the strongest nor the weakest of Ionesco's plays; it is surely, however, among the most memorable.

Set against the stuffy banality of a bourgeois household (Ionesco himself suggested the use of a set prepared for Henrik Ibsen's *Hedda Gabler*, 1890, English translation, 1891), *The Bald Soprano* begins with the dour, machine-voiced Mrs. Smith informing her husband that it is nine o'clock. The grandfather clock, however, has just struck seventeen times. Silent except for the regular clucking of his tongue, Smith puffs on his pipe as he reads the evening paper, held upside down. Mrs. Smith, seemingly oblivious to his lack of interest, continues to discuss the fine English food that they have eaten (including such anomalous dishes as quince-and-bean pie) and tell him the ages of their children. If Mrs. Smith's monologue seems increasingly surreal, the dialogue becomes even more so as Smith, still reading the paper, expresses amazement that the ages of the deceased are routinely printed in the papers, while those of newborns never are. Husband and wife then discuss a recent operation that the surgeon first performed on himself. Even so, the patient died.

A good doctor, opines Smith, should die with his patient, just as a captain should go down with his ship. Discussion of an apparent obituary for one Bobby Watson soon elicits the further information that the man has been dead for three years, that he left a truly well-preserved corpse, that his wife (also named Bobby Watson, as are their son and daughter) is unattractive because she is too dark, too fat, too pale, and too thin. All traveling salespeople, it seems, are also known as Bobby Watson, and vice versa.

Before long, the Smiths' maid interrupts to announce the arrival of their invited guests, Mr. and Mrs. Martin. Although introduced as husband and wife, the Martins (in what has since become one of the most famous scenes in contemporary drama) begin speaking to each other with all the tentative awkwardness of a pickup between strangers on a train. Gradually, expressing amazement with each passing coincidence, the Martins discover that they live in the same town, on the same street, in the same building, on the same floor, in the same apartment, and sleep in the same bed. Cleverly mocking every recognition scene known to conventional theater, Ionesco locks the couple in a passionate embrace, only to have the maid announce that the Martins are not husband and wife or even who they think they are, since her daughter and his daughter are not the same person, having eyes of different color on each side of the face.

Once admitted to the Smiths' parlor, the Martins join their hosts in what may well be the most effective parody of social interaction ever portrayed on the stage; all four participants hem and haw, clear their throats, and let one another's conversational gambits drop with a resounding thud. Ionesco's true intentions, however, clearly lie deeper than mere parody, and the conversation soon degenerates into a nightmare of cross-purposes interrupted (and complicated) by the arrival of an even more gratuitous personage, the Fire Chief.

The Chief, it seems, is making his rounds in search of possible fires; his arrival, meanwhile, has been preceded by a long discussion of whether the ringing of a doorbell indicates the presence of someone at the door. (The bell in fact sounds three times, at rather long intervals, before the Chief sees fit to show himself.) Once inside, the Chief avails himself of celebrity treatment to regale his hosts with a long, involved, and totally nonsensical story prefaced with the title, "The Head-Cold." The maid, attempting a story of her own, is pushed brutally offstage by the other characters and possibly beaten to death; in any event, she is not seen again.

Once the Chief has left, conversation among the four main characters resumes with a gabble of inapposite proverbs, soon degenerating into nonsense syllables shouted with great vehemence, simulating quite effectively the sounds of a genuine argument among four people. At the end, the syllables assume the regular rhythm of a chuffing locomotive, whereupon the curtain falls. A brief final scene recapitulates the first, with the Martins instead of the Smiths.

In its current and final form, *The Bald Soprano* incorporates many evolutionary changes said to have occurred in the course of production. At first, Ionesco admitted, he had no real idea of how to end the play, having once considered (and rejected) the arrival of armed "police" to clear the house of spectators. Later, he decided on a reprise of the opening scene with the Smiths, replacing them still later with the Martins to reinforce the notion of interchangeability already manifest in the Bobby Watson dialogue. Even the play's title is claimed as an addition, having occurred when an actor playing the Fire Chief in rehearsal misspoke the phrase "*institutrice blonde*" ("blonde schoolmistress") as "*cantatrice chauve*" (roughly, "bald primadonna" or "bald soprano"). Supposedly, the actress playing Mrs. Smith ad-libbed the line, "She still wears her hair the same way," and the hitherto untitled play was on its way. Although such an explanation may well be apocryphal, the fact remains that much of *The Bald Soprano* as it is now known was improvised in production, proving (among other things) the impressive fluidity of Ionesco's developing talent.

The Lesson • To those spectators falsely conditioned by the nonsense title of *The Bald Soprano*, the action of *The Lesson* may well have come as a rude shock. Although his first play calls for no vocalist, or even any bald person, *The Lesson* has very much to do with instruction, as seen in its most negative aspects. If knowledge is power, the play seems to be saying, it can also be used as a weapon, either political or sexual.

In fact, there is no evidence that the Professor of *The Lesson* really knows anything—except perhaps, on occasion, the techniques of psychological manipulation. His important-sounding lectures are by turns banal, nonsensical, irrelevant, and self-contradictory; yet the torrent of verbiage that pours forth from his mouth soon reduces his young, strong, confident Pupil to utter helplessness in anticipation of her inevitable death. Mild-mannered and tentative at the outset, the elderly Professor gains such confidence from the sound of his own voice that he is quite plausibly capable of murder, committed with an invisible knife made manifest by words.

Recapitulating the frequent use of nonsense dialogue in *The Bald Soprano*, Ionesco in *The Lesson* at first disorients the spectator with the Pupil who, armed merely with a schoolgirl's book bag, confidently announces her intention to pursue the "total doctorate"; even so, she is shaky on elementary geography and utterly unable to subtract, although she can multiply six-digit numbers in her head. When asked to account for the latter talent, she calmly replies that she has memorized all possible products. As in the earlier play, incipient tragedy is never far removed from comedy, and *The Lesson*, for all its sense of impending doom, is well provided with hilarious moments.

Despite obvious elements of political satire (increasingly evident toward the end of the play), the predominant tone of *The Lesson* is sexual. The Pupil, for all her apparent innocence, is a highly provocative figure only dimly aware of her powers. The Professor, helpless and seemingly tongue-tied in the presence of his acerbic Housekeeper, responds to the Pupil's implicit provocation with increasingly violent and eventually murderous aggression.

As the Housekeeper has warned him, "philology leads to the worst"; for Ionesco, "philology" here connotes not a "love of language" but a penchant pursued past the point of addiction. The Professor seems to exist only when, and because, he speaks. Language covers a multitude of probable sins, acquiring hypnotic powers quite beyond the scope of logic. For some, *The Lesson* symbolizes the inherently sexual nature of all teaching, which involves, at least in its intent, an act of penetration. Such an interpretation gathers further momentum from a Sartrean interpretation, whereby the Professor hides inauthentically behind his function in order to brutalize and terrorize a world that has long threatened him.

The Lesson retains such resonance as to resist simplistic attempts at explanation. For all its weaknesses (especially the anticlimactic ending), the play presents an arresting and still original deformation and reformation of human behavior and is one of Ionesco's best-realized expressions of a nightmarish vision.

The Chairs • Initially baffling even to those spectators familiar with *The Lesson* and *The Bald Soprano*, *The Chairs* broke new ground in the development of Ionesco's theater by introducing a poetic element of which his earlier plays had given little indication. Although connected to the earlier plays by nonsense elements, disconnected speech, and disorientation of the spectator, *The Chairs* establishes a thoughtful, elegiac tone that anticipates both *Exit the King* and the best plays of Beckett, whose *Waiting for Godot* was soon to be produced for the first time.

Like *The Lesson*, *The Chairs* vigorously rejects simplistic efforts at interpretation, although on the surface it might be said to be "about" love, marriage, aging, and, above all, the futility of all human endeavor. Both individually and as a pair, the nonagenarian couple with the main speaking parts recapitulate in their behavior all stages of human life, from babyhood to extreme old age. By turns pathetic and ridiculous, frequently sympathetic, the Old Man and the Old Woman represent as effectively as Hamm and Clov, of Beckett's *Endgame*, the human need to "mean something," even against insuperable odds.

Set inside a tower on a remote and sparsely populated island, *The Chairs* presents the old couple in what will be their final moments, as the Old Man prepares to leave his testament for all humanity. The testament, it seems, is in the form of a speech that the Old Man has prepared from the raw material of his long life, but which he feels unqualified to deliver in his own voice. For the momentous occasion, he has hired a professional Orator, who will deliver the speech to a carefully selected assemblage of invited dignitaries including the Emperor himself.

In time, the distinguished guests begin to arrive, greeted and seated by the delighted and understandably anxious old couple. The audience, however, never sees the guests, who are represented onstage by a rapidly growing number of empty chairs—hence the play's title. Gesturing and grimacing in a worthy parody of Marcel Proust's aristocratic hosts, the old couple continue to seat their invisible audience; the Orator, however, is quite visible, and as soon as the Emperor arrives (unseen), the action is ready to begin. Sure at last that he has not lived in vain, his message about to be delivered, the Old Man leaps to his death from a tower window, followed closely by his wife.

When the Orator rises to speak, however, he proves to be a deaf-mute (or at least tongue-tied). Turning at last to an available blackboard, the Orator fares hardly better, managing at best a meaningless gabble of words, letters, and fragments. Lest the spectator, however, leap to the conclusion that the Orator's audience has been hallucinated by the old couple, Ionesco calls in his script for crowd noises that, in production, tend to sound like a cross between applause and howls of derision. The audience, invisible or not, is still in evidence. *The Chairs* remains, like its predecessor, hauntingly enigmatic, reflecting back on the spectator his own attempts to determine the play's meaning.

The Killer • Following the belated success of *The Chairs*, Ionesco embarked on the most prolific phase of his career, producing more than a dozen short sketches and one-act plays as well as his first full-length plays, including *Amédée* and *Victims of Duty*. It was also during this period that the author's earliest and best-known work gave rise to the revisionist London controversy, involving (as did many similar disputes in the twentieth century) the social role of the writer as seen from the political Left.

By 1958, Ionesco stood persuasively accused (by Kenneth Tynan and others) of shunning his appropriate function in favor of nonsense theater, which is irrelevant by definition. Among the greater of ironies is that Ionesco, a man truly displaced by two world wars, gave evidence even in his earliest plays of a profound social conscience. Nevertheless, his deep-seated mistrust of political extremism on both sides left him peculiarly vulnerable to charges of political indifference. Like George Orwell before him, Ionesco aroused the ire of doctrinaire liberals by rejecting their proposed "solutions" as well as those offered from the Right.

In any event, it appears in retrospect that Ionesco may well have taken the criticism very much to heart, much as he professed not to in such documents as *Notes and Counter-Notes*. Toward the end of the 1950's Ionesco's plays seemed to strive increasingly for political relevance, with decidedly uneven results. In the strongest of these efforts, however, Ionesco retained his unique personal stamp with plays that resist any attempt to assign arbitrary political significance. *The Killer*, in particular, functions effectively as satire while going far deeper in its analysis of human aspirations and behavior. While waxing eloquent about the abuses of political power, *The Killer* also has much to say about the simple imperfectibility of human nature and the inevitability of death.

Partially set in a futuristic "Radiant City," probably inspired by the projections of the architect Le Corbusier, *The Killer* marks the first appearance of the protagonist Bérenger, a partially autobiographical Everyman-figure to be featured in several more plays of Ionesco's middle period. Arriving in Radiant City, which is surrounded by several darker neighborhoods, Bérenger is astounded to learn that most common problems and ailments have been banished from the area for good. His guide, the Architect (who also functions as police chief and coroner), explains that nothing has been left to chance, and that even the weather is controlled. Unfortunately, the streets are empty; eventually, the Architect explains to Bérenger that the inhabitants are hesitant to leave their homes for fear of an unknown killer, who lures people to their deaths by promising a glimpse of "the colonel's photograph."

Based on a short story in fact entitled "La Photo du colonel" ("The Colonel's Photograph"), *The Killer* quickly departs from simple satire in its deliberately uncertain distinction between the act of murder and the basic fact of death. If curiosity kills the cat, it doubtless kills people as well; whatever the "colonel's photograph" may indeed be like, it represents, among other things, the irrational element implicit in all human behavior. In French, the play's title suggests an unpaid, hence gratuitous killer, and in many respects the Killer differs little from the conventional figure of the Grim Reaper.

If death is inevitable, *The Killer* is not, however, without distinct political overtones. Employees of the state, it seems, enjoy guaranteed immunity from the Killer's assaults, a fact made painfully evident when Mlle Dany, the Architect's secretary and the woman of Bérenger's dreams, resigns her job only to fall victim soon after to the Killer. Another plainly political element is evident in the person of Mother Peep ("la mère Pipe"), a demagogue and rabble-rouser who has risen to prominence of sorts as keeper of the public geese. Divorced from the context of the play, the masterly scene depicting Mother Peep's rally might well be seen as one of the most powerful parodies of demagoguery and totalitarianism ever portrayed on the stage. Restored to context, however, the scene ultimately provides still further evidence of the absurd, together with the Killer himself. Political satire thus serves, for Ionesco, as the means to an end, rather than as an end in itself.

Motivated primarily by his desire to avenge Mlle Dany's apparently senseless murder, Bérenger sets off on a dogged search for the Killer, often appearing to be the only sane man (or indeed the only human being) in a world turned upside down. After adventures involving several cases of mistaken identity, Bérenger at last comes face to face with his quarry, an apparently feeble, one-eyed individual who, according to Ionesco, may or may not actually appear on the stage, according to the wishes of the individual director. In any case, the Killer has no real lines to speak, serving mainly as foil to Bérenger's impassioned, eloquent (and perhaps overlong) speech in defense of life, liberty, and the human race. As close to lyricism as Ionesco had thus far come in his career, Bérenger's speech in *The Killer* remains a powerful statement in defense of humanity; predictably, however, it falls on deaf ears, and Bérenger, out of options, offers himself freely to the Killer's brandished knife.

More ambitious in scope than any of Ionesco's earlier efforts for the stage, *The Killer* seemed to move his career into a new phase, partially satisfying those critics who had assailed his earlier work for its "irrelevance." It seems likely, however, that such critics may have seen primarily what they wanted to see; despite obvious political overtones, *The Killer* seems far closer to Ionesco's characteristic mode of expression than it may at the time have been supposed. In any case, it was not long before the critics were presented with a new object of study, the well-known and still controversial *Rhinoceros*.

Rhinoceros • First produced within a year after *The Killer* (to which it is related by the character of Bérenger), *Rhinoceros* remains the best-known and most frequently performed of Ionesco's later plays, quite probably for the wrong reasons. Although decidedly weaker than *The Killer*, *Rhinoceros* is not without its strengths; unfortunately, those strengths tend to be slighted by directors and spectators alike, in favor of those elements providing the play with its apparent "relevance."

Considering the heat generated at the height of the so-called London Controversy, it is perhaps not surprising that Ionesco proved more willing than usual to allow the attachment of literal significance to one of his more ambitious efforts. Unfortunately, the play itself, although up to Ionesco's usual standards, tends to collapse under the weight of "meaning" applied from without.

Last seen in *The Killer* as an eloquent advocate of human nature, Bérenger makes his entry in *Rhinoceros* in a decidedly more passive role, as an easygoing if rather morose fellow who would prefer, when possible, to be left alone. Indeed, he tries as long as possible to go about his business, despite the gathering invasion of rhinoceroses, whose bizarre trumpeting can be heard from the street below. Indeed, the device of the proliferating pachyderms is every bit as powerful and eloquent as that of a gratuitous murderer in the previous play.

Perceived at first as invaders from outside, the pachyderms are gradually seen to be emerging among the populace as well. A certain Mme Boeuf at first flees in terror from a trumpeting beast, only to recognize (somehow) in its voice the accents of her missing husband: She rides happily off on the animal's back in a parody of the traditional recognition scene rivaled only by the Martins of *The Bald Soprano*. Characters around Bérenger begin to talk and act strangely, finding the invaders handsome and their language beautiful, far more so than the "merely" human. It is not long before transformations from man to beast become an hourly occurrence, with the animals taking over local businesses and ultimately the broadcast media. At the time of the play's introduction, Ionesco readily admitted to obvious parallels between "rhinoceritis" and the rise of Nazi Germany from the decadent Weimar Republic. Unfortunately, his acknowledgment served to authorize a fixed interpretation of a play which, in true Ionesco fashion, is in its essence open-ended and fraught with ambiguities.

If staged without preconceptions as to meaning, *Rhinoceros* quickly emerges as one of Ionesco's more unsettling staged nightmares, less effective than *The Killer* but nearly as resonant as *The Lesson*. Unfortunately, deliberate efforts to present *Rhinoceros* as antifascist propaganda rob the play of one of its more haunting qualities, implicit in the characterization of Bérenger.

Quite unlike his earlier avatar in *The Killer*, the Bérenger of *Rhinoceros* is neither eloquent nor potentially heroic. Indeed, one of the major tensions latent in the play as written resides in the passivity of Bérenger, in his anguished uncertainty as to whether he *could* turn into a rhinoceros even if he so wished. His refusal to capitulate, articulated in the final scene and hailed by critics as proof of Ionesco's "message," emerges from the context of the play in accents not of heroism but of desperation. Bérenger alone remains the last human being on earth, less because he will not change than because he simply *cannot.*

If viewed with sufficient objectivity, *Rhinoceros* thus emerges as a chilling portrayal of an individual in a society, any society, ostracized by his or her fellows for reasons that cannot be fully comprehended. It is possible that future generations of actors and directors may well discover the latent subtext of *Rhinoceros* and restore the play to its rightful place among Ionesco's more disorienting nightmare visions. In the meantime, *Rhinoceros* remains hampered by its prevalent literal interpretation, far less effective as polemic than such overtly political plays as those of Bertolt Brecht or the later Adamov. Neither fish nor fowl, *Rhinoceros*, as commonly interpreted, can neither swim nor fly. To Ionesco's ultimate credit, however, it remains a better play than it seems.

Exit the King • Rivaled only by *The Killer*, *Exit the King* is perhaps the strongest and best realized of Ionesco's later plays, deserving more frequent revivals than it has received. Deceptively simple both in concept and in execution, *Exit the King* harks back to *The Killer* and *The Chairs* in its portrayal of a royal Bérenger awaiting death. Deftly compressing all of human history into a single life-experience, Ionesco presents a King Bérenger who, during several centuries of life and rule, has invented the airplane and the bicycle, has pseudonymously written all the plays and sonnets attributed to William Shakespeare, and has personally built all the major cities in Western Europe. By now, however, his kingdom is crumbling, its monuments are in ruins, and his rule is crippled by anarchy. The action of the play compresses some twenty years, indicated by Queen Marguerite's assertion that the king will be dead within an hour and a half, at the end of the play.

Inevitably reminiscent of Camus's *Caligula*, whose historically inspired imperial protagonist substitutes his own caprices for those of an incomprehensible natural order, Ionesco's King Bérenger suffers primarily from an awareness of the simple fact that people die and are not happy. Like the Old Man of *The Chairs*, Bérenger has lived and labored in vain; unlike the Old Man, he knows as much, vigorously protesting the unfairness of his fate. Resuming in his person the lives of all who have ever suffered, worked, or dreamed, Bérenger ultimately speaks in his anguish to the futility of all human endeavor given the eventuality of death, a finality as capricious as the actions of The Killer in the first of the Bérenger plays.

Surprisingly, in the light of its evident ambitions, *Exit the King* genuinely works, both as text and in production. Ponderousness of tone is avoided largely through Ionesco's choice of supporting characters; the king's protracted final moments are witnessed by both of his queens (one young and pretty, the other middle-aged and tart of tongue), a guard, and a Doctor who serves also as Astrologer and Chief Executioner. Among them, the characters provide for a strong infusion of humor, if never "comic relief." The aging Queen Marguerite, clearly descended from Mrs. Smith and from Madeleine of *Amédée*, continues the satire of marriage that runs as an undercurrent through many Ionesco plays; the younger Queen Marie, meanwhile, seems to represent maternal warmth as well as the promise of young love.

The Doctor, who has aided and abetted the king in many of his Promethean schemes, frequently provides a perfect foil for the king's thoroughly human grievances. In an evident parody of the political slogan "Every man a king," Ionesco presents a king who is indeed Everyman and whose life will be nullified as well as ended with his death. In the French title, the use of the reflexive construction reinforces the notion that death is a process rather than a mere event; the king, implies Ionesco, is dying—as are all men and women from the moment of their birth.

Exit the King remains among the most eloquent and economical of Ionesco's dramatic statements, surpassing most of his subsequent efforts. *Hunger and Thirst*, for all its innovative brilliance, is sententious and often confused; *Killing Game* reiterates what Ionesco had already said, and said better, in such earlier efforts as *The Killer* and *The Chairs*. Of Ionesco's later efforts, only *Man with Bags* approaches the concise statement and eloquent imagery to be found in such plays as *The Killer* and *Exit the King*.

Man with Bags • Based in large measure on nightmare visions already recorded in Ionesco's memoirs, *Man with Bags* ironically inverts, intentionally or not, the title and premise of Jean Anouilh's immensely popular 1937 play, *Le Voyageur sans bagage* (*Traveller Without Luggage*, 1959). Anouilh's play, in part a parody of the Oedipus theme, presents an amnesiac war veteran who, reunited with his true family after twenty years and countless false leads, seeks refuge in amnesia against a sordid past that he has no desire to reclaim. Rejecting the obviously valid claims of the Renaud family, the pseudonymous Gaston opts instead for outright fantasy, declaring that he is "washed clean" of his youth, and indeed of his identity. It remained for Ionesco, however, to explore even in his earliest efforts the horrific consequences that result when identity is lost or denied. Whether the individual likes it, identity (especially as retrieved through memory) is the only available proof of his existence. It therefore seemed quite fitting that Ionesco, nearly forty years after *Traveller Without Luggage*, should balance Anouilh's speculative fantasy with a highly convincing rebuttal.

Despite the strong infusion of dream elements in such earlier plays as *The Chairs, The Killer,* and *A Stroll in the Air, Man with Bags* is the first of Ionesco's efforts to be characterized by its author as a dream play. Ionesco, who, by the time of the play's introduction, was well acquainted with the precepts and procedures of Jungian psychoanalysis, readily conceded that his characters were in fact archetypes and that the play represented an attempt to explore human identity through dreams. No longer known as Bérenger, the autobiographical protagonist is identified simply as "The Man" or "No-man," the latter an obvious recollection of the pseudonym chosen by Odysseus during his encounter with the Cyclops. Another archetype strongly recalled by the protagonist in his adventures and behavior is that of the Wandering Jew. In a succession of scenes shifting wildly in space and time, the man travels resolutely in search of both his ancestry and his identity, accompanied only by the "luggage" of his memory.

Unlike such earlier dream plays as those of August Strindberg and those attempted by the Surrealists, *Man with Bags* abounds in the sharp, seemingly realistic detail to be found in actual dreams. Linked by the preconscious logic peculiar to the dream experience, the scenes are striking in their imagery and often memorable. In one, for example, an old woman converses animatedly with her long-lost mother; the actress playing the mother is in her young and vibrant twenties, the age at which the old woman last saw her. Political elements such as bureaucracy, war, and oppression are present in abundance, although portrayed (as usual in Ionesco's work) without emphasis, as yet another anomalous fact of life, such as death. As in real dreams, sexual fantasies are juxtaposed with philosophical and political ones.

In another memorable scene, the protagonist is propositioned by a married woman and accepts the offer in full view of her apparently willing husband, who agrees to keep an eye on the protagonist's luggage; the assignation then takes place in a public park ominously filled with armed guards. In the final scene, the man pauses to rest on one of his suitcases while the other characters rush about with their own luggage, vigorously pursuing the quest for identity of which the man himself has now grown tired. He does not, however, abandon or drop his own luggage; no doubt he will soon rise to his feet and continue as before. Memories, suggested Ionesco, remain the only proof that people have concerning the fact of their own individual passages through life.

Other major works

LONG FICTION: *Le Solitaire,* 1973 (*The Hermit,* 1974).

SHORT FICTION: *La Photo du colonel,* 1962 (*The Colonel's Photograph,* 1967).

SCREENPLAY: *La Vase,* 1970 (*The Mire,* 1973).

RADIO PLAY: *Le Salon de l'automobile,* 1952 (*The Motor Show,* 1963).

NONFICTION: *Nu,* 1934; *Notes et contre-notes,* 1962 (*Notes and Counter-Notes,* 1964); *Journal en miettes,* 1967 (*Fragments of a Journal,* 1968); *Présent passé passé présent,* 1968 (memoir; *Present Past Past Present,* 1972); *Un Homme en question,* 1979; *Le Blanc et le noir,* 1980; *Hugoliade,* 1982 (*Hugoliad: Or, The Grotesque and Tragic Life of Victor Hugo,* 1987); *La Quête intermittente,* 1988.

CHILDREN'S LITERATURE: *Story Number 1: For Children Under Three Years of Age,* 1969; *Story Number 2: For Children Under Three Years of Age,* 1970; *Story Number 3: For Children over Three Years of Age,* 1971; *Story Number 4: For Children over Three Years of Age,* 1975.

Bibliography

Coe, Richard N. *Ionesco: A Study of his Plays.* London: Methuen, 1971. The latest of several volumes written on Ionesco by the same critic beginning in 1961; the present volume includes a translation of the hitherto unpublished short play *The Niece-Wife.*

Esslin, Martin. *The Theater of the Absurd.* Reprint. Garden City, N.Y.: Doubleday, 1968. Esslin's ground-breaking study remains authoritative on Ionesco's theater and on its situation within the context of twentieth-century avant-garde drama.

Gaensbauer, Deborah B. *Eugène Ionseco Revisited.* New York: Twayne, 1996. Replaces an earlier volume (1972) by Allan Lewis in Twayne's World Authors Series; generally sound critical and historical presentation of Ionesco's dramatic canon and its legacy.

Lane, Nancy. *Understanding Eugène Ionesco.* Columbia: University of South Carolina Press, 1994. Published just before Ionesco's death, Lane's study is among the first to take note of Ionesco's corrected birth date and other biographical details; generally sound readings of the major plays.

Nottingham French Studies 35, no. 1 (1996). Edited by Steven Smith. A special Ionesco issue of the journal published by the University of Nottingham, collecting a dozen articles dealing with all aspects of the author's thought and theater. Contributors include David Bradby, Ingrid Coleman Chafee, Emmanuel Jacquart, and Rosette Lamont.

David B. Parsell

Ben Jonson

Born: London, England; June 11, 1573
Died: London, England; August 6, 1637

Principal drama • *The Isle of Dogs,* pr. 1597 (with Thomas Nashe; no longer extant);
The Case Is Altered, pr. 1597, pb. 1609; *Every Man in His Humour,* pr. 1598 (revised 1605),
pb. 1601 (revised 1616); *Hot Anger Soon Cold,* pr. 1598 (with Henry Chettle and Henry
Porter; no longer extant); *Every Man out of His Humour,* pr. 1599, pb. 1600; *The Page
of Plymouth,* pr. 1599 (with Thomas Dekker; no longer extant); *Robert the Second, King
of Scots,* pr. 1599 (with Henry Chettle and Thomas Dekker; no longer extant); *Cynthia's
Revels: Or, The Fountain of Self-Love,* pr. c. 1600-1601, pb. 1601; *Poetaster: Or, His Ar-
raignment,* pr. 1601, pb. 1602; *Sejanus His Fall,* pr. 1603, pb. 1605 (commonly known
as *Sejanus*); *Eastward Ho!,* pr., pb. 1605 (with George Chapman and John Marston);
Volpone: Or, The Fox, pr. 1605, pb. 1607; *Epicœne: Or, The Silent Woman,* pr. 1609,
pb. 1616; *The Alchemist,* pr. 1610, pb. 1612; *Catiline His Conspiracy,* pr., pb. 1611 (commonly known as *Catiline*); *Bartholomew Fair,* pr. 1614, pb. 1631; *The Devil Is an Ass,*
pr. 1616, pb. 1631; *The Staple of News,* pr. 1626, pb. 1631; *The New Inn: Or, The Light
Heart,* pr. 1629, pb. 1631; *The Magnetic Lady: Or, Humours Reconciled,* pr. 1632, pb. 1640;
A Tale of a Tub, pr. 1633, pb. 1640; *The Sad Shepherd: Or, A Tale of Robin Hood,* pb. 1640
(fragment)

Other literary forms • Ben Jonson was a masterful poet as well as a dramatist. His
poetry, with some justification, has the reputation of being remote from modern readers. A dedicated classicist, Jonson emphasized clarity of form and phrase over expression of emotion, and many of his poems seem to be exercises in cleverness and wit
rather than attempts to express an idea or image well. Others of his poems, however, re-
tain their power and vision: "To Celia," for example, has given the English language
the phrase "Drink to me only with thine eyes."

The difficulty of Jonson's poetry originates in large part in his very mastery of poetic form. Jonson was a student of literature, and he was a man of letters with few
equals in any era. He studied the poetic forms of classical Greek and Latin literature as
well as those of later European literature, and he used what he learned in his own
work. The result is a body of poetry that is very diverse, including salutations and love
poems, homilies and satires, epigrams and lyrics. Much of the poetry appeals primarily to academics because of its experimental qualities and its displays of technical virtuosity. Yet those who allow themselves to be put off by Jonson's prodigious intellectualism miss some of the finest verse in English.

Jonson was also a prodigious writer of masques—dramatic allegorical entertainments, usually prepared to celebrate special occasions and presented at court. Jonson's
masques have in common with his poetry technical achievement and, with much of his
occasional verse, a focus on the virtues, real and reputed, of nobility and royalty. Although the emphasis was on spectacle and celebration of the aristocracy, Jonson tried
to make his masques legitimate works of literature, and they have enjoyed increasing
critical attention in recent years.

Achievements • Ben Jonson was the foremost man of letters of his time. His knowledge of literature was combined with a passionate personality and a desire to be respected; the combination resulted in his efforts to elevate authors in the estimation of society. He endeavored to demonstrate the importance of literature in the lives of people and in their culture. Although he regarded his dramatic work as merely one facet of his literary life, he was determined that the playwright should receive the esteemed title of "poet." In the Elizabethan era, plays were regarded as unimportant public amusements; satires, sonnets, and narrative verse were expected to carry the heavy freight of ideas and art. Jonson worked to establish drama as a legitimate literary form by showing that it could be a conscious art with rules of organization that were as valid as those of more esteemed literary genres.

In 1616, Jonson published *The Workes of Benjamin Jonson*, including in the volume nine of his plays in addition to other writings. Never before had any author dared to give his plays the title "Works." The term "works" was usually reserved for profound philosophical treatises. Jonson was derided by some writers for being conceited and for trying to make plays seem important; even after his death, some traditionalists found his title difficult to accept. Further, Jonson promoted the cause of drama as high art by devoting much care to the publishing of the texts of his plays, thereby establishing a higher standard for published texts of dramas than had existed before. The publication of *The Workes of Benjamin Jonson* led at least indirectly to the important First Folio edition of William Shakespeare's plays.

Jonson's reputation as a dramatist is inextricably bound with that of Shakespeare. Although Jonson was esteemed above Shakespeare by most of his contemporaries, subsequent eras have elevated Shakespeare at Jonson's expense. Thus, although Jonson's comedies are wonderful and are well received by modern audiences, they are rarely performed. Shakespeare's poetry is better than Jonson's; his tragedies are more moving; his comedies are more diverse and have superior characterizations. To acknowledge Shakespeare's superiority is not to derogate Jonson's achievement; Shakespeare is alone atop the world's authors, but Jonson is not far below. In addition, Jonson's plays are superior to Shakespeare's in consistency of plot and structure. Had there been no William Shakespeare, there might today be Jonson festivals, and *Volpone* and *The Alchemist* might be the revered standards for college drama productions.

Biography • Tradition has it that Benjamin Jonson was born in 1572; literary historians put his birth in 1573, probably on June 11. His father, an Anglican minister, died about a month before Jonson was born.

(Library of Congress)

His mother married a master bricklayer in 1574; the family lived in Westminster. While growing up, Jonson attended Westminster School and became a student of William Camden, who was perhaps the greatest classicist and antiquarian of the Elizabethan and Jacobean ages. Jonson's interest in classical literature, his care in constructing what he wrote, and his respect for learning all have their origins in the teachings of Camden. Techniques for writing that Jonson used throughout his life were first learned from Camden, including the practice of writing out a prospective poem first in prose and then converting the prose to verse.

In about 1588, Jonson became an apprentice bricklayer. This part of his life became the subject of jokes and gibes in his later years, but he seems to have taken pride in his humble origins. His respect for achievement and general lack of respect for claims of importance based solely on heredity or accident may have had their roots in his own struggles as a lower-class laborer. He left his bricklaying work to join the army in its war against the Spanish in the Lowlands in 1591 or 1592. During his tenure in the army, he apparently served with some distinction; he claimed that he was the English champion in single combat against a Spanish champion and that he slew his opponent while the assembled armies watched. He was handy with swords and knives and was, when young, quite combative and physically intimidating.

Jonson eventually returned to England. Little is known of his activities until 1597, save that he married Anne Lewis on November 14, 1594. The marriage seems to have been unhappy. Before 1597, Jonson might have been an actor with a traveling troupe, many of whose members eked out marginal livings in the towns and hamlets of England. He was imprisoned in 1597 for having finished a play begun by Thomas Nashe; *The Isle of Dogs* was declared seditious by the Privy Council of the queen. The play, like most of Jonson's collaborations, has not been preserved. After a few weeks, Jonson was released from prison.

Jonson's career as a playwright began in earnest in 1598 after the production of *The Case Is Altered*, which was performed by a troupe of boys from the Chapel Royal. In that same year, *Every Man in His Humour*, the first of Jonson's important plays, was performed by William Shakespeare's company, the Lord Chamberlain's Men. Tradition has it that Shakespeare recognized Jonson's talent and persuaded the Lord Chamberlain's Men to stage the play. Although he admired Shakespeare, Jonson never regarded himself as principally a playwright, and therefore he never became a permanent shareholder in an acting company, as did Shakespeare. This enabled Jonson to maintain his artistic freedom but prevented him from earning the good living that Shakespeare and other shareholders enjoyed.

The year 1598 was a busy one for Jonson; he was again imprisoned, this time for killing an actor, Gabriel Spencer, in a duel on September 22. Jonson's property was confiscated, he was branded on the thumb, and he was to be executed, but he saved his life by pleading benefit of clergy, which he could do under ancient English law because he could read. While in prison, he was converted to Roman Catholicism, a faith he practiced until about 1608. In 1606, he was charged with seducing young people into Roman Catholicism; the charges were dropped when he converted back to Anglicanism.

Jonson pursued an active life as an author of plays, poetry, and treatises. His comedies were successful, but his tragedies were badly received. In 1603, Queen Elizabeth died and King James assumed the English throne. Jonson's *Entertainment at Athorpe* helped to launch him on a long career as a court poet. Also that year, his son Benjamin died at the age of six. Though Jonson was finding public acclaim and honor, his private life was miserable. He and his wife lived apart from 1602 to 1607, he lost his namesake son, and he grew obese. In 1605, he collaborated with John Marston and George Chapman on the rollicking comedy *Eastward Ho!* and was again imprisoned for a supposed slight to King James; the play made fun of Scots.

Jonson's plays *Volpone, Epicœne,* and *The Alchemist* enhanced his reputation among his literary peers; his court poetry and masques enhanced his status with King James. In 1616, he published *The Workes of Benjamin Jonson* and was awarded a pension by the king. The pension and Jonson's position as the leading literary figure in England in 1616 have encouraged many historians to call him an unofficial poet laureate, and he is usually honored as the first to fill that role in England. Until the death of King James in 1625, Jonson enjoyed his role as a favorite of the king and a respected author. His honors included a master of arts degree from the University of Oxford.

When Charles I assumed the throne, Jonson's status at court declined. The pension of wine and money was haphazardly delivered, and Jonson had difficulty pursuing his scholarly career because his lodgings burned down in 1623, and his books and papers were destroyed. He returned to playwriting with *The Staple of News* in 1626; the play was not as well received as his earlier comedies. In 1628, he suffered a stroke and was partially paralyzed. In 1629, his play *The New Inn* was staged by the King's Men and was a disaster. He continued to write until his death on August 6, 1637. He left unfinished the play *The Sad Shepherd,* which some critics admire. Although cranky, egotistical, and homely, Jonson retained much of his hold on the leading literary people of his time and was esteemed by younger authors even after his death. He is one of literature's most colorful figures. Combative, robust, and dedicated to his art, Jonson made major contributions to the development of English literature.

Analysis • Ben Jonson's dramatic canon is large, and most of the plays in it are worthy of long and careful study. He is best remembered for his comedies, which influenced comedy writing well into the eighteenth century and which remain entertaining. Jonson took Horace's maxim to heart—that to teach, a writer must first entertain—and he followed literary rules only so far as they enabled him to instruct and entertain his audience. By observing the neoclassical unities of time and space in his plays, Jonson gave his works a coherence often lacking in the comedies of his contemporaries: Loose ends are resolved, subplot and main plot are interwoven so that each enhances the other, and the conclusion of each play resolves the basic issues brought up during the action. Jonson's concern with entertaining makes most of his comedies delightful and attractive to modern audiences; his effort to instruct makes his plays substantial and meaningful.

From the beginning of his career as a playwright, Jonson was successful with comedy. His two attempts at tragedies are interesting as experiments but are unlikely to be successful with general audiences. His comedies are varied, ranging from the city to the countryside and including satires, comedies of manners, and farces. He was most successful when writing about city life, moralizing with good-natured humor.

Jonson's stature as a playwright is greater than current popular knowledge of him would indicate. Had Shakespeare lived at another time, Jonson would be the dramatic giant of his era. His comedies deserve to be performed more often than they are; his masterpieces play well before modern audiences, and even his minor plays have wit and ideas to recommend them. Jonson is a dramatist of the first rank.

Every Man in His Humour • Of his early comedies, *Every Man in His Humour* is the most important. Jonson's first significant popular success, it best represents those qualities that make some of his later plays great works of literature. Typical of a Jonsonian comedy, *Every Man in His Humour* has a complex interweaving of plots that creates an atmosphere of comic frenzy. Fools are duped, husbands fear cuckolding, wives suspect their husbands of having mistresses, fathers spy on sons, a servant plays tricks on everyone, and myriad disguises and social games confuse the characters. The audience is not left in confusion but is carefully let in on the nuances of the various plots.

The plot features Edward Knowell, who journeys to London to visit Wellbred, a wit whose devil-may-care behavior might get Edward into trouble. Old Knowell, Edward's father, follows his son to London in order to spy on him, and his servant Brainworm connives and plays tricks—as much to amuse himself as to gain anything. Subplots involve Captain Bobadill, a braggart soldier; Cob and Tib, the landlords of Bobadill; Kitely, a merchant; and Downright, Wellbred's plainspoken brother. The almost bewildering multiplicity of characters is typical of many of Jonson's plays. He borrows the plot of unwarranted suspicions from classical dramatists. Captain Bobadill is the miles gloriosus, the braggart soldier (usually a coward), a stock character in classical comedies. Brainworm is the conniving servant, another stock figure from classical comedies. Other characters also serve specific purposes: Downright is a shatterer of illusions—he points out the falseness in others. Edward Knowell is the romantic lead—a hero who retains his innocence in the middle of the turmoil of the plot. Kitely, Dame Kitely, Cob, and Tib provide much of the low comedy and serve to reflect the ridiculousness of the behavior of the main characters.

Although it shares many of the characteristics that typify Jonson's later comedies, *Every Man in His Humour* shows the dramatist still in the process of forging his mature style. He is still trying to reconcile his classical models to the traditions of English drama and to the tastes of his audience. The plot is loose, almost chaotic, and not as tightly controlled as those of *The Alchemist* and *Volpone.*

Volpone • "What a rare punishment/ Is avarice to itself," declares Volpone. At the heart of the complex play *Volpone* is the straightforward moral judgment that the evil one commits brings with it a suitable punishment. In *Volpone,* Jonson satirizes human nature and the baser impulses of humanity.

The play's characters pursue basely materialistic ideals, and in attaining their goals, they ensure their own downfall. Volpone begins the play with a monologue that is in itself a classic: "Good morning to the day; and next, my gold!/ Open the shrine that I may see my saint." His servant and partner in crime, Mosca, draws open a curtain and reveals piles of gold. Volpone has called the repository a "shrine" and the gold a "saint." As the rest of the monologue reveals, Volpone regards wealth with a religious fervor; gold, he asserts, is the "son of Sol"; it "giv'st all men tongues"; it "mak'st men do all things."

Volpone is not merely a clever faker, nor is his servant, Mosca. He is a devotee of an ideal, and as such he is at once more likable and more dangerous than an ordinary thief. He has the excuse that confidence men traditionally have had: that the greed of his victims is their undoing; if they were good people, he would be unable to cheat them. As long as he sticks to victimizing greedy people, he is spectacularly successful; the victims eagerly give him gold and jewels in the hope of gaining his fortune by having it left to them when he dies. When he seeks to "bed" innocent Celia, however, his empire of gold and deceit begins to crumble into its component parts of venality, lust, and spiritual morbidity.

Volpone is a captivating character. He is capable of wonderful flights of language and of clever intrigue, and he is a consummate actor; his strength is his knowledge of how much he can manipulate people into doing what he wants done; his weakness is his overweening pride—he revels too much in his ability to dupe his victims. By pretending to be an old, dying man, he helps convince his victims of his imminent death and of the possibility that one of them will inherit his wealth. They give him expensive gifts to ingratiate themselves with him. His accomplice, Mosca, is also a skilled actor, who can be obsequious one moment, gallant the next—all things to all people. Mosca convinces each victim that he is favored above all others in Volpone's will. The scheme is very successful, and there is much hilarity in the gulling of the lawyer Voltore (the vulture), the elderly Corbaccio (the crow), and the merchant and husband of Celia, Corvino (the raven). The actors should resemble their roles: Voltore is craven and menacing; Corbaccio is thin and leggy; and Corvino is quick-eyed and aggressive. There is exuberance in Volpone's shifts from boisterous and athletic man to bedridden old cripple, in Mosca's cheerful conniving, and in the duping of three socially prominent and nasty men. The subplot of Lord and Lady Politic Would-be heightens the comedy as Volpone, in his guise as cripple, endures Lady Would-be's endless talking and her willingness to surrender her virtue for his favor.

Volpone's gold-centered world would be thoroughly jolly if he were not right about gold's ability to influence people. His victims include innocents, such as Bonario, who is disinherited by his father, Corbaccio, so that Corbaccio can leave his wealth to Volpone in the hope that Volpone will reciprocate. Corvino values wealth above all else; he is a fitting worshiper at the shrine of gold, and he would sacrifice anything to the high priest Volpone in exchange for the promise of acquiring more wealth: Corvino even gives his jealously guarded and naïve wife, Celia, to the supposedly impotent Volpone; she is expected to sleep with him.

Underlying the gold-centered world is ugliness; under Volpone's dashing personality is bestiality; under Mosca's wit is spiritual paucity. Jonson shows this graphically. Volpone must pretend to be physically degenerated, yet the pretense mirrors the spiritual reality. As the play progresses, his performance becomes more extreme; eventually, he pretends to be nearly a corpse. The more complex his scheming becomes, the more wretched he must show himself to be. He is trapped in his world of gold; when he wants to leave his home to see what Celia looks like, he must disguise himself as a lowly mountebank. The physically vibrant Volpone is restricted to his gold and Mosca. When he reveals himself as ardent lover to the trapped Celia, his feigned physical degeneration emerges in his spiritual self, and he is doomed.

Volpone is a great play because it is a nearly perfect meshing of comedy, symbolism, suspense, and moralizing. Each change in any of its aspects is matched by changes in all. Its satiric targets are universals, including greed, moral idiocy, and the replacement of spiritual ideals with materialistic ones. Greed brings down most of the principal characters, including Mosca. Pride brings down Volpone; he cannot resist one more chance to display his brilliance. He pretends to be dead and to have left his fortune to Mosca, simply for the sake of seeing how his victims respond when they learn that he has left them nothing. Mosca, loyal only to the money, wants to keep all for himself. Gold turns the world upside down when made the focus of human endeavor: A husband gives his wife to another man; a father displaces his son; the just are made to look false; and a servant becomes master. Gold should serve its owner, and when Volpone enshrines it, he upsets the proper order of society.

The carnality of Volpone is discovered by Bonario, who was accidentally present during Volpone's near-rape of Celia because of one of Mosca's plots involving Corbaccio. In the ensuing trial, Volpone is presented to the court as a nearly dead old man who is incapable of molesting anyone. Voltore puts on his public mask of respectability and argues to the court that Bonario and Celia are liars and worse, and that those accused by them are honest and innocent. An important theme in the play is that of performance versus reality. Corbaccio properly *acts* the part of the kindly old gentleman. Corvino *plays* the honest merchant. Both are respected members of society. Yet just as the exuberant exterior of Volpone covers a decayed spirit, so, too, do the public personalities of Corbaccio, Corvino, and Voltore belie their evil. In a world in which gold is of paramount importance, such people can seem good; likewise, the truly honest and chaste Bonario and Celia can be made to seem conniving, greedy, and concupiscent.

Mosca almost gets the money. Corbaccio and Corvino almost escape with their reputations intact. Voltore almost wins a false case with his skillful arguments. Volpone cannot stand to lose his gold and cannot stand to see his victims succeed where he has failed. He reveals all to the court. The conclusion seems contrived—after all, the clever Volpone could start over and find new victims to gull—but it is thematically apt. No matter how often Volpone were to start over, his plotting would end the same way, because he worships a base and false god that cannot enrich his soul. The ending reveals the falseness in the principal characters and lays bare the emptiness of Volpone's world.

The use of the villain as protagonist can be found in the tragedies of Jonson's contemporaries. Shakespeare's Macbeth, for example, remains one of literature's most interesting villainous heroes. The use of a villain as protagonist in a comedy was more rare and may have come from classical comedies, in which conniving servants were often the most entertaining characters. Jonson created for himself a distinctive literary voice by using villains such as Volpone to carry his moral ideas; in *The Alchemist*, he exploited the same tension with equal success.

The Alchemist • Samuel Taylor Coleridge ranked the plot of *The Alchemist* among the three best in literature, along with those of Sophocles' *Oidipous Tyrannos* (c. 429 B.C.E.; *Oedipus Tyrannus*, 1715) and Henry Fielding's *Tom Jones* (1749). Like *Volpone*, the play is about people pretending to be what they are not. *The Alchemist*, however, goes a step further: Its characters seek to be transformed, to be made over into new people. The three characters who gull the others operate out of a house, and as in *Volpone*, the victims are brought to the house for fleecing. In contrast to the action of *Volpone*, however, the action of *The Alchemist* remains tightly focused on the house; society at large comes to the Blackfriars' house to be duped and cheated. Jeremy, the butler, goes by various names—usually Face, the conspirator. When his master leaves on a trip, he takes in Subtle, a down-on-his-luck swindler, and Doll Common, a prostitute. There is little pretense of a noble alliance, as in *Volpone*; these are criminals whose ignoble characters are never in doubt, although they, like their victims, aspire to become what they are not.

Part of the genius of the play is the fooling of the victimizers even as they prey on their victims. Doll Common plays the Queen of Faery for the stupid Dapper and a noblewoman for Sir Epicure Mammon. She throws herself into her roles with the hope that she will become—not simply pretend to be—a lady of noble character. Subtle forgets his recent destitution and begins to believe in his ability to transmute human character, even if his alchemical tricks cannot change matter. Face retains some sense of proportion as he shifts from one role to another, but even he hopes to become the important man in society that he cannot be while he remains a butler. These three quarrelsome rogues are laughable, but they also carry Jonson's moral freight: One must know oneself before a change in character is possible. All except the house's master, Lovewit, hope to be what they are not yet cannot change because they do not know themselves.

Dapper is a clerk who hopes to be a successful gambler; he hopes that Subtle, who poses as an alchemist, will be able to guarantee him good luck. Drugger is a silly shopkeeper who wants a guarantee of good business. Kastril is a country squire who wishes to become an urban wit. His sister, Dame Pliant, is an empty-headed, wealthy widow whose beautiful body hides an almost nonexistent personality. Tribulation, Wholesome, and Ananias are hypocritical Puritans who hope that Subtle will give them the philosophers' stone—which is reputed to have great alchemical powers to transmute—so that they will be able to rule the world. Sir Epicure Mammon (regarded by many critics as one of Jonson's greatest dramatic creations), egotistical and blind to his own weaknesses, wants the philosophers' stone so that he can become a kind of Volpone, ruling a materialistic realm in which he would be wonderful in his generosity and terrible in his appetites. Mammon is already living a fantasy, and he needs little encouragement from Subtle, Face, and Doll Common. The victims are motivated by greed and lust; their desires dictate the nature of their cozening.

The fun is in the increasingly complex machinations of the resourceful schemers. The satire is in the social roles of the victims, who range from clerk and shopkeeper to religious leader and gentleman. By the play's end, Surly, the friend of Mammon, has tried to reveal the schemers for what they are, but only Pliant believes him, and she believes whatever she is told. Mammon is in ardent pursuit of a prostitute in whom he sees noble ancestry; Wholesome and his aide Ananias are fearful of losing their chance to transform the world; Dapper is bound, gagged, and locked in a closet; and Subtle and Face are hopping from one deceit to another in order to keep their schemes balanced. Their small world is based on false understandings of self; no one understands who he really is. The hilarious confusion ends when Lovewit returns home and refuses to be fooled by Face's explanations.

Some critics argue that Lovewit is every bit as deluded as the other characters. They argue that the world of *The Alchemist* remains disordered at the play's finish. Yet Lovewit seems to see through Face's lies and games; he seems to know perfectly well what he is doing when he takes Pliant and her fortune for himself. While his remark to Face, "I will be rul'd by thee in any thing," can be taken to mean that master has yielded to servant, which would be a representation of disorder, it is more likely that Lovewit is expressing gratitude for the deliverance to him of Pliant, as his subsequent remarks suggest. He puts Face back in his place as servant; he puts Kastril in his proper place as his brother-in-law; and he handles the officers of the law and Tribulation and Mammon with confidence. He is in command of the problems created by Face, Subtle, and Doll Common almost from the moment he enters his home. Given the moral themes of the play, Lovewit's commanding presence provides a satisfying conclusion by showing a character who knows himself bringing order to the chaos brought on by fools.

Epicœne • Between *Volpone* and *The Alchemist,* Jonson wrote *Epicœne,* and after *The Alchemist* he wrote *Bartholomew Fair* and *The Devil Is an Ass.* The last-named work is an amusing play but not one of Jonson's best. The other two, however, rank among his most successful comedies. Unlike *Volpone* and *The Alchemist,* they involve broad social milieus. *Volpone* and *The Alchemist* present tight little worlds that parody reality; Volpone and Mosca rule theirs at the shrine of gold; Subtle, Face, and Doll Common are minor deities in the world encompassed by their house. In both plays, the outer world intrudes only to resolve their plots. In *Epicœne* and *Bartholomew Fair*, the larger world of Jacobean society appears on the stage.

Epicœne was written for a theatrical company made up entirely of boys, and the central conceit of the play turns on that aspect of its first performance, much as Shakespeare's *As You Like It* (pr. c. 1599-1600) has the young man playing Rosalind, a woman, pretend to be a woman pretending to be a man pretending to be a woman. Jonson's trick is to have Epicœne, played by a boy, turn out at play's end to be a boy. As in his other great comedies, false pretenses form one of the play's major themes. The duping of Morose, who loathes noise, draws in braggarts, pretentious women, and urbane wits. Coarse language, persistent lying, and brutality are revealed as the underlying traits of the supposedly refined and sophisticated members of polite society. In addition, Jonson calls into question the validity of sexual roles; Epicœne is called everything from the ideal woman to an Amazon—the boy who plays her fits easily into the society of women and is readily accepted by women until revealed as a boy.

Bartholomew Fair • *Bartholomew Fair* also deals in disguises and confused identities but is more cheerful than Jonson's other great comedies. The setting of a fair encourages varied action and characters, and Jonson evokes the robust nature of the fair by providing vigorous action and scenes that would be typical of the fairs of his day. The character Ursula is representative of the fair: She is the pig-woman, the operator of a stall that sells roast pig. Big, loud, and sweaty, she embodies the earthiness of the fair, which is noisy and hot with crowding people. The language of the characters is coarse, and they often use vulgarities. The effect is one of down-to-earth good humor and the happy-ending plot. This effect contrasts with *Epicœne*, which also features grossly vulgar language; its characters are supposedly refined, but they reflect their gutter minds in gutter language. Instead of being down-to-earth, much of the humor seems dirty.

Other major works

POETRY: *Poems*, 1601; *Epigrams*, 1616; *The Forest*, 1616; *Underwoods*, 1640.

NONFICTION: *The English Grammar*, 1640; *Timber: Or, Discoveries Made upon Men and Matter*, 1641.

TRANSLATION: *Horace His Art of Poetry*, 1640.

MISCELLANEOUS: *The Workes of Benjamin Jonson*, 1616; *The Works of Benjamin Jonson*, 1640-1641 (2 volumes).

Bibliography

Butler, Martin, ed. *Re-presenting Ben Jonson: Text, History, Performance*. New York: St. Martin's Press, 1999. An examination of the theater in the time of Jonson as well as of his works. Bibliography and index.

Cave, Richard, Elizabeth Schafer, and Brian Woolland, eds. *Ben Jonson and Theatre: Performance, Practice, and Theory*. New York: Routledge, 1999. A collection of essays dealing with the dramatic works of Jonson and the English theater of his time. Bibliography and index.

Dutton, Richard, ed. *Ben Jonson*. Longman Critical Readers. Harlow, England: Pearson Education, 2000. This study presents critical analysis and interpretation of Jonson's literary works. Bibliography and index.

Evans, Robert C., ed. *Ben Jonson's Major Plays: Summaries of Modern Monographs*. West Cornwall, Conn.: Locust Hill Press, 2000. A reference work containing abstracts and bibliographies of materials by and concerning Jonson. Bibliography and index.

Harp, Richard, and Stanley Stewart, eds. *The Cambridge Companion to Ben Jonson.* New York: Cambridge University Press, 2000. A companion to the playwright and his works.

Haynes, Jonathan. *The Social Relations of Jonson's Theatre.* New York: Cambridge University Press, 1992. A look at Jonson's dramatic works with emphasis on his political and social views. Bibliography and index.

Loxley, James. *The Complete Critical Guide to Ben Jonson.* New York: Routledge, 2002. A handbook designed to provide readers with critical analysis of Jonson's works. Bibliography and index.

Martin, Mathew R. *Between Theater and Philosophy: Skepticism in the Major City Comedies of Ben Jonson and Thomas Middleton.* Newark: University of Delaware Press, 2001. An examination of the dramatic works of Jonson and Thomas Middleton, with regard to their use of comedy. Bibliography and index.

Sanders, Julie. *Ben Jonson's Theatrical Republics.* New York: St. Martin's Press, 1998. An analysis of the political and social views of Jonson as they were manifested in his dramatic works. Bibliography and index.

Summers, Claude J., and Ted-Larry Pebworth. *Ben Jonson Revisited.* Rev. ed. Boston: Twayne, 1999. Though this book covers Jonson's nondramatic writings as well as his plays, it is an excellent starting point for understanding his drama. Each major play receives a full analysis, and Jonson's entire canon is placed in the context of its time. Bibliography and index.

Kirk H. Beetz,
updated by John R. Holmes

Tony Kushner

Born: New York, New York; July 16, 1956

Principal drama • *Yes Yes No No*, pr. 1985, pb. 1987 (children's play); *A Bright Room Called Day*, pr., pb. 1987; *Hydriotaphia: Or, The Death of Dr. Brown*, pr. 1987, pb. 2000; *Stella*, pr. 1987 (adaptation of Johann Wolfgang von Goethe's play); *The Illusion*, pr. 1988, pb. 1992 (adaptation of Pierre Corneille's play *L'Illusion comique*); *Widows*, pr. 1991 (with Ariel Dorfman; adaptation of Dorfman's novel); *Angels in America: A Gay Fantasia on National Themes (Part One: Millennium Approaches)*, pr. 1991, pb. 1992; *Angels in America: A Gay Fantasia on National Themes (Part Two: Perestroika)*, pr. 1992, pb. 1993, revised pb. 1996; *The Good Person of Setzuan*, pr. 1994 (adaptation of Bertolt Brecht's play); *Slavs! (Thinking About the Longstanding Problems of Virtue and Happiness)*, pr. 1994, pb. 1995; *A Dybbuk: Or, Between Two Worlds*, pr. 1997, pb. 1998 (adaptation of S. Ansky's play *The Dybbuk*); *Terminating: Or, Lass meine Schmerzen nicht verloren sein, Or, Ambivalence*, pr., pb. 1998 (adaptation of William Shakespeare's sonnet 75); *Death and Taxes: Hydriotaphia and Other Plays*, pb. 2000 (includes *Reverse Transcription*, *Hydriotaphia*, *G. David Schine in Hell*, *Notes on Akiba*, *Terminating*, and *East Coast Ode to Howard Jarvis*); *Homebody/Kabul*, pr. 2001, pb. 2002

Other literary forms • Tony Kushner is primarily known for his plays, although he has written a children's book, *Brundibar* (2002), and his thoughts are collected in *Tony Kushner in Conversation* (1998), edited by Robert Vorlicky.

Achievements • Tony Kushner won directing fellowships from the National Endowment of the Arts in 1985, 1987, and 1993. He received a playwriting fellowship from the New York State Council for the Arts in 1987. Kushner won the John Whiting Award from the Arts Council of Great Britain in 1990. Kushner's other awards include the Kennedy Center/ American Express New American Play Award in 1992 and the Will Glickham playwriting prize in 1992. *Angels in America* earned Kushner a Pulitzer Prize, two Tony Awards, two Drama Desk Awards, the *Evening Standard* Award, two Laurence Olivier Award Nominations, the New York Critics Circle Award, the Los Angeles Drama Critics Circle Award, and the Lambda Liberty Award for Drama.

In 1998, London's National Theatre selected *Angels in America* as one of the ten best plays of the twentieth century. Kushner's plays have been produced in more than thirty countries around the world and at the Mark Taper Forum, the New York Shakespeare Festival, New York Theatre Workshop, Hartford Stage Company, Berkeley Repertory Theatre, and the Los Angeles Theatre Center.

Biography • Tony Kushner was born in New York City in 1956, but the family soon moved to Lake Charles, Louisiana, so his parents, classical musicians, could pursue professional opportunities there. From an early age, Kushner's parents encouraged him to participate in music, literature, and the performing arts. Kushner's mother was also an actress, and he vividly recalls seeing his mother perform when he was only four or five years old, which made a powerful impression on him and probably inspired him to pursue a life in theater. His artistic and literary interests, his Jewish background, and his homosexuality set him apart from other children. In an interview with Richard Stayton of the *Los Angeles Times*, Kushner said that he has distinct memories of being gay since he was six. Kushner knew that he felt slightly different from most other boys. By the time he was eleven, Kushner had no doubts about his homosexuality.

However, Kushner kept his sexuality a secret throughout his college education at Columbia University in New York, even undergoing psychotherapy designed to make him heterosexual. Kushner eventually came out, or revealed his sexual orientation, to his family and friends. Coming out as a homosexual became a prominent theme in his writing, and many of his plays depict characters struggling with their sexuality. Kushner received his B.A.

Tony Kushner in 1993 (AP/Wide World Photos)

from Columbia in 1978, where he studied medieval literature, and he pursued an M.F.A. at New York University, where he studied directing. Kushner began working as a switchboard operator before his professional theater career took off with the production of *A Bright Room Called Day* in 1987 and the momentous hit, *Angels in America* in 1991. Kushner has served as an artist-in-residence and director at New York University, Yale, Princeton, the Julliard School of Drama, and at the St. Louis Repertory The ater.

Analysis • Tony Kushner has forged a new reputation as a spokesperson for change and progress during politically conservative times. In the early 1990's, his seven-hour, two-part Broadway production of *Angels in America* transformed him from an unknown gay Jewish activist into the most promising, highly acclaimed playwright of his generation, who insisted on the power of theater to convey important truths. In this work, Kushner is concerned with the moral responsibilities of people during war and politically repressive times. He insists on political messages in all of his plays, opposing the popular notions that Americans do not like politics and that entertainment cannot be political.

Although socialist politics and gay rights are not always mainstream topics, Kushner feels that artists need to be willing to take an issue that they feel passionately about and to address themselves to it extensively to build a consensus among groups. Kushner wants his plays to be part of a large political movement that teaches responsibility, honesty, social justice, and altruism. Kushner's plays are dark and speak about death, but they are full of hope for future change. He does not back away from difficult and unpopular social issues.

A Bright Room Called Day • Kushner's first important play was conceived during President Ronald Reagan's re-election in 1984, but its historical setting is 1932-1933 in the Weimar Republic of Germany before World War II. A close group of friends lose track of each other as they are forced into hiding during Adolf Hitler's rise to power. Kushner attempted to link the politics of Nazi Germany with the conservative Republican administration of Reagan, which caused many critics to complain about Kushner's implicit comparison of Reagan to Hitler, the Nazi totalitarian.

In one version of the play, a contemporary American character, Zillah Katz, moves to Berlin in the recently reunified Germany, where she lives in the apartment of Agnes Eggling, one of the original members of the German friends during World War II. Zillah and Agnes communicate to each other through dreams, though separated by forty years in time, and Zillah is inspired to political activism. Kushner raises the idea that all human actions are political.

Angels in America, Part One • This play initially came to life in a poem that Kushner wrote after finishing graduate studies at New York University. The poem was about gay men, Mormons, and the famous lawyer Roy Cohn. Originally conceived as a ninety-minute comedy, the play blossomed into two parts about the state of the United States and its struggles with sexual, racial, religious, and social issues such as the AIDS (acquired immunodeficiency syndrome) epidemic. *Angels in America* mixes reality and fantasy. Though it is filled with many different characters, Kushner designed *Angels in America* to be performed by eight actors each of whom plays several roles. This groundbreaking play focuses on three households in turmoil: a gay couple, Louis Ironson and Prior Walter, struggling with AIDS; another couple Harper Pitt and Joe Pitt, who is a Morman man coming to terms with his own sexuality; and the high-profile lawyer Roy Cohn, a historical person who died of AIDS in 1986. Cohn denied his homosexuality his whole life and persecuted gays. Cohn also helped Senator Joseph McCarthy persecute suspected members of the Communist Party in the 1950's.

The subtitle *Millennium Approaches* describes the impending doom that the character Prior feels when dealing with the deadly disease AIDS. Prior's illness heightens his sense of a coming apocalypse. Toward the conclusion of the play, a gloriously triumphant angel descends on Prior, rescuing him from death. Prior's lover Louis has abandoned him in cowardly fear of the illness. The angel tells Prior he has been selected to be a prophet: "Greetings, Prophet;/ The Great Work begins:/ The Messenger has arrived." The play's main statement is that the United States' response to the AIDS epidemic has been politicized and ineffective.

Angels in America, Part Two • This play continues the themes of the first part, but is a more somber play, getting its subtitle, *perestroika,* from Soviet president Mikhail Gorbachev's Russian word for the attempt at "restructuring" the nation's economic and social policies. The story of Prior's encounter with the angel continues. The angel tells Prior that God has abandoned his creation and that Prior has been anointed to resist modernity and return the world to the "good old days." Rejecting the authority granted him, Prior tells the angel that he is not a prophet and wants to be left alone to die in peace. Prior journeys to heaven to talk with God. The wondrous being that visited Prior at the end of Part One turns out to personify stagnancy or death, causing Prior to reject his commission. The lawyer Roy Cohn dies, but his spirit makes appearances later in the play, taking on the role of a lawyer for God. Even as he is dying, Roy

Cohn tries to manipulate the system and get special medical attention and trick the ghost of Ethel Rosenberg into singing him a lullaby.

At the play's conclusion, the major characters are gathered around the statue of the Bethesda angel in Central Park, where no water runs in the winter. Prior has been living with AIDS for five years, and he and his friends tell the story of the original fountain of Bethesda: When the millennium comes, everyone suffering in body or spirit who walks through the waters of the fountain will be healed and washed clean of pain. Prior and his friends represent a variety of religious and racial backgrounds and various sexual orientations. Even though the real angels seem incompetent and careless, the friends gathered at the Bethesda fountain represent a positive coalition working together to cure the ills of society. The *perestroika* of the subtitle speaks about the fundamental restructuring necessary in order to confront grave medical, social, and economic issues of the late twentieth century.

Slavs! • This play uses materials from the two-part *Angels* play, and it resembles the earlier play because of its interest in the matrix of social, economic, and political change resulting from the collapse of the Soviet Union. The play portrays the negative effects on people resulting from a lack of coherent leadership. The play begins on a frozen Moscow street in 1985, where two women discuss the failures of Soviet socialism. The character Aleksii Prelapsarianov, borrowed from the second part of *Angels in America*, is called "the world's oldest living Bolshevik" in *Slavs!* Prelapsarianov is concerned that the modern reformers do not have sufficient intellectual principles to guide them: "How are we to proceed without theory? Is it enough to reject the past, is it wise to move forward in this blind fashion, without the cold brilliant light of theory to guide the way?" Kushner makes a statement about the lack of direction in modern times. Socialism looks to the past in order to get the structure of the future, but modern restructuring does not have coherent theory to direct it.

The very last line of the play, "What is to be done?" is asked throughout the play. Despite the failure of communism and the discrediting of socialist theory, the capitalism of the West has failed to find an answer to social and economic injustice. The most emotional statement of this conundrum comes from the lips of Vodya Domik, an eight-year-old mute girl who died as a result of the Chernobyl nuclear reactor meltdown. She regains her voice along with a disheartened vision of the bitter reality of history: "Perhaps it is true that social justice, economic justice, equality, community, an end to master and slave, the withering away of the state: these are desirable but not realizable on the Earth."

A Dybbuk • The play is an adaptation of Sy Ansky's 1920 Yiddish play concerning the marriage of Leah, the daughter of a wealthy man who has pledged her to the son of another wealthy family. Leah experiences anguish and frustration because her true love is a penniless Yeshiva student named Khonen. Leah secretly returns Khonen's passion. When the father formally proclaims the appropriate husband for Leah, Khonen gets revenge by entering Leah's body as a "dybbuk," a Yiddish word meaning "a disturbed spirit" who takes possession of another's body. The father turns in frustration to the revered Rabbi of Miropol for an exorcism. However, the father finds himself under judgment by the rabbinical court. Long ago, the father had promised Leah to Khonen, but his greed blinded him to Leah's true desires when he tried to marry her to a rich young man. In the end, he pays for his vices by giving half of his wealth to the poor. Even the most unintended immoral act can have profound social consequences.

The play tries to foreshadow the forthcoming evils of the Holocaust in the closing epitaph.

Other major works

NONFICTION: *Tony Kushner in Conversation*, 1998 (Robert Vorlicky, editor).
CHILDREN'S LITERATURE: *Brundibar*, 2002 (illustrated by Maurice Sendak).
MISCELLANEOUS: *Thinking About the Longstanding Problems of Virtue and Happiness: Essays, a Play, Two Poems, and a Prayer*, 1995.

Bibliography

Bras, Per K. *Essays on Kushner's Angels*. Winnipeg, Canada: Blizzard Publishing, 1996. This collection of essays and an interview with the playwright discuss the impact of productions of *Angels in America* in regions and nations outside the United States, including Scandinavia, England, and Australia.
Fisher, James. *The Theater of Tony Kushner: Living Past Hope*. London: Routledge, 2001. A complete study of Kushner's work, Fisher's work covers all full-length, one-act, and adapted works by this Pulitzer Prize-winning dramatist. Fisher argues that Kushner is unusual among American playwrights because he believes that all theater is political. His plays explore the moral, social, religious, and political questions that shape the future of the United States in the world community.
Geis, Deborah R., and Steven F. Kruger. *Approaching the Millennium: Essays on "Angels in America."* Ann Arbor: University of Michigan Press, 1997. The book is divided into sections on Ronald Reagan's America and politics, identities in *Angels*, Kushner's theater, and *Angels* in performance contexts.
Osborn, M. Elizabeth, Terrence McNally, and Lanford Wilson. *The Way We Live Now: American Plays and the AIDS Crisis*. New York: Theatre Communications Group, 1990. Plays by a variety of contemporary playwrights including Susan Sontag, Harvey Fierstein, and Kushner demonstrate how the performing arts community has been devastated by the AIDS crisis.

Jonathan L. Thorndike

Pär Lagerkvist

Born: Växjö, Sweden; May 23, 1891
Died: Lidingö, Sweden; July 11, 1974

Principal drama • *Sista mänskan*, pb. 1917; *Den svåra stunden*, pr., pb. 1918 (*The Difficult Hour, I-III*, 1966); *Himlens hemlighet*, pb. 1919, pr. 1921 (*The Secret of Heaven*, 1966); *Den osynlige*, pb. 1923, pr. 1924; *Han som fick leva om sitt liv*, pr., pb. 1928 (*The Man Who Lived His Life Over*, 1971); *Konungen*, pb. 1932, pr. 1950 (*The King*, 1966); *Bödeln*, pb. 1933, pr. 1934 (adaptation of his novella; *The Hangman*, 1966); *Mannen utan själ*, pb. 1936, pr. 1938 (*The Man Without a Soul*, 1944); *Seger i mörker*, pb. 1939, pr. 1940; *Midsommardröm i fattighuset*, pr., pb. 1941 (*Midsummer Dream in the Workhouse*, 1953); *De vises sten*, pb. 1947, pr. 1948 (*The Philosopher's Stone*, 1966); *Låt människan leva*, pr., pb. 1949 (*Let Man Live*, 1951); *Barabbas*, pr., pb. 1953 (adaptation of his novel); *Dramatik*, pb. 1956 (3 volumes)

Other literary forms • Pär Lagerkvist is, outside Sweden, best known as a novelist. In his own country, he is highly esteemed both as a poet and as a novelist and is ranked second only to August Strindberg in Swedish drama (excluding the cinema). He is also the author of essays on drama, literature, and painting; prose poems; sketches; travel essays; and many short stories.

Achievements • As a Scandinavian playwright, Pär Lagerkvist now belongs to a triumvirate that includes Henrik Ibsen and August Strindberg. Thomas Buckman, the translator of seven of Lagerkvist's plays and of his essay on modern theater, recognizes him as having introduced "a new spirit of modernism" into drama. The scholar Alrik Gustafson, who was a friend and frequent guest of Lagerkvist, observed in 1951 that "Lagerkvist has placed his stamp so firmly on Swedish literary culture that a recent Scandinavian writes: 'If Swedish literature after 1914 may be expressed by a single name, that name must without question be Pär Lagerkvist.'" One may perhaps expect high praise from Scandinavians and from professors of Scandinavian studies, and indeed Martin Seymour-Smith, insisting that "Scandinavians overvalue their literature," says that "no better example of this habit could be found than in the vastly inflated reputation of Lagerkvist" and adds that in expressionist drama "his example has been disastrous."

This somewhat peevish appraisal is at least explicit on the magnitude of Lagerkvist's influence. For better or worse, Lagerkvist has been a real force in modern Swedish drama and literature. Richard B. Vowles, a critic of Lagerkvist's fiction, has written, fairly and noncommittally, "Between 1912 and 1918 he largely established the expressionist direction of Swedish modernism." It would be difficult to deny that Sweden's renowned film director Ingmar Bergman followed this direction. "Lagerkvist," according to Peter Cowie in his 1982 biography of Bergman, "is the only twentieth century Swedish artist whose religious preoccupations are on a par with Bergman's."

Lagerkvist's theme of the need for faith in a world unable to make proper provision for it is, again according to Cowie, "crucial to Bergman's films of the fifties, and in particular *The Seventh Seal* and *The Virgin Spring*." In his much-quoted praise of the novel

Barabbas (1950; English translation, 1951), which was subsequently dramatized, André Gide wrote, "It is the measure of Lagerkvist's success that he has managed so admirably to maintain his balance on a tightrope which stretches across the dark abyss that lies between the world of reality and the world of faith." Gide's statement may serve as a summary of the tension that informs Lagerkvist's drama; it is also evidence that appreciation of Lagerkvist is not limited to Scandinavia or to academe.

In the Scandinavian triumvirate there is, generally, in Ibsen a movement from psychological realism to symbolic naturalism, in Strindberg a movement from psychological naturalism to symbolic expressionism, and in Lagerkvist a movement from Strindbergian expressionism to metaphysical cubism. "Metaphysical" and "cubist" are terms that have become commonplace in Lagerkvist criticism. Others are visionary, anguished, spiritual, uncompromising, and honest. The term "moral" also appears in such criticism.

Lagerkvist's morality proved to be as unconventional as his religion (he identified himself as a religious atheist). In his work, simplistic notions of good and evil give way to the moral tension between love and evil, with "good" and "bad" being understood as functional opposites: Subject to moral tension, the individual becomes good *at*, or bad *at*, being a human (*människa*). The Lagerkvistian individual determines his own character, or ethical identity, by resolving this tension from within, by finding the kingdom of God, not in an external heaven or a prescriptive tradition but within the self. Existentialists would call this anguished search a quest for authenticity and an ethical imperative.

In his book *On Moral Fiction* (1978), John Gardner, attesting Lagerkvist's achievements as novelist and poet (to which must be added playwright), declared: "We have seen in recent years a few great novelists and poets like Pär Lagerkvist, who have interested themselves not only in the anguish of the social moment but also in a larger or at least more enduring problem: metaphysical anguish."

Biography • Pär Fabian Lagerkvist displayed his predisposition to independence in his very first appearance in print, a letter to the local newspaper in October, 1905, written when he was fourteen:

> Every schoolboy is surely aware of the hostility that exists, not only in Växiö but in other cities as well, between elementary- and secondary-school pupils. This hostility may appear to be insignificant, but it certainly is not; it is nothing other than the beginning of a pernicious class hatred in Sweden. For how easily does a boy from elementary school, who during his entire schooling grows accustomed to harboring the same hostility toward a secondary-school pupil that the socialists harbor toward the upper social classes, how easily does such a boy fall victim to pernicious socialism. Conversely, a secondary-school pupil can easily begin to hate not only the elementary-school students but also, when he is older and more mature, all members of the working class. Therefore, comrades, let's begin to lay aside this bad habit and rather try, in harmony, to further the best interests of our country. [*signed*] *A schoolboy.*

In five to seven years' time, Lagerkvist would become sufficiently amenable to socialism to lend his creative talents to the Social Democratic journals *Fram*, *Stormklockan*, and *Norskensflamman*.

Thirteen months after his debut in the local newspaper, he published a prose sketch entitled "Moderskärlek" and signed "Jagibus." It is a sentimental piece with a trace of

(© The Nobel Foundation)

bitterness over the emigration to the United States of which Småland had seen much during the last half of the nineteenth century.

The burgeoning of Lagerkvist's literary career coincides with the development of cubism from 1907 to 1914. In 1909 and 1910 he published thirteen poems under the pen name "Stig Stigson." The first work published in his own name was the poem "Kväll" ("Evening"), written in February, 1911, in honor of the poet Gustaf Fröding, who had recently died. In 1912, he published seven new poems, a copy of two hitherto unpublished Strindberg letters that he had discovered, a prose fantasy entitled "Gudstanken" ("God's Thought"), and his first novel, *Människor* (people).

Many of Lagerkvist's early works, particularly his poems, have a militant socialist focus that would give way by 1916 to his broader humanistic expressions of *längtan* (longing), *ångest* (anguish), and *kärlek* (love). Adumbrations of his plays and later novels are evident in "God's Thought," in which a Diana figure (to reappear in a 1960 novel), as a vestige of a dead religion, serves to turn a man toward the experience of his own being and, consequently, away from preoccupation with the supernatural, and in a 1912 poem, "Min Gud" ("My God"), which begins, "My god is a proud, defiant man/ — —my god is a child gone astray," asserts midway, "My god is what life has given me/ to mold into worship and belief," and concludes, "my god—my god—: he is I!—he is I!— — —."

Lagerkvist's maternal grandparents had been farm people, severely uncompromising in their fundamentalist religion. In their presence, Lagerkvist learned the cold terror of a religion of judgment. His father, Anders Johan Lagerkvist, a foreman at a railroad yard, and his mother, née Johanna Blad, were devout Christians, but their persuasion was marked more by the solace of the Gospel than by the rigidity of the Law. Ultimately, Lagerkvist abandoned the faith of both his grandparents and his parents.

In 1913, Lagerkvist published three poems and two prose sketches in *Stormklockan*, to which he also contributed twelve reviews, including his review of Fyodor Dostoevski's *Unizhennye i oskorblyonnye* (1861; *The Insulted and Injured*, 1887). His review article on Guillaume Apollinaire's *Les Peintres cubistes: Méditations esthétiques* (1913; *The Cubist Painters: Esthetic Meditations*, 1944) appeared in *Svenska dagbladet*. He also published that year *Två sagor om livet* (two tales of life, a pair of short stories) and his very important essay *Ordkonst och bildkonst* (*Literary Art and Pictorial Art*, 1982), which established his championship of cubism and helped to change the literary climate in Sweden. He saw cubism as greatly superior to impressionism and naturalism and developed the suggestion that the literary artist would do well to adhere to the mathematical technique and the structural principles of the cubist painter.

Lagerkvist passed his student-examination in Växjö at the age of nineteen, entitling him to wear the white *studentmössa* (student-cap), indicative of his eligibility for university study. He entered Uppsala University in 1911 but gave it up after a single term. *Människor* includes passages expressive of his dissatisfaction with student life. He carried on his studies independently. During the first half of 1913, he was in Paris, carefully appraising the theories and methods of French painting, particularly expressionism, Fauvism, and, as noted, cubism.

He lived in Denmark during World War I and recorded his bitter but lyric lament over the waste and inhumanity of war in *Järn och människor* (iron and men), a collection of five short stories published in 1915. In the next year, his first collection of poems appeared under the title of the poem that opens the collection, *Ångest*. The title, translated as "anguish," denotes a painfully intellectual emotion. Lagerkvist's first major renditions of the theme coincided with his residence in the country of Søren Kierkegaard, who had defined the existentialist concept of *ångest* as "a sympathetic antipathy and an antipathetic sympathy."

Lagerkvist developed a presentation of *ångest* as an intensified consciousness of *längtan* (longing). *Längtan* is common to both innocence (ignorance) and loss of innocence (awareness); it is in the loss of innocence that *längtan* becomes *ångest*. Both Lagerkvist and Kierkegaard see spirit as an intellectual emotion, as the imaginative awareness that is at once the source, the sustenance, and the identity of "anguish"; both see it as a synthesis of body and soul, a synthesis that spirit itself effects when it awakens from its own dream. Lagerkvist's *längtan* is Kierkegaard's *Aand . . . drømmende* (spirit . . . dreaming).

It was during this period in Denmark that Lagerkvist added to his independent curriculum a thoroughgoing study of drama. He concluded that modern theater, like modern literature, was seriously oppressed by naturalism; in "Modern teater: Synpunkter och angrepp" (1918; "Modern Theatre: Points of View and Attack," 1966), he criticized contemporary drama as vigorously as he had criticized contemporary literature in *Literary Art and Pictorial Art*, and his suggestion for its rejuvenation was much the same as the one he had made for literature—chiefly, mathematical construction and an application of the principles of cubist painting. He berated the naturalistic theater for its failure to express the time in which people were currently living, a time greatly in need of giving adequate expression to its *ångest*.

His first play, *Sista mänskan* (the last man), was published in 1917. Like his first novel, it was patently expressionistic, depressingly informed by the imagery of darkness, and presumably a failure. Lagerkvist never permitted any reprinting of *Människor*, and while he did not object to reprintings of *Sista mänskan*, he seems never to have sought or encouraged its production once he had achieved success with his subsequent plays. The number of plays he wrote is relatively small, thirteen in the thirty-six years from 1917 through 1953, with two of these being adaptations from his prose fiction. He published no dramatic works during the last twenty-one years of his life. The film production of his *Barabbas* in 1962 was essentially the work of others. Ibsen, having written twice that many plays in fifty-one years, remained active as a playwright until only seven years before his death. Strindberg, who wrote his last play only three years before his death, had completed forty-six plays in, at most, thirty-seven years.

By the time Lagerkvist had written his second and third plays, his second comprising three one-act plays and his third being a one-act play, he had succeeded August Brunius, his good friend and the author of the foreword to *Literary Art and Pictorial Art*, as art and drama critic for *Svenska dagbladet*. During 1918-1919, he wrote forty-six reviews for the newspaper. In 1922 he collected his thoughts on innocence, awareness, and spirit and wrote them down in "Myten om människorna" (the myth of humankind). This work deals with the beginning, as *Sista mänskan* deals with the end, of humankind. Only a fragment of it has been published. By 1925, Lagerkvist was well established as a significant figure in Swedish literature. In 1928, having successfully worked in all the literary genres that mark his canon, he received the prestigious literary prize awarded by Samfundet De Nio (The Committee of Nine).

Lagerkvist's most challenging works during the next decade were *Bödeln* (1933; *The Hangman*, 1936) and *Den knutna näven* (1934; *The Clenched Fist*, 1982), the latter written in conjuction with his travels to Greece and Palestine. In these works, he measures *ångest* against the problem of evil with which he had struggled in *Sista mänskan* and which he had elucidated in his collection of short stories *Onda sagor* (1924; evil tales). *The Hangman* is a lyric comment on the brutalism of fascist sovereignty; more important, it develops in sympathetic antipathy the theme of the necessity and persistence of evil. The subject is expanded in lyric essays in *The Clenched Fist* as Lagerkvist elaborates his version of Friedrich Nietzsche's Apollonian and Dionysian duality.

Unlike Nietzsche, Lagerkvist limits these motifs almost exclusively to morality, yet, like Nietzsche, he recognizes the positive and negative forces in each and the great dangers resulting from the ascendance of either one over the other. These themes receive masterful treatment in the novel *Dvärgen* (1944; *The Dwarf*, 1945) with its Apollonian artist-scientist Messer Bernardo, its Dionysian dwarf Piccoline, and its theme of inherent human evil.

Four years before publication of *The Dwarf*, Lagerkvist had succeeded to the chair of the deceased Verner von Heidenstam as a duly elected member of the Swedish Academy of Literature, that body of "immortals" that selects the winners of the Nobel Prize in Literature. Lagerkvist was himself nominated for the Nobel Prize in 1950, the year in which he published his novel *Barabbas*. André Gide had won the prize in 1947, T. S. Eliot in 1948. The 1949 prize was held over to 1950, the year of Lagerkvist's nomination; it was won by William Faulkner, for whom it is said Lagerkvist had cast his ballot, and the 1950 prize was awarded to Bertrand Russell. The 1951 prize was awarded to Pär Lagerkvist, the Uppsala University dropout who had received an honorary Ph.D. from the University of Gothenburg in 1941 and whose works became the subject of study at Uppsala. Lagerkvist's speech at the Nobel Prize ceremonies consisted of the aforementioned fragment from his 1922 composition "Myten om människorna."

From 1951 until his death in 1974, Lagerkvist published only six works—his ninth and last volume of poetry and five short novels. In 1977, his daughter Elin Lagerkvist published *Antecknat*, a collection of his notes, jottings, and diary entries, dating from 1906, and seven previously unpublished poems.

Analysis • *Ångest* is a subject that does not lend itself to comedy readily. Even the comedian Woody Allen had to move from farce to the seriocomic and serious in order to accommodate his attention to his Manhattanesque angst. Pär Lagerkvist's brooding seriousness—the Swedish word for it is *grubbel*—is rarely relieved in his work by a light touch or a comic lift. None of his plays is a comedy. Those that are not tragedies, or tragic, are, at their most positive level, hauntingly melancholy.

Sista mänskan • A good approach to his first play, *Sista mänskan*, is to see its world as the terminus of the world brought into being in "Myten om människorna," which begins, "Once upon a time there was a world." In "Myten om människorna," a man and a woman come to this world for a short visit. They make a home. The husband hunts and tills the soil. The wife bears three sons. One evening she tells her children about the other worlds she knows. When the youngest son dies, it is understood that he has gone to another world. The man and his wife grow old. After they die, their surviving sons feel great relief. Unbothered by further contemplation of other worlds, the two young men joyously go out to take possession of the earth, on which human life is burgeoning.

From this paradisiacal setting, Lagerkvist has excluded a creator and for the visit of Lucifer has substituted the event of death. The Adam and Eve of this myth have come from a heavenly realm where all was clear, bright, and glorious and where their love for each other was taken for granted. On earth, their love could not be taken for granted. It was a miracle, infinitely precious because it could not last. In their love and in their life on earth, they lost their knowledge of Heaven; it became a mystery. When the woman told her sons about the other world, she could not remember enough to satisfy her youngest, who, quite unlike his brothers, yearned for Heaven. In his yearning, he withers and dies, while his brothers revel in life on earth. There are two ideas expressed here. The first is that the price of earthly life is ignorance of Heaven; its corollary is that in the human presumption to know a no longer knowable Heaven, earthly life is wasted. The divinity of the other world separates the individual from the divinity within the self in proportion as the self yearns for the other world. The second idea is that loss of innocence is the price of human love and of the awakening of spirit in the physical consummation of that love.

The two ideas constitute the lesson that has not been learned in *Sista mänskan*, in which earth's last humans struggle for survival in the cold and the encroaching darkness of a world whose sun is dying. Adam and Eve have become Gama, a blind man, and Vyr, mother of a young boy named Ilja. Present also are a paralytic, a cripple, a leper, a redhead, old women, the last humans, the dead, and a chorus of suppliants. In the past, which is to say in the course of human history, Gama had raped Vyr, who in turn blinded him while he slept and then went off to live alone and bear and rear the son she had conceived. Blind Gama returns and attempts to love Vyr and her son without at first knowing that Vyr is the former victim of his lust and that Ilja is his son. Vyr desperately needs Gama's love, and Ilja hungers for the knowledge of what love is.

Gama and Vyr fall in love, but when Gama learns who Vyr is and that she was the one who blinded him, he strangles her. Ilja loses his desire to live and sinks to the ground. Gama, losing his sanity, calls out his son's name and sinks to the ground. In this short three-act play, Lagerkvist's pessimism is at its peak: He offers no hope that humankind will learn, not the meaning, but the lesson of life—namely, the need to stabilize evil by means of love. The meaning of life is something for each individual to determine through apprehending the divinity within the self.

Sista mänskan is Lagerkvist's expressionistic attempt to sustain what he considers to be Strindberg's rebellious renaissance in theatrical art. In "Modern Theatre," the 1918 essay in which he extols Strindberg's dramaturgy and condemns what he sees as Ibsen's tediously formalistic naturalism, Lagerkvist insists that modern theater should be true to its time, and he makes a statement that could pass for a description of the *mise en scène* of *The Last Man*: "At this time everything is torn apart, at loose ends, harsh, contradictory, with light and darkness irreconcilably opposed. And we must live within what encompasses us, in the time that is our own, feeling our way about in it and trying to understand."

The Difficult Hour, I-III • The expressionistic chiaroscuro of *Sista mänskan* is retained in *The Difficult Hour, I-III*, a more successful theatrical encounter with the lesson of life. The "difficult hour" is that critical moment at which life passes into death. Each of the one-act plays in this trilogy of death shows an individual—respectively, a young man, an old man, and a boy—learning the lesson of life during the moment in which he learns that he is dead. Although *The Difficult Hour, I-III* comprises three plays, it is a dramatic unit with a progressive lessening of the difficulty of the critical moment: The young man dies screaming in remorseful confusion; the old man dies in resignation; and the boy dies with full acceptance of his fate. Lagerkvist uses the image of physical deformity to symbolize human imperfection and limitation: a blind man, a paralytic, a cripple, and a leper in *Sista mänskan*; a hunchback and a dwarf in *The Difficult Hour, I-III*.

The Secret of Heaven • In the one-act play *The Secret of Heaven*, there is a blind man, a cripple, and a dwarf. Fate is represented by a man in tights who pulls the heads off dolls as indiscriminately as the spinning Parcae broke the threads of human lives. Religion takes the form of a man wearing a yarmulke who claims to understand everything except God. God appears, as he appears in the novella *Det eviga leendet* (1920; *The Eternal Smile*, 1934), in the person of an old man sawing wood. A young man asks the old woodsman for the meaning of everything and is told that meaning consists in the fact that everything whirls around (*Allting snurrar runt*). Later, when the young man receives the same answer from the man in the yarmulke, who adds a note of determinism by saying that everything must whirl around (*allting ska snurra runt*), he leaps into the void, screaming in frustration. The play's setting, which also reappears in *The Eternal Smile*, is Heaven, or eternity, wherein only God, darkness, and the dead are to be found.

Den osynlige • *Sista mänskan* and *The Difficult Hour, I-III* both exhibit what Wylie Sypher has called "cubist simultaneous perspective" in that both view human existence from the coextensive and intersecting planes of life and death and against the irreconcilable forces of light and darkness. In the three acts of his fourth play, *Den osynlige* (the invisible one), light and darkness are reconciled as the complements of a dualism. Like Aeschylus's *Oresteia* (458 B.C.E.; English translation, 1777), which discloses the mean between light and darkness and not the elimination of darkness in favor of light to be the proper object of human seeking, the play begins in darkness, wherein the voice of the Invisible One is heard, and ends in light, with the Invisible One identifying himself as *människoanden* (the human spirit), predicting his victory over and survival of Death, and dismissing Death.

The refrain of the play's third act is "God is dead." When Death asks the Invisible One if he is God, he says, "No, God is dead," and asserts that he, the human spirit, is alive. Two limited forces, tyranny and rebellion, personified respectively as the Administrator and the Hero, both come to an end: The Administrator is struck down by the Invisible One, and the Hero is mortally wounded in fighting for his beliefs. Death and the human spirit remain as the forces of opposition, which, in a type of Zoroastrian dualism, make the world go round, or ensure that everything whirls around. The Invisible One does emerge as God, not the eternal and external woodcutter, but the divinity resident in the heart of each human being.

The Man Who Lived His Life Over • *The Man Who Lived His Life Over* begins with a voice in darkness telling a dead man named Daniel that he may live again. Daniel is restored to his youth and his shoemaker's trade and determines that his second life will be the right one. It proves to be quite as bad as the first because again Daniel expects life, or God, to conform to his own true and unique identity. Daniel cannot really live, he can only exist because, looking for life to live him, he fails to make his life his own. The voice from the darkness proves to have been Death. God, as the human spirit, appears at the beginning of Daniel's second life in the form of an alcoholic man with a wooden leg who sells shoelaces. His name is Boman (Home-man or Living-man). He teaches Daniel how to make one's life one's own, but Daniel does not learn the lesson.

In his first life, Daniel had followed the dictates of passion—a course that led him to prison, convicted of the murder of a disreputable woman who flouted his desire. In his second life, he becomes a slave to conventional morality and drives his youngest son to suicide by refusing to let him carry on with the woman he loves, a woman of loose morals. The two lives are presented in simultaneity and from the simultaneous perspectives of a fantastic premise and a realistic setting, as Lagerkvist's cubism here supersedes his expressionism.

All three acts of *The Man Who Lived His Life Over* reverberate with the call for existentialist authenticity. In the first act, for example, Daniel tells Boman that "we live out something that has been thrown to us"; Boman quite agrees and is pleased with Daniel's insight into what Martin Heidegger had termed *Geworfenheit* (throwness) and adds that this thrown life "somehow becomes our own," that "we get used to it, and it becomes, so to speak, our self."

The King • Lagerkvist's sixth play, *The King*, in three acts, is a mythic drama concerning the ritual of a king's being reduced to beggary for one day, during which a member of the lowest class, in this case a criminal, rules as king. The criminal-king instigates a rebellion of his class against the upper classes and with its success assumes permanent power. The real king, as a member of the rebel horde, has been killed. Apart from its mythic information, the play is entirely conventional in structure and development. The image of deformity is retained, this time in a king's fool who is hunchbacked and a dwarf. The theme of authenticity is worked out as both the real king and the criminal-king realize their true selves in their changed roles. Historically, the play reflects the proletarian and God-is-dead movements: The new king commends a young man, whose life he has spared, for vowing to serve humankind after he, the king, has declared, "There are no divine laws any more." Stylistically, the play shares the simplicity and spareness of Lagerkvist's later narrative fiction.

The Hangman • A long one-act play adapted from his novella of the same title, *The Hangman* (also known as *The Executioner*), shows Lagerkvist at the peak of his talent as a dramatist. The play begins in a medieval tavern that later becomes a modern nightclub and the scene of a race riot with Nazi-like whites shooting and killing members of a black jazz band. There are three separate tableaux, each implicating the executioner, as a figure of evil, in an act of love. In the first, he lets a boy drink from his hand and thereby frees the boy from a curse. In the second, he saves the life of a woman whom he is to behead by marrying her and loving her. In the last, he presides over the Crucifixion of Christ, who calls him brother; the executioner then calls out that God is dead and that he himself is the living Christ whose task it has always been and always will be to shed blood as the means of relieving humankind of its burden of guilt.

The image of deformity is limited to blindness in *The Hangman* and, except for Deaf Anna in *Midsummer Dream in the Workhouse*, in Lagerkvist's last six plays. In two of those last six plays, *Seger i mörker* (victory in the dark) and *Barabbas*, there is not even a blind person, but both plays sustain and intensify Lagerkvist's expression of anguish at human blindness to human values.

The Man Without a Soul • *The Man Without a Soul* and *Seger i mörker*, in, respectively, five acts and four acts, are political dramas reminiscent of the Spanish civil war and other European events of the late 1930's. The man without a soul is the unfeeling murderer of a member of the political opposition. He enters into a relationship with a woman whom he learns is the mistress of the man he has killed. The knowledge of his evil coupled with his experience of love for the woman gives birth to his soul, or his authenticity, as the woman gives birth to her former lover's son. The woman dies in childbirth. The man, sentenced to death for deserting his comrades, dies in soul-birth as he goes to his execution in a flood of light with head uplifted.

Seger i mörker • *Seger i mörker* follows the mythic device of rival brothers. Robert Grant, stepbrother to Gabriel Fontan, the premier of a democratic government, conspires to overthrow the government and install a military dictatorship. He succeeds, but Gabriel gains a victory of the spirit as he, having been unfaithful to his wife, Stella, is reconciled with her before both are to be executed. They reaffirm their love and their faith in the political ideals they have shared. Robert, distraught over Stella's refusal to be spared, remains alone in the cell from which the husband and wife have been led to the firing squad, collapses on hearing the salvo, and crawls about like an animal as the sounds of airplanes and bombs draw ominously nearer and nearer. The darkness enshrouding Robert's victory is the darkness of the jungle.

Both these political dramas are as dramaturgically conventional and as formal as any of Ibsen's plays. The same is true of *The Philosopher's Stone*. At the same time, all three maintain and intensify Lagerkvist's constant themes of light and darkness, love and evil, individual authenticity, and the divinity of the human spirit. He reverts to Strindbergian expressionism in *Midsummer Dream in the Workhouse* and *Let Man Live*, but only as he nears the end of working his vein of drama.

Midsummer Dream in the Workhouse • *Midsummer Dream in the Workhouse*, with *The Difficult Hour, I-III, The Man Who Lived His Life Over*, and *The Hangman*, is the most successful of Lagerkvist's plays. *Midsummer Dream in the Workhouse* is a dream play in which Blind Jonas creates an imaginary world for a young Cecilia and manages to inhabit that world himself. If this play were to have an epigraph, it would be the words of Boman in *The Man Who Lived His Life Over*:

> Yes, we live as well as we can . . . this hard, hard life . . . we endure it . . . drag ourselves through it . . . day by day, year after year . . . as well as we are able to. . . . And we have our dreams, we have our dreams! Have you thought about that? Oh, there is generosity, there is generosity. . . . And we have our dreams.

Gustafson has written that in this play "Lagerkvist experiments with a strange blend of delicate dream elements and a coarse realism of situation and dialogue to produce a dramatic fantasy of haunting beauty."

The Philosopher's Stone • *The Philosopher's Stone* (literally, "the wise men's stone"; the pun on alchemy and the Magi of the New Testament is lost in translation) is Lagerkvist's longest play. Its four acts are somewhat marred by passages of awkward exposition and unengaging, lengthy dialogue. Albertus is an alchemist with faith in science but without religious faith. His wife, Maria, is a devout Christian. His friend Simonides is a dedicated rabbi, whose son Jacob wants to marry Albertus's daughter Catherine. Neither father approves of the marriage, which does not take place. Instead, Jacob is executed for killing a constable from whose hands he sought to rescue Catherine. Simonides and his followers are expelled from their ghetto. Catherine, to her mother's joy, decides to become a nun. Albertus lets the fire in his laboratory oven go out. Neither Albertus, obsessed with his chemical search for gold, nor Maria and Simonides, obsessed with their respective gods, foster the human love that Catherine and Jacob wished to consummate. Science and religion are not at odds in this play, although initially they seem to be. Actually, they prove to be unwitting coconspirators against the human spirit.

Let Man Live • From the conventional format of *The Philosopher's Stone*, Lagerkvist turns to a one-act recitative in *Let Man Live*. There are fourteen speakers: Judas Iscariot, who committed suicide, and thirteen who were executed: Richard, a seventeen-year-old radio operator killed while working for the underground; Joe, a black man who wanted to be a jazz saxophonist and who was lynched on suspicion of having danced with a white woman; Comtesse de la Roche-Montfaucon; a serf caught stealing meat; a witch who had had sexual intercourse with Satan; Giordano Bruno; an Inca chief killed by Christians; Jeanne d'Arc; Paolo and Francesca; a Christian martyr; Jesus; and Socrates. Each of the speakers addresses the audience directly and attests fidelity to his or her true self: Each has died as the price of having lived authentically. The plotless recitative ends with Paolo and Francesca calling on the audience to let humankind live. The work has been called an oratorio; it is also something of an oral chaconne.

Barabbas • Lagerkvist's dramatization of his novel *Barabbas* is cast in two acts, each divided into five scenes. The play opens and closes with a prospect of the three crosses on Golgotha. *Barabbas* is the story of an evil man redeemed by his authentic desire for a faith that he cannot achieve or understand and for a love that he cannot experience. At the end of both the novel and the play, Barabbas goes to his death physically with, but psychologically apart from, the Christians, whose Lord is love. Of the filmed *Barabbas*, it may be said that many of the scenes—the crucifixions, the eclipse of the sun, the copper-mine episode—and the character of Sahak are evocative of effects of Lagerkvist's novel and play, but such excesses as the needlessly complex scenario and the transformation of Barabbas into a gladiator are inconsistent with Lagerkvist's dark simplicity.

In the play *Barabbas*, the physical and psychological chiaroscuro and the titular character's groping for love do much to evoke the effects of *Sista mänskan*, but with *Barabbas*, Lagerkvist seems to have realized his intention with regard to those effects and seems also to have satisfied himself that he has done what he set out as a playwright to do. In *Sista mänskan*, there is this note on *Seger i mörker*: "Love is the one essential thing. All the other things are side effects. They have their importance as props—but love is the play itself." This note may be equivalent to a summary of Lagerkvist's intention as a playwright.

Other major works

LONG FICTION: *Människor*, 1912 (novella); *Det eviga leendet*, 1920 (novella; *The Eternal Smile*, 1934); *Gäst hos verkligheten*, 1925 (novella; *Guest of Reality*, 1936); *Bödeln*, 1933 (novella; *The Hangman*, 1936); *Dvärgen*, 1944 (*The Dwarf*, 1945); *Barabbas*, 1950 (English translation, 1951); *Sibyllan*, 1956 (*The Sibyl*, 1958); *Ahasverus död*, 1960 (*The Death of Ahasuerus*, 1962); *Pilgrim på havet*, 1962 (*Pilgrim at Sea*, 1964); *Det heliga landet*, 1964 (*The Holy Land*, 1966); *Pilgrimen*, 1966 (collective title for previous 3 novels); *Mariamne*, 1967 (*Herod and Mariamne*, 1968).

SHORT FICTION: *Två sagor om livet*, 1913; *Järn och människor*, 1915; *Onda sagor*, 1924; *Kämpande ande*, 1930; *I den tiden*, 1935; *The Eternal Smile and Other Stories*, 1954; *The Marriage Feast and Other Stories*, 1955; *Prosa I-V*, 1956; *The Eternal Smile: Three Stories*, 1971.

POETRY: *Ångest*, 1916; *Den lyckliges väg*, 1921; *Hjärtats sånger*, 1926; *Vid lägereld*, 1932; *Genius*, 1937; *Sång och strid*, 1940; *Dikter*, 1941; *Hemmet och stjärnan*, 1942; *Aftonland*, 1953 (*Evening Land*, 1975).

NONFICTION: *Ordkonst och bildkonst*, 1913 (*Literary Art and Pictorial Art*, 1982); *Teater*, 1918; "Modern teater: Synpunkter och angrepp," 1918 ("Modern Theatre: Points of View and Attack," 1966); *Det besegrade livet*, 1927; *Den knutna näven*, 1934 (*The Clenched Fist*, 1982); *Den befriade människan*, 1939; *Antecknat*, 1977.

MISCELLANEOUS: *Motiv*, 1914 (poetry, essays, and prose sketches); *Kaos*, 1919 (poetry and the play *The Secret of Heaven*); *Modern Theatre: Seven Plays and an Essay*, 1966; *Five Early Works*, 1989.

Bibliography

Scobbie, Irene. *Pär Lagerkvist: Gäst hos verkligheten.* 2d ed. Hull: Orton and Holmes, 1976. A study of Lagerkvist that focuses on his novel, *Guest of Reality.* Provides insights into the drama. Bibliography.

_____, ed. *Aspects of Modern Swedish Literature.* Rev. ed. Chester Springs, Pa.: Dufour Editions, 1999. Contains an in-depth study of Lagerkvist, among other writers.

Sjöberg, Leif. *Pär Lagerkvist.* New York: Columbia University Press, 1976. A study that combines biographical information on Lagerkvist with criticism of his works. Bibliography and index.

Spector, Robert Donald. *Pär Lagerkvist.* New York: Twayne, 1973. A basic biography of Lagerkvist that covers his life and works. Bibliography.

Warme, Lars G. *A History of Swedish Literature.* Lincoln: University of Nebraska Press, 1996. A scholarly study of Swedish literature that covers significant writers such as Lagerkvist.

White, Ray Lewis. *Pär Lagerkvist in America.* Atlantic Highlands, N.J.: Humanities Press, 1979. A look at the appreciation for Lagerkvist in the United States. Bibliography.

Roy Arthur Swanson

Carson McCullers

Born: Columbus, Georgia; February 19, 1917
Died: Nyack, New York; September 29, 1967

Principal drama • *The Member of the Wedding*, pr. 1950, pb. 1951 (adaptation of her novel); *The Square Root of Wonderful*, pr. 1957, pb. 1958

Other literary forms • Carson McCullers will be remembered primarily as a writer of fiction who experimented, with varying degrees of success, in the genres of drama, poetry, and the essay. She was one of the foremost of the remarkable generation of southern women writers who, in addition to McCullers, included Flannery O'Connor, Eudora Welty, and Katherine Anne Porter. With her fellow women writers, and with such southern male writers as William Faulkner, Truman Capote, and Tennessee Williams, McCullers shares an uncanny talent for capturing the grotesque. Her fictional world is peopled with the freaks of society: the physically handicapped, the emotionally disturbed, the alienated, the disenfranchised. This preoccupation with the bizarre earned for her a major place in the literary tradition known as the "southern gothic," a phrase used to describe the writers mentioned above and others who use gothic techniques and sensibilities in describing the South of the twentieth century.

Few have created a fictional South as successfully as has McCullers in her best fiction. Hers is a small-town South of mills and factories, of barren main streets lined with sad little shops and cafés, of intolerable summer heat and oppressive boredom. In her first and perhaps best novel, *The Heart Is a Lonely Hunter* (1940), she portrays a small southern town from the points of view of five of its residents: Mick Kelly, the confused adolescent heroine; Doctor Copeland, an embittered black physician whose youthful idealism has been destroyed; Jake Blount, an alcoholic drifter with Marxist leanings; Biff Brannon, the sexually disturbed owner of the café, where much of the novel's action takes place; and John Singer, the deaf-mute whose kindness, patience, and humanity to the other characters provide the moral center of the novel.

The themes of *The Heart Is a Lonely Hunter* are ones that McCullers never completely abandoned in her subsequent fiction and drama: the loneliness and isolation inherent in the human condition, the impossibility of complete reciprocity in a love relationship, the social injustice of a racially segregated South, and adolescence as a time of horrifying emotional and sexual confusion. In *Reflections in a Golden Eye* (1941), she explored sexual tension and jealousy among the denizens of a southern army post. *The Member of the Wedding* (1946), the novel she later adapted into the successful play of the same title, treats the delicate symbiotic relationship between a lonely adolescent girl, her seven-year-old cousin, and a black domestic. *The Ballad of the Sad Café*, first published in *Harper's Bazaar* in 1943 and later in a collection of McCullers's short works, is justifiably called one of the finest pieces of short fiction in American literature. It deals with another bizarre triangle, this one involving a masculine, sexually frigid, small-town heiress; her cousin, a hunchback dwarf; and her former husband, a worthless former convict with an old score to settle.

The four works of fiction mentioned above guarantee McCullers a permanent place among American writers of World War II and the postwar era. She also published more than a dozen short stories, most of which are not specifically set in the South. The best of them—"Wunderkind" (1936) and "A Tree. A Rock. A Cloud." (1942), for example—are proficiently executed exercises that demonstrate the sure control and balance so crucial to McCullers's longer fiction.

McCullers also wrote critical essays that betray a deep emotional and technical understanding of imaginative literature. Her small body of poetry, heavily influenced by the seventeenth century Metaphysicals, is consistently interesting. After McCullers's death, her sister, Margarita G. Smith, collected her previously uncollected short fiction, her literary criticism, and her poetry and essays in *The Mortgaged Heart* (1971).

Achievements • Carson McCullers's reputation as a playwright rests solely on the phenomenal success of one play, *The Member of the Wedding*, which she based on her novel of the same title. Her only other play, *The Square Root of Wonderful*, was a critical and popular failure and a professional disappointment from which McCullers never quite recovered. The very critics and theatergoers who hailed McCullers as a brilliant innovator in 1950 turned their backs on her in 1958. Flawed and uneven as her theatrical career was, however, McCullers deserves a special place among modern American playwrights, not only for what she achieved but also for what she attempted. With her friend Tennessee Williams, she was one of the first American playwrights to parlay a fragile, moody, nearly static vision of human frailty into solid commercial theater.

No one was more surprised by the success of *The Member of the Wedding* than McCullers herself. She had seen but a handful of plays in her life when Williams, with whom she was spending the summer of 1946 on Nantucket, suggested that she turn her novel into a play. Excited by the idea of writing in a new and unfamiliar genre and intrigued by Williams's sense that the novel had strong dramatic possibilities, McCullers spent that June calmly and steadily composing a draft of the play. Across the dining room table from her sat Williams, who was working on *Summer and Smoke*—it was the only time either of them was able to work with anyone else in the room. Despite Williams's willingness to help, McCullers steadfastly rejected her friend's advice, following instead her own creative instincts.

Though all odds were against it, the play was an immediate success when it opened on Broadway in January, 1950. Audiences gave the cast standing ovations, and the critics almost unanimously praised the work's grace, beauty, and timing. In the spring, *The Member of the Wedding* won two Donaldson Awards—as the best play of the season and as the best first Broadway play by an author—and the New York Drama Critics Circle Award for Best Play. McCullers was named Best Playwright of the Year and given a gold medal by the Theatre Club. *The Member of the Wedding* ran for 501 performances and grossed more than one million dollars on Broadway before enjoying a successful national tour.

This great acclaim, remarkable enough for a more conventional drama, is even more remarkable when one considers that *The Member of the Wedding* is a "mood play," dependent on emotion and feeling rather than on a standard plot. All three acts take place on one deliberately confining set, and much of the play's significant action happens offstage, "between acts," as it were. Indeed, even while praising the play, reviewers questioned whether it was a genuine drama at all. Like Williams's *The Glass Menagerie* (pr. 1944) and Arthur Miller's *Death of a Salesman* (pr. 1949)—significantly, the only two plays Carson McCullers had seen produced on Broadway before writing her hit–*The Member of the Wedding* is a play that subordinates plot to characterization, action to

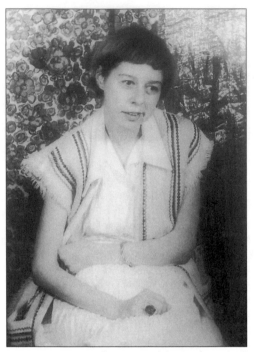

Carson McCullers in 1959 (Library of Congress)

the almost poetic accretion of psychic detail. That audiences would even sit through, let alone cheer, such a slow-moving piece of drama was a revelation to the theater world of 1950.

The success of *The Member of the Wedding* solved McCullers's chronic financial problems and earned for her a reputation as a gifted and innovative dramatist, but seven years of ill health and personal tragedy ensued before her next play, *The Square Root of Wonderful*, opened on Broadway in October, 1957. Plagued from the outset by personnel changes and by McCullers's incompetence at the kind of last-minute rewriting required by the theater, the play failed almost immediately. Neither McCullers nor director Jose Quintero could do anything to save it, and it closed after only forty-five performances. The disaster of *The Square Root of Wonderful* left McCullers severely depressed, so anxious had she been to repeat the triumph of *The Member of the Wedding*. Various physical ailments by then made it difficult for her to write at all, and she never again attempted writing for the theater.

Biography • Carson McCullers's life was one beset by serious illnesses and complex personal relationships. The last twenty years of her life were spent in the shadow of constant physical pain, but like her fellow southerner Flannery O'Connor, she continued working in spite of her handicaps, seldom complaining. She was married twice to the same man, an emotional cripple who drained her financially and psychically and who ultimately killed himself. That she left behind her a magnificent body of work and any number of devoted friends when she died at the tragically young age of fifty is a testament to the courage with which overwhelming obstacles can be overcome.

McCullers knew at first hand the small-town South that figures so prominently in her best writing. As the eldest of the three children of Lamar and Marguerite (Waters) Smith, Lula Carson Smith spent a normal middle-class childhood in the racially segregated mill town of Columbus, Georgia. Her father, like Mr. Kelly in *The Heart Is a Lonely Hunter* and Mr. Addams in *The Member of the Wedding*, was a jeweler who spent much of his time at work. Her mother, a lively, cultured woman and a strong influence throughout McCullers's life, encouraged her daughter's intellectual and artistic pursuits. By the age of fourteen, Carson Smith had dropped the Lula from her name and had announced her intention to become a concert pianist. She was by then practicing the piano several hours a day and taking lessons from Mary Tucker, the wife of an army colonel stationed at nearby Fort Benning. Her complex relationship with the Tucker family, at once giving her a sense of belonging and of estrangement, was later to provide material for the triangle theme of *The Member of the Wedding.* Like her heroine Frankie Addams, McCullers was fond of writing plays, casting them with family and friends, and staging them in her living room.

By the time she was graduated from high school, McCullers had already privately decided to become a writer rather than a musician. Inspired by the Russian realists and by the plays of Eugene O'Neill, McCullers had already tried her hand at both drama and fiction. The seventeen-year-old McCullers set out for New York City in September, 1934, with vague plans both to study music at the Juilliard School of Music and to study creative writing at Columbia University. By February, 1935, she had enrolled at Columbia, and the following September she enrolled in Sylvia Chatfield Bates's writing class at New York University.

During the summer of 1935, while she was vacationing in Georgia, a mutual friend introduced her to James Reeves McCullers, an army corporal stationed at Fort Benning. Reeves McCullers, like Carson, was interested in a career in letters. That he had neither the motivation nor the talent that enabled Carson to become a successful author was to be the source of much friction between them and a contributing factor to Reeves's eventual mental collapse. In 1936, Reeves left the army to join Carson in New York, and in September of 1937, they were married in the Smith home in Columbus.

By this time, McCullers had begun to undergo the cycles of illness and creativity that would characterize the rest of her life. Fatigued by the hectic pace of New York, she was forced to return to Georgia from time to time for peace and quiet, but her writing career had also taken off. Whit Burnett, with whom she had worked at Columbia, had published her story "Wunderkind" in the December, 1936, issue of his magazine *Story,* and she had begun to outline the plot of what would become her first novel, *The Heart Is a Lonely Hunter.* In the spring of 1939, while she was living with Reeves in Fayetteville, North Carolina, "The Mute" (as the novel was then called) was accepted by Houghton Mifflin. By autumn, she had completed a second manuscript, "Army Post" (later published as *Reflections in a Golden Eye*).

McCullers had long before vowed that when she would become a famous author, she would make New York her home. Feeling stifled in the South, their marriage in trouble, the McCullerses moved to New York only a few days after the publication of *The Heart Is a Lonely Hunter,* in June, 1940. The move, however, did nothing to improve their relationship. Carson, a sudden celebrity, was being courted by the literary world and making distinguished friends, among them W. H. Auden. That summer, as recipient of a fellowship to the Bread Loaf Writers Conference in Middlebury, Vermont, she came to know Wallace Stegner, Louis Untermeyer, and Eudora Welty.

It was not only Carson's increasing fame and Reeves's continued obscurity that placed stress on their relationship. Both were sexually naïve at the time of their marriage, and both were given to infatuations with members of their own sex. Though most of their homosexual relationships remained unconsummated, Carson's crush on the brilliant young Swiss emigrant Annemarie Clarac-Schwarzenbach was difficult for Reeves to tolerate. In September, 1940, Carson and Reeves separated. They were later divorced, only to remarry in 1945 when Reeves returned from action in World War II. For the rest of Reeves's life, they were to be alternately separated and reconciled. Their long and stormy relationship was ended only by Reeves's suicide in France in 1953.

When she separated from Reeves in the autumn of 1940, Carson accepted an invitation from her friend George Davis to move into a restored brownstone located in Brooklyn Heights. On establishing residence at 7 Middagh Street, she found herself in the midst of an unusual experiment in group housing; it later came to be known as February House. Besides her and Davis, the inhabitants included W. H. Auden, the striptease artist Gypsy Rose Lee, and, later, the composer Benjamin Britten and the writer Richard Wright and his family. McCullers made her home in this strange household intermittently for the next five years. When not traveling abroad, resting in Georgia, or spending time at Yaddo, the artists' colony in upstate New York, she played hostess in Brooklyn Heights to a distinguished group of celebrities from the literary and entertainment worlds, including Janet Flanner, Christopher Isherwood, Salvador Dalí, and Aaron Copland.

While in Georgia in February, 1941, McCullers suffered a stroke that left her partially blind and unable to walk for weeks. She would be victimized by such attacks for the rest of her life, and even after the first one, she never quite regained the kind of creative fervor of which she had once been capable. She was not to finish her next novel, *The Member of the Wedding*, until 1946, six years after she first started drafting it. Her final novel, *Clock Without Hands*, took her ten years to complete, not appearing until 1961. After 1947, as a result of the second severe stroke in a year, her left side was permanently paralyzed, and even the physical act of sitting at a typewriter was a challenge for her.

McCullers's Broadway career of the 1950's was, as has been noted, a source both of exhilaration and of disappointment for her. Nevertheless, her uneven career as a playwright brought her financial security, greater exposure than she had ever had before, and the fame she had craved since childhood. By the end of her life, she was an international literary celebrity, able to count among her personal friends the English poet Edith Sitwell and the Danish-born writer Isak Dinesen.

In 1958, severely depressed by Reeves's suicide in 1953, her mother's death in 1955, and the failure of her second play, McCullers sought professional psychiatric help from Dr. Mary Mercer, a therapist who was to care for McCullers until the author's death. Through the 1960's, McCullers was progressively less able and willing to leave the Nyack, New York, house that she had bought in 1951. She died there on September 29, 1967, of a cerebral hemorrhage.

Analysis • Though Carson McCullers's reputation as a playwright will never approach her reputation as a writer of fiction, it is her uniqueness in both genres that accounts for both her successes and her failures. Her first play succeeded because it defied conventions of plot and action; her second play failed in part because it too often mixed the modes of tragedy, comedy, and romance. It is no accident that three of her novels have been made into successful films, nor is it accidental that no less a playwright than Edward Albee adapted her novella *The Ballad of the Sad Café* for the stage. McCullers's dramatic sense was in every way original, and both her hit play and her failure demand acceptance on their own terms, quite apart from the whims of current theatrical convention and popular tastes.

The Member of the Wedding • Like the novel from which it was adapted, *The Member of the Wedding*, McCullers's first play, is a masterpiece of timing, mood, and character delineation. Insofar as there is a plot, it can be summarized as follows: Somewhere in the South, twelve-year-old Frankie Addams, a rebellious loner and a tomboy, secretly longs to belong to a group. Rejected by the girls at school, having recently lost her best friend, Frankie has no one to talk to except Berenice Sadie Brown, the black woman who cooks for Frankie and her father, and a seven-year-old cousin, John

Henry. When she discovers that her brother, Jarvis, is going to be married, Frankie decides to join him and his bride on their honeymoon and make her home with them in nearby Winter Hill, thus becoming once and for all a member—a member of the wedding.

Although Berenice tries to make her come to her senses, Frankie persists in her plan and makes a scene during the ceremony, begging the couple to take her with them. When they refuse, an agonized Frankie vows to run away from home. Sticking her father's pistol into the suitcase that she has already packed for the honeymoon, Frankie does leave, but it is later disclosed that she has spent the night in the alley behind her father's store. Chastened and somewhat resigned, she returns home, admitting that she had thought of committing suicide but then had changed her mind.

By the end of the play, which takes place several months after the wedding, life has changed for all three main characters. John Henry has died of meningitis; Berenice has given notice to Mr. Addams; and Frankie, having largely outgrown the adolescent identity crisis of the previous summer, has acquired a best friend and a beau, both of whom she had earlier hated. Although Frankie is undoubtedly much happier than she was at the beginning of the play, she has become a pretentious teenager, bereft of the poetry and passion of childhood. Berenice has lost not only John Henry but also her foster brother, Honey, who has hanged himself in jail. As the curtain falls on the third act, Berenice is alone onstage, quietly singing "His Eye Is on the Sparrow," the song that she had sung earlier to calm the tortured Frankie.

Most of the "action" of the play takes place offstage and is only later recounted through dialogue. The wedding and Frankie's tantrum occur in the living room of the Addams house, but the scene never moves from the kitchen: The audience is told about the wedding and about Frankie's disgrace by characters who move back and forth between the two rooms. Both Honey's and John Henry's deaths occur between scenes, as does Frankie's night in the alley. By thus deemphasizing dramatic action, McCullers is able to concentrate on the real issue of the play, the relationship among Frankie, Berenice, and John Henry.

By confining the action to one set, the kitchen and backyard of the Addams residence, the author effectively forces the audience to empathize with Frankie's desperate boredom and sense of confinement (and, perhaps, with Berenice's position in society as a black domestic). For much of the play, the three main characters are seated at the kitchen table, and this lack of movement lends the work the sense of paralysis, of inertia, that McCullers learned from the plays of Anton Chekhov and applied to the South of her childhood.

Frankie Addams is one of the most memorable adolescents in literature, at the same time an embodiment of the frustrations and contradictions inherent in adolescence and a strongly individual character. She yearns to belong to a group even as she shouts obscenities and threats to the members of the neighborhood girls' club. She is both masculine and feminine, a tomboy with a boy's haircut and dirty elbows who chooses a painfully vampish gown for her brother's wedding. McCullers skillfully exploits alternately comic and tragic aspects of Frankie's character. The audience must laugh at her histrionic declarations ("I am sick unto death!") but must also experience a strong identification with her sense of vulnerability and isolation ("I feel just exactly like somebody has peeled all the skin off me").

Caught between childhood and womanhood, Frankie is curious about both sexual and spiritual love. She claims to have been asked for a date by a soldier, only to wonder aloud "what you do on dates," and she is still capable of climbing into Berenice's lap to hear a lullaby. Frankie's body is fast maturing, but her emotions are slow in catching up.

Berenice Sadie Brown serves in the play as Frankie's main female role model (Frankie's own mother has died in childbirth), an embodiment of fully realized adult sexuality. As complex a character as Frankie, Berenice is much more than a servant: She is confessor, nurse, and storyteller. At forty-five, Berenice has been married four times but truly loved only her first husband—the remaining three she married in vain attempts to regain the bliss she enjoyed with Ludie Maxwell Freeman. Her search for love closely parallels Frankie's own, and despite their often antagonistic relationship, they share moments of spiritual harmony, as when they discuss the nature of love, a "thing known and not spoken."

Berenice also represents the position of the black in a segregated South; indeed, the issue of racism is very much present in *The Member of the Wedding* (as it is in *The Heart Is a Lonely Hunter* and *Clock Without Hands*), a fact that has often been overlooked by critics of both the novel and the play. Though she is the most influential adult in the world of the two white children, she is treated as a servant by the white adults. Berenice must deal not only with Frankie's growing pains but also with problems ultimately more grave: the funeral of an old black vegetable vendor and the arrest, imprisonment, and suicide of her foster brother, Honey.

Both Berenice and T. T. Williams, her beau, behave noticeably differently around white adults, while Honey, in a sense representative of a new generation of southern African Americans, refuses even to call Mr. Addams "sir." He is eventually jailed for knifing a white bartender who will not serve him. Honey's flight in the third act coincides with Frankie's own. Like Frankie, Honey is rebellious and frustrated, but unlike her, he is unable to find a place for himself in a hostile society. Death for Honey is preferable to confinement in the "nigger hole" or more "bowing and scraping" to white people.

If Honey's death in the third act symbolizes the end of Frankie the rebel, the death of John Henry represents the end of Frankie's childhood. Throughout the play, John Henry acts as a sort of idiot savant, uttering lines of great insight and demanding the plain truth from a hypocritical adult world. He asks Berenice why Mr. Addams has called Honey a nigger, and seems, ironically, incapable of understanding the nature of death. He is a link between Frankie and her childhood, a constant reminder of how recently she played with dolls (he gratefully accepts the doll that Jarvis has given Frankie as a gift after she rejects it). Frankie wants at once to be John Henry's playmate and to outgrow him. Though the transformed Frankie reacts coldly to John Henry's death, Berenice is devastated by it. She truly loved her "little boy," and she blames herself for having ignored his complaints of headaches in the first stages of his disease. John Henry dies a painful death, a victim who has done nothing to deserve his cruel fate.

The Member of the Wedding is a play about growing up, but it is also about the sacrifices that must be made before one can enter the adult world. Frankie is composed and even confident at the end of the play, but she has lost whatever sympathy she had for Berenice. Berenice is severely depressed by two deaths whose logic defies her. John Henry and Honey are dead, and the newlyweds are stationed in occupied Germany. When Berenice is left alone onstage at the end of the third act, holding John Henry's doll and singing a song whose truth the play has seriously questioned, the audience is forced to wonder with her whether the adult world of compromise and responsibility is worth entering.

The Square Root of Wonderful • McCullers stated in the author's preface to the published version of *The Square Root of Wonderful* that the lives and deaths of her mother and her husband in part compelled her to write the play. Marguerite Smith's grace, charm, and love of life emerge in the character of Mollie Lovejoy, while Phillip Lovejoy embodies all the tragic contradictions that led Reeves McCullers to alcoholism and suicide. Like so much of McCullers's work, the play concerns a love triangle: Mollie Lovejoy, who lives on an apple farm in suburban New York with her twelve-year-old son, Paris, has twice been married to Phillip Lovejoy, an alcoholic writer now confined to a sanatorium.

As the play opens, Mollie has only recently met John Tucker, a no-nonsense architect who is determined to wed her. Complications arise when Phillip Lovejoy unexpectedly returns to the farm, intent on a reconciliation with Mollie. His mother and his spinster sister are also on the scene, having come to New York from the South to visit Mollie and Paris and to see Phillip's new play (ironically, a failure).

The relationship between Phillip and Mollie has been a stormy one. The sexual attraction between them remains strong, and they sleep together on the night of Phillip's return, much to the chagrin of John Tucker. Still, Mollie cannot forget the years of drunken abuse she suffered at Phillip's hands. Physical abuse she could tolerate, but she decided to divorce him finally when he humiliated her by telling her that she used clichés. Mollie is clearly in a dilemma. In one of the play's most successful scenes, she admits to Paris that she loves both John and Phillip.

Phillip's problems, however, are manifold and insoluble. Clearly, he wants a reunion with Mollie so that she will protect him, as she once did, from his own self-destructive tendencies. When he at length realizes that Mollie will not return to him and, perhaps more important, that he will never again be able to write, he commits suicide by driving his car into a pond. With Phillip's death, Mollie is free to leave the apple farm and move to New York, and there is every reason to believe that she will eventually marry John Tucker.

Despite its commercial and critical failure, the play is perhaps worthy of more attention than it has received. At its best, it is a meditation on the nature of love. Mollie Lovejoy has always conceived of love as a sort of magic spell that is divorced from logic and free will. Her love for Phillip has brought her as much humiliation as happiness. From John Tucker, she learns that love can also be a matter of choice among mature adults. He uses the language of mathematics in describing his view of love to Paris: For John, humiliation is the square root of sin, while love is the square root of wonderful. The minor characters also provide interesting commentaries on the nature of love. Sister Lovejoy, the spinster librarian, lives in a world of fictional lovers drawn from the pages of books. Mother Lovejoy, while often a comic character, is at bottom a loveless woman who has spent her life humiliating her daughter.

The play's weaknesses, however, are many. The sure sense of timing that characterizes *The Member of the Wedding* is largely absent from *The Square Root of Wonderful*. The shifts in mood are less subtle than in the earlier play, and tragedy often follows too closely on the heels of comedy. The superb early morning scene in which Phillip Lovejoy says goodbye to his son, for example, is too rapidly undercut by a comic scene between Mother and Sister Lovejoy as they discuss Phillip's death. This tragicomic mixture of modes that McCullers executes so well in *The Member of the Wedding* goes awry in *The Square Root of Wonderful*, in part because none of the characters—except, perhaps, Phillip Lovejoy—is carefully enough drawn to elicit an audience's sympathy.

McCullers's best work is set in the South, not in upstate New York farmhouses. Her best work is also fiercely individual, completely defiant of convention and popular tastes. *The Square Root of Wonderful* fails largely because its author, in her eagerness to produce a second Broadway triumph, allowed producers, directors, and script doctors to strip it of the brilliant idiosyncracies that make *The Member of the Wedding* an American classic.

Other major works

LONG FICTION: *The Heart Is a Lonely Hunter*, 1940; *Reflections in a Golden Eye*, 1941; *The Ballad of the Sad Café*, 1943 (serial), 1951 (book); *The Member of the Wedding*, 1946; *Clock Without Hands*, 1961; *Carson McCullers, Complete Novels*, 2001.

SHORT FICTION: *The Ballad of the Sad Café: The Novels and Stories of Carson McCullers*, 1951; *The Ballad of the Sad Café and Collected Short Stories*, 1952, 1955; *The Shorter Novels and Stories of Carson McCullers*, 1972.

CHILDREN'S LITERATURE: *Sweet as a Pickle and Clean as a Pig*, 1964.

MISCELLANEOUS: *The Mortgaged Heart*, 1971 (short fiction, poetry, and essays; Margarita G. Smith, editor).

Bibliography

Bloom, Harold, ed. *Carson McCullers*. New York: Chelsea House, 1986. A collection of essays critically analyzing the works of McCullers. Bibliography and index.

Carr, Virginia Spencer. *The Lonely Hunter: A Biography of Carson McCullers*. New York: Carroll & Graf, 1985. A biography of McCullers that covers her life and work. Bibliography and index.

_____. *Understanding Carson McCullers*. Columbia: University of South Carolina Press, 1990. An examination of the works of McCullers. Bibliography and index.

Clark, Beverly Lyon, and Melvin J. Friedman, eds. *Critical Essays on Carson McCullers*. New York: G. K. Hall, 1996. Selected essays on McCullers that examine her life and work, with emphasis on her southern origins. Bibliography and index.

McDowell, Margaret M. *Carson McCullers*. Boston: Twayne, 1980. An analysis of McCullers's fiction and drama. Contains a brief chronology, a bibliography of works by and about McCullers, and an index.

Rich, Nancy B. *The Flowering Dream: The Historical Saga of Carson McCullers*. Chapel Hill, N.C.: Chapel Hill Press, 1999. An examination of McCullers's work, including her dramas. Bibliography.

Savigneau, Josyane. *Carson McCullers: A Life*. Boston: Houghton Mifflin, 2001. A biography of McCullers, looking at her works and her life, including her southern upbringing. Bibliography and index.

J. D. Daubs,
updated by Katherine Lederer

David Mamet

Born: Chicago, Illinois; November 30, 1947

Principal drama • *Camel*, pr. 1968; *Lakeboat*, pr. 1970, revised pr. 1980, pb. 1981; *Duck Variations*, pr. 1972, pb. 1977; *Sexual Perversity in Chicago*, pr. 1974, pb. 1977; *Squirrels*, pr. 1974, pb. 1982; *American Buffalo*, pr. 1975, pb. 1977; *Reunion*, pr. 1976, pb. 1979; *A Life in the Theatre*, pr., pb. 1977; *The Revenge of the Space Pandas*, pr. 1977, pb. 1978 (one act; children's play); *The Water Engine*, pr. 1977, pb. 1978; *Dark Pony*, pr. 1977, pb. 1979; *The Woods*, pr. 1977, pb. 1979; *Mr. Happiness*, pr., pb. 1978; *Lone Canoe*, pr. 1979 (music and lyrics by Alaric Jans); *The Sanctity of Marriage*, pr. 1979, pb. 1982; *Donny March*, pr. 1981; *The Poet and the Rent*, pr., pb. 1981 (children's play); *A Sermon*, pr., pb. 1981; *Short Plays and Monologues*, pb. 1981; *Edmond*, pr. 1982, pb. 1983; *Glengarry Glen Ross*, pr., pb. 1983; *The Disappearance of the Jews*, pr. 1983, pb. 1987 (one act); *Red River*, pr. 1983 (adaptation of Pierre Laville's play); *Goldberg Street: Short Plays and Monologues*, pb. 1985; *The Shawl*, pr., pb. 1985; *A Collection of Dramatic Sketches and Monologues*, pb. 1985; *Vint*, pr. 1985, pb. 1986 (adaptation of Anton Chekhov's short story); *The Cherry Orchard*, pr., pb. 1986 (adaptation of Chekhov's play); *Three Children's Plays*, pb. 1986; *Three Jewish Plays*, pb. 1987; *Speed-the-Plow*, pr., pb. 1988; *Uncle Vanya*, pr., pb. 1988 (adaptation of Chekhov's play); *Bobby Gould in Hell*, pr. 1989, pb. 1991 (one act); *Three Sisters*, pr., pb. 1990 (adaptation of Chekhov's play); *Oh Hell: Two One-Act Plays*, pb. 1991; *Oleanna*, pr. 1992, pb. 1993; *The Cryptogram*, pr., pb. 1994; *No One Will Be Immune: And Other Plays and Pieces*, pb. 1994; *Plays: One*, pb. 1994; *An Interview*, pr., pb. 1995 (one act); *Plays: Two*, pb. 1996; *Plays: Three*, pb. 1996; *The Old Neighborhood*, pr. 1997, pb. 1998 (includes *The Disappearance of the Jews*, *Jolly*, and *D.*); *Boston Marriage*, pr. 1999, pb. 2001; *Plays: Four*, pb. 2002

Other literary forms • While first and foremost a theatrician, David Mamet has also gained respect for his work in other literary forms. Perhaps Mamet's most popular contributions have been to Hollywood. His screenplays, which include *The Postman Always Rings Twice* (1981), *The Verdict* (1982), *The Untouchables* (1985), *House of Games* (1987), *Things Change* (1988), *Homicide* (1991), *Glengarry Glen Ross* (1992), *The Spanish Prisoner* (1997), *Wag the Dog* (1997), *The Heist* (2001), and *Hannibal* (2001), have been praised for their intriguing plots and monologues of cruelty. Mamet is also an accomplished director. He has directed many of his own best screenplays, from *House of Games* to *Homicide* and *The Spanish Prisoner*. Most scholars point to *House of Games*, with its ritualized forms of expiation, and *Glengarry Glen Ross*, with its dazzling repartee, as his best work in film. Finally, Mamet demonstrates his skill as an essayist in *Writing in Restaurants* (1986), a collection of essays that best spells out the playwright's theory of dramatic art as well as his sense of cultural poetics.

Achievements • David Mamet, winner of a Pulitzer Prize in 1984 (for his play *Glengarry Glen Ross*), two Obie Awards (1976, 1983), and two New York Drama Critics Circle Awards (1977, 1986) among many others, is regarded as a major voice in American drama and cinema. He animates his stage through language, a poetic idiolect that explores the relationship between public issue and private desires—and the effects of this

551

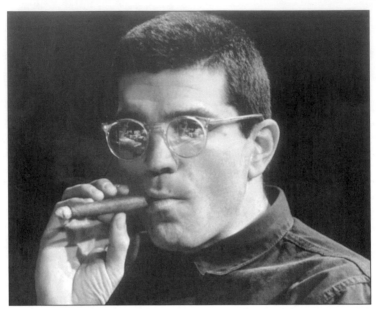

(Bridgitte Lacombe)

relationship on the individual's spirit. He is known for his wit and comedy, but beyond the streetwise dialogues lie more problematic concerns. The typical Mamet play presents the near-complete separation of the individual from genuine relationships. Mamet replicates human commitments and desires in demythicized forms: commodity fetishism, sexual negotiations and exploitations, botched crimes, physical assaults, fraudulent business transactions enacted by petty thieves masquerading as business associates, and human relationships whose only shared features are the presence of sex and the absence of love.

Although Mamet varies his plays in terms of plots and themes, he seems at his best when critiquing what he believes is a business ethic that has led to the corruption of both the social contract and his heroes' moral values. Mamet's major achievements, then, concern his use of language, his social examination of professional and private betrayals and alienation, and his ability to capture the anxieties of the individual—whether he or she is a small-time thief, a working-class person, or a Hollywood executive.

Biography • Born on the South Side of Chicago on November 30, 1947, David Alan Mamet became interested in the theater as a teenager. He worked at the Hull House Theatre and at Second City, one of Chicago's richest improvisational performance sites at the time, experiences that he recognized as having exerted an important influence on his language, characterizations, and plot structures. His mother, Lenore Silver, was a schoolteacher, his father, Bernard Mamet, a labor lawyer and minor semanticist, and though the parents' intellectual awareness of language plainly influenced their son, their divorce seems to have affected the young Mamet even more greatly.

After Mamet was exiled to what he saw as a sterile suburb of Chicago—Olympia Fields, his geographical move seemed all the more complicated because of his familial dislocations. His stepfather apparently (Mamet revealed in a 1992 essay entitled "The Rake") physically and psychologically abused the Mamet family, and it seems as if the world of the theater offered the playwright some form of reprieve and, later, recognition from a tension-filled youth. As a boy, Mamet also acted on television, an opportunity made possible by his uncle, who was the director of broadcasting for the Chicago Board of Rabbis. Mamet often was cast as a Jewish boy plagued by religious self-doubt and concerns.

After graduating from Francis Parker, a private school in downtown Chicago, Mamet attended Goddard College in Plainfield, Vermont, where he majored in theater and literature. At Goddard, he wrote his first play, *Camel*, which fulfilled his thesis requirement for graduation and was staged at the college in 1968. During his junior year (1968-1969), Mamet moved from Plainfield to New York City, where he studied acting at the Neighborhood Playhouse with Sanford Meisner, one of the founding members of the Group Theatre in the 1930's.

While his talents as an actor were minimal at best, Mamet's attention to idiolect and its cadence was greatly enhanced by Meisner. After earning his B.A. in literature in 1969, he worked in a truck factory, a canning plant, and a real estate office, and he labored as an office cleaner, a window washer, and a taxi driver. He also became a drama teacher for a year at the Marlboro College (1970-1971) and, after working at more odd jobs, returned to Goddard College as artist-in-residence (1971-1973). While at Goddard, he formed a group of actors that soon moved to Chicago as the St. Nicholas Theatre Company, for which he served as artistic director. Soon, Mamet's plays became regular fare within the burgeoning theater world in Chicago. Such small but influential theaters as the Body Politic, the Organic Theatre, and then the more established Goodman Theatre presented *Sexual Perversity in Chicago* and *American Buffalo*. In 1974, Mamet became a faculty member on the Illinois Arts Council and a year later a visiting lecturer at the University of Chicago. In 1976-1977, he became a teaching fellow at the Yale School of Drama.

Thus, the mid-1970's were pivotal years for the playwright. In 1975, *American Buffalo* opened at the Goodman Theatre and soon moved to the St. Nicholas Theatre; the play won a Joseph Jefferson Award for Outstanding Production, as did *Sexual Perversity in Chicago* that same year. Moreover, Mamet in 1975 finally saw his work staged in New York City: *Sexual Perversity* and *Duck Variations* opened at the St. Clement's Theatre and, in 1976, moved to the Off-Broadway Cherry Lane Theatre. In 1976, *American Buffalo* opened at the St. Clement's Theatre and Mamet won an Obie Award for *Sexual Perversity in Chicago* and *American Buffalo*.

No fewer than nine Mamet plays appeared in 1977 in theaters in New Haven, New York, Chicago, and, among other cities, London. *American Buffalo*, for which Mamet received the New York Drama Critics Circle Award, premiered on Broadway in 1977, starring Robert Duvall. In 1980, Al Pacino starred in a revival of *American Buffalo* in New Haven. Such successes confirmed Mamet's reputation as a new and vital theatrical voice in the United States.

Mamet has written more than thirty plays, a number of sketches, poetry, essays, children's plays, several important Chekhov adaptations, a book concerning film directing, and more than a dozen screenplays. He has also garnered many awards, including a Pulitzer Prize for *Glengarry Glen Ross* in 1986. Mamet in the 1990's has been honored for his brilliant use of language and characterizations that capture important aspects of American cultural poetics. His play *Oleanna*, which opened at the Orpheum Theatre in New York City in October, 1992, and featured William H. Macy and

Mamet's wife, British-born Rebecca Pidgeon, has only added to the dramatist's reputation for staging serious plays about serious matters.

Analysis • David Mamet is an ethicist. From his initial plays–*Camel, Lakeboat*—to those pivotal works that first brought him notoriety–*Sexual Perversity in Chicago, American Buffalo*—and from *Glengarry Glen Ross* to *Oleanna,* Mamet explores a delicate moral balance between private self-interests and larger public issues that shape modern culture. Indeed, Mamet is at his best when critiquing the tensions between his heroes' sense of public responsibility and their definition of private liberties. Throughout his theater, Mamet presents a dialectic that, on the one hand, recognizes the individual's right to pursue vigorously entrepreneurial interests, but that, on the other, acknowledges that in an ideal world, such private interests should, but do not, exist in equipoise with a civic sense and moral duty. This underlying tension produces in Mamet's protagonists divided loyalties. Such tension also gives his theater its particular unity of vision and ambivalent intensity.

Mamet has often mentioned that his views of the social contract have been greatly influenced by Thorstein Veblen's *The Theory of the Leisure Class* (1899), and such indebtedness in part accounts for Mamet's preoccupation with business as a sacramental world. Veblen's work, like Mamet's, underscores human action and response in terms of "pecuniary emulation," imperialist ownership, primitive sexual roles as first seen in ancient tribal communities, questions of honor, invidious comparisons, and the relationship between self-worth and wealth. Mamet is a theatrician of the ethical precisely because his characters, plots, and themes map out a predatory world in which only the fittest, and surely the greediest, might survive. Hence, Mamet's plays all are concerned with charting the moral relationship between the public issues of the nation and the private anxieties of its citizens.

Mamet seems at his best when dramatizing the way in which public issues, usually in the form of business transactions, permeate the individual's private sensibilities. "Business," for Mamet, becomes an expansive concept, including not only one's public, professional vocation but also one's private, personal existence—the problematic "business" of living itself. Under the guise of healthy competition and the right to pursue a contemporary version of the myth of the American Dream, Mamet's heroes too often conveniently twist such business savvy to suit their own selfish needs. Further, this examination of "business" suggests, for Mamet, that people live in a Macbethean world, where "fair is foul and foul is fair," where sharp business practice too often leads to corruption, where deception and stealing are simply regarded as being competitive within the American business world.

Mamet believes in the powers of the imagination and art to liberate, to create a liberal humanism. This is exactly what John in *A Life in the Theatre* and Karen in *Speed-the-Plow* believe. Such an attitude, however, clearly does not make sense, Mamet also implies throughout his theater, because there is little or no place for such romantic impulses in a hurly-burly business world. What makes Mamet's heroes so theatrically engaging to watch concerns an invisible inner drama, a subtextual crisis that haunts them: Underneath the character's hard-boiled, enameled public bravado lies a figure plagued with self-doubt and insecurities.

If Mamet's heroes try to come to some higher consciousness, as do Don in *American Buffalo*, Aaronow in *Glengarry Glen Ross*, and Karen in *Speed-the-Plow*, such valiant impulses to come to awareness are not ultimately to be realized. Many of Mamet's best characters—Bernie in *Sexual Perversity in Chicago* or Teach in *American Buffalo*—

simply seem unwilling or unable to understand what Mamet believes are the regenerative powers implicit in self-awareness and self-responsibility. Some of his characters— most of the men in *Lakeboat*, for example—do not seem to understand that any form of transcendent consciousness even exists as a possibility. Perhaps this explains why many Mamet heroes lack the capacity to celebrate any experience external to the self.

Typical Mamet heroes seem motivated only in sexual and financial terms, blinding themselves to the larger personal or societal implications of their exploits. To be sure, some Mamet characters exude a deeper awareness, as do the Father and Daughter in *Dark Pony*, Aaronow in *Glengarry Glen Ross*, or Karen in *Speed-the-Plow*. Others, moreover, come tantalizingly close to understanding their own essential self and the reason for their existence in a world of diminished possibilities; Lang in *The Water Engine* and Edmond in *Edmond* possess some degree of self-awareness, ineffectual as such awareness turns out to be for them.

Mamet's works, however, show a grimly deterministic theater in which his heroes are victims. Their victimization stems from outer forces—a ruthless business associate, an opportunistic executive, a petty thief—as well as from inner forces: the failure of self-reliance, the exaggerated claim that proves false, and characters' obsession with money that they will never see and with relationships that will never be fulfilling. Thus, throughout his career, Mamet investigates the relatedness of one's job, sense of fulfillment, and morality. The problem facing his characters, however, is that they struggle (and usually fail) to take responsibility, choosing instead to avoid honest communication or anything that might lead to an authentic encounter. Instead, Mamet's heroes often commit ethically perverse deeds that only further contribute to their own marginalization. In their efforts not to confuse public and private issues, Mamet's characters ironically distort the social contract to such an extent that humane values, communication, and love are reduced to barely felt forces.

Mamet's theater, in sum, repeatedly returns to broader social questions about communication and community. To be sure, not every Mamet drama includes verbal tirades and physical if not psychological violence. *Duck Variations*, *A Life in the Theatre*, *Reunion*, *The Woods*, and *The Shawl*—to cite plays spanning much of Mamet's career— appear as relatively quiet, meditative works whose plots and themes seem more interiorized. On the other hand, the playwright seems most comfortable, and at the height of his aesthetic power, when he replicates anger and betrayal, mystery and assault, and when he deepens social satire into private loss.

From *Sexual Perversity in Chicago* through at least *Speed-the-Plow*, relationships are as ephemeral as they are unsatisfying, and a brutalizing language seems to be an attempt by his heroes to mask, unsuccessfully, their primal insecurities. There are no villains in his theater—only individuals whose world of diminished possibilities and banalities defines and confines them. The detectable optimism found throughout much of *Writing in Restaurants*, a collection of essays that Mamet published in 1986 concerning his theory of art, seldom manifests itself in his theater. In a Mamet play, "things change" (to use the title of a Mamet screenplay), or perhaps things do not change, his characters remaining ossified spirits, divided against the self and the other, against home and their outer world.

Mamet *is* a theatrician of the ethical. His characters, sets, and overall situations, however, map out a predatory world in which genuine communication and authentic love remain distant forces. Hence, Barker's lines in *The Water Engine* ratify, Mamet suggests, the gulf between idea and reality:

And now we leave the Hall of Science, the hub of our Century of Progress Exposition. Science, yes, the greatest force for Good and Evil we possess. The Concrete Poetry of Humankind. Our thoughts, our dreams, our aspirations rendered into practical and useful forms. Our science is our self.

Such practicality, for Mamet, prefigures a kind of spiritual death on both a cultural and an individual level.

Mamet's following observation from *Writing in Restaurants* is hardly surprising: "As the Stoics said, either gods exist or they do not exist. If they exist, then, no doubt, things are unfolding as they should; if they do *not* exist, then why should we be reluctant to depart a world in which there are no gods?" This comment stands as the metaphysical question Mamet raises, and refuses to resolve, in his theater. The resolutions, whatever they may be, are left for the audience to ponder.

Duck Variations • Three early Mamet plays prefigure the issues discussed above. *Duck Variations* concerns Emil Varec and George S. Aronovitz, two men in their sixties sitting on a park bench, whose reflections and constant duologues reveal their attempt to come to terms with their own insignificance in the world. Built on numerous episodes, the play shows that the two men come too close to talking about their own finiteness, and so both replace honest conversation with banal talk, their way of avoiding their fear of death.

Lakeboat • In another early play, *Lakeboat,* Mamet presents life aboard the *T. Harrison,* a ship traveling through the Great Lakes. The men are leading death-in-life existences because their jobs have reduced their lives to deadening routines and habits. Built around fragments of conversation, the play presents ordinary men—Joe, Fred, and Fireman—leading desperate lives. To fill the void, they engage in endless talks that lead to no epiphany; like the ship, they simply sail through their lives.

Sexual Perversity in Chicago • *Sexual Perversity in Chicago* presents thirty-four scenes dealing with sex. The play opens in a singles' bar, where Bernard tells his friend Danny, in graphic detail, about his recent sexual encounter with a woman. Their conversations are carnivalesque dialogues filled with obscenities and dirty jokes. Deb and Joan, the central females in the drama, seem little better off, as Bernard's sexist remarks are matched by Joan's hostile response to Danny. Clearly in this play, Mamet outlines a world in which eros has been defleshed and a fundamental and anxiety-producing loneliness dominates. Near the end of the play, Danny and Bernard stare at women on the beach, and when one does not respond to Danny's coarse remarks, he screams obscenities, which outline the intensity of his frustration and his inability to deal with loss. Sexual encounters, devoid of any genuine love, account for the title and theme of this important work.

American Buffalo • These three earlier plays stand as examples of Mamet's interest in portraying people whose lives have almost been reduced to nothingness, a motif that he continues to refine in *American Buffalo, Glengarry Glen Ross, Speed-the-Plow,* and *Oleanna,* plays that most theatergoers and critics believe represent his best work.

American Buffalo concerns small-time thieves who find a buffalo nickel in Don's junk shop (where the play unwinds), motivating them to rob the man from whom Don supposedly purchased the coin. Don orchestrates the robbery plans, which the younger

Bob, who eats sugar, soda, and drugs, will try to accomplish. Teach, a nervous man with a swagger, insists that he, a man, do the job; Teach cannot believe that Don would let Bob, a boy, try such a robbery.

A long honor-among-thieves conversation ensues, in which Teach's lines brilliantly reflect Mamet's vision, a vision suggesting the extent to which ethics have been devalued and stealing has been elevated to the status of good business savvy. Free enterprise, Teach lectures Don, gives one the freedom "[t]o embark on Any . . . Course that he sees fit. . . . In order to secure his honest chance to make a profit." He quickly adds that this does not make him "a Commie" and that the "country's *founded* on this, Don. You know this."

The robbery never takes place, but near midnight, Bob returns with another buffalo nickel. Don seems embarrassed, and Teach becomes agitated, hitting the boy several times. Bob reveals that he bought the coveted nickel, made up the story about a rich coin collector, and suggested the burglary. Suddenly, whatever friendships exist among the men temporarily evaporate: Teach attacks Bob and trashes the entire junk shop. A precarious friendship, however, still remains. The play ends when Teach regains his composure and readies himself to take the injured Bob to the hospital; Bob and Don exchange apologies, and the curtain falls. If the characters do not realize how much they have buffaloed one another, the audience certainly does.

Glengarry Glen Ross • *Glengarry Glen Ross* extends Mamet's preoccupation with business as a sacramental world. The play dramatizes the high-pressure real estate profession as seen through the plight of small-time salesmen. Greed lies at the center of the play, for the characters' directing force in life is to secure sales leads, to close deals with clients, and to rise to the top of the board, the chart announcing which man in the sales force wins the ultimate prize—the Cadillac. The losers will simply be fired.

Glengarry Glen Ross, like *The Water Engine, Mr. Happiness,* and *American Buffalo,* relies on the myth of the American Dream as its ideological backdrop. The title refers to Florida swamps, not the Scottish Highlands, which indicates just how much the playwright wishes to make experience ironic in this drama. Whereas the characters in *Lakeboat, Reunion,* and even *The Shawl* lead lives of quiet desperation, those in *Glengarry Glen Ross* scream out two hours of obscenity-laced dialogue. Levene may be the most desperate, for his business failures of late lead him to crime: Through a Pinteresque unfolding of events, viewers learn that he robs his own office to secure precious sales leads. Moss is the most ruthless, masterminding the robbery while Aaronow simply seems bewildered by his cohorts' cheating. Williamson is the office manager, whose lack of sales experience and pettiness earn him the scorn of all. Ricky Roma, however, is different.

Roma emerges as the star of the sales team. He also appears as the most complex. Youthful, handsome, Roma exudes a certain panache that sets him apart from the others. Whereas the others talk about their past conquests and how, with luck (and deception), they will rise to the top of the sales board, Roma produces. If Levene and Moss radiate a frenetic pursuit of customers, Roma appears soft edged. Roma, indeed, nearly succeeds in swindling an unsuspecting customer, James Lingk, who nearly gets locked into buying suspect real estate. Ironically, Williamson reveals to Lingk the truth, and Roma loses his prized commission when Lingk cancels the deal. When Roma hears this, he screams obscenities at Williamson and adds: "You just cost me six thousand dollars. (*Pause.*) Six thousand dollars. And one Cadillac."

More than losing a sale, Roma loses what ethical perspective, if any, he possesses.

Roma cannot comprehend this. Like Levene and Moss, Roma has no conscience, no sense of the boundaries of business ethics. Like the characters throughout Mamet's theater, Roma and his colleagues distort language and action to justify their work. The play ends with Levene's arrest; Mamet suggests that, after Levene's and perhaps Moss's arrests, life will go on, business as usual.

Speed-the-Plow • *Speed-the-Plow* extends Mamet's business plays. Set in Hollywood, the play centers on Bobby Gould, the recently promoted head of production for a Hollywood film company, and Charlie Fox, a friend who shows him a "buddy prison" film script. They sense a hit because of a macho star who will fill the lead role. In a dialogue that by now is regarded as vintage Mamet, the two celebrate their future fame and money (that surely will be certified by casting the macho star in the film) through a litany of obscenities.

The plot thickens when they have to read a serious novel for cinematic possibilities and when a temporary secretary, Karen, enters and Charlie bets five hundred dollars to see if Bobby can seduce her. Karen, however, preaches the truth to Bobby ("Is it a good film?" she asks), who decides to replace the "buddy prison" script with a film based on a novel on radiation. An outraged Charlie verbally and physically assaults Bobby when he hears this and rages at Karen. After Karen says that she would not have gone to bed with Bobby, Charlie throws Karen out, and he and Bobby become friends again and produce the banal "buddy" film. A lack of trust animates this play, in which these Hollywood men are the spiritual kin of the men in *American Buffalo* and *Glengarry Glen Ross.*

Oleanna • *Oleanna*, a play that in part concerns sexual harassment, represents the playwright's response to the Anita F. Hill-Clarence Thomas controversy. In act 1, a male college professor, John, and a female student, Carol, are in his office, she there because of difficulties in understanding his class. John, who is under tenure review, offers to help. The complacent professor, who is happily married and is negotiating a deal on a house, listens as she confesses, "I don't *understand.* I don't understand what anything means . . . and I walk around. From morning til night: with this one thought in my head. I'm *stupid.*" He offers Carol some advice and a consoling hand. While the audience senses an impending catastrophe, act 1 gives little hint at—depending on one's point of view—just how distorted the interpretation of the seemingly innocuous events of the first act will become.

The hurly-burly of act 2, however, makes for sparkling drama. Carol registers a complaint, accusing the professor of sexism, classism, and sexual harassment. He calls her back to the office in a failed attempt to clear up any misunderstandings. For John, she is dealing with "accusations"; for Carol, he has to face "facts." A campus support group helps Carol, and the play presents her growing sense of power and John's loss of control over events for which he may or may not be responsible. By the final scene, John loses more than the house and tenure. The college suspends him, and he may be facing charges of rape. Reduced to a groveling, pathetic figure, John appears in stark contrast to the suddenly articulate and holier-than-thou Carol.

In *Oleanna*, Mamet returns to a world in which the gaps between words and deeds remain. The play is theatrically powerful precisely because its author never fills in such gaps. Instead, theatergoers might ask: Is Carol framing John? Are her accusations legitimate? Is Carol simply the first to have the courage to challenge a patronizing and, perhaps, womanizing male teacher? Is John so much a part of an inherently misogynistic world that he seems blithely unaware that his well-meaning actions are in fact highly sexist? Mamet invites viewers to respond to these and many other questions (issues of censorship, political correctness, battles of the sexes, representations of women in theater, and so on). Thus, this 1992 play continues Mamet's exploration of a world that remains a battleground of the sexes, where primal feelings of trust and rational human discourse between women and men remain problematic at best—if not impossible. The title of the play, taken from a folk song, alludes to a nineteenth century escapist vision of utopia. *Oleanna* reminds the audience of the impossibility of such vision.

The Cryptogram • Mamet's *The Cryptogram* concerns John, a ten-year-old boy who is afraid to fall asleep and who wonders where his father is. Donny, John's mother, expresses frustration throughout the play because she has often tried in vain to persuade John to go to sleep. On the first night in the play, John refuses to go to sleep, making the excuse that he is awaiting his father, who has promised to take him camping. Del, a friend of the family, who seems to be romantically linked with Donny, tries to calm John down and coax him to go to sleep, yet he also appears to be distracting the boy, trying to hide from him the fact that John's father has left the family for good. Del tells Donny and John about a camping trip he took with John's father the previous week, yet Donny discovers subsequently that the camping trip never took place and that the father was actually using Del's abode to commit adultery. Donny feels betrayed by Del, thus terminating any opportunity for Del to have a permanent romantic relationship with Donny, which had been possible with Donny's husband out of the picture.

A month later, feeling guilty that he has betrayed both Donny and John, Del gives John one of the boy's father's most prized possessions—his German pilot's knife. John, as usual, refuses to go to bed and only agrees to do so if he can sleep with a stadium blanket, which he cannot obtain because it is already packed (Donny, upset by her husband's decision to leave her and by Del's betrayal, is moving). Del gives John the knife as a memento of his father and also to cut the twine so that he can open the box containing the blanket. John takes the knife and walks toward the box, talking about voices that he hears in his bad dreams, voices that keep calling him. Hearing John say that the voices are calling him, Del hands him the knife and says, "Take the knife and go." The play ends chillingly as the audience is left to ponder what exactly John will do with the knife.

The play is entitled *The Cryptogram* because John keeps asking about his father and trying to solve the mystery surrounding his disappearance. Del and Donny refuse to tell him where his father is (actually, they, themselves, do not know) or that his father has left his mother, ending the marriage and breaking up the family structure. In fact, the conversations between Del and Donny are so cryptic that the audience experiences great difficulty in discerning what event has happened. The audience discovers that Del and Donny, the only characters who know what has transpired, keep secrets even from each other. However, it is Mamet's deft use of language that leads to the suspenseful nature of the mystery.

Although Mamet is a dramatist, his plays manifest that he is a poet. His plays are very much about language itself. In *The Cryptogram* as well as his other dramas, Mamet excels in his use of dialogue; he exhibits an excellent ear for dialogue, whether it involves the two adults in this play who strive to maintain their secret from John about his father's decision to leave the family, the working-class dialogue of Teach, Bob, and

Don in *American Buffalo*, or the middle-class realtors in *Glengarry Glen Ross*. Mamet adeptly uses dialogue to portray realistic characters with realistic language. In *The Cryptogram*, when Del asks John what he means when he mentions, "I could not sleep," John is confused because he believes that his comment is self-explanatory. Del denies that it is, remarking, "It means nothing other than the meaning you choose to assign to it." Del's comment concerns the power and the use of language, but it also is meant to confuse John.

The dialogue between Del and Donny is also telling. As in many of Mamet's plays, the characters know each other so well that they finish each other's sentences and interrupt each other, which leads to the confusion and the cryptic and suspenseful nature of the events. Language becomes a code. Mamet leaves it for the audience to figure out different strands in the play, such as the mystery of the torn blanket. The intensity builds in the last scene, which is evident by the increasing wrath of Donny as she attempts to persuade John to go to sleep and by John leaving with the knife, hearing voices that beckon him as he is without his male protector, his missing father.

Reunion • Two other Mamet plays that merit discussion are *Reunion*, a play whose title might better read as "disunion," and *Edmond*. In *Reunion*, Bernie tells Carol that, although he comes from a broken home, he is "a happy man" who works at "a good job," but his uneasiness remains, particularly when one sees the contemporary world in which he and Carol live: "It's a . . . jungle out there. And you got to learn the rules because *nobody's* going to learn them for you." Thus, true knowledge about the soul and the universe can, in Mamet's world, only be purchased, as the almost poetic lines continue: "Always the price. Whatever it is. And you gotta know it and be prepared to pay it if you don't want it to pass you by." Out of such everyday as well as sensory experiences, Mamet implies throughout his canon, emerge no epiphanies. Rather, his characters merely internalize the messy inconclusiveness of their misspent lives, without the reassurances of some higher consciousness.

Edmond • In *Edmond*, the title character is a racist, sexist, homophobic who leaves his "safe" marriage and embarks on an urban quest to find meaning to his fragmented world. Encountering violence, murder, sexual frustration, and so on, he winds up in jail, sodomized by his black cell mate. If Edmond learns anything from his quest, it is that he accepts his own plight as an acquiescent victim in the jail cell. He becomes the compliant partner with his cell mate.

Other major works

LONG FICTION: *The Village*, 1994; *The Old Religion*, 1997; *Wilson: A Consideration of the Sources*, 2000.

POETRY: *The Hero Pony*, 1990; *The Chinaman*, 1999.

SCREENPLAYS: *The Postman Always Rings Twice*, 1981 (adaptation of James M. Cain's novel); *The Verdict*, 1982 (adaptation of Barry Reed's novel); *The Untouchables*, 1985; *House of Games*, 1987; *Things Change*, 1988; *We're No Angels*, 1989; *Homicide*, 1991; *Glengarry Glen Ross*, 1992 (adaptation of his play); *Hoffa*, 1992; *Oleanna*, 1994 (adaptation of his play); *Vanya on 42nd Street*, 1994; *American Buffalo*, 1996 (adaptation of his play); *The Edge*, 1997; *The Spanish Prisoner*, 1997; *Wag the Dog*, 1997 (with Hilary Henkin; adaptation of Larry Beinhart's novel *American Hero*); *Ronin*, 1998 (credited as Richard Weisz); *The Winslow Boy*, 1999 (adaptation of Terrence Rattigan's play); *State and Main*, 2000; *The Heist*, 2001; *Hannibal*, 2001; *Lakeboat*, 2001 (adaptation of his play).

TELEPLAYS: *Five Television Plays,* 1990; *A Life in the Theatre,* 1993 (adaptation of his play); *Lansky,* 1999.

RADIO PLAYS: *Prairie du Chien,* 1978; *Cross Patch,* 1985; *Goldberg Street,* 1985.

NONFICTION: *Writing in Restaurants,* 1986; *Some Freaks,* 1989; *On Directing Film,* 1991; *The Cabin: Reminiscence and Diversions,* 1992; *The Village,* 1994; *A Whore's Profession: Notes and Essays,* 1994; *Make-Believe Town: Essays and Remembrances,* 1996; *True and False: Heresy and Common Sense for the Actor,* 1997; *Three Uses of the Knife: On the Nature and Purpose of Drama,* 1998; *Jafsie and John Henry: Essays on Hollywood, Bad Boys, and Six Hours of Perfect Poker,* 1999; *On Acting,* 1999.

CHILDREN'S LITERATURE: *The Owl,* 1987; *Warm and Cold,* 1988 (with Donald Sultan); *Passover,* 1995; *The Duck and the Goat,* 1996; *Bar Mitzvah,* 1999 (with Sultan); *Henrietta,* 1999.

Bibliography

Bigsby, C. W. E. *A Critical Introduction to Twentieth-Century American Drama: Beyond Broadway.* Vol. 3. Cambridge, England: Cambridge University Press, 1985. Bigsby devotes about forty pages to Mamet, whom he considers "a poet of loss." His analyses are as sensitive as they are challenging, and they are compulsory reading for anyone interested in Mamet. Includes a bibliography.

_____. *David Mamet.* London: Methuen, 1985. This first book-length study of Mamet is essential reading. Bigsby examines twelve plays and sees Mamet as "a moralist lamenting the collapse of public forum and private purpose, exposing a dessicated world in which the cadences of despair predominate." Contains a brief bibliography.

Carroll, Dennis. *David Mamet.* New York: St. Martin's Press, 1987. Carroll's discussions of Mamet's language are excellent, and he considers the plays in terms of business, sex, learning, and communion. This slender volume also contains a useful bibliography and chronology.

Dean, Anne. *David Mamet: Language as Dramatic Action.* Rutherford, N.J.: Fairleigh Dickinson University Press, 1990. In this perceptive study, Dean suggests that language describes, prescribes, defines, and confines Mamet's characters.

Hudgins, Christopher C., and Leslie Kane, eds. *Gender and Genre: Essays on David Mamet.* New York: Palgrave, 2001. This significant essay collection contains chapters on mothers in *American Buffalo* and *Speed-the-Plow,* gender and desire in *House of Games* and *Speed-the-Plow,* the women in *Edmond,* teaching in *Oleanna,* language and violence in *Oleanna,* and several other chapters. The book is very useful considering that the essays are very good and gender is a prevalent theme in Mamet's drama.

Kane, Leslie. *Weasels and Wisemen: Ethics and Ethnicity in the Work of David Mamet.* New York: Palgrave, 1999. This book, by a major authority on Mamet, covers issues such as morality and vice, as well as the influence of Jewish culture in his drama. Kane's book analyzes the theme of power in Mamet's drama, such as the relationship between power and ethics in his plays.

_____, ed. *David Mamet: A Casebook.* New York: Garland, 1992. The volume contains Kane's introduction, her two interviews, and her bibliography in addition to twelve essays by Ruby Cohn, Dennis Carroll, Steven H. Gale, Deborah R. Geis, Ann C. Hall, Christopher C. Hudgins, Michael Hinden, Pascale Hubert-Leiber, Matthew C. Roudané, Henry I. Schvey, and Hersh Zeifman. Contains a detailed annotated bibliography, an excellent chronology, and a thorough index.

_____. *David Mamet in Conversation.* Ann Arbor: University of Michigan Press, 2001. This book consists of interviews that Mamet has given, including some that have never appeared before in print. In these interviews, Mamet discusses his plays and films, as well as various themes such as sex, theatre, and dialogue. The interviews with Jim Lehrer and Charlie Rose are among the best in the book.

_____. *David Mamet's "Glengarry Glen Ross"*: Text and Performance. New York: Garland, 1996. This essay collection is essential for scholars and students who study this play. The essays concern the play as a detective story, the film version, anxiety, money, nostalgia, Levene's daughter, identity, and morality (this chapter also covers *Edmond*), and other themes. The book concludes with a very useful bibliography.

Matthew C. Roudané,
updated by Eric Sterling

Christopher Marlowe

Born: Canterbury, England; February 6, 1564
Died: Deptford, England; May 30, 1593

Principal drama • *Dido, Queen of Carthage*, pr. c. 1586-1587, pb. 1594 (with Thomas Nashe); *Tamburlaine the Great, Part I*, pr. c. 1587, pb. 1590 (commonly known as *Tamburlaine*); *Tamburlaine the Great, Part II*, pr. 1587, pb. 1590; *Doctor Faustus*, pr. c. 1588, pb. 1604; *The Jew of Malta*, pr. c. 1589, pb. 1633; *Edward II*, pr. c. 1592, pb. 1594; *The Massacre at Paris*, pr. 1593, pb. 1594(?); *Complete Plays*, pb. 1963

Other literary forms • Christopher Marlowe translated Lucan's *Bellum civile* (60-65 C.E.) as *Pharsalia* (1600) and Ovid's *Amores* (c. 20 B.C.E.) as *Elegies* (1595-1600) while still attending Cambridge (c. 1584-1587). The renderings of the *Elegies* are notable for their imaginative liveliness and rhetorical strength. They provide as well the earliest examples of the heroic couplet in English. *Hero and Leander* (1598), a long, erotic poem composed before 1593, is also indebted to Ovid. It is the best narrative of a group that includes William Shakespeare's *Venus and Adonis* (1593) and John Marston's *The Metamorphosis of Pigmalion's Image* (1598). The vogue for these Ovidian epyllions lasted for more than a decade, and Marlowe's reputation as a poet was confirmed on the basis of his contribution. He completed only the first two sestiads before his death, after which George Chapman continued and finished the poem.

Marlowe's brilliant heroic couplets create a world, in Eugene Ruoff's words, of "moonlight and mushrooms"; his lovers are the idealized figures of pastoral works, chanting lush and sensual hymns or laments. A sophisticated narrator—viewed by most critics as representing Marlowe's satiric viewpoint—manages to balance the sentimentalism of the lovers, giving the poem an ironic quality that is sustained throughout. This tone, however, is not a feature of Marlowe's famous lyric, "The Passionate Shepherd to His Love." First published in an anthology entitled *The Passionate Pilgrim* (1599), the poem is a beautiful evocation of the attractions of the pastoral world, a place where "melodious birds sing madrigals." Technically called an "invitation," "The Passionate Shepherd to His Love" became an extremely popular idyll and was often imitated or parodied by other writers.

One of the most intriguing responses, "The Nymph's Reply," was composed by Sir Walter Raleigh and published in *The Passionate Pilgrim*. Its worldly, skeptical attitude offers a contrast to the exuberance of Marlowe's lyric. Without a doubt, this pastoral piece, along with *Hero and Leander*, would have ensured Marlowe's reputation as a major literary figure even if he had never written a work intended for the stage.

Achievements • It is difficult to overestimate the poetic and dramatic achievement of Christopher Marlowe. Although his career was short (about six years), Marlowe wrote plays that appealed to an emerging popular audience and that strongly influenced other dramatists. The heroes of the plays have been called "overreachers" and "apostates," figures whom many critics believe reveal the defiance and cynicism of Marlowe himself. In addition to introducing these controversial, larger-than-life protagonists, Marlowe was also instrumental in fusing the elements of classical—and especially

Senecan—drama and native morality plays, thereby establishing a style that would be followed by many subsequent playwrights.

Doctor Faustus is the prime example of Marlowe's talent for combining classical satire and a conventional Elizabethan theme of humanity in a middle state, torn between the angel and the beast. The vitality of *Doctor Faustus, Tamburlaine the Great*, and Marlowe's other works can be traced as well to his facility for writing powerful yet musical blank verse. Indeed, so regular and forceful is his style that his verse has been described as "Marlowe's mighty line," and his achievement in blank verse no doubt influenced Shakespeare. It is apparent in such plays as *Richard II* (pr. c. 1595-1596), *The Merchant of Venice* (pr. c. 1596-1597), and *Othello, the Moor of Venice* (pr. 1604, rev. 1623) that Shakespeare was also inspired by certain of Marlowe's themes and plots.

Marlowe did not possess a patriotic spirit; his heroes are not Prince Hals but rather men similar to Shakespeare's Richard III. Yet he was sensitive to the range of passion in human nature. Many of Marlowe's characters reflect a true-to-life, even psychological complexity that preceding English playwrights had been incapable of demonstrating. Doctor Faustus's fear on the night he will lose his soul is beautifully portrayed in the memorable Latin line, adapted from Ovid's *Amores*, "O lente, lente currite noctis equi!" ("O slowly, slowly, run you horses of the night").

Barabas, villain-hero of *The Jew of Malta*, displays almost the same intensity of feeling as he rhapsodizes over his gold, his "infinite riches in a little room." Over the short span of his career, Marlowe moved away from the extravagant declamatory style of *Tamburlaine the Great* to a blank verse—notably in *Edward II*—that echoed the rhythm of elevated speech. It is difficult to predict what further advances there would have been in his style had he lived as long as Shakespeare. It is doubtful, however, that he would have changed so radically as to achieve universal popularity. His vision was satiric and therefore narrow; the themes and characters that he chose to write about lacked widespread appeal. Nevertheless, "Kit" Marlowe transformed the English stage from a platform for allegorical interludes or homespun slapstick into a forum for exploring the most controversial of human and social issues. Marlowe also established the poetic medium—vigorous blank verse—that would prove to be the dominant form of dramatic expression until the close of the Elizabethan Age.

Biography • Christopher Marlowe was born in Canterbury, England, in February, 1564. His father was a respected member of the tanners' and shoemakers' guild. Marlowe attended the King's School of Canterbury in 1579 and 1580 and in 1581 began study at Corpus Christi College, Cambridge. He was the recipient of a scholarship funded by Matthew Parker, archbishop of Canterbury. As a foundation scholar, Marlowe was expected to prepare for a post in the Church. In 1584, he took his bachelor of arts degree, after which he continued to hold his scholarship while studying for his master of arts degree. It appears that he would not have been granted his degree in 1587 except for the intervention of the queen's Privy Council. This body declared that Marlowe had done the government some service—probably as a spy in Reims, home of exiled English Roman Catholics—and ordered that he be granted his M.A. at the "next commencement."

Marlowe had no doubt been writing poetry while at Cambridge, and he probably decided to make his way in this profession in London. It is certain that he was there in 1589, because he was a resident of Newgate Prison during that year. He and a man named Thomas Watson were jailed for having murdered another man, although it appears that Watson actually did the killing. Three years later, in 1592, Marlowe was again in trouble with the law, being placed under a peace bond by two London constables. Clearly, the young writer and scholar did not move in the best of social circles, even though his patron was Thomas Walsingham and Sir Walter Raleigh was his close friend.

One of Marlowe's colleagues, a man with whom he once shared a room, was Thomas Kyd, who in May of 1593 was arrested, charged with atheism, and tortured. Kyd accused Marlowe of atheism, claiming that the heretical documents found in their room belonged to the latter. The Privy Council sent out an order for Marlowe's arrest (he was staying at the Walsingham estate), but instead of imprisoning him, the Council simply required that he report every day until the hearing.

That hearing never took place: Marlowe died within two weeks after his detainment. On May 30, after a bout of drinking at a tavern in Deptford, Marlowe quarreled with a companion named Ingram Frizer, who settled the account by stabbing the playwright. Those who believed the charge of atheism brought against him saw Marlowe's end as an example of God's justice. Others, however, speculated on the possibility that he was the victim of an assassination plot, spawned to eliminate a spy who may have known too much. This theory seems fanciful, but it had many contemporary adherents, as the details surrounding the murder do not adequately explain the facts. Whatever the cause, Marlowe's death marked the tragic end of a meteoric career on the public stage. As an innovator—and rebel—he challenged his fellow playwrights to achieve greater heights of creativity, and he left behind a rich legacy of plays and poems.

Analysis • Taken as a whole, Christopher Marlowe's canon represents a crucial step forward in the development of Elizabethan dramaturgy. Without him, there could not have been a Shakespeare or a John Webster, both of whom learned something of the art of popular melodrama from this master. It is lamentable that Marlowe's early death deprived audiences and subsequent critics of more examples of his poetic drama, drama that stirs both the heart and the mind.

Dido, Queen of Carthage • Marlowe probably began writing plays while he was a student at Cambridge. *Dido, Queen of Carthage*, which appeared in quarto form in 1594, was composed in collaboration with Thomas Nashe and was first performed by the children's company at the Chapel Royal. How much Nashe actually had to do with the work is conjectural; he may have only edited it for publication. The tragedy shows little evidence, however, of the playwright's later genius. It is closely tied to Vergil's *Aeneid* (c. 29-19 B.C.E.; English translation, 1553), with much of its blank verse qualifying as direct translation from the Latin. The characters are wooden and the action highly stylized, the result of an attempt to translate the material of epic into drama. The play impresses mainly through the force of its imagery.

Tamburlaine the Great, Part I • Sections of Marlowe's first popular theater success, *Tamburlaine the Great, Part I*, were probably sketched at Cambridge as well. First produced around 1587 (probably at an innyard), this exotic, bombastic piece won for its author considerable fame. His name was quickly cataloged with other so-called University Wits—men such as Robert Greene, John Lyly, and George Peele, whose dramas dominated the Elizabethan stage in the late 1580's. Marlowe's great dramatic epic was roughly based on the career of Timur Lenk (1336-1405), a Mongolian fighter who had led an army that defeated the Turks at Ankara in 1402. The defeat meant the salvation of Europe, an event that doubtless stimulated Marlowe's ironic vision. The playwright could have found the account of the audacious Scythian's career in many Latin and Italian sources, but his interest may have been first aroused after reading George Whetstone's *The English Mirror* (1586).

Tamburlaine emerges as an Olympian figure in Marlowe's hands. He begins as a lowly shepherd whose physical courage and captivating, defiant rhetoric take him to victories over apparently superior opponents. Although episodic, the plot does achieve a degree of tension as each successive opponent proves more difficult to overcome. Tamburlaine's first victim is a hereditary king named Mycetes, who underrates his adversary's strength and persuasiveness. The lieutenant who is sent to capture the upstart is suddenly and decisively won over to the rebel's side. Tamburlaine next outwits Cosroe, Mycetes' brother, who thinks he can use this untutored fighter to consolidate his own power. As the "bloody and insatiate Tamburlaine" kills him, Cosroe curses the turn of Fortune's Wheel that has cast him down. Even so, Marlowe believes not in the capricious goddess as the chief ruler of humankind but in a kind of Machiavellian system directed by the will of his larger-than-life hero.

A major test of Tamburlaine's will comes in his confrontation with Bajazeth, emperor of the Turks. Before the battle between the two warriors, there is a boasting bout between their two mistresses, Zenocrate and Zabina. The former, daughter to the Soldan of Egypt and in love with Tamburlaine, praises her beloved's strength and his destined glory. Both women also pray for the victory of their men, parallel actions that invite a comparison between the pairs of lovers. When Tamburlaine defeats Bajazeth, he takes the crown from Zabina's head and gives it to his queen—and "conqueror." Marlowe thereby demonstrates that the play qualifies as a monumental love story as well. Bajazeth is bound up and later thrown into a cage with his defeated queen; this contraption is then towed across the stage as part of Tamburlaine's victory procession. Before the final siege of Damascus, the city that houses Zenocrate's father, the Soldan, Tamburlaine unveils a magnificent banquet. During the festivities, he releases Bajazeth from his cage in order to use him as a footstool from which he will step onto his throne. This audacious touch of spectacle verifies Marlowe's aim of shocking his audience and displays contempt for the pride of rulers.

In the midst of this banquet, Tamburlaine orders his lieutenants to "hang our bloody colors by Damascus,/ Reflexing hues of blood upon their heads,/ While they walk quivering on their walls,/ Half dead for fear before they feel my wrath!" These threatening, boastful words are followed quickly by a change of colors to black, which signifies Tamburlaine's intention to destroy the city. He underscores this purpose by condemning four virgins, supplicants sent to assuage his anger, to their deaths on the spears of his horsemen. The destruction of the city soon follows, although the Soldan and the King of Arabia (to whom Zenocrate is still betrothed) lead out an army to do battle with their oppressor. While this battle takes place offstage, Bajazeth and Zabina are rolled in to deliver curses against their torturers. Wild from hunger and despair, Bajazeth asks his queen to fetch him something to drink; while she is away, he brains himself against the bars of the cage. Zabina, returning from her errand, finds her husband's battered corpse and follows his lead. The horror of this double suicide no doubt satisfied the popular audience's appetite for gore, an appetite that Marlowe fed lavishly in this play.

The finale of the first part depicts Tamburlaine's victory over the Soldan, who is spared because the victor plans to crown Zenocrate Queen of Persia. Meanwhile, her betrothed, the King of Arabia, dies from battle wounds; his death causes little conflict, however, in Zenocrate, who follows Tamburlaine as if he were indeed her conqueror, too. Now the lowly shepherd-turned-king declares a truce, buries his noble opponents with solemn rites, and prepares to marry his beloved in pomp and splendor. He appears to stand atop Fortune's Wheel, a startling example of the Machiavellian man of iron will to whom no leader or law is sacrosanct. There is little sense here that Tamburlaine is intended as an example of pride going before a fall. He has achieved stunning victories over foes who are as immoral as he is; most of them, including Bajazeth, emerge as fools who miscalculate or underrate Tamburlaine with fearful consequences. No doubt the popularity of the play is traceable to this fact and to the truth that most people nurture an amoral desire for fame or power that this hero fulfills with startling success.

Tamburlaine the Great, Part II • Part II shows Tamburlaine continuing on his road to conquest, securely characterizing himself as the scourge of God. As the play opens, Sigismund, Christian king of Hungary, and the pagan monarch Orcanes agree to a truce. This ceremony strikes one as ironic, as pagans and Christians swallow their pride in order to challenge and defeat the half-god who threatens them. In the meantime, Tamburlaine proudly surveys the fruits of Zenocrate's womb: three sons through whom he hopes to win immortality. One of the brood, however, is weak and unattracted by war; Calyphas seems devoted to his mother and to the blandishments of peace. His effeminate nature foreshadows Tamburlaine's decline and fall, revealing that his empire cannot survive his own death. Even though his two other sons exhibit natures cruel enough to match their father's, the flawed seed has obviously been planted.

The hastily forged truce is suddenly broken when Sigismund tears the document and turns his forces on Orcanes. Though Marlowe appears to be attacking the integrity of Christianity, he was in fact appealing to his audience's anti-Catholic sentiments. When Sigismund is wounded and dies, moreover, Orcanes announces that Christ has won a victory in defeating one so treacherous as Sigismund. While these events transpire on the battlefield, another death is about to take place in Tamburlaine's tent. Zenocrate has been in failing health, and her imminent death causes her husband to contemplate joining her. That he should entertain such a gesture at the height of his power confirms the depth of his love for Zenocrate. Her imploring words—"Live still, my lord! O, let my sovereign live!"—manage to stay his hand, but his pent-up rage cannot be restrained at her death. Shifting from a figure of gentleness and compassion in a moment's time, Tamburlaine orders the town in which she dies to be burned to the ground.

With the defeat of Sigismund, Orcanes emerges as a kingmaker, leading the grand procession at which Callapine, the avenging son of Bajazeth, vows to use his new crown as the means to conquer the lowly Scythian. This scene is succeeded by another ceremonial pageant, this one led by the mournful Tamburlaine and his sons carrying the coffin of Zenocrate. Her body will remain with the company wherever they go in battle. Determined to teach his sons the arts of war, Tamburlaine commences a lesson in besieging a fort. When Calyphas balks, afraid of wounding or death, an angry father lances his own arm and orders his sons to dip their hands in his blood. All of them comply, although Calyphas is moved to pity at this horrid sight. With this ritual, Marlowe underscores the tribal nature of his hero's family but at the same time implies that the letting of blood by Tamburlaine will not necessarily cure the "defect" in it.

The central battle in the second part pits Tamburlaine and his sons against Callapine and his crowned kings before Aleppo. In a preliminary verbal skirmish, Tamburlaine belittles Almeda, a traitor, who cowers behind Callapine's back when invited to take his crown. The scene is seriocomic as Almeda proves himself a coward before his kingly followers; his weakness is meant to parallel that of Calyphas, Tamburlaine's son. The latter remains behind in a tent playing cards while his two brothers earn martial honors on the battlefield. When they and their father enter, trailing the conquered Turkish monarchs behind them, Tamburlaine seizes his weakling son and stabs him. Among the many scenes of bloodshed Marlowe presents in the play, this is probably the most shocking and repulsive. Although he cites his role as God's scourge and this deed as "war's justice," Tamburlaine here reveals a self-destructive side of his nature that has not been evident before.

The audience does not have long to ponder the murder; the scene of horror is quickly followed by one of pageantry. Trebizon and Soria, two pagan kings, enter the stage drawing a chariot with Tamburlaine holding the reins. This spectacle is accompanied by the superhero's disdaining words: "Holla, ye pamper'd jades of Asia!/ What can ye draw but twenty miles a day,/ And have so proud a chariot at your heels,/ And such a coachman as great Tamburlaine?" The monarch-prisoners hurl curses at their captors as, like Bajazeth and Zabina, they are taunted unmercifully. Tamburlaine's soldiers are rewarded with Turkish concubines, after which the royal train heads toward Babylon for yet another bloody siege.

Before the walls of this ancient city, Tamburlaine calls on its governor to yield. (The scene recalls the negotiations before the walls of Damascus in Part I.) When he refuses, the lieutenants Techelles and Theridamas lead their soldiers in scaling the city's walls. The victory is quickly won, and Tamburlaine, dressed in black and driving his chariot, proudly announces the city's defeat. A quaking governor promises Tamburlaine abundant treasure if he will spare his life, but the conqueror disdains such bribes and has his victim hanged in chains from the walls. Theridamas shoots the governor while Tamburlaine proceeds to burn Muhammadan books in an open pit. Defying Mahomet to avenge his sacrilege if he has any power, Tamburlaine suddenly feels "distempered"; he recovers quickly, however, when he hears of Callapine's army advancing. Does Marlowe mean to imply that his hero's unexpected illness is punishment for his act of defiance? Although such an explicit moral lesson seems uncharacteristic, the connection between the two events appears to be more than a passing one.

The weakened Tamburlaine manages a final victory over Bajazeth's son, after which he produces a map that represents the extent of his conquests. With a trembling finger, he also directs his sons' attention to the remaining countries that they will be expected to conquer. Giving his crown to Theridamas (who later bestows it on Amyras) and turning his chariot over to his sons, Tamburlaine then calls for Zenocrate's hearse, beside which he stretches out to die. Before the mighty general's body is carried off, Amyras delivers the fitting eulogy:

> Meet heaven and earth, and here let all things end,
> For earth hath spent the pride of all her fruit,
> And heaven consum'd his choicest living fire:
> Let earth and heaven his timeless death deplore,
> For both their worths will equal him no more.

The death of the Scourge of Heaven follows no particular event; its suddenness only serves to underscore Tamburlaine's mortality. The audience is reminded of Alexander's demise in the midst of his glory. Because the chariot becomes such a dominant prop in the second part, Marlow may have likewise meant to suggest a parallel between his hero and Phaëthon, who in his pride fell from Jove's chariot because he could not control its course. Whatever the interpretation of this hero's fall, there can be little doubt that his mighty feats and his Senecan bombast made him an extremely popular—and awesome—figure on the Elizabethan stage.

The Jew of Malta • For his next play, *The Jew of Malta*, Marlowe also chose an antihero who poses a threat to the orderly rule of European society. As Tamburlaine had ruled by martial strength, Barabas (named to recall the thief whose place on the Cross was taken by Christ) hopes to dominate the world by his wealth. Although Marlowe depicts him as a grasping, evil man (to the delight of the anti-Semitic Elizabethan audience), Barabas holds one's interest as Richard III does—by the resourcefulness of his scheming. Just as Tamburlaine's audacity appeals to an unconscious desire for power, so Barabas's scorn for Christian morality probably appealed to the audience's wish to defy authority. He is not portrayed, however, as a sympathetic character, even though in the early stages of the play, the behavior of his Christian opponents toward him reveals their hypocrisy.

Faced with a threat from the powerful Turkish fleet, Ferneze, the Maltese governor, turns to Barabas for help in raising tribute money. While three of his colleagues agree to give up half of their estates and consent to baptism, Barabas refuses this arrangement, miscalculating the power and determination of the governor. Accompanied by a chorus of anti-Semitic remarks by the knights, Ferneze announces that he has already sent men to seize Barabas's property. He also declares that he intends to transform the Jew's mansion into a nunnery; this news further enrages Barabas, who curses them: "Take it to you, i' th' Devil's name." This scene highlights the hypocrisy of the Maltese; it also reveals the extent of Barabas's hatred for those among whom he has lived and worked. The audience has learned from the prologue spoken by Machiavel that the hero is one of his disciples and soon realizes that the subsequent action will show him "practicing" on his enemies.

When his daughter Abigail comes to recount angrily the takeover of their house, Barabas counsels patience, reminding her that he has hidden a fortune beneath its floorboards. In order to recover the money, he spawns a daring plan that requires his daughter to take vows as a means of entering the newly founded nunnery. In a heavily theatrical confrontation staged by Barabas, father accuses daughter of deserting him and their religion, while in an aside he tells her where to find the money. As Abigail is hurried into the mansion, she is spied by two young men, Mathias and Lodowick, both of whom fall in love with her—a rivalry that Barabas will later turn to his advantage. Later that night, Abigail appears on a balcony with Barabas's bags in her hands; she throws these down to him as he sees her and shouts: "O girl! O gold! O beauty! O my bliss!" This outburst illustrates the Jew's seriocomic nature, as he employs such impassioned speech to praise his gold. Eight years later, Shakespeare incorporated this trait into his characterization of Shylock in *The Merchant of Venice*.

In the square the next day, Barabas begins to practice in earnest against Ferneze. Ferneze's son Lodowick expresses his love for Abigail and is invited by Barabas to supper for a meeting with his "jewel." This dinner will prove Lodowick's undoing, as Barabas tells the audience in an aside. The Jew then proceeds to purchase the slave Ithamore, who will serve his master's will no matter what the command. In order to test the fellow, Barabas lists a remarkable catalog of evil deeds—including poisoning wells in nunneries—that he has supposedly committed. Ithamore responds by declaring himself in a league of villainy with the Jew: "We are villains both!—Both circumcised, we hate Christians both!" The slave aids his master by taking a forged challenge from Lodowick to Mathias, with whom Abigail is truly in love, even though her father has forced her to display affection for Lodowick. When the rivals meet to engage in a duel, Barabas is positioned above them, watching with pleasure as they kill each other.

Now, however, Ithamore and Abigail, whom he has told of the feigned challenge, know the extent of Barabas's treachery. In melodramatic fashion, the Jew decides that his daughter must die or she will reveal his deed. To kill her, he has Ithamore prepare a poisoned pot of rice to be "enjoyed" by all the nuns. To secure Ithamore's loyalty, Barabas promises him the whole of his inheritance, and he seems to adopt him as his son. The audience, however, knows from another aside that Barabas intends to kill his slave as well when the time is right.

Ithamore does his master's bidding, but before Abigail dies, she gives proof of her father's guilt to Friar Bernardine (depicted as a lustful clown), who vows to confront the Jew with it, accompanied by Friar Jacomo. Barabas outwits these two fellows, assuring them that he wishes to be converted; as he did with Lodowick and Mathias, he starts the two men quarreling with each other. By means of a clever ruse devised with the aid of Ithamore, he also eliminates these potential enemies. As each of his schemes proves successful, Barabas celebrates more openly and melodramatically. In this play, unlike *Tamburlaine the Great*, the audience senses that the hero-villain will soon go too far, tripping up on some unforeseen obstacle. The audience is meant to experience this sense of impending doom, especially after the murder of the innocent Abigail, who converted to Christianity before her death. This deed establishes a parallel between Barabas and the biblical Herod, another murderer of innocents.

Meanwhile, Ithamore, aided by a pimp and his whore, tries to blackmail his master to feed the whore's expensive tastes. Barabas resolves to kill them all. Disguised as a French musician, he comes to the party at which Ithamore and the others are drunkenly planning to destroy the Jew. Barabas plays and sings, then tosses to the revelers a bouquet that he has dusted with poison. They smell it and go ahead boldly in their plan to expose the Jew's actions. Before they die, they manage to tell Ferneze of Barabas's treachery; he and the others are led offstage, from where an officer quickly comes to tell of *all* of their deaths. The audience quickly learns, however, that Barabas has taken a sleeping potion and thus has deceived his enemies. Now intent on revenge, he joins forces with the besieging Turks, showing them a way into the city through a hidden tunnel.

With a suddenness of movement that imitates the Wheel of Fortune, Ferneze is defeated and Barabas is appointed governor of the island by the Turks. Rather than torturing and killing the former governor, as might be expected, Barabas offers to return his power and destroy the Turks if Ferneze will pay him, which Ferneze agrees to do. The Jew then invites Calymath to a feast in celebration of their great victory. Hard at work in the hall, Barabas constructs an elaborate trap that he plans to spring on Calymath with Ferneze's help. When the moment arrives, however, the Maltese governor cuts a rope that causes Barabas to fall into the trap, a large cauldron filled with boiling liquid. Ferneze then arrests the Turkish leader, telling him that his troops have been surprised and killed in the monastery where they were housed. Amid the shouts and curses of the Jew—"Damn's Christians, dogs, and Turkish infidels!"—the play ends in triumph for the Maltese citizens.

The Jew of Malta ends in the defeat of Machiavellian plotting. Even though he is a scheming villain throughout most of the action, however, Barabas might also be considered a near-tragic figure if one regards him as a man who degenerates in reaction to the evil done to him. In part, this reaction must follow from the behavior of Ferneze and Calymath; neither is morally superior to Barabas. He must honestly be described as the Elizabethan stereotype of a Jew, given to melodrama and sardonic humor. The audience feels no sympathy for him in his death, only a kind of relief that his destructive will has been defeated by someone capable of outwitting him. Although he finally overreaches himself, Barabas emerges as a totally fascinating villain, matched only by Shakespeare's Iago and Richard III.

The Massacre at Paris • In *The Massacre at Paris*, Marlowe depicts the episodic adventures of another antihero, the Guise, who is distinguishable from his predecessors only in representing the power of the Papacy. The character is based on a historical figure who was assassinated in 1588; the action recounts the infamous Saint Bartholomew's Day debacle of 1572, when hundreds of Huguenots were murdered by Roman Catholic forces. The succession of victims, whom the Guise orders murdered ostensibly to please the Church, makes the audience recoil from the character and his motives. Lacking any comic element in his nature, he qualifies as a parodied Machiavel intent on disrupting the reign of Henry III, a lecherous and inept leader. The Guise's soliloquies show him to be in quest of an "earthly crown," which he believes he deserves because of his superior will and intelligence. What makes him different from Tamburlaine is his inability to control his passions and the behavior of those closest to him. In critical situations, his rhetoric fails him. His wife's affair with the king's favorite cuckolds the Guise. Henry delights in making the sign of the horns at him in public. Enraged at being made a figure of public ridicule, he arranges to kill his rival, an act that all but ensures his fall.

The man who stands in opposition to both the Guise and Henry III is King Henry of Navarre. Although his speeches lack the fire and melodrama that mark the Guise's outbursts, Navarre champions a Catholicism that is anticlerical, even fundamentalist. He also defends the principle of king and country, which the Guise and Henry seem to have forgotten in their quest for power. To prove his antipapal views, Navarre joins forces with Queen Elizabeth in an alliance the rightness of which Marlowe underscores by having a dying Henry III embrace it. This bit of manipulation has led some critics to argue that with this play, Marlowe was returning to his own Christian faith and was rejecting the amoral position taken by Tamburlaine. It is dangerous, however, to infer an author's beliefs from those held by his characters; there is no corroborating evidence in this case. There can be little doubt that Navarre is intended to be seen as a heroic character unlike any encountered in the other plays. If he is not Prince Hal, he is certainly Bolingbroke, a man who acts on principle and proves effective.

Even though the confrontation between Navarre and the Guise has about it all the elements of exciting drama, *The Massacre at Paris* is ultimately disappointing. The Guise's philosophy of seeking out perilous situations in order to test his strength of will does hold one's attention for a while, but the play offers none of the heroic bombast of a Tamburlaine or witty audacity of a Barabas. There is a great deal of bloodshed on the stage and off, but there is no clear purpose for the murders, no sense in which they forward some particular end in the plot. To complicate matters, the text that has survived is garbled; no amount of reconstructing can account for the missing links. While Marlowe may have been attempting a new dramatic design (some textual critics suggest that the original version was twice as long), *The Massacre at Paris* in its present form cannot be regarded as achieving the degree of pathos necessary to call it a successful tragedy.

Edward II • In *Edward II*, however, such pathos can be found in the fateful careers of two men whose wills and hearts are sorely tested. Edward is presented as a man who is required to rule as king even though his weak nature disqualifies him from the task. As misfortune hounds him, he acquires humility and insight, which help to give him a more sympathetic personality than he has at the play's opening. He progresses toward self-understanding, and this transformation distinguishes him from more static characters such as Tamburlaine and Barabas. On the other hand, Mortimer, a man like Navarre who starts out professing deep concern for the destiny of his country, gradually loses the audience's sympathy as he becomes driven by ambition for the crown. This pattern of characterization charges *Edward II* with pathos of the kind Shakespeare would achieve in his tragedy *Richard II*, which was based on Marlowe's play and appeared a year after it.

Like Shakespeare, Marlowe turned to Raphael Holinshed's *Chronicles* (1577) to find the source material for *Edward II*. While earlier playwrights had attempted to transform the stuff of chronicle history into drama, Marlowe was the first to forge a dramatic design that is coherent and progressive. He presents a single theme—the struggle between Edward and his nobles—modulating it by means of the hero's victories and defeats. When Edward is finally overcome and the crown falls to his heir, he pursues Mortimer and his deceitful queen until revenge is won. In an ending unlike those of Marlowe's earlier plays, the accession of Edward III brings with it the promise of happier, more prosperous days. This exuberance at the close is a far cry from the condition of the state when the action begins. Gaveston, Edward's minion, seeks to divide his lover from the nobles not only for sexual reasons. He shows that he is ambitious and disdainful of his superiors. In an opening-scene confrontation (which Gaveston overhears), Edward defies the lords, announcing his intention to appoint Gaveston Lord High-Chamberlain. Edward's brother Kent at first supports him, telling the king to cut off the heads of those who challenge his authority. Yet by the close of the scene, when Edward has alienated the lords, the commons, and the bishops, Kent begins to wonder openly about his brother's ability to rule.

Mortimer, a man possessed by brashness, stands as the chief opponent to the king. He is begged by Queen Isabella not to move against the crown, even though she has been displaced by Gaveston. Mortimer is not alone in his opposition to the king's behavior. The archbishop of Canterbury joins the peers in composing a document that officially banishes Gaveston. Although Edward rages against this rebellious act, he soon realizes that to resist might well lead to his own deposing. He is trapped because he has placed love for his minion above his concern for England. It is significant in this regard that Gaveston is both low-born and a Frenchman, which qualified him as a true villain in the eyes of Elizabethan Englishmen. Before the two men part, expressing vows that sound like those of heterosexual lovers, Edward turns to Isabella, accusing her (at Gaveston's prompting) of being involved in an affair with Mortimer. Tortured by her husband's harsh, and for the moment untrue, words, Isabella approaches the lords and, with Mortimer's aid, persuade them to rescind the banishment order. Edward rejoices, suddenly announcing plans to marry Gaveston to his niece; his enthusiasm is not shared by Mortimer and his father, who see this as another move to entrench Gaveston in royal favor. The minion's success also breeds Machiavellian ambition in younger courtiers, the audience learns from a short interlude involving

Young Spencer and Baldock. This mirroring technique, by which lesser characters are observed copying the traits of the central figures, serves Marlowe's moral or instructive purposes in other plays as well.

When Gaveston returns in triumph, he expresses contempt for the "base, leaden earls" who greet him with a mocking recital of his newly acquired titles. Lancaster, then Mortimer and others, draw their swords and threaten Gaveston, an action that prompts Edward to order Mortimer from his court. A shouting match follows, sides are taken, and the earls set about planning how they will murder Gaveston. Fuel is added to the fire when Edward childishly refuses to ransom Mortimer's uncle, who has been captured by the Scots. (One can see in this episode parallels with the Hotspur-Henry IV quarrel in Shakespeare's *Henry IV, Part I*, pr. 1598.) Rejecting his brother Kent's sound advice to seek a truce with the lords, Edward declares his intention to be revenged on them all, plotting openly with Gaveston to be rid of his enemies. By allowing himself to be driven by anger, Edward exhibits his political naïveté: His threat against Mortimer also alienates the people, to whom he is a hero. Furthermore, as Marlowe makes clear, the lords frequently express their desire to expel the king's favorite, not the king. It is important to realize that the playwright does not present the homosexual affair in an exploitative way; rather, he wants the audience to understand how Edward's blind defense of his "friendship" makes it easy for his enemies to rally to the cause.

The lords finally decide to move openly against Gaveston, whose whereabouts Isabella reluctantly reveals. Isabella's position has been made increasingly difficult by the king's claim that she and young Mortimer are lovers. Now her action seems to confirm Edward's suspicions, even though she affirms her love for the king and her son. When Gaveston is overtaken by his enemies—one of whom compares him to Helen of Troy—he is accused of being a common thief, then given over to Warwick's custody, an act that ensures his death. Rather than solving the country's problems, however, the removal of Gaveston exacerbates them. Edward quickly embraces the support of Young Spencer and Baldock, his new favorites, while continuing to ignore the incursions of Scots marauders and of the French King Valois, who has invaded Normandy. Marlowe here paints a vivid picture of the collapse of the body politic from internal and external forces. Yet when the inevitable civil war breaks out, Edward wins, proceeding quickly to take revenge against those "traitors" who opposed him. In his rage, however, he makes another mistake; rather than killing Mortimer, he imprisons him in the Tower, where his ambition (or *virtu*) has an opportunity to flower. With the aid of Edward's disgruntled brother Kent, Mortimer escapes to France to seek aid—along with Isabella—to restore England to her former health. It now appears that Isabella and Mortimer have joined forces to place Prince Edward on the throne. Yet as they leave the French court with promises of support, the queen and the young climber appear to have their own interests, not those of the kingdom, at heart.

Not surprisingly, Edward is easily defeated in a second encounter with the lords, bolstered as they are by the troops of Mortimer and Isabella. Isabella immediately proclaims Prince Edward the new "warden" of the realm, then turns the question of Edward's fate over to the lords. It is at this point that Marlowe begins portraying the deposed king in a more sympathetic light. When he is captured by Leicester, Edward, along with Young Spencer and Baldock, is disguised and begging sanctuary from an abbot. In these perilous straits, he still refuses to denounce his friendship with obvious parasites.

As the bishop of Winchester asks for his crown, deeming the act for "England's good," Edward suddenly refuses to take it from his head, accusing Isabella and Mortimer of outright rebellion. What makes Edward such a pitiful figure here is his inability to comprehend his part in creating the circumstances of his fall. He regards himself as a wronged innocent surrounded by wolfish traitors; this self-blindness prevents him from acting wisely and in the country's best interests. Although he lacks the spiritual dimensions of Shakespeare's King Lear, his jealous possession of the crown represents the same childlike faith in the object, not in the qualities which it represents. This attitude and the behavior that it engenders—a self-dramatizing resignation—lead to Edward's death.

References to the Wheel of Fortune fill the final scenes of *Edward II*. Mortimer and Isabella appear to have reached the Wheel's top, as both actively plot Edward's death. Isabella emerges, however, as a mother determined to see her son ascend the throne, while Mortimer clearly plots to seize power for himself. He determines that the deposed king must die, but he will act through subordinates rather than directly. Mortimer's tactics represent the victory of Machiavellianism, as he proceeds to rule through plotting and hypocrisy. He has Prince Edward crowned, declaring himself to be protector, then sends Lightborn and Matrevis to murder Edward.

In a sad yet gruesome scene, the disheveled Edward is murdered in his jail bed when Lightborn places a table on top of him and jumps up and down on it. This horrible deed is quickly answered by Edward III, who arrests Mortimer, has him hanged and beheaded, and then places the head on his father's hearse. Isabella is sent to the Tower as the new king demonstrates the traits of strength and decisiveness that assure England's future glory. Edward III is a monarch who, like Shakespeare's Henry V, restores not only peace but also the values of patriotism and justice, which are necessary to the peaceful progress of the state.

In *Edward II*, Marlowe scores several successes. He creates a coherent play out of strands of historical material, lending pathos and poetic strength to the main character. He explores the depths of human emotions and depicts skillfully the ambiguous personalities of figures such as Isabella with consummate talent. He also reveals the effects of Machiavellianism in a personage, Mortimer, whose nature is more believable, less stereotyped, than those of Barabas or the Guise. These advances in dramaturgy not only lent tragic potency to *Edward II* but also prepared the way for Marlowe's most spectacular tragic achievement, *Doctor Faustus*.

Doctor Faustus • A major obstacle in the path of critics of Marlowe's most popular melodrama, however, is the state of the text. Not published until eleven years after the playwright's death, the play was modified by "doctors" who were paid to add certain effects and delete others. To complicate matters further, an enlarged quarto edition was published in 1616; this version features alterations that suggest it may have been printed from the promptbook. Today's text is largely the work of Sir Walter Greg, who attempted a reconstruction of the play based on the extant quartos.

The tragedy bears some resemblance to English morality interludes dealing with damnation and salvation. By selecting the Faustus myth, however, Marlowe was committed to portraying a story of damnation alone, with a hero who realizes too late the terrible consequences of selling his soul to the Devil. Indeed, the most impressive aspect of *Doctor Faustus* is its incisive treatment of the protagonist's tortured state of mind, which could easily be construed as an object lesson to sinners in the Elizabethan audience. Yet Marlowe was not preparing an interlude for the edification and instruction of simpleminded rustics. He was a daring, provocative artist exploring the character of a man who was legendary for his intellectual curiosity and for his intense desire to break the bonds of human knowledge and experience. However, *Doctor Faustus* does not contain any praise for the Christian religion and, therefore, is not a Christian morality play.

The character Doctor Faustus is closely related to Tamburlaine, another Marlovian hero whose desire for knowledge and power sent him on a spectacular quest. While Tamburlaine, however, is able to win the prize—if only for a brief time—Doctor Faustus in fact falls from the position of social and spiritual prominence he holds at the play's opening. He is a victim of a system he chooses to defy. In that act of defiance, he begins almost immediately to deteriorate into a fool. The stages of that decline are carefully, ironically traced by Marlowe, who seems to want the audience to regard his hero's striving as a futile gesture. The play's ending, with Faustus being led away by devils who torture and then dismember him, offers no optimistic vision to the audience. *Doctor Faustus* thus stands as Marlowe's most pessimistic play, a tragedy that instructs its spectators in the dangers and ultimate limitations of the human imagination.

The play's opening (after an induction by a Senecan Chorus) finds Faustus in his study rejecting the orthodox or conventional disciplines and hungering for the demigod status of a magician. Even though he is cautioned against incurring God's anger by the Good Angel, Faustus invites two magicians, Valdes and Cornelius, to dine with him. In an effective bit of mirroring, Marlowe invents a servant named Wagner, who mimics the behavior of his master by behaving condescendingly toward two scholars who have come to warn Faustus about practicing the "damn'd art." One is struck throughout the play by the concern shown for the hero by his friends.

When Doctor Faustus manages to cast a spell and call up his servant Mephostophilis, the audience should quickly realize that he has made a bad bargain. Lucifer's messenger tells him directly that he desires the magician's soul and that Faustus will possess only the power the devils choose to give him. Unfortunately, Faustus's pride blinds him to the reality of the contract, which he signs with his own blood. He must forfeit his soul after twenty-four years of magic. In a humorous parallel scene, Wagner, too, calls up spirits and purchases the services of a clown, the burlesque counterpart of Mephostophilis. The slapstick underplot makes clear the ironic point: The servants control their masters and not vice versa.

While the Good Angel urges Faustus to repent, he instead boldly defies God and mocks the existence of Hell. His haughtiness begins to weaken, however, when second thoughts about the contract start to plague him. Supposing himself to be beyond salvation, Faustus instead turns to Mephostophilis for answers to questions about the creation of humanity and the world. In place of answers, Mephostophilis offers evasions and sideshows, such as the procession of the Seven Deadly Sins. Again a comic scene echoes the main action as Robin the Clown steals his master's conjuring books and invites Dick to turn invisible with him, in which state they plan to visit the tavern and drink all they wish without paying. References to bills and nonpayment throw into relief the predicament of the hero, whose "bill" must be paid with his life. When the audience next encounters Faustus, he is in fact supposed to be invisible as he visits a papal banquet, where he daringly strikes the pope and plays sophomoric tricks on the cardinals. The appeal of such anti-Catholic skits to a Protestant audience is obvious; Marlowe reinforces that point when he has Faustus help rescue the rival Pope Bruno from imprisonment. Yet even though he succeeds in puncturing the vanity of Rome, Faustus also reveals himself to be a second-rate showman rather than the demigod he had hoped to become. Marlowe accomplishes this effect by depicting his hero first in the papal setting; then in Emperor Charles's court, placing the cuckold's horns on the heads of three courtiers; and finally in a tavern, where he tricks a horse-courser into believing he has pulled off Faustus's leg.

This foolery has been heavily criticized by commentators as nothing more than an attempt to divert the mechanicals. Some have argued that the scenes involving Robin and the other clowns were in fact added by subsequent playwrights. There can be little doubt, however, that many of these scenes are intended to underscore the hero's decline and to foreshadow later events. The horse-courser's pulling off of Faustus's "leg" and the subsequent purchase of a mare that turns out to be a bale of hay foreshadow the hero's final dismemberment and comment on the bad bargain that Faustus has made with Lucifer. As in plays such as Shakespeare's *Henry IV, Part I*, burlesque business in the underplot of *Doctor Faustus* provides a more informal way of appreciating the thematic significance of the main action.

Marlowe also exhibits his expertise in using conventions of the Elizabethan stage to reinforce his main themes. At the court of Emperor Charles, Faustus creates a dumb show that depicts Alexander defeating Darius, then giving the defeated king's crown to his paramour. (While this action is taking place, Mephostophilis places the cuckold's horns on the head of Benvolio, one of the courtiers who has challenged Faustus's authority.) The dumb show celebrates the victory of a great warrior and is obviously intended as an elaborate compliment to the emperor. Yet it also suggests how distant Faustus himself is from the noble stature of an Alexander; instead of performing great deeds—his original purpose—he can function only in the medium's role. This identity is reinforced in the climactic scene of the play, when Faustus requires Mephostophilis to conjure up Helen of Troy. She crosses the stage quickly, leaving Faustus unsatisfied. He is then approached by an old man who urges him to repent before it is too late. Stricken by these words and by his conscience, Faustus nearly commits suicide with a dagger that the invisible Mephostophilis conveniently places in his hand. The old man returns to stop him, but when he leaves the stage, Mephostophilis materializes and berates Faustus for his desperate attempt. Now believing himself beyond redemption and driven by desire, the magician calls again for Helen of Troy, whom he praises, kisses, and then leads away.

Several commentators believe this act of intercourse with a spirit (a succuba) damns Faustus unequivocally. His soul has become so corrupted as a result that it shares the demoniac spirit with the other devils. Marlowe, however, clearly wants his audience to believe that Faustus could save himself at any time should he decide to repent and ask forgiveness. The dilemma he faces is that he is torn between despair and faint hope; he never manages to decide on a course of action and take it.

This depiction of man as a battleground for the forces of good and evil looks back to the morality plays and ahead to plays of psychological complexity such as Shakespeare's *Hamlet, Prince of Denmark* (pr. c. 1600-1601). In the case of Doctor Faustus, the failure to repent allows Lucifer, Mephostophilis, and other devils to conjure up yet another vision, this time of a horror-filled Hell. Left alone on the stage, Faustus makes a pitiful attempt to slow the passage of time—"O, lente, lente, currite noctis equi!"—but now his magic has left him. This speech highlights one of the play's chief ironies: Twenty-four years have passed as quickly as twenty-four hours, the last one ticking away toward Faustus's doom. When the scholars who were Faustus's friends next enter, they find only his limbs, the grim remains of a man who thought himself to be a god. Hell turns out to be no fable for the damned hero. The hero of *Doctor Faustus*, Marlowe's major artistic and popular success, belongs with Marlowe's others by virtue of his defiance and his compelling rhetorical style.

Other major works

POETRY: *Hero and Leander*, 1598 (completed by George Chapman); "The Passionate Shepherd to His Love," 1599 (in *The Passionate Pilgrim*).

TRANSLATIONS: *Elegies*, 1595-1600 (of Ovid's *Amores*); *Pharsalia*, 1600 (of Lucan's *Bellum civile*).

MISCELLANEOUS: *The Works of Christopher Marlowe*, 1910, 1962 (C. F. Tucker Brooke, editor); *The Works and Life of Christopher Marlowe*, 1930-1933, 1966 (R. H. Case, editor); *The Complete Works of Christopher Marlowe*, 1973 (Fredson Bowers, editor).

Bibliography

Downie, J. A., and J. T. Parnell. *Constructing Christopher Marlowe.* New York: Cambridge University Press, 2000. This scholarly study contains essays on Marlowe's life and works. Includes bibliography and index.

Grantley, Darryll, and Peter Roberts, eds. *Christopher Marlowe and English Renaissance Culture.* Aldershot, Hants, England: Scholar Press, 1996. This collection of essays covers topics such as Marlowe and atheism and the staging of his plays and provides in-depth analysis of most of his plays. Bibliography and index.

Hopkins, Lisa. *Christopher Marlowe: A Literary Life.* New York: Palgrave, 2000. A study of Marlowe's career and what is known of his life. Hopkins focuses on Marlowe's skepticism toward colonialism, family, and religion.

Simkin, Stevie. *Marlowe: The Plays.* New York: Palgrave, 2001. Simkin provides in-depth analyses of Marlowe's dramas, major and minor. Bibliographical references and index.

_____. *A Preface to Marlowe.* New York: Longman, 2000. In addition to providing a biography of Marlowe, Simkin analyzes his major and minor plays, concluding with a chapter on Marlowe's influence on the theater. Bibliography and index.

Tauton, Nina. *Fifteen-nineties Drama and Militarism: Portrayals of War in Marlowe, Chapman, and Shakespeare's Henry V.* Aldershot, England: Ashgate, 2001. Tauton looks at war in the works of Marlowe, William Shakespeare, and George Chapman, writing in the late sixteenth century. Bibliography and index.

Tromly, Fred B. *Playing with Desire: Christopher Marlowe and the Art of Tantalization.* Buffalo, N.Y.: University of Toronto Press, 1998. Tromly discusses the dramatic works of Marlowe from the playwright's use of tantalization. Bibliographical references and index.

Trow, M. J., and Taliesin Trow. *Who Killed Kit Marlowe? A Contract to Murder in Elizabethan England.* Stroud, England: Sutton, 2001. This discussion focuses on Marlowe's mystery-shrouded death, providing both the evidence that is available and the many theories that exist. Bibliography and index.

Robert F. Willson, Jr.,
updated by Glenn Hopp

Thomas Middleton

Born: London, England; April 18, 1580 (baptized)
Died: Newington Butts, Surrey, England; July 4, 1627

Principal drama • *The Honest Whore, Part I,* pr., pb. 1604 (with Thomas Dekker); *The Family of Love,* pr. c. 1604-1607, pb. 1608; *The Phoenix,* pr. 1604, pb. 1607; *Your Five Gallants,* pr. 1604-1607, pb. 1608; *A Trick to Catch the Old One,* pr. c. 1605-1606, pb. 1608; *A Mad World, My Masters,* pr. c. 1606, pb. 1608; *Michaelmas Term,* pr. c. 1606, pb. 1607; *The Roaring Girl: Or, Moll Cutpurse,* pr. c. 1610, pb. 1611 (with Dekker); *The Witch,* pr. c. 1610, pb. 1778; *A Chaste Maid in Cheapside,* pr. 1611, pb. 1630; *No Wit, No Help Like a Woman's,* pr. c. 1613-1627, pb. 1657; *More Dissemblers Besides Women,* pr. c. 1615, pb. 1657; *A Fair Quarrel,* pr. c. 1615-1617, pb. 1617 (with William Rowley); *The Widow,* pr. c. 1616, pb. 1652 (with Ben Jonson and John Fletcher?); *The Major of Queenborough,* pr. c. 1616-1620, pb. 1661 (with Rowley); *The Old Law: Or, A New Way to Please You,* pr. c. 1618, pb. 1656 (with Rowley and Philip Massinger); *Anything for a Quiet Life,* pr. c. 1621, pb. 1662 (with John Webster?); *Women Beware Women,* pr. c. 1621-1627, pb. 1657; *The Changeling,* pr. 1622, pb. 1653 (with Rowley); *A Game at Chess,* pr. 1624, pb. 1625; *The Selected Plays of Thomas Middleton,* pb. 1978

Other literary forms • Thomas Middleton's nondramatic work includes a number of youthful, less accomplished works. He produced *The Wisdom of Solomon, Paraphrased* (1597), a poem based on the Book of Solomon; *Micro-cynicon* (1599), a volume of satiric poems; *The Ghost of Lucrece* (1600), a narrative poem; and *The Black Book* (1604) and *Father Hubburd's Tales* (1604), two satiric pamphlets, the latter of which includes poetry. Through the rest of his career, the main body of Middleton's writing that was not for the theater consisted of the lavish public or court entertainments known as masques, pageants, or shows. Middleton was the author of at least seven lord mayors' shows—huge allegorical spectacles honoring the city, performed outdoors using expensive sets and costumes. In 1603, he collaborated with Thomas Dekker and Ben Jonson on a coronation pageant, *The Magnificent Entertainment Given to King James,* and in 1625, he was in charge of a pageant to welcome Charles I to London after King James's death. Between 1604 and 1625, he wrote at least six other masques and entertainments for the court and for important occasions.

Achievements • Like most of the dramatists of his day, Thomas Middleton lived as a practicing man of the theater without apparent concern for claiming literary stature. As with William Shakespeare (but in contrast to Jonson), the evidence suggests that he cared little about having his works published. Apparently the success he sought was that of the playwright whose works were performed, not read. Yet his works do have stature, both in reading and in performance. He created a number of interesting and insightful comedies, several substantial tragicomedies, and the most fascinating political satire of the age.

Four of Middleton's comedies are frequently described as masterpieces, and two of his tragedies are considered great works. The four comedies, all dating from the first half of his career (1604-1613), are *A Chaste Maid in Cheapside; A Mad World, My Masters;*

The Roaring Girl; and *A Trick to Catch the Old One*. The two tragedies, both written later (1620-1627), are *The Changeling* and *Women Beware Women*. (To these might be added *The Revenger's Tragedy* of 1606-1607, generally attributed to Cyril Tourneur but believed by some critics to be Middleton's work.) Middleton is judged by some to be the third great playwright, after Shakespeare and Jonson, in a period notable for its abundance of gifted dramatists.

Biography • Very little is known about Thomas Middleton's life except what can be determined from legal and theater records. Middleton's father was a bricklayer but also a gentleman who acquired a sizable estate by buying London property. Middleton was born in 1580, and when he was five, his father died, leaving an estate of more than three hundred pounds to his wife. She then wisely placed the estate in trust to three advisers to protect herself and her children from fortune hunters. Soon, she married Thomas Harvey, an adventurer who had just returned from Sir Walter Raleigh's expedition to colonize Roanoke Island. Apparently, marrying Middleton's mother was also a business venture and apparently Harvey did not know about the trust; as a result, between 1587 and 1599 there was constant litigation as Harvey attempted to gain control of his wife's fortune. From the age of seven on, young Middleton was in the midst of an ugly family situation that undoubtedly encouraged his later bent for satire.

At eighteen, Middleton entered Oxford, where he studied for at least two years but left without taking a degree. By 1601, he had left Oxford for his new love, the theater, and in the following year was receiving payment from Philip Henslowe, the theater owner, for collaborations with Dekker and John Webster. About this time, Middleton married Mary Marbeck, the sister of an actor.

At first, Middleton was writing for the Lord Admiral's Men, but beginning in 1603, he began writing primarily for Paul's Boys and the Children of the Chapel Royal, two companies of professional "child" actors (actors in their early and middle teens). For the private indoor theater called the Blackfriars, which served a well-to-do, sophisticated audience, Middleton wrote a number of his most satiric and successful city comedies. During the years when Jonson wrote *Volpone* (pr. 1605) and when Shakespeare was approaching the end of his career, Middleton became established as one of the leading English playwrights.

Soon, Middleton was working more for the adult companies, especially the Prince's Men and the Lady Elizabeth's Men. He came to associate more with Dekker and Webster and with William Rowley and to write a broader type of comedy. Middleton suffered from indebtedness and had to struggle through lawsuits. By 1609, he was living at Newington Butts because it was close to the theater district, and he apparently lived there until his death. Beginning about 1613, Middleton turned increasingly to writing and producing lord mayor shows, and this led in 1620 to his appointment as city chronologer, by which time he was probably fairly well-to-do. During this period, he tried his hand at several tragicomedies, a genre made popular by Francis Beaumont and John Fletcher. Finally, in the 1620's came his two great tragedies, *The Changeling* and *Women Beware Women*.

In 1624, *A Game at Chess*, probably Middleton's last play, created a huge scandal. At the time, anger toward Roman Catholic Spain was especially high in England, and Middleton provided a focus for this sentiment. His play is an elaborate allegory in which a game of chess reflects the contemporary international situation. The play was a phenomenal success, drawing capacity crowds for nine days in succession, an unusually long run for the theater in that era. Finally, because of protests by the Spanish ambassador over the play's seditious nature, the Privy Council ordered the play closed down and, according to one report, had Middleton imprisoned. In any case, he was soon involved with overseeing the printing of the play, which was also very successful. Although *A Game at Chess* was probably very lucrative for Middleton, he left very little behind for his widow when he died three years later, at the age of forty-seven. Her death followed two weeks after his own.

Analysis • As is the case with many writers of the Elizabethan and Jacobean stage, Thomas Middleton's canon has never been definitively established. For several reasons, it is extremely difficult to determine what is his work: The concrete evidence is scanty. Many plays were published in pirated editions, and Middleton frequently collaborated in writing his plays. Many critics do not believe that Middleton has a distinct style. Indeed, T. S. Eliot, in an essay highly praising Middleton as an artist, went so far as to say that he felt no sense of a distinct personality unifying the plays: To Eliot, Middleton was simply a name connecting a number of works.

Although the controversy surrounding Middleton's authorship has not been resolved, the critical consensus is that there are stylistic and thematic patterns connecting those plays that are definitely by Middleton. In fact, the Victorians had already perceived a pattern in Middleton's plays: To them, Middleton's viewpoint was immoral. Modern criticism consistently rejects this reading but acknowledges that Middleton's subject matter was frequently low and often shocking and was presented with little apparent value judgment by the author. Middleton's comedies, usually set in the city and usually antiromantic, are pictures of lust, greed, and ambition. They are frequently called "realistic," and the term applies well in one sense. The modern reader must not expect consistent realism or naturalism in the modern sense, for, like all plays of the period, Middleton's plays employ many nonrealistic conventions. Still, they are realistic in that they are filled with the language and behavior of the least elegant characters of London—with the bravado of grocers and the gabble of grocers' wives, with the slang of whores and the cant of thieves, and with the equally unrefined attitudes and language of various gentlemen and gentlewomen, who are also hungry for gold and glamour. In all of this uproar, Middleton is remarkably detached. Authorial judgments are made, but they are implied through subtle ironies rather than directly stated.

Middleton worked at first with a comedy of humors in the tradition of Roman comedy and under the immediate influence of Jonson. In these early comedies, he developed an increasing interest in character, in the psychology of human behavior and particularly the psyche's response to sin. Often, Middleton's characters undergo startling but carefully prepared-for conversions as their sins overwhelm them. Also, he became fascinated with presenting contemporary London life from a woman's point of view: Middleton often placed female characters at the center of his plays. Consistent with his psychological interest, Middleton from the beginning stood apart from his characters, allowing them to speak and act with little authorial intrusion. Irony is an increasingly persistent effect in these plays, and it is often gained through the aside and the soliloquy. With these conventions, Middleton reveals inner fears and desires, often in conflict with a character's public pose. Middleton's detached, ironic stance and his intense psychological interest are even more apparent in the tragedies later in his career. In these plays in the tradition of Shakespeare, Webster, and John Ford, he continued to use sin and retribution, particularly sexual degradation, as major themes. As in his earlier plays, he typically blended prose with blank verse, a verse that is never ornate but that rises to eloquence when the scene demands it.

There is something particularly modern about Middleton's attitude toward his material; perhaps it is a moral relativism. This modernity shows up in his persistent exploration of the psyche's complexity and in the ironies through which this complexity is expressed. His characters cannot be dismissed or summarized easily—a disturbing fact to previous ages looking for more decisive, discriminating judgments. Yet to the modern age, this is the highest kind of morality, and for that reason, Middleton's reputation will probably endure.

The Roaring Girl • Written in collaboration by Middleton and Dekker, *The Roaring Girl* centers on a real-life London woman named Moll Frith. Moll was reputed to be a prostitute, bawd, and thief, but the playwrights present her as a woman of great spirit and virtue whose reputation is maligned by a petty, convention-bound society. In the play, as in real life, Moll dresses in men's clothes, smokes a pipe, and wears a sword. This unconventionality, the play suggests, leads to her spotted reputation. She is a roaring girl—a brash woman-about-town—but beneath this lack of femininity is a courageous, high-principled woman. Moll intervenes in the main plots and is involved in skirmishes with many of the characters, consistently displaying her ability to stand up for the oppressed and mistreated, most eloquently when they are women.

The main plot of *The Roaring Girl* involves a young man, Sebastian Wengrave, and a young woman, Mary Fitzallard, in love with each other but prevented from marrying because Sebastian's father, Sir Alexander Wengrave, wants a well-to-do daughter-in law. Sebastian plots to outwit his father: He will pretend to be in love with the infamous Moll, and when his small-minded father learns this, he will agree to the union with Mary simply to get rid of Moll. The plan temporarily backfires, however, because Sir Alexander at first reacts by employing a false-witted humor character named Ralph Trapdoor, "honest Ralph," to tempt Moll to theft and have her executed. Moll resists his temptations and instead exposes Trapdoor as a coward, ultimately eliciting a confession and an apology from him. She is also instrumental in helping Sebastian win Mary and even in bringing on a complete conversion of his father, who eventually sees Moll with the eyes of true judgment rather than through his willful prejudices.

Accompanying the main plot are two parallel stories of couples whose marriages are tested by callous gallants. One of these men, Laxton, leads on Mrs. Gallipot until she tricks her supremely gullible husband into giving thirty pounds to him. Ultimately, however, she becomes disgusted with her would-be seducer and denounces him to her husband, whose eyes are finally opened. Similarly, a "gentleman" named Goshawk tries to seduce Mrs. Openwork; her husband, however, is far shrewder than Gallipot. He outmaneuvers Goshawk, and together husband and wife expose Goshawk's lechery. In both of these plots, marriage survives its attackers, but the differences between the marriages are equally important. Given Gallipot's blindness and Mrs. Gallipot's lechery, their marriage survives largely because Laxton prefers money to sex. The Openworks' marriage, on the other hand, survives because of the intelligence and integrity of the marriage partners.

A major motif in *The Roaring Girl* is the reversal of gender stereotyping. Moll wears masculine clothes; Mary disguises herself in men's clothes; Mrs. Gallipot speaks scornfully of her "apron" husband; and Moll several times overcomes male antagonists by means of her sword and the manly art of bullying. These reversals of sex roles are one of the means of uniting the many elements of the play: They reveal that appearances count for little, that the reality of a person's character shows up only through certain kinds of trials. Such trials or tests are quite frequent in the play. For example, Openwork tests Goshawk's integrity, Goshawk tests Mrs. Openwork's virtue, and Laxton tests Mrs. Gallipot's. Moll's honesty is tried by Sir Alexander through Trapdoor, and Moll herself tests the courage and integrity of many characters. The play overturns conventional assumptions that men have a monopoly on courage and that all women are the daughters of Eve. Instead, the play implies that men and women must be judged carefully and on their individual merits. Throughout the play, Moll stands as a lively, unconventional, attractive woman—an ancestor of the Shavian heroine. She is the one shining example of integrity in the play and one of the great creations of the period.

A Chaste Maid in Cheapside • In contrast to *The Roaring Girl,* which was co-authored by Middleton and Dekker, *A Chaste Maid in Cheapside* was written by Middleton alone. Also, in contrast to the eponymous protagonist of *The Roaring Girl,* the "chaste maid" of the title is a minor character. The play focuses instead on several men—Allwit, Sir Walter Whorehound, and Yellowhammer—who embody the values of London's Cheapside district (an area notorious for its unchaste women—and men). The play is admirable for its complex interweaving of many plots and for Middleton's detached stance, which creates such effective satire.

Yellowhammer, a goldsmith, and his wife, Maudlin, have two children: One is sweet, silent Moll, the chaste maid of the title, and the other is Tim, a foolish young man who is overly impressed with himself for having done well in Latin at Cambridge. The parents' overriding concern is to "sell" their children to prosperous spouses. They plan to have Moll marry Sir Walter Whorehound (in spite of his last name), and they hope to marry Tim to Sir Walter's "niece" (even though, as they eventually learn, she is actually his cast-off whore). In the meantime, Allwit (a play on the term "wittol," a willing cuckold) has been living comfortably without working because he and his wife have been quite willing for wealthy Sir Walter to "keep" Mistress Allwit as his mistress. In fact, Allwit is quite content that Sir Walter has fathered all of Mistress Allwit's children. The central conflict in the play develops when Allwit learns that Sir Walter might marry Moll: Allwit must prevent this if he and his wife are to remain in Sir Walter's keep.

A romantic plot runs through the play: Moll and a penniless young gentleman, Touchwood Junior, want to marry, but her greedy father opposes the plan. Another plot involves Touchwood Senior, who is so sexually potent that his wife (and many other women as well) are continually bearing his children. As a result, he and his wife have agreed that they must separate for a time because of the expense of increasing the size of their family. Finally, a related plot involves Sir Oliver Kix and his lady, relatives of Sir Walter, who are miserable because they are childless.

The ways the plots develop and are resolved reveal their related purposes. Touchwood Senior generously fathers a child for Sir Oliver. This resembles the Allwit/Sir Walter arrangement but with the important exception that Sir Oliver has no idea that he is a cuckold. Because Sir Oliver and Lady Kix now have an heir, they take the place of their relative, Sir Walter, in line for the family fortune and thus ruin his chances to win Moll. Meanwhile, however, Sir Walter and Touchwood Junior have a sword fight because of Moll, in which Sir Walter is seriously wounded. Thinking that he is dying, Sir Walter undergoes a kind of deathbed conversion and delivers an angry sermon to Allwit, who callously throws his former benefactor out. Then, in a burlesque of a tragicomic ending, the characters assemble for what they believe is the funeral of Touchwood Junior (dead from the sword fight) and of Moll (dead of grief), but in the middle of the ceremony both characters arise from their coffins and reveal that they are married.

In the outcome of the play, a rough poetic justice operates. Touchwood Junior wins Moll, and Tim Yellowhammer finds himself married to Sir Walter's "niece," who is almost what he deserves. Although Sir Walter has repented and become a sort of moral spokesman, his rejection by Moll and his loss of fortune are a suitable penance for his earlier lechery. On the other hand, the treatment of Allwit violates the pattern. Throughout the play, he has served as a remarkably detached commentator on morals and manners. For example, in one sharply satiric scene, he delivers the author's cutting observations about the hypocrisy of the Puritan women when they come to the christening of the Allwit's child. This uncomfortable intimacy between the audience and such a character complicates the audience's judgment of him and at least disconcerts the audience as they condemn him. Ultimately, Allwit is left with a comfortable home and has begun to play the role he will adopt thereafter—that of the hypocritically "moral" citizen. At this point, Middleton chooses realism over a too-simplistic moralism: Although comedy demands a degree of poetic justice, life reminds one that degenerate behavior often goes unpunished.

The Changeling • Middleton's greatest and most frequently read play is *The Changeling*. Coming near the end of an extraordinary period in England drama, it is often described as the last great English tragedy. The play's psychological realism makes it particularly appealing to the modern temperament. *The Changeling* was written in collaboration with William Rowley, and scholars generally agreed that Rowley wrote almost all of the subplot, while Middleton wrote almost all of the main plot and was responsible for the unity of the whole.

Set in Spain, *The Changeling* centers on a young woman, Beatrice, who falls in love with one young man, Alsemero, whom she first meets five days after she has become betrothed to another man, Alonzo. Beatrice believes that fate has been unfair to her in causing her to find true love five days too late. She is desperate to break off the engagement to Alonzo but feels bound to its because of her father's insistence and because she would be dishonoring her vow. To resolve this dilemma, she exploits DeFlores, a poor gentleman employed as a servant to her father. Beatrice finds DeFlores physically repulsive, but DeFlores is passionately attracted to her. Noticing this, Beatrice flatters him into thinking that she finds him handsome and then easily persuades him to kill Alonzo. All along, she blindly assumes that payment in gold will satisfy him; she fails to see that DeFlores (whose name suggests "deflower") expects to have her as his reward.

For his own part, DeFlores, having seen that Beatrice can cold-bloodedly arrange her fiancé's murder, understandably assumes that she will no longer have scruples about yielding her virginity to him. This radical, but psychologically plausible, misunderstanding creates considerable tension until DeFlores must finally state the payment that will satisfy him. Beatrice is shocked that he would "murder her honor," at which DeFlores points to her moral blindness: "Push, you forget yourself!/ A woman dipped in blood, and talk of modesty?" DeFlores reminds her that she is now "the deed's creature," that her moral innocence is gone now that she has commissioned a murder. Beatrice first becomes furious and then kneels and implores him to spare her, but he stands triumphant over her, grandly declaring, "Can you weep fate from its determined purpose?/ So soon may you weep me."

Alsemero and Beatrice are soon married, but Alsemero, largely because he is obsessed with being sure of his wife's purity, proposes to administer a virginity test. Because she has been seduced by DeFlores, Beatrice is able to pass the test only by deception. She realizes that she will fail the next test, her wedding night, and she plots to have her maid Diaphanta take her place in the wedding bed for a few hours. Diaphanta stays too long; she is awakened by a fire in the house, started by DeFlores, who kills her in the ensuing confusion. At this point, Beatrice recognizes that she has come to love DeFlores, revealing, in the psychological terms of the play, that she has been reduced to his level. Finally, Alsemero discovers Beatrice and DeFlores together and confronts her as a whore. As the confessions at last come out, DeFlores kills Beatrice and then himself, and her husband and father are left with the horror of what has happened.

The subplot of *The Changeling* takes place in an insane asylum, where Alibius, who runs the madhouse, jealously keeps his wife, Isabella, closely guarded. Two inmates who are merely feigning madness, Antonio and Franciscus, and Lollio, Alibius's subordinate, all try to seduce Isabella. Although she has more of a motive for unfaithfulness than does Beatrice, she remains loyal to her vows and eventually shames her husband into treating her better. This subplot works as a comic contrast to the main action of the tragedy. Lollio unsuccessfully tries to use Isabella's apparent unfaithfulness to blackmail her into yielding to his lust, and the scene in which this occurs is pointedly placed between the two private meetings between Beatrice and DeFlores. On several occasions, the madmen in the asylum run across the stage shouting out their dangerously uncontrolled desires, provoking their keepers to use the whip on them. This image of uncontrolled human appetite held in check reflects on the main plot: Beatrice and DeFlores—and, arguably, Alsemero, because of his failure to honor Beatrice's betrothal—fail to check their own libidinous desires.

The main plot of *The Changeling* was based on a moralistic narrative by John Reynolds called *The Triumphs of God's Revenge Against the Crying and Execrable Sin of Willful and Premeditated Murder* (1621); Middleton's version makes changes that soften the harsh judgment of the original. In the source story, Beatrice is continuously self-possessed, but in the play she is pictured as distracted, out of control, moved by an overwhelming fate. She frequently allows this fate, operating through her willful temperament, to distort her sense of morality. Through a heavy use of the soliloquy and the aside, Middleton reveals the intense inner struggles and desires of his characters, particularly Beatrice and DeFlores. Ultimately, Beatrice is disgusted with her sinful behavior, even though, in contrast to many of the great figures of Shakespearean tragedy, she is not fully enlightened about her errors at the end; a part of her tragedy lies in her moral blindness. DeFlores, by contrast, gains less sympathy but, like Shakespeare's Macbeth, more stature by always behaving with his eyes open.

Women Beware Women • As in *The Changeling*, the characters in *Women Beware Women* are obsessed with lust; like Beatrice, they become totally degraded because of it. Also as in *The Changeling*, two plots borrowed from two distinct sources are woven together ingeniously, each one commenting on the other. The main plot deals with a marriage that at first seems wholesome, perhaps even romantic. Leantio, a Florentine businessman, has married a Venetian woman, Bianca, who appears not to regret having given up family riches for love. When he leaves her with his mother as her chaperone, the Duke of Florence sees the beautiful, foreign Bianca and desires her. In order to pander to their sovereign, a brother and sister, Hippolito and Livia, plot to bring the two women to their house so that the duke can seduce Bianca.

As Livia distracts Leantio's mother with a game of chess, Hippolito conducts Bianca on a tour of the house. Hippolito suddenly presents the duke to Bianca and leaves her alone with him. Bianca halfheartedly resists the duke but soon yields to his passionate wooing and his promises of wealth. While this is occurring, the chess game below provides brilliant ironic commentary on the seduction above. When Leantio returns, Bianca treats him scornfully and openly flaunts her new lover. Leantio strikes back by becoming the lover of Livia, who has developed a sudden passion for him.

The subplot presents the relationship between Hippolito and his niece Isabella, who at first seem to have a pure, loving friendship. When Hippolito tries to seduce his niece, however, Isabella rejects him in horror. As in the main plot, Livia intercedes to help her brother by telling Isabella a lie—that she is not really a blood relative of Hippolito. Relieved of the threat of incest, Isabella can now express her love for Hippolito. Thus far, Isabella is essentially an innocent victim, but she is not so innocent when she agrees to go ahead with an arranged marriage in order to cover her love affair. She is betrothed to a coarse, stupid man, the ward of a character named Guardiano.

Both plots revolve around women who appear to be virtuous but who quickly reveal their frailty. Isabella at first appears to be a foil to Bianca, but she is scarcely her moral superior. In both plots, Livia schemes to destroy a woman in order to please her brother. Eventually, Hippolito learns about Livia's relationship with Leantio and, strangely, defends her honor by fighting and killing him. In anguish, Livia retaliates by revealing Hippolito's relationship with his niece, and this brings on the series of revenges in the denouement. During a masque to celebrate the wedding of the duke to Bianca, fictitious violence turns out to be real revenge and suicide. At the end, death comes to Isabella, Guardiano, Livia, Hippolito, the duke, and Bianca.

As a summary of its plot suggests, *Women Beware Women* is a play of almost unrelieved horror and baseness. The play's only decent character, the cardinal, appears late in the action as a commentator on this baseness. Several of the main characters highlight their moral confusion by adopting moral poses in the midst of their depravity; Isabella's marriage with Guardiano's ward is an example of this defense mechanism, as is Hippolito's concern for his sister's honor even though at the time he is knowingly committing incest. Similarly, the lecherous duke deludes himself that he will become a virtuous person simply by marrying Bianca. At the center of the intrigue stands Livia, outwardly a good-humored, sociable woman but underneath a vastly dangerous person because of her extraordinary indifference to moral standards. Hippolito, as he dies, has some sense of what the tragedy has been about: "Lust and forgetfulness has [*sic*] been amongst us,/ And we are brought to nothing." Through this and other reminders near the end, and above all through the many ironies of the play, audiences are able to see the tremendous waste of healthy instincts destroyed by lust and ambition.

Other major works

POETRY: *The Wisdom of Solomon, Paraphrased*, 1597; *Micro-cynicon*, 1599; *The Ghost of Lucrece*, 1600.

MISCELLANEOUS: *The Magnificent Entertainment Given to King James*, 1603 (with Thomas Dekker and Ben Jonson); *The Black Book*, 1604; *Father Hubburd's Tales*, 1604 (includes poetry); *Sir Robert Sherley*, 1609; *The Works of Thomas Middleton*, 1885-1886 (8 volumes; A. H. Bullen, editor).

Bibliography

Brittin, Norman A. *Thomas Middleton.* New York: Twayne, 1972. Presents in a chronology and an introduction what little is known of Middleton's life, then marches through the generally accepted canon. The final chapter outlines the critical response to Middleton, and the annotated secondary bibliography is a good guide.

Chakravorty, Swapan. *Society and Politics in the Plays of Thomas Middleton.* New York: Oxford University Press, 1996. A look at the political and social world that surrounded Middleton and found its way into his plays. Bibliography and index.

Daileader, Celia R. *Eroticism on the Renaissance Stage: Transcendence, Desire, and the Limits of the Visible.* New York: Cambridge University Press, 1998. Daileader looks at the depiction of women and eroticism in the works of Middleton and Shakespeare. Bibliography and index.

Heinemann, Margot. *Puritanism and Theatre: Thomas Middleton and Opposition Drama Under the Early Stuarts.* New York: Cambridge University Press, 1980. Heinemann considers a series of problems: Why do Middleton's tragedies differ in tone from others of the period? Why did his work change so much over his career? How could *A Game at Chess* have been staged in the midst of a political crisis? Heinemann finds the answers in the plays' political settings.

Heller, Herbert Jack. *Penitent Brothellers: Grace, Sexuality, and Genre in Thomas Middleton's City Comedies.* Newark: University of Delaware Press, 2000. Heller looks at Calvinism, sex, and city and town life in Middleton's comedies. Bibliography and index.

Martin, Mathew R. *Between Theater and Philosophy: Skepticism in the Major City Comedies of Ben Jonson and Thomas Middleton.* Newark: University of Delaware Press, 2001. A scholarly study that looks at skepticism as it appeared in the comedic dramas of Middleton and Jonson. Bibliography and index.

Elliott A. Denniston,
updated by Frank Day

Arthur Miller

Born: New York, New York; October 17, 1915

Principal drama • *The Man Who Had All the Luck,* pr. 1944, pb. 1989; *All My Sons,* pr., pb. 1947; *Death of a Salesman,* pr., pb. 1949; *An Enemy of the People,* pr. 1950, pb. 1951 (adaptation of Henrik Ibsen's play); *The Crucible,* pr., pb. 1953; *A Memory of Two Mondays,* pr., pb. 1955; *A View from the Bridge,* pr., pb. 1955 (one-act version); *A View from the Bridge,* pr. 1956, pb. 1957 (two-act version); *Collected Plays,* pb. 1957 (includes *All My Sons, Death of a Salesman, The Crucible, A Memory of Two Mondays, A View from the Bridge*); *After the Fall,* pr., pb. 1964; *Incident at Vichy,* pr. 1964, pb. 1965; *The Price,* pr., pb. 1968; *The Creation of the World and Other Business,* pr. 1972, pb. 1973; *The American Clock,* pr. 1980, pb. 1982; *Arthur Miller's Collected Plays, Volume II,* pb. 1981 (includes *The Misfits, After the Fall, Incident at Vichy, The Price, The Creation of the World and Other Business, Playing for Time*); *The Archbishop's Ceiling,* pr., pb. 1984; *Two-Way Mirror,* pb. 1984; *Danger: Memory!,* pb. 1986, pr. 1988; *Plays: One,* pb. 1988; *Plays: Two,* pb. 1988; *Plays: Three,* pb. 1990; *The Ride Down Mt. Morgan,* pr. pb. 1991; *The Last Yankee,* pb. 1991, pr. 1993; *Broken Glass,* pr., pb. 1994; *Plays: Four,* pb. 1994; *Plays: Five,* pb. 1995; *Mr. Peter's Connections,* pr. 1998, pb. 1999

Other literary forms • Although Arthur Miller's major reputation is as a playwright, he has published reportage, *Situation Normal* (1944); a novel, *Focus* (1945); a novelized revision of his screenplay *The Misfits* (both 1961); a screenplay entitled *Everybody Wins* (1990); two collections of short stories, *I Don't Need You Any More* (1967) and *Homely Girl: A Life, and Other Stories* (1995); three book-length photo essays in collaboration with his wife, Ingeborg Morath, *In Russia* (1969), *In the Country* (1977), and *Chinese Encounters* (1979); and one television drama, aired in 1980, *Playing for Time.* Most studies of Miller's career neglect his nondramatic writing, even though he has demonstrated an impressive command of the short-story form and has proved himself remarkably adept at blending reportage, autobiography, and dramatic reflection in his later essay-length books, such as *"Salesman" in Beijing* (1984) and *Spain* (1987). All the important themes of his plays are explored in his nondramatic work, which also contains considerable comment on the nature of drama. *The Theater Essays of Arthur Miller* (1978), edited by Robert A. Martin, and *Conversations with Arthur Miller* (1987), edited by Matthew C. Roudané, are essential to an understanding of Miller's theory of drama, his career in the theater, his political views, and his work as a whole; as is his autobiography, *Timebends* (1987).

Achievements • Arthur Miller has been acclaimed as one of the most distinguished American dramatists since Eugene O'Neill, the father of modern American drama. Because of his direct engagement with political issues and with the theoretical concerns of contemporary drama, he has frequently been a significant spokesperson for his generation of writers. His reputation seems secure both nationally and internationally, and his plays continue to be performed live or through screenplay adaptations all over the world.

Miller successfully synthesized diverse dramatic styles and movements in the belief that a play should embody a delicate balance between the individual and society, between the singular personality and the polity, and between the separate and collective elements of life. Miller is a writer of social plays whose concern with the moral problems in American society led him to probe the psychological causes of behavior. He builds on the realist tradition of Henrik Ibsen in his exploration of the individual's conflict with society but also borrows Symbolist and expressionist techniques from Bertolt Brecht and others. He bases his plays on the assumption of an objective reality that is comprehensible as well as a subjective reality that makes life problematic and ambiguous. Therefore, all attempts to interpret his work from either an exclusively political or an exclusively psychological standpoint fail, for Miller regards his plays as indissoluble amalgamations of inner and outer realities.

Miller's achievement as a dramatist has been recognized with numerous awards. These include the Pulitzer Prize in 1944 for *Death of a Salesman*; the New York Drama Critics Circle Award for *All My Sons* in 1947 and for *Death of a Salesman* in 1949; the Antoinette Perry Award in 1949 for *Death of a Salesman* and for *The Crucible*. In 1956, Miller received an honorary Doctor of Humane Letters degree from the University of Michigan, and he was elected to the National Institute of Arts and Letters in 1958. During the 1990's, he received the William Ingle Festival Award for distinguished achievement in American theater and the Edward Albee Last Frontier Playwright Award. In 1998, Miller was named Distinguished Inaugural Senior Fellow of the American Academy in Berlin. In 1999, he received the Tony Award for Best Revival of a Play (*Death of a Salesman*) and in 2001 a National Endowment for the Humanities fellowship and the John H. Finley Award for Exemplary Service to New York City.

Biography • Arthur Miller grew up in New York City with an older brother and a younger sister. His father was a prosperous businessperson until the Crash of 1929, after which the family suffered through the Depression, a period that had a major impact on Miller's sense of himself, his family, and his society, and one that figures prominently in many of his dramas, essays, and stories. During the Depression, Miller drove trucks, unloaded cargoes, waited on tables, and worked as a clerk in a warehouse. These jobs brought him close to the kind of working-class characters who appear in his plays. His observation of his father's fall from financial security and of the way the people immediately around him had to struggle for even a modicum of dignity placed Miller in a position to probe individuals' tenuous hold on their place in society.

Although Miller had been a poor student in school, he was inspired

(Inge Morath/Magnum)

by Fyodor Dostoevski's implacable questioning of individual impulses and societal rules in *The Brothers Karamazov* (1879-1880), and eventually he was able to persuade the University of Michigan to admit him. Almost immediately he began to write plays that were to receive several Hopwood awards. If Miller was not exactly a Marxist during his college years (1934-1938), he was certainly a radical insofar as he believed that American society had to be made over, to be made fair to the masses of people who had been ruined by the Depression.

His early student plays contain sympathetic portrayals of student militants and union organizers as well as compassionate characterizations of small business owners and professional people caught in the economic and political tyranny of capitalism. In the fall of 1938, after his graduation from the University of Michigan with a bachelor of arts degree in English language and literature, Miller joined the Federal Theatre Project in New York City, for which he wrote numerous radio plays and scripts until 1943. Some of these works express his irrepressible interest in social and political issues. In 1940, Miller married Mary Grace Slattery, and a daughter, Jane, was born in 1944. They divorced in 1956.

From Miller's earliest student plays to *Death of a Salesman*, there is an evolution in his treatment of individuals in conflict with their society, a gradual realization of conflicts within individuals that both mirror the larger conflicts in society and define a core of singularity in the characters themselves. Undoubtedly, Miller's intense involvement in public affairs in the 1940's and 1950's—his support of various liberal and radical causes and his subsequent testimony about his political commitments before the House Committee on Un-American Activities in 1956 are two examples—reflected and reinforced his need to write social plays.

Miller's marriage to Marilyn Monroe in 1956, far from being the perplexing and amusing sideshow the press made of it, had a significant impact on his writing, not only by encouraging him to focus on female characters in ways he previously had not but also by stimulating him to enlarge on and reconsider the theme of innocence that he had adumbrated in earlier plays. After his divorce from Monroe in 1961, he wrote some of his finest plays and continued to participate in local, national, and international affairs—including two terms as international president of PEN, the worldwide writers' organization. He was a delegate to the Democratic conventions of 1968 and 1972. Miller married Ingeborg Morath, a Austrian-born photojournalist, in 1962, and the couple collaborated on several travel books. After serving as a lecturer at the University of Michigan in the mid-1970's, Miller retired to a large Connecticut estate, where he continued to write and where he indulged in such hobbies as carpentry and gardening. In 1997, he petitioned the Czech government to halt arrests of dissident writers. His international reputation expanded during the 1980's, when he directed *Death of a Salesman* in Beijing, China. Throughout the 1990's, Miller continued to receive numerous awards for distinguished achievement. In early 2002, his wife died.

Analysis • A back injury prevented Arthur Miller from serving in the armed forces during World War II, but in characteristic fashion, he became involved in the war effort by gathering material for a screenplay, "The Story of GI Joe," which was never filmed but instead became the basis of his book *Situation Normal*, in which he reported on army camps in the United States and on soldiers' attitudes toward the war in which they were preparing to fight. For the most part, the soldiers had no great interest in the democratic principles for which Miller believed the war was fought, but he elevated one war hero, Watson, to a representative position as a figure whose intensely avowed loyalty to his company represents the democratic solidarity many others cannot articulate. Miller admitted candidly the skepticism of Watson's company commander, who doubted Watson's wholehearted commitment to rejoin his fellow soldiers in one of the most dangerous theaters of the war: "The company pride that made him do the great things he did do is gone now and he is left unattached, an individual," who yearns for—yet probably fears—returning to men he knows he will never see again. Thus, *Situation Normal* was transformed into the drama of how Miller's innocent convictions about the war were challenged by psychological and social complexities; indeed, the book is informed by a crisis of conviction that Miller did not fully recognize until the writing of *After the Fall* and *Incident at Vichy*.

The Man Who Had All the Luck • Even in an early play, *The Man Who Had All the Luck*—Miller's first Broadway production—there is some awareness of the dangers inherent in the innocent attitude of characters such as David Frieber, who insists that the world conform to what his employer, Shory, calls "the awards of some cloudy court of justice." At twenty, Frieber is still a child, Shory suggests, and Frieber admits that he does not know what he is supposed to be. He believes that he must somehow earn everything that comes to him. That good fortune and the complex interplay of societal forces he cannot control also contribute significantly to his success is an idea that disturbs him. In his quest to become self-made, he withdraws from society, from his family, and ultimately from himself. In the midst of his guilty obsession with the fact that others have aided him, he is unable to see that he has already demonstrated his resourcefulness. In his delusion that he can measure himself, he gives up everything he owns and starts a new business. Frieber's lunacy seems somewhat forced—much too strident, making it all too obvious that Miller has a point to prove. Moreover, Frieber's quasi-philosophical declamations disturb what is otherwise rather well-executed midwestern dialogue.

All My Sons • Miller comes even closer to fluent dialogue and carefully crafted dramatic structure in *All My Sons*, his first Broadway success and the first play he deemed mature enough to include in his *Collected Plays* of 1957. Critics have long admired the playwright's suspenseful handling of the Keller family's burden: the father's permitting defective parts to remain in warplanes that subsequently crash. Not only does Joe Keller fail to recognize his social responsibility, but also he allows his business partner to take the blame and serve the prison term for the crime.

Gradually, events combine to strip Keller of his rationalizations. He argues that he never believed that the cracked engine heads would be installed and that he never admitted his mistake because it would have driven him out of business at the age of sixty-one, when he would not have another chance to "make something" for his family, his highest priority. "If there's something bigger than that I'll put a bullet in my head!" he exclaims. He also claims that other businessmen behaved no differently during the war and that Larry, his son who died flying a warplane, would have approved of his actions: "He understood the way the world is made. He listened to me," Keller contends. He maintains these arguments, however, as a man who has clearly been challenged by his surviving son, Chris, who questions his father's very humanity when the full truth of Joe's irresponsibility is exposed: "What the hell are you? You're not even an animal, no animal kills his own, what are you?"

Joe Keller's tough, resilient character crumbles quickly after Larry's former fiancée, Ann, discloses Larry's last letter, in which he expresses his intention to crash his plane in shame over his father's culpability. The play turns somewhat melodramatic with Joe's reversal of viewpoint, his discovery of his social responsibility, and his human loss in the deaths of the young fliers. His statement, "They were all my sons," depends heavily on Larry's self-abnegating idealism and on other contrived plot devices, as Leonard Moss instructively points out. Miller resorts to the theatrical trick of the last-minute revelation rather than relying on character development.

Nevertheless, the logic of destroying Joe's innocent disregard of the world at large—he is not so much deeply cynical as he is profoundly unaware of the ties that must hold society together—is compelling, especially because he cries for moral direction. "What do I do? he asks his wife, Kate, thus strengthening Chris's imperative that his father reckon the consequences of his terrible moral oversight. If audiences are still gripped by the final events of *All My Sons*, it is because the play's early scenes convincingly dramatize familiar aspects of family and community, with characters who know one another very well, who are quick to respond to the nuances of conversation and to what is unspoken but clearly implied.

What disables Miller's plays before *Death of a Salesman* is not so much an inadequate understanding of dramatic form; rather, both his dramatic and nondramatic prose lack artistic tact. He tends to overstate social problems, to give otherwise inarticulate characters such as Lawrence Newman in the novel *Focus* an inappropriately self-conscious language that is meant to identify their cumulative awareness of societal sickness—in Newman's case, of anti-Semitism. Like so much of Miller's writing, however, *Focus* transcends its faults because of its author's incisive portrayal of events that relentlessly push Newman to the brink of self-knowledge.

Death of a Salesman • In *Death of a Salesman*—originally entitled "The Inside of His Head"—Miller brilliantly solves the problem of revealing his main character's inner discord, rendering Willy Loman as solid as the society in which he tries to sell himself. Indeed, many critics believe that Miller has never surpassed his achievement in this play, which stands as his breakthrough work, distinguished by an extremely long Broadway run, by many revivals, and by many theater awards, including the Pulitzer Prize in 1949. *Death of a Salesman* seems destined to remain an American classic and a standard text in American classrooms.

Willy Loman desperately wants to believe that he has succeeded, that he is "well liked" as a great salesman, a fine father, and a devoted husband. That he has not really attracted the admiration and popularity at which he has aimed is evident, however, in the weariness that belabors him from the beginning of the play. At the age of sixty-three, nearing retirement, Willy dreads confronting the conclusion that his life has gone offtrack, just like the automobile he cannot keep from driving off the road. His mind wanders because he has lost control: He has trouble keeping up with the bills; he feels hemmed in at home by huge, towering apartment buildings; his sales are slipping drastically; and his sons have thwarted his hope for their success.

Earlier in his career, Miller might have made a good but unremarkable play out of Willy's dilemma, a drama about how American society has misled him and stuffed him with unrealizable dreams until a conflict between social structures and individual desires becomes inevitable. Instead, Miller learned from the mistakes in his earlier plays not to divide individual and social realities too neatly or too simply, so that in *Death of a Salesman*, he created a great play that is not merely about a victim of society.

Willy is not easily categorized; he is both simple and complex. On the one hand, he has all the modern conveniences that stamp him as a product of society; on the other hand, he is not content to be simply another social component. As he tells Linda, his wife, who tries to soothe his sense of failure, "some people accomplish something." "A man has got to add up to something," he assures his brother, Uncle Ben. Willy resists the idea that his life has been processed for him—like the processed American cheese he angrily rejects for Swiss, his favorite. Still, he wonders, "How can they whip cheese?" and thus he can be diverted from self-scrutiny to the trivialities of postwar consumer society.

Willy worries that he talks too much, that he is fat and unattractive, but he also brags about his persuasive abilities, his knack for knowing how to please people. Similarly, he alternately regards his son Biff as a bum and as having "greatness"; Willy's automobile is alternately the finest of its kind and a piece of junk. Willy is a mass of contradictions who asks why he is "always being contradicted." He has never been able to sort himself out, to be certain of his course in life. He is insulted when his friend Charley offers him a job, because the job offer and Charley's self-assured demeanor—he keeps asking Willy when will he grow up—remind Willy of Uncle Ben, a man who is "utterly certain of his destiny," who once extended to Willy a tremendous opportunity in Alaska, an opportunity Willy rejected with regret in favor of a salesperson's career. He lives with the might-have-been of the past as though it were his present and even confuses Charley with Ben. As a result, scenes from Willy's past and present follow— and indeed pursue—one another successively in a fuguelike fashion that shows his awareness of his failure to progress.

There is a grandeur in Willy's dreams of success; his self-deceptions are derived from his genuine perceptions of life's great possibilities, which are like the big sales he has always hoped to make. This is why Linda abets his penchant for self-aggrandizement. She knows that he has not been a successful salesperson, but she tempers his faults: "You don't talk too much, you're just lively." At the same time, she is utterly believable as a housewife who has to know how much money her husband has brought home from work. After Willy exaggerates his sales from one trip, Linda quietly but firmly brings him back to reality by simply asking, "How much did you do?"—a question that becomes more pointed if the actress playing the role delicately emphasizes the word "did."

When the play is read aloud, there is an uncanny power in some of its simplest and seemingly pedestrian lines, lines that capture the nuances and innuendos of colloquial language. This subtly effective dialogue is enhanced by a powerful use of human gesture that distinguishes *Death of a Salesman* as a completely realizable stage drama. Toward the end of the play, for example, after Biff, "at the peak of his fury," bluntly tells Willy, "Pop, I'm nothing!" Biff relents, breaks down, sobs, and holds on to Willy, "who dumbly fumbles for Biff's face." This brief intimate encounter encapsulates everything that can be learned about Willy and Biff and about the play's import, for the son renounces the father's ridiculous belief in the son's superiority even as the son clings to the father for support. While Biff rejects Willy, he embraces him and has to explain himself to Willy, who is "astonished" and at first does not know how to interpret his son's holding on to him. Willy does not understand why Biff is crying. Willy has always been blind to Biff's needs, has always "fumbled" their relationship, yet—as so often— Willy transforms Biff's words of rejection into an affirmation. The Biff who leans on him is the son who "likes me!" Willy exclaims, after their close but momentary contact. This fleeting instance of family solidarity, however, cannot overcome the abiding family conflicts and misunderstandings, epitomized by Willy's delusion that the insurance money accrued from his suicide will finally make him the good provider, the person who furthers his son's magnificent future.

An Enemy of the People • Miller followed *Death of a Salesman* with his 1951 adaptation of Henrik Ibsen's *En folkefiende* (pb. 1882; *An Enemy of the People*, 1890). Miller transforms Ibsen's language into American idioms and shortens the play to emphasize the impact of Dr. Stockmann's confrontation with his community, which will not acknowledge its polluted water, its own moral and political corruption. Stockmann's battle against public opinion clearly foreshadows John Proctor's struggle with his society's self-inflicted evil in *The Crucible*. *The Crucible* is far more complex than Miller's adaptation of Ibsen's play, however, because Proctor is much more complicated than Stockmann, and the motivations of the Puritans are not as easily fathomed as those of Stockmann's townspeople, who are primarily worried about their economic welfare. Even so, *An Enemy of the People* prefigures the fundamental questions raised in *The Crucible* about the value of human dignity and individuality and the kind of justice one can expect from a majority culture, especially when that culture begins to doubt its own coherence.

The Crucible • With incisive historical summaries, Miller, in *The Crucible*, characterizes the community of Salem, Massachusetts, in 1692, which has been beset by property disputes, by a slackening in religious fervor, and by an increasing lack of trust among its citizens. Rather than face their inner turmoil, some of Salem's citizens search for scapegoats, for people who can take on the society's sense of defeat and frustration, who can be punished, and who can carry away by means of their execution the society's burden of guilt. In short, the Puritans seek signs of the devil and devil-worship in their midst in order to dissolve their own dissension. Although John Proctor, like Stockmann, speaks against his community's blindness to the true causes of its corruption, he does not share to the same degree Stockmann's naïveté, youthful outrage at injustice, and virtually pure innocence as a dissident. On the contrary, Proctor eventually opposes the witch-hunt, because he accepts his own part in having made that hysterical clamor for scapegoats possible.

Proctor knows that he has not acted quickly enough to expose Abigail, the chief instigator of the witch-hunt, because he has feared his own exposure as an adulterer. What finally exercises his conscience is not simply that he had previously given way to his lust for Abigail but that he had deluded himself into thinking he no longer cared for her and had even reprimanded his wife, Elizabeth, for failing to forgive him. Elizabeth is unbending but not without cause, for she intuits her husband's tender feelings toward Abigail and suspects that he refuses to know his own mind. Proctor almost relinquishes his good name by confessing to witchery, until he realizes that however deep his guilt and responsibility may be for the community's corruption, he cannot surrender his integrity, his cherished individuality. Like Willy Loman, Proctor reaffirms his own name—"I am John Proctor!"—and prefers his own crucible to his society's severe test of him for its redemption.

The Crucible is not only Proctor's play, however, and as important as its moral and political implications are—it was first received as a parable on McCarthyism and the 1950's hysteria over communism in the United States—it deserves analysis as a dramatic whole in the same way that *Death of a Salesman* does. In Miller's superb creation of scenes that require a company of carefully choreographed actors and actresses, he is able to dramatize an entire society and to show the interplay of individual and group psychology. Proctor would not be regarded as such a powerful personality were it not for the full panoply of personalities out of which he emerges. In this respect, *The Crucible* has a finer equilibrium as a social play than does *Death of a Salesman*, which is inescapably dominated by Willy Loman's consciousness.

Miller's accomplished use of the Puritans' formal idioms suggests their rigid judgments of one another. Perhaps he even exaggerates the archaisms of their language in order to stress the gravity of their worldview, although at the same time, he dramatizes a childishness in their readiness to credit the workings of witchcraft. There is a great deal of humor, for example, in one of the play's early scenes, in which Mrs. Putnam's energetic entrance explodes the seriousness of reports that the Reverend Parris's child, Betty, has been bewitched. Mrs. Putnam, every bit as excited as a child, immediately glances at Betty and wonders, "How high did she fly, how high?" The simple, naïve directness of these words catches the audience up in a kind of enthusiasm for the marvelous that will soon infect Abigail and her female followers as well as the whole society of Salem. By varying his speakers' styles to conform to the precise demands of each dramatic situation, Miller wins the audience's absolute confidence in the psychological reality of his characters.

A Memory of Two Mondays • Miller's excursion into the Puritan past was followed by the writing of two one-act plays, *A Memory of Two Mondays* and *A View from the Bridge* (later revised as a two-act play), both of which he regarded as having arisen from his personal experience, although it took him some time to discover the autobiographical elements of the latter play. *A Memory of Two Mondays* covers the Depression period before Miller's admission to the University of Michigan, and the play centers on the discrepancy between human needs and work requirements. Kenneth, the most melancholy character in the play, also has the greatest feeling for life and for its poetry. In the end, however, he has forgotten the poems he recites to Bert, the only character who escapes the tedium of the automobile parts warehouse, who will read the great books and save enough money to go to college. The other characters remain very much imprisoned in their everyday lives. Bert's leavetaking is hardly noticed, even though he lingers in obvious need of making more out of his friendships at the warehouse than others are willing to acknowledge. Earlier, he and Kenneth had washed the windows of the warehouse to get a clear look at the world in which they were situated; now Kenneth is a drunk and Bert must stand apart, like his author, remembering the meaning of what others have already forgotten because of the demands of their jobs. Although *A Memory of Two Mondays* is one of Miller's minor achievements, it is also one of his most perfectly executed dramas in that the impulse to rescue significance from Bert's departure is sensitively qualified by the consciousness of human loss.

A View from the Bridge • Miller's one-act version of *A View from the Bridge* is also a memory play—in this case based on a story he had heard and pondered for several years. Eddie Carbone, a longshoreman, is driven to violate the most sacred ties of trust that bind his community by his compulsion to possess his niece, Catherine—a compulsion that he denies and displaces by conceiving an unreasoning dislike for his wife's young relative, Rodolpho, an illegal immigrant whom Eddie has agreed to harbor. Eddie implies that Rodolpho is a homosexual, an unnatural man who will marry Catherine merely to make his stay in the country legal. Eddie's desperate need to have Catherine becomes so uncontrollable that, when she and Rodolpho make plans to marry, he informs on Rodolpho and his brother, Marco, who are apprehended in circumstances that expose Eddie to his neighborhood as an informer. In Marco's view, Eddie must be confronted with his subhuman behavior. In words reminiscent of Chris's charge in *All My Sons* that his father is not human, Marco calls Eddie an animal who must abase himself. "You go on your knees to me!" Marco commands Eddie, while Eddie expects Marco to give him back his "good name." They fight, and Eddie dies, stabbed by Marco with the former's own knife. In a sense, Eddie has stabbed himself; the play has shown all along that Eddie's mortal wound has been self-inflicted.

Eddie's cry for self-respect recalls similar pleas by Willy Loman and John Proctor, and the concern in *A View from the Bridge* with informing and betrayal of friendships and blood ties echoes themes from Miller's student plays through *The Crucible*, foreshadowing not only his own refusal to "name names" in his testimony before the House Committee on Un-American Activities but also Quentin's fundamental exploration of many different kinds of betrayal in *After the Fall*. Yet Miller first wrote *A View from the Bridge* as if he were aloof from its central story, as if it were a parable that he did not understand. He even provides a narrator, Alfieri, an attorney who ruminates over the significance of the story as Miller admits he had done in writing the play.

The one-act version of *A View from the Bridge* seems aloof from the audience as well. There is very little attempt to probe the characters' psychology, so that what Miller gains in dramatic force by presenting events swiftly and starkly, he loses in the audience's inability to empathize with circumscribed characters. Miller acknowledges these faults and notes that the two-act version more fully develops his characters' psychology, particularly that of Eddie's wife, Beatrice. Catherine, too, is a much-improved character in the two-act version. She tentatively expresses her divided feelings about Eddie, whereas in the one-act version, she is far less self-searching, almost woodenly immune to his passion. In the two-act, she desires to appease Eddie's growing fears of her approaching adulthood. She loves him for his devotion to her, but her childlike behavior, as Beatrice points out to her, only encourages his possessiveness. Thus, Catherine tries gradually to separate herself from Eddie so that she can attain full maturity. As a result, Eddie's rigid refusal to admit his perverse passion for Catherine, even when Beatrice confronts him with it, makes him singularly willful and more particularly responsible for his tragedy than is the case in the one-act version, in which all the characters, except Alfieri, are rather helplessly impelled by events. In this respect, Rodolpho is a more credible suitor for Catherine in the two-act version because he is somewhat more commanding (she pleads with him, "I don't know anything, teach me, Rodolpho, hold me") in capturing her love and therefore a stronger counterweight to Eddie's authority.

A View from the Bridge in two acts still does not overcome all the play's weaknesses. For example, Alfieri, like many narrators in drama, seems somewhat intrusive in his use of elevated language to wrest an overarching meaning from characters and events, even though he is an active participant in some fine scenes. Nevertheless, the play is as beautifully written and moving as any of Miller's major works, and its main character is almost as powerfully drawn as Willy Loman and John Proctor, who, like Eddie Carbone, will not "settle for half"—will not be content with less than their lives' joy. Because of an ample sense of self, they allow themselves, in Alfieri's words, "to be wholly known."

An interlude • Miller arrived at an impasse upon his completion of the two-act version of *A View from the Bridge*, which was successfully produced in England in 1956, and he did not have another new work staged until 1964. Various explanations have been offered for this long gap in his dramatic production—including his marriage to Marilyn Monroe, the attendant publicity that interfered with his working life, and the trying and time-consuming process of defending his political activities. Of crucial importance, however, seems to have been his feeling that what he had been working for in his plays had not been sufficiently understood by his public. At any rate, he wrote several plays that did not satisfy him, a number of short stories, and a screenplay, *The Misfits*, that was subsequently revised as a novel. He may have turned to other literary forms from a belief that he had temporarily exhausted what had been an evolving sense of dramatic structure. Nondramatic prose seems to have permitted him to explore certain themes and narrative viewpoints that he had not been able to incorporate fully in *A View from the Bridge*, for his next produced play, *After the Fall*, successfully fuses narrative and dramatic discourse in the figure of its central character, Quentin, who constantly forces the audience into the explicit position of auditors rather than into the intermittent role of eavesdroppers addressed by a narrator as in *A View from the Bridge*.

After the Fall • How does one live in a world beset by death? This question is relentlessly probed in *After the Fall*, with its concentration-camp tower serving as one of the central metaphors for the human betrayal of life. As was so often true in the camps, the characters in *After the Fall* are divided against themselves. Not only can kind men kill, but also intelligent men can act like idiots, and Maggie—innocent in so many ways—is horribly transformed into a hater of life. Quentin, who is Maggie's momentary stay against confusion, witnesses "things falling apart" and wonders, "Were they ever whole?" He proves to be incapable of protecting Maggie, so concerned is he with his own survival. In the very act of saving her from her pills—from her death—he defends himself by strangling her, suffocating her just as surely as the pills would have done. He discovers the limits of his own love for Maggie, and Maggie sees his human incapacity for unconditional love as a betrayal, just as Quentin interprets the limitations of his mother's love as a betrayal of him.

Thus, for Maggie, Quentin comes at "the end of a long, long line" of men who have degraded her, betrayed her, killed her. He is, in other words, an accomplice in the general evil of the world, and therefore his presence as an "accomplice" in the ultimate evil that is the concentration camp is not altogether unfitting. He has been his mother's accomplice in the degradation of his father and an accomplice in the death of his friend, Lou, who sensed that Quentin could not wholeheartedly defend his reputation and that he was not, in fact, a true friend. Quentin craves his own safety, and he feels the guilt of the survivor as the concentration-camp tower "blazes into life."

Maggie has no identity to hold back, no reserves of self to compensate for her disappointment in Quentin. She thinks of herself as "nothing" and hopes to please everyone by becoming "all love." (The metaphor's abstractness virtually ensures her inability to develop a defined self.) Ironically, her generosity eats her up—people eat her up— because she does not possess the normal defenses of a separate ego. Maggie requires from Quentin the same selflessness she represents. She wants him to look at her "out of [his] *self*." Quentin has abetted her by acting more like a child than an adult. Like William Faulkner's Quentin Compson in *The Sound and the Fury* (1929), Miller's Quentin is an idealist and something of a Puritan; he romanticizes Maggie's innocence and believes that she must be saved from herself and from a corrupt world. In some ways, he seems as thoroughly innocent as Quentin Compson's brother Benjy, an idiot—the word itself is applied to Miller's protagonist more than once, and it recurs obsessively as he recalls how others have employed the term to deny and attack one another. No more than Benjy or Maggie can Quentin accept the separateness of the adult world of his mother, his friends, and his wives.

These failures of love, of human connection, force Quentin to reexamine the moments of hopefulness that recur, one might say, idiotically—for no apparently sensible reason—throughout the play. From the concentration-camp tower and on "the mountain of skulls" where no one can be "innocent again," Quentin observes the "fallen Maggie," who once seemed like a proof of victory, and he realizes that his brothers both died in and built the camp, that Maggie's fall is his fall, and that without that fall he would have no hope, for hope in the real world is "not in some garden of wax fruit and painted trees, that lie of Eden," but in the knowledge of human destructiveness, of human idiocy, which will not go away and so must be taken to heart. In the full knowledge of his failures, Quentin embraces his life at the end of the play, whereas Maggie is seen rising from the floor "webbed in with her demons, trying to awake."

Maggie's partial consciousness reflects her inability to take full responsibility for her life, to see that she was not simply a victim but in charge of her emotions. The hardest thing Quentin must do is reverse the force of the play's dominant metaphor, making the idiot serve not as a rejection of the broken, fragmented facts of life but as an acceptance of the flawed face of all people. That reversal of rejection is accomplished by saying hello to Holga, his third partner in life, who has provided the dream—the metaphor, in truth—of how lives such as Quentin's ("Why do I make such stupid statements!") and Maggie's ("I'm a joke that brings in money") can tentatively approach redemption.

After the Fall sometimes suffers from a vagueness of rhetoric and from overstatement, so that Quentin's confessions overwhelm the dramatic action and diminish the substantiality of other characters. Miller restrains Quentin's verbosity in the revised stage version quoted here (printed in 1964, the same year as the production of the original stage version, available in *Collected Plays, Volume II*). A television adaptation (1974) removes nearly all of Quentin's verbiage, but in none of these versions is Miller entirely successful in balancing Quentin's subjective and objective realities. Edward Murray argues, for example, that not all scenes are consistently staged "in the mind, thought, and memory of Quentin," as the play would have it. Hence it is difficult to find a "warrant," a certifiable viewpoint, for some of the play's action. In *Death of a Salesman*, on the contrary, the audience is compelled to move in and out of Willy's mind and is thereby able to comprehend his reality both subjectively and objectively. In part, Murray's objection may be met by carefully following Quentin's struggle to *know* his past, not simply to repossess it as Willy does. How does one achieve a viewpoint, Quentin asks, when there is no objective basis on which to recreate one's past? In the disagreements over Quentin's motives (some critics emphasize his self-criticism, others his self-exculpation), Miller adumbrates an ambiguity of viewpoint explored more successfully in *The Price*.

Incident at Vichy • Some reviewers of the first production of *Incident at Vichy* mistook it as a message play and faulted Miller not only for his didacticism but also for teaching a lesson already learned about Nazism and people's inhumanity toward others. It is a very talky drama, and given the various arguments advanced, it is easy to regard the characters as representative figures rather than as whole personalities. That this is not the case, however, is evident in the play's refusal to locate a winning argument, a resolution of the crisis of conviction besetting each character as his most cherished opinions are found wanting, are exposed as contradictory and self-serving.

Even Leduc, who does a large amount of the debunking, discovers that he is not free of self-aggrandizing illusions. The Major reveals Leduc's privileged sense of himself, and Von Berg forces on him a pass to freedom, which he must take at the cost of another's imprisonment. Von Berg's self-abnegating act of love for another man—although a moving statement of his belief that there are people in the world who would sacrifice themselves rather than permit evil to be done to others—is not dramatized as a final answer to the self-interested pleas of the other characters, however, and it does not cause the reversal of belief Miller coerced from Joe Keller after his son Larry's suicide in *All My Sons*. On the contrary, Von Berg is faced at the end of the play with an uncomprehending Major, a man who scorns gestures of self-sacrifice, except insofar as he is "an idealist" who ironically sacrifices himself for the perpetuation of the totalitarian system he serves.

For all the characters, then, Vichy France during World War II is a place of detention where their self-justifications are demolished as they await their turns in the examination room, in which their release or their final fate in the concentration camps will be determined. Like Quentin, they are all vulnerable to the suspicion that they have not lived in "good faith." In other words, it is their questionable integrity, not their shaky ideas, that is ultimately at stake. *Incident at Vichy* is Miller's most existential play, in the sense that there is no exit from the dilemmas it portrays, no consoling truths to which characters can cling permanently; instead, there are only approximations of the truth, certain accurate perceptions, but there is nothing like the requiem, the coda, the summing up to be found in *Death of a Salesman, The Crucible,* and *A View from the Bridge.*

The Price • In *The Price,* Miller combines the best features of *After the Fall* and *Incident at Vichy.* Once again, the issue of coming to others in "good faith" is paramount, as Esther realizes in characterizing the surprise appearance of her husband Victor's brother, Walter. Walter returns to their boyhood apartment, where Victor is selling the family possessions because the building has been condemned. Walter has not seen his brother in sixteen years and wants to explain to him why he chose such an independent course, why he failed to support their father as Victor had done, to the detriment of his career.

The immensely successful Walter feels stymied by the past and suggests that he and Victor took "seemingly different roads out of the same trap" created by their father's pose of helplessness after the failure of his business in the Crash of 1929. While Victor chose to "invent" a life of self-sacrifice, Walter chose to adopt a career of self-advancement. "We're like two halves of the same guy," Walter insists. His point is well taken in terms of Miller's dramatic development, for Victor and Walter are also opposite sides of Quentin, whose family background is somewhat similar to theirs and who engages in similar debates with himself concerning the calls of self-denial and self-preferment; indeed, like Quentin, Victor and Walter are having what is essentially an argument with themselves in front of auditors (Esther and the furniture dealer, Gregory Solomon).

Because Walter and Victor can go over the same ground of the past, their recollections are both arguable and utterly convincing as parallel but divergent interpretations. Thus, the audience responds to one character's point of view in the context of the other's and follows precisely the process by which these characters form their histories. Walter excuses himself by showing that in objective terms his father was not helpless; he had four thousand dollars he asked Walter to invest for him. Walter rejects the vision of family harmony that Victor worked so steadily to maintain; there was no love between their mother and father, only a business arrangement, as Walter brutally reveals with vivid memories of how their mother failed to support their father in his terrible need. Victor dismisses Walter's narrowly conceived interpretation of his father and their family. "A system broke down," he reminds Walter, referring to the Crash, "did I invent that?" Victor fights against Walter's simplification of their father's psychology. Embedded in Victor's words is an echo of Miller's original title for *Death of a Salesman*: "What about the inside of his head? The man was ashamed to go into the street!"

In the dialogue between these "archetypal brothers," as Neil Carson calls them, the nature of individual psychology and social reality, which Miller explores in all of his plays, is debated, and nowhere is that exploration more finely balanced, more convincingly conceived, than in *The Price*, where the two brothers—for all of their representativeness—steadfastly remain individual and irreconcilable. Moreover, the other two characters, Esther and Solomon (a kibitzer who is Miller's funniest and wisest creation), are just as credibly presented, as they mediate between the hard positions held by Victor and Walter. Esther is one of Miller's most complex female characters, as her lyric memory at the end of the play demonstrates, for her wistful words richly embody all the wonderful promise of a life gone sour, just as Solomon's last actions—he is listening to a "laughing record" from the 1920's, "sprawling in the chair, laughing with tears in his eyes, howling helplessly to the air"—recall all the characters' hilarious and painful memories, leaving the audience perfectly poised in this drama of life's alternative expressions.

The Creation of the World and Other Business • *The Creation of the World and Other Business*—with its archetypal brothers (Cain and Abel), its battle between God and Lucifer (who stand as the alternatives between which Adam and Eve must choose), its feel for human beings in a state of natural but problematic innocence, and its grappling with injustice—is an inevitable outgrowth of themes Miller has pursued throughout his career. When the play first appeared, however, it startled reviewers with its departure from Miller's realistic, domestic settings. They did not receive it favorably, and the play failed in its initial Broadway production, which is unfortunate, because it contains some of Miller's shrewdest writing and a surprisingly innovative rendition of the Edenic myth.

The play's humor saves it from becoming a ponderous retelling of the familiar biblical account. The wide-ranging use of idiomatic expressions in English, Yiddish, and French mixed with the English of the Authorized Version of the Bible sets up a fascinating juxtaposition between the traditional story and the contemporary language that gives the whole play an uncanny freshness and irreverence. God calls Adam and Eve "my two idiotic darlings," and the profoundly comic nature of their moral and sexual education gradually acquires credibility. Would not the experience of being the first man and woman constitute the first comedy as well as the first tragedy? This is the question Miller appears to have posed for himself in this play, for Adam and Eve do not know what to do. Not having a history of feelings about God, about humanity, and about their sexuality, they must discover their sentiments about all of these things, and Lucifer would like to show them the shortcuts, to rationalize life, to avoid conflict before it begins. In order to follow him, however, Adam and Eve must accept the primacy of intellect over love.

Later plays • Several of Miller's later plays, including *The American Clock*, *The Archbishop's Ceiling*, and *Danger: Memory!*, proved far more successful in London than in New York, a fact the playwright attributed at one point to the discomfort his American producers felt in dealing with "psychopolitical themes." Deeply cognizant of the dangers of social coercion and excessive conformity, Miller continued to hunger for the sense of community he described in one of his books of photo essays, *In Russia*:

> No one who goes to the theater in Russia can fail to be struck by the audience. . . . It is as though there were still a sort of community in this country, for the feeling transcends mere admiration for professionals doing their work well. It is as though art were a communal utterance, a kind of speech which everyone present is delivering together.

Other major works

LONG FICTION: *Focus*, 1945; *The Misfits*, 1961.

SHORT FICTION: *I Don't Need You Any More*, 1967; *Homely Girl: A Life, and Other Stories*, 1995.

SCREENPLAYS: *The Misfits*, 1961; *Everybody Wins*, 1990; *The Crucible*, 1996.

TELEPLAY: *Playing for Time*, 1980.

NONFICTION: *Situation Normal*, 1944; *In Russia*, 1969 (photo essay; with Inge Morath); *In the Country*, 1977 (photo essay; with Morath); *The Theater Essays of Arthur Miller*, 1978, revised and expanded 1996 (Robert A. Martin, editor); *Chinese Encounters*, 1979 (photo essay; with Morath); *"Salesman" in Beijing*, 1984; *Conversations with Arthur Miller*, 1987 (Matthew C. Roudané, editor); *Spain*, 1987; *Timebends: A Life*, 1987; *Arthur Miller and Company*, 1990 (Christopher Bigsby, editor); *The Crucible in History and Other Essays*, 2000; *Echoes Down the Corridor: Collected Essays, 1947-2000*, 2000; *On Politics and the Art of Acting*, 2001.

CHILDREN'S LITERATURE: *Jane's Blanket*, 1963.

MISCELLANEOUS: *The Portable Arthur Miller*, 1995 (Christopher Bigsby, editor).

Bibliography

Bigsby, C. W. E. *File on Miller*. New York: Methuen, 1987. Contains a detailed, up-to-date chronology, synopses of the major and minor plays and of the drama on television and radio, and excerpts from nonfiction writing, with each section accompanied by critical commentary. Also includes a comprehensive bibliography of Miller's essays, interviews, and secondary sources (collections of essays, articles, chapters in books, and book-length studies).

Bigsby, Christopher, ed. *The Cambridge Companion to Arthur Miller*. Cambridge, England: Cambridge University Press, 1997. Contains a detailed chronology, an essay on the tradition of social drama, and chapters on the early plays, the major plays, and Arthur Miller in each of the decades from the 1960's through the 1990's. There follow chapters on Miller's involvement with cinema, his fiction, and his relationship with criticism and critics. Includes a bibliographic essay and an index.

Bloom, Harold, ed. *Arthur Miller*. New York: Chelsea House, 1987. This volume consists of essays on Miller's major drama from *All My Sons* to *The American Clock*, a brief introduction discussing Miller's significance, a chronology, a bibliography, and an index. Includes important early essays (Raymond Williams and Tom F. Driver on the playwright's strengths and weaknesses) and later criticism by Neil Carson, C. W. E. Bigsby, and E. Miller Buddick.

_____, ed. *Arthur Miller's "Death of a Salesman."* New York: Chelsea House, 1988. Contains critical discussions published between 1963 and 1987, a chronology of Miller's life, a comprehensive bibliography of books and articles, and an index. In spite of reservations about Miller's importance as a writer, Bloom explains in his introduction how the play "achieves true aesthetic dignity" and discusses the particular merits of the essays in this collection.

Murphy, Brenda. *Miller: Death of a Salesman.* Cambridge, England: Cambridge University Press, 1995. This comprehensive treatment of Miller's play *Death of a Salesman* discusses its Broadway production, productions in English and in other languages, and media productions. Also provides a production chronology, a discography, a videography, and an extensive bibliography and index.

Schleuter, June, and James K. Flanagan. *Arthur Miller.* New York: Frederick Ungar, 1987. Contains a comprehensive narrative chronology, a thorough first chapter on Miller's literature and life to 1985, chapter-length discussions of his major plays (including *The Archbishop's Ceiling*), and a concluding chapter on his later one-act plays. Extensive notes, bibliography of Miller's work in all genres, select secondary bibliography of books and articles, and index.

Carl Rollyson,
updated by Victoria Price

Yukio Mishima

Kimitake Hiraoka

Born: Tokyo, Japan; January 14, 1925
Died: Tokyo, Japan; November 25, 1970

Principal drama • *Kantan,* wr. 1950, pb. 1956 (English translation, 1957); *Yoro no himawari,* pr., pb. 1953 (*Twilight Sunflower,* 1958); *Dōjōji,* pb. 1953 (English translation, 1966); *Aya no tsuzumi,* pr. 1955, pb. 1956 (*The Damask Drum,* 1957); *Aoi no ue,* pr., pb. 1956 (*The Lady Aoi,* 1957); *Hanjo,* pb. 1956 (English translation, 1957); *Sotoba Komachi,* pb. 1956 (English translation, 1957); *Kindai nōgakushū,* pb. 1956 (includes *Kantan, The Damask Drum, The Lady Aoi, Hanjo,* and *Sotoba Komachi; Five Modern Nō Plays,* 1957); *Tōka no kiku,* pr., pb. 1961; *Sado kōshaku fujin,* pr., pb. 1965 (*Madame de Sade,* 1967); *Suzakuke no metsubō,* pr., pb. 1967; *Waga tomo Hittorā, pb. 1968, pr. 1969 (My Friend Hitler,* 1977); *Chinsetsu yumiharizuki,* pr., pb. 1969

Other literary forms • Yukio Mishima was a critic, an essayist, and a poet (though largely unpublished in the latter genre) as well as a dramatist. His aesthetic is carefully set forth in *Taiyō to tetsu* (1968; *Sun and Steel,* 1970) and *Hagakure nyumon* (1967; *On Hagakure,* 1977). No doubt, however, he is best known as one of Japan's most accomplished and prolific novelists of the immediate post-World War II period, and it is as a novelist that he will be known to future generations. His major novels include *Kamen no kokuhaku* (1949; *Confessions of a Mask,* 1958), *Kinkakuji* (1956; *The Temple of the Golden Pavilion,* 1959), *Gogo no eikō* (1963; *The Sailor Who Fell from Grace with the Sea,* 1965), and his tetralogy, *Hōjō no umi,* published between 1969 and 1971, and translated into English between 1972 and 1974 as *The Sea of Fertility: A Cycle of Four Novels,* comprising *Haru no yuki* (1969; *Spring Snow,* 1972), *Homba* (1969; *Runaway Horses,* 1973), *Akatsuki no tera* (1970; *The Temple of Dawn,* 1973), and *Tennin gosui* (1971; *The Decay of the Angel,* 1974). In addition to the above-named works and several other significant novels, Mishima published some fine short fiction and a large quantity of other writings, ranging from literary criticism to slick formula fiction produced strictly to maintain his expensive lifestyle.

Achievements • The paradoxical Yukio Mishima brought to the West an awareness of modern Japan both as a unique culture and as a lively leader in the world, as a nation with much in common between its individuals and those of other cultures and an appreciation of the complexities of contemporary life. Most important, perhaps, he drew attention to human problems and human verities that stretch across the entirety of history. It was appropriate that he chose for much of his drama the ancient and classical Nō form as base, as its ultimate concerns are based in timelessness.

The young Mishima early gained the attention of the established novelist Yasunari Kawabata. Kawabata, winner of the Nobel Prize in Literature in 1968, was to be an advocate of Mishima's work throughout his career. He participated in Mishima's wedding to Yoko Sugiyama on June 1, 1958, and himself committed suicide seventeen months after Mishima. It was Kawabata who said of Mishima's work, "Such a writer appears once in three hundred years."

Biography • Yukio Mishima was born Kimitake Hiraoka, the son of a government bureaucrat. Mishima's life was unusual from the outset. His physically ill grandmother, Natsuko, virtually kidnapped the firstborn of her son Azusa and his wife, Shizue, sequestering the child in her quarters. The young Mishima lived with her, enduring that strained situation. When he was ready for the seventh grade, however, she allowed him to move back to his parents' section of the house. Mishima said that as early as the age of five, he learned to prefer an imaginary world, often of violence, to the real world. As early as the age of four he was to begin a pattern of falling in love with pictures in books. A favorite picture was of Joan of Arc, whom he assumed to be a male. Mishima candidly reported that his first erotic arousal occurred when he was looking at a photograph of Guido Reni's portrait of Saint Sebastian pierced by arrows.

Yukio Mishima at his home in Tokyo, Japan, in September, 1966 (AP/Wide World Photos)

Mishima attended the exclusive Peer's School in Tokyo. He was too young for the draft in early World War II but was called up later, only to fail the physical, and so returned to work in the aircraft factory where he had been employed. Fame was to come to him following the publication of the novel *Confessions of a Mask*. He complemented his writing of plays and novels by creating his own persona, pursuing bodybuilding and mastering English. Mishima visited the United States on a world tour, which included Latin America and Greece, in 1951 and 1952. This trip was to be the first of several journeys to the United States, including one in 1957 and another, with his wife, Yoko, in 1960.

Mishima and his wife had two children by the early 1960's. By the middle of the decade, he was probably the best-known living Japanese with the exception of the emperor. Mishima was frequently a nominee for the Nobel Prize; one of his champions is said to have been the then-United Nations Secretary General, Dag Hammarskjöld. Nevertheless, in 1968, it was his mentor Kawabata who was named Nobel laureate for literature. Mishima was disappointed but nevertheless often appeared in public with his very shy teacher to help Kawabata cope with his unwanted fame. Among Mishima's other close friends were novelist Kōbō Abe, Kabuki actor Utaemon Nakamura, critic-historian Donald Keene, writer-film-producer Donald Richie, and popular female impersonator Akihiro Maruyama.

On November 25, 1970, after delivering the last book of his tetralogy, *The Decay of the Angel*, to his publisher, Mishima, accompanied by a select squad of his Shield Society (a handpicked private legion of just under one hundred university men), seized the Eastern Military Headquarters in downtown Tokyo, spoke to the troops, urging an overthrow of the current government and a return of absolute power to the emperor, and then committed ritual suicide (seppuku). He was in his forty-fifth year.

Analysis • Yukio Mishima's dramatic works share with his others a concern with action in the face of the void. His conviction that every act is necessarily a political act is a significant one, and it provides a unifying force in the plays, as does his conviction that, in things great or small, any action, ultimately, is better than no action. This constant often leads to tortured situations reminiscent of Jean-Paul Sartre. Indeed, it is easy to see why Mishima preferred Sartre to Albert Camus, philosophically, despite Mishima's dislike of the political Left and his outright contempt for bureaucracy.

Mishima favored modern adaptation to extend great art through all time. Donald Keene, one of his foremost translators, has noted that Mishima believed that his modern Nō plays should be as effective in a performance in Central Park as on a traditional Nō stage. This belief reminds one of William Butler Yeats's conviction that set properties and cast were too complex if all could not be fitted into a taxi, brought to a destination, and performed in a private home.

Mishima's negative critics point to the stiff nature of characters, as well as the restricted action in his conventional plays, claiming that he was overly influenced by the French period drama of Jean Racine. These so-called drawbacks, however, served a larger purpose in *Madame de Sade* and *My Friend Hitler*, which may be compared to the dramas of Aeschylus and Sophocles, in which unspeakable, bloody, or violent acts are described rather than acted onstage.

Flawlessly educated, Mishima had perfect command of the classical as well as the modern Japanese language. His grasp of Eastern and Western literature was equaled by few, if any, of his peers. The same was true of his understanding of history and politics, as well as philosophy. Jean Cocteau, whom he met in Paris, and Oscar Wilde were two writers who exercised great influence on him. Both, like Mishima, were flamboyant public figures. One is reminded that Mishima's experiment with becoming a boxer parallels Cocteau's becoming the manager of a professional prizefighter. Mishima also was interested in the multifaceted Italian writer Gabriele D'Annunzio, who not only wrote in a number of forms but also shared an interest in the martyrdom of Saint Sebastian and who became a military activist and daring airplane pilot. Mishima himself was eventually to help train Japanese self-defense force troops in parachute jumping (a skill that he taught himself), in addition to forming and financing his own small, private army, dedicated to the protection of the emperor.

The plays published in *Five Modern Nō Plays*, written between 1950 and 1955, have been performed, in various groupings, by a number of small theater groups throughout the United States. *Sotoba Komachi*, *The Lady Aoi*, and *Hanjo* have probably been acted more frequently than *The Damask Drum* and *Kantan*. Similarities discovered in opposites and the dictatorship of desire—even beyond the grave—and the agonies attendant thereto are the motivating force behind them all.

Sotoba Komachi • In *Sotoba Komachi*, the primary characters are an arrogant Poet (who remains nameless) and an ugly Old Woman, who is soon to be discovered by the audience as Komachi, the formerly devastating beauty, reincarnated. Beauty and torment are welded in all the works of Mishima. Komachi historically tormented her suitor, refusing to give herself unless courted for one hundred nights. The suitor died on the ninety-ninth night.

Both of the primary characters are developed sympathetically. The Poet, who at first harshly tells the Old Woman, whom he stumbles on in the park late at night, that someone as old and vile as she should leave that spot for young lovers, is destined to change his insult that she is "a profanation." When Komachi tells him that she is ninety-nine years old, he recoils yet again, though he is drawn to look at her more closely. During the course of their exchange, the park empties, and Komachi reminisces about her love for Captain Fukakusa eighty years previously. Here Mishima is freer still with his modernization of the classic Komachi and introduces an onstage flashback to a ball at which Fukakusa was courting Komachi—but Viennese waltzes, not Japanese music, provide background as various couples appear and discuss the romance of Komachi and her captain.

The audience suddenly realizes that fate is destined to repeat itself as the Poet begins to see the Old Woman as absolutely beautiful and begins to pay court to her. Komachi's hundredth night has again come around. To her credit, she tries to warn the young man, but he is totally enthralled by his new vision of her. The play, carried by Mishima's powerful dialogue, at once masterful in its timing and economical but eloquent in its progress, concludes with his dying and Komachi's acceptance of "a hundred more years to wait," as she returns to counting cigarette butts garnered that day. She is seen at the final curtain as she was when the curtain rose. The play is classic Mishima—including his obsessive interest in cycles, despite his personal disclaimer of belief in reincarnation. His claimed belief in active nihilism is seldom more accurately manifested than in this koanlike play.

Bondage to an emotional state and/or obsession is a frequent theme for Mishima and probably goes back even to his preadolescent intoxication with Reni's portrait of Saint Sebastian, ultimately leading to a commissioned series of portraits of himself in various dying situations—including one of himself as Saint Sebastian, arms bound above his head and arrows appearing to protrude from his torso. In *The Damask Drum* and *Hanjo* such pain and torture are enacted at an essentially intellectual-emotional level. *The Lady Aoi* also works at that level but features spirit possession, torture of a physical sort, and murder, too.

The Damask Drum • *The Damask Drum* centers on an old janitor, Iwakichi, who falls madly and impossibly in love with a woman whom he has never met but has observed across the alley from the office building where he cleans. He has spied her repeatedly in a fashionable dress shop just across the way. Iwakichi confesses to the clerk Kayoko that he must have sent the mystery lady thirty unanswered love letters, in addition to seventy more that he has burned after writing. (The mystery of the hundredth occasion reminds one of *Sotoba Komachi*.) After their exchange, Iwakichi and Kayoko continue to spy on the adjacent office and observe the activity there during their night shift. Eventually tiring, Kayoko takes her leave of the old man, carrying with her yet another love letter for the mystery lady from him. Across the way, three sophisticated male customers and the proprietress of the shop discuss the old man's obsessive passion. The proprietress confesses that she has used the old man's letters as wipers for her dog's combs, never showing them to Mrs. Hanako Tsukioka, who is the object of the old man's passion. The girl Kayoko arrives with the thirtieth letter, which they read aloud.

The discourse that follows concerns questions of romance, the erotic, and fashion—then returns to the old man, whom they decide to discipline for his cheeky courtship. They contrive to give Iwakichi a stage prop, a drum that is made of damask and therefore soundless. The drum is accompanied by a note that hints that Mrs. Tsukioka will grant the old man her favors when she hears the drum beating. On his failure to be heard, as they laugh at him from across the alley, Iwakichi commits suicide by jumping from his window ledge. Stage lighting soon indicates that night has come, and Mrs. Tsukioka is "back" at the scene to meet the ghost of Iwakichi. Now it is their turn to speak of love and its flaws. Responding to her challenge, yet again, to make the drum sound, the ghost pounds away, only to fall into despair on the hundredth beat and disappear. "I would have heard if he had only struck it once more," avers the lady—less kind and less intelligent than the earlier Komachi but less cruel than Rokujō in *The Lady Aoi*.

The Lady Aoi • In *The Lady Aoi* there are but four characters, the three major ones being Aoi, her husband, Hiraku, and Lady Rokujō. The action opens in a hospital, which, it seems, may use sexual therapy. This element is intended by Mishima to shock. Though Mishima was hostile to the theories of Sigmund Freud and his disciples, he was keenly, if unhappily, aware of their influence on the twentieth century; hence, that influence appears in this modern version of a tale from the Genji cycle. Spirit possession is the mainspring of this intense play's action, which presents an effective story of love and of hate growing from betrayed love. Not the Genji figure, Hiraku, but his chosen, Aoi, is killed by the spirit of Rokujō, whose ability to manifest in both spirit and person is stunningly effective in this jarring masterwork.

Kantan • *Kantan*, the earliest of the five plays in the collection, is perhaps the least effective of Mishima's Nō plays. Although it may remind one of Eugène Ionesco's *L'Avenir est dans les œufs: Ou, Il Faut de tout pour faire un monde* (pr. 1953; *The Future Is in Eggs: Or, It Takes All Sorts to Make a World*, 1960), or perhaps of the works of Harold Pinter or Samuel Beckett, the dialogue does not always cohere, and one is not quite sure if this incoherence is the playwright's intention. *Kantan* does contain some delightful whimsy, and dreams and near-romps abound as eighteen-year-old Jirō imagines that he becomes a dictator and power broker. He awakens to a new love for real life and his doting nurse, Kiku, as magical flowers burst into bloom everywhere. *Kantan* is the stuff of opera or ballet and should be splendidly adaptable to such works.

Hanjo • The homoerotic theme is dominant in *Hanjo*, one of the most powerful and economical of Mishima's works. True to Mishima's desire, it could well be played in any theater in the world—or even in Central Park. *Hanjo* is a drama of love and alienation, in which the loyal, long-suffering lesbian wins. Hanako, a beautiful girl, has gone mad after being deserted by her handsome lover, Yoshio. She is taken off the streets, loved (and painted) and nurtured by a middle-aged artist, Jitsuko Honda. Jitsuko's idyll is jeopardized by a newspaper story, telling of her rescue of the girl and even providing her name and address. Her worst fears are soon realized, for Yoshio sees the story and subsequently finds them. His identification of Hanako is confirmed by matching a pair of fans that they had exchanged as symbols of undying loyalty. A brutal psychological battle between Yoshio and Jitsuko ensues, and which Jitsuko presumes that she has lost. Yet the tables turn when Hanako insists to the young man, "You are not Yoshio. Your face is dead." She maintains this claim and eventually dismisses him. Jitsuko is gentle in dealing with Yoshio in his defeat but cannot resist exultantly exclaiming "Oh, wonderful life!" when he finally has gone.

Dōjōji • It is in the Nō play *Dōjōji*, which first found print amid nine short stories of the volume *Manatsu no shi* (1953; *Death in Midsummer and Other Stories*, 1966), that Mishima perhaps stands more revealed than in any of his other plays, in the person of a young lady named Kiyoko. (It may be worth noting that Mishima's female characters tend to have more dimensions than his men—unlike those of Ernest Hemingway, with whom he is often paralleled.)

Dōjōji's other characters are the Antique Dealer and the Apartment House Superintendent (both unnamed), and five nondescript men and women patrons of the antique shop. The setting is "a room in what is in fact a secondhand furniture shop, though it is so filled with antiques—both Oriental and Occidental—that it might properly be called a museum." Like the classical version of this Nō play, Mishima's version involves unabated passion. In the traditional play, *Kanegamisaki* (the cape of the temple bell), a hermit is loved by a stunning beauty. Rejecting her, he takes refuge by hiding under the huge Dōjōji temple bell. Crazed by her desire for him, she transforms herself into a great and outraged serpent whose fire burns the ungrateful hermit as it coils around the bell.

Mishima's Kiyoko, a dancer, keeps to the passion with something of a plot reversal suitable to modern times. She desires a huge wardrobe (with, appropriately, the form of a bell carved into its doors) from the antique shop. The cabinet is about to be sold to the highest bidder among a number of interested, affluent parties, but the sale is spoiled by Kiyoko telling of the murder of a young lover who hid inside—obviously unsuccessfully—from a jealous husband.

After the potential buyers have been driven away, Kiyoko reveals to the Dealer that indeed a man had died inside the wardrobe, but that it was her lover, Yasushi, who jilted her for an older woman because she (Kiyoko) was too beautiful. Yasushi chose to hide in the wardrobe to avoid the world, to live and, in fact, to die there (suicide is suggested). Kiyoko browbeats the Dealer but still cannot afford the wardrobe. She leaps inside and locks herself in, crying out that she will disfigure her features with acid. Panic ensues, but when she finally emerges, her face is unchanged. It is at the very end of the play that Mishima and his character seem to merge. Kiyoko says, "Nothing can bother me, no matter what happens. Who do you suppose can wound me now?" Soon the Dealer replies, "You'll be ruined, your heart will be torn to shreds. You'll end up no longer able to feel anything." To this Kiyoko replies, "Still, nothing that happens can ever change my face."

Longer plays • The longer and more conventional plays, *Madame de Sade* and *My Friend Hitler*, have much in common. Like many plays, for all but an unusually specialized or attentive audience, they may be deemed to read better than they play. Ironically, this gives them a point in common with traditional Nō, which some prefer to have explicated rather than to attend. More traditional critics claim that the plays are sometimes overwhelmed by dialogue at the expense of action.

In these two plays, the most horrible acts of violence and violation are described in frequently long, descriptive speeches, in which the actors simply face off and deliver— hence it is easy to lose a sense of outrage. Yet, as noted above, one may compare this type of play with the classical Greek drama, in which the violence was described instead of witnessed.

Madame de Sade • *Madame de Sade*, the first of these two plays of the theater of tirade, was finished in 1965 and played successfully in Tokyo, opening in November of
that year. Its five characters are all female. They are Renée, Sade's wife; Mme de
Montreuil, her mother; Anne, her younger sister; Baronesse de Simiane; the cruel
Comtesse de Saint-Fonde; and Charlotte, who is housekeeper to the Montreuils. Much
of the main debate of the play swings between the decadent Saint-Fonde, who states
that God is both lazy and decrepit after proclaiming herself "utterly bored with the ar-
tifices of love and the nasty machinations . . . even my own bad reputation." She describes love as a mixture of honey and ashes, announcing that she has concluded that
the highly religious Montreuil was correct earlier when describing the truth as "whips
and sweets, that's all."

The fascinating exchanges and revelations proceed, often staggering in their implications. The third and final act, following a major soliloquy of Renée, ends after embracing the notion that Sade embodies the cruel essence of reality; the arrival of the
Marquis de Sade, himself, is heralded by a knock at the door. The maid describes the
bloated, down-at-heels, albeit dignified appearance of the man, who has been long in
prison. Renée, Madame de Sade, seeming to have arrived at a sudden decision, stuns
the audience by announcing her decision to "never see him again." As the maid leaves
to communicate this to the Marquis de Sade, the curtain falls. Remarkable as it is, there
is a classic Zen koanlike quality to this play; a rap on the head by the playwright in the
role as Zen master—and the audience is left to find the truth on its own.

My Friend Hitler • *My Friend Hitler*, also in three acts, has as its characters Adolf Hitler, the arms magnate Alfried Krupp, the SA Captain Ernst Roehm, and left-wing Nazi
Gregor Strasser. The play is set on the infamous "night of long knives," when, in late
June and early July of 1934, Hitler gave his blessing to the SS, led by Hermann Göring,
Heinrich Himmler, Rudolf Hess, Joseph Goebbels, and others, to liquidate all leadership of the rival SA paramilitary organization. The SA, a less elite, though larger,
group of Hitler's backers, was headed by Captain Roehm, who believed himself to be
Hitler's best friend. The leftist Strasser, who also helped in Hitler's rise to power, has
become unable to tolerate Hitler's leadership, while Roehm, like many of his men a
motorcycle-riding, hard-drinking bully, believes that Nazi leadership will soften unless it rests on a continual revolution. The dialogue between them is spirited and fascinating, as is that between Hitler and Krupp, the only man before whom Hitler trembles.

Donald Richie calls the work an "allegory in iron," and that it is. It ran successfully
in Tokyo in January, 1969, but has not been presented in English except as laboratory
theater at St. Andrews College in 1982, in the Hiroaki Sato translation. Again,
Mishima—who said that he could never identify with Hitler, though he had some sympathy for Benito Mussolini—leaves the spectator with tense irresolution at the play's
end. As gunfire continues in the background, signaling the continuing execution of SA
leaders, Hitler, now recovered from his terror of the intimidating Krupp, accepts the
latter's congratulations for cutting down both the Left and the Right, walking to center
stage to state, "Yes, government must take the middle road."

Other major works

LONG FICTION: *Kamen no kokuhaku*, 1949 (*Confessions of a Mask*, 1958); *Kinjiki*, 1951,
and *Higyo*, 1953 (combined as *Forbidden Colors*, 1968); *Shiosai*, 1954 (*The Sound of Waves*,
1956); *Kinkakuji*, 1956 (*The Temple of the Golden Pavilion*, 1959); *Kyōko no ie*, 1959; *Utage*

no ato, 1960 (*After the Banquet*, 1963); *Gogo no eikō*, 1963 (*The Sailor Who Fell from Grace with the Sea*, 1965); *Haru no yuki*, 1969 (*Spring Snow*, 1972); *Homba*, 1969 (*Runaway Horses*, 1973); *Akatsuki no tera*, 1970 (*The Temple of Dawn*, 1973); *Tennin gosui*, 1971 (*The Decay of the Angel*, 1974); *Hōjō no umi*, 1969-1971 (collective title for previous four novels; *The Sea of Fertility: A Cycle of Four Novels*, 1972-1974).

SHORT FICTION: *Kaibutsu*, 1950; *Tōnorikai*, 1951; *Manatsu no shi*, 1953 (*Death in Midsummer and Other Stories*, 1966).

NONFICTION: *Hagakure nyumōn*, 1967 (*The Way of the Samurai*, 1977); *Taiyō to tetsu*, 1968 (*Sun and Steel*, 1970); *Yukio Mishima on "Hagakure": The Samurai Ethic and Modern Japan*, 1978.

EDITED TEXT: *New Writing in Japan*, 1972 (with Geoffrey Bownas).

MISCELLANEOUS: *Hanazakari no mori*, 1944 (short fiction and plays); *Eirei no Koe*, 1966 (short fiction and essays).

Bibliography

Miller, Henry. *Reflections on the Death of Mishima*. Santa Barbara, Calif.: Capra, 1972. A noted author's comments on the death of Mishima.

Napier, Susan Jolliffe. *Escape from the Wasteland: Romanticism and Realism in the Fiction of Mishima Yukio and Oe Kenzaburo*. Cambridge, Mass.: Harvard University Press, 1991. A look at romanticism and realism in the works of Mishima and Kenzaburo Oe. Bibliography and index.

Nathan, John. *Mishima: A Biography*. 1974. Reprint. Cambridge, Mass.: Da Capo Press, 2000. The classic biography of Mishima, with a new preface by Nathan. Index.

Scott-Stokes, Henry. *The Life and Death of Yukio Mishima*. Rev ed. New York: Noonday Press, 1995. The revised edition of Scott-Stokes's 1974 biography of Mishima, covering his life and works. Bibliography and index.

Starrs, Roy. *Deadly Dialectics: Sex, Violence, and Nihilism in the World of Yukio Mishima*. Honolulu: University of Hawaii Press, 1994. A study of Mishima's literary works, with emphasis on his philosophy.

Wolfe, Peter. *Yukio Mishima*. New York: Continuum, 1989. A basic biography of Mishima that covers his life and works. Index.

Yourcenar, Marguerite. *Mishima: A Vision of the Void*. Chicago: University of Chicago Press, 2001. This edition of a biography of Mishima published in 1986 contains a foreword by Donald Richie, a well-known critic and Japan expert.

Ronald H. Bayes

Molière

Jean-Baptiste Poquelin

Born: Paris, France; January 15, 1622 (baptized)
Died: Paris, France; February 17, 1673

Principal drama • *L'Étourdi: Ou, Les Contre-temps*, pr. 1653, pb. 1663 (verse play; *The Blunderer*, 1678); *Le Dépit amoureux*, pr. 1656, pb. 1663 (adaptation of Niccolò Secchi's *L'Interessé; The Love-Tiff*, 1930); *Les Précieuses ridicules*, pr. 1659, pb. 1660 (*The Affected Young Ladies*, 1732); *L'École des maris*, pr., pb. 1661 (verse play; *The School for Husbands*, 1732); *L'École des femmes*, pr. 1662, pb. 1663 (verse play; *The School for Wives*, 1732); *La Critique de "L'École des femmes,"* pr., pb. 1663 (*The Critique of "The School for Wives,"* 1957); *L'Impromptu de Versailles*, pr. 1663, pb. 1682 (*The Versailles Impromptu*, 1714); *Tartuffe: Ou, L'Imposteur*, pr. 1664, revised pr. 1667, pb. 1669 (verse play; English translation, 1732); *Dom Juan: Ou, Le Festin de Pierre*, pr. 1665, pb. 1682 (*Don Juan*, 1755); *L'Amour médecin*, pr. 1665, pb. 1666 (*Love's the Best Doctor*, 1755); *Le Misanthrope*, pr. 1666, pb. 1667 (verse play; *The Misanthrope*, 1709); *Le Médecin malgré lui*, pr., pb. 1666 (*The Doctor in Spite of Himself*, 1672); *Amphitryon*, pr., pb. 1668 (verse play; English translation, 1755); *L'Avare*, pr. 1668, pb. 1669 (*The Miser*, 1672); *Le Bourgeois Gentilhomme*, pr. 1670, pb. 1671 (*The Would-Be Gentleman*, 1675); *Les Fourberies de Scapin*, pr., pb. 1671 (*The Cheats of Scapin*, 1701); *Les Femmes savantes*, pr., pb. 1672 (verse play; *The Learned Ladies*, pr., pb. 1693); *Le Malade imaginaire*, pr. 1673, pb. 1674 (*The Imaginary Invalid*, 1732; also known as *The Hypochondriac*); *Dramatic Works*, pb. 1875-1876 (3 volumes); *The Plays of Molière*, pb. 1926 (8 volumes)

Other literary forms • Molière is known only for his plays.

Achievements • Molière possessed a brilliant imagination, constantly creating new characters and easily moving from one type of comedy to another. His imagination was, however, carefully controlled through reason, by which he avoided excess. Reality is the point of departure for his wildest creations, and his comedies owe their depth to his keen observation of humanity. When Molière began writing for the theater there was little comedy, except for that of Pierre Corneille's first works, and what there was leaned heavily toward the extravagant. Molière soon realized that, more than any other genre, comedy required a basis in truth. Consequently, he was not particularly concerned with original subjects or careful plots, but rather with the portrayal of manners and the study of character.

Therefore, Molière made free use of any subject or plot that came his way, borrowing in whole or in part from earlier French works of any genre, or from Latin, Italian, and Spanish sources. Although he was capable of devising clever plots, he believed that simple ones were better if the audience was to concentrate on the substance of the play. As for denouements, any or none would do, once he had said what he intended.

Molière was thoroughly familiar with the milieus of his day and represented them all faithfully as settings for his characters and their foibles. What interested Molière more than sociological truth, however, was universal truth. His precious ladies, pedants, and nouveaux riches could be of any era. More important than a wealth of exterior detail was this portrayal of universal types. These were to replace the conventional figures—boastful captains, scheming parasites, sweet ingenues, young lovers, and the like—of traditional comedy. Despite their universality, however, Molière's characters were not created according to simple formulas. On the contrary, they are complex to an extreme, each possessing the general traits of the type observed and abstracted by Molière from reality, yet endowed with enough of the particulars to make each a real human being. There is no one stock servant in Molière's work, but a series of individualized servants. His Miser is a lover as well. The Hypocrite is also a lecher. Molière's dramatic universe is a very real one.

Molière made special use of those of his observations that could make the spectator laugh at humanity. Although the comedy almost always contains a serious meaning, its forms are extremely varied, and its tones range from the most farcical to the most subtle, all arranged with the utmost skill during the course of a single play. Thus, the spectator may remain unaware of how disagreeable a subject is until, the performance over, he reflects on it further. Especially telling is Molière's device of making certain characters repeat words and gestures that reveal the vice or passion that controls each. By this technique, the characters are reduced almost to the status of machines and thus inspire, not sympathy or pity, but ridicule.

Molière believed that human nature was basically good and sensible, and he opposed any artificial constraints placed on it. Such constraints came not from society, which is a collection of human natures whose discipline reasonable people accept; rather, they had their source in perverse individuals who conformed neither to human nature nor to society. Molière has been criticized for excessive optimism and conformism, but however conservative his solutions to the problems that he posed, there can be no doubt that he was forthright and courageous in posing them.

Biography • Very little is known of the personal life of Molière, born Jean-Baptiste Poquelin. He left no diary, no memoirs, no correspondence, no autobiography. The first biography, J.-L. Le Gallois Grimarest's *Vie de Monsieur de Molière* (1705), is interesting, but it was not published until thirty-two years after Molière's death, and is therefore considered questionable by most modern scholars. Anything written by his contemporaries was polemical in nature.

Molière was baptized January 15, 1622, on the rue Saint-Honoré. He was of a good bourgeois family that had recently come to Paris from Beauvais. His father was a merchant and "upholsterer by appointment of the King," having received the title from his brother. Molière's mother died in 1632, and his father soon remarried, only to become a widower again in 1636.

Between 1632 and 1639, Molière attended the Collège de Clermont, studied law in Orléans, and became a lawyer. In addition, in 1637, his father arranged for his son to succeed him in his official charge. Molière was not much interested in the law, however, and his practice was not brisk, nor was he inclined to follow in his father's footsteps.

It is said that Molière's grandfather often took him to the Hôtel de Bourgogne to see French tragedy and Italian comedy. Around 1640, Molière probably met Tiberio Fiurelli, known as Scaramouche in the Italian theater, and became closely associated with the Béjart family. Its members were involved in the arts, particularly theater, and were somewhat eccentric, but they lived in the fashionable Marais section of Paris and had some good connections. Their oldest daughter, Madeleine, known as an actress, was the sometime mistress of the Baron de Modène and mother of a child recognized by him. At a time when "actor" and "outlaw" were considered synonymous by many, Molière chose the life of the theater. He was giving up the security and respectability offered him, not only by the right to succeed his father, but also by the legal profession. At first, he chose not to write for the theater, instead pursuing a career as an actor.

The Illustre Théâtre was founded in 1643 by the Béjarts and other actors, including Molière, not for profit at first but simply for their entertainment and that of the bourgeoisie of Paris. The troupe was under the protection of Gaston, the duke of Orléans, brother of Louis XIII, who did not always remember to pay his actors. They rented and appointed a former tennis court as a theater, opened their doors in 1644, and were soon in serious financial difficulty. Marie Hervé, mother of the Béjart girls, helped her children and Molière, who had by then taken this name and was head of the troupe. Despite all measures, matters grew worse. In 1645, Molière was sued by numerous creditors and experienced a brief sojourn in debtors' prison. He had made many friends among Parisian men of letters and their noble patrons, however, and formulated his philosophy of the theater. He had not wasted his time.

On his release from prison, Molière decided to leave Paris to try his luck in another troupe. Madeleine soon joined him. At the behest of a number of dramatic authors, the duke of Épernon received Molière, Madeleine, and her brother and sister into his troupe. They toured the provinces under the direction of Charles Dufresne until 1650, when the duke withdrew his support and Dufresne left the troupe. Molière assumed leadership during this awkward time, but in 1652 the troupe found a new patron in the prince of Conti. Again, the intercession of men of letters in Paris had been instrumental. The prince was an enlightened man who enjoyed such company, and he came to prize Molière's intelligence and culture highly. Unfortunately, the prince's spiritual advisers persuaded him to lead a more austere life, and in 1657 he withdrew his patronage.

(Library of Congress)

By this time, the troupe was doing well artistically and financially. It contained a number of artists who were or would become celebrated. A fine actor, Molière was an equally fine director. He was a hard taskmaster but earned his actors' respect and affection, and the turnover in his troupe was always remarkably low.

The players decided that, after a lengthy sojourn in Rouen, they would spend the winter of 1658 in Paris, which they had revisited sporadically, maintaining numerous contacts. In Paris, they rented the Marais Theatre for eighteen months and were granted the protection of Philippe, duke of Orléans, who paid them no more faithfully than had

Gaston. On October 24, 1658, they played Corneille's *Nicomède* (pr., pb. 1651; English translation, 1671) and then Molière's *The Love-Tiff* before Louis XIV. The king was so pleased with Molière's work that he accorded the troupe the use of the Petit-Bourbon on the days that the Italians did not play there. They performed in the fine hall there until 1660, when, for unknown reason, they moved to a smaller theater that was badly in need of repairs. Despite all efforts, the theater remained a makeshift affair. The troupe remained there, more or less permanently, until 1671, when it relocated to the Palais-Royal, which was properly remodeled and appointed.

The old Corneillean repertoire was no longer successful. Moreover, there was considerable bias on the part of good dramatic authors against offering their works to any troupe until 1667, when Corneille allowed *Attila* (English translation, 1960) to be mounted at the Petit-Bourbon, and 1670, when he gave Molière *Tite et Bérénice* to perform. Molière had found it necessary to create his own repertoire, a task that he had already begun in a modest way in the provinces. His comedies were well received, and the troupe seemed firmly established. The players at the Hôtel de Bourgogne and the Marais became increasingly more disgruntled. The triumph of *The Affected Young Ladies* in 1659 brought its author the active enmity of his rivals as well as the admiration of his public. Molière would never leave Paris again. His most important plays remained to be written. They were to win for him the highest praise, his contemporaries' and posterity's, and engage him in the fiercest of polemics with certain factions.

Molière was a short, rather ugly man with severe curvature of the spine, and he was by nature serious and somewhat taciturn. Nevertheless, his great art and talent brought him many friends, admirers, and patrons, and he enjoyed their company. He especially enjoyed being received by the notables of his day, whose invitations he insisted on reciprocating rather elegantly. During his life he had several mistresses, usually actresses, beginning with Madeleine Béjart, with whom he had a lifelong association, although he was not the most attentive of lovers.

At about the age of forty, Molière married pretty Armande Béjart, then about seventeen years of age and said variously to be Madeleine's sister or daughter (perhaps by Molière). As was to be expected, their life was not a happy one. He was jealous of her as he had been of no other, and she seems to have given him considerable cause. Three children were born during their marriage, but Esprit-Madeleine was the only one to whom he was greatly attached and perhaps the only one that he fathered. Despite all vicissitudes, he continued to love Armande, and she was with him when he died in 1673.

Molière's had always been a generous nature, emotionally as well as financially. Temperamental, not easy to live with, and always willing to engage in fierce polemic, he was nevertheless very forgiving. He was known not only to reconcile with but also to lend substantial sums of money to former enemies.

Louis XIV was Molière's greatest patron, showering him with money and favors and protecting him from powerful enemies. After 1665, Molière's group was known as "the King's troupe," a name preferred to that of the Hôtel de Bourgogne, and was requested to perform at Versailles, Saint-Germain, and Chambord. For inexplicable reasons, Jean-Baptiste Lully, the Florentine composer and sometime collaborator with Molière, became Louis's favorite with respect to theatrical entertainment in 1672, only one year before Molière's death. Although he had protected Molière in some extremely delicate situations, the king now preferred Lully's frivolous productions to Molière's masterpieces, and he granted the Italian exclusive rights over all works in which he had had a part. In vain, Molière tried legal means to oppose Louis's will. Fortunately, he had long had important protectors at court, such as the king's sister-in-law, Henriette d'Angleterre, and the prince of Conti, as well as numerous influential friends in various Parisian circles, including men of letters such as Nicholas Boileau.

After some initial difficulties concerning Lully's rights and the search for another composer, *The Imaginary Invalid*, originally created for the court, was a success at the Palais-Royal. Despite his ill health, Molière played the title role. It was during the fourth performance that he fell seriously and visibly ill; however, the show continued because the prince of Conti and other notables were in the audience and the actors needed to work. After the performance, Molière was taken home, where his hemorrhaging grew worse. His wife was called, and his servants tried to find a priest who would come to an actor's deathbed. When one finally arrived an hour later, Molière was dead.

Analysis • Molière's first comedies were composed of elements borrowed from a variety of comic genres, high and low, ancient and modern, foreign and domestic. In each, he revealed considerable skill in development of character, observation of manners, construction of plot, or a combination of all these laced with much amusing physical activity. There was little original invention until *The Affected Young Ladies*, which was a *petite comédie*, a short farce designed to be performed after a longer serious work, but a farce containing satire of the excesses of certain manners of the day. Still specializing in the farce, of which he would remain a master, Molière continued his search for originality. *The School for Husbands*, in three acts, is the first of his plays to add a social thesis, however disguised by humorous treatment, to the observation of manners and character.

The School for Wives • *The School for Wives*, Molière's first major play, centers on the vain Arnolphe, who has taken the aristocratic name of M. de la Souche. Hoping to acquire the peace and happiness of a conjugal life in his old age, he wishes to marry his young ward, Agnès, who is being reared in solitude and ignorance. He praises the virtues of this unnatural form of education to his friend, Chrysalde, who protests against his plan in the name of common sense. Meanwhile, Horace, the son of Oronte, a great friend of Arnolphe, has fallen in love with Agnès and has even been successful in communicating with her. He confides in Arnolphe himself, whom he does not know by the name of de la Souche, and of whose role as guardian and jailer he is unaware.

In act 2, Arnolphe, after scolding his servants, Alain and Georgette, for having allowed Horace to enter the house, questions Agnès. She is innocent and docile and willingly gives him the details of her meeting with Horace, who has moved her, she admits ingenuously. Arnolphe decides to marry Agnès without delay and orders her to throw stones at the suitor if he dares to declare himself. In act 3, Arnolphe lectures Agnès further and makes her read the disagreeable "Maxims on Marriage"; later, Horace reports to Arnolphe the vain precautions taken by the jealous old man: Agnès had thrown Horace a stone, but only after attaching a love note to it.

As act 4 reveals, Arnolphe is prepared to fight for Agnès and issues orders to his servants accordingly. Nevertheless, Horace informs him that he has been able to visit Agnès and that he intends to elope with her during the night. Arnolphe calls for the notary to draw up a marriage contract and plans an ambush for Horace. In the fifth and final act, Horace is surprised by Alain and Georgette and severely beaten. Feigning death, he succeeds in abducting Agnès but foolishly entrusts her to Arnolphe, whom he still does not connect with the jealous old man. Arnolphe's declarations of love do not touch Agnès, however, who now knows what true love is. Agnès's father, who opportunely returns from America, allows her to marry Horace.

In five acts, this *grande comédie* exemplifies the formula that Molière had developed for his theater through a series of shorter pieces. As in *The School for Husbands*, the theme is the proper education of young women. The setting is a real one drawn from contemporary society. Arnolphe and Chrysalde are French bourgeois; Alain and Georgette are French peasants. At the same time, all the characters are highly personalized. Agnès is a remarkable portrait of a young woman who, acting on her instincts, becomes aware of her love for Horace and becomes aware of herself as a person. Arnolphe, the principal character, is both ridiculous, because of his obsession to keep Agnès in ignorance and be master of the house, and tragic, because of his unrequited love for Agnès and his despair at losing her, which ennobles him. In part through Chrysalde, one of his numerous mouthpieces, and in part through a conventional denouement, Molière reveals an important tenet of his philosophy: It is stupid and dangerous to try to suppress natural emotion, for it always wins out in the end.

The Critique of "The School for Wives" • *The School for Wives* was so successful as to earn for its author additional favors from the king and more polemics from diverse factions. Supported by Louis and the *honnêtes gens*, Molière responded to his enemies' attacks in *The Critique of "The School for Wives,"* a one-act play in prose, by means of a series of caricatures and his definition of art as the portrayal of truth. The setting is Uranie's salon, where a discussion of Molière's play is taking place. Célimène, a *précieuse*, attacks Molière's immorality and vulgarity, and is in turn attacked by Uranie for her affected prudery. The marquis criticizes the play for having made the common people laugh, whereupon Dorante defends their common sense and good judgment. The pedant Lysidas considers the play an insignificant piece that cannot be compared with serious plays. He casts doubt on the judgment of the court in applauding Molière's work, for it breaks all the rules of art. Once again, it is Dorante who acts as the author's spokesman by stating that comedy is as difficult as tragedy to create and more true to life. For him the greatest rule is to please, and he sides with the court in its approbation of *The School for Wives*. Molière's enemies were not stilled; they counterattacked with other short plays, accusing him of being too personal, impious, and immoral in his private life.

The Versailles Impromptu • At the insistence of the king this time, Molière wrote another one-act piece in prose, *The Versailles Impromptu*, performed for Louis in October of 1663. Molière represents himself as director and actor in the midst of a rehearsal for a play to be given before the king. Having mocked the actors of the Hôtel de Bourgogne, Molière proceeds to give each of his players advice appropriate to his role and defends his theater, whose goal is to depict manners, not personalities. Whatever his enemies may say of his work does not disturb him, but he forbids them to intrude on his privacy. The piece concludes with an announcement from the king postponing the performance of the play under rehearsal.

Tartuffe • *Tartuffe*, perhaps the most controversial of Molière's comedies, was first given in its original version, now lost, as a part of *Les Plaisirs de l'île enchantée*, a week of the most extravagant entertainment offered by Louis XIV at Versailles in 1664 in honor of Louise de la Vallière. *Tartuffe* (then titled *Tartuffe: Ou, L'Hypocrite*) not only gave rise to another fierce polemic, but also was finally banned by the king at the insistence of the Company of the Blessed Sacrament, a secret society dedicated to reform-ing manners, who were concerned that Molière had them in mind when he presented his hypocrite as a cleric. Molière modified and expanded the play from three to five acts, and Louis authorized its performance (entitled *L'Imposteur*) at the Palais-Royal in 1667. Although Molière had made the hypocrite a layperson and softened his satire, the police and the Archbishop of Paris took advantage of the king's trip to Flanders to shut down the successful play. After more efforts by Molière and Louis, the comedy was again authorized in 1669 and performed triumphantly as *Tartuffe: Ou, L'Imposteur*.

As the play begins, Mme Pernelle, pleased that her son, Orgon, has welcomed such a pious man into his household, roundly criticizes each member of the family who ac-cuses Tartuffe of hypocrisy, including the outspoken servant Dorine. Returning from the country, Orgon inquires most solicitously about Tartuffe's health (not his wife's) and gives his brother-in-law, Cléante, an evasive answer regarding the proposed mar-riage of his daughter to Valère.

Complications develop in act 2: Despite Mariane's dislike for Tartuffe, Orgon wants his daughter to marry him rather than the man whom she loves and who loves her. Dorine's remonstrances are of no avail with Orgon, and she comforts the timid Mariane and settles the lovers' quarrel that Orgon's wishes have incited. In act 3, Orgon's son Damis tries to intervene also, but Dorine makes him promise to leave matters to his stepmother, Elmire. The latter sends for Tartuffe, who finally appears. The young woman begs him to give up Mariane. The hypocrite takes advantage of the situation to try to seduce Elmire, who agrees not to reveal his scandalous behavior if he will favor the marriage of Mariane and Valère, but Damis, who overhears everything from a nearby closet, informs his father. Tartuffe feigns humility and deceives Orgon, who turns against his son and makes Tartuffe his heir.

Tartuffe is evasive when, in act 4, Cléante begs him to reconcile Orgon and Damis. Orgon wishes to hasten his daughter's wedding to Tartuffe despite the protests of Cléante and Mariane. In order to disabuse her husband, Elmire has him hide under a table, summons Tartuffe, and pretends to respond to his passion. Finally understand-ing that he has been tricked by an impostor, Orgon comes out of his hiding place and orders Tartuffe to leave the house. The hypocrite abandons his mask and threatens Orgon, for the house belongs to him now.

The concluding act brings about the anticipated reversal. Orgon regrets having turned all his worldly possessions over to Tartuffe, including a strongbox containing the papers entrusted to him by a friend who is in political trouble. Mme Pernelle con-tinues to have faith in Tartuffe when M. Loyal arrives with a court order to evict Orgon. Valère offers to help Orgon escape, for the incriminating strongbox has been turned over to the king's officers. Tartuffe appears in person with an officer to have Orgon arrested, but it is Tartuffe who is arrested instead; the king had been alerted to the impostor's fraudulent activities and knew of Orgon's services to the royal cause during the rebellion of the Fronde. The *deus ex machina* ending finds the king praised and Valère and Mariane about to be married.

In *Tartuffe*, Molière claimed to attack hypocrisy only and took pains to have Cléante, his spokesman, distinguish carefully between true and false piety. Despite praise of the former, the only avowed Christians in the work, Orgon and his mother, are depicted as ridiculous, whereas the principal characters shown in a good light, Elmire and Cléante, are not religious persons. The emphasis in *Tartuffe* is clearly on hu-man rather than divine wisdom, very much in the spirit of the eighteenth century philosophes.

Tartuffe's is a skillful plot that maintains interest in its theme, the rise and fall of a religious hypocrite, from the lively, realistic exposition to the unlikely denouement. It is the perfect model of a comedy of character as well. Although all the characters are complex, drawn from life, it is Tartuffe who stands out, not only for his hypocrisy, but his keen intelligence, strong will, and great powers of dissimulation. For all his cleverness, however, he has a weakness, his sensuality coupled with greed, and this brutal passion causes his downfall.

Don Juan • Between 1664 and 1669, Molière produced ten comedies in addition to reworking *Tartuffe*. Among them was *Don Juan*, whose Spanish subject had become popular in Italy and France. Molière's version, a five-act play in prose, was very successful, but again, he was opposed by the religious faction. No doubt the libertine's cynicism, his perverse seduction, his impious "articles of faith," and his unrepentant sins were shocking to audiences of the time. Still more shocking was his novel recourse to hypocrisy in the last act, although in the end Don Juan remains an unregenerate sinner and is led off to Hell.

As the play begins, Don Juan informs his valet, Sganarelle, that his happiness consists in seducing all women without becoming attached to any. Elvire, whom he has abandoned, attempts in vain to win him back. Shipwrecked on the coast during a storm, Don Juan and Sganarelle are taken in by some peasants. There, Don Juan seduces two young women, whom he deceives with promises of marriage. Pursued by Elvire's brothers, he hides in the forest with Sganarelle.

In act 3, to the horror of his valet, Don Juan explains his "articles of faith," which may be summarized as "two and two are four." He meets a poor man and tries to bribe him with alms to blaspheme. Then he saves the life of one of Elvire's brothers. In an act of bravado, he invites the statue of a Commander whom he killed in the past to dine; the statue accepts with a gesture.

In the fourth act, Don Juan is insolent to his father, Don Louis, who rebukes him for his scandalous life, and he remains insensitive to the prayers of Elvire, who, before retiring to a convent, would like to bring him to repentance. He sits down to dine, and the statue appears to remind him of his invitation. Sganarelle is terrified, but Don Juan retains his composure.

In the final act, Don Juan, having pretended to repent before his father, explains to Sganarelle that henceforth he intends to wear the mask of a hypocrite; it is in this manner also that he responds to the challenge of Elvire's brothers. At this point, a ghost appears to tell Don Juan that he has only a moment in which to repent if he wishes divine mercy. Hardhearted, he mocks this warning. The Commander's statue arrives, takes him by the hand, and Don Juan is engulfed in the invisible flames of Hell.

At first glance, *Don Juan* does not seem to be related to its author's earlier works. Molière did wish to try something new. The play requires several changes of scene and machinery to achieve stage effects. It includes the supernatural along with the realistic, phantoms and an animated statue along with peasants drawn from real life. Similarly, the comedy of the almost burlesque scene with M. Dimanche alternates with the tragic qualities of Don Louis's vehement speech to his son.

Yet this work is related to Molière's serious concerns. For the first time in the succession of versions of the Don Juan story, the principal character is not only debauched but also a hypocrite. As long as he is a seducer and blasphemer, divine mercy will spare him; when in the last act he pretends to be converted, he goes too far, and divine patience is exhausted. While in *Tartuffe* it is the king who intervenes to punish the hyp-

ocrite, in *Don Juan* it is Heaven. Molière thus uses another occasion to attack his enemies' false piety, but again religion, false or sincere, finds itself in a weak position.
Atheism is defended by a vicious but intelligent and charming aristocrat, whereas the
defender of religion is a sensible yet somewhat obtuse valet.

The Misanthrope • A five-act comedy in verse, *The Misanthrope*, on which Molière
had been working since 1664, finally appeared in 1666. Although well received by the
intellectual elite, the work did not enjoy great favor with the general public, who preferred Molière's farces, comedies with music and ballet, and satire.

In the salon of a young widow, Célimène, whom he awaits, the misanthropic
Alceste rails to his friend, the indulgent Philinte, against the worldly hypocrisy that
makes him detest humankind. Nevertheless, he loves the coquettish Célimène. Oronte
asks Alceste for his opinion of a love sonnet that he has composed. Reticent at first,
Alceste finally blurts out his opinion of the piece, which he finds detestable. Furious,
Oronte withdraws, followed by Alceste and Philinte, who leave together.

As act 2 begins, Alceste has brought Célimène home, where he reproaches her for
her fickleness and tries to make her declare her love. The arrival of two dandies,
Acaste and Clitandre, suitors of Célimène, interrupts the scene between the lovers.
Philinte and Eliante, Célimène's cousin, arrive, and a conversation takes place in
which the young widow draws satiric portraits of friends in their absence. Célimène's
clever but biting tongue makes Alceste indignant, and he is not spared her witty attacks. Alceste must leave, for he is being sued by Oronte because of his critical judgment of the sonnet.

In act 3, Acaste and Clitandre make a pact: The one who can first give clear proof of
Célimène's love for him shall be declared the winner. During a visit with Arsinoë,
Célimène is provoked by her guest's innuendos regarding her flirtations into giving
the prude her comeuppance. Her vanity wounded, Arsinoë tries in vain to charm
Alceste, but she succeeds in troubling him with regard to Célimène's love, offering to
furnish him evidence that she is betraying him.

The fourth act adds further complications. When Philinte tells Eliante how Alceste
and Oronte have patched up their differences, she reveals her admiration for the misanthrope's heroic sincerity; in turn, Philinte declares his love to her. Alceste, however,
arrives in a rage, for Arsinoë has produced a note written by Célimène to Oronte.
Alceste offers his heart to Eliante, and, when Célimène appears, he heaps reproach on
her. Lying artfully, she justifies herself and triumphs over Alceste, who loves her more
than ever despite shame for his weakness. Her explanation is interrupted by the arrival
of the burlesque valet, Dubois, with the news that Alceste has lost an important lawsuit
and risks arrest.

The conclusion plays against comic conventions. Alceste decides to leave society,
against Philinte's advice, and he wants to know if Célimène is ready to accompany
him. She arrives with Oronte, and when the two suitors demand that she choose between them, she is embarrassed and asks Eliante, who refuses, to judge. When Acaste
and Clitandre appear and read notes that make it clear to all how false Célimène has
been with her several suitors, her salon is deserted. Only Alceste remains to offer himself if she will follow him. She accepts him as a husband but refuses to leave Paris.
Alceste will not marry her under these conditions, and, as Eliante agrees to marry
Philinte, he prepares to go to his retreat alone.

Unlike most of Molière's plays, which take place in a bourgeois setting, *The Misanthrope* depicts the aristocracy of the period. The often crude humor of an earlier time

has been replaced by refined manners. An elegant elite frequents Célimène's salon where visiting, conversation, and gallantry are the preferred diversions. The charming young widow's guests reveal their wit by improvising verbal portraits, engaging in subtle analyses of amorous themes, and judging one another's latest verses. Molière reveals, however, that beneath this society's brilliant exterior there lies mediocrity and profound hypocrisy: Polite manners thinly veil coldness; the art of conversation consists of clever but malicious gossip or sarcastic repartee between supposed friends; gallantry is coupled with contempt for women and love.

The Misanthrope is a love story, too, told as it is ending. From the first scene between Alceste and Célimène one knows that they are incompatible, for they disagree on everything, especially love, which for her is only flirtation, for him total commitment. Love has blinded Alceste, and he indulges himself in the hope of reforming Célimène, until he begins to suspect that he has been betrayed. He then scorns Célimène, and he scorns himself for being unable to stifle his passion. When he is certain that Célimène does not love him, he rejects her as being unworthy of him and takes refuge in voluntary exile. Contrary to the traditions of comedy, the lovers separate at the end.

Finally, *The Misanthrope* is a perfect comedy of character. The characters' features are less striking than those found in *Tartuffe*, but they are more delicately modeled. Alceste, whose soul is noble, has a disagreeable temperament. He is the opposite of Philinte, who is a man of the world, outwardly indulgent to his fellows, although he really despises them. In contrast to Célimène, the eternal coquette, young, beautiful, and witty, but heartless, stand the wise Eliante and the prudish Arsinoë. Among the secondary figures at whom Molière points the finger of ridicule, Oronte, the would-be poet whose vanity leads him to commit nasty, cowardly acts, is outstanding.

Each age sees *The Misanthrope* differently, according to its own preoccupations, and discovers a new wealth of emotions and ideas. Whereas the seventeenth century found Alceste odd and ridiculous, later periods have appreciated his heroic and pathetic side.

Later works • Molière's career changed direction when, in 1669, the ban on *Tartuffe* was finally lifted. He felt vindicated, and he took care thereafter not to write highly controversial works. Charged with the organization of royal entertainments, he produced the farces and comedies with music and dance that had always won for him general acclaim, as well as a number of novel pieces, often in collaboration with Lully and on one occasion with Corneille. There was, as always, much satire, but of politically powerless types. For example, because of his ill health, Molière found doctors an increasingly favorite object of his attacks.

The actor and director • Molière's worst enemies admitted that he was an extraordinary comedic actor. Despite the efforts of traditionalists to make him fit a classical mold, it is more accurate to say that he followed Gallic and Italian traditions. Not only did Molière know Scaramouche but also he was on familiar terms with the whole Italian troupe and their work; he imitated the costumes and traits of both Scaramouche and Sganarelle. Above all, he learned the art of caricature and mime, long popular in France and so necessary for the Italians in a foreign country, and applied their synthetic approach to re-create life in his theaters. Molière developed a stylized walk, posture, and facial expression by which he became known to his public for many years in whatever role he played. There were important modifications from time to time, depending on the roles and changes in Molière's physical condition, but his basic philosophy remained the same.

Molière governed his troupe with cordial familiarity and firm authority. He was a most exacting director at a time when directing had not advanced far, and he made fine actors and actresses of mediocre talents. As has been noted, Molière's first efforts to recruit a repertoire met with small success; he was obliged to create his own, one that served as a model closely followed by his successors for many years. Among Molière's many duties was that of keeping order among the spectators in his theater, not always an easy task at the time. It seems that Molière was as successful on this count as on the many others required to create the national theater in France that is his glory.

Bibliography

Calder, Andrew. *Molière: The Theory and Practice of Comedy*. Atlantic Highlands, N.J.: Athlone Press, 1993. An analysis of the comedic dramas of Molière. Bibliography and index.

Carmody, James Patrick. *Rereading Molière: Mise en scène from Antoine to Vitez*. Ann Arbor: University of Michigan Press, 1993. An examination of the production of Molière's plays and their stage history. Bibliography and index.

Finn, Thomas P. *Molière's Spanish Connection: Seventeenth Century Spanish Theatrical Influence on Imaginary Identity in Molière*. New York: Peter Lang, 2001. A look at the influence of Spanish drama on identity in the works of Molière. Bibliography and index.

Kroen, Sheryl. *Politics and Theater: The Crisis of Legitimacy in Restoration France, 1815-1830*. Berkeley: University of California Press, 2000. This look at Restoration France examines Molière's *Tartuffe* and its influence. Bibliography and index.

Lalande, Roxanne Decker. *Intruders in the Play World: The Dynamics of Gender in Molière's Comedies*. Madison, N.J.: Fairleigh Dickinson University Press, 1996. A critical analysis of Molière's plays from the perspective of gender. Bibliography and index.

Norman, Larry F. *The Public Mirror: Molière and the Social Commerce of Depiction*. Chicago: University of Chicago Press, 1999. Norman examines depiction in the plays of Molière. Bibliography and index.

Scott, Virginia. *Molière: A Theatrical Life*. New York: Cambridge University Press, 2000. A biography of the dramatist that examines his life as a member of the theater rather than as man of letters. Bibliography and index.

Richard A. Mazzara

Sean O'Casey

John Casey

Born: Dublin, Ireland; March 30, 1880
Died: Torquay, England; September 18, 1964

Principal drama • *The Shadow of a Gunman*, pr. 1923, pb. 1925; *Cathleen Listens In*, pr. 1923, pb. 1962; *Juno and the Paycock*, pr. 1924, pb. 1925; *Nannie's Night Out*, pr. 1924, pb. 1962 (one act); *Two Plays*, pb. 1925 (includes *The Shadow of a Gunman* and *Juno and the Paycock*); *The Plough and the Stars*, pr., pb. 1926; *The Silver Tassie*, pb. 1928, pr. 1929; *Within the Gates*, pb. 1933, pr. 1934; *A Pound on Demand*, pb. 1934, pr. 1947 (one act); *The End of the Beginning*, pb. 1934, pr. 1937 (one act); *Five Irish Plays*, pb. 1935; *The Star Turns Red*, pr., pb. 1940; *Purple Dust*, pb. 1940, pr. 1944; *Red Roses for Me*, pb. 1942, pr. 1943; *Oak Leaves and Lavender: Or, A World on Wallpaper*, pb. 1946, pr. 1947; *Cock-a-Doodle Dandy*, pr., pb. 1949; *Collected Plays*, pb. 1949-1951 (4 volumes; includes *Cock-a-Doodle Dandy, Bedtime Story, Hall of Healing, Time to Go*); *Bedtime Story*, pb. 1951, pr. 1952; *Hall of Healing*, pr. 1951, pr. 1952 (one act); *Time to Go*, pb. 1951, pr. 1952 (one act); *The Bishop's Bonfire*, pr., pb. 1955; *Selected Plays of Sean O'Casey*, pb. 1956; *Five One-Act Plays*, pb. 1958, 1990; *The Drums of Father Ned*, pr. 1959, pb. 1960; *Behind the Green Curtains*, pb. 1961, pr. 1962; *Figure in the Night*, pb. 1961, pr. 1962 (one act); *The Moon Shines on Kylenamoe*, pb. 1961, pr. 1962 (one act); *Three More Plays*, pb. 1965; *The Complete Plays of Sean O'Casey*, pb. 1984

Other literary forms • Along with his drama, Sean O'Casey wrote verse, political tracts, historical sketches, essays, dramatic criticism, short stories, and an extensive six-volume autobiography: *I Knock at the Door* (1939), *Pictures in the Hallway* (1942), *Drums Under the Windows* (1945), *Inishfallen, Fare Thee Well* (1949), *Rose and Crown* (1952), and *Sunset and Evening Star* (1954). The autobiography is also available in a two-volume edition, *Mirror in My House* (1956). Early in his career, O'Casey published two volumes of poetry: *Songs of the Wren* (1918) and *More Wren Songs* (1918). His political pamphlets include *The Story of Thomas Ashe* (1918), *The Sacrifice of Thomas Ashe* (1918), and *The Story of the Irish Citizen Army* (1919). O'Casey's two essay collections are *The Flying Wasp* (1937) and *The Green Crow* (1956). His essays, criticism, short stories, and verse have been collected in several anthologies, including *Windfalls* (1934), *Feathers from the Green Crow: Sean O'Casey, 1905-1925* (1962), *Under a Colored Cap* (1963), and *Blasts and Benedictions* (1967).

Achievements • Poet, playwright, essayist, and short-story writer Sean O'Casey stands as one of the major figures of the Irish Literary Renaissance. Though he began his career as a playwright late in life, he still managed to complete more than twenty plays, a six-volume autobiography, and numerous short stories and essays before his death in 1964. Along with the works of John Millington Synge, Lady Augusta Gregory, and William Butler Yeats, his plays sustained the Abbey Theatre during its early years, accounting for its greatest commercial successes, and they are still among the most popular works in the Abbey Theatre's repertory.

During his career, O'Casey moved beyond the confines of dramatic realism to create a new style of expressionism in Anglo-Irish theater. In this regard, he is among the most original and innovative of modern European playwrights. Perhaps only the epic realism of Bertolt Brecht's works rivals the sheer spectacle and vitality of O'Casey's stage. Though his early plays have continued in repertory, these later plays, especially, deserve to be performed more often, despite the demands of their Irish dialect and their variety of song-and-dance material. That they are not reflects the impoverishment of the modern stage, for O'Casey was a master of theatrical entertainment.

Biography • The youngest child in a large Irish Protestant family of modest means, Sean O'Casey was born John Casey in Dublin on March 30, 1880. He was the third child in his family to be named John; two of his siblings with that name had died in infancy. Later, in his twenties, after he had become an Irish nationalist and a member of the Gaelic League, he adopted the Gaelic version of his name, Sean O'Cathasaigh (pronounced O'Casey). O'Casey's father, Michael Casey, who came from a farming family in Limerick, worked as a clerk for the Anglican Irish Church Missions. He went to Dublin as a young man and married Susan Archer, of a respectable auctioneer's family. Michael Casey was a literate man with a good library of English classics, while O'Casey's mother was a woman of great fortitude and devotion to her children, especially her youngest, whom she sheltered because of his physical frailty and a severe eye affliction, which left his vision permanently impaired. Even in the difficult period after her husband's death, she maintained her respectability and encouraged her children to enter professions.

Michael Casey died after a protracted illness on September 6, 1886, when his youngest son was only six. With the loss of his income, the family started a gradual decline into poverty. The Caseys were forced to move to cheaper lodgings in a Dublin dockside neighborhood. There, O'Casey started to associate with working-class Roman Catholic boys who attended the local parochial school. He had been enrolled at St. Mary's National School, where his sister Isabella taught, but when he reached the age of fourteen, his schooling came to an end. His family needed the extra income, so he began to work as a stock boy with a Dublin hardware firm. Though out of school, O'Casey continued his interest in books, and he certainly learned to read before the age of sixteen, contrary to what he later reported to Lady Gregory.

O'Casey became active in the Church of Ireland during this time and was confirmed at the age of seventeen. In his free time, he read William Shakespeare and the Irish playwright Dion Boucicault. He also attended the Mechanics' Theatre with his brother Isaac and even acted in at least one production. His love of drama was strengthened by these early productions, and after the group was later reorganized as the Abbey Theatre, he would see two of his early plays produced there in 1923.

In 1902, O'Casey began work as a laborer on the Great Northern Railway of Ireland, where he was employed for the next ten years. His budding interest in Irish nationalism led him to join the Gaelic League, learn the Irish language, and change his name. Within a short time, he was also a member of the Irish Republican Brotherhood. Through these associations, O'Casey began to shape his identity as Irish nationalist, laborer, and political activist. His interest in writing also emerged as he joined the St. Lawrence O'Toole Club, a local literary society. Above all, he forged the commitment to Irish nationalism that would occupy him for the next twenty years.

O'Casey joined the Irish Transport and General Workers Union in 1909 and was dismissed from his job later that year for refusing to sign a nonstrike pledge during the railway strike. Left unemployed, he turned increasingly to politics while he supported himself as a laborer in the building trade. From his perspective, socialism began to look attractive as an alternative to British economic domination of Ireland. The six-month Dublin labor lockout of 1913 hardened his political views, as he helped organize a relief fund for destitute families. Becoming more militant, he drafted part of the constitution for the Irish Citizen Army, though recuperation from an operation and personal doubts kept him from taking part in the weeklong insurrection of Easter, 1916. Instead, he wrote poems, pamphlets, and broadsides in support of the Irish cause.

His mother and sister died in 1918, leaving O'Casey to board temporarily with the family of his brother Michael. This period marked a low point in O'Casey's fortunes because he was out of work and was forced to accept the charity of others. Yet he was determined to write. In 1921, while living in a small flat, he started work on his three Dublin plays: *The Shadow of a Gunman, Juno and the Paycock*, and *The Plough and the Stars*. O'Casey reached the age of forty-three before *The Shadow of a Gunman* was finally produced, in April, 1923, but his career as a playwright had finally begun. *Juno and the Paycock* followed in March, 1924, and *The Plough and the Stars*, two years later.

O'Casey's Dublin play *The Plough and the Stars* presented such an unflattering view of the Easter Week uprising of 1916 that the audience rioted when it opened at the Abbey Theatre in February, 1926. Yeats stood up before the mob and defended the play, but O'Casey was embittered by its hostile reception and decided shortly afterward to leave Ireland for voluntary exile in England.

In 1926, O'Casey won the Hawthornden Prize for *Juno and the Paycock*, and he left for London that spring to accept the award in person. There, he hoped to find greater artistic freedom as a playwright. During his first three years in London, he was introduced to George Bernard Shaw, had his portrait painted by Augustus John, and met the talented and attractive actress Eileen Reynolds (stage name Carey), whom he married on September 23, 1927. They were to enjoy a long and mutually supportive marriage for thirty-seven years, with their three children, Breon, Niall, and Shivaun. Marriage and life in London apparently had a salutary effect on O'Casey's imagination, for he began to work almost immediately after their marriage on the expressionistic play *The Silver Tassie*, which marked a clear departure from his earlier work.

O'Casey had been attracted to socialism as early as 1911, during the Irish railway strike, but the economic hardships of the 1930's and the rise of Fascism drove him further to the left, to the point of tacitly accepting communism and serving as a member of the advisory board of the London *Daily Worker*. He also became increasingly anticlerical in regard to Ireland, viewing the Roman Catholic prelacy as the oppressor of the Irish people. After World War II, O'Casey spoke out vigorously in favor of the Soviet Union. He opposed the arms race and urged nuclear disarmament.

In 1954, O'Casey moved with his family from London to the resort town of St. Marychurch, Torquay, in Devon. There, in 1956, the family suffered a deep personal loss when the younger son, Niall, died of leukemia. In his mid-seventies when this misfortune occurred, virtually blind and suffering from constant pain, O'Casey still possessed the strength of character to write a moving tribute to his son, "Under a Greenwood Tree He Died," and to continue his playwriting. Friends remembered him from these last years as a thin, sharp-faced man with a gay spirit and an enchanting Irish brogue, who was usually dressed in a warm turtleneck sweater and one of the brightly colored caps that his daughter had knit for him.

The last decade of O'Casey's life showed an increasing American interest in his work and brought him numerous awards and honors, most of which he declined, including an appointment as Commander of the Order of the British Empire and several honorary doctorates from the Universities of Durham and Exeter and from Trinity College, Dublin. His eightieth birthday was celebrated with much fanfare. After suffering a heart attack, O'Casey died in Torquay on September 18, 1964, at the age of eighty-four.

Analysis • In "O'Casey's Credo," an essay that appeared in *The New York Times* and was written in 1958 for the opening of an American production of *Cock-a-Doodle Dandy*, Sean O'Casey remarked that "the first thing I try to do is to make a play live: live as a part of life, and live in its own right as a work of drama." This concern with the vitality of his plays marked O'Casey's craftsmanship as a playwright throughout his career. "Every character, every life," he continued, "[has] something to say, comic or serious, and to say it well [is] not an easy thing to do." To express this vitality through his characters' actions and dialogue was O'Casey's goal as a dramatist. All of his plays share the blend of comic, serious, and poetic imagination that O'Casey believed should meld in any play worth staging.

O'Casey's three periods • O'Casey's plays fall into three periods: the early naturalistic tragicomedies, the expressionistic plays of the middle period, and the exuberant, satiric comedies that mark his later work. O'Casey was forty-three years old when his first play, *The Shadow of a Gunman*, was accepted by the Abbey Theatre. Behind him lay four apprentice plays and more than twenty years of hard experience in Dublin as a laborer, nationalist, and political organizer. He might easily have failed to develop his talent but for the encouragement of Lady Augusta Gregory, Yeats, and Lennox Robinson, who read his early scripts and urged him to continue writing. O'Casey was drawn to the theater as a social medium—as the best way for him to express the impact on Dublin's poor of Ireland's struggle for independence.

O'Casey's first play, *The Shadow of a Gunman*, opened at the Abbey Theatre in April, 1923, and ran for only a few performances, but its modest success encouraged O'Casey to submit *Juno and the Paycock* and *The Plough and the Stars* within the next three years. O'Casey had lived through the bitter period when Ireland was torn first by insurrection and later by the bloody struggle between the Irish Republican Army and the notorious Black and Tans. In these plays, his Dublin trilogy, he expresses disillusionment and bitterness about the way in which the Irish struggle for independence degenerated into fratricidal bloodshed. Together, these plays present a chronicle history of the Irish conflict between 1916 and 1921. Naturalistic in style and approach, they are noted, as critics have remarked, for their tragicomic tone, their vivid depictions of Dublin tenement dwellers, and their lively and colorful speech.

The second period of O'Casey's playwriting career began after he left Dublin for London in 1926. Up to this point, he had been an Irish playwright writing for a national theater, but the response to *The Plough and the Stars*, which provoked a riot at the Abbey Theatre when it opened, may have led him to recognize the limitations of conventional dramatic realism. Seeking ways to expand his artistic vision, O'Casey turned to the expressionistic mode in his next play, *The Silver Tassie*. Inspired by a London coal vendor's song, this ambitious play about World War I incorporates songs, chants, ritualistic scenes, allegorized characters, and stylized sets. The play's action alternates between Dublin and the front as O'Casey depicts the cost of war for all the young men who departed as heroes and returned as cripples and invalids.

Like John Millington Synge before him, O'Casey opened new possibilities for Irish theater, but unfortunately, the Abbey Theatre was unwilling to accept his stylistic innovations. When O'Casey submitted *The Silver Tassie* to the Abbey Theatre in 1928, Yeats rejected it with a sharply worded reply that initiated a bitter exchange; the two were finally reconciled in 1935. Yeats attacked the play for its alleged introduction of propaganda into the theater, for, despite his own experiments with Japanese Nō theater, he was curiously unreceptive to O'Casey's attempts to move beyond dramatic realism. O'Casey did not aspire to a "pure" art of theater or cherish a dramatic theory, as did Yeats. Instead, he merely intended to expand the range of tragicomedy using the devices of expressionism. He hoped to use the exuberance of music-hall entertainment—its melodrama, boisterous comedy, burlesque, and farce—to animate serious drama, just as Shakespeare had woven comic interludes into even his most somber tragedies.

After the rejection of *The Silver Tassie* by the Abbey Theatre, O'Casey turned to a London producer to stage the play. Henceforth, he was to be a playwright without a permanent theater, often forced to publish his plays before they were staged and to depend on commercial productions of varying quality. Though *The Silver Tassie* enjoyed only a mixed success, O'Casey was committed to expressionism as an artistic direction, and his plays during the next decade show the gradual development of this style.

The 1930's were a period of diversity for O'Casey. Besides writing several one-act plays and the full-length morality play *Within the Gates*, he published drama reviews and short stories and began his six-volume autobiography. In his drama reviews and criticism, O'Casey defended other contemporary, experimental playwrights and called for the use of a wider range of theatrical techniques and for a drama criticism receptive to these innovations. He attacked the British critics' taste for the light drawing-room comedies of Noël Coward and the general lack of variety in the London theater. By this time he had also become a committed left-wing thinker who actively sympathized with communist causes. His political ideology is evident in two plays of this period, *The Star Turns Red* and *Oak Leaves and Lavender*. Unfortunately, art and politics did not mix well for O'Casey, and these are largely inferior works.

Perhaps O'Casey came to realize the limits of ideological drama, or he may simply have grown tired of the war theme, for in the most successful plays of his middle period, he returned to an Irish setting, combining expressionistic techniques with traditional Irish characters, scenes, songs, and material. Also written during the war years, *Purple Dust* and *Red Roses for Me* show the refinement of expressionistic techniques that O'Casey had introduced in *The Silver Tassie* almost fifteen years earlier. These two plays demonstrate the range and quality of O'Casey's mature lyric imagination as he animates his stage with the song, pageantry, and spectacle of the Elizabethan theater. As he later observed about his plays, "Like [James] Joyce, it is only through an Irish scene that my imagination can weave a way."

The third period of O'Casey's career reflects a further enhancement of his artistic vision through a series of exuberant comic fantasies dramatizing the conflict between the affirmative and repressive forces in Irish culture. Here, he sharpened his critique of the provincialism, clericalism, materialism, and restrictive religious morality that he perceived in modern Irish life. Starting with *Cock-a-Doodle Dandy*, which O'Casey regarded as his favorite, and continuing with *The Bishop's Bonfire*, *The Drums of Father Ned*, and *Behind the Green Curtains*, the plays of this period mark the height of his mature achievement. In these late plays, O'Casey perfected his distinctive blend of broad comedy, farce, song, fantasy, dance, satire, and melodrama. As his favorite dramatists, William Shakespeare and Dion Boucicault, had done before him, O'Casey made his plays infinitely richer and more varied than conventional realistic drama. His expressionism became a medium for his lyricism and gaiety of spirit. This determination to broaden the range of contemporary theater perhaps marks O'Casey's most distinctive contribution to the modern stage.

In his long and productive career, O'Casey reanimated the Anglo-Irish theater with a blend of tragicomedy, fantasy, and farce that drew from Elizabethan drama, the music hall, and expressionism to create a vibrant and innovative form of dramatic theater. Though his plays have been criticized for lacking a "pure" dramatic form, his vigorous mixture of theatrical elements has stood in marked contrast to other trends in contemporary theater through its sheer power of entertainment and affirmation. O'Casey had the creative power and vision to transcend the limitations of dramatic theory. His genius was for theatrical vitality rather than pure dramatic art.

The Shadow of a Gunman • O'Casey's first play to be accepted by the Abbey Theatre, *The Shadow of a Gunman,* is a two-act tragicomedy set in a Dublin tenement during the May, 1920, struggle between the Irish Republican Army (IRA) and the British Black and Tans. Two hapless young Irishmen, Seumas Shields (a Catholic peddler) and Donal Davoren (a poet manqué) are drawn into the guerrilla warfare when other residents mistake them for IRA fighters and a friend accidentally leaves a bag of terrorist bombs in their rooms. Davoren, the would-be poet, enjoys the hero-worship of his neighbors and the affection of young Minnie Powell, while he writes poor imitations of Percy Bysshe Shelley and pretends to be an insurgent. O'Casey uses the contrast between the self-deceiving appearance and the reality of the two men to debunk romantic myths of Irish heroism and valor. Shields and Davoren are both antiheroes, ordinary men who instinctively shun violence and try to live the semblance of normal lives amid the conflict. This antiheroic theme is the source of both comedy and pathos, for while Shields and Davoren act as cowards, Minnie behaves heroically. In act 2, when British soldiers arrive to search the apartments for snipers or weapons, she volunteers to hide the bag of bombs in her room and is discovered and captured. Sacrificing herself for a sham ideal, she is shot while trying to escape from the British, as Shields and Davoren, who form "the shadow of a gunman," cower in their rooms, terrified of the gunfire.

Juno and the Paycock • *Juno and the Paycock* is set in 1922 during the period of continued civil war after the Irish Free State had been established. The scene is once again a Dublin tenement, and the play depicts the misfortunes of the Boyle family, impoverished Dubliners temporarily lifted out of their squalor by a spurious legacy, which they quickly squander. This three-act tragicomedy parallels domestic and civil chaos; the Boyles struggle against the disintegration of their family, while outside the provisional Irish Republican Army continues its resistance against the Dublin government.

"Captain" Jack Boyle and "Joxer" Daley are among O'Casey's most memorable characters. The Captain struts from apartment to pub, accompanied by the ingratiating Joxer, embellishing on his past adventures, complaining about his hard luck, and deftly avoiding responsibility, while his wife, Juno, struggles both to work and to keep house. As the play progresses, their crippled son, Johnny, becomes an IRA informer, and their daughter, Mary, falls in love with the young lawyer who brings the family news of their supposed inheritance. Despite these misfortunes, the play generates rich humor from the garrulous, irresponsible behavior of the Captain and Joxer, who belong to a long tradition of the stage Irishman and the braggart soldier. Once their inheritance is discovered to be a sham, the family's fortunes swiftly disintegrate, as their furniture is repossessed, Johnny is shot by the IRA, and Mary is left pregnant and deserted by her lover. By the end of the play, bitter and defeated, Juno and Mary mourn Johnny's death, while the Captain and Joxer stagger in, drunk and lugubrious, to lament "the terrible state o' chassis" of the world.

The Plough and the Stars • The title for O'Casey's *The Plough and the Stars* is taken from the original flag of the Irish Citizen Army, with its working-class symbols, but the focus is once again the folly and futility of war. This four-act tragicomedy is set before and during the Easter, 1916, uprising in Dublin and dramatizes the mixed motives of idealism, vanity, and folly that inspired Irish nationalism. The action in the play alternates between a Dublin boardinghouse and the streets and pubs of the city. It dramatizes the trauma of war in separating a young couple, Jack and Nora Clitheroe, recently married. When the call for the uprising takes place, Jack hurries to join his compatriots, while Nora desperately tries to prevent him from leaving and then wanders through the strife-torn city in search of him. After the battle, the city is filled with looters, and O'Casey creates some memorable scenes of rioters fighting over their plunder. The various boarders at the Clitheroes's boardinghouse represent differing attitudes toward the insurrection, from patriotism to scorn. By the end of the play, Dublin is in flames and Jack has died heroically, although Nora, who has lost her baby, cannot be told. Her neighbor, the Unionist Bessie Burgess, is fatally shot by the British while nursing Nora, and the play ends with British soldiers drinking tea in the rooms they have just ransacked.

The Silver Tassie • In style and technique, *The Silver Tassie* marks a clear departure from O'Casey's earlier plays. Though he retains the tragicomic mode, he turns from a realistic to an expressionistic mode to convey the horrors of modern warfare. Symbols and abstractions of war bode large in this play, particularly in act 2, as O'Casey attempts to move his art beyond dramatic realism to a more poetic theater. The protagonist, Harry Heegan, leaves for the front in act 1 after he has won the Silver Tassie, or victory cup, for his Avondale Football Club. He departs as a hero, victorious and in love with Jessie Taite, and returns a crippled, embittered veteran, having lost his youth, vitality, and love. Act 2 invokes the carnage of the front through chant and ritual; an allegorical figure, the Croucher, dominates the action, while Harry is wounded in battle. Act 3 shifts to the army hospital during Harry's recuperation from his injuries, and act 4 brings him back to a dance at the Avondale Football Club. Now a wheelchair invalid, and having lost Jessie to his friend Barney, he drinks the bitter cup of loss and smashes the Silver Tassie on the floor. The dramatic action is quite simple, but O'Casey's expressionistic treatment makes this a powerful and compelling play.

Purple Dust • After a period of unsuccessful propaganda plays, O'Casey's next significant play was *Purple Dust*. He called the play a "wayward comedy," though perhaps it is closer in form to a rollicking farce—a humorous confrontation between the English and the Irish national characters reminiscent of George Bernard Shaw's *John Bull's Other Island* (pr. 1904, pb. 1907). The play is set in the Irish countryside, where two wealthy English dupes, Cyril Poges and Basil Stokes, try to restore a dilapidated Tudor mansion in Clune na Geera. O'Casey's "stage Englishmen" are thwarted by their bungling mismanagement and by the unpredictable Irish weather. By the end of the play, their young Irish mistresses have run off with two Irish workmen and the mansion is about to be destroyed by a flood. Once again, the English are defeated in their attempt to dominate Ireland economically, and, as the title suggests, the pair are left in the ruins of their romantic and extravagant obsession with the "purple dust" of Tudor Ireland.

Red Roses for Me • The most autobiographical of O'Casey's plays, *Red Roses for Me*, presents a romantic, nostalgic evocation of his early manhood in Dublin. The protagonist, Ayamonn Breydon, is a young Protestant railway worker who helps organize a strike in the Dublin yards to win a small wage increase. Ayamonn is in love with a timid Catholic girl, Sheila Moorneen, who, along with Ayamonn's mother, begs him to give up the strike, but Ayamonn is determined that the strike will occur, and he is killed in the labor violence that follows. Before his death, however, he enjoys a moment of ecstatic vision, as, from a bridge across the Liffey, he envisions Dublin transfigured from its drab dullness to a golden radiance. This magnificent scene and the rich language of the play save it from becoming a mere propaganda piece for the cause of Labour.

Cock-a-Doodle Dandy • O'Casey often remarked that he considered *Cock-a-Doodle Dandy* his best play, although it is by no means the easiest to produce. Reminiscent of the fantastic comedies of Aristophanes, this play features a life-size apocalyptic Cock who comes to banish religious bigotry and puritanism from the small Irish village of Nyadnanave, inciting a series of magical and mysterious events. The village priest and older men are sure the Cock represents some malign spirit, though the young women, especially, are attracted to it. O'Casey himself commented that "the Cock is the joyful, active spirit of life as it weaves a way through the Irish scene." In three long scenes, the play presents a parable of the Irish spirit in conflict, torn between the powers of affirmation and negation, as the puritanical Father Domineer musters the village forces of superstition, ignorance, and fear to suppress dance and merriment and, ultimately, to banish the most attractive young women from the region. Unfortunately, the enchantment of the Cock does not prevail in this play, although O'Casey implies that the spirit of human joy is irrepressible.

The Bishop's Bonfire • O'Casey continues his anticlerical theme in *The Bishop's Bonfire*, a satirical farce in which Bishop Bill Mullarky's visit to his hometown is marked by a ritual book-burning of objectionable literature. The forces of piety and respectability are once more in control, as Councillor Reiligan, the richest man in the village, prepares his house to welcome the bishop, while both the upper and lower classes celebrate the homecoming in their own ways. The pompous Reiligan also interferes with his daughters' happiness by preventing them from marrying the men they love because he thinks these men are not respectable enough. Much of the play is farcical or melodramatic, particularly the death scene at the end of the play, in which Fooraun Reiligan is shot by her suitor, Manus Moanroe, when she discovers that he is stealing church funds from her house. Her suicide note absolves him, however, as the sight of burning books welcomes the bishop home.

The Drums of Father Ned • O'Casey's continuing satire of Irish morality irritated many of his compatriots, and the controversy surrounding his next play, *The Drums of Father Ned*, seems like a parody of the play itself in a strange instance of life imitating art. Set in the village of Doonavale during the Tostal, or national arts festival, the play depicts the healing of an old feud between two prosperous families, the Binningtons and the McGilligans, when their son and daughter fall in love during play rehearsals. A short "Prerumble," or one-act prelude, reenacts the feud between Alderman Binnington and Councillor McGilligan, enemies since the Irish Civil War, who will talk with each other only about business matters. Through the evocative power of the "drums" of Father Ned, a life-affirming country priest, the families are reconciled, and joy and love of life are restored to the village of Doonavale during the Tostal celebration. Ironically, this seemingly innocuous comedy was scheduled to be performed at the 1958 Dublin Tostal until it was withdrawn at the behest of the archbishop of Dublin, who refused to celebrate Mass at the festival if works by O'Casey, Joyce, or Samuel Beckett were performed. The spirit of negation prevailed, unfortunately, and the festival continued without the works of three principal Irish artists.

Other major works

POETRY: *Songs of the Wren,* 1918; *More Wren Songs,* 1918.

NONFICTION: *The Story of Thomas Ashe,* 1918; *The Sacrifice of Thomas Ashe,* 1918; *The Story of the Irish Citizen Army,* 1919; *The Flying Wasp,* 1937; *I Knock at the Door,* 1939 (autobiography); *Pictures in the Hallway,* 1942 (autobiography); *Drums Under the Windows,* 1945 (autobiography); *Inishfallen, Fare Thee Well,* 1949 (autobiography); *Rose and Crown,* 1952 (autobiography); *Sunset and Evening Star,* 1954 (autobiography); *Mirror in My House,* 1956 (2 volumes; reissue of 6 volumes of autobiography above); *The Green Crow,* 1956; *Under a Colored Cap,* 1963; *Blasts and Benedictions,* 1967; *The Letters of Sean O'Casey,* 1975, 1978 (3 volumes; David Krause, editor).

MISCELLANEOUS: *Windfalls,* 1934 (includes essays, plays, poems, and stories); *Feathers from the Green Crow: Sean O'Casey, 1905-1925,* 1962 (includes essays, plays, poems, and stories); *The Sean O'Casey Reader: Plays, Autobiographies, Opinions,* 1968 (Brooks Atkinson, editor).

Bibliography

Ayling, Ronald, and Michael J. Durkan. *Sean O'Casey: A Bibliography.* London: Macmillan, 1978. This volume is considered to be the standard bibliographic source on O'Casey's work and the critical reaction to it.

Kearney, Colbert. *The Glamour of Grammar: Orality and Politics and the Emergence of Sean O'Casey.* Westport, Conn.: Greenwood Press, 2000. A study of the Irishness of the literary language of O'Casey, especially his early works.

Krause, David. *Sean O'Casey: The Man and His Work.* 2d ed. New York: Macmillan, 1975. An enlarged edition of an earlier and useful scholarly study. Krause examines O'Casey's life, drama, and experiences in the theatrical world.

Mikhail, E. H. *Sean O'Casey and His Critics: An Annotated Bibliography.* Metuchen, N.J.: Scarecrow Press, 1985. Mikhail's bibliography is the finest later survey of available sources on Ireland's most celebrated playwright.

Mitchell, Jack. *The Essential O'Casey: A Study of the Twelve Major Plays of Sean O'Casey.* New York: International Publishers, 1980. This volume provides a handy summary of O'Casey's most popular works.

O'Connor, Garry. *Sean O'Casey: A Life.* New York: Atheneum, 1988. The best and most readable biography, especially useful on the playwright's rise, through self-education and life as a Dublin laborer, to a major role in the 1916 Easter Rebellion and his Abbey Theatre productions.

Andrew J. Angyal,
updated by Peter C. Holloran

Clifford Odets

Born: Philadelphia, Pennsylvania; July 18, 1906
Died: Los Angeles, California; August 14, 1963

Principal drama · *Waiting for Lefty*, pr., pb. 1935 (one act); *Till the Day I Die*, pr., pb. 1935; *Awake and Sing!*, pr., pb. 1935; *Paradise Lost*, pr. 1935, pb. 1936; *I Can't Sleep*, pr. 1935, pb. 1936; *Golden Boy*, pr., pb. 1937; *Rocket to the Moon*, pr. 1938, pb. 1939; *Six Plays of Clifford Odets*, pb. 1939 (revised as *"Waiting for Lefty" and Other Plays*, 1993); *Night Music*, pr., pb. 1940; *Clash by Night*, pr. 1941, pb. 1942; *The Russian People*, pr. 1942, pb. 1946 (adaptation of Konstantin Simonov's play *The Russians*); *The Big Knife*, pr., pb. 1949; *The Country Girl*, pr. 1950, pb. 1951; *The Flowering Peach*, pr., pb. 1954

Other literary forms · Clifford Odets is also known for his screenplays, which include *The General Died at Dawn* (1936), an adaptation of Charles G. Booth's novel; *Blockade* (1938); *None but the Lonely Heart* (1944), an adaptation of Richard Llewellyn's novel; *Deadline at Dawn* (1946), an adaptation of William Irish's novel; *Humoresque* (1946), an adaptation of Fanny Hurst's story, with Zachary Gold; *The Sweet Smell of Success* (1957), an adaptation, with Ernest Lehman, of Lehman's novel; *The Story on Page One* (1960); and *Wild in the Country* (1961), an adaptation of J. R. Salamanca's novel *The Lost Country*.

Achievements · In the spring of 1935, Clifford Odets, a young playwright thitherto unknown, had the heady experience of seeing three of his plays produced in New York. Overnight, he was hailed as the rising star of American drama. *Waiting for Lefty*, a timely tour de force dealing specifically with the strike of New York taxicab drivers but more broadly with the stressful socioeconomic situation in which many working people found themselves during the Great Depression, was a pioneering effort in proletarian drama that made its point by presenting six vignettes around a controlling theme and by involving the audience directly in the play's action—it is the audience that gives the strike call in the play's dramatically intense ending. By March, 1935, the play had been brought to Broadway to play as part of a double bill with *Till the Day I Die*, written quickly as an accompaniment to it. By July, 1935, *Waiting for Lefty* had been performed in thirty cities across the United States.

On February 19, 1935, the Group Theatre brought *Awake and Sing!* to Broadway some weeks after *Waiting for Lefty* had first gained its widespread popular acclaim, and this warm play of middle-class Jewish family life clearly established its author as a significant and effective playwright.

If ever a dramatist were right for his time, the young Odets was right for the 1930's. A nonconformist with a strong sense of outrage at social injustice, Odets drifted into various acting and radio jobs after he dropped out of high school at age seventeen. During this period, Odets learned a great deal about the struggle to survive and about theater. It was his association with the Group Theatre that gave Odets an identity, a satisfying surrogate family, and the motivation that he had until then been lacking. The Group Theatre, an outgrowth of the Depression, was to become the compelling force in the spirit and structure of Odets's best work, the plays from *Waiting for Lefty* through

Paradise Lost, excluding only the somewhat inconsequential *Till the Day I Die*. His plays reflected the philosophy of the Group Theatre that there should be no stars; in these early plays, Odets discovered and experimented with the theme of nonfulfillment, which was to be the controlling theme of most of his writing.

The Depression gave Odets a strong subject, and when it ended, he had difficulty finding subjects about which he could write with the force and conviction of his early work. The Odets who could convincingly argue the case of young lovers unable to marry because of the economic pressures of the Depression was a much less persuasive social protester when, more than a decade later, in *The Big Knife*, he attacked Hollywood's exploitation of Charlie Castle, an actor who had a fourteen-year contract for four million dollars. The social conditions out of which Odets's best artistic achievement grew had largely ceased to exist by 1940, and he was never able to find another theme with which he could identify so fully or in quite the same way as he had with the themes that the Depression provided him. While his last three plays are dramatically sound and compelling, Odets was always forced to work in his own enormous shadow, and his public demanded more of him than he could deliver in his later years.

Biography • Clifford Odets was born in Philadelphia to a twenty-year-old Lithuanian immigrant, Louis J. Odets, and his nineteen-year-old wife, Pearl Geisinger Odets, who had come to the United States from Romania, often called "Austria" by the Geisingers. Odets was the first of three children, and he was closer in many ways to his Aunt Esther and her husband than he was to his sickly, chronically depressed mother and somewhat combative father. "Tante Esther," as he called her, had been just enough older than her sister Pearl when they arrived in the United States that she remembered Yiddish and was able to speak it. Her husband, Israel Rossman, read Yiddish newspapers, and in the Rossman household, the young Odets was exposed to cadences of language that were absent from his parents' home and that he was to use effectively in dialogue throughout his career. Indeed, Odets was more successful than any playwright of his time in capturing the speech cadences and intonations of Jewish Americans.

Odets's father rose quickly to middle-class status. By the early 1920's, Louis Odets was owner of a print shop in the Bronx. As the fortunes of the family improved, however, Odets began to feel spiritually alienated from the bourgeois values of his parents. He was moving gradually into what would be his vocation by affiliating himself with such theatrical groups as the Drawing-Room Players, Harry Kemp's Poets' Theatre, the Mae Desmond Stock Company, and, for a short time in 1929, the Theatre Guild. It was not until 1931, however, that he found his spiritual home in the newly formed Group Theatre. His writing was to be shaped by the philosophy of the Group Theatre, in which, as Harold Clurman wrote in *The Fervent Years*, "there were to be no stars . . . not for the negative purpose of avoiding distinction, but because all distinction . . . was to be embodied in the production as a whole." Odets's plays, reflecting this philosophy, generally contain no starring roles, but rather six or eight substantial roles of essentially equal importance.

With his meteoric rise to fame in 1935, Odets's commitment to the Group Theatre grew, and as the group faced financial difficulties, Odets reluctantly became a Hollywood screenwriter, primarily to earn enough money to keep it from financial collapse. Some argue that Odets compromised his talent by writing for the screen, that he was never again able to write with the force and the conviction that he had demonstrated before "selling out" to Hollywood. Although it is evident that he never again wrote as well as he had in the 1930's, it is overly simplistic to attribute Odets's artistic decline to any single causal factor. The times in which he lived and crucial events in his own life, including his 1937 marriage to and subsequent divorce in 1941 from Austrian film star Luise Rainer, both contributed to Odets's artistic decline in the early 1940's.

Odets's middle range of plays—*Rocket to the Moon, Night Music,* and *Clash by Night*—deal largely with questions of love, personal isolation, and nonfulfillment. None reaches the artistic level of the earlier plays. In the seven-year hiatus between *Clash by Night* and the 1949 production of *The Big Knife,* Odets produced three screenplays and an adaptation of Konstantin Simonov's *The Russians,* a propaganda piece. Odets was unable to recapture in his later plays the freshness and the authentic social anger of his early plays.

When he was called before the House Committee on Un-American Activities in 1952, Odets admitted to having been a member of the Communist Party "from toward the end of 1934 to the middle of 1935, covering anywhere from six to eight months." Never a very convinced party member, Odets favored having a third major political party in the United States but was quickly disenchanted with the rigidity of the Communist Party and dismissed it as a reasonable vehicle for dealing with the social problems that perplexed him.

Odets's last stage play, *The Flowering Peach,* reflects its author's newly found interest in the biblical heritage of the Jewish people. A redaction of the Noah story, *The Flowering Peach* is warm and sensitive, reminiscent in its family orientation of *Awake and Sing!* It is a play of resignation rather than of revolution.

In the last decade of his life, Odets produced little, although in the last year of his life he was working on an ambitious project to write four of the thirteen scripts for *The Richard Boone Show,* a dramatic television series. Odets had completed three of the four scripts he was to write before he succumbed to cancer in Los Angeles on August 14, 1963. The year after Odets's death, the musical version of *Golden Boy,* on which he had been working with William Gibson, reached Broadway.

Analysis • In an interview with Arthur Wagner conducted two years before Clifford Odets's death but not published in *Harper's Magazine* until September of 1966, Odets told Wagner, "The question is really not one of knowing how to write so much as knowing how to connect with yourself so that the writing is, so to speak, born affiliated with yourself." When he was dealing with the pressing social problems of the 1930's, which were times of great national pain that spilled over into the lives of individuals and into the conduct of families, Odets was connecting with himself. He was writing from deep personal conviction intensified by moral outrage at a society that could do no better for its members than to allow the economic and social dissolution that the Depression brought.

Waiting for Lefty • Economic and social determinism is significantly present in all of Odets's major plays, and *Waiting for Lefty* is no exception. Despite its brevity, it makes eloquent statements on a broad range of topics, ranging from family life to anti-Semitism to collective bargaining to the ecological irresponsibility of capitalist producers of poison gas. The overwhelming question posed by the play is whether workers should have control over their own destinies, a question that recurs in Odets's later plays. Although the last curtain leaves no doubt about the answer Odets proposes, it is clear that the social and economic pressure under which his characters are laboring will not magically disappear.

As often happens with social drama, *Waiting for Lefty*, which Brooks Atkinson called "fiercely dramatic in the theater," has become, as Michael Mendelsohn wrote, "as dead as last year's newspaper." This earliest of Odets's plays, an agitprop piece written in great haste to be presented at workers' meetings, was to catapult its author into public recognition and to offer him the opportunity to become a successful Broadway playwright.

Waiting for Lefty was intended to be a play about "the stormbirds of the working class"; the play is more accurately described as being about "declassed members of the middle class," as John Howard Lawson contends. The principals in the play are from various walks of life. They have two things in common: They are taxicab drivers, and they earn their living in this way because the Depression has made it impossible for them to follow other pursuits. The drivers and those close to them are examples of men with thwarted ambitions and broken dreams; external economic forces are determining their lives. They meet to consider whether they should strike, and as the strike is discussed, various drivers tell their stories in the several vignettes of which the play is composed. Mendelsohn rightly perceived that the play succeeds dramatically because of its "interplay between personal lives and collective action." Odets was himself middle-class, his audiences were middle-class, and the play is essentially middle-class, despite Odets's polemics to the contrary. This accounts for the play's initial success with its audiences. A middle-class audience could feel empathy with middle-class protagonists who had been brought to the level of the working class by the Depression.

Till the Day I Die • *Waiting for Lefty*, which plays in less than an hour, was too short to be taken to Broadway as an evening's entertainment. The play and its writer were in great demand with all sorts of political groups, and the publicity generated by the play made producers eager to bring it to Broadway, where *Awake and Sing!* had just opened. In order to round out an evening of theater, Odets wrote *Till the Day I Die*, one of the early anti-Nazi plays to appear on Broadway. The play, which focuses on the situation of communists in Adolf Hitler's Germany, is somewhat trivial, although in it one can recognize the beginning of themes that Odets was to develop later. For example, the protagonist, Ernst Tausig, is brought in for questioning by the storm troopers, who smash his right hand with a rifle butt. This leads eventually to amputation, a particularly difficult outcome for Ernst, who is a violinist. (Similarly, in *Golden Boy*, Joe Bonaparte is a promising violinist, but he destroys his hands by becoming a prizewinning boxer, led into this activity by economic necessity rather than by choice.) Ernst Tausig commits suicide, finally, and if any ray of hope is offered, it is a questionable one: Ernst's mistress, Tilly, is pregnant and presumably will produce a child who will carry on. What this child is likely to become in Hitler's Germany is doubtful. *Till the Day I Die* was dashed off in five days, and the play is less than convincing. As a curtain opener for *Waiting for Lefty*, it served its commercial purposes at the expense of artistic integrity; its value is historical rather than artistic.

Awake and Sing! • The backdrop of the Depression pervades *Awake and Sing!* Those who expected another play with the political fervor and intense anger of *Waiting for Lefty* found instead that *Awake and Sing!* was an accurate view of Jewish family life and of the effect of the Depression on three generations of the Berger family, all living under one roof. The play focuses primarily on the two members of the youngest generation, Ralph and Hennie. Both are thwarted because of the economic pressures under which they live. Hennie is trapped in a marriage contrived by her mother, who cannot bear the thought of her daughter mothering an illegitimate child. Her brother, Ralph, the idealist, can proclaim, "We don't want life printed on dollar bills," but his whole existence is so economically determined that he has little control over his life. The grandfather, Jacob, also an idealist, complains, "This is a house? Marx said it—abolish such families." Jacob commits suicide in the end, leaving to Ralph the small legacy that his insurance policy will provide: a slender but unconvincing thread of hope. Bessie Berger, the mother of the household, lives in fear that her family will collapse and her home be taken away: "They threw out a family on Dawson Street today. All the furniture on the sidewalk. A fine old woman with gray hair." Ever concerned with appearances, Bessie proclaims ingenuously, "I like my house to look respectable," and acts to keep it that way no matter what deceptions she must engage in to maintain the appearance. Odets is at his best in *Awake and Sing!* He is close to his blood ties: He knows his characters, and the play exudes authenticity.

Paradise Lost • Speaking of *Awake and Sing!*, Odets said that his "interest was not in the presentation of an individual's problems, but in those of a whole class." One must bear this statement in mind when approaching *Paradise Lost*, in which the trials visited on the Gordon family are so numerous and so close together in time that they put one in mind of the most melodramatic of soap operas. In this play, which, like *Awake and Sing!*, is Chekhovian in its characterization and structure, Odets deals with an upper-middle-class family caught in the grip of the Depression.

As the threat of economic annihilation closes in on the Gordons, Leo, the father, loses his business, largely through the deception of an unscrupulous partner. One of his sons, Julie, is dying of encephalitis. The other son, Ben, a former Olympic runner, is felled by a policeman's bullets in a chase following a robbery he committed in order to get money for his wife and family. Leo's daughter, Pearl, frustrated in her musical and personal ambitions, becomes a virtual recluse. Ultimately, the family is evicted when Leo's business plunges into bankruptcy.

Odets considered *Paradise Lost* his most profound play. Most of the critics did not agree, with even such perceptive commentators as Joseph Wood Krutch suggesting that the play was a mere burlesque of *Awake and Sing!* Few could see through the melodrama and sentimentality of *Paradise Lost* to what Odets was struggling to communicate. Harold Clurman, writing in his introduction to the published version of the play, contended quite correctly that it is about middle-class people who have the "bewildering perception that everything [they intimately believe] is being denied by the actual conditions of contemporary society." Metaphorically, the play, like *Waiting for Lefty* and *Awake and Sing!*, is about an entire class of people who are being wiped out by the Depression. The Bergers represent the lower range of this class; the Gordons, the upper range. The middle class, upper or lower, is being dragged down by economic conditions over which they have no control. As in most of his plays, Odets wrote in *Paradise Lost* about blocked aspirations. The theme of nonfulfillment controls the play, whose only shred of hope comes in Leo's final lengthy oration, which, in the face of such encompassing despair, is somewhat out of place and unconvincing.

The play, nevertheless, has strong vignettes, the best of which are found in the portrayal of Sam Katz, Leo's dishonest business partner. Sam, sexually impotent, blames his long-suffering wife for their childlessness. Sam's impotence can be taken to represent a general lack of the strength and will that might enable him to live as he desires. His wife-mother, Bertha, endures his taunts and his humiliation, comforting him at the end and calling him "a good boy." In Sam and Bertha, Odets was beginning to develop the characters who emerged more fully developed as Ben and Belle in *Rocket to the Moon* and who reappeared in a somewhat different form in *The Country Girl*. His concern with a weak man in a childless marriage to a woman whose maternal feelings are directed at her spouse pervades these three plays.

Golden Boy • In *Golden Boy*, Joe Bonaparte's artistic nature and his desire to be a concert violinist are at odds with the economic realities of his life. Bonaparte goes into boxing to make money, and in so doing, he ruins his sensitive hands and destroys any possibility that he might ultimately achieve his artistic goal. On a metaphoric level, Odets is suggesting quite cynically a philosophy that Moe Axelrod espoused in *Awake and Sing!*: "One thing to get another." Life kills the dreamer, the artist, in the same way that Odets's father had done everything in his power to make his son practical, to kill the dreamer in him.

Harold Clurman called *Golden Boy* Odets's most subjective play. Odets held the play in some contempt, claiming to have written the play to be a hit in order to keep the Group Theatre together. *Golden Boy*, however, shows commendable control and artistic maturation. If one can overcome the early incongruity of a boxer who is also a sensitive violinist, the rest of the play is plausible and well made. Joe Bonaparte, the "golden boy" of the play's title, falls victim to what Gerald Weales called "the disintegration brought on by success." Joe makes the difficult decision to abandon his musical career in order to pursue a career in championship boxing. Ironically, he wins the championship fight but, in so doing, kills his opponent and forecloses all hope of returning to his music.

Joe grows increasingly alienated from his society as he realizes that he has sold out. His trainer cautions him, "Your heart ain't in fighting . . . your *hate* is." Joe changes in the course of the play from a youth who is sensitive about being cross-eyed to a necessarily hardened figure: Sensitivity, an asset for a musician, is a liability for a boxer. Ultimately, Joe becomes a piece of property (this theme recurs forcefully in *The Big Knife*). Joe gets his Duesenberg, a clear and visible symbol of economic success, but he dies when the car crashes, a conclusion with a dramatic impact not unlike that left on audiences who learn at the end of *Waiting for Lefty* that Lefty has been found shot to death in an alley. Whereas the news of Lefty's death forces the taxicab drivers to rise to action, the news of Joe Bonaparte's death leaves audiences with a dull, pervasive ache for the human condition.

Golden Boy was Odets's first drama to underplay the Yiddish-English dialect of his earlier work. In this departure, one sees a playwright trying to broaden his range, trying to reduce his dependence on his Jewish heritage. *Rocket to the Moon, Night Music*, and *Clash by Night* represented a new direction for Odets. The years in which these plays were written were those during which Odets was married to and divorced from Luise Rainer, and the plays themselves are much concerned with questions of love and marriage. *Night Music* is concerned with young love and the effects of economic uncertainty on it, while the other two are concerned with romantic triangles. Odets is tentative in these plays. His personal concerns have shifted from those of an artist struggling to establish himself and to survive during the Depression to those of someone who is concerned primarily with the tensions that two people experience in a love relationship and in marriage.

Rocket to the Moon • *Rocket to the Moon* is an unfocused drama about the tedious dalliance of a middle-aged dentist with Cleo, his receptionist. Unfortunately, Odets allowed himself to be sidetracked in this play, concentrating more on Ben Stark, the dentist, than on Cleo, the receptionist, who could have been drawn with sufficient psychological complexity to bring some intensity into the drama. The sensitivity with which Odets portrayed Sam and Bertha Katz in *Paradise Lost* was not repeated in *Rocket to the Moon*, although Ben and Belle indisputably resemble Sam and Bertha. This play is at best tawdry and represents an artistic setback for its author. Odets was at this time able neither to distance himself sufficiently from his own problems to practice his profession at its highest level, nor to use his own suffering and confusion to enrich his art. Some of Odets's remarkable ability to sketch characters is, nevertheless, evident in *Rocket to the Moon.* Belle's father, Mr. Prince, is drawn with great skill, and in him one sees a bit of what Odets was beginning to fancy himself to be—someone who had gained material security but who was essentially unloved. When Mr. Prince suggests that Cleo might marry him, she rejects the offer, saying, "Next week I'll buy myself a dog."

Night Music • The theme of *Night Music* is homelessness. Steve Takis, the protagonist, is known as "Suitcase Steve" because he always carries a suitcase with him and constantly moves from place to place. He has been sent East on an incredible errand to pick up two apes for a Hollywood film studio and to accompany them back to the West Coast. One of the apes snatches a gold locket from Fay Tucker, the police become involved, and Steve is arrested and then released, his apes being held as security. He approaches Fay with indignation for the trouble she has caused him, and, predictably, the two fall in love. The play's most sympathetic character, Detective A. L. Rosenberg, helps the couple, but Rosenberg, the symbol of good in a hostile world, is dying of cancer. The play's didacticism overcomes its warmth and its occasional gentle tenderness. The symbols are heavy-handed, and the interesting themes of personal isolation, homelessness, and loneliness, which had been themes of some prominence in all of Odets's earlier plays, here seem completely trivial.

Clash by Night • *Clash by Night* was written as Odets's marriage fell apart and as the Group Theatre was reaching the point of disbanding. Between the time the play opened out of town and the time it opened on Broadway, the Japanese had bombed Pearl Harbor and national attention was on more serious matters than the sordid love triangle around which this play revolves. *Clash by Night* is about Mae Wilenski and her lackluster husband, Jerry.

Mae is bored with her life, and before the end of act 1, she is involved in a love affair with Earl Pfeiffer, a boarder in the Wilenski household. The action plays out quite slowly, each act being interlarded with echoes of Odets's social fervor; in a subplot, for example, Joe and Peggy have been engaged for two years and are unable to marry because Joe works only three days a week, a situation rather unconvincing to audiences in a society gearing up for war and recruiting every available able-bodied citizen to work in defense jobs. Ultimately, Jerry is led by jealousy to murder Earl, an interesting outcome in this love triangle involving two men and a woman as opposed to the two women-one man triangle in *Rocket to the Moon.* Whereas Belle takes Ben back, perhaps to nurture him but more likely to torture him for the rest of his days, Jerry must strike out in a manly way and seek vengeance through killing his rival.

The Big Knife • A seven-year gap separated *Clash by Night* from Odets's next Broadway production, *The Big Knife.* The play focuses on Hollywood's exploitation of Charlie Castle, an actor who has just been offered a fourteen-year movie contract worth four million dollars. Charlie, however, does not wish to sign. Like Joe Bonaparte in *Golden Boy*, he is in danger of becoming merely a piece of property, and Charlie recoils from allowing the studio to own him. The complication is that Charlie was involved in a fatal hit-and-run accident for which he and the studio have permitted his publicity man, Buddy Bliss, to take the rap. The studio now attempts to force Charlie to sign the contract under threat of revealing the real facts of the accident. In a sense, Odets was back to arguing the worker-management conflict with which he first dealt in *Waiting for Lefty*; the argument against management is somewhat less convincing, however, when management is paying the worker as handsomely as it is here, even though the principle may be similar.

The play sheds some light on the false standards of Hollywood society, presenting interesting scenes that spotlight such realities of Hollywood life as the control that gossip columnists have over actors' lives. Charlie Castle calls free speech "the highest-priced luxury in this country today," and he attacks the superficiality of Hollywood relationships by saying, "I'll bet you don't know why we all wear these beautiful, expensive ties in Hollywood. . . . It's a military tactic—we hope you won't notice our faces." Odets thus gave vent to the resentment that had been growing in him during the decade since he first went to Hollywood as a screenwriter. *The Big Knife* is tightly structured, and its dramatic intensity is at times superb, but its basic premise is difficult to accept, and Charlie Castle's suicide at the end is more melodramatic than artistically valid.

The Country Girl • *The Country Girl* followed *The Big Knife* in 1950, and in it Odets revived some of the controlling ideas of his earlier plays. The protagonist, Frank Elgin, is an aging actor who has fallen on hard times, largely because of his alcoholism, brought about by the accidental death of his young son, for which he blames himself. Frank's wife, Georgie, is a wife-mother recalling Bertha Katz and Belle Stark. Bernie Dodd, a director, has given Frank one last chance for a comeback. He insists that if Frank begins drinking again, he will dismiss him immediately. Bernie, who first detests Georgie, later is strongly attracted to her, creating a love triangle. This love triangle differs from Odets's previous ones, however, in that Georgie and Bernie are ironically united in their efforts to rehabilitate Frank. The psychological complexity of the play makes it conceptually stronger than *Rocket to the Moon* or *Clash by Night*.

In numerous rewrites, the role of Georgie was drastically changed from that of a nagging wife to that of a firm but understanding and supportive marriage partner. The love relationship that grows between Georgie and Bernie is the timeworn love-hate relationship. Frank remains largely oblivious to it until near the end of the last act. In the end, despite lapses along the way, Frank succeeds in acting his part well and in paving the way for the comeback toward which he has been struggling. The role of Frank provides a challenging vehicle for an actor to play a weak, insecure character, a pathological liar who successfully undergoes a difficult rehabilitation. Still, Frank's triumph at the end, accompanied by Georgie's decision to stay with him, leaves doubts in the minds of the audience. Throughout the play, Georgie's relationship to Frank has been based on her providing strength for a weak husband. If Frank has overcome his weakness, one must seriously question whether the relationship will give Georgie what she needs. If he has not overcome his weakness, then they are back exactly where they began. Odets himself viewed *The Country Girl* as a theater piece and disparaged the play's artistry, although he was pleased with certain technical aspects of it, especially the much-revised ending.

The Flowering Peach • In his last play, *The Flowering Peach*, Odets returned to his blood sources. The family in the play, reminiscent of the Bergers in *Awake and Sing!*, speaks in the Yiddish-English dialect of Odets's earlier characters. *The Flowering Peach* is a version of the Noah story and largely concerns Noah, to whom God appears in a dream, predicting the Flood; Noah's attempts to build the Ark; and his conflicts with his son, Japheth, who, even when he comes to believe the truth of his father's dream, refuses to enter the Ark as a protest against a cruel God who would destroy the earth. Japheth finds himself on the Ark only because his father knocks him out and has him carried aboard. Once there, the father-son conflict, the conflict between faith and reason, again erupts. Japheth is convinced that the Ark should have a rudder; his father is equally convinced that God will direct the Ark as He intends.

The Flowering Peach is a warm and satisfying play. In it, Odets again explores the family as a unit, and he does so with sensitivity and with a sentimentality that, in this play, is not unbecoming. The dialogue is easy and natural, and tensions are reduced by the inclusion of amusing wisecracks. *The Flowering Peach* was nominated for the Pulitzer Prize, the first time that such recognition had come to an Odets play, but the Pulitzer Prize's advisory board overruled the jurors and gave the prize for the 1954-1955 season to Tennessee Williams for his *Cat on a Hot Tin Roof*. *The Flowering Peach*, a play of great affirmation, has yet to receive the recognition that many believe it deserves.

Odets wrote to Eugene Gross, "Nothing moves me so much as human aspirations blocked, nothing enrages me like waste. I am for use as opposed to abuse." All of his plays, with the possible exception of *The Flowering Peach*, have a deep and controlling concern with the question of blocked aspirations, and this persistent concern with a universal human problem gives Odets's work a lasting value, despite the dated topical themes of many of his plays.

Other major works

SCREENPLAYS: *The General Died at Dawn*, 1936 (adaptation of Charles G. Booth's novel); *Blockade*, 1938; *None but the Lonely Heart*, 1944 (adaptation of Richard Llewellyn's novel); *Deadline at Dawn*, 1946 (adaptation of William Irish's novel); *Humoresque*, 1946 (with Zachary Gold; adaptation of Fannie Hurst's story); *The Sweet Smell of Success*, 1957 (with Ernest Lehman; adaptation of Lehman's novel); *The Story on Page One*, 1960 (directed by Odets); *Wild in the Country*, 1961 (adaptation of J. R. Salamanca's novel *The Lost Country*).

NONFICTION: *The Time Is Ripe: The 1940 Journal of Clifford Odets*, 1988.

Bibliography

Brenman-Gibson, Margaret. *Clifford Odets: American Playwright; the Years from 1906-1940*. New York: Applause, 2001. This biography of Odets focuses on the earlier part of his career, which many would argue was the better part.

Cantor, Hal. *Clifford Odets: Playwright-Poet*. Lanham, Md.: Scarecrow Press, 2000. Rather than examining Odets from a political or biographical perspective, Cantor concentrates on eleven of his plays, reading closely and identifying common themes. He emphasizes Odets's poetic style and also notes Odets's influence on American theater. Bibliography and index.

Cooperman, Robert. *Clifford Odets: An Annotated Bibliography, 1935-1989*. Westport, Conn.: Meckler, 1990. A useful bibliographic essay evaluates the listed entries, which are divided into primary works (plays, screenplays, teleplays, articles, journals, and diaries), critical studies (on individual plays and politics, and on the Group

Theatre), and information on the House Committee on Un-American Activities. Includes a brief chronology and an index.

Demastes, William W. *Clifford Odets: A Research and Production Sourcebook.* New York: Greenwood Press, 1991. The book's main features are summaries of characters and plots, along with overviews of the critical reception of Odets's stage and radio plays. Includes a brief chronology, a biographical essay, a bibliography of Odets's primary works (with unpublished archival sources), an annotated secondary bibliography (1935-1990), a list of major productions, and an index.

Miller, Gabriel. *Clifford Odets.* New York: Continuum, 1989. Critical of the narrow interpretations of Odets as a political playwright of the 1930's, Miller focuses primarily on the published plays, arranged thematically around several "visions": Chekhovian, tragic, romantic, melodramatic, and political. The interest centers on both experimentation with form and the evolution of Odets's "significant thematic and social concerns." Index.

_____, ed. *Critical Essays on Clifford Odets.* Boston: G. K. Hall, 1991. This anthology includes ten reviews of Odets's productions (from *Waiting for Lefty* to *The Flowering Peach*), two 1930's evaluations of Odets, three interviews with Odets dating from the 1950's and 1960's, and a collection of essays, most reprinted from earlier books. The introduction provides an evaluative chronological overview of primary and secondary sources.

R. Baird Shuman,
updated by Elsie Galbreath Haley

Eugene O'Neill

Born: New York, New York; October 16, 1888
Died: Boston, Massachusetts; November 27, 1953

Principal drama • *Bound East for Cardiff,* wr. 1913-1914, pr. 1916, pb. 1919; *Thirst, and Other One-Act Plays,* pb. 1914; *Chris Christophersen,* wr. 1919, pb. 1982 (revised as *Anna Christie*); *Beyond the Horizon,* pr., pb. 1920; *The Emperor Jones,* pr. 1920, pb. 1921; *Anna Christie,* pr. 1921, pb. 1923; *The Hairy Ape,* pr., pb. 1922; *All God's Chillun Got Wings,* pr., pb. 1924; *Complete Works,* pb. 1924 (2 volumes); *Desire Under the Elms,* pr. 1924, pb. 1925; *The Great God Brown,* pr., pb. 1926; *Lazarus Laughed,* pb. 1927, pr. 1928; *Strange Interlude,* pr., pb. 1928; *Mourning Becomes Electra,* pr., pb. 1931 (includes *Homecoming, The Hunted,* and *The Haunted*); *Nine Plays,* pb. 1932; *Ah, Wilderness!,* pr., pb. 1933; *Plays,* pb. 1941 (3 volumes), pb. 1955 (revised); *The Iceman Cometh,* pr., pb. 1946; *A Moon for the Misbegotten,* pr. 1947, pb. 1952; *Long Day's Journey into Night,* pr., pb. 1956; *Later Plays,* pb. 1967; *The Calms of Capricorn,* pb. 1981 (with Donald Gallup); *The Complete Plays,* pb. 1988 (3 volumes); *Ten "Lost" Plays,* pb. 1995; *Early Plays,* pb. 2001

Other literary forms • Although primarily known for his plays, Eugene O'Neill also wrote poetry and a large amount of correspondence, collected in several volumes and published posthumously. Among these are *"The Theatre We Worked For": The Letters of Eugene O'Neill to Kenneth MacGowan* (1982), edited by Jackson R. Bryer and Ruth M. Alvarez and containing an introductory essay by Travis Bogard; *"Love and Admiration and Respect": The O'Neill-Commins Correspondence* (1986), edited by Dorothy Commins; and *"As Ever, Gene": The Letters of Eugene O'Neill to George Jean Nathan* (1987), edited by Nancy L. Roberts and Arthur W. Roberts. O'Neill's poems were published in *Poems, 1912-1944* (1979) and were edited by Donald Gallup. His unpublished or unfamiliar writings were published in *The Unknown O'Neill* (1988), edited by Travis Bogard.

Achievements • Eugene O'Neill has been called, rightly, the father of modern American drama, not only because he was the first major American playwright but also because of the influence of his work on the development of American theater and on other dramatists. In addition to achieving both popular success and critical acclaim in the United States, O'Neill has achieved an international reputation. Produced throughout the world, his plays are the subject of countless critical books and articles. In many of his plays, O'Neill employed traditional themes such as the quest, while in others he treated subjects that had gone largely unexamined on the American stage, particularly subjects concerning human psychology.

Although many of O'Neill's works are now universally acclaimed, initial critical reaction to the emotional content of some of these plays was mixed. In addition to breaking new ground in theme and subject matter, O'Neill was innovative in his use of technical elements of the theater. He experimented with such devices as masks, "asides," and even the stage itself as vehicles to further themes. Moreover, in an effort to achieve for the drama the broad temporal spectrum of the novel, he experimented with dramatic time, presenting two of his works in trilogies of nine acts each. Although some of O'Neill's dramatic and theatrical experiments were less well received than others, his reputation is now secure; his plays continue to be widely produced throughout the world, both on the stage and on film, because they speak to the human experience that is shared by all.

Biography • Eugene Gladstone O'Neill's parents were James O'Neill, an actor imprisoned by the material success of his role as the Count of Monte Cristo, and Ellen Quinlan O'Neill, a romantic and idealistic woman similarly trapped for much of her life by an addiction to morphine. The complex psychologies of O'Neill's parents and his brother, and the relationships among all the family members, figure significantly as subjects of many of O'Neill's best plays, particularly *Long Day's Journey into Night.*

Educated in Roman Catholic schools, O'Neill entered Princeton University in 1906 but left before a year was over. His travels in 1910 and 1911 to South America and England provided background for his early plays of the sea, several of which he wrote during a six-month hospitalization for tuberculosis in 1912. The following year, he participated in George Pierce Baker's Workshop 47 at Harvard University, where he formally studied playwriting. O'Neill was married three times: to Kathleen Jenkins in 1909, to Agnes Boulton in 1918, and to Carlotta Monterey in 1929. He had three children: Eugene, Jr., who was born to the first marriage and who committed suicide in 1950; and Shane and Oona, who were born to the second marriage. O'Neill won four Pulitzer Prizes for his plays: in 1920 for *Beyond the Horizon,* in 1922 for *Anna Christie,* in 1928 for *Strange Interlude,* and in 1957 for *Long Day's Journey into Night.* In 1936, he was awarded the Nobel Prize in Literature. Although ill for the last seventeen years of his life, O'Neill wrote several of his finest plays during that period.

Analysis • Eugene O'Neill has often been criticized for his choice of characters, for their aberrant psychologies, and for their emotionalism. Certainly he dealt with emotions, but he did so because he believed that emotions were a better guide than thoughts in the search for truth. The struggles of his characters frequently take place, therefore, within themselves, so that there is little real action performed on the stage. Victories, consequently, are in the mind, not quantifiable. The ephemeral nature of such victories has been, for some critics, insufficient.

The popularity of O'Neill's work, however, continues to grow. His plays have been performed throughout the world and transformed into film and opera because they concern truths of human existence. For O'Neill, life *is* a tragedy—but human beings have the resources with

(© The Nobel Foundation)

which to confront it. The dramatic presentation of that struggle was O'Neill's life-work.

The Emperor Jones • Although O'Neill was fortunate in having several of his earliest plays produced, his first real success was *The Emperor Jones*, produced by the Provincetown Players in 1920. The play was an immense success for the small theater, for O'Neill, and for Charles Gilpin, who performed as America's first black tragic hero in a role later played by Paul Robeson. Devoted to the final hours in the life of Brutus Jones, a former convict who, in the course of two years, comes to be emperor of an island in the West Indies, O'Neill's expressionist play won immediate acclaim, both popular and critical.

The form of the play is particularly interesting, for it is composed essentially of one act with eight scenes. The six interior monologue scenes take place in the forest and in Jones's mind and are peopled by the ghosts and phantoms that plague Jones. These six scenes are enveloped by opening and closing scenes that occur outside the forest and that present real characters. The movement of the play is thus a journey from the civilized world into the primitive world of the forest and of the mind, and a journey for Jones to self-knowledge and to death.

The play's expository opening scene reveals that Jones, who arrived on the island two years earlier as a stowaway and who has come to rule the island, has exploited the natives and has enriched himself by manipulation, thievery, and cruel taxation. As a consequence, he has become so hated that the natives have withdrawn into the hills to stage a revolution. Jones believes, however, that he is prepared for all possibilities: Should he need to escape suddenly, he has hidden food and has learned the paths of the forest. He has also removed vast amounts of money from the island to a safe place. As he explains, he has learned from white people to steal big, and he proudly asserts that he makes his own good luck by using his brain.

Jones has also created among the islanders a mystique and a mythology for himself; distancing himself completely from the natives, whom he terms "bush niggers" and to whom he feels vastly superior, Jones has propagated the myth that he is magically protected from lead bullets and can be killed only by one of silver. Furthermore, having made for himself a silver bullet that he carries as the sixth in his gun, he has spread the companion tale that he is invulnerable to native assaults because he is the only man big enough to kill himself. Having learned that the natives are rebelling, he congratulates himself on his precautions, boasts about how easy it is to outwit them, and makes his way to the forest through which he must go that night in order to meet the boat that will take him to safety.

When, in the second scene, Jones reaches the edge of the forest, the audience begins to see some of O'Neill's experimental techniques. The edge of the forest, O'Neill tells the audience, is a "wall of darkness dividing the world," a point at which Jones begins to understand the uselessness of his precautions: He cannot find his store of food, and more important, he is not even sure where he is, exactly. When the little Formless Fears appear, amorphous, black, child-size shapes that, with low sounds of laughter, advance writhingly toward him, he is terrified and fires a shot at them.

Jones reveals his thought processes through a continuing monologue, a technique that seems to reflect the influence of August Strindberg on O'Neill. Jones's monologue, which continues throughout the six forest scenes, reveals at this point his fear at having disclosed his location and his determination to make it through the forest. In addition, he begins to have, within his monologue, a dialogue with himself, a dialogue that symbolically suggests a duality within him, a dissociation between mind and body and between outer bravado and inner fear. The steadily increasing beat of the drum, which had begun with his departure from the palace in the first act, reflects Jones's heightened emotional state and conveys not only the buildup of tension in him but also that in the distant natives.

This first forest scene and the five that follow present a series of vignettes that derive both from Jones's own life and mind and from the racial memory, or collective unconscious. Having first encountered the Formless Fears, he comes next on Jeff, the Pullman porter he killed with a razor in a fight over a crap game and for whose death he went to prison. Both furious and terrified, Jones fires his second bullet into the ghost, who disappears as the drumbeat's tempo once again increases. When, in the fourth scene, Jones reaches a wide road that he does not recognize, his outer appearance is beginning to deteriorate: His glorious uniform is torn and dirty, and he removes his coat and his spurs for comfort. Castigating himself for his belief in ghosts, he reminds himself that he is civilized, not like "dese ign'rent black niggers heah." He is nearly paralyzed with fright, however, when he sees another apparition, a chain gang with a guard who forces Jones to join the prisoners. When the guard beats Jones with his whip, Jones, reenacting his actual break from prison, fires his third bullet into the guard's back.

These first three forest scenes, concerned with aspects of Jones's own life, represent troublesome elements from his individual consciousness. Making him aware of the evil to which he has committed himself, they are important stages in his journey to self-knowledge. Moreover, they indicate, beyond a doubt, the true criminality of his nature. The following scenes, concerned with aspects of his racial memory, present elements that are part of the collective unconscious and thereby reveal some of the cultural forces that have made him what he is.

In the fifth scene, in a clearing in the forest, Jones comes on a dead stump that looks like an auction block. His appearance further deteriorating, his pants torn and ragged, he removes his battered shoes; the outer symbols of his exalted position, and of his difference from the natives, are virtually gone. As he sends an agonized prayer to Jesus, admitting his wrongdoing and acknowledging that as emperor he is getting "mighty low," he is suddenly surrounded by a group of southern aristocrats of the 1850's who are waiting for a group of slaves to come in. To Jones's utter horror, the auctioneer compels Jones to stand on the auction block; when he is bought, Jones, suddenly coming to life and resisting this treatment, angrily pulls out his gun and fires at both the auctioneer and his purchaser, using his last two lead bullets, as the drum quickens and the scene fades.

The sixth scene goes back to a time preceding the fifth; Jones finds himself in a clearing so overhung by trees that it appears as the hold of a ship. By this time, Jones's clothes have been so torn that he is wearing only a loincloth. Discovering that he is among two rows of blacks who moan desolately as they sway back and forth, Jones finds himself inadvertently joining in their chorus of despair, crying out even more loudly than they. Having used all his lead bullets, he has nothing with which to dispatch them, since he needs his silver bullet for luck, for self-preservation.

Jones is obliged, then, as he was obliged to recommit his crimes, to enter into the racial experience of slavery, to feel the grief and desperation of his ancestors. Unable to disperse this scene, Jones simply walks into the seventh and last of the forest scenes, which takes him to an even earlier time. Coming on an ancient altar by the river, Jones instinctively bows, even as he wonders why he does so. Although he prays for the

Christian God's protection, what appears is a witch doctor whose dance and incantations hypnotize Jones and force his participation in an ancient and mysterious ritual. O'Neill's stage directions indicate that Jones is expected at this point to sacrifice himself to the forces of evil, to the forces that have governed his life and that are now represented by a huge crocodile emerging from the river. Urged onward by the witch doctor and unable to stop himself from moving toward the crocodile, Jones, in a last act of desperate defiance, shoots the crocodile with his last bullet—the silver bullet.

The last act at the edge of the forest, an act that serves as an epilogue, is almost anticlimactic, describing how the natives enter the forest to kill the dazed Jones, who has wandered back (full circle) to the spot where he entered. The audience knows, however, that Jones has symbolically killed himself, destroying his evil and his identity with his own silver bullet. It is, moreover, particularly appropriate that the natives shoot Jones with silver bullets, bullets they have made out of melted money.

The journey into the forest has been for Jones a journey to death, but it has also been a journey to understanding. He has come not only to understand the evil of his own life but also to destroy it symbolically by destroying the crocodile with the bullet that affirms his identity. In effect, he is obliged to confront his true nature when the structure he has created for himself collapses. He has also come, however, to understand both his membership in his race and his connection with those natives to whom he felt so superior. By being forced to undergo the primitive experiences of his people, he is able to move from individuation into the group, into an awareness of the experiences common to his race. He is able to return, by means of this backward and inward journey, to his essential self, the self he had denied out of greed and egotism.

O'Neill in this way presents Jones as both a criminal and a victim, as a man whose own character and personality help to create his fate but whose racial and cultural experiences have also shaped him. Part of the play's tragedy, though, is that the knowledge Jones gains is insufficient to save his life. Nevertheless, as the trader, Smithers, concludes at the end of the play, the Emperor Jones "died in the 'eighth o' style, any'ow."

With this play, O'Neill established himself as an important and innovative American playwright. The play is also notable for its lack of autobiographical elements. It is an imaginative creation based on a blend of folktale and psychology that permitted O'Neill to enter the racial memory of another.

Desire Under the Elms • A play differing considerably in kind is *Desire Under the Elms*, first performed by the Provincetown Players in 1924 and perhaps one of O'Neill's most representative works. It reflects a number of the influences that worked significantly on him, including the Bible and classical mythology. It treats several of his favorite subjects, including the tension-ridden family, antimaterialism, and individuals' participation in creating their own fate; and although the play was initially received with considerable skepticism and disapproval (it was banned in both Boston and England), its critical reputation and its popular acceptance have steadily increased with time, and it continues to be produced for appreciative contemporary audiences.

The play is set on a New England farm in the mid-nineteenth century, a thematically important setting. Just as the New England land is rocky, unyielding, and difficult to manage, so is old Ephraim Cabot, who owns the farm, and so is the Puritan ethos that governs the lives of this patriarch and those around him. Accompanying this symbolism of hardness and coldness in the land and in Ephraim is the emotional symbolism associated with the farmhouse: O'Neill's set directions specify that the farmhouse is flanked by "two enormous elms" that "brood oppressively over the house," that "appear to protect and at the same time subdue," and that possess "a sinister maternity in their aspect, a crushing, jealous absorption." Clearly symbolic of Ephraim's dead second wife, and typifying both her physical and mental exhaustion and her unavenged spirit, the elms are also symbolic of the restrictive nature of New England farm life. In signifying that restriction, they are symbolic also of Ephraim, who exercises a jealous and unrelentingly selfish control over everything and everyone within his reach.

When the play opens, Ephraim is away from the farm on a trip, during which he marries Abbie Putnam, a young widow. By means of the marriage, Ephraim can prove his continuing virility and vigor and, he believes, achieve his paramount desire: to perpetuate his power and his hold over the land. His three grown sons, Simeon and Peter, children of Ephraim's first wife, and the sensitive Eben, son of Ephraim's second wife, dislike and distrust their father and recognize that his marriage to Abbie ensures that none of them will satisfy their desire to inherit the farm. One of the French naturalist writers whose work influenced O'Neill was Émile Zola, and this play seems to be particularly evocative of Zola's *La Terre* (1887; *The Soil*, 1888; also as *Earth*, 1954) in dealing with the human greed for land. This shared desire for land, however, is not the only desire with which the play is concerned. Ephraim, who sees himself as an extension of the Old Testament God, desires to maintain his power forever. Abbie, who marries because of her initial desire for security, comes later to desire love instead, as does Eben, who initially desires revenge on his father for working his mother to death. Although Simeon and Peter also hope for a share in the farm, they are happy to accept Eben's offer to buy them off, realizing that their expectations, because of their father's new marriage, will probably go unrealized.

The play establishes in the first act the many violent tensions existing between father and son. Blaming his father for the death of his mother, Eben also believes his father is cheating him out of the farm. Moreover, although Eben insists that he is like his mother and denies any similarity to his father and although Ephraim likewise considers his son weak and spineless, it is one of the play's ironies that father and son are in fact much alike, as indicated symbolically by the fact that both patronize the same local prostitute. More significant, however, both father and son are governed by strong emotions: Both are quick to anger, stubborn, vengeful, proud, and hard, and both are the victims of seething animal passions that are covered by only a thin veneer of civilization. The psychologically normal conflict between any father and son is thus intensified by their temperamental similarities, and when Abbie, the catalyst, appears as the stepmother who is closer in age to son than to father, the stage is indeed set for a depiction of violent emotions that result in great tragedy.

Because they both desire the farm, Abbie and Eben initially hate and mistrust each other, but their harsh and cruel behavior toward each other is counterpointed by a growing physical desire between them, a reflection, perhaps, of O'Neill's interest in the classical myths of Oedipus and Phaedra. O'Neill's use of a divided set permits the audience to watch this desire growing as they see simultaneously into the bedroom of Eben, as he moves half-unconsciously toward the wall beyond which Abbie stands, and into the bedroom of Ephraim and Abbie, where they continue to hope for the son who will fulfill Ephraim's desire and ensure Abbie's security. As the obvious but unspoken passion between Abbie and Eben mounts and the house grows correspondingly cold, Ephraim is driven to find solace in the barn, among the animals, where it is warm—an opportunity that Abbie uses to seduce Eben in the parlor, where the restless spirit of Eben's mother seems to be concentrated.

This lovemaking between stepmother and son, teetering as it does on the brink of incest, was, as one might expect, an aspect of the play to which censors objected. Abbie is, after all, Eben's stepmother, and she uses her "maternal" relationship to Eben as a means of seduction. At the same time that she vows to kiss him "pure," as if she were his mother, she passionately blurts out that loving him like a mother "hain't enuf," and that "it's got to be that and more." As O'Neill explains in his stage directions, there is in her "a horribly frank mixture of lust and mother love." One further motive for Abbie that O'Neill leaves uncertain is her need to produce a son for Ephraim. It is one of the fine ambiguities of the play that viewers are unable to decide whether Abbie seduces Eben out of greed for the land, out of maternal caring, out of physical lust, or out of genuine love for him. Eben is moved by similarly discordant motives, by both a real desire for Abbie and a desire to avenge his mother by taking his father's woman. He senses his mother's spirit leaving the house and returning to her grave, finally at peace. Eben indicates his understanding of and his satisfaction with the retributive nature of this act the next morning when he offers his hand to his father, remarking to the uncomprehending Ephraim that they are now "quits."

Yet, despite the deliberate calculation with which this love affair begins, Abbie and Eben come in time genuinely to love each other. What was initially, at least in part, a mutually self-serving and opportunistic seduction results in the first warm human relationship the farm has seen. There is, however, no way for the drama to end happily, even though, at the beginning of the third act, all have attained what they at one time desired: Ephraim has a son to prove his virility, Abbie has earned the farm by providing that son, and Eben has avenged his mother. These desires are, to Abbie and Eben, at least, no longer of prime importance, and the party Ephraim gives to celebrate the birth of "his" son serves as an ironic backdrop to the play's tragic climax.

Ephraim, flushed with liquor and pride at producing a son at seventy-six and oblivious to the knowing sneers of the townspeople, in a brutal physical and emotional confrontation with Eben gloats that Abbie wanted a child only to preempt Eben's claim to the farm. Believing that Abbie has seduced him only in order to become pregnant and cheat him, Eben turns violently against her, telling her that he hates her and wishes their son dead. The half-crazed Abbie, hysterically wishing to restore the time when Eben loved her and confusedly identifying the child as the cause of Eben's present hate, smothers the child in its cradle in an appalling inversion of the myth of Medea: Whereas Medea murders her children as an act of revenge against her faithless husband, Abbie murders her child in order to recapture the lost love of Eben. Eben, however, does not respond with love, but with horror and revulsion, and he runs for the sheriff to arrest her. Returning before the sheriff, Eben in a change of heart acknowledges his own guilt and reaffirms his love for Abbie. The play ends with their mutual expression of love as they are taken off by the sheriff, who ironically remarks, with admiration, that "it's a jim-dandy farm."

The play seems, then, to be unmitigatedly naturalistic and pessimistic as the lovers go off to be hanged and as Ephraim is left alone with his farm. Yet O'Neill poses the possibility of a spiritual victory in the play: Although the desire to possess has dominated their lives, Abbie and Eben are freed of that desire at the end—even though their victory is to be short-lived. It is also possible to see a victory over the forces of evil embodied in Puritanism and in the New England patriarchal society, because, even though Eben reacts initially to his father's announcement and to the baby's murder with all the violent self-righteousness one would expect of his father, he comes to transcend this attitude and to acknowledge both his love for Abbie and his own guilt. Although Abbie and Eben have lost everything in the worldly sense, in finding love and faith in each other they do perhaps escape, however briefly and symbolically, from the brooding, confining New England elms.

In this play, O'Neill seems to return to the naturalism that informed his early plays of the sea. His characters are presented as bewildered, struggling beings, blown about like leaves in the gutter, compelled by the external forces of fate, chance, and environment and by the internal workings of their physical nature. It is indeed difficult for these characters to win, but for O'Neill, the salient point is that, in struggling, his characters can transcend their fate.

The Iceman Cometh • The critics, who had difficulty with *Desire Under the Elms* because of its objectionable subject matter, were also troubled by *The Iceman Cometh*, but for different reasons; many considered the latter play unhealthy, pessimistic, and morbid in its depiction of the wasted lives of the habitués of Harry Hope's New York saloon, modeled after those in which O'Neill spent considerable time in 1911 and in 1914-1919. A key theme in the play, and a recurring theme in O'Neill's dramas, is the power and the necessity of illusion to give meaning to life. O'Neill develops this theme through expository conversation and monologues because there is very little onstage action during the two-day period that the play's four acts encompass. Containing both comic and tragic elements, the play, set in 1912, takes place entirely in the back room of Harry Hope's bar, where the regulars gather.

The play opens on a gathering of regulars to await the arrival of Hickey, a hardware salesperson who is the most successful among them and who comes to the bar for periodic drunks, particularly on the occasion of Harry Hope's birthday, when he funds a great drunken party for the regulars. Himself unfaithful to his wife, Hickey maintains a running gag that his apparently saintly wife must, in his absence, be having an affair with the iceman. Hickey and all the other characters live in a world of illusion, a world that ignores today: They all look backward to yesterday, to what they once were or to what their rosy rewriting of history now tells them they once were, just as they look forward to an equally rosy and improbable tomorrow. The illusion that they all have a future is part of the pipe dream each has, a pipe dream essential to their lives that helps them "keep up the appearances of life." Although these people really have, in Robert Frost's words, "nothing to look backward to with pride" and "nothing to look forward to with hope," they somehow manage to live, to survive in the bleak, drunken world they inhabit, because they possess the illusion that they have a yesterday about which they can feel pride and a tomorrow about which they can hope. That illusion enables them to ignore the dark reality that is their today. Moreover, because they understand one another's illusions and accept them, they can be sympathetic to and tolerant of one another's failings as well as of their own.

Among the characters who frequent the bar are Larry Slade, an elderly anarchist who believes he is uninvolved in life and who claims he wants only to die; Joe Mott, an African American who plans to open a gambling house one day; Piet Wetjoen, a former Boer War commander who believes he can return home; Pat McGloin, who plans to return soon to the police force; Harry Hope, a former Tammany politician who believes he will someday leave his saloon and walk the ward; Willie Oban, previously of Harvard Law School, who plans one day to go to the district attorney and get a law job; Rocky, the night bartender, who, because he works as a bartender, believes that he is not a pimp, even though he "manages" and takes money from two prostitutes; Margie and Pearl, Rocky's two "girls," who make the fine distinction that they are tarts but not whores—because they don't have a pimp; Chuck, the day bartender, who believes he will go on the wagon, marry Cora, and buy a farm in the country; and Cora, who shares Chuck's dream and who also believes that he will forgive her for making her living as a prostitute. Into the circle of regulars comes the eighteen-year-old Don Parritt, whose mother, part of the anarchist movement, is on trial out West for a bombing.

Although many of these regulars stay up all night in the saloon to await Hickey, his arrival is disappointing and strangely troubling: When he appears, he is not the same as before. For one thing, he fails to make his usual joke about his wife and the iceman, and for another, he no longer drinks; he explains that he no longer needs it after he threw away "the damned lying pipe dream" that had made him feel miserable. Moreover, he wants very much to save his friends by persuading them to be honest, to stop lying about themselves, and to stop kidding themselves about their tomorrows. He believes that by giving up their illusions, they can attain peace and contentment, and he systematically embarks on a campaign to make them admit the truth about their pasts and to do immediately what they have always said they will do in the future—even though Hickey knows that they will fail. Hickey insists that if one faces reality and kills one's dreams, then those dreams will not be there to nag or to cause guilt, not haunted by yesterday and not fooling oneself about tomorrow. Then, Hickey believes, his friends will have peace, as he does.

As a result of his campaign, however, the friendly and tolerant atmosphere of the bar wears dangerously thin as the friends, stripped of their protective illusions and their defense mechanisms, become not only sober but also nervous, irritable, and belligerent with one another. Harry's birthday party is a flop, spoiled by fights and bad feeling and finally by Hickey's announcement that his wife is dead. Moreover, the peace that Hickey predicts will come, as an effect of facing reality, does not, even though the characters, with varying degrees of reluctance, attempt to give up their dreams, to leave the bar—actually as well as symbolically—and to face reality. Instead of providing them with peace, the act of facing reality robs them of tolerance for one another and therefore of companionship, of tolerance for themselves and therefore of self-respect, of hope for the future and therefore of happiness. As a result of Hickey's efforts to save them from their illusions, as a result of his forcing them to face their tomorrows and to fail, the habitués of Harry Hope's bar are miserable—quarrelsome, despondent, and hateful toward themselves and one another. Even alcohol loses its kick; it seems to have "no life in it," and they can no longer even pass out.

Hickey is genuinely puzzled by these results because his expectation was that, once they had "killed tomorrow," they would have "licked the game of life." The play's fourth act, which begins by further demonstrating the unpleasantness that has derived from exposure to reality, centers on Hickey's revelation of his new philosophy and how he acted out this philosophy in his marriage, finally murdering his wife. He killed her, he says, to give her peace by ending her pipe dream that he would one day be better, that he would stop drinking and whoring. Continually making vows to her that he was unable to keep, he was then obliged to feel guilty because his wife was continually hurt and disappointed. Juxtaposed to Hickey's story of love and guilt is Parritt's parallel narrative disclosing his betrayal of his mother. The two stories reach a climax when Parritt confesses that he betrayed the movement because he hated his mother as Hickey confesses that after killing his wife he laughed and called her a "damned bitch." Unable to live with what he has admitted, Hickey seizes on the explanation that he must have been insane—insane, that is, to laugh at his wife's death, because everyone surely knows that he has always loved her, and if he laughed at her death, then he must have been insane.

The other characters seize on this explanation as well, because it means they can disregard what he has said before, reestablish their illusions, and thereby once again live with one another and themselves. Don Parritt, however, apparently unable to live with his betrayal of his mother and the reality that his betrayal was motivated by hate, commits suicide by jumping off the fire escape, as, in a sense, does Hickey by calling the police to come for him. He and Parritt, facing the reality about themselves, must destroy themselves because of the pain of that reality. In truth, Hickey hated his wife because she represented his conscience, because although she always forgave him, she also always expected him to try to be better, which he simply did not wish to do. When for one brief moment he admits the truth, that he wanted and was glad to be free of the burden of this conscience, he is unable to live with that truth and he immediately rationalizes that he must have been insane. He thus proves that illusion is, in fact, necessary, in order to accept oneself and in order to live not only with others in the world but also with the reality that death, the iceman, does indeed "cometh."

The play, then, while pessimistic in delineating human weaknesses, seems to hold out the possibility that those weaknesses can be transcended so long as life exists. O'Neill suggests that, in order for life to exist, there must be hope—and hope, very often, is created from illusion. Although Hickey is termed a "nihilist" at one point in the play, he serves, through the dramatic revelation of his own example, to reinforce the necessity, and the positive power, of illusion.

Other major works

POETRY: *Poems, 1912-1944,* 1979 (Donald Gallup, editor).

NONFICTION: *"The Theatre We Worked For": The Letters of Eugene O'Neill to Kenneth MacGowan,* 1982 (Jackson R. Bryer and Ruth M. Alvarez, editors); *"Love and Admiration and Respect": The O'Neill-Commins Correspondence,* 1986 (Dorothy Commins, editor); *"As Ever, Gene": The Letters of Eugene O'Neill to George Jean Nathan,* 1987 (Nancy L. Roberts and Arthur W. Roberts, editors); *Selected Letters of Eugene O'Neill,* 1988 (Travis Bogard and Bryer, editors); *A Wind Is Rising: The Correspondence of Agnes Boulton and Eugene O'Neill,* 2000 (William Davies King, editor).

MISCELLANEOUS: *The Unknown O'Neill: Unpublished or Unfamiliar Writings of Eugene O'Neill,* 1988 (Travis Bogard, editor).

Bibliography

Bloom, Harold, ed. *Eugene O'Neill.* New York: Chelsea House, 1987. As part of the Modern Critical Views series, this collection includes essays by Lionel Trilling, Doris Falk, Arnold Goldman, Robert Lee, Travis Boyard, Thomas Van Laan, Jean Chathia, C. W. Bigsby, and Michael Manheim, arranged in chronological order by their original publication dates. Bloom describes them as representative of the "best criticism available." The theoretical slant is thematic and philosophical, with detailed characters and plot analyses. Contains a brief bibliography.

Brietzke, Zander. *The Aesthetics of Failure: Dynamic Structure in the Plays of Eugene O'Neill.* Jefferson, N.C.: McFarland, 2001. A controversial but insightful study of O'Neill's literary theory, with particular attention to his "anti-theater" approach to character development and storytelling.

Manheim, Michael, ed. *The Cambridge Companion to Eugene O'Neill.* New York: Cambridge University Press, 1998. A comprehensive reference work that contains a wealth of information on the life and works of O'Neill. Bibliography and index.

Moorton, Richard F., Jr., ed. *Eugene O'Neill's Century.* New York: Greenwood Press, 1991. This collection includes excerpts from more than seventeen plays and collected notes, as well as articles ranging from Spencer Golub's semiotic analysis of *Long Day's Journey into Night* to biographical and psychological analyses by Lowell Swortzell, Jane Torrey, Georgia Nugent, Jeffrey Elliott Sands, and Linda Herr. Some essays focus on how and why O'Neill's extensive stage directions have influenced dramatic practice. Six pages of works cited and thirteen pages of index are useful for scholars.

Ranald, Margaret Loftus. *The Eugene O'Neill Companion.* Westport, Conn.: Greenwood Press, 1984. The author has arranged in alphabetical order a complete compendium of plays, synopses, production histories, characters, personal and professional acquaintances, and critical analysis. Three appendices include a chronology of plays, adaptations, and a critical overview. Twenty-eight pages of notes and thirty-seven index pages make this work an invaluable, encyclopedia resource and guide to further study of O'Neill's work.

Robinson, James A. *Eugene O'Neill and Oriental Thought: A Divided Vision.* Carbondale: Southern Illinois University Press, 1982. Taking a philosophical approach to O'Neill's work, Robinson's 186-page work is a scholarly, detailed analysis of possible connections between O'Neill's plays and Oriental mysticism, particularly Hindu, Buddhist, and Daoist belief systems. The bibliography and index offer more information on philosophy and religions of the East than on O'Neill, but Robinson's analysis of individual plays, such as *The Great God Brown, Lazarus Laughed, The Iceman Cometh,* and *Long Day's Journey into Night,* sheds new light on the often-stated view of O'Neill's drama as "religious" and "romantic."

Sheaffer, Louis. *O'Neill.* 2 vols. Boston: Little, Brown, 1968-1973. This two-part biography is considered the most complete work on O'Neill's life, and it stands as a model for the genre of literary biography. Including recollections by a variety of O'Neill's colleagues and friends, this work reads smoothly and effectively combines scholarship and human interest. Generally acknowledged as both sympathetic and trustworthy. Notes, index.

Wainscott, Ronald H. *Staging O'Neill: The Experimental Years, 1920-1934.* New Haven, Conn.: Yale University Press, 1988. This highly scholarly yet accessible historical work chronicles the production of O'Neill's plays and the profound influence of his work on American theater practice. Written in a lively style, it is the most detailed work of its kind on O'Neill, although others may have greater scope.

Evelyn S. Newlyn,
updated by Rebecca Bell-Metereau

Joe Orton

Born: Leicester, England; January 1, 1933
Died: London, England; August 9, 1967

Principal drama • *The Ruffian on the Stair*, pr. 1964 (radio play), pr. 1966 (staged), pb. 1967 (one act); *Entertaining Mr. Sloane*, pr., pb. 1964; *The Good and Faithful Servant*, wr. 1964, pr. 1967 (staged and televised), pb. 1970 (one act); *Loot*, pr. 1965, pb. 1967; *The Erpingham Camp*, pr. 1966 (televised), pr. 1967 (staged), pb. 1967 (one act); *Funeral Games*, pr. 1968 (televised), pr. 1970 (staged), pb. 1970 (as television script; one act); *What the Butler Saw*, pr., pb. 1969; *The Complete Plays*, pb. 1976

Other literary forms • Joe Orton's novel *Head to Toe* (originally entitled "The Vision of Gombold Proval") was published posthumously in 1971. *Up Against It*, a screenplay written for the Beatles, was published in 1979, although it was never produced. He also collaborated on several novels with Kenneth Halliwell, entitled "The Last Days of Sodom," "Priapus in the Shrubbery," and "The Mechanical Womb"; these were never published.

Achievements • Joe Orton's meteoric rise as a dramatist during the mid-1960's in Britain was the result of the unique and frequently outrageous tone and style of his plays. Called "the master farceur of his age" by John Lahr and "the Oscar Wilde of Welfare State gentility" by Ronald Bryden, Orton made a radical break with the currently popular naturalistic drama of John Osborne and Arnold Wesker. He was instead influenced by Samuel Beckett and Harold Pinter, although he rapidly moved away from Pinter's "comedy of menace" to experiment with farce and the brittle epigrammatic style of Oscar Wilde.

The verbal wit, aggressive sexuality, and black humor of Orton's dramas created a new critical term, "Ortonesque," to describe his own style and that of his imitators. The critical reaction to Orton's drama was and remains mixed; the middle-class audiences that Orton worked so hard to affront frequently reacted with horror and shock to his plays, as did many reviewers. Playwrights as varied as Pinter and Terence Rattigan, however, were impressed by Orton. *Loot* won the best play of 1966 award from the *Evening Standard* and was voted the best play of 1966 by *Plays and Players*. Orton's body of work is small, consisting of four one-act plays and three full-length dramas, but he gained an international reputation before his premature death. At the time of his murder, he had begun work on a play tentatively entitled "Prick Up Your Ears," a farce about King Edward VII's coronation.

Biography • John Kingsley Orton (who later changed his name to Joe Orton to avoid any confusion with playwright John Osborne) was born to William and Elsie Orton in a working-class area of Leicester, England. After failing the eleven-plus examination, he enrolled in Clark's College, a commercial school where one of his teachers described him as "semiliterate." Seeing the theater as a way to escape the drudgery of the menial jobs he was forced to take, Orton joined the Leicester Dramatic Society in 1949 and acted in several small roles in other amateur theatrical groups. In 1950, he was accepted to study at the Royal Academy of Dramatic Art, which he entered in 1951. It was there that he met a fellow student-actor, Kenneth Halliwell, who became Orton's friend, lover, and roommate for the rest of his life.

After receiving his diploma from the Royal Academy of Dramatic Art, Orton worked briefly as an assistant stage manager for the Ipswich Repertory Company and then rejoined Halliwell in London in 1953. They began collaborating on a series of novels, all of which were turned down for publication. In 1959, Orton, aided by Halliwell, began stealing and defacing books from the Islington and Hampstead libraries. Orton, who would remove the photographs and illustrations from the books and then replace them with his own creations, would also write false blurbs and summaries; after replacing the books on the shelves, he would stand and watch people's reactions to his pranks. In 1962, Orton and Halliwell were arrested and convicted of theft and malicious damage, and both men were sentenced to six months in jail. The jail sentence was a turning point in Orton's life, for it brought him a new sense of detachment from his own writing that had been lacking before this experience. After his release, he began writing plays and no longer collaborated to any great degree with Halliwell.

Orton's sudden fame and fortune during his brief career from 1963 to 1967 put a tremendous strain on his relationship with Halliwell, who, older and better educated than Orton, had considered himself the real creative artist. Deeply resentful of Orton's literary success and sexual promiscuity, Halliwell became more and more deeply depressed and neurotic. On August 9, 1967, a chauffeur who had come to drive Orton to an appointment to discuss his screenplay, *Up Against It*, discovered the bodies of Orton and Halliwell. Halliwell had beaten Orton to death with hammer blows to his head and then committed suicide with sleeping pills. Orton's murder, which was so similar in fashion to many of the events of his plays, made him even more famous in death than in life.

Analysis • Joe Orton's career was launched by the British Broadcasting Corporation's acceptance of his first play, *The Ruffian on the Stair*. By the time the drama was broadcast in 1964, however, Orton had already achieved fame with the successful West End production of *Entertaining Mr. Sloane*. Orton revised *The Ruffian on the Stair* for its stage production in 1966; the revised version is less derivative of Harold Pinter's *The Room* (pr. 1957), although it still shows Orton's early debt to Pinter's techniques.

The Ruffian on the Stair • This one-act play involves three characters: Joyce, a former prostitute; Mike, a thief; and Wilson, the "intruder" who arrives at Joyce and Mike's apartment ostensibly searching for a room to rent. During the course of the play, Wilson reveals that he has had a homosexual relationship with his own brother, whom Mike has recently killed.

Wilson's plan is to force Mike to kill him by pretending to sleep with Joyce; in this way, he hopes that Mike will be brought to justice for the murder. Wilson's plan succeeds, and the drama concludes with Mike comforting Joyce, who is weeping not over Wilson's murder but over the death of her goldfish. The play shows Orton, still strongly influenced by Pinter, moving toward the kind of verbal style that would characterize *Entertaining Mr. Sloane*—a style in which characters use media-influenced language to mask their real thoughts and emotions. The emotional sterility of the characters is reflected in the debased, meaningless language of cliché and the popular press, which they use almost exclusively. Although the play suffers from an ending that appears to be arbitrarily forced on the action, *The Ruffian on the Stair* does show Orton's talent with dialogue and his ability to create a degree of emotional tension among his characters.

Entertaining Mr. Sloane • Orton's first full-length drama was *Entertaining Mr. Sloane*, a three-act play that showed that the playwright had made important advancements beyond *The Ruffian on the Stair*. In much firmer control of his material in this play, Orton perfected his characters' use of media-influenced language and cliché. In addition, he was able to construct a relationship among the characters that made the play's ending believable and inevitable, a problem he had been unable to solve satisfactorily in *The Ruffian on the Stair*.

In *Entertaining Mr. Sloane*, Kath and Ed, Kath's brother, battle for control and possession of Sloane, Kath's young lodger. The double meaning of the play's title becomes clear as the play progresses, for the insidious Sloane is at first wooed and entertained by Kath and Ed and later must provide entertainment in the form of sexual favors for both of them when they become witnesses to his second murder. At the beginning of the play, Sloane takes a room in Kath's house, where she lives with her father, Kemp. Kemp soon recognizes Sloane as the young man who murdered his employer two years earlier. Kath, a middle-aged woman who coyly plays the role of Sloane's "Mamma" while brazenly seducing him at the end of the first act, soon finds herself pregnant by Sloane. Sloane is also being pursued, in a less obvious fashion, by Ed, who gives him a job as his chauffeur. When Kemp threatens to expose Sloane as a murderer, Sloane accidentally kills him and is then at the mercy of Kath and Ed, who both want to possess him exclusively. The brother and sister finally agree to share Sloane, each taking him for six months at a time. Sloane, who at the play's beginning was able to control Kath and Ed completely, is quickly reduced to an object.

Orton insisted that the play should be acted as realistically as possible so that the characters would not degenerate into caricatures or stereotypes. "What I wanted to do in *Sloane*," said Orton, "was to break down all the sexual compartments that people have." Kath and Ed are deadly serious about their designs on the young lodger, and Orton resisted the two male leads being played as effeminate homosexuals, just as he did not wish Kath to be played as a nymphomaniac. Instead, the play is about individual personalities who are constantly maneuvering in their attempts to gain power. Despite the play's realism, however, *Entertaining Mr. Sloane* is, like several of Orton's later dramas, reflexive in the sense that the characters are aware of their own theatricality. Orton also uses the rhetoric of the detective film in the play, just as he would parody the genre of farce in later dramas.

Present throughout the play is Orton's fascination with a debased language that functions to obscure the characters' real thoughts and deeds. John Lahr argues that Orton's dialogue reveals the "sensory overload" of the effects of the media on the individual—what he calls "an eclectic brew of rhythms and idioms which captured and commented on the mutation of language." *Entertaining Mr. Sloane* is the best example of Orton's search for what he described as his "collage" literary style: His characters mix the language of newspaper headlines, scandal sheets, advertising, and cliché in a comical and meaningless speech that nevertheless manages to communicate their obsessions and desires. Pinter's influence is still present in *Entertaining Mr. Sloane*, but Orton's success with the play led him in new directions as a dramatist. His work became increasingly more outrageous and farcical as a result of the self-confidence he gained because of the success of *Entertaining Mr. Sloane*.

The Good and Faithful Servant • Orton's next play, *The Good and Faithful Servant*, was written in 1964 and appeared on television and stage in 1967. It was Orton's first full-scale attack on authority and convention, represented in this case by the company from which the main character, Buchanan, is retiring after fifty years of service. At the time of his retirement, Buchanan is stripped of his uniform and given an electric clock and toaster, neither of which works. Buchanan also encounters Edith Anderson, an elderly maid who is working for the firm and who turns out to have given birth to their illegitimate twins many years ago. The one-act play concerns Buchanan's adjustment to his retirement, his marriage to Edith, and the relationship between his grandson, Ray, and Debbie, who is pregnant with Ray's illegitimate child.

Buchanan's broken-down physical condition is reflective of what his lifelong service to the company has given him. Although he claims to have led "a useful and constructive life," he breaks down coughing at the end of this statement and, in addition to needing glasses and a hearing aid, has also lost an arm in the service of the firm. Buchanan's pitiful reverence for the company is shared by the other employees. Edith is thrilled because she was able to sweep out the canteen one day in the distant past, and Buchanan states that the "high point" of his life came when he appeared in the company's magazine. He also reverentially mentions that he was "almost Staff" and actually opened the door to the chairman of the board on one occasion. Buchanan's death at the end of the play, which occurs after his disillusionment with the party for the elderly, which culminates in his smashing of the toaster and clock with a hammer, is ironically counterpointed by Ray's induction into the corporate life after having been forced by the company's representative, Mrs. Vealfoy, into marrying Debbie. Just as illegitimacy is handed down from generation to generation in the play, so is the grinding and mindless service to a corporation that remains an abstraction to its employees.

Mrs. Vealfoy is the voice both of the corporate mentality and of the social conformity that it uses to manipulate its workers. She advises Ray to "say 'yes' as often as possible. . . . I always do. . . . Always," and she organizes the darkly comic party for the retired workers in scene 16, forcing the dispirited elderly people to sing songs containing the word "happy" while a woman collapses and dies in the background. Mrs. Vealfoy's genial intrusiveness and blind faith in the rightness of the company's policies structure *The Good and Faithful Servant*, which is Orton's most naturalistic assault on the world of authority and convention that he would lampoon in a much more anarchic and farcical style in his later drama.

Loot • In his novel *Head to Toe*, Orton said that "To be destructive, words had to be irrefutable. . . . Print was less effective than the spoken word because the blast was greater; eyes could ignore, slide past, dangerous verbs or nouns. But if you could lock the enemy into a room somewhere and fire the sentences at them, you would get a sort of seismic disturbance." Not surprisingly, Orton turned from fiction to the theater, where he could attack his audience directly with words, for Orton considered his audience to be his enemy. He chose farce as the most appropriate genre to create a "seismic disturbance," to disturb his audience's conventions and expectations. *Loot* was the first full-length play in which he allowed his taste for anarchic farce a free rein, and if it sometimes too exuberantly celebrates a farcical, outrageous, and topsy-turvy world of madness and corruption, it also shows Orton discovering the proper vehicle for his talent. Farce, observes John Lahr, is an act of "literary aggression," and Orton used farce in order to vent his own anger and to assault a society that he believed to be hypocritical and stultifying. In his farces, he sought what he called in *Head to Toe* a "particularly dangerous collection of words" which could "explode," creating "shock waves [which] were capable of killing centuries afterwards."

In *Loot*, Orton mercilessly lampoons authority, represented most clearly in the play by Detective Truscott. Truscott, who comes to the home of Mr. McLeavy, whose wife has just died, is investigating a theft in which Hal, McLeavy's son, has been involved. McLeavy, the only character in the play with any real respect for authority, is also the only "innocent" character; ironically, it is McLeavy who at the play's conclusion is arrested for a "crime" that Truscott refuses to define.

McLeavy's faith in authority is naïve and pitiful. Early in the play, he says that he likes "to be of assistance to authority" and that public servants can be relied on to behave themselves: "As a good citizen I ignore the stories which bring officialdom into disrepute." All the events of the play work to underscore the irony of McLeavy's blind trust in "officialdom," and his statement in act 2 that "my personal freedom must be sacrificed" so that Truscott can continue with his investigation becomes chillingly significant later in the play.

McLeavy's amazement at his own arrest at the conclusion of the play leads to his incredulous comment, "You can't do this. I've always been a law-abiding citizen. The police are for the protection of ordinary people." Truscott's reply, that he does not understand where McLeavy has picked up "such slogans," sums up Orton's view of authority and justice: The conventional law and order of society is merely a mask for corruption, intolerance, and irrationality. As a result, most of the play's references to authority are couched in clichés that render the characters' speeches ludicrous. Fay, the young nurse who has just murdered McLeavy's wife for her money, reacts similarly to McLeavy when she is threatened with arrest: "I'm innocent till I'm proved guilty. This is a free country. The law is impartial." Truscott's response is reminiscent of his reply to McLeavy: "Who's been filling your head with that rubbish?"

As *What the Butler Saw* would later parody farce, *Loot* parodies the detective novel and film. Truscott's comical conclusion that Fay shot her husband at the Hermitage Private Hotel because one of her wedding rings has a roughness associated with "powder burns and salt" shows Orton mocking the detective story's emphasis on rational thinking and deductive reasoning. The world of *Loot* is instead one of madness and illogic in which relationships among people alter rapidly; there is no core of stability or predictability.

McLeavy finally asks Truscott, "Is the world mad? Tell me it's not"; his question is answered by Truscott's statement that "I'm not paid to quarrel with accepted facts." *Loot* shows that mysteries cannot be solved, for mysteries only lead to further mystification: Truscott tells the group that "the process by which the police arrive at the solution to a mystery is, in itself, a mystery." In *Loot*, the plot becomes more rather than less complicated as it progresses; the true "criminals" are allowed to go free while the "detective" becomes part of the crime. Fay's final statement in the play, "We must keep up appearances," articulates an important theme: The world is composed of masks, false identities, and lies that exist not to conceal reality but to compensate for its nonexistence. There are only appearances, and the characters who can most effectively manipulate appearance are the most successful. McLeavy's worship of authority reflects his ignorance of appearances. He assumes that those in power are what they claim to be, and he pays the price.

The Erpingham Camp • In *The Erpingham Camp*, Orton continues to attack authority and convention and to develop the brilliantly epigrammatic style that culminated in *What the Butler Saw*. Much less naturalistic even than *Loot*, *The Erpingham Camp* is a one-act play composed of eleven short scenes. Its setting is a holiday camp in which chaos and anarchy erupt in what initially appears to be a rigidly organized situation controlled by the proud entrepreneur Erpingham. He is the major symbol of authority in the play and, like Orton's other authority figures, has false notions about the predictability and rational nature of the world. Early in the play, he tells an employee, "We live in a rational world, Riley"; the rest of the drama functions to destroy the validity of this statement.

Problems begin when Riley, who is organizing an evening of entertainment, slaps Eileen, a pregnant woman who is screaming hysterically. Although Riley's action is an attempt to make her stop screaming, a melee ensues and the campers begin, in Erpingham's phrase, to "destroy property," which results in Erpingham refusing to feed them an evening meal. "We've no time for hedonists here. My camp is a pure camp," Erpingham had said earlier, and he tries to punish his "underlings" in an effort to control their behavior. Erpingham, whose usual advice in any situation is to "consult the manual," is unable to understand or deal with the campers' rage and replies to their pleas for food with the statement, "You have no rights. You have certain privileges which can be withdrawn. I am withdrawing them."

Physical and verbal violence breaks out after this incident, with two groups of campers battling for their own "approach" to the situation. Lou and Ted, a right-wing young couple who claim to have met outside the Young Conservatives, call for moderation, remaining "within the law," and adherence to "page twenty of the Civil Defense Booklet." Kenny and Eileen, a working-class couple resentful of Lou and Ted's "advantages," instead want to take the "means of supply" into their own hands and encourage the campers to break into the food stores, screaming, "Have a bash, I say. Have a bash for the pregnant woman next door!"

The play becomes increasingly anarchic and unrealistic until it concludes with Erpingham falling to his death down a hole in the floor. Attending at the funeral is the Padre, who has just returned from a court appearance in which he has been accused of molesting a young girl and who ironically notes, "As the little foxes gnaw at the roots of the vine, so anarchy weakens the fibers of society." The play ends with one of Orton's most famous epigrams, the Padre's statement that "it's Life that defeats the Christian Church. She's always been well-equipped to deal with Death." Although his themes in this play are similar to the dramas of the past, particularly the attacks on political and clerical authority, convention, and corruption, *The Erpingham Camp* shows Orton's increasing confidence in his ability to write anarchic farce in the epigrammatic style and was an important step in his movement away from naturalistic drama.

What the Butler Saw • Orton's last completed drama, *What the Butler Saw*, was not performed until after his death, and as a result the play did not undergo final rewrites by the playwright. Nevertheless, *What the Butler Saw* is Orton's most accomplished work. The play is a celebration of irrationality that also parodies the farce form by comically exaggerating its structure and characteristics: An absurdist genre is parodically made even more absurd. C. W. E. Bigsby suggests that the "byzantine complexities of the plot of *What the Butler Saw* can be seen as a deliberate attempt to parody the very structure of farce itself," and certainly the play's intricate plot makes summary almost impossible.

Like Orton's earlier work, *What the Butler Saw* attacks authority and tradition. In this drama, Dr. Rance, a government representative who has come to Dr. Prentice's mental clinic to be "given details" about its operations, at first appears to be the voice of conventional authority that wishes to suppress the forces of chaos. Although Rance represents the "Commissioners," however, he is also a spokesperson for unreason, mentioning to Dr. Prentice that he is a representative of "Her Majesty's Government. Your immediate superiors in madness," and opining that "the higher reaches of the

Civil Service are recruited entirely from corpses or madmen." In *What the Butler Saw*, Orton's questioning of authority goes beyond that of religious or governmental institutions; here, he tries to destroy the very foundations of logic, reason, and predictability on which his audience's assumptions are based.

One of the most important themes of the play is the very thin line of demarcation between the sane and the insane. The setting is a madhouse in which no actual "insane" patients ever appear; rather, it is the ostensibly sane inhabitants, particularly the psychologists, who are mad. Rance tells the policeman Match that they are in a madhouse where "unusual behavior" is the prerogative of everyone: "We've no privileged class here. It's democratic lunacy we practice." "Democratic lunacy" aptly describes the world of *What the Butler Saw*, in which sanity and insanity are relative conditions that depend entirely on perspective. "The sane appear as strange to the mad as the mad to the sane," Rance tells Dr. Prentice in a statement that echoes the play's epigraph, drawn from Cyril Tourneur's play *The Revenger's Tragedy* (pr. 1606-1607): "Surely we're all mad people, and they/ Whom we think are, are not." Rance tells Mrs. Prentice that her husband's behavior is "so ridiculous one might suspect him of being sane," a Wildean paradox that sums up Orton's view that sanity and insanity are actually mirror images of one another.

In this play, sanity is dependent on a rejection of all evidence of reality; Rance, after denying that the blood on Mrs. Prentice's hand is "real" while admitting that he sees it, says, "I'm a scientist. I state facts, I cannot be expected to provide explanations. Reject any para-normal phenomena. It's the only way to remain sane." Because reality *is* madness, sanity can exist only when reality is denied. In a sense, however, madness is to be preferred to sanity, for Rance tells Geraldine Barclay that the fact that her mind has "given way" will be an invaluable aid in her efforts to "come to terms with twentieth century living." In a world in which irrationality and farcical absurdity rule, the most effective defense is insanity.

Orton's characters also lack any firm sense of their individual identities. Identities and sexes are exchanged with dizzying rapidity, with the result that the characters begin to lose their sense of who and what they are. Nicholas Beckett, in an attempt to verify his own existence, tells Rance, "If [my] pain is real I must be real," a statement Rance counters with the observation that "I'd rather not get involved in metaphysical speculation." Rance prefers to construct elaborate and illogical premises on which he bases even more outrageously illogical theories, at one point noting his own "law" that the "relations of apparitions are also apparitions." In *What the Butler Saw*, characters are much like "apparitions" who disappear and reemerge as different people; lacking any core of intrinsic identity, they are capable of endless psychic transformations. This lack of immutable identity, however, is not necessarily a negative characteristic: Like madness, fluidity of identity is a means of survival.

What the Butler Saw posits a universe in which irrationality must rule because all premises are illogical, erroneous, or nonexistent. Rance's comically incorrect "theories" about the reasons for Geraldine Barclay's neuroses and Dr. Prentice's madness are blatant fictions that have, as he is well aware, no relationship to reality. In the play, there is no actual "reality" because there is no truth. Geraldine asserts to Dr. Prentice, "We must tell the truth!" and is answered, "That's a thoroughly defeatist attitude." Rance's repeated admonishments to characters to "face facts" is ironic in this context, and near the end of the play, he admits to Geraldine, who is still trying to discover the "truth" about her situation, "It's much too late to tell the truth," a statement that could have been uttered at the play's beginning.

Indeed, Rance is adept at creating theories that satisfy his imagination much more than any simple truth could. When confronted with an actual "fact," such as Dr. Prentice's attack on Mrs. Prentice, he dismisses it by saying, "Oh, that was a mere physical act with no special psychological significance." Rance, entranced with Freudian symbols and theoretical interpretations, sees the madness around him as culminating in the "final chapters" of his planned documentary novel, which will include "incest, buggery, outrageous women, and strange love-cults catering to depraved appetites. Rance's fictive reworking of the "plot" of the drama is similar to the artistic process, and Orton the dramatist creates a character who imaginatively and fictively revels in the madness around him, just as Orton used his own chaotic lifestyle as fodder for his art. His early death ended a career that had, perhaps, only begun to approach its maturity. It is impossible to speculate, given his rapid development as a playwright, in which directions he might have gone.

Other major works

LONG FICTION: *Head to Toe*, 1971; *Between Us Girls*, 1988 (wr. 1957); *"Lord Cucumber"* and *"The Boy Hairdresser": Two Novels*, 1999 (*Lord Cucumber*, wr. 1960; *The Boy Hairdresser*, wr. 1954).

NONFICTION: *The Orton Diaries*, 1986, expanded 1996 (John Lahr, editor).

SCREENPLAY: *Up Against It*, 1979.

Bibliography

Bigsby, C. W. E. *Joe Orton*. London: Methuen, 1982. This brief study contends that Orton developed a style of anarchic farce that was deliberately subversive, not only of the authority figures appearing in his plays but also of language itself and conventionalities of plot and character. Bigsby also relates Orton's work to developments in postmodern literature and contemporary art. Notes, bibliography.

Charney, Maurice. *Joe Orton*. London: Macmillan, 1984. This introductory overview of Orton's work concisely assesses not only all of his plays but also his novel *Head to Toe* and his unproduced screenplay for the Beatles, *Up Against It*. The final chapter offers a useful definition of "the Ortonesque." Photographs, notes, bibliography.

Lahr, John. *Prick Up Your Ears: The Biography of Joe Orton*. 1978. Reprint. Berkeley: University of California Press, 2000. This definitive biography of the playwright, based in part on Orton's diaries, is indispensable to any study of Orton's work. It is not only a readable, detailed study of his life but also an insightful critical appreciation of the plays. The biography was the basis of a feature film of the same name, directed by Stephen Frears and released in 1987. Photographs, notes.

Rusinko, Susan. *Joe Orton*. New York: Twayne, 1995. A basic biography of Orton that covers his life and works. Bibliography and index.

Shepherd, Simon. *Because We're Queers: The Life and Crimes of Kenneth Halliwell and Joe Orton*. Boston: Alyson, 1989. A biography that covers the lives of Orton and his partner Halliwell. Bibliography.

Zarhy-Levo, Yael. *The Theatrical Critic as Cultural Agent: Constructing Pinter, Orton, and Stoppard as Absurdist Playwrights*. New York: Peter Lang, 2001. A look at the connection between absurdism and the theatrical works of Orton, Harold Pinter, and Tom Stoppard. Bibliography and index.

Angela Hague,
updated by William Hutchings

John Osborne

Born: London, England; December 12, 1929
Died: Shropshire, England; December 24, 1994

Principal drama • *Look Back in Anger*, pr. 1956, pb. 1957; *The Entertainer*, pr., pb. 1957 (music by John Addison); *Epitaph for George Dillon*, pr., pb. 1958 (with Anthony Creighton); *The World of Paul Slickey*, pr., pb. 1959 (music by Christopher Whelen); *Luther*, pr., pb. 1961; *Plays for England: The Blood of the Bambergs and Under Plain Cover*, pr. 1962, pb. 1963; *Inadmissible Evidence*, pr. 1964, pb. 1965; *A Bond Honored*, pr., pb. 1966 (adaptation of Lope de Vega's play *La fianza satistecna*); *A Patriot for Me*, pr., pb. 1966; *The Hotel in Amsterdam*, pr., pb. 1968; *Time Present*, pr., pb. 1968; *A Sense of Detachment*, pr. 1972, pb. 1973; *Hedda Gabler*, pr., pb. 1972 (adaptation of Henrik Ibsen's play); *A Place Calling Itself Rome*, pb. 1973 (adaptation of William Shakespeare's play *Coriolanus*); *Four Plays*, pb. 1973; *The Picture of Dorian Gray*, pb. 1973, pr. 1975 (adaptation of Oscar Wilde's novel); *West of Suez*, pr., pb. 1973; *Watch It Come Down*, pb. 1975, pr. 1976; *Déjàvu*, pb. 1991, pr. 1992; *Plays*, pb. 1993-1998 (3 volumes); *Four Plays*, pb. 2000

Other literary forms • John Osborne's considerable output includes, besides his plays, a comparatively unsuccessful musical comedy about a gossip columnist with a dual personality, *The World of Paul Slickey*, and a series of dramatic scripts for television: *A Subject of Scandal and Concern* (1960, originally *A Matter of Scandal and Concern*); *The Right Prospectus* (1970); *Very Like a Whale* (1971); *The Gift of Friendship* (1972); *Ms.: Or, Jill and Jack* (1974, later published as *Jill and Jack*); *The End of Me Old Cigar* (1975); *Try a Little Tenderness* (1978); and *You're Not Watching Me, Mummy* (1980). He adapted several plays and a novel for the stage and wrote the screenplays for several of his own plays. His adaptation of *Tom Jones* (1963) from Henry Fielding's novel earned for him an Academy Award in 1964. He also wrote *A Better Class of Person: An Autobiography, 1929-1956* (1981), and the second volume, titled *Almost a Gentleman: An Autobiography, Volume Two, 1955-1966* (1991), covering his life to 1966.

Achievements • John Osborne's most generous critics credit him with having transformed the English stage on a single night: May 8, 1956, when *Look Back in Anger* opened at the Royal Court Theatre. He is celebrated as the principal voice among England's Angry Young Men of the 1950's and 1960's, who railed vindictively against Edwardian dinosaurs and the empty-headed bourgeoisie; it should be noted, however, that his antiheroes rebel against their own frustrations and futility more than they do in the service of any substantial social or political reform. Indeed, they betray their envy of the stability and the "historical legitimacy" of the very generation they condemn. Perhaps Osborne's most profound influence has been his leadership in bringing authenticity into contemporary English theater; a member of what has loosely been defined as the kitchen-sink school, he helped institute a new receptivity to social issues, naturalistic characterization, and the vernacular, thereby revitalizing a theater scene that had been dominated by the verse elevations of T. S. Eliot and Christopher Fry and the commercial conventionality of Terence Rattigan.

In addition to his achievements as a playwright, Osborne was also an accomplished actor, director, and screenwriter. Testimonies to his popular and critical successes include three *Evening Standard* awards (1956, 1965, 1968), two New York Drama Critics Circle Awards (1958, 1965), a Tony (1963), and an Oscar (1964). In the last twenty years of his life, Osborne devoted much of his energy to television plays for the British Broadcasting Corporation. Although some saw this as a confirmation of dwindling artistic resources, Osborne's reputation as a prime mover of the postwar English stage held secure. He created some of the most arresting roles in twentieth century drama, and his career-long indictment of complacency is evident in every "lesson of feeling" he delivered to his audiences.

Biography • John Osborne grew up in Fulham, Ventnor, and Surrey, leading a suburban childhood in somewhat less dire circumstances than one's preconception of Jimmy Porter's alter ego would lead one to expect. In fact, every class subtlety between "upper-lower" and "lower-middle" was represented in his own extended family; Osborne's autobiography traces, with a gusto bordering on the vengeful, the Welsh and Cockney sides of his family, and characterizes, in the spirit of English low comedy, their attempts to sustain outworn Edwardian amenities after having "come down in the world." His father was an advertising copywriter who suffered long spells of illness, and his mother was a barmaid, but the family tree included many connections to the music hall and the theater. (Grandfather Grove, for example, would be revived in the form of Billy Rice in *The Entertainer.*)

Osborne was an only child, rather sickly and bookish. His most vivid memories of adolescence include listening in the air-raid shelter to German bombers and suffering the abuse of bullies at school. Eventually, he went to a boarding school, St. Michael's, and after being expelled for striking back at the headmaster, turned toward journalism as a reporter for a trade journal, *Gas World*. After a failed engagement, he joined a struggling touring company, with which he gained his first experience in acting and playwriting, including an artistic and sexual collaboration with an older actress. The most important result of this picaresque period for the young Osborne was that he realized his ear for speech and developed his ambition to write for the stage. The early 1950's led him into the vital world of provincial repertory—the background for *Epitaph for George Dillon*—and ultimately, to the acceptance of *Look Back in Anger* by George Devine and the English Stage Company. Thus began a prolific career that established Osborne as an influence on the style and subject of contemporary English theater, rivaled only by Harold Pinter. He was married four times, to Pamela Lane (1951-1957), actress Mary Ure (1957-1963), writer Penelope Gilliatt (1963-1968), and actress Jill Bennett, whom he married in 1968. He had one child. Osborne was a member of the Royal Society of Arts, and in 1970, he received an honorary doctorate from the Royal College of Art in London.

In the mid-1970's, after two decades of steady production for the stage, Osborne substantially reduced his playwriting, though he continued to turn out television dramas. Other than occasional adaptations, such as the 1991 televised revision (produced as a stage work in 1975) of Oscar Wilde's *The Picture of Dorian Gray* and an hour-long profile on British television's South Bank Show, Osborne was not highly visible on the theater scene in these later decades of his life. His 1991 play, *Déjàvu*, which opened at the Comedy Theater in London to mixed reviews, was his first major new work to appear on the London stage in more than fifteen years. The 1991 publication of the second volume of Osborne's autobiography, *Almost a Gentleman*, brought his memoirs up to the mid-1960's and kept his name in the news for a short time. He died in 1994 at the age of sixty-five.

Analysis • When the much-heralded John Osborne hero tore into an entire generation yet had no prospect for viable change, he discovered his own nakedness and vulnerability. He was inevitably a man in limbo, caught between nostalgia for the settled order of the past and hope for an idealized future he could not possibly identify. His rage was directed against his own inadequacy, not simply against that of his society. Because it was ineffectual, protesting against the ills of society became primarily a ritual complaint of the self against its own limitations.

Every Osborne play deals with reality's raids on self-esteem. His characters, even those who are most hostile to outworn conventions, are all in search of some private realm where they can operate with distinction. Sadly, that very search, which leads to isolation and denies communication, is as important a contributor to the contemporary malaise as is any governing body or social system. Angry young men and scornful old men, alike, feel disaffiliated and frustrated by the meager roles they occupy, but their greatest failure comes from not making a commitment to anything other than the justification of those feelings. Osborne wrote of a world that is immune to meaningful achievement. The degree to which his characters can move beyond complaint toward some constructive alternative that welcomes other people is the best measure of their heroism.

Look Back in Anger • *Look Back in Anger* is less specifically about rebellion than it is about the inertia that overcomes someone when he feels helpless to rebel. To excuse his own inanition, Jimmy Porter cries that there are no "good, brave causes left"; in fact, he daily rails against dozens of enemies—the bomb, advertisers, the church, politicians, aristocrats, cinema audiences, and others—until one realizes that the problem is that there are *too many* causes worth fighting for, and their sheer magnitude renders Jimmy impotent. His anger, his irreverence, and his castigating wit are all an imposture, an attempt to shield himself from his failure to take meaningful action. While he pricks the illusions and damns the lethargy of those around him, he himself holds fast to the sense that only he suffers, that his anger betokens spiritual superiority over Alison, who irons incessantly and who only desires peace, and over Cliff, who buries his head in the newspaper and who only desires comfortable seclusion in the Porters' flat. However justifiable his charges against the other characters, Jimmy's anger is less a mark of privilege than it is a standing joke—part of the "Sunday ritual."

Jimmy at times seems almost envious of those he attacks. The man for whom he professes the greatest resentment, Colonel Redfern, is an illusion-ridden, displaced Edwardian whom Jimmy prefers to see as the tyrannical father from whose clutches he saved Alison; nevertheless, the colonel at least had a golden age, whereas Jimmy agitates in a vacuum. Similarly, Helena, Alison's posh actress-friend, inspires in Jimmy equal portions of spite and sexual desire; he not only brings this officious snob down from her pedestal but also makes a place for her in his home after Alison's departure. Even Alison's political brother, Nigel, "the chinless wonder," whose vagueness Jimmy loves to attack, reflects on Jimmy's personal lack of commitment.

The point is that Jimmy cannot afford to see himself as in any way implicated by his own attacks. He resents everyone else's desperate evasion of suffering—he goes so far as to wish that Alison should witness the death of a baby, thereby unwittingly previewing her fate—but he, too, tends to leave the scene at times of crisis, going off to play his horn in the other room, for example, when Alison returns to confront the "traitorous" Helena. At this crucial juncture, Helena decides to opt out of the mess. Rather than risk dirtying her soul, she spouts convenient clichés about doing the decent thing and thus escapes her guilt. Alison's return is itself a compromise made in order to reaffirm the only security she has ever had. To say that Jimmy Porter proves any more willing to handle the pain and difficulty of being alive, however, is to ignore the fact that his has been an exclusive self-interest throughout the play. He is childishly arrogant rather than righteously indignant. So long as some woman is there to iron his clothes, he will not be bothered about his responsibilities to either Alison or Helena. (After all, he reasons, by leaving him, they have betrayed his "love," and so they deserve little more than scorn.) The image that concludes the play—Jimmy and Alison huddled together in a game of bears and squirrels—marks a final repudiation of the complications of adult life. "Let's pretend we're human" is Jimmy's original suggestion at the beginning of *Look Back in Anger*, but the consequences of human thought and feeling are too great; only within the limited arrangement of a "brainless" love game can either of them function at the end of the play.

Look Back in Anger portrays a world that lacks opportunities for meaningful achievement. Jimmy Porter loses his glibness and sarcasm as the "cruel steel traps" of the world close in on him; he trades in his anger for anesthesia. Ironically, even more obsolete than Colonel Redfern's visions of bygone days is Jimmy's own anger; Helena suggests that he really belongs "in the middle of the French Revolution," when glory was available. Jimmy Porter, who embodies the failures of his society, can support no cause other than that of the self in retreat. An impotent reformer and would-be martyr, he is consumed by a burning rage that finds no outlet.

The Entertainer • Osborne's society is one that seems immune to creativity and inimical to full humanity. In *The Entertainer*, Archie Rice looks back on the past nobility of the music hall (his is now a tawdry striptease joint) and forward to the barren legacy he has to offer his alienated children, and he wonders where all the "real people" have gone. Like Colonel Redfern, he is an anachronism, a personification of degraded values, as exemplified by his adherence to a dead art. He lacks even the satisfaction of the dying Billy Rice, who can at least withdraw into memories of free pudding with a pint of beer and respectable women in elegant dresses. Instead, Archie must console himself as best he can with a pitiful affair, his "little round world of light" onstage, and the conviction that at least he has "had a go at life."

The music hall structure of "turns" on a bill is imitated in the structure of the play itself. In this way, the story of the Rice family becomes an elaborate sketch, including overture, comic patter, heartrending interludes, and skits of love and death. Like the music hall, which has been corrupted by nudity and obscenity, the family unit, once a bastion of British dignity, has fallen on hard times. Phoebe, Archie's wife, indulges her husband's adulteries and failures and seeks shelter in local movie houses (another degraded art form). His son Frank is a conscientious objector who can only manage a "relationship substitute" with his father. His daughter Jean is also estranged from her parents, as she nurses the pain of a failed engagement and teaches an art class to children she loathes. In short, the younger generation is embittered by an inheritance of disappointment and ruined values, and Archie is incapable of communicating with them naturally and openly. He chooses, rather, to relate to them through a contrived performance, as he would to one of his vulgar audiences. In the place of intimacy, there is cajolement and manipulation, so that it becomes impossible for characters to distinguish sincerity from routine, confession from monologue.

"Everybody's all right," croons Archie, and the central tension of *The Entertainer* is that between his efforts to sustain happiness, Britishness, the welfare state, and the state of his private little world, all by sheer theatricality, and the steady deconstruction of those myths. The final blows are the deaths of Billy Rice and young Mick, the one seeming to pass away out of his own irrelevance to the contemporary world, and the other killed in an otherworldly war. The result is shell shock. All that Archie can turn to is a quiet drink and a few awkward old songs in the faded spotlight. Like *Look Back in Anger*, which concludes with a desperate desire for mindless retreat, *The Entertainer* shows the responses to crisis as the familiar patter and the old soft shoe.

Luther • *Luther* was both a departure from and an expansion of familiar themes for Osborne. The move from contemporary middle-class England to sixteenth century Germany makes *Luther* seem an anomalous experiment, but Osborne was once again concerned with the psychology of a sensitive man who prefers to escape the world rather than cope with the burden of mammoth causes that he finds overwhelming. Luther is a direct ancestor of Jimmy Porter: He is frightened by the implications of his own anger. The realization of God's enormous task sends him into an epileptic fit. By embracing a monastic alternative, Luther can rationalize, at least temporarily, his divestment of the trappings and complications of secular life in the protective bosom of the Lord. The Augustinian order is the religious equivalent of the psychological refuges in Osborne's previous plays.

It is not God alone who castigates Luther for his retreat. Luther's father, a practical and rather blasphemous man of the world, argues that his son, who could have been a fine lawyer, has chosen to run away from such a challenge and is now "abusing his youth with fear and humiliation." Luther's response is that his father is narrow-minded and blind to the glory of God, but the indictment still plagues Luther. The other brothers, too, laugh at the intensity of his "over-stimulated conscience"; Brother Weinand says Luther always speaks "as if lightning were just about to strike" behind him. Even Luther's sleep is infested by demons, and his days are soured by constipation and vomiting. Having entered the monastery to find security and certainty, Luther is instead faced with weakness and doubt. Not only does he fail to forge his soul into a human equivalent of sanctuary, but he also finds his worst traits are exaggerated within this restricted arena. As Staupitz will advise him years later, his fanaticism does not guarantee the order's potency, it simply renders it ridiculous. It is paranoia, not faith, that underlies Luther's devotion.

One can appreciate the fact that, despite Luther's ultimate role as world-shaker, he is not a social revolutionary. He consistently sides with the forces of law and order during the Peasants' Revolt. Although he prefers to drink to his own conscience instead of to the pope, he is equally disdainful of the "empty" rampage of revolution, which he deems an affront to what is truly Christian. In short, Luther has never learned the last tool of good works—to hate his own will—and his one-man crusade in the play is not so much against Satan as it is against the devilish fears in his own heart.

It is ironic that Luther contributes to the dismantling of the fortress that Cajetan calls a representation of the perfect unity of the world because Luther has never desired anything more than its unassailable safety. As he tries to bargain with God, he insists, "This cause is not mine but yours. For myself, I've no business to be dealing with the great lords of the world. I want to be still, in peace, and alone." *Luther* concludes with the hero crawling into a substitute sanctuary, in the form of marriage to a nun, Katherina von Bora. One is left with a weary man cradling his sleeping son in his arms and praying that God grant both of them sweet dreams. Luther is no different from Osborne's wholly fictional creations in that he is the one who appears to be most afflicted by the fires he has ignited; the fact that Luther is far more successful in having an effect on the world at large than is Jimmy Porter does not free him from the sense that all he has "ever managed to do is convert everything into stench and dying and peril."

Inadmissible Evidence • *Inadmissible Evidence* resumed Osborne's contention that one can suffer more personal damage from one's own attempts to insulate oneself than from those things—a hostile world, a guilty past, or simply other people—from which one desires insulation. Bill Maitland is an attorney who undergoes a play-long cross-examination about the quality of his own life. Although his detestation of computerized, deculturalized, dehumanized society may in part explain his callousness and conceit, it does not justify his personal inadequacies or his inability to maintain meaningful relationships. The most damaging evidence against him is that, however virulently he argues that the world has discarded him, he appears to be the instrument of his own isolation, and this is what he cannot admit to himself.

The play records Maitland's last hours in a process of collapse. It opens in a "dream-court," in which he conducts an anxious, helpless defense; when he awakens to his real world, he is no longer capable of handling the trials there. Like so many of Osborne's main characters, Maitland turns to rhetoric to defend himself and to convince himself of his own existence. With a lawyer's expertise, he spins convoluted monologues. He proposes to obscure, if he cannot eliminate, the ambiguous "wicked, bawdy and scandalous object" of which he stands accused: a life lived at a distance.

Inadmissible Evidence has the effect of a one-man play, for Maitland is so manipulative and exploitative that other characters in the play are reduced to two-dimensional fact files, existing solely as embodiments of reactions toward Maitland. Their limited existence is a result of his incapacity for engaging in relationships of any real complexity or depth. What he sees as betrayal by his friends and family—one by one they appear in his office or call up to confirm their desertion—is, from another perspective, Maitland's steady disappearance into solipsism. Having treated everyone with the same cynical caution, he grows to feel more and more "like something in a capsule in space, weightless, unable to touch anything or do anything, like a groping baby in a removed, putrefying womb." He is losing the control he once exerted over people both sexually and professionally, and now he cannot stem the tide of their retreat. Eventually, not even taxis notice him, and the newspapers feature the replacement of lawyers by computers that will render them obsolete. Ironically, the sentence for the crime of a practiced detachment is a suffocating anonymity.

Maitland's last clients serve as the most effective witnesses for the "prosecution." The women who complain of the callousness and the adulteries of their men come for legal counsel, but their function in the play is to force Maitland to recognize his own crimes in those of their men. (That all the women are played by one actress seems to insist on their symbolic status; they represent a single indictment.) Maitland can no longer escape into his work, for his work presents further evidence against him. He becomes indistinguishable from his last client, the self-consumed Mr. Maples, who also wants to avoid the ugly issues he has helped to create for himself.

The play ends in plea bargaining. It is no longer possible to keep from being "found out" (his fear in the opening dream sequence), so Maitland considers changing his plea to guilty in order possibly to mitigate the judgment against him. Perhaps he can salvage something by warning his daughter not to make the same mistakes and messes he did. Unfortunately, it may simply be too late to avoid his sentence; after all, can his daughter take to heart the didactic instruction of a man who has shown her nothing but insincerity? *Inadmissible Evidence* leaves one with the image of a man repenting his sins in solitary confinement.

A new focus • Osborne never deserted the theme of life's failure to measure up to human desires, and of people's unwitting contribution to that failure by virtue of the self-interest that underlies their complaints. Thus, for example, does Pamela in *Time Present* take up the gauntlet from Jimmy Porter, ridiculing the tawdriness and banality of the 1960's, the drugs, hippies, happenings, and the need to be "cool," with the same fervor that Jimmy railed against the uninspiring prospects of life in the 1950's. Osborne's later approach to this theme, however, was from the point of view of the conservative forces that were the target of the younger heroes of his earlier plays. This approach was not so much the inevitable by-product of an aging playwright's political reassessment as it was a change of focus that intensified his argument. In other words, the materially comfortable Establishment and the stolid aristocracy are as dissatisfied as the disenfranchised younger generation. In *West of Suez*, the first play designating this new focus, the shift from self-righteous anger to anxious unsettledness denotes not only nostalgia for the past and dissatisfaction with the present but also a fear of the future.

West of Suez • *West of Suez* examines yet another cramped refuge: In this case, it is the garden of a villa in the West Indies meant to serve as a retreat from the "cold, uncertain tides and striving pavements. And the marriage of anxieties." What had been intended as a reservation for the vestiges of the old British Empire is instead proof of its degradation. The Suez Canal is closed; the dreams of the empire it once exemplified are choked. The fiction cannot survive unless those who maintain it do so miles away from the reality, "in the West, among the non-descripts of the Bahamas."

Like their literary predecessors, Colonel Redfern and Billy Rice, the nostalgia-ridden members of this "exclusive circle" have been trivialized into comedy. A brigadier is reduced to domestic chores; the aged writer, Wyatt Gillman, gives an interview "like a wounded imperial bull being baited by a member of the lesser breeds"; social gatherings are contaminated by hippies, homosexuals, and tourists. The only defense against this invasion is boorish prejudice, which the traditionalists exhibit throughout the play.

The offspring of their obsolescence, represented by Edward and Frederica, are saddled with a useless legacy, and their marriage encompasses the tension and disappointment of people who must live vicariously on other people's distant memories. Edward immerses himself in pathology because it affords him uncompromised detachment, and Frederica finds her self-possession in a kind of sneering sophistication. Their conversations are nothing more than highly stylized verbal exercises designed to take their minds off the supreme boredom of their lives. In a sense, they aspire to the state of blissful self-importance of Wyatt Gillman, the extreme version of which must be senility.

Modern life is not something in which the couple would choose to involve themselves, but their island home is no escape from vulgarity. Tourists litter the place, cheapening it with their very presence, and the native blacks are charmless and sullen. Finally, there is the anarchist-hippie Jed, something of a reincarnation of Jimmy Porter, who lambastes the befuddled aristocrats with curses and threats of violence. His heavy-handed assault summarizes their ineffectuality, their pathetic irrelevance to the real world, while also demonstrating the ugliness of that world and almost justifying aristocratic stereotypes of the undignified lower classes. The response of Wyatt Gillman to all of this is to ask to go to bed, but there is no hiding from Jed's vicious prophecy. Wyatt is murdered at the end of *West of Suez* by a band of natives. Nothing is sacred anymore, especially not the memory of colonial power and prestige. Wyatt's children, friends, and associates, all of whom have staked claims in a world that no longer exists, stand over his corpse in stupefaction.

Déjàvu • In 1992, Osborne returned to the London stage with *Déjàvu*, which brought *Look Back in Anger*'s Jimmy Porter back to life after two and a half decades. In *Déjàvu*, Jimmy, now a middle-aged drunk, still vents his spleen at all those around him. Few critics, though, thought that the new incarnation matched the power of the original.

Other major works

SCREENPLAYS: *Look Back in Anger*, 1959 (with Nigel Kneale; adaptation of his stage play); *The Entertainer*, 1960 (with Kneale; adaptation of his stage play); *Tom Jones*, 1963 (adaptation of Henry Fielding's novel); *Inadmissible Evidence*, 1968 (adaptation of his stage play); *The Charge of the Light Brigade*, 1968 (with Charles Wood).

TELEPLAYS: *A Subject of Scandal and Concern*, 1960 (originally as *A Matter of Scandal and Concern*); *The Right Prospectus*, 1970; *Very Like a Whale*, 1971; *The Gift of Friendship*, 1972; *Ms.: Or, Jill and Jack*, 1974 (later published as *Jill and Jack*); *The End of Me Old Cigar*, 1975; *Try a Little Tenderness*, 1978; *You're Not Watching Me, Mummy*, 1980; *A Better Class of Person*, 1985; *God Rot Tunbridge Wells*, 1985; *The Picture of Dorian Gray*, 1991 (adaptation of Oscar Wilde's novel).

NONFICTION: *A Better Class of Person: An Autobiography, 1929-1956*, 1981; *Almost a Gentleman: An Autobiography, Volume Two: 1955-1966*, 1991; *Damn You, England: Collected Prose*, 1994.

Bibliography

Banham, Martin. *Osborne.* Edinburgh, Scotland: Oliver and Boyd, 1969. Contains discerning essays on *Look Back in Anger*, *The Entertainer*, and nine other plays, discussed around the thesis statement that "most of Osborne's targets are very clearly observed, defined, and, through his frontal assault, shaken to their foundations." Rich with material for further inquiry, especially when compared with later work. Complemented by a list of first British productions and a select bibliography.

Brien, Alan. "Snot or Not?" Review of *Almost a Gentleman*. *New Statesman Society* 4 (November 15, 1991): 47. In this review of Osborne's second volume of his autobiography, Brien's premise is that an "autobiography is not history. It is a form of entertainment." He finds Osborne's work hostile but valuable. Brien was one of the few defenders of Osborne's aggressively straightforward second volume.

Denison, Patricia D., ed. *John Osborne: A Casebook.* New York: Garland, 1997. Several essays critically examine Osborne's body of work, focusing on his form and technique, the construction of gender, and the relationships between his life and plays.

Ferrar, Harold. *John Osborne.* New York: Columbia University Press, 1973. This booklet on Osborne's first fifteen years of output notes that Jimmy Porter (in *Look Back in*

Anger) is a portrait of "the body politic: one either defensively dismisses him or confronts the political implications of his protest and the social etiology of his anguish." Discusses *A Bond Honored, The Hotel in Amsterdam,* and other more obscure works. Brief select bibliography.

Gilleman, Luc. *John Osborne: Vituperative Artist.* New York: Routledge, 2002. Provides criticism and analysis of Osborne's life and works. Bibliography and index.

Hayman, Ronald. *John Osborne.* New York: Frederick Ungar, 1972. The World Dramatists series specializes in a factual overview, with play-by-play chapters, copious notes on stage productions, cast lists (here, both of London and New York premieres and productions), and a careful chronology. The introduction speaks of Osborne's ability to "epitomize something important about England today, not just by expressing moods and stating attitudes but by summing up the condition that the country is in, almost personifying it." Index.

Hinchliffe, Arnold P. *British Theatre, 1950-1970.* Totowa, N.J.: Rowman and Littlefield, 1974. The best book for putting Osborne in the context of the total revolutionary movement in British and European theater, and written when the movement was preparing for the second wave of playwrights. Particularly articulate on European influences, the Theater of the Absurd, and the relation of a national theater to the themes of Osborne and his contemporaries. Select bibliography but no index.

_____. *John Osborne.* Boston: Twayne, 1984. A general introduction to Osborne, with an oddly dated discussion of his most influential works, and not much new. Chronology, index, and bibliography.

Arthur M. Saltzman,
updated by Thomas J. Taylor
and Robert McClenaghan

Suzan-Lori Parks

Born: Fort Knox, Kentucky; May 10, 1963

Principal drama • *The Sinner's Place*, pr. 1984, pb. 1995; *Betting on the Dust Commander*, pr. 1987, pb. 1995; *Imperceptible Mutabilities in the Third Kingdom*, pr. 1989, pb. 1995; *The Death of the Last Black Man in the Whole Entire World*, pr. 1990, pb. 1995; *Devotees in the Garden of Love*, pr. 1991, pb. 1995; *The America Play*, pr. 1993, pb. 1995; *The America Play and Other Works*, pb. 1995; *Venus*, pr. 1996, pb. 1997; *In the Blood*, pr. 1999, pb. 2000; *Fucking A*, pr. 2000, pb. 2001; *The Red Letter Plays*, pb. 2001 (includes *In the Blood* and *Fucking A*); *Topdog/Underdog*, pr., pb. 2001

Other literary forms • Though her literary reputation rests primarily on her dramatic writing, Suzan-Lori Parks has also written several screenplays: *Anemone Me*, an independent film released in New York in 1990, *Girl 6*, directed by Spike Lee and released in 1996, and two scripts for Jodie Foster and Danny Glover. Parks has also written several essays that have been published in theater journals.

Achievements • Suzan-Lori Parks produced her first play, *The Sinner's Place*, in 1984, as a student at Mount Holyoke College. Her second, *Betting on the Dust Commander*, debuted in a Brooklyn garage in 1987, with Parks purchasing five folding chairs to accommodate the audience. From these modest beginnings, Parks has become one of the most celebrated American playwrights of her generation. *Imperceptible Mutabilities in the Third Kingdom*, produced in 1989, earned Parks her first Obie Award for best new American play, and *The New York Times* named her the year's most promising playwright. Parks received her second Obie, for *Venus*, in 1996. Her next play, *In the Blood*, was a Pulitzer Prize finalist in 2000.

Parks has received numerous fellowships and grants, including the Guggenheim Fellowship in 2000 and the MacArthur Foundation Fellowship in 2001. In 2002, Parks became only the fourth African American and the first African American woman to receive the Pulitzer Prize in drama for her play *Topdog/Underdog*. She has taught at the University of Michigan, Yale University, and New York University. She also served as writer-in-residence at the New School for Social Research (now New School University) in New York from 1991 to 1992. In 2000, Parks became director of the Audrey Skirball Kernis Theatre Projects Writing for Performance program at the California Institute of the Arts.

Biography • Suzan-Lori Parks was born in Fort Knox, Kentucky, in 1963, the daughter of a career army officer. She spent her early childhood in several cities across the United States and lived in Germany, where she attended high school. She began writing short stories as a third grader and continued to focus on prose writing until her undergraduate years at Mount Holyoke College in Massachusetts. There, she met the distinguished author and essayist James Baldwin, who recognized her gift for dialogue and suggested that she explore drama.

Parks wrote her first play, *The Sinner's Place*, in 1984 as a student at Mount Holyoke.

Though she earned an honors citation for her work, the college's theater department refused to stage the play. Parks graduated with honors in 1985 and moved to London for a year to study acting. *Betting on the Dust Commander*, her first play to be produced in New York City, debuted in 1987. Two years later, Parks received an Obie Award for *Imperceptible Mutabilities in the Third Kingdom*, and *The New York Times* named Parks the most promising playwright of 1989.

Following the successful production of *The Death of the Last Black Man in the Whole Entire World* at the Brooklyn Arts Council's BACA Downtown Theatre in 1990, Parks produced her next two plays, *Devotees in the Garden of Love* and *The America Play* on smaller stages in Lexington, Kentucky, and Dallas, Texas, respectively. *The America Play* later opened Off-Broadway at the Joseph Papp Public Theatre in New

(AP/Wide World Photos)

York City in 1994. Parks earned a second Obie Award in 1996, for her play *Venus*, which also debuted at the Joseph Papp Public Theatre. Also in 1996, Parks wrote the screenplay for director Spike Lee's film *Girl 6*.

The productions of *In the Blood*, which was nominated for the Pulitzer Prize in Drama in 2000, and *Fucking A*, both of which draw on elements in Nathaniel Hawthorne's classic novel, *The Scarlet Letter* (1850), continued to earn Parks wide critical acclaim. She received the prestigious Guggenheim Fellowship in 2000 and the MacArthur Fellowship (called the genius grant) in 2001. Parks's growing reputation as a brilliant young playwright reached new heights in 2001 with the production of *Topdog/Underdog*. The play opened on July 22, 2001, at the Joseph Papp Public Theatre in New York City to rave reviews and earned Parks the Pulitzer Prize in drama in 2002, distinguishing her as the first African American woman and only the fourth African American to win the award. *Topdog/Underdog* opened on Broadway in April of 2002, the first Broadway opening for an African American woman since Ntozake Shange, whose *for colored girls who have considered suicide/since the rainbow is enuf* opened in 1976.

"I think it's a great moment for all African-American women writers," Parks has explained about becoming the first African American woman to receive the Pulitzer Prize in drama. "And anytime America recognizes a member of a certain group for excellence—one that has not traditionally been recognized—it's a great moment for American culture." Parks married Paul Oscher, a blues musician, in 2001, and joined the faculty of the California Institute of the Arts in Valencia, California, as the director of the Audrey Skirball Kernis Theatre Projects Writing for Performance program.

Analysis • "I am obsessed with resurrecting," Suzan-Lori Parks explained in a 1996 interview, "with bringing up the dead . . . and hearing their stories as they come into my head." Parks has often described the characters she creates as independent beings, as voices that relate their stories to her. Rather than writing them into existence, Parks allows the characters to speak themselves into being. Drawing on history, myth, and fantasy, she populates her plays with conventional and unconventional characters whose stories excavate the past in order to expose the truths and misconceptions about African American and American history. "Every play I write is about love and distance. And time," she explained in 1994. "And from that we can get things like history." She elaborates further in her essay "Possession," collected in *The America Play and Other Works*. "Through each line of text, I'm rewriting the Time Line—creating history where it is and always was but has not yet been divined."

Language plays a vital role in this creation of history. Using what she calls "rep and rev" (repetition and revision), Parks often employs language as a musical refrain, with characters repeating phrases throughout her plays, the repetition of which adds different shades of meaning. In *Topdog/Underdog*, Booth rehearses his three-card monte street routine, addressing his imaginary audience: "Watch me close watch me close now: who-see-thuh-red-card-who-see-the-red-card?" As the words recur at various points in the play, they take on the quality of a chant, or a chorus that signifies the building tension between the brothers.

The question of identity in Parks's drama, as self-awareness and the identification of an individual within a group, is of central importance. As characters attempt to identify themselves, they must destroy the false identities and histories that have been attributed to them. In *Imperceptible Mutabilities in the Third Kingdom*, the characters Mona, Chona, and Verona, whose names have been changed to Molly, Charlene, and Veronica, meditate on the apparent mutability of their characters. "Once there was uh me named Mona who wondered what she'd be like if no one was watchin," Mona/Molly says. The Foundling Father of Parks's *The America Play*, whose setting is the Great Pit of History, is obsessed by Abraham Lincoln and decides to reenact his assassination in a traveling show. Like the character of Lincoln in *Topdog/Underdog*, who earns his living by reenacting Abraham Lincoln's assassination in a local arcade, the Foundling Father is a captive of history.

Imperceptible Mutabilities in the Third Kingdom • Rather than separating her first major play into traditional acts, Parks creates four separate stories that provide a nonlinear and sometimes surreal look at aspects of the African American experience in her *Imperceptible Mutabilities in the Third Kingdom*.

"Snails," the first section of the play, looks at a contemporary group of women who possess two names, one they have chosen and another that has been imposed on them. The second section, "Third Kingdom," re-creates the tragic Middle Passage, through which enslaved Africans journeyed on their way to America, and the details of which are narrated by characters like Kin-Seer, Us-Seer, and Over-Seer. "Open House," the third section, depicts the life of Aretha Saxon, a black servant/slave in the household of the white Saxon family. Aretha's departure from the family is occasioned by the removal with pliers of all of her teeth. The play's final section, "Greeks," is a modern interpretation of Homer's *Odyssey* (c. 750 B.C.E.; English translation, 1614), with Mr. Seargant Smith in the role of Odysseus. Hoping to earn "his Distinction" in the army, Seargant Smith spends most of his life away from his family, who await his return and the honor he hopes to bring back with him.

The four stories in *Imperceptible Mutabilities in the Third Kingdom* depict characters whose identity and culture are marginalized by others. From the three women in "Snails," whose identities are studied and inevitably altered by the invasive Lutsky, to Miss Faith's extraction of Aretha Saxon's teeth in an act that functions metaphorically as a means of extracting Aretha from the Saxon family history, Parks dramatizes the struggle of African Americans against cultural, historical, and linguistic sabotoge. A critical and popular success, *Imperceptible Mutabilities in the Third Kingdom* earned Parks her first Obie Award for best new American play. *The New York Times* also named her 1989's most promising young playwright.

Venus • *Venus* received mixed reviews for its portrayal of an African woman whose unconventional physiognomy becomes the basis for her exhibition in a traveling side-show in Europe. Parks based her play on a historical character, Saartjie Baartman, a South African woman whose body was displayed publicly in London and Paris in the early nineteenth century. Dubbed the Hottentot Venus, Baartman became a popular spectacle for white audiences who were fascinated and revolted by her appearance. After her death, Baartman's sexual organs and buttocks were preserved and housed in the Musée de l'Homme in Paris until the late twentieth century.

As the play opens, Venus is a popular attraction in Mother Showman's traveling show of Nine Human Wonders in London. Because slavery has been outlawed in England, Mother Showman's captivity of Venus sparks a debate about whether such exhibitions constitute slavery. Venus eventually escapes to Paris, where she falls under the influence of the Baron Docteur, who falls in love with Venus but also assures his colleagues that he intends to make her the object of scientific study. A twisted custody battle ensues as Mother Showman and Baron Docteur fight over who has the right to exhibit Venus.

In the character of Venus, Parks explores the objectification of human beings, and particularly African Americans, whose humanity was denied in the nineteenth century (and beyond) on the basis of pseudoscientific theories that reinforced prejudices against physical and cultural difference. Venus, a woman who desires to be treated with love and respect, becomes an oddity in a circus sideshow, reduced to little more in the public consciousness than her "great heathen buttocks."

In the Blood • A modern interpretation of Nathaniel Hawthorne's novel *The Scarlet Letter, In the Blood* depicts a homeless woman's struggle to care for herself and her family. Hester, La Negrita, and her five children, all from different fathers, live under a bridge, making what little money they have from collecting cans. Hester spends much of her time practicing her writing (she knows only the letter *A*). As her health declines, Hester appeals for assistance to a street doctor, her welfare case worker, a former lover and father of her first child, and eventually a local reverend, who is the father of her youngest child.

The actors who portray Hester's five children also double as adult characters. In a series of stage confessions that resemble the chorus of a Greek tragedy, these characters (Amiga Gringa, Chilli, The Doctor, The Welfare Lady, and Reverend D) explain the ways in which they have taken advantage of Hester, who has been sexually exploited by almost everyone whom she knows.

In the Blood is a hopeless tale of a woman undone by poverty and a social system that cannot meet her needs. Individuals in a position to help Hester can think only of how to use her. The word "slut," scrawled on the wall of Hester's makeshift home under the bridge in the play's opening scene, serves a purpose similar to Hawthorne's scarlet letter on Hester Prynne's chest. Both Hesters are defined almost exclusively by what their societies perceive as aberrant sexuality. When every means of salvation is exhausted, Hester is left, in the final scene of the play, with the word "slut," this time on the lips of her oldest child. Hester's murder of her son Jabber at the end of the play functions as an attempt to efface the word, and the identification, both of which have followed her throughout the play. A critical and popular success, *In the Blood* was named a finalist for the 2000 Pulitzer Prize in Drama.

Topdog/Underdog • Departing from the unorthodox staging and characterization of her previous plays, Parks presents what appears on the surface to be a traditional tale of sibling rivalry in *Topdog/Underdog*, which opened at the Joseph Papp Public Theatre on July 22, 2001, and opened on Broadway at the Ambassador Theatre in New York less than a year later. However, Parks links the struggle of her two characters, named Lincoln and Booth, to more complex and historical struggles of race, family, and identity.

The two brothers, Lincoln and Booth, share a seedy urban apartment. Lincoln, a former street hustler whose skill at the card game three-card monte is legendary, now works at an arcade where he impersonates Abraham Lincoln for patrons who pay money to reenact his assassination. Booth, who aspires to his brother's greatness at three-card monte, relies on Lincoln's paychecks and whatever he can steal to make ends meet.

As Lincoln and Booth, so named as a joke by their father, try to plan for their future, they confront the realities of the past: their abandonment by their parents and the buried animosities toward each other. In the play's final scene, Booth flies into a rage when Lincoln bests him at three-card monte, thereby winning the family legacy (five hundred dollars rolled in a stocking) left to each son when their parents fled. Lincoln's violent end is foreshadowed by his job at the arcade and by his and Booth's names. How each brother accepts and realizes the roles imposed by family history, circumstance, and the inherent opposition of their names, however, makes the play a deeply compelling one. In 2002, shortly after its debut on Broadway, *Topdog/Underdog* earned Parks the Pulitzer Prize in drama.

Other major works
    SCREENPLAYS: *Anemone Me*, 1990; *Girl 6*, 1996.
    RADIO PLAYS: *Pickling*, 1990; *The Third Kingdom*, 1990; *Locomotive*, 1991.

Bibliography
Frieze, James. "*Imperceptible Mutabilities in the Third Kingdom*: Suzan-Lori Parks and the Shared Struggle to Perceive." *Modern Drama* 41, no. 4 (Winter, 1998): 523. Frieze provides a detailed analysis of Parks's Obie Award-winning play, emphasizing the significance of identity in shaping the actions and thoughts of the play's characters.
Garrett, Shawn-Marie. "The Possession of Suzan-Lori Parks." *American Theatre* 17, no. 8 (October, 2000): 22. This essay provides some background on Parks's beginnings as a playwright and her unconventional approach to the writing process. Garrett provides a good overview of Parks's development as a playwright and the historical, political, and racial forces that inform her work.
Parks, Suzan-Lori. *The America Play and Other Works*. New York: Theatre Communications Group, 1995. This volume combines a sampling of Parks's early plays, includ-

ing *Betting on the Dust Commander* and *Devotees in the Garden of Love*, with three essays that provide insight on the aims and methods of Parks's writing.

Pochoda, Elizabeth. "I See Thuh Black Card . . . ?" *Nation* 274, no. 20 (May 27, 2002): 36. A review of Parks's *Topdog/Underdog*, following its Broadway debut at the Ambassador Theatre in New York, which touches on the major themes of the Pulitzer Prize-winning play.

Wilmer, S. E. "Restaging the Nation: The Work of Suzan-Lori Parks." *Modern Drama* 43, no. 3 (Fall, 2000): 442. Examines the postmodern elements of Parks's drama and provides analysis of most of her major plays.

Philip Bader

Arthur Wing Pinero

Born: London, England; May 24, 1855
Died: London, England; November 23, 1934

Principal drama • *£200 a Year*, pr. 1877; *Two Can Play at That Game*, pr. 1877; *La Comète: Or, Two Hearts*, pr. 1878; *Daisy's Escape*, pr. 1879; *Bygones*, pr. 1880; *Hester's Mystery*, pr. 1880, pb. 1893; *The Money Spinner*, pr. 1880, pb. 1900; *Imprudence*, pr. 1881; *The Squire*, pr., pb. 1881; *Girls and Boys*, pr. 1882; *Lords and Commons*, pr. 1883; *The Rector*, pr. 1883; *The Rocket*, pr. 1883, pb. 1905; *Low Water*, pr. 1884, pb. 1905; *The Ironmaster*, pr. 1884 (adaptation of George Ohnet's play *Le Maître de forges*); *In Chancery*, pr. 1884, pb. 1905; *The Magistrate*, pr. 1885, pb. 1892; *Mayfair*, pr. 1885 (adaptation of Victorien Sardou's play *Maison neuve*); *The Hobby Horse*, pr. 1886, pb. 1892; *The School Mistress*, pr. 1886, pb. 1894; *Dandy Dick*, pr. 1887, pb. 1893; *Sweet Lavender*, pr. 1888, pb. 1893; *The Weaker Sex*, pr. 1888, pb. 1894; *The Profligate*, pr. 1889, pb. 1892; *The Cabinet Minister*, pr. 1890, pb. 1891; *The Plays of Arthur W. Pinero*, pb. 1891-1915 (25 volumes); *Lady Bountiful*, pr. 1891, pb. 1892; *The Times*, pr., pb. 1891; *The Amazons*, pr. 1893, pb. 1905; *The Second Mrs. Tanqueray*, pr. 1893, pb. 1895; *The Benefit of the Doubt*, pr. 1895, pb. 1896; *The Notorious Mrs. Ebbsmith*, pr., pb. 1895; *The Princess and the Butterfly: Or, The Fantastics*, pr. 1897, pb. 1898; *The Beauty Stone*, pr., pb. 1898 (libretto, with J. Comyns Carr; music by Sir Arthur Sullivan); *Trelawny of the "Wells,"* pr., pb. 1898; *The Gay Lord Quex*, pr. 1899, pb. 1900; *Iris*, pr. 1901, pb. 1902; *Letty*, pr. 1903, pb. 1904; *A Wife Without a Smile*, pr. 1904, pb. 1905; *His House in Order*, pr., pb. 1906; *The Thunderbolt*, pr. 1908, pb. 1909; *Mid-Channel*, pr. 1909, pb. 1910; *Preserving Mr. Panmure*, pr. 1911, pb. 1912; *The "Mind the Paint" Girl*, pr. 1912, pb. 1913; *The Widow of Wasdale Head*, pr. 1912, pb. 1924; *Playgoers*, pr., pb. 1913; *The Big Drum*, pr., pb. 1915; *Mr. Livermore's Dream*, pb. 1916, pr. 1917; *Social Plays*, pb. 1917-1922 (4 volumes); *The Freaks: An Idyll of Suburbia*, pr. 1918, pb. 1922; *Monica's Blue Boy*, pb. 1918 (ballet-pantomime; music by Frederick Cowen); *Quick Work*, pr. 1919; *A Seat in the Park*, pr., pb. 1922; *The Enchanted Cottage*, pr., pb. 1922; *A Private Room*, pr., pb. 1928; *Dr. Harmer's Holiday*, pr. 1930, pb. 1931; *A Cold June*, pb. 1931, pr. 1932; *Three Plays*, pb. 1985; *"Trelawny of the 'Wells'" and Other Plays*, pb. 1995

Other literary forms • Unlike his great contemporary George Bernard Shaw, Arthur Wing Pinero wrote very little other than plays. His nondramatic works consist of less than a dozen essays and the collected letters. The essays contain comments on theatrical technique, appreciations and criticisms of his fellow playwrights, retrospective accounts of the late nineteenth century London stage, and vignettes of his own life in the theater. The letters constitute a more substantial document; written in a style that varies from the businesslike to the witty and urbane, they provide invaluable glimpses of London theatrical life during the several decades in which Pinero was a dominant figure in British drama.

Achievements • During his extraordinarily productive career, Arthur Wing Pinero wrote more than fifty plays, nearly all of which were produced and most of which were popular successes. Although his reputation is no longer what it once was, during the last two decades of the nineteenth century and the first decade of the twentieth, he was one of Britain's most acclaimed playwrights. His prolific output was the financial mainstay of many a London theater, and his plays brought him both great wealth and international fame. The foremost performers of his day acted the roles he created, often achieving triumphs that they could never again equal. Nothing in the career of Edward Terry, for example, could match his popularity as Dick Phenyl, the amiable drunkard of *Sweet Lavender.*

Pinero achieved success in a variety of dramatic forms. He wrote a series of farces for the Court Theatre that brought that institution from the brink of financial collapse to immediate prosperity. The first of these, *The Magistrate,* set a London record by running for more than three hundred consecutive performances. The play is still occasionally revived, a retitled version having been produced in London as recently as 1983. His sentimental comedies were also immensely popular, especially *Sweet Lavender,* which outdid even *The Magistrate* with an unprecedented first run of 684 performances. More historically important were Pinero's problem plays, which demonstrated that drama with a serious social purpose could succeed on the nineteenth century British stage. Such plays as *The Profligate, The Second Mrs. Tanqueray,* and *The Notorious Mrs. Ebbsmith* lack the intellectual subtlety and dramatic power of the works of Shaw, but they did help to prepare the way for Shaw. Although Pinero never challenged his audience's social assumptions as directly as Shaw did, he showed that British playgoers were willing to think as well as to be entertained.

Another of Pinero's accomplishments was his successful advocacy, along with Henry Arthur Jones, of dramatic realism. An admirer from his youth of Thomas William Robertson's cup-and-saucer drama, Pinero wrote in a colloquial rather than a declamatory style and avoided extreme melodramatic flourishes. Like Robertson, he drew his characters and plots from ordinary life, especially the life of the upper-middle class. He made meticulous use of place references and of speech mannerisms to establish dramatic verisimilitude, and because of its greater naturalness for the performance of social drama, he preferred the three-walled-box stage to all other arrangements. As director of his own plays, he insisted that his actors avoid artificiality in the delivery of their lines, a practice that helped rid the theater of its last vestiges of bombast. Pinero's determination that his plays not be distorted during their preparation for performance induced him, in fact, to exert complete directorial control over the final product, and the key place of the director in modern theater owes much to Pinero's thoroughness.

The extreme care with which Pinero created his realistic effects did not preclude the occurrence in his plays of sentimental and sensational moments reminiscent of melodrama. Indeed, sentiment and surprise are vital elements in most, if not all, of Pinero's works, but these elements develop with a logical inevitability from character portrayal and plot construction rather than springing up, as they so often do in melodrama, with inappropriate suddenness. Unfortunately, the plot construction necessary to bring about some of the effects at which Pinero aimed is not as realistic as other aspects of his writing, and his plots often seem contrived. In imitation of Eugène Scribe, Victorien Sardou, and Alexandre Dumas, *fils,* Pinero was a writer of well-made plays, plays that Shaw compared to "cats'-cradles, clockwork mice, mechanical rabbits, and the like." Such plays relied heavily on compressed exposition through convenient exchanges of letters and unlikely conversations between characters. Their well-made plots contained obtrusive foreshadowings of later events, especially of the startling, but carefully prepared-for, plot reversal. They then moved to their inevitable denouement, in which every plot complication was resolved and every uncertainty clarified.

Although Pinero's fusion of realism, sentiment, and plot contrivance may sound like an unpromising amalgam, the craftsmanship with which he drew these elements together suited the taste of his audiences well enough to make him the most popular playwright in the English-speaking world for more than two decades and to earn for him, in 1909, a knighthood—the second to be granted to a playwright for his contributions to the theater; no one but W. S. Gilbert had been so honored previously. Moreover, the conventions of popular theater that Pinero helped shape are not drastically different from the conventions that exist today. It would take very little rewriting to transform *The Magistrate* into the most up-to-date of situation comedies, and it would take only slightly more effort to make *Sweet Lavender* a believable contemporary screen romance. For his considerable contributions to popular theater, then, and for his pioneering efforts in serious social drama, Pinero is worthy of more attention than he has, in the past, received.

Biography • Sir Arthur Wing Pinero was born into an upper-middle-class family in London, England, on May 24, 1855. He was the youngest child and only son of Lucy Daines Pinero and John Daniel Pinero, a couple described by Pinero's biographer, Wilbur Dunkel, as "liberal-minded." Pinero's maternal ancestors were of long-established English stock. His paternal forebears, whose name was originally Pinheiro, were Portuguese Jewish immigrants who had arrived in England in the early eighteenth century.

Pinero's parents were frequent theatergoers, and one of his earliest memories was of attending a Grecian Theatre pantomime with his parents and his sisters, Frances and Mary. Very early, too, he discovered the wonders of Sadler's Wells, where, for a mere eighteen pence, he could indulge his growing fascination with plays and actors. His parents never objected to this fascination, but it was always understood that Arthur, like his father and his grandfather, would become a lawyer.

Because of family financial difficulties, Pinero was removed from school and began his legal apprenticeship at age ten. He worked in his father's law office, without great enthusiasm, until his father's retirement in 1870 and then found employment as a library clerk. He soon left that job to accept a position in a solicitor's office, but he felt no more interest in the law while working for his new employer in Lincoln's Inn Fields than he had felt while working for his father in Great James Street.

Meanwhile, Pinero's fascination with the theater continued to increase: He discovered Thomas William Robertson's dramas at the Prince of Wales's Theatre and became absorbed in the new theatrical realism. He learned much that would later be of great use to him from Marie Wilton's purposely understated productions of Robertson's plays, and he began to haunt the street outside the David Garrick Club in hopes of catching an occasional glimpse of the performers he so much admired. He wrote plays that no theater manager would produce, took elocution lessons that intensified his interest in the actor's art, and decided finally to seek a theatrical career of his own.

In 1874, soon after the death of his father, Pinero became an extra with the Edinburgh Theatre Royal. A year later, he moved on to Liverpool, where Wilkie Collins saw him and secured for him a part in his newest play, *Miss Gwilt*, which opened at the Globe Theatre, London, in April of 1876. Henry Irving liked Pinero's unpretentious style of acting and offered him the role of Claudius in a Lyceum Theatre tour of William Shakespeare's *Hamlet, Prince of Denmark* (pr. c. 1600-1601). Pinero accepted the part and spent most of the next five years performing in various Lyceum Theatre productions.

Pinero also succeeded for the first time in having one of his own plays produced. In October of 1877, *£200 a Year* was performed as a curtain raiser at the Globe Theatre, which borrowed him back from the Lyceum for the evening to play the male lead. During the next three years, five more of his plays were produced, with varying degrees of success, followed at last by his first undeniable hit, *The Money Spinner*, which opened in Manchester during November of 1880 and moved to London the following January. His next several plays also turned a profit, and he retired from acting in 1882 to dedicate himself fully to the creation of new works for the stage.

Pinero's work habits were almost compulsive in their regularity, and even after marrying Myra Holme, a widowed actress, in 1883, he refused to deviate from his accustomed writing schedule. Between teatime and breakfast, he wrote and slept, a routine that he maintained with stubborn perseverance and that helped him turn out an amazing number of plays. Many of these early efforts were farces, farce being the first dramatic form of which Pinero was an acknowledged master. *The Rocket* and *In Chancery*, which premiered in December of 1883 and December of 1884 respectively, brought Pinero considerable success, but it was with the opening of *The Magistrate*, the first of the Court farces, on March 21, 1885, that his reputation soared. During the next several years, he supplied the Court Theatre with four more farces, *The School Mistress*, *Dandy Dick*, *The Cabinet Minister*, and *The Amazons*, all of which were resoundingly popular.

In this same period, Pinero was also writing sentimental comedies and had begun to experiment with the problem play. *Sweet Lavender* commenced its record first run on March 21, 1888, and the more modestly successful but equally sentimental *Lady Bountiful* opened on March 7, 1891. The first of the significant problem plays, *The Profligate*, premiered in the spring of 1889 and caused a considerable critical stir. The play was hailed for its daring treatment of a serious social theme, and hope was expressed that further plays of the same sort, from Pinero or from others, might soon appear.

This hope was realized on May 27, 1893, with the premiere of *The Second Mrs. Tanqueray*, Pinero's most acclaimed play. Pinero had dedicated a year of his life to putting the play together and another several months to getting it staged. Despite Pinero's prodigious reputation, none of the London theater managers was at first willing to touch it. Finally, with some reluctance, George Alexander accepted it for production at the St. James's Theatre and cast an unknown actress, Mrs. Patrick Campbell, in the title role of Paula Tanqueray. In a part that was later to provide triumphs for Sarah Bernhardt, Eleonora Duse, and Ethel Barrymore, Mrs. Campbell was brilliant, and the play was an unqualified critical and popular success. It was compared favorably to Dumas's *Camille* (pr. 1852) and was declared to be superior to every English drama since the time of Richard Brinsley Sheridan.

For the next fifteen years, Pinero was at the top of his profession. Theaters clamored for his work, his plays were performed throughout the world, and nearly everything he wrote gained an enthusiastic reception. There were occasional failures, such as *The Princess and the Butterfly* and the ill-advised Sir Arthur Sullivan collaboration, *The Beauty Stone*, but the successes far outnumbered the infrequent lapses. When Pinero's knighthood was announced in 1909, there were few to cavil. After all, his two most recent plays, *His House in Order* (which earned for him an astounding £50,000) and *The Thunderbolt*, were among his very best works, and the immediately following *Mid-Channel* was equally fine.

Preserving Mr. Panmure, however, was not so fine, and *The "Mind the Paint" Girl* was booed. The materials Pinero was shaping were not so very different from those he had used in the past, but he had begun to lose his craftsman's touch, and his audience's interests had begun to shift in ways he could not understand. He was becoming old-fashioned, and try as he might, he could never regain the knack for creating successful plays.

The last twenty-five years of Pinero's life were marked by a gradual decline. He wrote fewer and fewer plays, and they received less and less attention. He remained financially prosperous, but he was no longer the theatrical lion that he had once been. The death of his wife in 1919 reduced his creative energies still more, and when he died in London on November 23, 1934, it had been many years since he had experienced a theatrical triumph.

Analysis • Because of its earnest self-importance and prudish restrictiveness, Victorian England was as ripe for comic deflation as the Rome of Plautus, and few of his contemporaries were as skillful as Arthur Wing Pinero at producing subversive, farcical laughter. In the typical Pinero farce, the young and uninhibited gain the upper hand over their proper, authoritarian elders with dazzling ease. In the course of the play, the well established and the vain, the powerful and the pompous are teased and tormented until nothing remains of their cherished propriety but a sheepish grin. All of this is accomplished without rancor, however, and even the figures of fun are treated with warmhearted sympathy.

The Magistrate • In *The Magistrate*, the primary victims of comic deflation are the mock-heroically named Aeneas Posket, a stuffy but charitable police magistrate who fills his household with those convicted in his court, and his deceiving second wife, Agatha. The instigator of their discomfiture is Agatha's delightfully irresponsible son, Cis Farringdon. The unlikely premise on which the plot depends is that, out of vanity and a desire to catch a second husband, Agatha has subtracted five years from her own age and five years from that of her son, thereby convincing both Aeneas and Cis that she is thirty-one and that Cis is fourteen. As she explains to her sister Charlotte in one of Pinero's contrived expository dialogues, "If I am only thirty-one now, my boy couldn't have been born nineteen years ago, and if he could, he oughtn't to have been, because, on my own showing, I wasn't married till four years later." Because she lives in a society that has taught her that no man is likely to propose to a middle-aged woman and that no respectable woman has a child out of wedlock, Agatha has set a trap both for herself and for her unsuspecting husband.

The trap is sprung by Cis, who, despite believing himself to be fourteen, cannot help acting nineteen. He flirts with his sixteen-year-old music teacher, gambles quite skillfully, and lures his dignified stepfather, at a key moment, into a night of carousing. The carousing is made possible through Pinero's use of another of his favorite plot contrivances, the fortuitous arrival of important letters. One of these letters announces an upcoming visit by Colonel Lukyn, a friend of Agatha's first husband, who will be sure to expose Agatha's deceit unless she intercepts him. A second letter informs Agatha of the sickness of a friend, Lady Adelaide Jenkins, which gives Agatha the excuse she needs to leave the house in quest of Colonel Lukyn. A third contains an overdue bill for charges incurred by Cis and his friends at the Hotel des Princes, a bill that Cis decides to manipulate his stepfather into paying. The fourth, whose significance in Pinero's jigsaw puzzle plot becomes clear only later in the play, declares the intention of Charlotte's straitlaced, sententious fiancé, Captain Horace Vale, to break off their engagement because of the impulsive Charlotte's flirtation with another man.

What the characters are unaware of is that all of them are headed for the same place, the Hotel des Princes, where the intricately prepared comic reversal awaits them. Cis is there to get his bill paid for him and to have a good time; Aeneas is there to see his wondrous new fourteen-year-old son in his unlikely natural habitat; Colonel Lukyn is there to visit old haunts; Captain Vale is there because he knows Colonel Lukyn; Agatha is there to plead for Lukyn's silence; and Charlotte is there because Agatha is.

Pinero milks the scenes that follow for all of their humorous possibilities, and in the process, he puts his dignified characters through absurd torments. The proper Captain Vale, for example, is asked to step onto a rickety balcony during a torrential rainstorm when Agatha and Charlotte request a private meeting with the colonel. He later creeps back into the room, soaked to the skin and wearing a bedraggled, oversized hat, mistakenly handed to him by Lukyn, and hides behind a curtain. In the meantime, the colonel has peppered his speech with so many babbling asides about his poor friend on the balcony that Agatha suspects him of suffering the aftereffects of sunstroke. Nevertheless, she does win his pledge to keep her secret, and the three sit down to dinner, while the grumbling, half-starved captain acts as a disembodied waiter from behind the curtain.

After an absurd discovery scene in which Vale, visible to the audience, converses from his hiding place with the principals, Pinero begins the true humbling of his characters. As Vale and Charlotte attempt a reconciliation and as the infuriated Agatha realizes for the first time that the voices from the next room are those of her husband and her son—both of whom, like Agatha herself, have lied about their plans for the evening— the hotel is raided for serving food and drink after hours. Aeneas, the ostensible upholder of the laws, and Cis escape by leaping through a window and falling through a roof, while the magistrate's wife and her three companions are dragged off to jail.

After several hours of running from the authorities, Aeneas again becomes a figure of authority himself and prepares, as best he can, to judge the wrongdoings of others. What a shock it is, however, when he finds that the first case before him involves his wife's friend, Colonel Lukyn, and three of Lukyn's comrades. In a face-to-face interview with the colonel before the trial begins, Aeneas refuses to give special treatment to any of the four, not even the two ladies, and he exclaims, in righteous indignation, "I am listening, sir, to the guiding voice of Mrs. Posket—that newly-made wife still blushing from the embarrassment of her second marriage, and that voice says, 'Strike for the sanctity of hearth and home, for the credit of the wives of England—no mercy!'" The result is that he hears the four malefactors plead guilty to exactly the crime he himself has committed and sentences them to seven days in jail, at the very moment that his wife, who has lied about her identity, pulls back her veil.

In a play of this sort, in which self-righteousness and rigid social conventions are held up to ridicule, the appropriate conclusion is a liberating relaxation of the rules, and Pinero chooses just such a conclusion for *The Magistrate*. Mr. Bullamy, Aeneas's fellow magistrate, finds a way of skirting the letter of the law and secures the prisoners' release. The warring parties, much chastened by their experiences, are reconciled, and every concealed truth is revealed. Pinero even makes use of that most ancient symbol of reconciliation, a marriage, to bring the play to an end. Aeneas agrees to bless the upcoming union of the music teacher and Cis, who was fourteen yesterday but is nineteen today, especially if the two will accept his gift of a thousand pounds and take themselves off to Canada.

Sweet Lavender • Pinero's most successful sentimental comedy, *Sweet Lavender*, also makes use of ego deflation to bring its characters to their senses, but here laughter is less important than pathos for winning the audience's approval of the playwright's resolution of his plot. The play centers on one of the themes dealt with in *The Magistrate*, the sometimes rocky progress of love, but *Sweet Lavender* manages to explore much more dangerous ground without giving the impression of considering controversial materials. Essentially, the play asks whether one should follow the dictates of one's heart or the expectations of society when choosing a spouse; the emphatic, and unabashedly maudlin, answer is that, if it is sensitive to innocence and virtue, the heart is the better guide.

The exposition is again handled through convenient conversations, but this time with less artificiality than in *The Magistrate*. From these conversations, the audience learns that Clement Hale, a law student and the adopted son of wealthy banker Geoffrey Wedderburn, is sharing rooms with Dick Phenyl, a drunken but kindly barrister, and that Clement loves Lavender Rolt, the young daughter of housekeeper Ruth Rolt. He has not yet told Lavender of his love, and Dick Phenyl is convinced that such a declaration would destroy Clement's future. The simple, poverty-stricken young lady is an unworthy match for Clement, he argues, and Mr. Wedderburn expects Clement to marry his niece, Minnie Gilfillian. Dick himself is very familiar with poverty and failure and would hate to see his young friend ruin his own expectations.

From Lavender's first entrance, however, Pinero makes it clear that she and Clement are destined for each other and that whatever snobbishness interferes with their union is unjust and must be overcome. Barriers of rank and wealth are of no consequence when two people are as well matched as Clement and Lavender, and the audience is in perfect sympathy with the two lovers when Clement, early in the play, proposes marriage and Lavender accepts him. Their decision to marry is so obviously right that the Wedderburns and anyone who sides with them must be convinced of their error in resisting such a perfect union.

Dick Phenyl is the first to be won over. An impractical romantic himself, and for that very reason an admirable character, he quickly succumbs to the sentiment of the situation and acts as the lovers' ally. Minnie becomes a collaborator with equal ease; her love for Clement is more nearly sisterly affection than passion, and besides, she herself is too busy flouting social conventions by playing the coquette with an upstart American to worry about a lost match with Clement.

Mr. Wedderburn and his sister, Mrs. Gilfillian, are more stubborn in their interference, and it is only after both have been humbled that the marriage can occur. In one of his most extreme reversal scenes, Pinero has Wedderburn deliver an ultimatum to Clement to abandon Lavender or be cut off without a cent at the very moment when his own ruin is about to be announced. Barely has Clement reaffirmed his loyalty to Lavender and Wedderburn cursed him as a penniless fool when Dick Phenyl carries in a telegram that tells of the collapse of Mr. Wedderburn's bank. At the same instant, Ruth Rolt appears at the door, and Wedderburn stares at her in shock. He has just been using himself as an example of a man who escaped the consequences of an improvident love affair by leaving the woman he loved; that woman was Ruth.

In fact, the young lady whom Wedderburn has branded as unworthy of his stepson is Wedderburn's own daughter, and the poverty for which he despised her becomes, temporarily, his own. Mrs. Gilfillian, who performs the housekeeping tasks once taken care of by the Rolts, is also drawn down, by necessity, to the level of those whom she has scorned. Both learn respect for their erstwhile inferiors and drop all objection to Clement's marriage to Lavender. Mrs. Rolt, who had taken Lavender away out of fear that her daughter would either enter an incestuous marriage or have to be told the closely guarded secret of her illegitimacy, also relents when she discovers that Clement is an adopted son and that Mr. Wedderburn, who still loves her, will never reveal the truth. Finally, Dick Phenyl crowns the play's triumphant ending when he announces that he has it in his power to restore Mr. Wedderburn's bank to solvency. He knew of the bank's collapse because he had been informed of his unexpected inheritance of the estate of his Uncle George, all of whose money had been placed in Mr. Wedderburn's bank. By withdrawing his claim to the money, he can put the bank back on its feet. With this announcement, the play comes to its ecstatic conclusion.

Despite the play's popular success, Pinero was well aware that *Sweet Lavender* is artistically flawed. It slips perilously close to pure melodrama, and its fairy-tale ending is outrageously contrived. Shakespearean comedy contains elements as unlikely as those found here, but as many commentators have pointed out, such plays as *The Winter's Tale* (pr. c.1610-1611) and *As You Like It* (pr. c.1599-1600) make no claims to verisimilitude, whereas *Sweet Lavender* purports to be realistic. The incompatibility that exists between its real and its contrived elements hurts the play's artistic integrity.

Nevertheless, *Sweet Lavender* does contain elements of serious drama, however flawed it may be. In its contrast of happy and unhappy couples, it attempts to make a statement about male sexual irresponsibility and about the double standard that allows such irresponsibility to flourish. The victimizing male is forced to see the consequences of his insensitivity to the abandoned female, and he feels appropriately ashamed. A more idealistic male is then permitted to right the wrongs of the past by treating the virginal female with proper love and respect.

The Profligate • Such a neatly symmetrical combination of parts, however, is not often reflective of the complexities and compromises of real life. Of much deeper human interest is the use Pinero makes of the same four character types in his fascinating, but again flawed, problem play, *The Profligate*. Here, innocence is married to experience, and the virginal female to the victimizing male, while the idealistic male and the abandoned female move into and out of their lives, sometimes in troublesome ways.

Hugh Murray, a thirty-year-old solicitor, is selflessly in love with Leslie Brundenell, a naïve but charming schoolgirl. Unfortunately for Hugh, "a pale, thoughtful, resolute-looking man," Leslie has fallen in love with the gallant and worldly Dunstan Renshaw, the sort of man that Hugh himself admits to be more often successful with the ladies than men of his own kind. Leslie and Dunstan are to be married, and Hugh has agreed to be best man at their wedding, but he has second thoughts about his participation in the ceremony when Dunstan's friend Lord Dangars drops by to pick up his latest divorce decree. After all, how could the friend of such a libertine as Dangars, a friend whose past is probably as shameful as Dangars's own, behave honorably toward the innocent Miss Brundenell? Hugh will not actively interfere with the young couple's union, but he will also not help it take place.

Almost as soon as the wedding party departs, Janet Preece appears, a woman in search of her seducer. He had called himself Lawrence Kenward when he had known her in the country, but Janet is well aware that that name was as false as the man himself. She wants Hugh Murray to help her find him, and when he guesses the man's identity, he agrees.

If the audience is unfamiliar enough with Pinero's use of foreshadowing not to have discovered that Lawrence Kenward is Dunstan Renshaw, Murray makes that fact explicit during a later conversation with Renshaw. Leslie and Dunstan have been living together blissfully in an Italian villa for several weeks when Murray arrives to warn Renshaw of his danger. He has compromised his professional ethics for a month by concealing what he knows from Janet Preece, but the secret will soon be out, and for Leslie's sake, Dunstan had best be prepared.

Unfortunately, when the secret does come out, Dunstan is not the least prepared, and the results are disastrous. In a series of coincidences as unlikely as the events which bring the characters in *The Magistrate* together at the Hotel des Princes, Janet, Leslie, Dunstan, and Lord Dangars suddenly find themselves in a distressing confrontation at the Italian villa. Janet has been stranded at the villa by her former employer and has confessed her sordid past to the kindly Leslie, who has nursed her through a serious illness. Soon thereafter, Dunstan returns from a visit with Lord Dangars. Dangars has accompanied Dunstan to the villa, since Dangars's latest fiancée, who is Leslie's closest friend and the daughter of Janet's former employer, is staying there. When Janet sees the two approaching, she shouts, "It's the man—the man!" and Leslie's imagination does the rest. In order to protect her affianced friend, she prepares for Lord Dangars's unmasking and unmasks her own husband instead. Despite Dunstan's pleas for mercy, Leslie leaves him, and Dunstan commits suicide.

This summary of events seems to support the frequently enunciated interpretation of the play as an attack on the double standard, which makes its point by punishing the erring male as severely as the more conventional moral tale punishes the erring female. According to this view, then, men ought to guard their honor as diligently as women do, for who knows what the eventual consequences of sin may be? Such an interpretation undervalues the play's complexity.

First, Dunstan is not destroyed by his sin but by the moral rigidity of his wife. Dunstan has been cruel in his abandoning of Janet Preece, and it was his lust that led him astray, but he has changed since that premarital adventure and has become worthy of Leslie's love. Because of her own upbringing as an overprotected Victorian young lady, however, Leslie cannot see this and classes Dunstan with the play's one true profligate, Lord Dangars. So serious is this inability to discriminate, in fact, that, in the moment of her greatest distress over the discovery of Dunstan's past, Leslie loses the power to protect her close friend from the truly dangerous male, and Dangars escorts his reluctant fiancée from the stage. Furthermore, human sexuality is not as one-sided as Leslie assumes, and in a startling confession toward the end of the play, Janet admits to having been the sexual aggressor in her affair with Dunstan, a confession that Leslie dismisses without considering its implications. She does finally forgive Dunstan, however, and in the final scene of the play, she exhibits a sadder but deeper humanity than she possessed at the play's beginning. Unfortunately, the man to whom she speaks her forgiveness has already taken his life.

The Second Mrs. Tanqueray • The dialogue in *The Profligate* is too wooden and a number of the scenes too sensational for the play to be a fully successful work of art. In *The Second Mrs. Tanqueray*, Pinero largely solved such aesthetic problems to produce what is generally regarded as his masterpiece. The play again concerns Victorian sexual mores, and it again centers on the confrontation between innocence and experience, with innocence once more learning the lesson of tolerance and humanity too late.

In the play's opening act, which contains some of Pinero's most skillfully handled exposition and foreshadowing, Aubrey Tanqueray is bidding a tentative farewell to the friends of his single life, to whom he announces that tomorrow he will be married for the second time. The first Mrs. Tanqueray had been "one of your cold sort . . . all marble arms and black velvet." She had had no lack of Victorian respectability, but sexually, "She *was* an iceberg! As for kissing, the mere contact would have given him chapped lips." The second Mrs. Tanqueray will be different; just how different is implied by Aubrey's uncertainty that his friends will continue to socialize with him after the marriage has occurred. It is also implied by the discomfort with which he listens to the account given by his best friend, Cayley Drummle, of Sir George Orreyed's marriage to a woman of low repute. The best people will cut him dead, Cayley asserts. The man should have known better.

At the end of the act, when the men have left, the audience is introduced directly to the future Paula Tanqueray and indirectly to her pure and innocent opposite, Aubrey's daughter Ellean. Paula, who has been the mistress of many men, has arrived at an outrageously late hour to deliver a letter to Aubrey containing an account of her various sexual escapades. She wants Aubrey to enter married life with no illusions about his wife's past, but Aubrey assures her that he has no doubts about the wisdom of marrying her and gallantly burns the letter. She begs him to be sure, very sure, of what he feels; reminds him of the suicide of one of her close friends; and leaves him for the evening. He then opens a letter from his daughter, who has treated him with the same bloodless coldness as her mother had done before her, and discovers that Ellean has suddenly decided to leave the convent in which she has been educated in order to come home to her father. The potential difficulties of his decision are immediately obvious. How can such a creature of the spirit as Ellean and such a creature of the flesh as Paula be brought under the same roof without tragic results? How, in the age of Victoria, can the soul and the body be reconciled?

The confrontation between the two women develops gradually and occurs, ironically enough, after they appear to have made peace. During the first days of their acquaintance, Paula is constantly attempting to win Ellean's friendship and is constantly being treated with a maddening, dutiful politeness. Paula's self-respect is totally dependent on being accepted and understood by Aubrey's virginal daughter, a fact of which Aubrey himself is partially aware, and when that acceptance and understanding are not forthcoming, Paula lashes out at those around her. As Aubrey had feared, he and Paula have not been received into polite society, and their ostracism has intensified Paula's contradictory feelings of shame and anger. She wants very much to be an untainted woman, and despite the power of her personality, a power that sometimes suggests a Phaedra or a Hedda Gabler, she has a deep need for approval. If Ellean, the embodiment of the purity she herself had once possessed, can love her, all will be well.

For that to occur, however, each woman needs to learn something about the other's attitude toward human relationships. That reeducation takes place for Ellean when she accompanies Aubrey's friend, Mrs. Cortelyon, on a trip to Paris, a trip that Paula mistakenly assumes is intended to separate her forever from her stepdaughter. Paula's own reeducation occurs when, in retaliation for the carrying off of Ellean and in direct defiance of her husband's wishes, she invites the Orreyeds to visit. Lady Orreyed had been a close friend during their days as mistresses to the wealthy, and Paula has frequently expressed a desire to see her again.

What she sees, however, is a vulgar gold digger who has married a stupid drunkard and who seems well on her way to bankrupting him. The married Paula Tanqueray is no more like Lady Orreyed than the married Dunstan Renshaw is like Lord Dangars, but after watching Lady Orreyed in action, Paula can hardly fail to see why anyone whose situation even superficially resembles Lady Orreyed's might have difficulty winning her way into the hearts of the respectable and the well-to-do. Sexual prudery is part of the problem, but not the whole problem.

The more drastic transformation has taken place in Ellean. This cold, spiritual young lady has experienced a sexual awakening, and the drives that have determined so much of Paula's life are suddenly comprehensible to her. While in Paris, she has fallen in love. The young man is reputed to have had a wild youth, but he has since performed an act of heroism in India, and no one is more dashing and handsome. She now understands and accepts Paula, or seems to, and she kisses her in acknowledgment of their shared womanhood. At last, Paula is happy.

Then the catastrophe occurs. Ellean's sweetheart was once Paula's sweetheart, and out of a false sense of duty, Paula informs Aubrey. Aubrey forbids Ellean to see him again. Ellean guesses the reason, and her love for Paula becomes hatred. In response, Paula surrenders to the sense of worthlessness that society has tried for so long to force on her and kills herself. Ellean hears "the fall" of this fallen woman's body and runs to tell her father, crying out as she does so, "But I know—I helped to kill her. If I had only been merciful!"

The Second Mrs. Tanqueray exhibits Pinero's talents at their best, but it also suggests why Pinero is not praised today as enthusiastically as he once was. His craftsmanship is there for all to see, no matter in which literary epoch they live, but his serious social statements come through in their full power only when one is familiar with their Victorian context. His pronouncements lack the ring of lasting truth of the words of a Shakespeare or a Shaw, whatever he might have taught his Victorian (and later his Edwardian) audiences. Nevertheless, he helped to prepare the way for modern English social drama, and he perfected many of the techniques of modern popular drama, accomplishments that assure his place in British dramatic history.

Other major work

NONFICTION: *The Collected Letters of Sir Arthur Pinero*, 1974 (J. P. Wearing, editor).

Bibliography

Beerbohm, Max. *Around Theatres*. London: Rupert Hart-Davies, 1953. A collection of theater pieces by one of England's most brilliant and perceptive writers and cartoonists. Contains reviews of four Pinero plays, *The School Mistress, Iris, Letty*, and *The Notorious Mrs. Ebbsmith*, valuable precisely because Beerbohm wrote them after he succeeded George Bernard Shaw as drama critic for the *Saturday Review*.

Dawick, John. *Pinero: A Theatrical Life*. Niwot: University Press of Colorado, 1993. Dawick provides a look at Pinero's long history with the theater. Contains bibliography and index.

Griffin, Penny. *Arthur Wing Pinero and Henry Arthur Jones*. New York: St. Martin's Press, 1991. Griffin examines English drama in the late nineteenth and early twentieth centuries, focusing on a comparison of the works of Pinero and Henry Arthur Jones. Bibliography and index.

Lazenby, Walter. *Arthur Wing Pinero*. New York: Twayne, 1972. A basic look at the life and works of Pinero. Bibliography.

Shaw, G. B. *Dramatic Opinions and Essays*. 2 vols. New York: Brentano's, 1907. These reviews, published when Shaw was still a drama critic, remain the most perceptive ever written about Pinero. Despite Pinero's extraordinary popularity, Shaw exposed the conventionality of the playwright's ideas and his inability to come to grips with the situations he had created.

Smith, Leslie. *Modern British Farce: A Selective Study of British Farce from Pinero to the Present Day*. Totowa, N.J.: Barnes and Noble, 1989. Smith examines British farce, with emphasis on Pinero and his legacy. Bibliography and index.

Robert H. O'Connor,
updated by Mildred C. Kuner

Harold Pinter

Born: London, England; October 10, 1930

Principal drama • *The Room,* pr. 1957, pb. 1960 (one act); *The Birthday Party,* pr. 1958, pb. 1959; *The Dumb Waiter,* pr. 1959 (in German), pr., pb. 1960 (in English; one act); *The Caretaker,* pr., pb. 1960; *The Collection,* pr. 1961, pb. 1963; *"A Slight Ache" and Other Plays,* pb. 1961; *The Lover,* pr., pb. 1963 (one act); *The Homecoming,* pr., pb. 1965; *Tea Party,* pb. 1965, pr. 1965 (televised), pr. 1968 (staged); *The Basement,* pb. 1967, pr. 1967 (televised), pr. 1968 (staged); *Landscape,* pb. 1968, pr. 1968 (radio play), pr. 1969 (staged; one act); *Silence,* pr., pb. 1969 (one act); *Old Times,* pr., pb. 1971; *No Man's Land,* pr., pb. 1975; *Plays,* pb. 1975-1981, revised pb. 1991-1998 (4 volumes); *Betrayal,* pr., pb. 1978; *The Hothouse,* pr., pb. 1980 (wr. 1958); *Family Voices,* pr., pb. 1981; *Other Places: Three Plays,* pr., pb. 1982 (includes *Family Voices, Victoria Station,* and *A Kind of Alaska;* revised in 1984, includes *One for the Road* and deletes *Family Voices*); *Mountain Language,* pr., pb. 1988; *The New World Order,* pr. 1991; *Party Time,* pr., pb. 1991; *Moonlight,* pr., pb. 1993; *Ashes to Ashes,* pb. 1996; *The Dwarfs and Nine Revue Sketches,* pb. 1999; *Celebration,* pr., pb. 2000; *Remembrance of Things Past,* pr., pb. 2000 (with Di Trevis; adaptation of Marcel Proust's novel); *Press Conference,* pr., pb. 2002 (sketch)

Other literary forms • In addition to his works for the stage, Harold Pinter has published poetry and a few short stories in magazines. Early in his writing career, he contributed poems to *Poetry London* under the pseudonym Harold Pinta. He has written a number of radio plays as well as screenplays adapted from his own works and those of other writers. In 1972, Pinter was approached by Joseph Losey, who had directed the films made from Pinter's screenplays *The Servant* (1963), *Accident* (1967), and *The Go-Between* (1971), with the idea of adapting Marcel Proust's *À la recherche du temps perdu* (1913-1927; *Remembrance of Things Past,* 1922-1931, 1981) for the screen. The task of turning Proust's monumental seven-volume novel into a workable screenplay was daunting, and although the screenplay was published in 1977, the film was never made. However, Pinter has written that the time devoted to the Proust project was the best working year of his life. Three collections of Pinter's screenplays were published in 2000, and a collection of his prose and poetry, *Various Voices: Prose, Poetry, Politics, 1948-1998,* was published in 1998.

Achievements • Harold Pinter has won many awards, including the *Evening Standard* Award (1960, for *The Caretaker*), the Italia Prize (1963, for the television version of *The Lover*), the British Film Academy Award (1965, for *The Pumpkin Eater*), and the Commonwealth Award (1981). He has a long list of honorary degrees, and he was elected an Honorary Fellow in the Modern Language Association in 1970. Pinter has also been decorated by his government: He was named a Commander of the Order of the British Empire (CBE) in 1966 and a Companion of Honour in 2002.

Biography • Harold Pinter was born October 10, 1930, in England, the son of a hard-working Jewish tailor whose business eventually failed. Pinter grew up in a rundown working-class area, full of railroad yards and bad-smelling factories. When World

(R. Jones)

War II broke out in 1939, Pinter, like most London children, was evacuated to the countryside to be safe from the German bombing. Living in the countryside or by the sea
was not, for Pinter, as idyllic as it might have been: "I was quite a morose little boy." He
returned to London before the end of the war and remembers seeing V-2 rockets flying
overhead and his backyard in flames. After the war ended, the violence did not cease;
anti-Semitism was strong in his neighborhood, and Jews were frequently threatened.
Perhaps these early brushes with war and violence decided him; when he was eighteen
and eligible for National Service, he declared himself a conscientious objector. He was
afraid he would be jailed, but in fact, he was merely fined. In grammar school, he was a
sprinter and set a record for the hundred-yard dash. He was also an actor in school
plays, playing Macbeth and Romeo, and he received a grant in 1948 to study acting at
the Royal Academy of Dramatic Art.

Pinter did not stay at the Academy long, however, and spent the next year tramping
the streets. He published a few poems in literary magazines (he was only nineteen
when the first were published) and got an acting job with a Shakespearean company
touring Ireland; other acting jobs followed. He met the actress Vivien Merchant and
married her in 1956; she was to perform in a number of his plays. They were divorced
in 1980, and in November of that year Pinter married Lady Antonia Fraser, a highly regarded writer of historical biographies and one of England's great beauties. The match
of the famous, working-class playwright and the beautiful, aristocratic biographer was
the object of much attention in London literary circles and in the popular press. Pinter
had one son, Daniel, from his first marriage.

In 1957, a friend of Pinter who was studying directing at Bristol University told him
he needed a play, and Pinter wrote *The Room* for him in four afternoons. The play was
performed and was favorably reviewed by Harold Hobson in the *Sunday Times*. Pinter
seemed to have found himself. Immediately after writing *The Room*, he wrote *The Birthday Party* and *The Dumb Waiter*. The plays were performed, and though Hobson continued to champion him, many drama critics gave the plays scathing reviews. *The Birthday
Party* closed after a week. In the following years, though Pinter's plays continued to be

attacked, they also continued to be revived and performed, and his work began to receive considerable critical attention. After his play *The Caretaker* became his first commercial success, Pinter emerged as a productive and versatile writer for stage and screen, as well as a political activist and spokesperson for the arts in general.

In 1989, he came to the United States to direct his play *Mountain Language*. Directing his own and others' work and acting in such touring shows as *Old Times* (with Liv Ullmann, in 1986), he was to become very well respected in the theater community. His film work includes, in addition to adaptations of his plays, *The Handmaid's Tale* (1990; adapted from Margaret Atwood's novel), *The Heat of the Day* (1990; based on Elizabeth Bowen's novel), and original works such as *Reunion* (1989).

Politically and culturally, Pinter protested the imprisonment of writers through his activities with the International Association of Poets, Playwrights, Editors, Essayists, and Novelists (PEN Club), donated proceeds to Václav Havel, protested against the Margaret Thatcher government in Great Britain and U.S. involvement in Central and South America, founded the Arts for Nicaragua Fund, delivered a speech by Salman Rushdie while the writer was in hiding, and raised funds for famine relief in Ethiopia. In 1990, he organized a celebration in honor of Samuel Beckett at the National Theatre. During the 1990's, Pinter became less active as a playwright.

Analysis • Harold Pinter is sometimes associated with the generation of British playwrights who emerged in the 1950's and are known as the Angry Young Men. His first plays, with their dingy, working-class settings and surface naturalism, seemed to link Pinter with this group, but only the surface of his plays is naturalistic; most of a Pinter play takes place beneath the surface. His closest affinities are with a more centrally important movement, the Theater of the Absurd. As a young man, before he started writing plays, the works of Franz Kafka and Samuel Beckett made a great impression on Pinter. Like Kafka, Pinter portrays the absurdity of human existence with a loving attention to detail that creates the deceptive naturalism of his surfaces.

It is particularly with the meticulously rendered, tape-recorder-accurate language of his characters that Pinter pulls the naturalistic and absurdist strands of his drama all together. The language of his characters, bumbling, repetitive, circular, is actually more realistic—more like actual human speech—than the precise and rhetorically patterned dialogue found in what is considered to be "realistic" drama. Yet that actual language of human beings, when isolated on the stage, underlines the absurdity of human aspirations and becomes both wonderfully comic and pathetic as it marks the stages of human beings' inability to communicate what is most important to them. Pinter, however, is more than an accurate recorder of speech; he is also a poet. The language of his characters, for all of their inarticulateness, is finally profoundly communicative of the human condition. What makes Pinter one of the most important modern British dramatists is his consummate skill as a dramatist; the fact that in language and pattern he is a poet, especially a poet of contemporary language, both its spoken expression and its expressive silences; and his existential insight into human beings' place in the universe, which connects him with the most profound writers and thinkers of his time.

The Room • Pinter's first play, *The Room*, contained a number of features that were to become his hallmarks. The play is set in a single small room, the characters warm and secure within but threatened by cold and death from without. *The Room* is overtly symbolic, more so than Pinter's later work, but the setting and characters are, for the most part, realistic. Rose sits in the cheap flat making endless cups of tea, wrapping a muffler around her man before she lets him go out into the cold; her husband, Bert, drives a van. Under the naturalistic veneer, however, the play has a murky, almost expression- istic atmosphere. The room is Rose's living space on earth. If she stays within, she is warm and safe. Outside, it is so cold it is "murder," she says. She opens the door, and there, waiting to come in, is the new generation, a young couple named Mr. and Mrs. Sands (the sands of time? Mr. Sands's name is Tod, which in German means "death"). They are looking for an apartment and have heard that Rose's apartment is empty. "This room is occupied," she insists, obviously upset at this premonition of her depar- ture. A man has been staying in the basement. She imagines it to be wet and cold there, a place where no one would stand much of a chance. The man wants to see her.

Again the door opens, to reveal a terrifying intruder from the outside. He comes in. He is a black man—the color of death—and he is blind, tapping in with his stick, blind as death is when claiming its victims from the ranks of the good or the bad. "Your fa- ther wants you to come home," he tells her. Rose's husband comes in at this moment, shrieks "Lice!" and immediately attacks the man, tipping him out of his chair and kick- ing him in the head until he is motionless. On the naturalistic level of the play, the ac- tion seems motivated by racist hatred, perhaps, but at the symbolic level, Bert seems to have recognized death and instinctively engages it in battle, as later Pinter characters kick out violently against their fate. It is, however, to no avail: Rose has been struck blind, already infected by her approaching death.

While this summary stresses the symbolic dimension of the play, it is Pinter's genius to achieve such symbolic resonance at the same time that he maintains an eerily natu- ralistic surface—although less so in this first play than in later plays. Critics have ob- jected to the heavy-handedness, the overt symbolism, of the blind black man, and characters with similar roles in later plays are more subtly drawn.

The Birthday Party • *The Birthday Party* was Pinter's first full-length play; in effect, it is a much fuller and more skillful working out of the elements already present in *The Room*. The scene once more is restricted to a single room, the dining room of a seedy seaside guesthouse. Meg, the landlady, and Petey, her husband, who has a menial job outside the hotel, resemble Rose and her husband of *The Room*. Meg is especially like Rose in her suffocating motherliness. In this play, however, she is no longer the main character. That role has been taken by Stanley, the only boarder of the house, who has been there for a year. He is pinned to the house, afraid to go out, feeling that intruders from outside are menacing bringers of death. Although he is in his late thirties, he is be- ing kept by Meg as a spoiled little boy. He sleeps late in the morning, and when he co- mes down to breakfast, he complains querulously about everything she fixes for him. He is unshaven and unwashed, still wearing his pajamas.

What is enacted symbolically by Stan's refusal to leave the house is his fear of going out and engaging life, his fear that an acceptance of life—meaning going outside, hav- ing a job, having normal sexual relations with a woman his age—would also mean ac- cepting his eventual death. He is refusing to live in an absurd world that exacts so high a price for life. It is an untenable position, and his refusal to live as an adult human be- ing has left him a wrinkled and aging child. Further, it does him no good to remain in the house: If he does not go out into the world, the world will come in to him. In fact, he hears that two men have come to town and that they are going to stay at the guest- house. He knows at once that they have come for him and is thrown into a panic. In the meantime, Meg decides that it is his birthday and gives him a present. The unintentionally chilling reminder of his aging is cut across by the present itself, a child's toy drum, which Stan begins beating frenziedly as the first act ends.

The symbolic action, though more complex, resembles that of *The Room*: What is new is the much finer texture of the realistic surface of the play. The relationship between Stan and his surrogate mother, Meg, beautifully handled, is both comic and sad—comic because it is ridiculous for this nearly middle-aged man to be mothered so excessively and to behave so much like a spoiled child; sad because one believes in both Meg and Stan as human beings. Both comedy and pathos, realism and symbolic undercurrents, grow out of the fully developed language of the dialogue. Its richness, its circumlocution—all elements that have come to be called "Pinteresque"—are evident even in this early play.

It is obvious that the two men who come, Goldberg and McCann, have indeed come for Stan. There is no concealment between them and Stan. He is rude to them and tries to order them out. They make it equally clear to him that he is not to leave the premises. McCann is gloomy and taciturn; Goldberg, the senior partner, is glib and falsely jovial. His language is a wonderfully comic—and sinister—blend of politicians' clichés, shallow philosophy, and gangster argot. There is a brilliant scene when they first confront Stan, cross-examining him with a dizzying landslide of insane questions ("Why did you kill your wife? . . . Why did you never get married? . . . Why do you pick your nose?") that finally leaves him screaming, and he kicks Goldberg in the stomach, just as the husband in *The Room* kicks the blind black man. It is too late, however, for they have already taken his glasses, and he has had his first taste of the blindness of death.

Meg comes in, and they stop scuffling, the two henchmen putting on a show of joviality. They begin to have a birthday party for Stan. Lulu, a pretty but rather vulgar young woman, is invited. Lulu in the past has frequently invited Stan to go outside walking with her, but he has refused. She and Goldberg hit it off together, and she ends up in his lap kissing him as everyone at the party drinks heavily. They begin a drunken game of blindman's buff—"If you're touched, then you're blind"—and the recurring image of blindness serves as a foretaste of death. McCann, wearing the blindfold, comes over and touches Stan, so that it is Stan's turn to be "blind." To make sure, McCann breaks Stan's glasses. The drunken Stan stumbles over to Meg and suddenly begins strangling her. They rush over to stop him, and suddenly the power goes out. In the darkness, Stan rushes around, avoiding them, giggling. The terrified Lulu faints, and when someone briefly turns on a flashlight, the audience sees that Stan has Lulu spread-eagled on the table and is on top of her.

With his mortality approaching him anyway, then, Stan, buoyed up by drink, makes a desperate effort to get out of the house, out of his entrapment in sterile childhood. He struggles to strangle the mother who is suffocating him and to have a sexual relationship with an appropriate female—a taste of the life he has denied himself in order to escape paying the debt, death. It is too late. In the morning, a nearly catatonic Stan is brought downstairs by the two henchmen. He has been washed and shaved and dressed in a suit, as if for burial. A black limousine waits outside the door. Petey, Meg's husband, makes a halfhearted attempt to save Stan from the henchmen, but to still his protests, they need only invite him to come along. One is reminded of the medieval morality play *Everyman*. When Death is carrying off Everyman, Everyman's friends and family promise to be true to him and help him in any way, but the moment they are invited to come with him, they find some excuse to stay behind.

The play in some ways points one back to other possible intentions in *The Room*.

Perhaps Rose, like Stan, has denied life. Afraid to go out in the cold, she does not escape having the cold come in after her. What she has lost is the pleasure she might have had in actively engaging life. Her husband, for example, comes home after a cold, wintry day out driving his van and talks with almost sexual relish about the pleasure he has had in masterfully controlling his van through all the dangers of his route.

The Dumb Waiter • *The Dumb Waiter* has much in common with *The Room* and *The Birthday Party*. Again, the setting is a single room in which the characters sit, nervously waiting for an ominous presence from the outside. The two characters are a pair of assassins, sent from place to place, job to job, to kill people. They are, then, rather like McCann and Goldberg of *The Birthday Party*. What is interesting is that the cast of *The Birthday Party* has been collapsed into only these two, for they are not only the killers who come from outside, they are also the victims who wait nervously inside. While they wait in an anonymous room for their final directions on their new job, a job in which everything begins to go wrong, they pass the time by talking. The conversation ranges from reports of what one character is reading in the paper to discussions of how to prepare their tea, but in this oblique fashion it begins circling around to much more pressing speculations on the nature of their lives, questions with which these semiliterate thugs are poorly equipped to deal. The dialogue is quite comical at first, the verbal sparring between the two Cockneys handled with Pinter's customary assurance, but the play is also witty in a more intellectual, allusive manner.

In the opening scene, a number of direct allusions are made to Beckett's play, *En attendant Godot* (pb. 1952, pr. 1953; *Waiting for Godot*, 1954). There is, for example, a great deal of comic business made over putting on and taking off shoes and shaking things out of them, and at one point a character walks to the apron, looks over the audience, and says, "I wouldn't like to live in this dump." Ben and Gus (like Didi and Gogo) are waiting, with varying amounts of patience and impatience, for the arrival of a mysterious presence to reveal the meaning of things to them—the person who makes all the arrangements and sends them out on their jobs. Also Beckettian is the way an entire life is described in the most minimal terms: "I mean, you come into a place when it's still dark, you come into a room you've never seen before, you sleep all day, you do your job, and then you go away in the night."

These parallels are intentional: *The Dumb Waiter* is Pinter's urban, Cockney version of *Waiting for Godot*. In *Waiting for Godot*, there was at least a tree; here, there is only a squalid room, with no windows, in the basement of an old restaurant. The two characters do not have any intellectual or poetic aspirations, as do the two characters representing humankind in Beckett's play. In Beckett's play, Godot's name suggests at least a remnant of belief in a benevolent, loving God—if only by parody. *The Dumb Waiter* lacks even such a remnant. The name of Gus and Ben's boss, Wilson, is deliberately lacking in any allegorical resonance. Further, Wilson is depicted as being increasingly arbitrary in his treatment of them, even though they have been faithful and pride themselves on their reliability. If God exists in this contemporary world, he is God as a fascist.

Early in the play, mysteriously, an envelope slides under the outside door. It contains twelve matches. Is a benevolent power giving them fire, the great civilizing agent, to help them stave off chaos? They use the matches to light a fire under their kettle, but a moment later, the gas fails, and they have no tea. It is not benevolence, but the power of chance, which rules their absurd world, as soon becomes manifest. There is a dumb-waiter in the room. A tray comes down to them from upstairs. They open the dumbwaiter and take it out. There is a message, ordering an elaborate meal. They do not know what to do, and a moment later the tray goes back upstairs. They are quite worried. When it comes down again, ordering an even more elaborate meal, they desperately fill it with everything they have—biscuits, tea, potato chips. A message comes down telling them that it is not good enough.

Earlier in the play, Ben had read to Gus items from the newspaper, accounts of bizarre accidents and killings, and they had been astounded that such things could go on. The popular press represented their access—from their safe room—to the absurd goings-on in the arbitrary world outside. They try to go back to remarking on the news items now, but they are no longer really interested in the news from outside, because now the absurd has invaded their safe room. They have passed all of their tests, they have been reliable and faithful on the job—yet absurdity is still with them. Their good behavior has not, after all, been able to save them. Ben, the senior partner, falls back on what has been successful for him before: He follows instructions more and more rigidly, becoming increasingly punctilious over the least detail of formal instructions. Gus, who from the beginning has shown himself to be more sensitive, reacts in a quite different way. He begins questioning the absurdity; he begins, to Ben's horror, to question authority.

Gus's first questions have to do with his job. He does not have the luxury of being a guiltless victim, such as the two tramps in *Waiting for Godot*. He lives in his modern society by being a part of its violence. Others die that he may live and hold his place in the world. This has already been bothering him, and when he finds out that on top of his burden of guilt, he will not even be treated fairly by authority, he begins to rebel; he criticizes Ben, his superior, and even shouts angrily up the dumbwaiter shaft. He wanders off stage left to get a glass of water. Then Ben is notified by the authority that the person he is to kill is coming in the door at stage right (to the audience's left). He shouts for Gus, his partner, to come help him.

The door at stage right flies open. Ben levels his revolver. It is Gus, thrust in, his coat and tie and revolver stripped from him, to stand there, stooped and awkward; he slowly looks up to meet Ben's eyes. The play ends there, but it is clear that Ben, who, faced with absurdity, reacts by following orders all the more unquestioningly, will shoot his partner. He will be the ostensible winner, the survivor, although in an absurd world, what can really be won? He will in the end be nothing. When Gus spoke earlier about coming in at night, doing a job, and leaving at night—a realistic statement but also a metaphor of a human being's life—he went on to say that he wanted a window, a bit of a view, before he left. His perceptions of absurdity and guilt, a first step toward moral choice, constitute his bit of a view, his wresting of some meaning out of life.

The Caretaker · *The Caretaker*, generally considered to be Pinter's greatest play, is in many ways an even more complex permutation of the elements that were developed in his first few plays. Though *The Caretaker* is much more realistic on the surface than the earlier plays and has much less overt violence, it retains its tie with absurdist theater in the fact that it readily lends itself to allegorical interpretation. The setting, again, is a single room, and once more, it is made clear that at least a degree of security exists within the room, and that outside, in the endlessly rainy weather, there is little chance for survival. Davies, the old tramp, is the man struggling to stay in the room, but he is ultimately thrown out to his destruction. The two young men, the brothers Aston and Mick, though in much more subtle and complex ways, occupy the role of the killers. It is they who throw Davies out.

The setting is a run-down room in an old house, with a leaky roof and piles of miscellaneous junk stacked everywhere. As the scene opens, Mick, the younger brother, is scrutinizing the room. He hears a door slam and voices offstage, and he quietly exits. Aston, the older brother, enters. He has brought Davies, the old tramp, along. It is revealed that Aston had found him in a fight, had saved him from a bad beating, and is now taking him into his house and giving him a place to sleep. Davies is the worst kind of garrulous old man, puffed up with self-importance, constantly justifying himself, and running down everyone else, especially blacks and aliens. Aston seems kindly, ingenuous, almost a bit simple. Davies, who is wearing old sandals, says he needs shoes. Aston immediately rummages through his things and brings out a solid pair of shoes to give him. Davies regards them very critically and rejects them as too narrow, throwing them aside.

In a nice bit of theatercraft on Pinter's part, the audience initially tends to see the play from the kindly Aston's point of view and wonders why he has taken in this tiresome and ungrateful old bum. Very shortly, however, as Aston begins to act more strangely and as his brother Mick shows his own erratic and unpredictable behavior, the audience slowly realizes that it is seeing the play from Davies' point of view—that Davies, disagreeable as he is, is Everyman.

Davies, who is shabby and bad-smelling, continues truculently to insist on his personal worth. He evidently does this no matter what the cost. He lost his job, which he sorely needed, and got in the fight, which might have killed him, because he was asked to carry out a bucket of slops when he had been hired to sweep up. He also values himself for not being a black or an alien and therefore, he believes, having a higher place in the scheme of things. He is rude and choosy when Aston offers him gifts. Obviously, however, these are all pathetic attempts by a man with nothing to preserve but a certain dignity. When Aston goes out the next morning, Davies is incredulous that Aston lets him remain behind, actually trusting him in the room alone. In other words, Davies knows that his position is low, but he desperately wants to keep it above the very bottom. It is all he has left.

Aston, though apparently kindly, is very strange. He goes out every day and buys more worthless junk to pile up in the room. He is constantly tinkering with electric appliances, though obviously without a clue as to how to fix them. He plans eventually to fix up the room but obviously, from day to day, is accomplishing nothing. When he leaves, Mick comes in. If Aston is slow in everything he does, Mick is dazzlingly quick. He deluges Davies with torrents of language, holds Davies completely in his power, and torments him with words—threats alternating with attractive-sounding offers. It is his house, it turns out, in which Aston merely lives. Both Mick and Aston, at different times, offer Davies the job of being caretaker of the house. The offer is tempting.

Davies keeps saying he needs shoes so he can get down to Sidcup and pick up his papers and get his life sorted out. Yet as he refuses offers of shoes, it becomes clear that he does not want to go; he wants to remain in this room, which, for all of its shortcomings, is at least out of the rain. One night, in a long monologue, the usually taciturn Aston tells Davies about the time he was committed to an asylum and given shock treatment. Davies, who knows that he is himself near the bottom, only marginally above the blacks, now decides that, being sane, he is also above Aston. Although Aston has befriended him and put him up, and Mick has only offered him extravagant promises, Davies decides he will be Mick's man and perhaps work to ease out Aston.

Aston has been waking Davies up in the middle of the night, complaining that his muttering and groaning make it impossible to sleep. Davies is fed up with this treatment, and the next time Aston wakes him up, Davies explodes and tells him that he is crazy and should go back to the asylum, and that he, Davies, and Mick will start running things—perhaps Aston had better leave. It is a typical outburst from Davies, overstepping himself, but he relies on Mick—though Mick has been erratic and unpredictable in the past—to back him up. At this point, Aston tells Davies that he had better look for a place somewhere else, and Davies is forced to leave. Davies comes back the next day to the room when only Mick is there, but Mick turns on him savagely, and Davies realizes he has been had. Aston comes in, and Mick exits. All Davies' truculence is gone, and he begs Aston to take him back, but Aston ignores him, and it is clear that Davies must depart.

The play is moving enough only on its surface, by turns comic, ominous, perhaps even approaching the tragic. It does not remain at the surface, however, but pushes toward allegorical interpretation. There are many possible readings of the play, none of which necessarily excludes the others. Martin Esslin, in *The Peopled Wound: The Work of Harold Pinter* (1970), sees the play as an Oedipal confrontation: The father lords it over the sons while he has the power, but when he gets too old to defend himself, their covert antagonism against him comes to the surface, and they destroy him, throwing out the old generation so that the new generation has room in which to live. An even older archetype, however, might fit the play more closely. A kindly God puts together a world for man and invites him to come live in it. Man, rather than being grateful, as he ought, becomes puffed up with self-importance and lets a tempting Satan (Mick) convince him that he, humankind, is the equal of God; as a result, he is thrown out of his paradise. Pinter has updated his allegory. It is a rather trashy and rundown paradise, a Cockney paradise in a London slum.

Obviously, the temptation and fall, the ejection from paradise, is a pattern that can be read into many stories. There is evidence in the text, however, that Pinter intended this particular reading. Aston is referred to in terms that would suggest such an interpretation. "There was someone walking about on the roof the other night," Davies says. "It must have been him." Aston is the giver of all necessary things—a roof, money, bread. When Davies wakes in the morning, he is startled to find that Aston is sitting smiling at him. Davies, characteristically, immediately begins complaining that Aston's gifts are not enough. Aston gives him bread but no knife with which to cut it (reminiscent of Wilson, in *The Dumb Waiter*, sending the two men matches to light the stove but providing no gas for the stove); gives him shoes with unmatching shoelaces; and does not give him a clock.

Aston's curious life history suggests an identification with Christ. He tells Davies that he used to talk to everyone, and he thought they listened, and that it was all right. He used to have hallucinations, in which he would see everything very clearly. When he had something to say, he would tell the others, but some lie got spread about him, and they took him away, and gave him shock treatment (the Crucifixion?), after which he was no longer able to work or get his thoughts together. After his long confessional monologue to Davies, Aston seldom speaks to him again, and Davies feels deserted. In suggestive words, Davies says: "Christ! That bastard, he ain't even listening to me!" By this time, Davies has also deserted Aston. He listens to Mick, forgetting Mick's previous bad treatment of him and forgetting Aston's many kindnesses to him.

It is a hopeless situation for Davies, because Aston does indeed seem feckless and unstable; Mick seems to own the world now, and in a world of increasing absurdity, Davies has to make his decision, has to struggle for survival and some sort of existential sense of personal value. In the final scene before Davies' expulsion, Mick and Aston meet briefly and smile faintly, and there is almost, for the moment, the hint of collusion between them, as if God and the Devil worked in concert to destroy humankind, as if, working together, they were indeed the two hit men sent out to annihilate humankind after human beings' brief sojourn in an absurd world.

The Caretaker carries to full maturity the themes and techniques that Pinter first adumbrated in *The Room* and developed over his next few plays. With its characters, its allegory, and its brilliant language and stagecraft, it is a quintessentially Pinteresque play, the perfection of all he was feeling his way toward as a playwright. Thereafter, he had to change direction if he were going to avoid merely imitating himself. He felt increasingly that he "couldn't any longer stay in the room with this bunch of people who opened doors and came in and went out." He changed his milieu, writing plays with middle-class characters, leaving behind the Cockney language of the first plays but demonstrating that he had just as accurate an ear for the absurdities and banalities of middle-class speech and could hear just as clearly what was trying to be said under the affectations of its language.

The Homecoming • *The Homecoming*, perhaps the most Kafkaesque of Pinter's plays, firmly established his dramatic idiom as unique. In the play, a professor who has been teaching in the United States returns to his London home so that his wife might meet his father and his brothers. He is greeted with oblique suggestions of enmity and sexual overtures toward his wife. In the end, the detached professor (like so many of Kafka's passive protagonists) acquiesces when his wife announces her decision to move in with the father and the two brothers.

Later plays • With plays such as *Landscape* and *Silence*, Pinter began working with more lyrical language. In *One for the Road, Mountain Language*, and *The New World Order*, Pinter began writing overtly political works that reflected his growing activism as a self-styled "citizen of the world." In each new direction he has taken, he has continued to show that the essence of Pinter is not one or another easily imitated mannerism, but rather his poetic brilliance with language, his flawless stagecraft, and his insights into the human condition.

In February, 2002, nine of Pinter's sketches, none longer than ten minutes, were performed at the Lyttleton Theatre. Seven dated from around 1959, but "Tess" was two years old, and "Press Conference" was new. "Tess" is a slight work featuring a smiling lady from a comically disreputable upper-crust family. In "Press Conference," Pinter himself (battling cancer and chemotherapy) played the lead, a Minister of Culture who was recently head of the secret police. This sketch reveals the same skepticism of, even hostility toward, supposedly democratic governments as reflected in *One for the Road* and *Ashes to Ashes*. During the press conference, the urbane Minister blandly announces what his response will be to those people who resist the free market. Their women will be raped, and their children will be killed or abducted. Dissent will not be tolerated. The journalists greet the Minister's program with chuckles and applause. In the latter part of his career, Pinter appears to draw little distinction between governments of the capitalistic West and brutal dictatorships elsewhere in the world.

Other major works

LONG FICTION: *The Dwarfs*, 1990.

POETRY: *Poems*, 1968 (Alan Clodd, editor); *I Know the Place*, 1979; *Ten Early Poems*, 1992.

SCREENPLAYS: *The Servant*, 1963; *The Guest*, 1964; *The Pumpkin Eater*, 1964; *The Quiller Memorandum*, 1966 (adaptation of Adam Hall's novel); *Accident*, 1967; *The Birthday Party*, 1968 (adaptation of his play); *The Go-between*, 1971; *The Homecoming*, 1971 (adaptation of his play); *The Last Tycoon*, 1976 (adaptation of F. Scott Fitzgerald's novel); *Proust: A Screenplay*, 1977; *The French Lieutenant's Woman*, 1981 (adaptation of John Fowles's novel); *Betrayal*, 1983 (adaptation of his play); *Turtle Diary*, 1985; *Reunion*, 1989; *The Handmaid's Tale*, 1990 (adaptation of Margaret Atwood's novel); *The Heat of the Day*, 1990 (adaptation of Elizabeth Bowen's novel); *The Comfort of Strangers*, 1991; *Party Time*, 1991 (adaptation of his play); *The Remains of the Day*, 1991 (adaptation of Kazuo Ishiguro's novel); *The Trial*, 1992 (adaptation of Franz Kafka's novel); *Collected Screenplays*, 2000 (3 volumes).

NONFICTION: *Pinter at Sixty*, 1993; *Conversations with Pinter*, 1996.

EDITED TEXT: *One Hundred Poems by One Hundred Poets*, 1991 (with Geoffrey Godbert and Anthony Astbury).

MISCELLANEOUS: *Various Voices: Prose, Poetry, Politics, 1948-1998*, 1998.

Bibliography

Billington, Michael. *The Life and Work of Harold Pinter*. New York: Faber and Faber, 2001. This 432-page update of a 1997 study covers the life of Pinter and provides critical analysis of his major works.

Burkman, Katherine H. *The Dramatic World of Harold Pinter: Its Basis in Ritual*. Columbus: Ohio State University Press, 1971. A fairly early study dealing with mythic structures in the stylized staging of Pinter's work, especially *The Birthday Party* (viewed as an agon) and *The Caretaker*, "a poignant portrayal of man's self-destructive nature, his seeming compulsion to live his life in the image of the cruel ritual of the priesthood of Nemi." Bibliography and index.

Dukore, Bernard F. *Harold Pinter*. 2d ed. London: Macmillan, 1988. An updating of Dukore's earlier 1982 work, this study serves as a condensation of the essential critical vision: the sense of menace, the acknowledgment of the absurd, struggles with realism, the nature of power, and the place of memory. Notes Pinter's "minimalist theorizing." Bibliography; index of proper names and play titles.

Gale, Steven H. *Butter's Going Up: A Critical Analysis of Harold Pinter's Work*. Durham, N.C.: Duke University Press, 1977. After a brief biographical chapter, Gale examines "the comedies of menace," a group of Pinter's plays that "collectively . . . defines the themes and establishes the techniques which will be basic in all of his works." Following chapters analyze the metaphor of "the room" and sum up Pinter's writing patterns over a long and varied career. Contains lists of first performances, casts and directors, productions directed by Pinter, and several other valuable appendices. Strong chronology, annotated bibliography (including select reviews), and index.

Gordon, Lois, ed. *Harold Pinter: A Casebook*. New York: Garland, 1990. Honoring Pinter on his sixtieth birthday, this collection of insightful essays is a good source for later plays and revisionist criticism on earlier plays. Best is Gordon's "observation," full of contemporary information, of Pinter's 1989 visit to the United States, where the playwright came to stage *Mountain Language*, among other projects. Appendix of photographs from Pauline Flanagan's collection, select bibliography, and valuable index to all articles.

Gussow, Mel. *Conversations with Pinter*. New York: Grove/Atlantic, 1996. The playwright discusses his technique and aesthetic.

Merritt, Susan Hollis. *Pinter in Play: Critical Strategies and the Plays of Harold Pinter.* Durham, N.C.: Duke University Press, 1990. Centering her discussion on "criticism as strategy" and comparing criticism to "playing" in Pinter's work, Merritt puts a postmodern twist to her study. Divided into "Perspectives on Pinter's Critical Evolution," "Some Strategies of Pinter Critics," and "Social Relations of Critical and Cultural Change," this work is a major statement, sophisticated and astute. Supplemented by a list of works cited and an index.

Morrison, Kristin. *Canters and Chronicles: The Use of Narrative in the Plays of Samuel Beckett and Harold Pinter.* Chicago: University of Chicago Press, 1996. Compares narrative movement and, especially, Pinter's absurdist approach to dialogue with that of his early idol.

Quigley, Austin E. *The Pinter Problem.* Princeton, N.J.: Princeton University Press, 1975. This early study of Pinter's "problems of identity, illusion, menace, and verification" is the first to examine the contradiction between the concrete and the abstract approaches to understanding Pinter's work, up to *Landscape.* Bibliography and index of proper names only.

Thompson, David T. *Pinter: The Player's Playwright.* New York: Schocken Books, 1985. Taking a performance approach, and starting from Pinter's own acting career, this short but information-packed work helps get the plays off the page and onto the stage. Subtleties of movement and dialogue, and Pinter's concentration on "the positioning of characters" in the stage picture, are well discussed, with theatrical examples throughout. Claims more attention should be paid to stage directions. Includes a list of plays acted by Pinter in the 1950's and a good index.

Norman Lavers, updated by Thomas J. Taylor
and Patrick Adcock

Luigi Pirandello

Born: Girgenti (now Agrigento), Sicily, Italy; June 28, 1867
Died: Rome, Italy; December 10, 1936

Principal drama • *La morsa*, pb. as *L'epilogo*, 1898, pr. 1910 (*The Vise*, 1928); *Scamandro*, pb. 1909, pr. 1928; *Lumìe di Sicilia*, pr. 1910, pb. 1911 (*Sicilian Limes*, 1921); *Il dovere del medico*, pb. 1912, pr. 1913 (*The Doctor's Duty*, 1928); *Se non così . . .*, pr. 1915, pb. 1916; *All'uscita*, pr. 1916, pb. 1922 (*At the Gate*, 1928); *Liolà*, pr. 1916, pb. 1917 (English translation, 1952); *Pensaci, Giacomino!*, pr. 1916, pb. 1917; *Il berretto a sonagli*, pr. 1917, pb. 1920 (*Cap and Bells*, 1957); *Così è (se vi pare)*, pr. 1917, pb. 1918 (*Right You Are [If You Think So]*, 1922); *La giara*, pr. 1917, pb. 1925 (*The Jar*, 1928); *Il piacere dell'onestà*, pr. 1917, pb. 1918 (*The Pleasure of Honesty*, 1923); *Il giuoco delle parti*, pr. 1918, pb. 1919 (*The Rules of the Game*, 1959); *Ma non è una cosa seria*, pr. 1918, pb. 1919; *La patente*, pb. 1918, pr. 1919 (*The License*, 1964); *L'innesto*, pr. 1919, pb. 1921; *L'uomo, la bestia, e la virtù*, pr., pb. 1919 (*Man, Beast, and Virtue*, 1989); *Come prima, meglio di prima*, pr. 1920, pb. 1921; *La Signora Morli, una e due*, pr. 1920, pb. 1922; *Tutto per bene*, pr., pb. 1920 (*All for the Best*, 1960); *Sei personaggi in cerca d'autore*, pr., pb. 1921 (*Six Characters in Search of an Author*, 1922); *Enrico IV*, pr., pb. 1922 (*Henry IV*, 1923); *L'imbecille*, pr. 1922, pb. 1926 (*The Imbecile*, 1928); *Vestire gli ignudi*, pr. 1922, pb. 1923 (*Naked*, 1924); *L'altro figlio*, pr. 1923, pb. 1925 (*The House with the Column*, 1928); *L'uomo dal fiore in bocca*, pr. 1923, pb. 1926 (*The Man with the Flower in His Mouth*, 1928); *La vita che ti diedi*, pr. 1923, pb. 1924 (*The Life I Gave You*, 1959); *Ciascuno a suo modo*, pr., pb. 1924 (*Each in His Own Way*, 1923); *Sagra del Signore della nave*, pb. 1924, pr. 1925 (*Our Lord of the Ship*, 1928), *Diana e la Tuda*, Swiss pr. 1926, pr., pb. 1927 (*Diana and Tudo*, 1950); *L'amica della mogli*, pr., pb. 1927 (*The Wives' Friend*, 1949); *Bellavita*, pr. 1927, pb. 1928 (English translation, 1964); *La nuova colonia*, pr., pb. 1928 (*The New Colony*, 1958); *Lazzaro*, pr., pb. 1929 (*Lazarus*, 1952); *O di uno o di nessuno*, pr., pb. 1929; *Sogno (ma forse no)*, pb. 1929, pr. 1936 (*I'm Dreaming, But Am I?*, 1964); *Come tu mi vuoi*, pr., pb. 1930 (*As You Desire Me*, 1931); *Questa sera si recita a soggetto*, pr., pb. 1930 (*Tonight We Improvise*, 1932); *I giganti della montagna*, act 1 pb. 1931, act 2 pb. 1934, act 3 pr. 1937 (*The Mountain Giants*, 1958); *Trovarsi*, pr., pb. 1932 (*To Find Oneself*, 1943); *Quando si è qualcuno*, pr. 1933 (*When Someone Is Somebody*, 1958); *La favola del figlio cambiato*, pr., pb. 1934; *Non si sa come*, pr. 1934, pb. 1935 (*No One Knows How*, 1960); *Naked Masks: Five Plays*, pb. 1952

Other literary forms • Luigi Pirandello wrote seven novels, more than three hundred short stories, a number of critical essays, and six volumes of poetry. The standard edition of his works, *Opere* (1966), published by Mondadori in Milan, consists of six volumes, including *Novelle per un anno* (1956-1957); *Tutti i romanzi* (1957); *Maschere nude* (1958); and *Saggi, poesie, scritti vari* (1960).

Achievements • Italy's most acclaimed modern writer, Luigi Pirandello is known in the United States primarily for three or four of his forty-four plays, written between 1917 and 1924 and collected by Eric Bentley in *Naked Masks* (1952). Of these plays, *Six Characters in Search of an Author* has earned for Pirandello a reputation as a major figure in the development of modern drama. Assessing the impact of that play's 1923 produc-

697

tion in Paris, Georges Neveux remarked that "the entire theatre of an era came out of the womb of that play." Another critic affirmed Pirandello's seminal importance by referring to his plays as the symbolic beginning of a new form of drama, for which the phrase "after Pirandello" has become a critical shorthand.

Critics who have tired of plays that explore the theme of reality and illusion have complained that Pirandello is more philosopher than playwright, but his plays endure as theatrically surprising and provocative contributions to the modern stage. Himself influenced by Luigi Chiarelli and the *teatro del grottesco*, Pirandello in turn has influenced virtually every playwright of reputation writing since the 1920's, including Jean-Paul Sartre, Albert Camus, Samuel Beckett, Eugène Ionesco, Eugene O'Neill, Harold Pinter, Edward Albee, Thornton Wilder, Jack Gelber, Jean Anouilh, Jean Giraudoux, and Jean Genet. With Beckett, Pirandello stands as the most influential playwright of this century.

Biography • Luigi Pirandello was born on June 28, 1867, at Villa del Caos in Girgenti (now Agrigento), Sicily, and moved to Palermo with his family when he was fourteen. Son of an owner of sulfur mines, Pirandello entered into an arranged marriage in 1894 with Maria Antonietta Portulano, the daughter of one of his father's business associates. Their first son, Stefano (named after Pirandello's father), was born a year later; Lietta, a daughter, was born in 1897, and Fausto, a son, in 1899. In 1903, when his father's mines were flooded and Pirandello's assets were lost, his wife suffered a shock that progressed into paranoia, finally necessitating her confinement in a nursing home (where she remained for forty years). Until 1919, however, when he consented to the transfer, Pirandello cared for his wife at home, an experience that undoubtedly stimulated the writer's preoccupation with the distinctions between sanity and madness.

Pirandello was a well-educated man, who studied at the universities of Palermo, Rome, and Bonn. In 1891, he completed a dissertation on his native Sicilian dialect, receiving the Doctor of Philosophy degree from Bonn. In 1898, he accepted a position as a professor of Italian at a normal school, Istituto Superiore di Magistero Femminile, in Rome. Ten years later, he was given that institution's chair in Italian language.

Pirandello published his first poems as early as 1883; he wrote his first play, "Gli uccelli dell'alto" (birds that fly), in 1886; his first novel, *L'esclusa* (*The Outcast*, 1925) in 1901;

(© The Nobel Foundation)

and he published his first collection of short stories, *Amori senza amore* (loves without love), in 1894. Until the early 1920's, Pirandello's work was known primarily in Italy. He gained international recognition, however, with performances of *Six Characters in Search of an Author* in Rome, London, New York City, Paris, Vienna, and Berlin between 1921 and 1924. Also active as the first director of the Teatro d'arte di Roma, Pirandello toured Europe, North America, and South America between 1924 and 1928. Pirandello's frequent travel was followed by residences in Paris and Berlin and by a period of intense creativity. Two years before his death of pneumonia in Rome on December 10, 1936, Pirandello was awarded the Nobel Prize in Literature.

Analysis • In *Each in His Own Way*, Luigi Pirandello playfully has one of his characters ask another to justify his incessant "harping on this illusion and reality string." So persistent is Pirandello's dramatic examination of the multiplicity of personality, the nature of truth, and the interplay between life and art that the term "Pirandellian" has become synonymous with the complexities that result from any attempt to define the fluid line between what is illusory and what is real. In his inquiry into the nature of truth, Pirandello constructs and demolishes layers of illusion, probing the multiple perceptions and identities of his characters to reveal yet conceal the "naked mask." In his fascination with his own power as artist-creator, he dramatizes the dialectic between the fluid, spontaneous, sprawling nature of life and the fixed, predictable, and contained nature of art.

The typical Pirandellian character—Signora Ponza in *Right You Are (If You Think So)*, for example, or Leone in *The Rules of the Game*—presents himself through both "mask" and "face," a dichotomy that is more generally reflected in the playwright's treatment of theater as both illusory and real. For Pirandello, character creation involves a less-than-subtle but endlessly clever interplay among the psychological, the social, and the theatrical, which consistently reiterates the playwright's preoccupation with the multiple facets of reality and illusion.

The relationship between reality and illusion provided Pirandello with a seemingly inexhaustible fund of dramatic material. In part this is a tribute to his creative imagination, but it also suggests that this theme is not merely one among others, one that—as some critics have charged—has been worn out through overuse. Rather, the very nature of theater ensures that this theme will be forever fresh in the hands of a playwright who, like Pirandello, has the audacity to make it new.

Right You Are (If You Think So) • *Right You Are (If You Think So)*, also known as *It Is So! (If You Think So)*, is at once a traditional melodrama and a clever investigation into the nature of truth. The dramatic question propelling the play's action involves the identity of Signora Ponza, the woman whom Signor Ponza claims is his second wife and Signora Frola claims is her daughter. A group of curious members of the community into which the trio has recently moved is determined to discover the truth and, in a series of revelations, is led to believe first Signor Ponza and then Signora Frola. In order for either to be believed, however, the other must be thought to be mentally unstable. Signor Ponza's story is that Signora Frola was the mother of his first wife, who died, but for her sake he has continued the pretense that his present wife is her daughter. Signora Frola's story is that the woman is indeed her daughter and that during the daughter's illness, which necessitated her stay at a nursing home, Signor Ponza went mad. Believing that his wife had died, he refused to accept her as his wife on her return, marrying her a second time as though she were another woman. The two claims are logically irreconcilable: Signora Ponza cannot be both Ponza's second wife and Signora Frola's daughter.

The neatly constructed plot unfolds gradually as each new piece of information is revealed. Instead of adding to what has already been established, however, each new bit of information invalidates what was previously believed, leaving the town gossips, as well as the audience, suspicious and unsure. The promise of relief by forthcoming official records from the trio's previous residence is short-lived, for an earthquake has destroyed all evidence. Encouraged by Laudisi, who is amused by the others' insistence on one truth when he knows there may be several, the townspeople confront the veiled Signora Ponza herself, who reveals that she is both Signor Ponza's second wife and Signora Frola's daughter. The reply satisfies no one but Laudisi, but it is, as Signora Ponza understands, the only solution that compassion will allow.

In his monograph on *Modernism in Modern Drama* (1966), Joseph Wood Krutch speaks of Pirandello as making the most crucial denial of all: the denial of the existence of a continuous, identifiable self. The play, however, is less a modern skeptic's dramatization of the dissolution of self than it is a forceful suggestion that truth is not an external, objective fact but an internal, psychological reality. In demonstrating dramatically that Signora Ponza is both women, depending on what her perceiver chooses her to be, *Right You Are (If You Think So)* sets the stage for Pirandello's subsequent, more complex inquiries into the nature of reality and illusion.

Six Characters in Search of an Author • The first of a trilogy of stage plays that includes *Each in His Own Way* and *Tonight We Improvise, Six Characters in Search of an Author* is a spectacularly theatrical play that leaves its audience as confused as the Stage Manager and Actors whom a family of Characters interrupts, hoping that they will dramatize its story. Those Characters—the Father, his estranged wife, his son, and three stepchildren—claim to have been created by an author who, having given them life, has abandoned them. Driven by the need for self-actualization, the Father insists on enacting—or living—the family's story onstage, which the Characters do in increasingly provocative episodes that culminate in the drowning of one child and the suicide of another.

Some years earlier, when the couple had only one child, the Father recognized the attraction his wife had for an employee, so he sent the two of them off to live in a common-law relationship that resulted in three children. A number of years later, the Father visits Madame Pace's brothel, where the Stepdaughter has been forced, by poverty, to work, and he then becomes her client. The Father insists that the Mother's interruption of the encounter and the discovery of the young woman's identity prevented a consummation, but the Stepdaughter's bitterness hints otherwise.

The family's intensely emotional story constitutes the dramatic center of the play, but the play's greatest interest rests in the interplay among the dimensions of reality and fiction it presents. Although the Characters insist that they are living, not reenacting, their story, the Stage Manager believes otherwise. His attempt to cast the Actors as the Characters, however, results in a patently false performance, lending curious authenticity to the presumably fictive Characters. For the Characters, the script, though unfinished, is their destiny, compelling them to define themselves through what their author has created and constantly to live their story and their suffering.

As drama, *Six Characters in Search of an Author* is exceptionally self-conscious, dramatizing not only the relationship between reality and illusion in a philosophical sense but also the process of character creation. The play boldly presents character in the making, from the author's conception through the independent, seemingly autonomous transformations that each character undergoes before achieving full realization. When the Actors play the Characters, it becomes evident that their interpretation of character does not coincide with that of the author, thus making the actor a participant in the creation as well. Still, the Father, who feels confident that he knows his own essential nature, argues that the fictive character's life is fixed and identifiable, unlike the human life, which changes daily.

In his preface to the play, Pirandello speaks of how the Characters surfaced in his imagination one day, but how, finding no special meaning in them, he decided to abandon them. The Characters, though, remained, virtually demanding that they live and making Pirandello realize it was no longer in his power to deny them life. Thereafter, they chose their own time to reappear in his imagination, each time enticing him to give them a story, until Pirandello found himself obsessed with them. It was then that he had the idea of dramatizing this peculiar, but artistically typical, situation itself, to present the autonomy of these dramatic characters. The result, he remarks, was a combination of "tragic and comic, fantastic and realistic" that finally suggested the conflict between an ever-changing life and a fixed, immutable form.

Pirandello's manipulative powers are at their best in this play, which ends with the Actors, as well as the audience, questioning whether the deaths of the children are real, and hence a onetime occurrence, or fictive, and hence performable night after night. The unsettling ending is a fitting climax to the ongoing dialectic between reality and illusion and life and art that the Characters' invasion of the Actors' stage has caused.

Henry IV • A play as provocative dramatically and philosophically as *Six Characters in Search of an Author, Henry IV* introduces an unnamed protagonist who, some twenty years earlier, suffered a fall during a masquerade party. Dressed as Henry IV at the time, he has since lived his life as though he were the eleventh century German king, with a host of retainers who support the pretense. The protagonist repeatedly replays one particular incident in the life of the historical king, Henry's penitent journey to Canossa, where he knelt before Pope Gregory VII. At the masquerade, the woman whom the protagonist loved, Donna Matilda, was dressed as Matilda of Canossa, and she has remained that figure in the mind of the madman.

Early in the play, Donna Matilda, along with four others—Carlo Di Nolli, the protagonist's nephew; Frida, Donna Matilda's daughter and Carlo's fiancée; Belcredi, the rival for Donna Matilda's affection; and Dionysius Genoni, a physician—visit the throne room, intending to administer a treatment that they hope will restore the protagonist's memory. Through dressing the young woman as her mother in masquerade twenty years earlier, then presenting her along with the older woman, who has aged, they hope to telescope time and shock the protagonist into sanity. The group does not know, however, that the protagonist recovered his memory after twelve years and has for the past eight years only pretended to be Henry IV.

The plan proceeds and backfires. When the protagonist sees the young woman looking exactly as her mother did twenty years earlier, he loses his sense of certainty in his sanity; thinking the younger woman to be Donna Matilda, he becomes obsessed with her, as he had been years before with her mother. As with the earlier play, the ending leaves the visitors and the audience questioning whether the final event occurs in the realm of reality or illusion, whether Henry IV is sane or insane when, in an act of revenge, he slays Belcredi. Either way, the protagonist must now remain in an "eternal masquerade," permanently fixed in the identity of Henry IV. The love triangle is central to *Henry IV*, just as the family's story was to *Six Characters in Search of an Author*, but as with the earlier drama, the play's contribution to dramatic innovation rests in the philosophical and artistic questions that it raises.

Henry IV is perhaps the richest of Pirandello's plays in its treatment of the complexity of identity, for each of its characters possesses at least two distinct selves. In the case of Donna Matilda, the character moves among several identities as the action shifts from the distant past to the recent past to the present. Which of these several selves she is at any given moment depends on the director of the play-within-the-play, Henry IV. If the protagonist is playing the penitent, Donna Matilda must assume the role within that scenario. So also might Donna Matilda be the young woman of twenty years earlier, whom the masquerading protagonist loved, or the middle-aged woman of the present, depending on the protagonist's perception of her. The protagonist is well aware of his manipulative powers and of the superiority that his position grants him. When the protagonist pretends to be mad, he is fully conscious that his role is an illusion, but he sustains the role to amuse and protect himself. Even when he is actually mad, though, he is curiously superior to the others, for then he is so totally committed to his one, fixed identity as Henry IV that for him no distinction exists between the mask and the face.

Henry IV's madness and sanity also serve to suggest the division between life and art that so fascinated Pirandello. As the playwright remarks in his 1908 essay, *L'umorismo* (revised 1920; partial translation *On Humor*, 1966; complete translation, 1974), we are constantly trying to stop the continuous flow of life and to fix it in determinate forms. In *Henry IV*, the protagonist, unlike the others in the play, succeeds through his self-created fiction, which, in its immunity to time, belies his own graying hair. Yet in his success, the protagonist has sacrificed the spontaneity that only the "continuous flow" of which Pirandello speaks can offer. The ongoing dialectic between motion and form that characterizes life is exemplified in the play's final moments, when Frida steps out of the picture frame where she posed as the youthful Donna Matilda and the protagonist embraces her, in a ground swell of emotion that has been suppressed for twenty years. Within moments, however, the protagonist loses the possibility of embracing the pure life that Frida symbolizes, for in slaying Belcredi, he must reclaim and perpetuate his fictive role.

Each in His Own Way • Though less often performed in the United States than the three plays discussed above, *Each in His Own Way* exemplifies the theatrical innovation on which Pirandello's fame rests. In this play, the audience itself is involved in the action, informing the already complex dialectic between the fictive and the real with yet another dimension. The play being performed is presumably based on the recent scandal involving Amelia Moreno, an actress who betrayed her sculptor fiancé, Giacomo La Vela, by running off with Baron Nuti, leading the distraught sculptor to suicide. Onstage, two men attempt to blame the dramatic counterparts of the three involved in the love triangle. As with *Right You Are (If You Think So)*, the audience vacillates between believing first one person and then another, but here the playwright has added reversals that leave the audience uncertain as to whether the young woman, Amelia Moreno, is to be blamed. At the moment when she has been vindicated, she appears to take full responsibility and to apologize. The first-act curtain falls in a seeming intermission, but before the audience can parade out into the lobby, the "intermission" begins to take form onstage, which is now set as a theater with audience members and critics discussing the Pirandello play. In a wonderful invasion of this already unusual performance, a woman who is apparently Amelia Moreno rushes onstage to protest this intrusion of her privacy.

Act 2 begins with Amelia and the man for whom she left her artist fiancé arguing, embracing, then going off together as the guilty pair. Again, the curtain falls and is raised on the intermission set, and Amelia Moreno rushes onstage to protest. This time, however, the audience witnesses a presumably real-life scene among the characters on whom the drama is based. In a clever reversal, Pirandello has set up a situation in which life imitates art rather than the other way around. The annoyed actors refuse to perform the third act, and the play ends, presumably incomplete but having perfectly achieved Pirandello's goal.

Other major works

LONG FICTION: *L'esclusa,* 1901 (*The Outcast,* 1925); *Il turno,* 1902 (*The Merry-Go-Round of Love,* 1964); *Il fu Mattia Pascal,* 1904 (*The Late Mattia Pascal,* 1923); *Suo marito,* 1911 (*Her Husband,* 2000); *I vecchi e i giovani,* 1913 (*The Old and the Young,* 1928); *Si gira . . . ,* 1916 (*Shoot! The Notebooks of Serafino Gubbio, Cinematograph Operator,* 1926); *Uno, nessuno, centomila,* 1925 (*One, None and a Hundred Thousand,* 1933); *Tutti i romanzi,* 1941 (collected novels).

SHORT FICTION: *Amori senza amore,* 1894; *Beffe della morte e della vita,* 1902-1903 (2 volumes); *Quando'ero matto . . . ,* 1902; *Bianche e nere,* 1904; *Erma bifronte,* 1906; *La vita nuda,* 1910; *Terzetti,* 1912; *Le due maschere,* 1914; *Erba del nostro orto,* 1915; *La trappola,* 1915; *E domani, lunedì,* 1917; *Un cavallo nella luna,* 1918; *Berecche e la guerra,* 1919; *Il carnevale dei morti,* 1919; *A Horse in the Moon and Twelve Short Stories,* 1932; *Better Think Twice About It! and Twelve Other Stories,* 1933; *The Naked Truth and Eleven Other Stories,* 1934; *Four Tales,* 1939; *The Medals and Other Stories,* 1939; *Short Stories,* 1959; *The Merry-Go-Round of Love and Selected Stories,* 1964; *Selected Stories,* 1964; *Short Stories,* 1964.

POETRY: *Mal giocondo,* 1889; *Pasqua di Gea,* 1891; *Pier Gudrò,* 1894; *Elegie renane,* 1895; *Elegie romane,* 1896 (translation of Johann von Goethe's *Römische Elegien*); *Scamandro,* 1909 (dramatic poem); *Fuori de chiave,* 1912; *Saggi,* 1939.

NONFICTION: *Arte e scienze,* 1908; *L'umorismo,* 1908, revised 1920 (partial translation *On Humor,* 1966; complete translation, 1974); *Saggi,* 1939.

MISCELLANEOUS: *Opere,* 1966.

Bibliography

Alessio, A., D. Pietropaolo, and G. Sanguinetti-Katz, eds. Ottawa, Ont.: Canadian Society for Italian Studies, 1992. A selection from the proceedings of the International Conference on Pirandello and the Modern Theatre, held in Toronto in November, 1990. Bibliography.

Bassanese, Fiora A. *Understanding Luigi Pirandello.* Columbia: University of South Carolina Press, 1997. In her scholarly examination of Pirandello's works, Bassanese looks at the question of reality and illusion, focusing on *Right You Are (If You Think So)* and *Henry IV.* Bibliography and index.

Biasin, Gian-Paolo, and Manuela Gieri, eds. *Luigi Pirandello: Contemporary Perspectives.* Buffalo: University of Toronto Press, 1999. This collection of essays provides modern perspectives on the work of Pirandello, including his quest for truth, his use of theater-within-the-theater, and use of characters and actors on the stage.

Dashwood, Julie, ed. *Luigi Pirandello: The Theater of Paradox.* Lewiston, N.Y.: Edwin Mellen Press, 1996. This volume examines the works of Pirandello, particularly his creation of paradoxical scenes in his drama. Bibliography and index.

O'Grady, Deidre. *Piave, Boito, Pirandello: From Romantic Realism to Modernism.* Lewiston, N.Y.: Edwin Mellen Press, 2000. O'Grady traces the development of Italian literature, from romantic realism to modernism, examining the works of Pirandello, Arrigo Boito, and Francesco Maria Piave, among others. Bibliography and index.

Parilla, Catherine Arturi. *A Theory for Reading Dramatic Texts: Selected Plays by Pirandello and García Lorca.* New York: P. Lang, 1995. Parilla contrasts and compares Pirandello and Federico García Lorca, focusing on Pirandello's *Six Characters in Search of an Author* and *Henry IV* and García Lorca's *Yerma* (pr. 1934; English translation, 1941) and *La casa de Bernarda Alba* (wr. 1936, pr., pb. 1945; *The House of Bernarda Alba,* 1947).

Stella, M. John. *Self and Self-compromise in the Narratives of Pirandello and Moravia.* New York: P. Lang, 2000. Stella examines the concept of self in literature, comparing and contrasting the works of Pirandello and Alberto Moravia.

June Schlueter

Plautus

Born: Sarsina, Umbria (now in Italy); c. 254 b.c.e.
Died: Rome; 184 b.c.e.

Principal drama • External evidence suggests the following order for the plays of Plautus, but it is possible to give exact dates to only two of his plays: *Asinaria* (*The Comedy of Asses*, 1774); *Mercator* (*The Merchant*, 1767); *Miles gloriosus* (*The Braggart Warrior*, 1767); *Cistellaria* (*The Casket*, 1774); *Stichus*, 200 b.c.e. (English translation, 1774); *Aulularia* (*The Pot of Gold*, 1767); *Curculio* (English translation, 1774); *Mostellaria* (*The Haunted House*, 1774); *Poenulus* (*The Carthaginian*, 1774); *Pseudolus*, 191 b.c.e. (English translation, 1774); *Epidicus* (English translation, 1694); *Bacchides* (*The Two Bacchides*, 1774); *Rudens* (*The Rope*, 1694); *Captivi* (*The Captives*, 1767); *Trinummus* (*The Three-penny Day*, 1767); *Truculentus* (English translation, 1774); *Amphitruo* (*Amphitryon*, 1694); *Menaechmi* (*The Twin Menaechmi*, 1595); *Persa* (*The Girl from Persia*, 1774); *Casina* (English translation, 1774); *The Comedies*, pb. 1769-1774 (5 volumes); *Works*, pb. 1928-1938 (5 volumes); *Plautus: The Comedies*, pb. 1995 (4 volumes)

Other literary forms • Plautus is remembered only for his plays.

Achievements • Writing in the second century c.e., Aulus Gellius recorded that 130 plays of Plautus were in circulation, of which twenty-one were agreed on by all as genuine plays of Plautus, at least according to Marcus Terentius Varro, the most respected scholar of the first century b.c.e. It is this set of twenty-one that survives, though the twenty-first, the *Vidularia* (*The Tale of a Travelling Bag*), is only four pages of fragments. In addition to the twenty complete plays, fragmentary lines from thirty-two plays ascribed to Plautus survive in the form of quotations in other writers' works.

Partly through merit and partly through fortune, Plautus stands as the fountainhead of comic drama. A central fact is that each play of Plautus is rendered from a Greek original; twice the prologue identifies which play of which Greek author Plautus is adapting or rendering. None of the Greek originals survives. In fact, until Menander's *Dyskolos* (317 b.c.e.; *The Bad-Tempered Man*, 1921; also known as *The Grouch*) surfaced in a papyrus codex in the twentieth century, no Greek New Comedy survived at all. The work of Plautus—with the six similar plays of his countryman Terence—therefore represents an entire ancient genre and an unmatched source for modern drama. The contemporary critical wisdom is that the course of drama went from Euripidean tragicomedy to Greek New Comedy to Plautus to modern drama.

Old Comedy refers to Aristophanes, whose plots are mythic and fantastic; the humor is bisexual and flatulent and ad hominem. For New Comedy, perhaps "boy meets girl" is the most succinct description. This is Plautus's work in the main: His plots involve mortals, not gods, and though the humor may still be "indecent," it is human rather than ad hominem. Plautus's contemporary Gnaeus Naevius demonstrated that Rome was no market for Old Comedy: Assaying its ad hominem humor, he was jailed for calumny. Old Comedy is represented in Plautus by *Amphitryon*, a mythic burlesque.

What Roman stylists appreciated about Plautus was savor. Aulus Gellius uses a verb of tasting to define what is "Plautine." A line could "taste" like Plautus. This taste was a salty, direct simplicity, peppered with wordplay. Plautine Latin style has even been recognized, among scholars of Saint Jerome, as an influential factor in the Latin Vulgate. Saint Jerome's versions are marked by a boisterous energy and a breadth of both meters and subject matter.

On the larger scale of dramatic structure, the firmest evidence for Plautus's originality lies in the prologue of Terence's *Andria* (166 B.C.E.; English translation, 1598). From it, readers learn that Menander's *Andria* and *Perinthie* "differed more in speech and style than in plot," and that Terence took what he liked from the latter into his version of the former. When this was objected to as contamination of the original, Terence offered the precedent of Plautus in his defense. That Plautus was known to have mixed two plays into one strongly suggests that he was eclectically building, rather than simply translating, plays. Such weaving has been recognized in *The Braggart Warrior* and in *The Carthaginian.*

Plautus's material has been a gold mine for William Shakespeare, Molière, Henry Fielding, and others who have done unto Plautus as he did unto his Greek sources. Plautus, or Plautine material, still "plays," as the success of *The Boys from Syracuse* (1938) and *A Funny Thing Happened on the Way to the Forum* (1962) attests. *The Boys from Syracuse,* a musical by Richard Rodgers and Lorenz Hart, follows Plautus's *The Twin Menaechmi* much more closely than did Shakespeare's *The Comedy of Errors* (pr. c. 1592-1594). *A Funny Thing Happened on the Way to the Forum* weaves together many Plautine plots, scenes, and ideas, principally from *Casina, The Haunted House, The Braggart Warrior,* and *Pseudolus.* The character names "Miles Gloriosus" and "Pseudolus" in fact pay homage to these last two sources.

Mapping the scope of Plautus's originality vis-à-vis his sources is an abiding scholarly quest. Though this will not be settled, it can be comprehended. Reading or viewing one of the two musicals named above helps, given familiarity with Plautus as a starting point, to understand the adaptive process. Some adaptive concept of Plautus's originality is necessary: Axiomatically, pure translation of past drama produced for another culture would not play. It must be adapted to its own audience or that audience would walk away from it—which in fact happened the first two times Terence tried to present his *Hecyra* (165 B.C.E.; *The Mother-in-Law,* 1598). There is no record of an audience walking away from Plautus.

Biography • The life of Titus Maccius Plautus is known from three ancient notices, two chance remarks in the works of Cicero, and a paragraph in Gellius's *Noctes Atticae* (c. 180 C.E.; *Attic Nights,* 1927). While contending that old age is pleasant if intellectually productive, Cicero observes "how pleased . . . Plautus must have been with the *Truculentus,* with the *Pseudolus!*" The passage shows how flimsy a construction the life of Plautus must be: The original production notice, the *didascalia,* has survived for the *Pseudolus.* This provides the firm date 191 B.C.E. From Cicero, one can infer that Plautus was old in 191 B.C.E. The traditional date for his birth, 254 B.C.E., is owing to nothing more and arbitrarily defines "old" as the age of sixty-three.

Several details of Plautus's life come to light in Gellius's *Attic Nights*:

> Varro and others relate that he wrote the *Saturio* and the *Addictus,* and a third one which I can't remember, while working in a bakery turning a pushmill. The money he had saved working as a stage carpenter he had lost in business, and he came back to Rome looking for a living.

Supposing that Varro was correct, Plautus first made a living as a stage carpenter. In that period, he would have been working on the Latin plays of a Greek slave named Livius Andronicus. This raises a point of contrast with the mainstream of Latin literature: Plautus was not an independently wealthy man writing in the leisure time that wealth afforded but a professional. As such, his market consisted of four Roman officials, called aediles, whose purview included organization and supervision of the public games, which were public holidays with public entertainments. Around the year 240 B.C.E., one aedile saw an intellectual and satisfyingly economical way of fulfilling his duties: Drama would not, like some other entertainments, cost the lives of perhaps half the trained personnel each performance. Livius Andronicus, the slave of Marcus Livius Salinator, was engaged to produce a Latinized script of a Greek play. Drama in Rome thus was established on a large scale. Building sets for these early hybrids was Plautus's apprenticeship. After the failure of his business enterprise, Plautus's ticket out of drudgery was the realization that he could sell plays to the aediles as competently as Andronicus, who may, in fact, have bought Plautus's freedom—Plautus did end up a freedman. After three sales, Plautus was free, if Varro is right.

The remaining relevant passage in Cicero names the consuls for the year Plautus died, giving a certain date, 184 B.C.E., for his death.

Analysis • New Comedy is characterized by a program filled with certain stock roles. First, there is the *adulescens*, or youth. He is fickle, he is incompetent, he is in love; his father is rich and away on business. The *adulescens'* modern acme is P. G. Wodehouse's Bertie Wooster. The *senex*, or old man, is befuddled, doddering, philandering, and irascible. He strikes terror in the heart of his son, the *adulescens*, and lives in terror of his wife, the *matrona*. The *scortum*, or courtesan, sometimes has a house of her own, and it is next door. Or she is owned by the *leno*, always a practical businessman. The money that the youth must pay to the *leno* comes from the *danista*, the moneylender, who will demand payment. The driving force is the essential character, *servus callidus*, the clever slave.

The slave extemporizes intermediary solutions, finds ways for the youths, dupes the old men, and runs a gauntlet between them, for satisfying the young master means a whipping at the hands of the old one. The braggart soldier, *miles gloriosus*, rival for the hand of the maiden, is no match for him, even with an army. *Virgo*, the maiden, was kidnapped in early childhood but has kept with her always the tokens of her last day of freedom. These serve as the sufficient proofs of her identity: She is recognized as the freeborn daughter of a good family. This is the recognition scene, *recognitio*, which is New Comedy's counterpart to the *deus ex machina* of tragedy in that it solves the insoluble and brings the play to its end. Where it is used, it makes the slave girl eligible to marry the *adulescens*.

Of the plays described below, the relative uniqueness of *Amphitryon*, a holdover from an earlier age of drama; *Casina*, with melded *adulescens-senex* and vicarious father-son rivalry; and *The Twin Menaechmi*, a comedy of mistaken identity, argues against the sameness of all Roman comedy, or at least of all Plautine comedy. Of these plays, *The Haunted House* most closely follows the type, with most of the stock characters appearing in their stock situations. A sustained metaphor from musical composition best answers the question of the perceived sameness, the question of Plautus's originality with regard to his Greek sources, and the matter of Plautus's place in the art of drama.

When one thinks of Plautus's originality, one should think of Johannes Brahms composing the *Academic Festival Overture*. He incorporated student songs into it, with the song "Gaudeamus Igitur" for climax. The audience knows that the song is old; that someone else wrote the melody; that the selection, orchestration, and the overture itself are Brahms. The matter of perceived sameness and the position of Plautus in the history of drama are both picked up in the inevitable question which the dilettante has ready for the contemporary composer, "You know what that reminds me of?" There are only eight notes in the scale. Plautus's stock characters, *senex, matrona, adulescens, virgo, scortum, danista,* and *miles gloriosus,* are taken from life and resound all its centers and epicenters: family, love, power, money, and biological urges.

Amphitryon • Though the above must serve as the *dramatis personae* and prologue for the twenty surviving plays, it would be misleading if from it one were to expect a sameness about them. *Amphitryon,* in fact, is not a New Comedy. Mercury, speaking the introduction, first calls it tragedy (the audience scowls), then comedy, then mixes them to call it tragicomedy. The title character of *Amphitryon* suggests divine ribaldry and mortal tragedy: He is the father of Heracles, or rather, the cuckolded husband whom Jupiter displaced for a night to sire the future hero and god. Its burlesque of myth and its adultery of a married woman make it unique in Roman comedy. It fulfills Mercury's promise and is a sampling of the breadth in Plautus, who does not always write a simple variation of the boy-meets-girl story.

The Captives • There is a thrill of the newness of the whole art in Plautus. *The Captives* is a very human comedy with the triumph in the end, not of lust, but of family, in the loyalty of slave to master and the reuniting of father and son. The prologue warns—or boasts—of the difference from the expected: "It is not the same as the others: no indecent, unrepeatable lines, no pimps, no whores, not even a braggart soldier."

Casina • Alone of the plays, *Casina* has a prologue that stems from a much later Roman production in a time that looks on Plautus as ancient, is nostalgic about him, and speaks of *Casina* as a perennial favorite. This comedy will show, then, what noble Romans on a holiday appreciated. *Casina* opens with two slaves, Olympio and Chalinus, challenging each other over the hand of Casina, a foundling reared in the house as a slave, who is now sixteen years old. Cleustrata, the lady of the house, knows that her husband, Lysidamus, wants Olympio, the overseer of his farm, to wed Casina, so he can, with Olympio winking, slake his "love," as he calls it, for Casina. Part of the comedy is that the old man is in the role of the *adulescens* and is as unable as the inexperienced youth to discern between lust and love. Cleustrata would have the slave Chalinus, armor-bearer to her son, marry Casina. It is understood that Cleustrata's son would then cuckold the groom. Father and son are thus vicarious rivals for the same woman. Lysidamus settles the issue by lot. His choice, Olympio, wins. Lysidamus next arranges an overnight detour for the wedding party on the route to the farm: The neighbor and his entire family are to spend the night in Lysidamus's house, to leave the house next door vacant for Lysidamus's seigneurial wedding night with Casina. The slave Chalinus overhears this detour plot and relates it to Cleustrata.

A novelty here is a nonstock character, the clever matron: Cleustrata arranges a series of contretemps to vex and foil her errant husband. The series begins with neighborly altercations and culminates in the dressing and veiling of vengeful Chalinus as the bride. This results in bruises, puns, and bawdy jokes as the two intending husbands first conduct the "bride" away and then report their ardor-cooling experiences as each man attempts to be first with "Casina." Their reports are the climax of the play.

The resolution is that the husband, foiled, is forgiven by the *matrona*. Casina, the object of all desiring, never appears. Nor in fact does the son, Euthynicus: A closing speaker, in two lines before the request for applause, says that Casina will be acknowledged as the neighbor's daughter and will marry the master's son. Here Plautus has not even bothered to dramatize the *recognitio*; in asking the audience to pretend that he did, he practically boasts of not bothering with the typical fare. The play is Plautus at his salty and language-twisting best.

The untranslatability of puns makes them, by definition, a measure of Plautine originality and individual contribution. He crowds them thickly. In *Casina*, as Olympio and Lysidamus conduct the "bride," Lysidamus exclaims in pain, "She almost spread me out with her elbow!" Response: "Therefore she wants to go to bed." "Cubito" means "with an elbow," and "cubitum" is a supine form meaning "to go to bed."

The Twin Menaechmi • Shakespeare's favorite play by Plautus, if imitation is the sincerest form of flattery, is *The Twin Menaechmi*. Before the action begins, twin sons, Menaechmus and Sosicles, were born to a Sicilian merchant. During a business trip to Italy, this merchant and his son Menaechmus became separated at the public games. The lost Menaechmus was adopted by a man from Epidamnus. The grieving father died of a broken heart, leaving a grandfather to rear Sosicles, whom he renamed Menaechmus after the lost twin. As the play opens, the renamed Menaechmus, grown to maturity, has searched the world for the lost Menaechmus and is disembarking at the home of Epidamnus. The Epidamnian twin, heir to his stepfather's estate, is an established householder and henpecked husband. His heart belongs to the girl next door, a professional woman named Erotium. Her lines of greeting are laden with M's. It is not simply that Erotium is greeting Menaechmus: Plautus typically crams a courtesan's greeting lines with M's: "Mmmmmmm." It is part of his art.

The local Menaechmus appropriates his wife's best dress and gives it to Erotium. This dress becomes an Ariadne's thread that winds through the labyrinth of the play, an audience guide to the action. At each turning, the wrong Menaechmus possesses it, whether it is a ticket to a good time or a lightning rod to attract trouble. Finally, the twin Menaechmi are onstage together, and the clever slave who proves to them that they are brothers wins his freedom.

The Haunted House • *The Twin Menaechmi* is a jewel, complete and artistic in its balanced neatness. If such quality were everywhere maintained, it would be insufficiently appreciated, and some Plautine jewels lack such complete settings. *The Haunted House*, at least two scenes of which are reworked in *A Funny Thing Happened on the Way to the Forum*, has a scene deserving of comic immortality, but it nevertheless limps. Tranio, the clever slave, is left in charge of the master's son while the master is absent on a long trip. A slave in charge of a young adult free citizen? The situation is an impossible one, comic in itself. Unhindered by Tranio, the *adulescens* has embarked on a nonstop party, has fallen in love with a slave girl, borrowed money from a *danista*, and bought the slave girl from her pimp. He gives her freedom. Amid his revelry, lovemaking, and the dunning administered by the *danista*, the breathless news comes from the harbor: His father is back.

Tranio keeps the *senex* away for the moment by convincing him that his house is haunted. Tranio explains the moneylender's inopportune dun by adding that because the haunt has made their house uninhabitable, his son had to go into debt to buy another one. One lie requires another, leading one scholar most aptly to call *The Haunted House* a house of cards, as the metaphor suggests onlookers just waiting to see which additional pasteboard will make the whole structure collapse.

Tranio claims to have bought the neighbor's house, and he must now lie to the *senex* next door: His master wants to inspect the house, to model his own remodeling after it. The tour of the house is the heart of the comedy. Once inside, Tranio takes the two old men—and the audience—in with their own bamboozling. He asks them to admire the painting of the two old donkeys being led around by the crow. Where? The two old men do not see any such painting, but the audience sees the play, and there is, clear as life, such a picture before them. Tranio, when the inevitable occurs, takes refuge at an altar. After much worthwhile comic repartee, there comes along a young man bringing the end of the play with him: As he had just slept off a drunk when the news came, the partiers selected him to face the returning father, suggesting that the others are in no condition to speak to anyone. He entreats the angry *senex* by stages first to forgive his son and then his rascal slave.

Bibliography

McCarthy, Kathleen. *Slaves, Masters, and the Art of Authority in Plautine Comedy.* Princeton, N.J.: Princeton University Press, 2000. A look at the relation of slaves to their masters, with emphasis on the work of Plautus. Bibliography and index.

Moore, Timothy. *The Theater of Plautus: Playing to the Audience.* Austin: University of Texas Press, 1998. A study of Plautus that focuses on his endeavors to adapt works to suit his audience's taste and culture. Bibliography and indexes.

Riehle, Wolfgang. *Shakespeare, Plautus, and the Humanist Tradition.* Rochester, N.Y.: D. S. Brewer, 1990. A comparison of William Shakespeare and Plautus, examining Plautus's influence on Shakespeare. Bibliography and index.

Slater, Niall W. *Plautus in Performance: The Theater of the Mind.* Amsterdam: Harwood Academic, 2000. This study focuses on the production of the plays of Plautus. Bibliography and index.

Sutton, Dana Ferrin. *Ancient Comedy: The War of the Generations.* New York: Twayne, 1993. An examination of early comedy that looks at Plautus, Aristophanes, Menander, and Terence.

Thomas N. Winter

J. B. Priestley

Born: Bradford, England; September 13, 1894
Died: Stratford-upon-Avon, England; August 14, 1984

Principal drama • *The Good Companions*, pr. 1931, pb. 1935 (adaptation of his novel, with Edward Knoblock); *Dangerous Corner*, pr., pb. 1932; *The Roundabout*, pr. 1932, pb. 1933; *Laburnum Grove*, pr. 1933, pb. 1934; *Eden End*, pr., pb. 1934; *Cornelius*, pr., pb. 1935; *Duet in Floodlight*, pr., pb. 1935; *Bees on the Boat Deck*, pr., pb. 1936; *Spring Tide*, pr., pb. 1936 (with George Billam); *People at Sea*, pr., pb. 1937; *Time and the Conways*, pr., pb. 1937; *I Have Been Here Before*, pr., pb. 1937; *Music at Night*, pr. 1938, pb. 1947; *Mystery at Greenfingers*, pr., pb. 1938; *When We Are Married*, pr., pb. 1938; *Johnson over Jordan*, pr., pb. 1939; *The Long Mirror*, pr., pb. 1940; *Goodnight, Children*, pr., pb. 1942; *They Came to a City*, pr. 1943, pb. 1944; *Desert Highway*, pr., pb. 1944; *The Golden Fleece*, pr. 1944, pb. 1948; *How Are They at Home?*, pr., pb. 1944; *An Inspector Calls*, pr. 1946, pb. 1947; *Ever Since Paradise*, pr. 1946, pb. 1950; *The Linden Tree*, pr. 1947, pb. 1948; *The Rose and Crown*, pb. 1947 (one act); *The High Toby*, pb. 1948 (for puppet theater); *Home Is Tomorrow*, pr. 1948, pb. 1949; *The Plays of J. B. Priestley*, pb. 1948-1950 (3 volumes); *Summer Day's Dream*, pr. 1949, pb. 1950; *Bright Shadow*, pr., pb. 1950; *Seven Plays of J. B. Priestley*, pb. 1950; *Dragon's Mouth*, pr., pb. 1952 (with Jacquetta Hawkes); *Treasure on Pelican*, pr. 1952, pb. 1953; *Mother's Day*, pb. 1953 (one act); *Private Rooms*, pb. 1953 (one act); *Try It Again*, pb. 1953 (one act); *A Glass of Bitter*, pb. 1954 (one act); *The White Countess*, pr. 1954 (with Hawkes); *The Scandalous Affair of Mr. Kettle and Mrs. Moon*, pr., pb. 1955; *These Our Actors*, pr. 1956; *The Glass Cage*, pr. 1957, pb. 1958; *The Pavilion of Masks*, pr. 1963; *A Severed Head*, pr. 1963, pb. 1964 (with Iris Murdoch; adaptation of Murdoch's novel); *An Inspector Calls and Other Plays*, pb. 2001

Other literary forms • J. B. Priestley's plays may be his most lasting contribution to literature, yet as a consummate man of letters, he mastered many genres in a canon consisting of nearly two hundred works. Beginning his writing career as critic and essayist on subjects ranging from William Shakespeare to Thomas Love Peacock, from the art of conversation to political theory, Priestley became a household name in 1929 with the extraordinarily popular success of *The Good Companions*, a picaresque novel about a concert party, which, translated into many languages, was an international best-seller.

In all, Priestly wrote more than thirty novels, eighteen books of essays and autobiography, numerous works of social commentary and history, accounts of his travels, philosophical conjectures on the nature of time, even morale-boosting propaganda during World War II, as well as an occasional screenplay and an opera libretto. Poetry was the only genre he neglected, after publishing, at his own expense, a single slim volume of verse in 1918, *The Chapman of Rhymes*. He was a popular professional writer, vitally concerned with every aspect of human life, and no subject escaped his scrutiny. As a result, the gruff, pipe-smoking Yorkshireman held a unique position in English letters as a highly respected sage who was also a man of the people.

For more than half a century, he remained loyal to a single publishing house, William Heinemann, which brought out nearly all of his massive output in various genres. Heinemann published single editions of most of his plays as well as thematically linked

collections of two, three, and four
plays. Heinemann's major collection
of his drama, consisting of twenty-
one of his plays, both comedies and
dramas, was published as *The Plays
of J. B. Priestley* in three volumes
from 1948 to 1950.

Achievements • J. B. Priestley's
achievements as a dramatist out-
shine his work as a novelist. If he
was a mainstream figure, albeit a minor one, in a vastly rich period of the
English novel, in drama, he was the
single serious English writer of the
first half of the twentieth century,
bridging the gap between George
Bernard Shaw and John Osborne.
Only Sean O'Casey, an Irishman
like Shaw, had a reputation as dramatist greater than Priestley's in the
same period. The plays of John Gals-
worthy were quickly dated, while
much of the work of Sir James Barrie,
aside from the 1904 production of
the immortal *Peter Pan*, was too cloy-
ing to survive its own generation.

(Library of Congress)

The plays of W. Somerset Maugham and Noël Coward may have been more successful
with contemporary audiences, but they remain monuments to triviality rather than attempts to illuminate the plight of twentieth century humankind.

Priestley's focus was England and the Englishman, not the aristocrats and idle wast-
rels who people Maugham's and Coward's elegant drawing rooms but the middle
classes, the workers—the backbone of the country, England's defenders and its hope
for a workable future. Priestley was an optimist who believed that human beings working in and for the community can overcome any obstacle. A socialist, he firmly believed throughout a long career that the golden world in which he grew up before
World War I could be reestablished once people rid themselves of sloth and greed and
willingly accept responsibility for others. His view, which may seem overly romantic
to modern readers, was fueled by a belief in a quasi-scientific theory of the coexistence
of all time, popularized by J. W. Dunne in *An Experiment with Time* (1927), and was tempered by a clear-sightedness concerning his compatriots' failings, which may have
caused a decline in his popularity at home after World War II at the same time that his
plays were embraced in the communist world.

Priestly was offered a knighthood and a life peerage but insisted on remaining a
man of the people and refused them. In 1973, however, he received the conferment of
the Freedom of the City of Bradford. In 1977, he accepted membership in the Order of
Merit, a prestigious honor limited to twenty-four living Britons, privately expressing
the opinion that it had come too late to bring him satisfaction for very long. Nevertheless, Priestley lived to enjoy the honor for seven years.

After attempting comedies of manners in such works as *The Roundabout* and *Duet in Floodlight* but rejecting the mode as a shallow one, Priestley revealed that the influences on his drama were more Continental than native. Specifically, he attempted to demonstrate, like dramatist Henrik Ibsen, that the present is the inevitable result of the deeds and actions of one's past. The present, in turn, inevitably colors the future. Here, too, the reader can detect the effect of theorizing about time as a fourth dimension in which human beings live.

The single most important influence on Priestley's drama, however, was the dramatist Anton Chekhov. Like Chekhov's dramas, Priestley's best plays capture and sustain an elegiac atmosphere in which imperfect individuals lose their way but also touch others and their families with love. Again like Chekhov, the dramatist could love his characters despite their failings, but unlike Chekhov, Priestley did not always successfully universalize his situations. Whereas *Vishnyovy sad* (pr., pb. 1904; *The Cherry Orchard*, 1908) becomes a metaphor reaching beyond Russia to evoke a world, *Eden End* remains a view of provincial England. As a result, Priestley never touched American audiences as he did his own people. Nevertheless, in such plays as *Eden End*, *Cornelius*, and *The Linden Tree*, Priestley evoked a sense of loss more subtly than any dramatist since Chekhov.

Exploring the family circle in such early plays as *Laburnum Grove* and *Eden End*, Priestley eventually widened his focus to the nation as family in *They Came to a City* and *How Are They at Home?* and inevitably to the world as family in *Home Is Tomorrow* and *Summer Day's Dream*. The unifying thread through these works is the Jungian concept of the unity of all human beings, a concept most clearly expressed in such innovative plays as *Johnson over Jordan* and *Music at Night*, works that enabled Priestley to handle time and place in the fluid manner of the expressionists. Priestley, however, denied that his work was expressionistic; he preferred to believe instead that his theory of coexisting time, in which persons are at all times beyond mere chronological time, proved that expressionist "distortion" does not take place in his work.

Priestley's experimental dramas, again influenced by Continental writers, as well as his insistence on thrusting the common person to the very center of the stage in his realistic plays, were important blows in freeing the English theater from a stultifying conservatism. Never losing sight of the fact that a dramatist must be able to entertain his audience, Priestley found the way to make audiences think as well, to face hard truths about themselves, and to confront these truths with love rather than with anger. Although the Angry Young Men who came after him mistakenly thought him to be, as Osborne has stated, an Edwardian relic, Priestley's plays are in fact precursors of their own. Their concerns were his before them, but his voice was gentler and, unlike theirs, forgiving.

Biography • Bradford, once the wool-merchandizing center of northern England, provided the perfect atmosphere for a budding writer. A commercial hub on a more human scale than sprawling London, the city nurtured the arts. There were two theaters, two music halls, a concert hall visited by the world's most renowned musicians, play-reading societies, arts clubs, a good library, and a local paper that accepted contributions from young writers. Nearby were the Yorkshire dales, providing solace from the city's bustle. John Boynton Priestley, encouraged by his Socialist schoolmaster father and his kindly stepmother, took advantage of all that his native city had to offer. He lived a culturally rich childhood balanced by long weekend walks on the moors. The environment of his home, where his father led discussions on the arts, education, and politics, stimulated him as well. To Richard Pendlebury, his English master, Priestley attributed his awakening interest in literature and his early desire to be a writer.

Priestley furtively wrote poetry and short stories in his notebooks during the days he spent as a junior clerk in a wool firm. Unable to concentrate on commerce, he began placing his pieces in popular London weekly magazines. In 1913, he became a regular contributor to *The Bradford Pioneer*, a Labour weekly, with a cultural column he called "Round the Hearth."

World War I interrupted a tranquil, idyllic, if directionless, existence, and, in 1914, Priestley enlisted in the duke of Wellington's West Riding Regiment. Shipped to France, he was wounded near Souchez and returned to England. In 1917, after his recuperation, he received a commission as lieutenant. Back in France, Priestley, along with several members of his Devon Regiment, was gassed. In his writing, he hardly mentioned the wartime horrors that he witnessed and suffered, yet World War I remains the key to an understanding of his work. Priestley never shed his sense of waste and loss. The war spelled an end to a simpler life, which, in retrospect, always seemed to him a better life. The world he was brought up to inhabit no longer existed, and Priestley's own boyish innocence died with it. Much of his work was a romantic attempt to recapture the vitalizing spirit of an earlier time, of a world in harmony.

After three unsatisfying years at Cambridge, from 1919 to 1922, where he studied literature, history, and political science, Priestley abandoned plans for a teaching career and moved to London to try his luck as a freelance writer. At the time, he and his wife, Pat Tempest, whom he married in 1919, were expecting their first child. Aided by J. C. Squire, who ran *The London Mercury*, he established himself as essayist and critic. In 1925, after a long illness, his first wife died. A year later, he married Mary (Holland) Wyndham Lewis. As a result of the two marriages, Priestley had five children: four daughters and a son.

The almost immediate worldwide success of *The Good Companions* in 1929 made it possible for Priestley to live the life he had chosen, that of a professional writer. He began to travel widely at home and abroad to find new subjects to explore and entered the world of the commercial theater, which had seemed, until his success, too much of a risk for a family man. Beginning a new phase of his career in 1931 with the adaptation (in collaboration with Edward Knoblock) of *The Good Companions*, the novel that had won for him fame and a newfound security, Priestley achieved theatrical success on his own a year later with a well-crafted melodrama, *Dangerous Corner*, which was soon produced around the world. Shortly afterward, he formed a company for the production of his own work. In addition to writing various types of plays, Priestley occasionally directed them as well, and even acted in one, *When We Are Married*, while a leading actor was indisposed. For a time Priestley thought of himself as primarily a dramatist, but in later life, he left the theater to concentrate again on novels and essays.

Priestley became one of his nation's most beloved figures during World War II, rivaling Sir Winston Churchill in popularity, with the weekly broadcasts of his "Postscripts" for the British Broadcasting Company. These began in 1940 after Dunkirk and ended the next year when the Germans launched their blitz on London. The talks stirred a nation and comforted those who, like Priestley, hoped that a better world would be the outcome of this devastating war.

In 1952, Priestley divorced his second wife and a year later married Jacquetta Hawkes, the distinguished anthropologist with whom he occasionally collaborated. The two lived in a gracious Georgian home, Kissing Tree House, in Alveston, just outside Stratford-upon-Avon. After a short illness in 1984, he died in his home one month before his ninetieth birthday.

Analysis • Much of J. B. Priestley's drama explores the oneness of all human beings. That notion leads the dramatist to view individuals as members of a charmed or magic circle. The circle is continually broken, but Priestley, the essential optimist, believed that the circle can and must be mended as people accept responsibility for their fellow human beings. The family, then, with its temporary victories, its too frequently dashed dreams, its individuals pulling the circle out of shape only to have it reshaped by the family's wiser members, becomes the microcosm of the world. That world, however, is continually buffeted by time. Priestley therefore viewed the family through a multiple time perspective. He was conscious of time past, time present, even future time. Occasionally he enabled an especially perceptive character to understand his place in flowing time, but he always led his audience to an awareness that all time is one. Even in an early commercial success such as the melodramatic *Dangerous Corner*, Priestley implied that a family shattered by the sordid past deeds of one of its members can find life anew. It need not be bound by the past, and a new awareness in the present may even reshape a past. The return to the beginning and a second chance for the characters of *Dangerous Corner*, though perhaps a mere theatrical gimmick in this early play, foreshadows Priestley's more thoughtful view of the Family of Man in time in *Eden End, Time and the Conways, Johnson over Jordan,* and *An Inspector Calls.*

Eden End • Time provides *Eden End* its richest dimension. Eschewing the gimmickry of *Dangerous Corner*'s celebrated time twist, Priestley made extraordinary use of dramatic irony in *Eden End*, a realistic family drama set in 1912. Not only are his characters about to lose their innocence but also an entire world is about to be plunged into the horrors of a war from which it can never recover. As characters speak of a better time to come, the audience is fully aware of darkening shadows on the horizon. Time itself evokes *Eden End*'s autumnal atmosphere, making the play a threnody for a glorious but doomed world, which must inevitably give way to a material, technological advancement, spelling the end of the safe and sane values of love and loyalty and the quiet pleasures of a life lived in the service of others. As the Kirby family inevitably breaks apart, Eden comes to an end.

The widower Dr. Kirby, a general practitioner who has always longed for something more from his career, is suffering from a heart condition that will soon kill him. He has with him in Eden End, in northern England, his younger daughter, Lilian, who serves as his housekeeper, and crotchety old Sarah, who was nurse to his three children and has been retained beyond her years of usefulness. Expected to arrive is Wilfred, the youngest of the children, home on leave from the British West Africa Company. However, an unexpected arrival, Stella, Lilian's older sister and the family prodigal, disrupts a stable family situation. Stella had left the limited horizons of Eden End to pursue an unsuccessful career as an actress. Aware now that the only happy period in her life was her youth in Eden End, she learns before the play ends that one's youth cannot be recaptured; to expect miracles is a pointless pastime. Eden End can no longer be for her the haven she has imagined, and she must return to the actress's life of tiring railway journeys, uncomfortable lodgings, and dusty dressing rooms.

Before her departure, which signals a return to normalcy for the others, Stella attempts to rekindle the love of Geoffrey Farant, who runs a nearby estate. Lilian, however, herself interested in Geoffrey, retaliates by bringing Charlie Appleby, another second-rate actor and Stella's estranged husband, to Eden End to confront her. On learning that Stella is married, Geoffrey plans to relocate in New Zealand, inadvertently dashing the hopes of Lilian, who has for many years been quietly contemplating a home of her own with the man she loves. Reconciled, Stella and Charlie make a seemingly futile attempt to renew their life together, while Wilfred, frustrated by an aborted relationship with a local barmaid, takes his disappointment back with him to Nigeria, where he will wait patiently for his next unfulfilling leave.

Knowing that his own death is approaching, Dr. Kirby ironically comforts himself with the mistaken notion of a bright future that he believes life holds in store for his children and for the baby he has just delivered. If no dreams come true, if life holds only the promise of hardship and heartbreak in Eden End, it is left to Charlie Appleby to proclaim the reward that life offers to all. That he is inebriated at the time does not diminish the truth of his observation that life is full of wonder. Pain is part of life's wonder, and humankind is the richer for experiencing it, especially in those moments in which the experience is shared with others. Dr. Kirby is not the failure he believes himself to be, but a good man who has shared the life of family and community.

In a brief critical study, *Anton Chekhov* (1970), Priestley makes clear his admiration and affection for the plays of the Russian master, and in *Eden End* he demonstrates that he has been an apt pupil. Priestly's method is Chekhov's own as he sustains a mood dependent on depth of characterization and wealth of detail. Stella incorporates the qualities of Madame Ranevskaya of *The Cherry Orchard*, Nina of *Chayka* (pr. 1896, rev. pr. 1898; *The Seagull*, 1909), and Elena of *Dyadya Vanya* (pb. 1897; *Uncle Vanya*, 1914) as she tries to win the man loved by her more practical sister Lilian, who recalls *Uncle Vanya*'s Sonia and Varya of *The Cherry Orchard*. Lilian even has a brief exchange with Geoffrey Farant in which, like Varya and Lopakhin, they avoid any discussion of their personal relationship by talking about the weather instead. Wilfred is as much the idle dreamer as Gaev, and Dr. Kirby recalls a number of Chekhov's sad and wise doctors. Like old Firs, Sarah emphasizes a bewildering, rapidly changing world. She still thinks of her charges as children and fails to come to terms with the technology of motorcars and phonographs. When the others go off to the station at the play's end, Sarah, like Firs, is left behind and ignores the ringing telephone that replaces Chekhov's breaking string.

Despite the similarities, however, *Eden End* is no mere imitation of Chekhov. The play exquisitely evokes the life of provincial England in the second decade of the twentieth century, and English audiences, deeply moved by it, responded enthusiastically. The minute details of English life in another era, however, may finally work against the play's achieving universality, and it has not found favor abroad. Acknowledging that Chekhov has influenced many English dramatists, Priestley himself suggested that he and others were better for that influence. *Eden End* ranks among the finest plays of the Chekhovian mode.

Time and the Conways • Priestley, who called himself "a Time haunted man," inevitably turned again to time as the controlling factor in human life in *Time and the Conways*, a play highly influenced by the theories of Dunne. In *An Experiment with Time*, Dunne, the designer of Great Britain's first military aircraft, attempts to explain the experience of precognition, that sense of déjà vu in which human beings, through the distortion of dream, receive foreknowledge of future events displaced in time. Dunne's quasi-scientific theory provides for a series of observers within every person existing in a series of times. To a person's ordinary self, Observer One, the fourth dimension appears as time. The self within dreams, however, is Observer Two, to whom the fifth dimension appears as time. Unlike the three-dimensional outlook of Observer One, Observer Two has a four-dimensional outlook that enables him or her to receive images from the coexisting times of past and future. Part of the appeal of Dunne's so-called theory of Serialism is its provision for immortality: Observer One dies in time one but lives on within Observer Two in time two, and so on to "infinite regression." *Time and the Conways* is Priestley's rendering of abstruse theory into poignantly effective literature. Revisiting the world of his own past, he infuses it with an awareness of the effects of time on all human beings, a sense of waste and loss tempered with a note of hope and an intimation of immortality.

The play begins in 1919 in the Conway home, in a prosperous suburb of a manufacturing town, where a party is under way to celebrate Kay's twenty-first birthday. An aspiring novelist, Kay is joined by her widowed mother, five brothers and sisters, friends, and neighbors. With the war ended, all of them look forward to a bright future. Madge is eager to be part of a new Socialist order; Robin, home from the Royal Air Force, expects to make his fortune in car sales; Hazel, the family beauty, awaits her Prince Charming, while Carol, the youngest, is bursting with an overflowing sense of life. Alan, a clerk in the Rate Office and the only member of the family with no great hopes or plans, is the most contented of the lot as he savors what seems to the others to be merely a humdrum existence. Once their game of charades is over and the costumes are put away, everyone goes into the next room to hear Mrs. Conway's rendering of Robert Schumann's "Der Nussbaum." Kay, however, returns to the sitting room. She cannot let go of this moment of blissful happiness, the happiest moment any of the young Conways will ever experience. Sitting on a window seat, her head bathed in moonlight, Kay, with the special sensitivity of the artist, is about to be granted a vision of her family's future as the curtain falls on the first act.

The action of act 2 seems to be continuous as the rising curtain reveals Kay in the same position. When Alan enters and turns on the lights, however, it is obvious that several years have passed. It is again Kay's birthday, but the year is 1937, the year in which the play was written, and Kay is now forty. Act 2, as Priestley explained it, is Kay's precognition or glimpse of the future. In terms of Dunne's Serialism, her Observer Two sees what will happen to her Observer One.

Mrs. Conway, as impractical as Madame Ranevskaya, has called her children together to discuss her financial difficulties but has attempted to turn the homecoming into a party. Her children, however, are not in a party mood this time. Kay, no celebrated novelist, merely a hack journalist, is involved in an unhappy affair with a married man. Madge is an embittered schoolmistress, and Robin is unable to hold on to a job. He has frittered away much of the family funds and has deserted his wife and children. Hazel, too, has changed. Married to a wealthy mill owner who resents the family for snubbing him years before when he had first come to town, she is terrified of her husband. Conspicuously absent from the family group is Carol. On the threshold of life in the first act, she has been dead for sixteen years in the second.

The air is full of insult, accusation, and recrimination. Once the others have gone their separate ways, a miserable Kay tells her brother Alan that life seems pointless to her now as she remembers the happiness of their younger days. At forty, she is constantly aware of every tick of the clock, of that great devil in the universe called time. Alan, still the one stable element in the family, manages to soothe her. She is again alone at the window as the act ends.

Act 3 continues the action of act 1. Mrs. Conway can be heard singing as Kay is again discovered at the window. It is again 1919 and her twenty-first birthday. The events of act 2 have not yet taken place; life has not yet exacted its toll. Kay, however, has an awareness the others do not share. For her and for the audience, act 3 has a terrible poignancy as the carefree Conways unwittingly plant the seeds of their future unhappiness and destroy one another in ignorance and innocence. The doomed Carol tells the rest how full her life will be. She will act, paint, travel, but the point of it all, she explains with Priestley's acquiescence, is to live. Moved, Kay begins to cry and asks Alan for comforting words. As the play ends, Alan replies that one day he will have something to tell her that may comfort her.

What Kay needs to hear, what Alan will tell her in eighteen years, he has already told her at the end of Kay's precognitive vision that is act 2—that all human beings are at any moment only a cross-section of their real selves. At the end of their lives, they are all of themselves in all of their times and may find themselves in yet another time that is another kind of dream. If the ideas are Dunne's, Priestley transcends theory in a profoundly moving play that affords insight into a person's plight in a bewildering age and offers an audience something to cling to in the midst of the pain of life. Pseudoscientific explanations are beside the point.

The play is no bag of tricks, as some critics have complained, with a third act where the second ought to be. Performed chronologically, the three acts would not have the meaningful impact that Priestley's dramatic irony unleashes. In *Time and the Conways*, Priestley revealed himself as innovator, liberating the stage from the limiting convention of realism, paving the way for such later works as Harold Pinter's 1971 production of *Old Times* and his 1975 production of *No Man's Land*, in which past and present coexist on the stage.

Johnson over Jordan • The enthusiastic acceptance and understanding of *Time and the Conways* convinced Priestley that audiences were ready for more daring experimentation, that he could challenge himself and them with the form and content of untried materials. In *Johnson over Jordan*, which he called "a biographical morality play," Priestley made maximal use of all the resources the theater offered in a drama stressing the timelessness that was one of his favorite themes. The play calls for intricate musical effects requiring a full orchestra, even ballet sequences, as characters are taken outside time and presented four-dimensionally.

Influenced by the Tibetan Book of the Dead, Priestley was especially struck by an account of the Bardo, a dreamlike state after death, filled with hallucinatory visions. *Johnson over Jordan* is an attempt to simplify the complex Bardo into a Westernized version in which Robert Johnson, an English Everyman, moves back and forth in time examining the quality of the life he has just departed.

The manager of a small business firm, Johnson cannot let go of his material concerns even after death. He wanders through a distorted landscape of documents, ledgers, and tax forms, a nightmare world with which he cannot cope. Like the officer in August Strindberg's *A Dream Play*, he becomes a schoolboy again, confused by life's contradictions, reminded of his petty deeds and thoughtless actions. Eventually he takes refuge, like Ibsen's Peer Gynt in the land of the trolls, in the Jungle Hot Spot. Here, he confronts his animal self as he mingles with men and women in grotesque, piglike masks. A mysterious figure, who, like Peer's Button Moulder, reappears throughout his spiritual journey, directs him on to the Inn at the End of the World. All who have illuminated Johnson's mind and touched his heart, members of his immediate family and characters from beloved books, reappear to him through a window at the inn. He recognizes his wife, like Peer's Solveig, as Eternal Woman. His love for her, stronger than material desires, is a lasting one that makes him finally aware of life's wonders and its prosaic joys. At last Johnson, acknowledging himself a less than perfect being, is granted entry into an unknown universe.

Despite a now legendary performance by Sir Ralph Richardson, effective music by Benjamin Britten, and inventive choreography by Antony Tudor, *Johnson over Jordan* failed to find its audience. To some extent Priestley attributed that failure to the critics who dwelled on the work's expressionistic style, frightening away its potential audience. Priestley's own view of the expressionistic theater is that it is peopled entirely by symbolic figures and flattened characters. In the case of *Johnson over Jordan*, he believed, the realistic portrayal of the protagonist, despite the distorted trappings of his environment, made a mockery of the dreaded label. His own explanation of what he was attempting, however—to make use of objective form to present material that was deeply subjective—suggests that the work in fact derives from the expressionist tradition. Like those of expressionist drama, the characters, apart from Johnson himself, are types. All, Johnson among them, speak a heightened language, and the play, in its exploration of a dreamworld devoid of time and space, deals abstractly with a basic expressionist theme—the worth of human beings. The play's very theatricality is the measure of its achievement. Without becoming a commercial success, *Johnson over Jordan* was a landmark occasion in a London theater long resistant to dynamic change. It encouraged others to press on with efforts to expand the limits of a too confining stage.

An Inspector Calls • Priestley's work for the theater during World War II expressed his lifelong theme of commitment to community. Plays such as *Desert Highway* and *How Are They at Home?* appear to have been written more from a sense of duty than from a spark of creativity, but one play of the war years stands apart from the rest. Written during the last winter of the war, *An Inspector Calls* was first performed by two Soviet theater companies in Moscow at a time when no London theater was available for its production.

When the play was produced at home in 1946, in a weighty production full of realistic detail, it was dismissed with indifference. Priestley believed that acclaim with which Russian audiences had greeted it resulted from a more sympathetic symbolic production. There were no walls to the set, only an illuminated acting area. The symbolic setting made the audience aware that the play concerned more than its immediate and continuous action, was in fact concerned with the history of a generation that had just come through a worldwide conflagration. Sharing with *Dangerous Corner* the form of a conventional melodrama, *An Inspector Calls* is a committed social drama that focuses on one man's family while insisting inevitably on the Family of Man.

On an evening in 1912 in an industrial city in the North Midlands, the Birlings are celebrating their daughter Sheila's engagement to Gerald Croft. The coming wedding will signal the merger of Birling and Company and Crofts Limited. Dashing the festive mood of the occasion is the visit of an Inspector Goole, new to the district, to announce the death that evening of a young woman, Eva Smith, who swallowed a disinfectant and died in agony in the infirmary. One by one the Birlings are shown a photograph of the girl, and each recognizes her. By the time Goole departs, everyone is implicated in the girl's death. Birling had fired her for her part in a strike at his factory, and Sheila had had her discharged from a dress shop for impertinence. Croft, who knew her as Daisy Renton, had made her his mistress for a time, but she had later become pregnant by Birling's son Eric. When she had asked for assistance from a charity organization, she had been denied by the interviewing committee, chaired by Mrs. Birling. Frustrated at every turn, she had committed suicide.

The Birling children are shaken by Goole's statement that the world is full of Eva Smiths, and that everyone is responsible for his or her own destiny. The elder Birlings and Croft, on the other hand, are more concerned with their reputations and with covering up the scandal than they are convinced of their guilt and responsibility. It even occurs to them that they may have been shown different photos, that Eva Smith and Daisy Renton may not have been the same girl. Checking with the police a few minutes later, they are overjoyed to learn that there is no Inspector Goole on the force and that no girl has died in the infirmary. Believing that they have been the victims of an elaborate hoax, they prepare to carry on as before, much to the dismay of Sheila and Eric. Suddenly the phone rings, and Birling reports his telephone conversation to the others. The police have just informed him that a girl has died on the way to the infirmary after swallowing disinfectant. An inspector is on his way to ask some questions. The curtain abruptly falls on five stunned characters.

In one of Priestley's tautest and best-crafted works, what seems to be a realistic drama suddenly moves outside time. No particular time theory is under illustration here. Instead, time reinforces the notion that human beings must take responsibility for their actions and their consequences. In the present, individuals prepare their future. Even Inspector Goole is taken outside time. Is he police officer or imposter? Perhaps he is the very embodiment of the Birlings' collective guilt, which has been called forth by their need to account for their actions.

Like *Eden End, An Inspector Calls* is set in 1912, enabling the dramatist to make astonishing use of dramatic irony. The Birlings' world, like the Kirbys', is about to disintegrate. The Kirbys were victims of their own innocence, but the Birlings, no innocents, have caused the demise of their comfortable world through a lack of compassion, a disregard for those members of their community less fortunate than themselves. Priestley added a further dimension to the play, which he wrote as World War II was ending, by setting it on the eve of World War I. When will humankind benefit, he was asking, from the lessons of the past?

Later plays • Priestley's wartime despair eventually gave way to a cautious optimism, despite the uncertainties of the future, in such later plays as *Summer Day's Dream* and *The Linden Tree*. After collaborating with Iris Murdoch on a successful adaptation of her novel *A Severed Head* in 1963, he abandoned the theater.

Other major works

LONG FICTION: *Adam in Moonshine*, 1927; *Benighted*, 1927; *Farthing Hall*, 1929 (with Hugh Walpole); *The Good Companions*, 1929; *Angel Pavement*, 1930; *Faraway*, 1932; *I'll Tell You Everything*, 1933 (with George Bullett); *Wonder Hero*, 1933; *They Walk in the City: The Lovers in the Stone Forest*, 1936; *The Doomsday Men: An Adventure*, 1938; *Let the People Sing*, 1939; *Blackout in Gretley: A Story of—and for—Wartime*, 1942; *Daylight on Saturday: A Novel About an Aircraft Factory*, 1943; *Three Men in New Suits*, 1945; *Bright Day*, 1946; *Jenny Villiers: A Story of the Theatre*, 1947; *Festival at Farbridge*, 1951 (published in the United States as *Festival*); *Low Notes on a High Level: A Frolic*, 1954; *The Magicians*, 1954; *Saturn over the Water: An Account of His Adventures in London, South America, and Australia by Tim Bedford, Painter, Edited with Some Preliminary and Concluding Remarks by Henry Sulgrave and Here Presented to the Reading Public*, 1961; *The Thirty-first of June: A Tale of*

True Love, Enterprise, and Progress in the Arthurian and Ad-Atomic Ages, 1961; *The Shape of Sleep: A Topical Tale*, 1962; *Sir Michael and Sir George: A Tale of COMSA and DISCUS and the New Elizabethans*, 1964 (also known as *Sir Michael and Sir George: A Comedy of New Elizabethans*); *Lost Empires: Being Richard Herncastle's Account of His Life on the Variety Stage from November, 1913, to August, 1914, Together with a Prologue and Epilogue*, 1965; *Salt Is Leaving*, 1966; *It's an Old Country*, 1967; *The Image Men: "Out of Town" and "London End,"* 1968; *The Carfitt Crisis*, 1975; *Found, Lost, Found: Or, The English Way of Life*, 1976; *My Three Favorite Novels*, 1978.

SHORT FICTION: *The Town Major of Miraucourt*, 1930; *Going Up: Stories and Sketches*, 1950; *The Other Place and Other Stories of the Same Sort*, 1953; *The Carfitt Crisis and Two Other Stories*, 1975.

POETRY: *The Chapman of Rhymes*, 1918.

SCREENPLAY: *Last Holiday*, 1950.

NONFICTION: *Brief Diversions: Being Tales, Travesties, and Epigrams*, 1922; *Papers from Lilliput*, 1922; *I for One*, 1923; *Figures in Modern Literature*, 1924; *Fools and Philosophers: A Gallery of Comic Figures from English Literature*, 1925 (published in the United States as *The English Comic Characters*); *George Meredith*, 1926; *Talking: An Essay*, 1926; *The English Novel*, 1927, 1935, 1974; *Open House: A Book of Essays*, 1927; *Thomas Love Peacock*, 1927; *Too Many People and Other Reflections*, 1928; *Apes and Angels: A Book of Essays*, 1928; *The Balconinny and Other Essays*, 1929 (published in the United States as *The Balconinny*, 1931); *English Humour*, 1929, 1976; *The Lost Generation: An Armistice Day Article*, 1932; *Self-Selected Essays*, 1932; *Albert Goes Through*, 1933; *English Journey: Being a Rambling but Truthful Account of What One Man Saw and Heard and Felt and Thought During a Journey Through England During the Autumn of the Year 1933*, 1934; *Four-in-Hand*, 1934; *Midnight on the Desert: A Chapter of Autobiography*, 1937 (published in the United States as *Midnight on the Desert: Being an Excursion into Autobiography During a Winter in America, 1935-1936*, 1937); *Rain upon Godshill: A Further Chapter of Autobiography*, 1939; *Britain Speaks*, 1940; *Postscripts*, 1940 (radio talks); *Out of the People*, 1941; *Britain at War*, 1942; *British Women Go to War*, 1943; *The Man-Power Story*, 1943; *Here Are Your Answers*, 1944; *The New Citizen*, 1944; *Letter to a Returning Serviceman*, 1945; *Russian Journey*, 1946; *The Secret Dream: An Essay on Britain, America, and Russia*, 1946; *The Arts Under Socialism: Being a Lecture Given to the Fabian Society, with a Postscript on What Government Should Do for the Arts Here and Now*, 1947; *Theatre Outlook*, 1947; *Delight*, 1949; *Journey Down a Rainbow*, 1955 (with Jacquetta Hawkes); *All About Ourselves and Other Essays*, 1956; *The Writer in a Changing Society*, 1956; *The Art of the Dramatist: A Lecture Together with Appendices and Discursive Notes*, 1957; *The Bodley Head Leacock*, 1957; *Thoughts in the Wilderness*, 1957; *Topside: Or, The Future of England, a Dialogue*, 1958; *The Story of Theatre*, 1959; *Literature and Western Man*, 1960; *William Hazlitt*, 1960; *Charles Dickens: A Pictorial Biography*, 1962; *Margin Released: A Writer's Reminiscences and Reflections*, 1962; *The English Comic Characters*, 1963; *Man and Time*, 1964; *The Moments and Other Pieces*, 1966; *All England Listened: J. B. Priestley's Wartime Broadcasts*, 1968; *Essays of Five Decades*, 1968 (Susan Cooper, editor); *Trumpets over the Sea: Being a Rambling and Egotistical Account of the London Symphony Orchestra's Engagement at Daytona Beach, Florida, in July-August, 1967*, 1968; *The Prince of Pleasure and His Regency, 1811-1820*, 1969; *Anton Chekhov*, 1970; *The Edwardians*, 1970; *Over the Long High Wall: Some Reflections and Speculations on Life, Death, and Time*, 1972; *Victoria's Heyday*, 1972; *The English*, 1973; *Outcries and Asides*, 1974; *A Visit to New Zealand, Particular Pleasures: Being a Personal Record of Some Varied Arts and Many Different Artists*, 1974; *The Happy Dream: An Essay*, 1976; *Instead of the Trees*, 1977 (autobiography).

CHILDREN'S LITERATURE: *Snoggle*, 1972.

EDITED TEXTS: *Essayist Past and Present: A Selection of English Essays*, 1925; *Tom Moore's Diary: A Selection*, 1925; *The Book of Bodley Head Verse*, 1926; *The Female Spectator: Selections from Mrs. Eliza Heywood's Periodical, 1744-1746*, 1929; *Our Nation's Heritage*, 1939; *Scenes of London Life, from "Sketches by Boz" by Charles Dickens*, 1947; *The Best of Leacock*, 1957; *Four English Novels*, 1960; *Four English Biographies*, 1961; *Adventures in English Literature*, 1963; *An Everyman Anthology*, 1966.

Bibliography

Atkins, John. *J. B. Priestley: The Last of the Sages*. New York: Riverrun Press, 1981. Atkins's attempt to illustrate Priestley's development as essayist, critic, novelist, dramatist, autobiographer, social commentator, historian, and travel writer in a "leap-frogging method" leads inevitably to overlapping and repetition. The 309-page book is most useful on the political, social, and economic background of the late 1920's and 1930's, the period of Priestley's most significant contributions to literature.

Brome, Vincent. *J. B. Priestley*. London: Hamish Hamilton, 1988. Brome offers an affectionate but candid portrait of the writer in public and private life. Brome rightly argues that the prolific writer has been denied his proper niche by overly harsh critics who do not deal fairly with those who write for a wide, general audience. Brome points to the popularization of Carl Jung's theories as an important aspect of Priestley's work.

Cook, Judith. *Priestley*. London: Bloomsbury, 1997. Cook provides a biography of Priestley, examining both his prose and dramatic works. Includes bibliography and index.

DeVitis, A. A., and Albert E. Kalson. *J. B. Priestley*. Boston: Twayne, 1980. After a biographical chapter that includes a discussion of Priestley's time theories, the 257-page book divides into two sections, the first half dealing with Priestley as novelist, the latter half dealing with Priestley as dramatist. All Priestley's works in the two genres are discussed, the more significant ones in some detail. Includes a chronology of the important events in the writer's life and a useful bibliography.

Gray, Dulcie. *J. B. Priestley*. Stroud, England: Sutton, 2000. This volume in the Sutton Pocket Biographies series provides a concise look at Priestley's life and many works. Includes bibliography.

Klein, Holger. *J. B. Priestley's Plays*. New York: St. Martin's Press, 1988. Klein states that his goal is "to further an understanding" of Priestley's "dramatic objectives and methods," but his seeming inability to differentiate between Priestley the serious dramatist and Priestley the occasional hack working to order occasionally invalidates his findings in the confusing first section of the book that deals with dramatic structure. Klein's study is more useful in its latter half in its discussion of Priestley's ideas concerning contemporary issues, pointing especially to *The Linden Tree* as the dramatist's condemnation of Great Britain's post-World War II malaise.

Albert E. Kalson

Jean Racine

Born: La Ferté-Milon, France; December, 1639
Died: Paris, France; April 21, 1699

Principal drama • *La Thébaïde: Ou, Les Frères ennemis*, pr., pb. 1664 (*The Theban Brothers*, 1723); *Alexandre le Grand*, pr. 1665, pb. 1666 (*Alexander the Great*, 1714); *Andromaque*, pr. 1667, pb. 1668 (*Andromache*, 1674); *Les Plaideurs*, pr. 1668, pb. 1669 (*The Litigants*, 1715); *Britannicus*, pr. 1669, pb. 1670 (English translation, 1714); *Bérénice*, pr. 1670, pb. 1671 (English translation, 1676); *Bajazet*, pr., pb. 1672 (English translation, 1717); *Mithridate*, pr., pb. 1673 (*Mithridates*, 1926); *Iphigénie*, pr. 1674, pb. 1675 (*Iphigenia in Aulis*, 1700); *Phèdre*, pr., pb. 1677 (*Phaedra*, 1701); *Idylle sur la paix*, pb. 1685 (libretto, with Jean-Baptiste Lully); *Esther*, pr., pb. 1689 (English translation, 1715); *Athalie*, pr., pb. 1691 (*Athaliah*, 1722); *The Dramatic Works of Jean Racine*, pb. 1889; *The Best Plays of Racine*, pb. 1936; *Five Plays*, pb. 1960; *The Complete Plays*, pb. 1967

Other literary forms • Jean Racine's reputation rests on a relatively limited body of dramatic works. Nevertheless, Racine published a number of other works during his literary career. Among these are several odes celebrating Louis XIV in the early 1660's; a polemical letter attacking his Jansenist mentors in 1666; a collection of religious poems, *Cantiques spirituels* (1694); and an unfinished defense of the Jansenists, *Abrégé de l'histoire de Port-Royal* (1742, 1767). To accompany his plays, Racine also wrote critical prefaces in which he vigorously defended himself against his detractors.

Achievements • Racinian tragedy is the supreme expression of French seventeenth century classical literature, a period called *le grand siècle* (the grand century), a golden age of French art, literature, and architecture. This cultural efflorescence centered on the Sun King, Louis XIV, whom the ambitious Jean Racine assiduously courted. For the playwright, the famous rules of French drama were not fetters that hampered the full realization of his genius but rather intrinsic elements of what only can be called the Racinian "tone." Racine offers, as he states in the preface to *Britannicus*, "A simple action, charged with little subject matter, necessary in an action which must occur in a single day, and which, moving forward by degrees, is sustained only by the interests, the sentiments, and the passions of the characters." The simplicity, violence, and elegance of Racine's style create a tone of "majestic sadness" (an expression of Racine) concerning the human condition. His noble and grandiose protagonists confront their tragic destiny with lucidity and humanity. The result is a fusion of psychological realism and a restrained grandeur that is the soul of classical art.

Like all great artists, Racine has enjoyed periods of adulation alternating with periods of scorn and derision. In his own century, he rapidly eclipsed Pierre Corneille's renown with apparently simple plays in which pathos and emotion replaced Corneillian intellectuality and complexity. It is significant that the great codifier of French classicism, Nicolas Boileau, defined tragedy according to the Racinian model in his *L'Art poétique* (1674). The struggle between disciples of Corneille and Racine continued in the eighteenth century, but most commentators looked on Racinian tragedy as a model of perfection. Its adherence to the rules of reason and nature, according to the Age of Voltaire, made it the quintessence of the French spirit.

With the rise of Romanticism in the nineteenth century, however, a polemical criticism developed that declared that the slavish imitation of the Racinian model had impeded the evolution of French theater in the eighteenth century. This reaction saw Racine as too cramped by convention and courtly etiquette to permit a true depiction of human emotions. Later in the century, however, a new nationalistic fervor elevated Racine to the status of a national idol, the epitome of *le grand siècle*. In numerous and varied studies, the twentieth century, for the most part, rescued Racine from the purely historical approach of the preceding century. Most recent studies adopt a sociological, theological, or psychoanalytical premise that serves to elucidate Racine's life and work. Thus, Racine's plays emerge as an expression of Jansenist theology, a firm rejection of the baroque style, or as a genuine reflection of Racine's psyche. Other studies have focused on the recurrent elements and structural patterns that are then used to define Racine's work.

Biography • Born in December, 1639, to a bourgeois family of La Ferté-Milon (about forty miles northeast of Paris), Jean Racine was left an orphan at the age of four and was adopted by his paternal grandmother. In 1649, his penurious grandmother sought refuge at the celebrated center of Jansenism, Port-Royal, where Racine received an excellent education in Latin as well as Greek. Jansenism, which upheld the doctrine of predestination and insisted on the helplessness of humankind without divine grace, can be described as a kind of Calvinistic Catholicism. Denying free will and practicing a very rigorous code of morality, the Jansenists reproved the more relaxed tenets of the dominant and rival Jesuits. Although many critics have focused on a Jansenist orientation in the plays, it is uncertain whether Racine was a Jansenist during his literary career or indeed whether his teachers actually inculcated their theology in their pupils.

After four years at Port-Royal, Racine spent two years at the Collège de Beauvais, then three more at Port-Royal, and finally completed his education in Paris at the Collège d'Harcourt. Racine's austere and scholarly masters (called *solitaires*, the solitary persons) introduced the young Racine to the Bible and ancient literature. In an age in which education was based on Latin, Racine was fortunate to acquire a thorough knowledge of Greek. He read in the original ancient Greek tragedy, notably Sophocles and Euripides, and most critics point to the Hellenistic simplicity and the mysterious force of destiny so characteristic of Racine's plays. In Paris, the ambitious Racine wrote poetry and cultivated many literary acquaintances. His first published piece, an ode in honor of Louis XIV's marriage, appeared in 1660, and earned for Racine a small royal gratification. Racine's first play, "L'Amasie," now lost, was rejected; a second attempt at the theater, "Théagène et Chariclée," remained unfinished. Torn between worldly ambition and the lingering influence of Port-Royal, which condemned a literary career as frivolous and sinful, Racine spent an unhappy year in southern France, at Uzès, where he had hoped to gain an ecclesiastic sinecure. His decision to return to Paris in 1663 was rewarded by some literary success; the publication of several poems put Racine on a list of royal pensioners.

Although Racine's first two dramatic ventures did not reach the stage, they brought him into closer contact with Molière, who, as director of an important theatrical troupe—the Théâtre du Marais—was to premiere Racine's first two performed dramas, *The Theban Brothers*, a success, though a mediocre one, and *Alexander the Great*, an

instant popular success. After several performances, Racine, apparently feeling that Molière's troupe was misinterpreting *Alexander the Great*, gave the play to the rival, more prestigious troupe of the Hôtel de Bourgogne without informing Molière, an act of ingratitude characteristic of Racine's overwhelming desire to arrive as a dramatist. This ambition also explains his break with his Jansenist mentors at Port-Royal. Realizing that the Jansenists, deeply suspect as dissenters by the government, would never help him in his literary career, Racine took great care to dissociate himself from the *solitaires* in two sarcastic letters (one of which was published) attacking Port-Royal, which had condemned a writer as a "public poisoner."

In 1667, Racine was secretly married to Thérèse Du Parc, a famous actress whom he had lured away from Molière's troupe. In the same year, *Andromache* premiered, with Du Parc in the leading role. The popular and critical acclaim of what is considered Racine's first masterpiece helped him to replace the aging Pierre Corneille as supreme French tragedian. Racine's triumph occasioned a series of personal and critical attacks from the partisans of Corneille, initiating a prolonged and bitter polemic. After his only comedy *The Litigants*, Racine responded to his detractors with *Britannicus*, called by some a Corneillian tragedy because of its Roman subject and political emphasis. In the play's preface, Racine virulently attacked his adversary. Racine's next play, *Bérénice*, was performed in direct competition with Corneille's *Tite et Bérénice* (1670), over which Racine's version won a clear victory. Elected to the French Academy in 1673 and finding himself in possession of a growing fortune and elevated social standing, Racine continued to present a string of hits when in 1677 he produced *Phaedra*, which, because of a rival play on the same subject, appeared at first to be a failure. The superiority of the Racine play asserted itself, however, and *Phaedra* became a huge success.

At the age of thirty-seven, at the height of his renown, Racine retired from the theater, a retirement he thought definitive at the time. Much speculation has centered on this withdrawal. Historians emphasize a reconciliation with Port-Royal or simply a reasoned career move: Just married to Catherine de Romanet (with whom he had seven children), and appointed with Nicolas Boileau to the lucrative position of the king's historiographer, Racine, ever the shrewd courtier, may simply have decided that higher social elevation and greater security would come if he abandoned the theater. At any rate, Racine led the life of a courtier, a permanent resident at Versailles, in constant contact with Louis XIV, while remaining the best-known and most popular playwright in France.

In 1689, Racine made a modest return to the stage, composing, at the request of the king's morganatic wife, Mme de Maintenon, *Esther*, a biblical drama to be performed by the young ladies at the school at Saint-Cyr. In 1691, he composed another sacred drama, *Athaliah*, also for Saint-Cyr. Written and performed for an extremely limited audience of courtiers, Racine's last two plays are nevertheless judged masterpieces by most critics. Racine developed closer ties to Jansenism in his last years, composing the unfinished "Abrégé de l'histoire de Port-Royal"; he died in April, 1699, and was buried at the feet of a former master at Port-Royal. A destitute orphan at his origins, Racine died "fabulously rich." Biographers see contradictory images of the man: a calculating, cruel arriviste and courtier in opposition to the pious family man of the later years.

Analysis • The outer form of Racinian tragedy differs little from that of his predecessors. His five-act plays are written in regular twelve-syllable Alexandrine verse; Jean Racine adheres to the three unities of time, place, and action, to the concept of *bienséance*, which prohibited vulgarity of language and overt violence on the stage, and to the required "unity of tone," a sustained elegance and dignity proper to tragedy. The concept of *gloire*, which informs the work of Corneille, however, is modified in Racine. An exulted self-esteem and worldly fame arising from the exercise of total freedom, *gloire* in Racine loses its compelling force. Whereas in Corneille, the hero achieves self-realization through the domination of his or her love, the hero in Racine accepts fully this passion and the destiny that it entails. The dependent, yet far from weak, lover in Racine knows and acknowledges that he or she cannot exist without the beloved. This "demolition of the hero" reveals a new psychological realism that spurns the illusory ambition of complete self-mastery and independence. From a social and historical viewpoint, this new perspective bears witness to the decline of the ancient aristocratic ideals after the subjugation of the nobility during the absolutist regime of Louis XIV.

Andromache • Although famous after the resounding success of *Alexander the Great* in 1665, Racine created in his next play, *Andromache*, what is unanimously called his first true masterpiece. This play presented something new to contemporary audiences: love as an overwhelming, ultimately destructive passion in both men and women, who, under its sway, are bereft of honor, pride, resolve, and self-control. This play proved beyond doubt that Corneillian heroism was *passé*, and Racine was generally hailed as the great man's successor despite vehement criticisms leveled at the play by Corneille's supporters.

Evoking the epic grandeur of Vergil's *Aeneid* (c. 29-19 B.C.E.; English translation, 1553), *Andromache*, set at the court of Pyrrhus in Epirus, opens with Oreste sent by the vengeful and fearful Greeks to demand Hector's son, Astyanax, who has been held captive by Pyrrhus since the Fall of Troy one year earlier. Because of his passionate love for the captive Andromache, Pyrrhus refuses to deliver the boy to the Greeks. He intends to use Astyanax as blackmail: He will turn him over to the Greeks if Andromache does not marry him. Oreste, ostensibly on a diplomatic mission, has other motives for visiting Epirus: He loves Hermione, Pyrrhus's betrothed, whom Pyrrhus has neglected because of his passion for Andromache. Oreste hopes that his mission will fail so that he will be able to persuade Hermione to renounce the unfaithful Pyrrhus and return with him to Greece. Pyrrhus's blackmail means that the entire situation revolves on Andromache's decision: If she accepts his offer, he will reject Hermione, thus making her available to Oreste; if she refuses, Pyrrhus will accept

Hermione, Andromache will lose Astyanax—the last vestige of her dead husband Hector—and Oreste will lose all hope of winning Hermione.

While Andromache ponders this momentous decision, Pyrrhus, angered by her hesitations, has a change of heart. He will fulfill his official duty by marrying Hermione and delivering Astyanax to the Greeks. Thinking that he must now yield Hermione to Pyrrhus, Oreste is disconsolate when he learns of this. Andromache is in despair; Hermione, who is apparently triumphant, exults. The depth of Pyrrhus's passion, however, forces him to weaken. In a fateful interview with Andromache, he again falls under her spell, allowing her more time to choose between marrying him or losing her son. Andromache's long-awaited decision emerges at the beginning of act 4: To save her son, she will marry Pyrrhus, then commit suicide. Neglected once again, Hermione, in a jealous rage, demands that Oreste murder the double-dealing Pyrrhus. In act 5, scene 3, the deed is done; Oreste, believing that this act has earned for him possession of Hermione, is astounded when she bitterly blames him for the murder of her beloved Pyrrhus. He goes mad after learning that Hermione has killed herself over the body of Pyrrhus. Of the four principal characters, Andromache, the Trojan captive, alone survives, indeed triumphs, at the play's close, for she has assured the survival of her son, and, as widow of Pyrrhus, assumes control over Epirus.

The outward simplicity of the play's plot structure belies the complex psychology at work. Because the action of the play is psychological, time and space play no role: Racine has made use of the unities to create a taut work that concentrates on the emotional crisis provoked by Oreste's arrival. Once this occurs, the dominant emotions of the individuals affected inexorably lead to the final catastrophe. Aside from the Greeks' demand, revealed in act 1, scene 1, no external event influences the emotional interplay among the four protagonists. The three Greek characters are at the mercy of their passions: Pyrrhus, son of the great Achilles, is a horribly tormented king who, almost despite himself, is ready to sacrifice all for Andromache. Oreste, son of Agamemnon, whose incipient madness is suggested in the opening scene, actually hopes that his diplomatic mission will fail so that he might win Hermione. Hermione, daughter of the beautiful and celebrated Helen, is overwhelmed by Pyrrhus's rejection of her. She, like Oreste and Pyrrhus, can rule neither her heart nor her mind.

Illumined by the grandeur that was Troy, Andromache, however, does not belong to the psychological universe of the Greek characters. Her fidelity to her destroyed city and above all to her dead husband, Hector, both incarnate in the person of Astyanax (who never appears onstage, thereby reinforcing his value as symbol), is the keystone of her complex character. Her dilemma—to marry Pyrrhus or to see her son die—entails in each case treason against Troy. Her solution, which, she says, the spirit of Hector has ordered, constitutes a heroic self-sacrifice in the name of a higher value.

The irony of Andromache's triumph—a captive who imposes her will on the others—reflects the more general theme of revenge in the play. Troy, in the person of Andromache, avenges itself on its Greek enemies. Repeated allusions to the destruction of Troy and to its hero Hector reinforce this interpretation. The means of revenge is the insurmountable power of passion. Pyrrhus, a cruel warrior who played a major role in Troy's final destruction, now suffers the intolerable pangs of unrequited love as well as remorse for his murderous barbarism at Troy. The seemingly conventional image of love's flame is rejuvenated by Racine to evoke Troy's revenge on Pyrrhus; he is *"Brûlé de plus de feux que je n'en allumai"* ("Burned by more fires than I lit"). Just as he had burned Troy in a passion of hatred, he himself now "burns" in a passion of love that Andromache's eyes have kindled within him. Racine's mastery of imagery and vocabulary is also apparent in what one critic calls the "poetics of the glance": The eyes of the lover can only imperfectly "grasp" the beloved, yet the latter's eyes maintain an inescapable power over he who loves.

The situation in which one character has absolute physical control over another, yet loves passionately and without recompense the same character, exists in many of Racine's plays. The main structure of Racinian tragedy appears to be based on a relationship of force and authority. As a consequence, a trial of strength lies at the foundation of his theater. Although the characters in *Andromache*—and in this they are characteristically Racinian—appear to be carried away with their emotions, they arrive at essential decisions lucidly: Pyrrhus, in wishing to marry a Trojan captive, knows very well that he is disowning his country and repudiating his past deeds as well as those of his father Achilles. Like Oreste, he accepts fully his passion and its tragic consequences. His acquiescence to blind destiny constitutes his self-realization. Unlike the autonomous, strong-willed heroes of Corneille, Racinian heroes enjoy no genuine freedom.

The Litigants • *The Litigants*, Racine's only comedy, is an anomaly in his rather unified tragic works, and for this reason it has been relatively neglected by scholars. A scathing satire of the French legal system, the play exhibits, by its parodies, puns, and acrobatic versification, Racine's mastery of language and poetry.

Britannicus • The huge success of *Andromache* prompted the partisans of Corneille to charge that Racine was merely a poet of love and tenderness and that he would never master the more significant historical and political subjects of Corneille's drama. To answer these criticisms, Racine presented *Britannicus*, a political play of jealousy and ambition set in Nero's Rome. At first a failure, *Britannicus* later established itself; it ranks third, after *Phaedra* and *Andromache*, in the number of performances at the Comédie-Française.

As in *Andromache*, the plot is rather simple. Intending to continue her own rule, Agrippine, mother of Néron, has put her own son on the throne in place of Britannicus, its rightful heir. Néron, however, does not prove to be the obedient and docile son: At the opening of the action, he has just abducted the young princess Junie, whom Agrippine had intended for Britannicus, and with whom Néron, finding himself in a loveless political marriage, has fallen in love. Junie loves Britannicus, which Néron will not tolerate: In a famous scene (act 2, scene 6), the hidden Néron watches as Junie, under his command, must reject the stunned Britannicus. At a critical moment in his infamous career, Néron oscillates between two antithetical political conceptions: Burrhus counsels a policy based on morality, respect of law, and trust in the basic virtue of the people, whereas the Machiavellian Narcisse maintains that Néron must subdue the capricious mob and all those who oppose him. Warned by Narcisse, Néron discovers that Junie, aided by Agrippine, has been able to inform Britannicus of the real reason for her rejection. In this key scene (act 3, scene 8), Néron has the defiant Britannicus arrested on the spot while Agrippine and Junie are put under house arrest.

In act 4, Narcisse finally prevails over Burrhus: Néron makes the momentous decision to murder his rival and to marry Junie. In act 5, during a feast of reconciliation, Britannicus is poisoned. Junie flees to the Vestal Virgins: Agrippine curses Néron, who lapses into a despair verging on madness. The play thus closes just as Néron is beginning his murderous career. Racine in his preface describes the play as the depiction of a *monstre naissant*, a nascent monster. The political conflict among Néron, Agrippine, and Britannicus ends with Néron's victory: He now has the absolute power required for a reign of tyranny and terror.

Like other Racinian heroes, Néron is predestined, determined by heredity to sadistic cruelty and madness. External circumstances converge to force him to reveal this fatality to all. In the course of the play, Néron's behavior is unpredictable—which undoubtedly creates great suspense—yet the logic of his actions becomes clear after the entire plot unfolds: Néron unmasks himself, revealing the true character that had been hidden during his three years of rule before the opening of the play. The image of the glance, so important in *Andromache*, also emerges in *Britannicus*: Néron seeks to seize and possess another by means of his eyes (act 2, scene 6, for example); his constant avoidance of Agrippine's formidable presence, his desire to escape her glance and its influence, stress the power of the eyes. Despite his efforts to escape his mother's tutelage, Néron never succeeds in gaining control over others or events: His adviser Narcisse is killed by a mob, and Junie escapes.

Inasmuch as Néron is probably the play's most dynamic, interesting character, critics have questioned its title. Britannicus is a courageous, noble, yet extremely naïve and imprudent young man whose political ineptitude makes his murder inevitable. Yet in his preface, Racine insisted on the innocence of Britannicus. A sympathetic character who, through political machinations cannot inherit his rightful place, arouses the compassion and pity of the audience: hence the title of the play.

With the longest role in the play, Agrippine presents an intelligent, proud, unscrupulous, and hugely ambitious woman, a typically formidable Racinian heroine. Her fall is inextricably tied to the death of Britannicus, and, as such, it forms a major subject of the play. She is the outsider, rejected by the young lovers as well as her newly independent son. Just as Pyrrhus in *Andromache* is torn between Hermione and Andromache, Néron is torn between Agrippine and Junie. In both cases the male character loves, and is rejected by, the gentler woman; each is trying to escape from a domineering, violent woman, a possessive fiancé in one play, a possessive mother in the other. The basic structure of an all-powerful protagonist (Néron) who loves a weaker character (Junie), who in turn has other emotional loyalties, also obtains in this play.

Bérénice • Racine's success continued in the 1670's. His next play, *Bérénice*, is remarkable for its extreme simplicity. In his preface, the author expresses his thoughts on simplicity of action: "There are some who think that this simplicity [of *Bérénice*] is evidence of little inventiveness. They don't believe that, on the contrary, all inventiveness lies in making something from nothing." Written, apparently, as a challenge to Corneille's *Tite et Bérénice* (pr. 1670), this play contains only three main characters and their confidants, whose roles are minor. Set in ancient Rome, the action is intimate: The new emperor Tite, whose father Vespasien has recently died, has loved the queen of Palestine, Bérénice, for five years. Although he wishes to marry her, the Senate opposes the marriage of a head of state with a foreign queen. After much pain and hesitation, Tite sacrifices Bérénice and his love to the reason of state. Thus a strangely Corneillian denouement, in which duty triumphs over passion, closes this most Racinian of Racine's dramas; it is in effect a play of personal sacrifice, quite different in this respect from Racine's other works.

Bajazet • After creating a play in which nothing happens, Racine in *Bajazet*, his next work, presented the violent, even sadistic world of the Turkish court in the 1630's. *Bajazet* was Racine's first play published without a polemical, apologetic preface, suggesting, perhaps, that his self-confidence was increasing. Full of suspense, court intrigues, and bloody passions, *Bajazet*, like *Andromache* and *Britannicus*, depicts a character (Roxane) whose power of life or death over another character (Bajazet) is mocked by the enslaving power of love. Roxane swings violently between love and hatred—allied emotions in the complex of Racinian passion—depending on whether she believes that Bajazet returns her love or not and finally has him killed. Despite her cruelty and deceit, Roxane remains a pathetic figure: All of her power cannot erase the fact that her happiness is utterly dependent on Bajazet. Although set in an exotic locale, *Bajazet*, like Racine's other plays, is a psychological study revealing the eternal truth of the human heart.

Mithridates • A huge success from its first performance, *Mithridates*, Racine's only serious play with what could be called a happy ending, enjoyed the acclaim of the court, the city, and even of the Corneille clique. Set in Rome, the work depicts the cagey, longtime foe of the Romans, Mithridates, at the end of his life. The relatively involved plot and large number of dramatic surprises or *coups de théâtre*, the heroic apotheosis of Mithridates, whose generosity wins over others who had feared and despised him, and generally strong characters who put duty before sentiment, mark this play among all Racine's works as the most strongly influenced by Corneille.

Iphigenia in Aulis • Racine's next play, *Iphigenia in Aulis*, once again demonstrated his supremacy on the French stage. Returning to Greek myth for his subject matter, Racine imitated Euripides' *Iphigeneia ē en Aulidi* (405 B.C.E.; *Iphigenia in Aulis*, 1782). It was necessary, however, to adapt the ancient story to the tastes of the seventeenth century French audience. To accomplish this, Racine invented the character of Eriphile, who, because of an ambiguity in the oracle that apparently demands the sacrifice of Iphigenia before the Greek fleet can depart for Troy, is substituted for her and dies on the altar, thus allowing the Greeks to continue their voyage. By substituting a more *vraisemblance*—or verisimilar—denouement for the miraculous ending of Euripides, Racine satisfied the demand for *bienséance* (propriety or decorum), for the treacherous and ungrateful Eriphile is much less sympathetic than the virtuous Iphigenia. The enormous suspense generated just before the audience learns that Iphigenia is saved attests Racine's skill in plot construction. Alternately savage and lyric, *Iphigenia in Aulis* has been called Racine's most Homeric play.

Phaedra • Racine's greatest masterpiece, easily his most celebrated play, *Phaedra*, was presented in January, 1677, at the same time as a competing "Phaedra." Jacques Pradon had composed a rival *Phèdre et Hippolyte* (competing authors often wrote in direct competition), which was at first more successful. After several months, however, Racine's *Phaedra* surpassed Pradon's in popular acclaim. That the play was the inaugural performance of the Comédie-Française in 1680 confirmed its appeal. As in *Iphigenia in Aulis*, in *Phaedra*, the mythic element dominates; humanity is in eternal opposition to the seemingly perfidious gods.

At the opening of the play, Thésée, king of Troezen, has been absent for six months. The king's son Hippolyte, apparently concerned about his father, wishes to leave Troezen in search of Thésée. In fact, other reasons motivate Hippolyte's departure: his love for Aricie, whom Thésée has forbidden him to marry because of her link to the rebellious Pallantides, and his desire to flee the overt hatred of his stepmother Phaedra. After Hippolyte's revelation that he loves Aricie, a dying Phaedra takes the stage and confesses to her confidante Oenone that she loves Hippolyte and that her enmity toward him has been a means of avoiding an unwilling declaration of her love. A peripeteia closes the first act: News (Aricie calls it "incredible") arrives that Thésée is dead. This external event effects profound changes in the internal situation: Hippolyte is now free to woo Aricie, and Phaedra can now pursue Hippolyte without fear of incest and adultery.

On the urging of Oenone, Phaedra determines to speak privately to Hippolyte on a political pretext relating to the rights of succession. In perhaps the most famous scene in French classical theater (act 2, scene 5), Phaedra, carried away by her passion, declares her love. While Hippolyte stands dumbfounded, Phaedra seizes his sword, thinking to kill herself but does not. In act 3, the humiliated, rejected Phaedra oscillates between love and hatred for Hippolyte. In her confused state, against the advice of Oenone, she decides to use political blackmail to gain Hippolyte's love. Devastating news then arrives: Thésée is alive. The desperate and helpless Phaedra, fearful that Hippolyte will tell his father of her incestuous love, is persuaded by Oenone that she must accuse Hippolyte of attempting to seduce her before he can reveal the truth. Putting herself in the hands of Oenone, Phaedra greets Thésée coldly, refusing to accept his sincere affection. Stunned and suspicious, Thésée demands an explanation from Hippolyte, who has naïvely vowed never to reveal Phaedra's shame to his father.

This oath puts Hippolyte in an untenable position, for he has no effective means of defending himself against Oenone's lies. The violent, vengeful, and quick-tempered Thésée is convinced by Hippolyte's sword, left in the hands of Phaedra after act 2, scene 5, and by his son's diffident behavior. In a stormy interview, Thésée asks Neptune to wreak vengeance on his son; in an attempt at self-defense, Hippolyte confesses his real love for Aricie, which Thésée judges a cowardly ruse. Phaedra, who now realizes that Hippolyte is in mortal danger, resolves to reveal the truth to Thésée. Her regret and pity, however, change to furious hatred and jealousy when Thésée tells her that Hippolyte told him that he loves Aricie. This news makes her continue to hide the truth. Although Thésée begins to guess that Hippolyte was not lying, inexorable destiny is played out in act 5. Hippolyte kills a sea monster sent by Neptune, but then Neptune himself causes the horses of Hippolyte's chariot to stampede, killing the innocent young hero. Overwhelmed by the enormity of her crime, Phaedra poisons herself. Right before she dies, Phaedra finally tells the truth; the desolate Thésée determines to protect the bereft Aricie.

A malevolent destiny hovers over the action of *Phaedra*. A descendant of the Sun, daughter of Minos and Pasiphaé, Phaedra bears the curse of Venus. Her mother's indomitable passion for the White Bull of Crete, the issue of this passion, the Minotaur and its Labyrinth, the doomed love of Phaedra's sister Ariadne for Thésée—all figure prominently in the play and serve as background to the fateful, "monstrous" passion of Phaedra for Hippolyte. The gods in *Phaedra*, if one wishes to consider them such (they have been interpreted as symbols for humanity's unbridled passions), emerge as incomprehensible powers with no moral purpose. Phaedra, who wishes to die throughout the play, knows that escape from her anguish is impossible, for her own father Minos sits as judge at the gates of Hades. Racine presents a universe in which the innocent are punished for uncommitted crimes, in which people are forced by the gods to commit crimes for which they will suffer eternal torment. Such a universe seems absurd; it is truly a tragic vision of the human condition.

True to the Aristotelian concept of the tragic hero, Racine emphasized in his preface that Phaedra is "neither totally guilty nor totally innocent." Victim of an unrelenting divine vengeance, Phaedra condemns herself for a passion to which she has never yielded. She feels herself responsible for a love over which she has absolutely no control. Phaedra aspires to good, but the gods force her to submit to evil. Both Phaedra and Hippolyte view their respective passions as a *mal*, a kind of sickness that destroys sovereign reason and thus transforms he who loves. Racinian passion is inimical to self-control and equilibrium, a monster that destroys independence and harmony.

Critics have frequently declared that *Phaedra* summarizes all Racine's drama. The universality of the play, its unremitting depiction of human nature aspiring to virtue but condemned to vice, has undoubtedly contributed to its status as Racine's crowning achievement. The play poses the fundamental problem of liberty. Predetermined, whether by the gods, heredity, or other forces, humanity is unable to escape the monsters that pursue it. Nevertheless, humankind never ceases to assume responsibility and thus affirms an illusory freedom. Phaedra's awareness of her crime and its shame constitutes, perhaps, a kind of individual liberty and tragic grandeur.

Key words and images converge in the play to reinforce the major themes and conflict. Poison plays a central role as symbol for the fatal passion that courses through the veins of Phaedra. A complex network of images relating to light and darkness also pervades the work. Unable to face her formidable ancestor the Sun, Phaedra retreats from the accusing light of purity and innocence like a furtive nocturnal creature; Phaedra's desire for darkness evokes not only her shame but also her wish to discover in death eternal darkness. Hippolyte and Aricie, however, share an innocence and purity that revel in the light: "Every day rose clear and serene for them," whereas Phaedra says of herself: "I hid from the day, I fled from the light." *Phaedra* is also a play of monsters: The fruit of Pasiphaé's passion, the Minotaur, was destroyed by the heroic monster-killer Thésée, whom Hippolyte wishes to emulate. Hippolyte kills the sea monster sent by Neptune, yet dies a victim of Phaedra, whose love, like that of her mother for the White Bull, is against nature, monstrous.

Esther and **Athaliah** • After *Phaedra*, twelve years passed before Racine's next play. Whatever the true reasons for his long silence, it is clear that he became reconciled with his Jansenist masters at Port-Royal. Racine's second wife, whom he married in 1677, the year of *Phaedra*, never read her husband's tragedies; their seven children received a most austere Jansenist upbringing. Racine's last two plays, *Esther* and *Athaliah*, attest the piety of his later years; overtly didactic, both derive from the Old Testament. Although some scholars have hesitated to view these religious plays as integral components of Racine's work, all agree that both obviously bear the imprint of Racine; many consider *Athaliah* one of his best plays.

Other major works
POETRY: *Cantiques spirituels*, 1694.
NONFICTION: *Abrégé de l'histoire de Port-Royal*, 1742 (first part), 1767 (full text).

Bibliography
Barthes, Roland. *On Racine*. 1983. Reprint. Berkeley: University of California Press, 1992. A French scholar discusses Racine's tragedies. Bibliography and index.
Caldicott, Edric, and Derval Conroy, eds. *Racine: The Power and the Pleasure*. Dublin, Ireland: University College Dublin Press, 2001. This study examines the concepts of power and pleasure in Racine's dramas.

Goodkin, Richard E. *Birth Marks: The Tragedy of Primogeniture in Pierre Corneille, Thomas Corneille, and Jean Racine.* Philadelphia: University of Pennsylvania Press, 2000. Goodkin examines the works of Racine and the two Corneilles, placing special emphasis on their treatments of primogeniture.

Hawcroft, Michael. *Word as Action: Racine, Rhetoric, and Theatrical Language.* New York: Oxford University Press, 1992. Hawcroft examines Racine's use of language in his dramatic works. Bibliography and indexes.

Parish, Richard. *Racine: The Limits of Tragedy.* Seattle, Wash.: Papers on French Seventeenth Century Literature, 1993. An examination of the tragedies written by Racine. Bibliography.

Phillips, Henry. *Racine: Language and Theatre.* Durham, England: University of Durham, 1994. A look at the language of Racine and how he used it in his dramas. Bibliography.

Tobin, Ronald W. *Jean Racine Revisited.* New York: Twayne, 1999. A basic biography of Racine that covers his life and works. Bibliography and index.

Robert T. Corum, Jr.

Terence Rattigan

Born: London, England; June 10, 1911
Died: Bermuda; November 30, 1977

Principal drama • *First Episode*, pr. 1933; *French Without Tears*, pr. 1936, pb. 1937; *Flare Path*, pr., pb. 1942; *While the Sun Shines*, pr. 1943, pb. 1944; *Love in Idleness*, pr. 1944, pb. 1945 (also as *O Mistress Mine*, pr., pb. 1946); *The Winslow Boy*, pr., pb. 1946; *Playbill: "The Browning Version" and "Harlequinade,"* pr. 1948, pb. 1949 (2 one-acts); *Adventure Story*, pr. 1949, pb. 1950; *The Deep Blue Sea*, pr., pb. 1952; *The Collected Plays of Terence Rattigan*, pb. 1953-1978 (4 volumes; Hamish Hamilton, editor); *The Sleeping Prince*, pr. 1953, pb. 1954; *Separate Tables: "Table by the Window" and "Table Number Seven,"* pr. 1954, pb. 1955 (two playlets; commonly known as *Separate Tables*); *Ross*, pr., pb. 1960; *Man and Boy*, pr., pb. 1963; *A Bequest to the Nation*, pr., pb. 1970 (adaptation of Rattigan's teleplay *Nelson*, pr. 1964); *In Praise of Love: "Before Dawn" and "After Lydia,"* pb. 1973, pr. 1974 (as *In Praise of Love*); *Cause Célèbre*, pr. 1977, pb. 1978 (adaptation of his radio play); *Plays*, pb. 1981-1985 (2 volumes)

Other literary forms • Terence Rattigan wrote many screenplays, including a number of adaptations of his own plays. For the film of *The Browning Version*, he won the 1951 Cannes Film Festival Award for best screenplay. In 1958, the screenplay of *Separate Tables*, adapted from Rattigan's play in collaboration with John Gay, was nominated for an Academy Award. The triumvirate of Rattigan, cowriter/producer Anatole de Grunwald, and director Anthony Asquith created a number of films, including *Quiet Wedding* (1941, based on Esther McCracken's play), *English Without Tears* (1944, based on *French Without Tears*; also as *Her Man Gilbey*), *The Way to the Stars* (1945; also as *Johnny in the Clouds*, 1946), *While the Sun Shines* (1946, adapted from Rattigan's play), and *The Winslow Boy* (1948, adapted from Rattigan's play).

The films were significant contributions to Great Britain's postwar film renaissance. *The Sound Barrier* (1952; also as *Breaking the Sound Barrier*), from Rattigan's screenplay, is considered by some aficionados the finest film ever made about aviation. His best-known films are probably *Separate Tables* (for which David Niven won an Academy Award as Best Actor), *The Prince and the Showgirl* (1957, starring Marilyn Monroe and Sir Laurence Olivier in the adaptation of Rattigan's stage comedy *The Sleeping Prince*), and *The VIPs* (1963, with an all-star cast headed by Elizabeth Taylor and Richard Burton).

Of Rattigan's seven original television scripts and one radio script, *The Final Test* (1951) was released as a film in 1954; *Nelson—A Portrait in Miniature* (1964) was adapted as the play *A Bequest to the Nation* in 1970, with the film version appearing in 1973 under that title; and the radio script *Cause Célèbre* (1975) was adapted for the stage.

Rattigan also wrote numerous theoretical essays. Most important to his career were "Concerning the Play of Ideas" and "The Play of Ideas," both published in 1950 in *The New Statesman and Nation*, and the prefaces he wrote for the first three volumes of *The Collected Plays*, published by Hamish Hamilton. In *The New Statesman and Nation*, Rattigan defended story and character—as opposed to intellectual debate and propagandizing—as the timeless values of drama. He was rebutted, wholly or partly, by

James Bridie, Benn Levy, Peter Ustinov, Sean O'Casey, Christopher Fry, and George Bernard Shaw.

In his second and third prefaces, Rattigan invented a prototypical theatergoer, Aunt Edna, intended as a humorous salute to the good common sense of audiences throughout the ages but attacked as evidence of his own pandering to lowbrow sensibilities. His theoretical essays are too gentlemanly in tone to persuade with the sheer moral fervor of Shaw's, yet Rattigan was as sincere in his convictions and as true to his own values. His championship of the craft of playwriting and of the judgment of the dedicated theatergoer, his exploration in his first preface of the significance of dramatic implication, his musings in American newspaper articles on why plays suffer a "sea change" when produced in foreign countries, and his concept of the "farce of character" (in a 1947 *Strand* magazine article) are all valuable contributions to the literature of dramatic theory.

Achievements • The first author ever to have had two plays (*French Without Tears* and *While the Sun Shines*) run for more than one thousand performances each on London's West End, Terence Rattigan was one of the most commercially successful playwrights in theater history. With striking versatility, he achieved his goal of moving audiences to laughter or tears in romantic comedy, comedy of manners, farce, fantasy, history plays, courtroom drama, and dramas about troubled middle-class characters. He also attracted many of the finest acting and directing talents of his period. Roles in Rattigan plays made stars of such young actors as Rex Harrison, Paul Scofield, and Kenneth More, and enhanced the careers of such luminaries as Dame Peggy Ashcroft, Sir Laurence Olivier, Sir Alec Guinness, Margaret Sullivan, Margaret Leighton, and Alfred Lunt and Lynn Fontanne (a couple who had enjoyed the longest run of their stage careers in the American version of *Love in Idleness*).

Rattigan's success, however, was often held against him by critics, who did not bother to look beyond the polished surfaces of his plays. Failing to grasp the depth of psychological insight and the serious themes that usually characterized even his light comedies, most critics rated him as a good boulevard playwright at best. During the 1950's and the 1960's, the heyday of the Angry Young Men and the Theater of the Absurd, Rattigan's work was derided as representing the establishment culture that younger playwrights and critics sought to demolish. London revivals of five of his plays between

(AP/Wide World Photos)

1970 and 1977, the year of Rattigan's death, led to a greater appreciation of his worth. With the widely hailed National Theatre's production of *Playbill* in 1980 and the Roundabout Theatre Company's acclaimed New York revivals of *The Winslow Boy* in 1980 and *The Browning Version* in 1982, Rattigan began to be recognized as an artist of high stature.

Biography • Terence Mervyn Rattigan was born in Kensington, London, on June 10, 1911, to William Frank Rattigan and Vera Houston Rattigan, ten days before the coronation of George V. His father, a career diplomat, was a minor functionary in the coronation and his mother missed the ceremony because of her confinement. Forty-two years later, when Rattigan wrote his sophisticated fantasy *The Sleeping Prince* as a *pièce d'occasion* for Elizabeth II's coronation, he said that he used George V's coronation for the background of the play as a present to his mother for having missed the real thing.

Both of Rattigan's parents came from distinguished families of Irish lawyers, a heritage that fascinated Rattigan and showed itself not only in the characters of the lawyers in *The Winslow Boy* and *Cause Célèbre* but also in such scenes as the hotel residents' "trial" of Major Pollock in *Table Number Seven*. Rattigan's father, who failed in his own career and was pensioned off in 1922, hoped that Rattigan would find a career in the diplomatic service.

From early boyhood, however, when his parents first took him to the theater, Rattigan was determined to be a playwright. He hoarded his allowance and sneaked off to the theater, began writing plays at eleven, and read plays avidly while on scholarship at Harrow from 1925 to 1930. At Oxford on a history scholarship, he acted, wrote criticism for the *Cherwell*, and collaborated with fellow student Philip Heimann on a play about Oxonian high jinks and their sad consequences entitled *First Episode*, which enjoyed respectful reviews and a brief run on the West End in the 1933-1934 season. On the strength of this success, he persuaded his father to give him a modest allowance to enable him to write for two years, at the end of which he either would be a successful playwright or would bow to his parents' wishes for his career.

Rattigan's Oxford years were far from wasted; his reading of history helped inspire his studies of Alexander the Great (*Adventure Story*, 1949), T. E. Lawrence (*Ross*), and Lord Nelson (*A Bequest to the Nation*), and summers spent taking language courses in Germany and France prompted *French Without Tears*, whose spectacular success enabled Rattigan to win his career gamble with his father. From then until the last decade of his life, even though he suffered his share of flops and personal sorrows, Rattigan was depicted in the press as fortune's favorite, an image enlarged by his exceptional good looks and elegant lifestyle.

Virtually all of Rattigan's work was influenced directly or indirectly by his personal experience. Several of his wartime plays and film scripts, for example, grew out of his service as a Royal Air Force flight lieutenant. *In Praise of Love* was dually inspired by his friendship with Rex Harrison and Harrison's wife, Kay Kendall, when she was dying of leukemia and by a false diagnosis of leukemia in Rattigan himself in 1962. Examples of more pervasive influences are his parents' unhappy marriage, his attempts to love and be loyal to both his mother and his father, and his own homosexuality. Rattigan's comedies and dramas often feature compassionate portraits of mismatched couples, bewildered youths in contention with their elders, and individuals tortured by sexual repression, deviation, or frustration. Rattigan's protagonists generally meet their problems with the dignity and courage that he brought to his own life, particularly during his two-year battle with bone cancer. After a self-imposed seven-year exile to write film scripts during the period of his greatest vilification by younger critics and colleagues, Rattigan lived to see himself welcomed back into the British theater community with his knighthood in 1971, the beginning of his artistic renaissance through revivals of his earlier plays, and the positive reception of a new work, *Cause Célèbre*, only months before his death.

Analysis • In a 1962 *Theatre Arts* interview, Terence Rattigan told John Simon that playwrights were born Ibsenites or Chekhovians and that he was the former longing to be the latter. In fact, he blended the influences of both. Like Henrik Ibsen in his problem plays, Rattigan reshaped the Scribean well-made play to his own ends, imbuing it with psychological complexity and moral passion. Unlike Ibsen, he seldom allowed his characters to debate ideas and issues, taking instead a firm stand against ideological drama. Like Anton Chekhov, Rattigan focused on the personal problems of predominantly middle-class characters who are left with no neat solutions; his comedies end with a respite instead of a celebration; his dramas, with a delicate balance of losses and gains. Rattigan's characters are, like Chekhov's, bound in a rich tapestry: Their fates are to varying degrees interrelated, but their essential aloneness is poignantly conveyed. Unlike Ibsen or Chekhov, Rattigan was not a radical innovator, and as yet there is no evidence of his direct influence on successors. Each of Rattigan's plays displays innovative touches, however, and the body of his work reveals an artist with a distinct personal vision that he expressed in both the content and the form of his plays.

Rattigan's attacks on doctrinaire drama and his dismissal by most critics as an ideologically empty playwright are ironic, for his work is deeply ideological. His pervading theme is a passionate defense of the most oppressed minority throughout history: the individual. In a 1982 *Contemporary Review* retrospective, a writer recalled Rattigan's saying: "People should care about people, and I've some doubts that the ideologists do. They may care about the starving millions, but they're not worried too much about those millions' particular concerns." Rattigan was.

All but three of his plays are set in the twentieth century, most in the period from the 1930's to the 1960's. Rattigan captured the bewilderment of people living in a world without a firm moral and social structure to give them a sense of place and security. Theirs is a stark existence in which confusion and loneliness predominate, compounded by stale ideas and conventions. The philosophical idea Rattigan implicitly condemned throughout his work was the mind-body dichotomy, or the belief that human beings' physical and spiritual natures are irreconcilable, that one can be satisfied only at the expense of the other, and that spiritual love is superior to physical love. The social conventions Rattigan most abhorred were the prohibition against expressing emotion and the ostracism of individuals for deviating from various norms. His plays show that the individual's best resources are self-reliance and self-respect, understanding and compassion for others, and the healing bonds of kindness and friendship.

Rattigan's characters are influenced by outside factors, but all have a range of choice in their values and actions. His plots delineate the cause-and-effect relationship between the nature of the values that individuals pursue, evade, or betray and their psychological and existential well-being. The form of a Rattigan play is determined by and inseparable from its content. In a *Daily Telegraph* tribute after the playwright's death, William Douglas-Home likened the beauty of Rattigan's structures to those of classical architecture and the symphony. The *Contemporary Review* writer stated that Rattigan's plays have "'good bones'—a prime requisite for aging well." The sinews of his plays are his extraordinarily rich dialogue—naturalistic but so precisely stylized that a few simple words can, as Harold Hobson frequently pointed out, convey a world of meaning. Rattigan's personal signature on the form and content of his work may be seen by surveying one play from each of the five decades of his playwriting career.

French Without Tears • Even when one recalls that Rattigan had been writing plays diligently from the age of eleven, the artistic wholeness of *French Without Tears*, his first produced solo effort, seems remarkable. In varying degrees, the characteristics of his body of work are all present in this early work.

The innovative element of this romantic comedy is Rattigan's reversal of the cliché of a femme fatale who turns friends into enemies. At a small language program in France, several young Englishmen try to learn French while one student's alluring sister, Diana, tries to distract them. She entraps Kit, much to the distress of the French tutor's daughter, Jacqueline, and then entices a newly arrived, more mature naval commander. Alan, a diplomat's son yearning to be a novelist (an autobiographical touch), feigns indifference to Diana, cheers Kit, and ridicules the Commander. In a scene reminiscent of the Elyot-Victor clash in Noël Coward's *Private Lives* (pr. 1930), Kit and the Commander fight until they discover that Diana has used the same "line" on them. They unite in friendship, accompanied by Alan, and confront Diana with her perfidy. She confounds them all by declaring that she really loves Alan. Kit turns to Jacqueline, and Diana chases Alan as he, taking the Commander's advice, bolts to London to tell his father that he is taking up writing instead of diplomacy. Although structured on the Chekhovian model of short scenes between groups of characters, building up a central situation through accumulation of detail, the plot has the vitality of a mixed-doubles grudge match in tennis, with changes of partners topped by one player taking off after the referee.

The play examines the relationship of love and sex at a depth unusual in light comedy. Alan and Kit are caught in the mind-body dichotomy, desiring an attractive girl with little character and feeling only friendship for the plainer but more worthy Jacqueline. At the end, she and Kit decide timidly to see if love and friendship, sex and liking, can mix. For all of his sophisticated airs, Alan is a little English gentleman who can sail only calm waters. He feels comfortable in friendship with Jacqueline but panics over Diana, afraid of sex and of having his emotions aroused.

Friendship is a bond bridging social and economic gaps and changing people's lives throughout Rattigan's work. When they stop fighting with the Commander, Kit and Alan discover that he is not the stodgy figure they mocked but a sensitive and sensible man. This revelation is also an instance of Rattigan showing characters as individuals, not types. He accomplishes this with Diana in a sequence in which she admits to Jacqueline that she cannot give up the chase because she knows that men can only love but never like her.

Rattigan's use of dramatic implication is illustrated by a short scene in which Alan describes the plot of his rejected novel to Kit and the Commander. His story not only mirrors the conflict between his listeners and its resolution but also foreshadows the war clouds gathering around the students—a point reinforced by other touches in the play. Historically, the comedy is a sunny look at the youth of a generation soon to fight World War II. Rattigan's biographers, Michael Darlow and Gillian Hodson, cite *French Without Tears* as the best comedy of the 1930's and the representative British play of that decade.

Playbill • In spite of the success of his war drama *Flare Path*, his comedy of manners and romance *Love in Idleness*, and his courtroom-like drama set entirely in a drawing room, *The Winslow Boy*, Rattigan had difficulty finding a producer for *Playbill*. Most managements thought bills of one-acts commercial folly. T. C. Worsley noted in a *London Magazine* essay that Rattigan's defense of the artistic integrity of the one-act form and his reintroduction of it to the West End after the war proved boons to his successors.

Though *The Browning Version* and *Harlequinade* are often produced separately, their coupling in *Playbill* represents an artistic design. The overall structure is psychological, encompassing studies of vastly different personalities—the severely repressed and the flamboyantly theatrical. They are embodied in plots ingeniously similar enough—in each play, errors from the past press on the protagonists—to highlight the contrast between psychologies.

The Browning Version, which won the Ellen Terry Award for best play of 1948, probes a psychological state that Rattigan had used as a leitmotif of characterization in his earlier plays. As Kay Nolte Smith pointed out in a 1971 *Objectivist* essay, the drama's theme is the tragedy of emotional repression. This is Rattigan's most original theme, and a difficult one to dramatize. His genius lay in making the causes and effects of repression intelligible and dramatic in a classically severe plot, without the use of soliloquy, of a narrator or *raisonneur* figure to offer explanations, or even of the word "repression."

The setting is the living room of a schoolmaster's apartment at a British boy's school. Andrew Crocker-Harris, once a brilliant and idealistic Greek master but now a dessicated pedant, is retiring early because of ill health. Visits by his young successor, the Headmaster, a pupil, and a colleague, and constant taunts by his sexually and socially frustrated wife, recall Crocker-Harris to his hopes and failures as a teacher and as a husband. Two gestures of kindness—the pupil's parting gift of Robert Browning's version of Aeschylus's *Agamemnōn* (458 B.C.E.; *Agamemnon*, 1777) and the colleague's offer of friendship—help Crocker-Harris to overcome what he calls his state of being a spiritual corpse, to break with his wife and to assert himself to the Headmaster. The play's penultimate line, when Crocker-Harris claims from the Headmaster his right to speak last at a school ceremony, "I am of opinion that occasionally an anti-climax can be surprisingly effective," is a characteristic Rattigan understatement, conveying his protagonist's recovery of self-respect in a simple phrase. Reviewing a 1976 London revival in the *Sunday Times*, Harold Hobson called *The Browning Version* "a masterpiece if ever there was one, the best one-act in the language."

Crocker-Harris was inspired partly by Rattigan's Greek master at Harrow. The famed acting team playing an aging Romeo and Juliet, whose dress rehearsal is interrupted by unwelcome visitors in *Harlequinade*, bore resemblances to Alfred Lunt and Lynn Fontanne, with whom Rattigan had worked so closely on *Love in Idleness*. The focus is on the Romeo, a quintessential actor-manager oblivious of events outside the theater, who embodies Rattigan's theory that farce may be based on character. The comedy has been compared favorably with George Villiers's *The Rehearsal* (pr. 1671, pb. 1672), Richard Brinsley Sheridan's *The Critic: Or, A Tragedy Rehearsed* (pr. 1779), and Arthur Wing Pinero's *Trelawny of the "Wells"* (pr., pb. 1898) as a classic play about theater life.

The Deep Blue Sea • Though usually cited as one of Rattigan's finest works, *The Deep Blue Sea* has yet to be fully appreciated. Eleven years before the women's movement began with the publication of Betty Friedan's *The Feminine Mystique* (1963), Rattigan produced a prescient drama about the effects of a woman's "raised consciousness."

The play is structured like a thriller, beginning with a landlady's discovery of Hester Collyer, unconscious from a suicide attempt, in a run-down London boardinghouse. Hester no longer feels worthy or desirous of living; gradually, the action reveals why. Daughter of a clergyman, wife of a judge honored with knighthood, she has fallen passionately in love with a feckless younger man and run off with him. A war pilot who has never found an equivalent challenge in civilian life, Freddie Page loves Hester in his way but is incapable of returning her ardor sexually or emotionally, and determines to leave rather than ruin Hester's life further. Hester's loving husband, Sir William, views her attachment as an ignoble but pardonable sex obsession and wants her to return to being his companionable wife.

Hester's sexual awakening with Freddie has released her need for more intense relationships than either man can offer. She feels deep shame at the pain she has caused, terror at the prospect of losing Freddie, and anger at the religious and societal view— pressed by her background, Sir William, and a young neighbor—that spiritual love is superior to physical. Another neighbor, a former doctor who lost his license and bears his disgrace with dignity, is able from his perspective as a social outcast to help Hester view herself as a worthy individual. In the end, after saying goodbye to her husband and lover, Hester takes her first step toward independence by lighting the gas heater she may still decide to use to escape life. *The Deep Blue Sea* was ahead of its time not only in Rattigan's sympathetic portrait of a woman who must virtually start life again almost at middle age, but also in his equally compassionate portrayals of men who are bewildered, wounded, and threatened by women's changing needs.

The Adventure Story and **Ross** • Rattigan applied principles of craftsmanship from the well-made play to the epic form with impressive results. Although his portraits of Alexander the Great in *Adventure Story* and T. E. Lawrence in *Ross* are marred by earnest but ultimately unconvincing attempts to explain each man's motivations, Rattigan captures the personal charisma of both figures and the sweep of their lives through world history with narrative mastery.

Like *Adventure Story*, *Ross* traces the psychological destruction of a brilliant military leader. The first three scenes dramatize Lawrence's attempt to find peace after World War I as a Royal Air Force aircraftman enlisted under the pseudonym of Ross. Recognized and awaiting expulsion, he drifts into a malarial dream that becomes a bridge to scenes depicting the wartime exploits that made him famous but sickened him spiritually. He is torn by exulting in his triumphs while wading through carnage to achieve them and then destroyed psychologically by being awakened to his homosexual and masochistic tendencies in his (offstage) beating and rape by Turkish soldiers. Lawrence had trusted in the supremacy of his will and cannot face the realization that behind his will are not strength and integrity but inclinations that shame him. In the end, he decides to seek sanctuary in the service again under another assumed name.

In terms of Rattigan's attempt to integrate an expansive narrative structure with a comprehensive character study, *Ross* is his most complex and ambitious play. There is a density in its texture because of the sheer weight of material it encompasses. Rattigan had to explain the British, Arab, and Turkish positions during the World War I Middle Eastern conflict while simultaneously exploring the inner conflicts of a character who is both a man of action and a deeply repressed, tormented intellectual. Without narration, Rattigan was able to organize his mass of material in theatrical terms, judiciously balancing humor, suspense, and pathos.

In Praise of Love • The last third of *In Praise of Love*, Rattigan's penultimate play, contains some of his finest writing. About an East European war refugee dying of leukemia, her apparently callous British husband, their sensitive son, and an old family friend, the work is structured as a psychological suspense story. Two-thirds of the play are devoted to creating a negative picture of the husband as a childish, boorish, selfish man. The wife confides her illness to the friend because she fears boring her husband, as she thinks she once bored him with her refugee tales, and tries to reconcile the contentious husband and son, both of whom she adores. In a *coup de théâtre*, the husband is forced to tell the friend that he has known of his wife's illness all along and is determined to keep it from her lest she relive her wartime anticipation of death at any moment. His callousness, once a habit, is now a mask he dons to foster the illusion that all is normal. He finds the mask torturous to wear because he has realized how much he loves his wife yet cannot tell her. He remarks that the English people's worst vice is their refusal to admit to their emotions.

Rattigan's condemnation of emotional repression is explicit in *In Praise of Love*, but particularly noteworthy in the play is the most daring use he ever made of implication. Rattigan's dramas are all dotted with comic dialogue and business that further his goals without undercutting the seriousness of his subjects. With *In Praise of Love*, he used comic dialogue and action throughout to build a picture of a household under almost unbearable emotional pressure, a household in which characters use banter to mask their own feelings and to try to spare the feelings of others. The contrast between the characters' veneer and the depth of their love and grief is profoundly poignant.

On Rattigan's death in 1977, the *Guardian*'s Michael Billington, representative of a post-Angry-Young-Man generation of theater critics, maintained that Rattigan was misunderstood as an exemplar of the cool and gentlemanly school of English playwriting: "The real truth is that his plays are a remorseless attack on English emotional inhibition, and a moving plea for affection and kindness and understanding in the everyday business of life. . . . Few dramatists [in the twentieth] century have written with more understanding about the human heart." Giving evidence that this revaluation is not confined to British critics, Susan Rusinko concludes in her 1983 study of Rattigan for Twayne's English Authors series: "Polished without being slick, natural without untidiness, Rattigan's art has given firm shape to the mid-twentieth century mainstream of English life, chronicling the sweeping changes in the moods and attitudes of the time, as [did] Chekhov for his time."

Other major works

SCREENPLAYS: *Quiet Wedding*, 1941 (based on Esther McCracken's play); *English Without Tears*, 1944 (with Anatole de Grunwald; also known as *Her Man Gilbey*); *The Way to the Stars*, 1945 (with de Grunwald; also known as *Johnny in the Clouds*); *While the Sun Shines*, 1946; *The Winslow Boy*, 1948 (with de Grunwald); *Bond Street*, 1948; *Brighton Rock*, 1948 (later as *Young Scarface*; with Graham Greene; based on Greene's novel); *The Browning Version*, 1951; *The Sound Barrier*, 1952 (also known as *Breaking the Sound Barrier*); *The Final Test*, 1954; *The Prince and the Showgirl*, 1957 (adaptation of *The Sleeping Prince*); *Separate Tables*, 1958 (with John Gay; adaptation of Rattigan's play); *The VIPs*, 1963; *The Yellow Rolls-Royce*, 1965; *A Bequest to the Nation*, 1973.

TELEPLAYS: *The Final Test,* 1951; *Heart to Heart,* 1964; *Nelson—A Portrait in Miniature,* 1964.

RADIO PLAY: *Cause Célèbre,* 1975.

Bibliography

Darlow, Michael, and Gillian Hodson. *Terence Rattigan: The Man and His Work.* London: Quartet Books, 1979. A 360-page critical biography, thoroughly researched, using archives from the British Broadcasting Corporation. In this eminently readable narrative of Rattigan, his plays, and their times—all three led inexorably to one another—the authors write with authority and with permission from Rattigan to reveal much of what he had been unable to write about directly in his own plays. Includes photographs, a bibliography, a list of British and American opening dates and casts, and an index.

O'Connor, Sean. *Straight Acting: Popular Gay Drama from Wilde to Rattigan.* Washington, D.C.: Cassell, 1998. A look at homosexuality and literature that traces gay writers from Oscar Wilde and W. Somerset Maugham to more modern writers such as Noël Coward and Terence Rattigan. Bibliography and index.

Rusinko, Susan. *Terence Rattigan.* Boston: Twayne, 1983. A chronological summary-analysis of the complete stage, film, and television plays, analyzing Rattigan's major plays, from his early sunny comedies to his later dramas about dysfunctional families in a dysfunctional society. Photograph, chronology, bibliography, index.

Wansell, Geoffrey. *Terence Rattigan.* New York: St. Martin's Press, 1997. A biography of the British dramatist that covers his works for the stage as well as those for television and the movie theater. Bibliography and index.

Young, B. A. *The Rattigan Version: The Theatre of Character.* New York: Atheneum, 1988. A personal memoir by an author who knew Rattigan. Leisurely in pace and impressionistic in style, it raises some questions, as in the descriptions of Rattigan's manner of throwing "his dialogue down on the page, caring only for its gist rather than its style." Includes index, cast lists, and photographs that tell their own story.

Holly Hill,
updated by Susan Rusinko

Edmond Rostand

Born: Marseilles, France; April 1, 1868
Died: Paris, France; December 2, 1918

Principal drama • *Le Gant rouge*, pr., pb. 1888 (with Henry Lee); *Les Romanesques*, pr., 1894, pb. 1917 (verse play; *The Romantics*, 1899); *La Princesse lointaine*, pr. 1895, pb. 1908 (verse play; *The Far Princess*, 1899); *La Samaritaine*, pr. 1897, pb. 1898 (verse play; *The Woman of Samaria*, 1921); *Cyrano de Bergerac*, pr. 1897, pb. 1898 (verse play; English translation, 1898); *L'Aiglon*, pr., pb. 1900 (verse play; *The Eaglet*, 1898); *Chantecler*, pr., pb. 1910 (verse play; *Chanticleer*, 1910); *La Dernière Nuit de Don Juan*, pb. 1921, pr. 1922 (verse play; *The Last Night of Don Juan*, 1929); *Plays of Edmond Rostand*, pb. 1921

Other literary forms • Although his greatest success was as a dramatist, Edmond Rostand was first of all a poet. All of his plays are written in verse, and despite his real flair for dramatic situations, it is the wit and lyricism of his verse that raise his best plays above the level of ordinary melodrama. His first published work was a volume of poetry, *Les Musardises* (1890). The title is untranslatable. Its basic meaning is "daydreams," but in a preface, Rostand explained that he also meant to evoke a kind of melancholy—*muzer*, in the Walloon dialect, meaning "to be sad"—as well as the source of poetic inspiration—the Muse. He published two later volumes of verse, *Le Cantique de l'aile* (1910; the canticle of the wing), including a paean to the first aviators, and *Le Vol de la Marseillaise* (1914; the flight of the Marseillaise), a collection of patriotic poems inspired by World War I. He wrote little prose, but a boyhood essay on Honoré d'Urfé and Émile Zola, which won for him first prize in a contest sponsored by the Academy of Moral and Political Sciences of Marseilles, proved important because it introduced him to the strain in French literature known as *préciosité*, of which d'Urfé's work was a classic expression. Rostand's speech on his induction into the Académie Française is also revealing; in it, he discusses the notion of *panache*, the "spirit of bravura" central to his masterpiece, *Cyrano de Bergerac*.

Achievements • Edmond Rostand is remembered, and will probably continue to be remembered, exclusively as the author of a single play, *Cyrano de Bergerac*. Its first production, in Paris in 1897, was greeted with wild enthusiasm (the ovation on opening night lasted almost an hour) and made the twenty-nine-year-old author famous overnight. His popularity did not diminish during his lifetime, and he became the youngest man ever elected to the Académie Française, but most of his plays are marred by sentimentality and have not been much revived since his death. Only one, *The Eaglet*, enjoyed a reception comparable to that of *Cyrano de Bergerac*, but this was partly because of the popularity of its theme (the fate of Napoleon II) among Rostand's contemporaries, and partly because of the acting of Sarah Bernhardt, who appeared in the title role. Rostand cannot be said to have influenced subsequent French drama, for his style was anachronistic in his own day, a reaction against what was perceived as the pessimism of the realistic theater. *Cyrano de Bergerac*, however, has proved to be a perennial favorite on the world stage and has been translated into languages as disparate as Turkish, Russian, Hebrew, and Japanese. In addition, a musical comedy, *The Fantasticks*, based on

The Romantics, ran at an Off-Broadway theater from 1960 to 2002 and has been produced in fifty-seven countries.

Biography • Edmond Eugène Alexis Rostand was born into an upper-middle-class
family with deep roots in the south of France that can be traced back to the sixteenth
century. His father, Eugène, and his paternal uncle Alexis were distinguished econo-
mists who also managed to cultivate their gifts for poetry and music, respectively:
Eugène translated Catullus and wrote the librettos for Alexis's oratorios. The young
Rostand was a shy and studious child who loved to read and play with marionettes; his
favorite authors were Sir Walter Scott and Alexandre Dumas, *père*. During long summer vacations in the Pyrenees, he developed a deep attachment for the region; there he
also wrote his first poems. After completing primary school and six years at the Marseilles Lycée, he was sent to the Collège Stanislas in Paris to complete his secondary education. His teachers there introduced him to the work of William Shakespeare, Johann
Wolfgang von Goethe, and Alfred de Musset (some echoes of Musset's comedies may
be detected in *The Romantics* and *The Far Princess*). Rostand's other literary heroes were
Miguel de Cervantes and Victor Hugo.

Untouched by the naturalists and Symbolists, he was not drawn into any of the literary circles of Paris. Through his future wife, Rosemonde Gérard, he made the acquaintance of the poet Leconte de Lisle, her godfather, but received no encouragement from
him. At his father's urging, he began to study law while making his first attempts at
playwriting. *Le Gant rouge* (the red glove), a comedy written in collaboration with
Henry Lee, his future brother-in-law, was staged in 1888 but was not well received. *Les
Musardises* met with mixed reviews in 1890. In the same year Rostand married Gérard,
who was herself a poet (her collection *Les Pipeaux* was published in 1889). According to
Rostand's biographer Émile Ripert, Gérard was responsible in large measure for
bringing her husband's work to the attention of the public. A perfectionist, Rostand re-
vised his work repeatedly and was reluctant to publish. The couple had two sons,
Maurice, a dramatist, and Jean, an eminent biologist. With *The Romantics* and *The Far
Princess*, Rostand gained some recognition. The former play won for him the Toirac
Prize, and the latter, the friendship and admiration of Sarah Bernhardt, who produced
the work and played the princess. The title role of *The Woman of Samaria* was created
especially for Bernhardt.

The appearance of *Cyrano de Bergerac* proved a watershed in the poet's life; from that
time until his death, he was a famous man, besieged by admirers and, as Ripert notes,
acutely conscious of his "spiritual mission" as poet, patriot, and idealist. In spite of the
nationalist tendency observable in *The Eaglet* (Rostand's father was a Bonapartist),
Rostand did not support the nationalist parties of his day and, in fact, risked his popularity by maintaining the innocence of Alfred Dreyfus. In politics as in literature, he refused to align himself with a particular movement; he admired quixotic daring against
all odds—the bravura of Cyrano—wherever he saw it, and wrote poems in praise of
both the Greeks and the Boers in their bids for independence.

Rostand was plagued by recurrent pulmonary infections, and, after the success of
The Eaglet, he moved with his family to Cambo in the foothills of the Pyrenees, where
the weather and the relative privacy were better for his health. He returned to Paris for
short periods only—for example, to deliver an acceptance speech at the Académie
Française in 1903 and to supervise the staging of *Chanticleer*. Even in Cambo, where he
built a villa and lived in semiretirement for the remainder of his life, the mantle of unofficial poet laureate weighed heavily on him. He was forced to hire a secretary to an-

swer the flood of mail he received, and he spent ten years revising *Chanticleer*, for fear of disappointing his public (the play was only a partial success). A compulsive worker who suffered from insomnia, Rostand was a rather distant father to his two sons. As Maurice Rostand put it, "Glory makes homes empty." By contrast, he corresponded with hundreds of young soldiers during World War I and visited others in the trenches. The war cast a deep gloom over his last years, during which he wrote a collection of labored patriotic verse and *The Last Night of Don Juan*, which he termed a "dramatic poem." The latter was staged in 1922, four years after his death, but without success. He died of pneumonia on December 2, 1918, shortly after the Armistice.

Analysis • Despite his debt to the romantics, the strain in French literature to which Edmond Rostand really belongs is that of *préciosité*, "precious" or elaborately refined writing, usually on the subject of love. An outstanding trait of *préciosité* is the prominence it gives to form, often at the expense of content. Therefore, Rostand wrote his dramas in the regular rhymed couplets of the classical and romantic French theater, even insisting on *rime riche* in the manner of the Parnassian poet Théodore de Banville. His diction and imagery were equally studied and at times rather farfetched. When deployed with wit and grace, as in his best plays, this fastidious technique served Rostand well, but it was not equally suited to all the subjects he treated.

At heart, Rostand—like most of his protagonists—was an idealist who shunned what he saw as the negativism of modern literature. Like Edwin Arlington Robinson's Miniver Cheevy, he was in a real sense "born too late"; only instead of drinking as Miniver did, he "kept on writing" in his own vein, oblivious of his naturalist and Symbolist contemporaries. He was at his best, however, when he tempered his romantic flights with a dose of humor or with a trace of the irony that characterized his own age. Therefore, his masterpiece, *Cyrano de Bergerac*, takes as its hero a seventeenth century wit (himself a *précieux*) whose tendency to take himself too seriously is perfectly tempered by his ludicrous appearance. In Cyrano, Rostand was able to fuse his idealism and his polished wit in a character who is by turns heroic and comical—to resounding dramatic effect.

Indeed, Rostand was not only a meticulous versifier but also a man of considerable dramatic gifts. In particular, he knew how to vary the moods of successive scenes and achieve striking stage effects with surprise reversals. He was also capable of clever plot development, as his best plays, *Cyrano de Bergerac* and *The Romantics*, demonstrate. Yet because his characters are only sketchily developed, their actions can appear insufficiently motivated, and the interplay of character and action characteristic of most great drama is missing. Nor is there a structure of ideas in Rostand's plays that might compensate for this shallowness of characterization. In his dramatic effects, as in his verbal craftsmanship, he is above all a superb entertainer—albeit an idealistic one.

Indeed, *préciosité* is, in essence, a form of highly refined entertainment. It is not a school but rather a tendency that runs through much of French poetry, though its heyday was in the early seventeenth century. (Its origins may be traced to the courtly lyrics of the troubadors, and it is visible in the poetry of the sixteenth century "Pléïade" as well as in that of the nineteenth century Parnassians.) The context in which the seventeenth century *précieux* flourished was that of the salons, exclusive social circles that noble and, later, bourgeois women gathered about themselves. The members of such circles met to discuss literary topics and often to compete with one another in actual poetic contests. One of Rostand's best poems, a period piece called *La Journée d'une précieuse* (1898; a day in the life of a précieuse), describes such a contest, in which the requirement is to compose a *rondeau* with rhymes in -*al* and -*oche* "to accompany the gift of a seal of rock-crystal." Rostand's poem manages to poke gentle fun at the extravagances of his heroine and her salon while conveying some of the genuine wit and charm that such circles fostered.

In most of the salons, wit and worldly graces were prized above true erudition; writers of a "precious" cast tended to seek new, entertaining ways of saying things rather than new things to say. In general this is true of Rostand, whose imagery, diction, and versification all display the studied (*recherché*) quality proper to the *précieux*. Rostand's decision to write verse dramas in the last decade of the nineteenth and the first decade of the twentieth centuries was itself a relative anachronism (the realistic theater confined itself to prose) and as such called attention to his virtuosity. He allowed himself romantic license in his use of the Alexandrine (the twelve-syllable line that had been the medium for classical French drama): Enjambments are frequent, and single lines are routinely divided among three, four, or even more different characters. Even in crowd scenes, however, there are no lapses into prose, and the effect is often that of a tour de force.

Such a tour de force works well when the theme is love or bravado, as in the famous balcony scene or in Cyrano's duel with the Vicomte de Valvert, during which he composes a *ballade*, finishing off his opponent at the end of the refrain; it is less successful when more banal topics are involved, and especially when, as in *Chanticleer*, the necessary suspension of disbelief cannot be maintained: Twentieth century farm animals cannot be made to speak heroic couplets except in farce, and Rostand exceeds the limits of his form by freighting the play with serious themes. Even in plays set in a distant or legendary past, such as *The Far Princess* and *The Woman of Samaria*, there are lapses of taste, for the finely chiseled lines and *rime riche* (rhyme involving not only the last syllable of a word but also the preceding consonant or syllable) can easily ring false outside certain contexts. The same may be said of Rostand's diction, which—largely as a result of his insistence on "rich" rhyme—includes rare and occasionally grotesque words, some of them coinages. These qualities suit the burlesque scenes to perfection but give a labored or awkward tone to some serious scenes, especially in *The Far Princess*.

Where imagery is concerned, Rostand is a true *précieux*, working best on the small scale of the individual line or speech; his recurrent or governing images are often banal (thus light is symbolic of glory, wings of daring or aspiration, lilies of chastity, and roses of fulfilled love). Even these can be effective in specific contexts—when, for example, the "Far Princess," Mélissinde, acknowledges that the strong yet overrefined scent of the lilies with which she surrounds herself may reinforce her own "solitary pride." By insisting that the stage be strewn with lilies, however—to be exchanged for roses in act 3, when Mélissinde has fallen in love with Bertrand—Rostand makes the symbolism too emphatic and obvious. Granted that hyperbole or exaggeration is also a feature of the "precious" style, this overworking is a temptation to which Rostand, like many *précieux*, succumbs all too readily. One of his loveliest images compares the Samaritan woman's gesture, as she balances a water jar on her head with one hand, to the jar itself with its graceful handle; yet instead of letting the image stand on its own, he goes on to freight it with a grandiloquence ("Immortal splendor of this rustic grace!") and a sentimentality beneath which it all but founders.

The far-fetched quality proper to "precious" imagery makes it most appropriate to, and effective in, burlesque or self-consciously witty passages. Here Rostand is in his element and can make the sparks fly. Perhaps the most famous example is the "nose tirade" in act 1 of *Cyrano de Bergerac*, in which the hero puts a man who has insulted him to scorn by improving on the insult. Instead of saying baldly, "You have a very big nose," the man might have compared the nose to a peninsula, a scissors-case, a conch, a monument—even, "when it bleeds, the Red Sea!" This kind of virtuosity is already visible in Rostand's early poem, "Charivari à la lune" (mock-serenade for the moon, in *Les Musardises*), which compares the moon to scores of different objects, including a cymbal, a mushroom, an egg, and a fingernail. More striking than the images themselves is the grace and wit with which Rostand arranges them: At first, each quatrain encompasses a single image, then two, then four, until the last frenetic strophe of the "serenade" is made to hold eight different images. Lapsing into Alexandrines, the poet admits that he is out of breath and hopes for a response from the moon—but all he hears is an ironic, "Go on!" Here as elsewhere, wit is Rostand's great redeeming grace, the pinprick deflating what otherwise might become intolerably artificial and hollow.

This is not to deny Rostand's properly dramatic talents. Even his most sentimental plays contain effective scenes, in which a sense of dramatic movement is sustained by artful development or sudden reversals. Thus, the woman of Samaria, recognizing Jesus as the Messiah, bursts into the same profane love song with which she had approached the well; thus Metternich, entering the Duke of Reichstadt's bedroom late at night, is confronted by a French grenadier standing guard and half believes for a moment that Napoleon is occupying the palace as he had twenty years earlier. Indeed, the entire plot of *The Romantics* is built on a double reversal of romantic conventions, which Rostand arranges to maximum theatrical effect.

The Romantics • *The Romantics* might be described as an anti-*Romeo and Juliet* (pr. c. 1595-1596; deliberately so on Rostand's part—as it opens, the hero is reading Romeo's speech from the balcony scene). In the first act, two fathers foster an attachment between their children, Sylvette and Percinet, by pretending to be mortal enemies; like Ovid's Pyramus and Thisbe, the young couple meet in secret by the wall dividing the two estates. The fathers put a contrived end to their contrived hatred by hiring a knockabout named Straforel to stage an "abduction" of Sylvette, whom Percinet "rescues." As act 2 opens, the wall is down and the marriage, imminent, but a second (and this time realistic) reversal is in store: The fathers, finding each other's daily company irritating, are on the way to becoming enemies in earnest. They find it still harder to bear the condescension of their children, who believe that their own romantic ideal has won the day over the obtuse self-interest of their elders.

At last unable to contain themselves, the fathers tell Sylvette the truth; she tries to hide it from Percinet but finds herself losing interest in his romantic excesses, which now strike her as pretentious and hollow. Then Percinet stumbles on Straforel's bill for the "abduction" (a masterfully comic touch, including items such as "Rumpled clothing, ten francs; Hurt pride, forty"). Though their first reaction is to reaffirm their love, which they insist is real even if their situation has been false, they soon quarrel, and Percinet runs off to seek "real" adventure. Straforel, who has yet to be paid, decides to patch it up between the two; he begins by proposing a real elopement to Sylvette, describing the hardships she will face in terms that make her long for a quiet life with Percinet. Meanwhile, her fiancé returns, disenchanted by his brushes with "adventure" in the form of barmaids and thugs, and the two lovers are reconciled.

As can be seen from this summary, the plot is clever, and Rostand unfolds it artfully, making the most of every reversal. He also maintains a consistent tone throughout the poetic dialogue—light and graceful, as in *La Journée d'une précieuse*, with exactly the right shade of gentle irony. After *Cyrano de Bergerac*, *The Romantics* is the play of

Rostand that holds up best for a modern-day audience. This is largely a result of the universal appeal of its stock characters, which can be traced back as far as Menander (young lovers, burlesque fathers, jacks-of-all-trades), but it is also attributable to the essential modernity of the play's theme: the ironic unmasking of romantic ideals. The fact that Rostand arranges a happy ending—in effect, a kind of *re*-masking—makes it all the more stageworthy; it is a comedy in the classical mold. Yet it portrays middle-class disillusionment in a manner that rings true.

In this respect, *The Romantics* is unique among Rostand's plays. Most of the time, he prided himself on resisting the disillusionment of his contemporaries, choosing as heroes men whose great aim in life was to distinguish themselves. The means to this end differ considerably from play to play (poetry, fidelity in love, even, in *Chanticleer*, a rooster's crowing), yet in each case the hero justifies his endeavor by maintaining its value on an ideal plane. The distinction he seeks is not so much public recognition— though most of Rostand's heroes crave recognition as well—but rather the singularity of the romantic idealist, often purchased at the price of loneliness and self-doubt. Love is also an important theme in the plays, but it is always subordinate to the hero's struggle for distinction and is tinged with the idealism of that struggle. Hence the platonic character of the great "love affairs" in Rostand—Jaufré Rudel and Mélissinde, Cyrano and Roxane. (An extreme example can be seen in the Samaritan woman's response to Jesus, who replaces the imperfect former objects of her love.) Even Rostand's Don Juan exhibits no real sensuality; the reasons he gives for a lifetime of seduction are all intellectual, amounting to perverted or negative ideals.

It is in his idealism, which stems from the nineteenth century romantics, that Rostand least resembles the seventeenth century *précieux*; for while the latter also engaged in platonic love affairs and professed a consuming interest in "things of the spirit," the salons in which they sought to distinguish themselves were above all social circles, little courts formed in emulation of the royal court. As such, they could be stepping-stones to worldly recognition and influence. The emphasis on form in the writings of the *précieux* thus stems from a desire to please; theirs is the art of the courtier. Rostand was far more ambivalent in his attitude toward the public for which he wrote. Though anxious lest he disappoint his audience, he believed that the poet's mission was not only to please but also to inspire. This sense of mission unfortunately had a pernicious effect on his last works, replacing the easy grace of *The Romantics* with an uneven tone that fluctuates between heavy humor and preachiness. In *Cyrano de Bergerac*, however, Rostand managed to strike the perfect compromise between his *préciosité* and his idealism.

Cyrano de Bergerac • Never was his sense of properly theatrical values keener than in *Cyrano de Bergerac*. The plot moves briskly, keeping the audience amused while engaging its sympathies in favor of the hero, then building to a double climax of considerable pathos. Each of the five acts has a dramatic unity of its own, yet together the acts form an almost seamless whole. A poet and soldier of uncompromising ideals, Cyrano has been cursed with an outlandish nose that he himself freely ridicules but will allow no one else to mention. His bravado dominates the first act, in which he composes a *ballade* while fighting a duel then goes alone to face one hundred men whom he learns are waiting to ambush his friend Lignière.

There is one person, however, before whom Cyrano trembles: his cousin Roxane, whom he secretly loves but fears to woo because of his ugliness. He is on tenterhooks when, in the second act, she asks to meet with him in private and confesses that she is in love; but it emerges that her infatuation is for Christian de Neuvillette, a new member of Cyrano's company in the Guards, and whom she wants her cousin to befriend and protect. This Cyrano resolutely promises to do, though he warns Roxane—herself a *précieuse*—that Christian, with whom she has never spoken, may prove a fool for all of his beauty. When this prediction turns out to be true, Cyrano takes his self-sacrifice a step further and offers to coach Christian, providing him with witty and tender words that enchant Roxane.

In act 3, Christian tries to speak for himself, but his awkwardness offends Roxane; in an attempt to put things right again, Cyrano has him call her to her balcony, and he himself addresses her from the shadows below. Overcome with emotion, he pours out his heart—still in Christian's name—and Roxane arranges a secret wedding for that very night, during which time Cyrano stands guard, detaining yet another of Roxane's suitors, the powerful Count de Guiche. Enraged, the count dispatches the Guards to the siege of Arras; in act 4, Roxane manages to join them there, drawn by the beauty of "Christian's" daily letters. When Roxane tells Christian that she would love him even if he were ugly, Christian urges Cyrano to tell her the truth, but a few minutes later Christian is killed, and Cyrano resolves to keep the secret. It is not until the end of act 5 (which takes place fourteen years later) that he reveals the truth, half involuntarily, on the verge of his own death.

What makes the play so compelling is the thoroughly romantic contrast between the "inner" and "outer" man: Like the dwarf Triboulet (the original of Giuseppe Verdi's Rigoletto) in Victor Hugo's play *Le Roi s'amuse* (1832; *The King Amuses Himself*, 1842), Cyrano may be tender and passionate in spite of his ridiculous face. (Similarly, in *The Eaglet*, the Duke of Reichstadt may be considered "a great prince" although he accomplishes nothing.) The weakness of Rostand's work is that the singularity of the soul that he claims for his heroes is merely assumed, never substantiated by depth or complexity of characterization. Even Cyrano, his most successful creation, is incompletely developed. One has only to ask what it is that Roxane loves in Cyrano (or, still more pointedly, what it is that Cyrano loves in Roxane) to realize that Rostand never tells. Roxane learned to love Cyrano's "soul," she says, by reading his letters, yet the only real taste that the audience gets of his eloquence is the balcony scene, in which form (witty phrasing, precious imagery) predominates and the real poignancy stems from the contrast—of which Roxane is unaware—between the beauty of Cyrano's words and the ugliness of his face.

In fact, as a survey of his other plays reveals, Rostand had only a limited repertory of characters, types to which he reverted again and again: the romantic idealist, usually his protagonist; the desirable but fickle woman, confused about what qualities are worth loving; and the hard-headed realist, who serves as foil and often friend to the hero. Because his dramas hinged on these ideal types, Rostand sought exotic settings such as twelfth century Tripoli or seventeenth century Paris; he himself admitted that he set *Chanticleer* in a barnyard because no contemporary human setting would suit his purpose.

Much of Rostand's purpose becomes clear if one compares his Cyrano with the real Cyrano, Savinien de Cyrano de Bergerac, whose life is well documented and many of whose writings survive. The greatest surprise is to discover that this Cyrano would in fact have made a very good contemporary hero—or antihero: He gave up a military career in disgust after being wounded twice; he changed sides (possibly for pay) during the Fronde, the struggle between some nobles and the regent Cardinal Mazarin; and he almost certainly died of syphilis (like Rostand's Cyrano, he was also struck on the head by a log, but this preceded his death by some time and may have been an accident rather than an ambush). Admittedly, the real Cyrano was a man of the seventeenth century as well: An avowed "libertine" or freethinker, he is said to have returned to the faith on his deathbed, at the urging of his friend Lebret and his relative, Mother Marguérite of Jesus.

Rostand, however, did not want a seventeenth century hero any more than he wanted a twenty-first century one. His Cyrano is larger than life—a great lover and a great fighter, a man of immutable ideals, impossible courage, and matchless wit. He lacks psychological depth and plausibility precisely because the ideal that Rostand would have him sustain has something inhuman about it. Why, the audience may ask, does Cyrano remain silent for fourteen years? If it were out of loyalty to Christian, he betrays his friend just as surely by speaking at the end of that time as he would have by speaking at the beginning—and, in the meantime, he has deprived not only himself but also Roxane of happiness. The answer Rostand would have given, to judge by his other plays and poems, is that the essence of Cyrano's (and Roxane's) love was not denied but preserved by his silence: There could be no disillusionment, no imperfection, in such an idealized passion. This means that Roxane, too, must be something less than a real woman, because she also is expected to be something more; as Charles Pujos puts it, "The beloved has to remain unpolluted to the very end, since she represents an Idea more than she does a woman, and only the [author's] symbolic intention can justify that."

Given its wholly platonic conception of love, how does the play continue to hold the stage in the late twentieth century? In fairness to Rostand, it must be added that questions such as that of Cyrano's silence suggest themselves to a reader sooner than they do to a spectator, and perhaps to a spectator only after the play is finished. It should also be noted that Rostand has always found his most ardent admirers among the young, who see in Cyrano the courageous nonconformist and the tragic lover. Because of the play's wit, its carefully articulated plot, and the delicate balance it maintains between idealism and *préciosité*, *Cyrano de Bergerac* is a superb dramatic entertainment. As such, it will probably remain a perennial favorite with theatergoers around the world.

Other major works

POETRY: *Les Musardises*, 1890; *La Journée d'une précieuse*, 1898; *Le Cantique de l'aile*, 1910; *Le Vol de la Marseillaise*, 1914.

Bibliography
Amoia, Alba della Fazia. *Edmond Rostand*. Boston: Twayne, 1978. In this concise biography, Amoia discusses Rostand's life and works. Bibliography and index.

Chweh, Crystal R., ed. *Readings on "Cyrano de Bergerac."* Literary Companion to World Literature series. San Diego, Calif.: Greenhaven Press, 2001. This book of essays, intended for young adults, presents literary criticism of Rostand's best-known work.

Freeman, E. J. *Edmond Rostand, Cyrano de Bergerac*. Glasgow, Scotland: University of Glasgow French and German Publications, 1995. Freeman looks at Rostand and his most popular work. Bibliography.

Lillian Doherty